# WEBSTER'S LEGAL SECRETARIES HANDBOOK

*A Merriam-Webster*®

# WEBSTER'S LEGAL SECRETARIES HANDBOOK

COLEEN K. WITHGOTT • General Editor
AUSTIN G. ANDERSON • Consulting Editor

Merriam-Webster Inc., Publishers
Springfield, Massachusetts 01102

Copyright © 1981 by Merriam-Webster Inc.
Philippines Copyright 1981 by Merriam-Webster Inc.

Library of Congress Cataloging in Publication Data
Main entry under title:

Webster's legal secretaries handbook.

    Bibliography: p.
    Includes index.
    1. Legal secretaries—United States—Handbooks,
manuals, etc.   I. Withgott, Coleen K., 1937–
II. Anderson, Austin G., 1931–   III. Title:
Legal secretaries handbook.
KF319.W42      651'.934      81-11014
ISBN 0-87779-034-5

Printed and bound in the United States of America

91011RRD908988

Design/Carolyn McHenry
Illustration/Julie A. Collier; Carolyn McHenry
Index/Eva Weber

# CONTRIBUTORS

AUSTIN G. ANDERSON, JD
Director, Institute of Continuing Legal
Education
University of Michigan, Ann Arbor

CLEIJO J. BATES, PLS
Legal Assistant
Stafford, Rosenbaum, Rieser & Hansen
Madison, Wisconsin

ROGER W. DOW, MEd
Associate Director of Curriculum
Heald Colleges
San Francisco, California

THOMAS MORE GRIFFIN
Legal Filing Consultant
Legal Fil-Ease
Washington, D.C.

JOHN G. IEZZI, CPA
General Manager
McGuire, Woods & Battle
Richmond, Virginia

LORRAINE A. KULPA, LLB, MSLS, MBA
Legal Staff Management Information Systems
Attorney-in-Charge
General Motors Corporation
Detroit, Michigan

SHERYL L. LINDSELL, MS
Instructor of English and Business
Taylor Business Institute
Paramus, New Jersey

FRANCES J. MAHAN, PhD
Associate Professor
Bryant College
Smithfield, Rhode Island

EUNICE MILLER
Facilities Manager
Naman, Howell, Smith, Lee &
Muldrow, P.C.
Waco, Texas

DOROTHY MANGUM, PLS
Legal Administrative Assistant
Republic National Life Insurance Company
Dallas, Texas

ESTELLE M. SHERRY, MS
Assistant Professor
Greater Hartford Community College
Hartford, Connecticut

HERBERT S. SCHWAB, LLB
Management Consultant to Law Firms
Westlake Village, California

WILLOUGHBY ANN WALSHE
Executive Editor, Word Processing &
Information Systems
Executive Editor, Information & Word
Processing Report
Geyer-McAllister Publications, Inc.
New York City

COLEEN WITHGOTT, MS
Merriam-Webster Inc.

SANDRA YOST, PLS
Legal Secretary
Braud, Warner, Neppl & Westensee, Ltd.
Rock Island, Illinois

# TABLE OF CONTENTS

Acknowledgments
The individuals and groups listed alphabetically below gave
valuable assistance during the development and production
of this book, and to them we express our gratitude:

All-State Legal Supply Company
Mountainside, New Jersey

James J. Barden, JD
Bay Path Junior College
Longmeadow, Massachusetts

Julius Blumberg, Inc.
New York City

The Colwell Company
Champaign, Illinois

Hobbs & Warren, Inc.
Publishers Standard Legal Forms
Boston

Betty Kirby, PLS
Past President
Texas Association of Legal Secretaries

Law Publications, Inc.
Los Angeles

Marjorie A. Miller
Association of Legal Administrators

Richard S. Milstein, JD
Ely, King, Corcoran, Milstein & Beaudry
Springfield, Massachusetts

Rosemont Forms
Bryn Mawr, Pennsylvania

Safeguard Business Systems, Inc.
Fort Washington, Pennsylvania

Marie Gould Seaton, MEd
Bay Path Junior College
Longmeadow, Massachusetts

Ross A. Sussman
LAWDEX—Shafer & Feld, Inc.
Minneapolis, Minnesota

Western Union Corporation
Corporate Communications Department
Upper Saddle River, New Jersey

# PREFACE

The book that you are reading is a product of Merriam-Webster Inc., publisher of the Merriam-Webster dictionaries and reference books. *Webster's Legal Secretaries Handbook* is the result of Merriam's collaboration with 15 specialists in the fields of law, law office management, records administration, financial administration, business education, word processing, and law libraries—and, of course, in the legal secretarial field. The combined experience and technical expertise of these specialists have produced the 18 chapters in the book.

**Direction and scope**  *Webster's Legal Secretaries Handbook* is directed to legal secretaries and legal assistants who are employed or expect to be employed in a law firm. The book concerns itself mainly with the *administrative* procedures and responsibilities that these people are expected to carry out. Other books exist for the purpose of explaining specific legal procedures in detail; this one goes into detail on the organization and administration of a law office. Some of the very important topics of interest to practicing legal secretaries and assistants are these: telephone techniques, reminder systems, records management, accounting systems, the use of printed forms, arranging out-of-town trips for the attorney, setting up meetings, and managing a small law library.

Office supervisors, transcribers, and typists employed by large law firms and the legal departments of corporations will also find the book useful. These readers will be particularly interested in the material devoted to the writing of effective English, the typing of correspondence, dictation/transcription systems and techniques, and office copying equipment.

In addition, the book is directed to those readers enrolled in legal secretarial programs and to those considering reentry into the profession. Chapter 2 introduces the reader to career opportunities in different types of law offices, then takes the reader through every major step in the preemployment process. The proper ways of presenting oneself to a prospective employer by telephone, by letter, by résumé, and in person are explained. *Webster's Legal Secretaries Handbook* is a useful reference source not only for students but also for instructors who are preparing course outlines and lectures in legal secretarial studies.

It is equally important to mention the material in this book that is of interest to lawyers themselves: the questions listed in Chapter 3 for offices considering the purchase of a private telephone system, and those in Chapter 16 that should be asked before purchasing a copier; the discussion of financial management in Chapter 7; the guidelines in Chapter 8 for improving one's dictation techniques; the overview of text-editing machines and their special uses in Chapter 15; and the detailed discussion of English grammar and usage in Chapter 9.

**Textual organization**  Each chapter is introduced by its own table of contents listing in numerical order all of its major sections. In turn, the subsections of the chapters are introduced by highly visible boldface subheadings that alert the reader to the particular topics under discussion. When specific data are sought, one need only consult the detailed Index which will guide one quickly to the desired information. Furthermore, the text is copiously illustrated with diagrams, charts, tables, lists, and numerous facsimiles that offer abundant information in a concise, readable form.

**Special features**  This book is committed to a realistic, detailed presentation of the administrative functions performed in a lawyer's office. It takes into account the realities that face its readers from day to day: scheduling clients, storing and retrieving records, transcription problems, arranging a suddenly scheduled meeting—to name only a few. The book provides tested, workable problem-solving tips and procedures tailored to the practice of a sole proprietor as well as the larger law firm.

Chapter 18, The Law Library, merits special attention. Authored by an experienced law librarian and law library journal editor, the chapter first provides a comprehensive yet manageable survey of the sources most commonly researched by lawyers and checked by secretaries to verity citations. It also offers useful guidance to the legal secretary who manages a small law library.

Chapter 15, Text-editing Systems in Law Offices, is another outstanding feature of the book. In it, a word-processing specialist with a background in law office management provides an up-to-date overview of the equipment that is available to law offices and discusses how this equipment is used in specific legal applications.

Accurate, coherent—even attractive—written communication continues to be vitally important to lawyers and their secretaries. The written word is the lawyer's chief product, and communications sent from the office go a long way toward determining the lawyer's professional image. For this reason, more than 160 pages have been devoted to legal writing, business writing, and correspondence styles. Chapter 9, for example, contains guides listing many rules for the use of capitalization, italics, numerals, and punctuation in both general and legal writing. Each rule is exemplified by at least one verbal illustration. Further chapters provide specific advice on the format, punctuation, and typewriting of correspondence, client documents, and court documents.

A lawyer's practice can run smoothly only insofar as the staff members understand, accept, and carry out all assigned tasks competently and with minimal supervision. *Webster's Legal Secretaries Handbook* has been written to help you accomplish this goal.

**Editorial Credits**   *Webster's Legal Secretaries Handbook,* like other Merriam-Webster publications, represents a collective effort. It would therefore be ungracious and unfair not to recognize those Merriam staff members who have contributed greatly to the value of the book. Former staff member Anne H. Soukhanov provided the initial outlines of the book and suggested its scope and direction. Dr. Frederick C. Mish, Editorial Director, reviewed the entire manuscript, offered sound advice, and gave valuable guidance throughout the project. John M. Morse, Assistant Editor, directed the book through the stages of typesetting and printing. Claire O. Cody, Secretary to the President, and Helene A. Gingold, Editorial Department Secretary, prepared the typewritten facsimiles. The manuscript was typed by Barbara Winkler, Georgette Boucher, and Joan Lancour under the direction of Gloria J. Afflitto.

The Editors

# 1

CHAPTER ONE

# AMERICAN LAW AND THE JUDICIAL SYSTEM

## CONTENTS

# 1.1

## AN OVERVIEW OF AMERICAN LAW

The legal secretary is aware of the existence of law long before entering the law office. The contact has been made in many ways—driving an automobile at a prescribed speed limit, registering to vote in an election, taking out a marriage license, applying for a divorce, or purchasing food or clothing the production of which was regulated by one or more government agencies. In your position as legal secretary, it will be helpful if you are familiar with the origins of the law, the agencies that administer and interpret the law, and the individuals who interpret or administer the law. The legal documents prepared in your law office will have greater meaning if you can relate client to legal matter and legal matter to court or agency.

Although laws affect much of what we do and how we do it, rarely do we think of what law is. In simplest terms, laws are the rules and principles of conduct which are recognized, applied, and enforced by a court. A more formal definition of law, but one which nonetheless makes the same basic statement, is "that which must be obeyed and followed by citizens subject to sanctions or legal consequences." Matter of Koenig v. Flynn, 258 N.Y. 292, 301, 179 N.E. 705, 707 (1932).

Emphasizing the institutional aspects of law and the origin of laws, one can say that a law is a statute, bill, rule, or constitutional provision that, according to *Black's Law Dictionary*, includes the "body of principles, standards and rules promulgated by government," be it by executive decree, court decision, or legislative enactment.

If there is a single word which may be used to describe the philosophy of law and legal relations, it is *jurisprudence*. It differs from *justice*, which Black's defines as "the constant and perpetual disposition of legal matters to render every man his due." It is justice which is sought by the party bringing a dispute to a court and which is expected by all parties to the dispute. Jurisprudence, on the other hand, is a formal analytical science dealing with the principles on which legal rules are based.

## CIVIL AND COMMON LAW SYSTEMS

The two primary sources of American law are the civil law system and the common law system. The civil law system may be traced back to the Roman law from which most European law systems originated. It was brought to the Western Hemisphere by the French, Spanish, and Portuguese. The civil law system as it exists in Europe is the result of Napoleon Bonaparte's efforts; he provided for the drafting of the Code Civil or Code Napoleon, which restated the earlier principles of Roman law in more modern terms.

The common law system which developed in England is based on precedent. It incorporates no formal code; instead, the courts build the law by attempting to follow earlier recorded decisions in deciding subsequent cases.

Louisiana in the United States and Quebec in Canada are examples of political entities which apply the Code Civil as it developed in North America. Other jurisdictions in the United States and Canada follow the common law system.

## CLASSIFICATIONS OF LAW

Law may be classified in several ways: by type (written and common law), by source (constitutional, statutory, and case law), by the parties involved (public and private law), by substance (civil and criminal law), and by function (substantive and adjective law). Each of these classifications is discussed in the paragraphs that follow.

**Written law**   The two principal types of law are written law and common law. Written law, which is also known as *statutory law*, is defined in *Ballentine's Law Dictionary* as "law which is written in statutes, ordinances, by-laws, treaties and written constitutions." Written law covers federal and state constitutions and statutes and ordinances adopted by counties, cities, townships, and villages. It is written in the attempt to anticipate problems and disputes and provide for their solutions. The written law is laid down by a legislative body without regard to a particular dispute between two parties.

**Common law**   Common law is the law made by courts. It is also known as *case law* because it derives from judicial decisions of certain cases rather than from written statutes. Common law is more formally defined in *Black's Law Dictionary* as the law which "comprises the body of those principles and rules of action, relating to the government and security of persons and property, which derive their authority solely from usages and customs of immemorial antiquity, or from the judgments and decrees of the courts recognizing, affirming, and enforcing such usages and customs . . . ." This definition encompasses common law as it evolved in England and as it was passed on into American law. Prior to the development of written law, controversies were decided on the basis of established customs. If there were no established customs, judges decided a case on the basis of what they considered to be right and wrong. As these decisions began to be recorded, judges looked for guidance to the decision in a prior case that had similar facts. This is known as the *doctrine of precedents*. Another term for the concept of relying on precedent is *stare decisis*, which means "to stand by (previous) decisions." The doctrine of precedents is important because it provides for consistency in the application of common law and offers some assurance to a person seeking relief in the courts as to the rules of the game.

**Equity law**   A review of the common law is not complete without examining *equity law*. Equity has been summarized in Gifis' *Law Dictionary* as law which

developed as a separate body of law in England in reaction to the inability of the common law courts, in their strict adherence to rigid writs and forms of action, to entertain or provide a remedy for every injury. The King therefore established the high court of chancery, the purpose of which was to do justice between parties in those cases where the common law would give no or inadequate redress. Equity law to a large extent was formulated in maxims, . . . meaning that equity will derive a means to achieve a lawful result when legal procedure is inadequate.

Although a few states still have separate courts of equity and courts of law, most jurisdictions have merged the two bodies of law. While the historical justifications for equity law are declining, equity techniques continue to provide unusual and personal remedies for legal disputes of a civil nature. Two of the most familiar equity decrees are the *injunction* and *specific performance*. An injunction restrains a party from doing something which would cause irreparable harm if not enjoined or temporarily halted. For example, an injunction may order a manufacturer to stop dumping certain chemicals into a river. Specific performance requires the performance of a duty agreed on in a contract or other agreement. Both decrees are laid down by a court.

**Constitutional law**   A constitution is the basic framework for a legal system. It defines basic principles of law and delegates authority to various officials and agencies.

The United States Constitution is the supreme law of the United States. No other law or statute may impose upon its provisions. The Constitution provides in Article VI, Section 2 that it "shall be the supreme Law of the Land; and the Judges in every State shall be bound thereby, any Thing in the Constitution or Laws of any State to the Contrary notwithstanding." Nothing could be clearer than that.

The United States Constitution is divided into three parts. The first part, the original text of the Constitution, divides governmental power among the three branches of government (legislative, executive, and judicial) and between the federal and state governments. Powers not reserved by the United States Constitution reside with the states.

The second part of the Constitution is the Bill of Rights, which consists of the first ten amendments. The first nine amendments provide for and protect individual freedoms including freedom of religion, speech, press, assembly, and petition for redress of grievances. Other protections afforded are the ability to keep arms, the freedom from unreasonable search and seizure, and the right to speedy and public jury trial in criminal cases and jury trial in civil cases. These have been among the most widely debated concepts in constitutional law.

The third part of the Constitution—the amendments which have been added to the Constitution over the past 200 years—reflects the efforts to keep it current with respect to changing social and political needs. These amendments cover a wide range of subjects. The Thirteenth Amendment abolished slavery in 1865. The Fifteenth, Nineteenth, Twenty-fourth, and Twenty-sixth Amendments extended the right to vote. The Eighteenth Amendment prohibited the manufacture and sale of intoxicating beverages, and the Twenty-first Amendment repealed the Eighteenth Amendment.

Article V of the Constitution defines how amendments to the Constitution may be made: "The Congress, whenever two thirds of both Houses shall deem it necessary, shall propose Amendments . . . or, on the Application of the Legislatures of two thirds of the several States, shall call a Convention for proposing Amendments, which . . . shall be valid . . . when ratified by the Legislatures of three fourths of the several States, or by Conventions, in three fourths thereof . . . ."

States also have constitutions, which are often more detailed than the United States Constitution. Constitutions are further discussed on page 5.

**Statutory law**   Statutes are enacted by legislatures to regulate areas within the legislature's jurisdiction.

The U.S. Congress (by authority of Article I, Section 8 of the U.S. Constitution) has reserved to itself the power to regulate certain activities including patents, trademarks, copyrights, federal taxation, customs matters, the postal system, admiralty matters, bankruptcy, and diplomatic matters. It has the exclusive right to pass laws affecting these subjects. Congress also has power to pass legislation not specifically reserved to it by the Constitution, such as labor laws, pollution control laws, and laws in many other areas.

Laws passed by Congress must be signed into law by the President. These laws are published annually in the *Statutes at Large* and eventually compiled in the *United States Code* (U.S.C.), an official government publication, and the *United States Code Annotated* (U.S.C.A.), a commercial publication. To facilitate finding a statute, this Code is organized into 50 titles or subject areas. When a citation to one of these titles is made, the title number appears first. For example, 50 U.S.C. § 1511 cites to Title 50 (War and National Defense), Section 1511 of the *United States Code*.

### Titles of United States Code and United States Code Annotated

1. General Provisions
2. The Congress
3. The President
4. Flag and Seal, Seat of Government, and the States
5. Government Organization and Employees
6. Surety Bonds
7. Agriculture
8. Aliens and Nationality
9. Arbitration
10. Armed Forces
11. Bankruptcy
12. Banks and Banking
13. Census
14. Coast Guard
15. Commerce and Trade
16. Conservation
17. Copyrights
18. Crimes and Criminal Procedure
19. Customs Duties
20. Education
21. Food and Drugs
22. Foreign Relations and Intercourse
23. Highways
24. Hospitals and Asylums
25. Indians
26. Internal Revenue Code
27. Intoxicating Liquors
28. Judiciary and Judicial Procedure
29. Labor
30. Mineral Lands and Mining
31. Money and Finance
32. National Guard
33. Navigation and Navigable Waters
34. Navy (Eliminated by the enactment of Title 10)
35. Patents
36. Patriotic Societies and Observances
37. Pay and Allowances of the Uniformed Services
38. Veterans' Benefits
39. Postal Service
40. Public Buildings, Property, and Works
41. Public Contracts
42. The Public Health and Welfare
43. Public Lands
44. Public Printing and Documents
45. Railroads
46. Shipping
47. Telegraphs, Telephones, and Radiotelegraphs
48. Territories and Insular Possessions
49. Transportation
50. War and National Defense

Each year the legislative body in each state passes many laws which are then approved by the governor. The exact titles of the session laws—that is, the collections of statutes passed in each session of the legislature—vary, as do the titles given to the compilations of laws. Statutory compilations, which are collections of all the laws in force in a particular state, are ordinarily known as codes, revisions, or annotations. In Michigan, for example, they are known as *Michigan Compiled Laws Annotated* (Mich. Comp. Laws Ann.). In Minnesota, they are called *Minnesota Statutes Annotated* (Minn. Stat. Ann.), while in North Dakota they are called the *North Dakota Century Code* (N.D. Cent. Code).

All of the statutes for a particular state are published in annotated form by a private law-book publisher. The annotations will include legislative history, prior laws on the subject, applicable case law, references to law review articles, and other pertinent information. Statutory compilations are kept up to date by cumulative supplements.

**Case law**    Constitutional law, statutory law, and case law are the three primary sources of American law. Case law has been defined as the "aggregate of reported cases as forming a body of jurisprudence, or the law of a particular subject as evidenced or formed by the adjudged cases, in distinction to statutes and other sources of law" (*Black's Law Dictionary*). This means that as a court decides and reports its decision concerning a particular suit, this reported case becomes part of the body of law and is consulted in later cases involving similar problems.

Case law consists of reported decisions of both federal and state courts. These decisions may be divided into three primary categories: (1) interpretation of the United States Constitution and the various state constitutions, (2) interpretation of federal and state statutes, and (3) decisions based on British and American precedents involving matters in which no apparent constitution or statutory enactment applies.

**Relationship of constitutions, statutes, and the courts**    A doctrine known as the federal supremacy doctrine declares any federal law or constitutional provision to be dominant when a state and a federal interest are at odds. Federal laws must comply only with the federal constitution, but the laws of any state must comply with provisions of both the state constitution and the U.S. Constitution. In a clash between a federal and a state law, the federal law would prevail.

Ordinarily when a state legislature has spoken clearly on a subject through the passage of a law signed by the governor, the courts will not overrule the legislature. However, if a state legislature were to pass a law in violation of the state constitution—for example, a law requiring that all textbooks be submitted to a review board—the appellate court in the state could declare the law unconstitutional.

Except in the matter of constitutionality of laws or statutes, the legislative body has the last word. Courts will, however, interpret statutes and supply legal principles when no rule exists. Once the court decides what the legislature intended, the court's ruling has as much validity and importance as the statute itself, and it becomes part of the case law on the subject.

**Public and private law**    Another classification of laws evolving from both constitutional and statutory sources is based on the scope of the laws, i.e., on the parties to whom they apply. This classification includes public and private law. "Statutes may be called public because the rights conferred are of general application, while laws known as private affect few or selected individuals or localities." Garner v. Teamsters, Chauffeurs and Helpers Local Union No. 776, 346 U.S. 485, 494 (1953).

Private law governs the relationship between private citizens. Disputes may involve property, contracts, negligence, wills, and any number of other matters. Occasionally, as in marriage and divorce, the state may be involved indirectly but, as it is not itself a litigant, the matter remains one of private law.

Public law is a branch of law concerned with regulating the relations of individuals among themselves and with the government as well as the organization and conduct of government itself. It "concerns the interests of the public at large . . . [it] may be a general, local, or special law." Haas v. Hancock County, 183 Miss. 365, 370, 184 So. 812, 813 (1938). Public law disputes involve the state or its agencies in a direct manner. Usually the state is a litigant; it is often the plaintiff, the party bringing the suit to court. Examples of public law are municipal law, township law, criminal law, admiralty law, securities law, social security law, and aviation law.

When individual laws are referred to, however, there is a different kind of distinction between public and private laws. Specifically, a private law is a law which affects only selected individuals or localities, while a public law affects the welfare of the whole governed unit. A private law provides a kind of exception to the public rule.

**Administrative law**    Administrative law has become a major part of public law. Administrative law comprises the rules and regulations framed and enforced by an administrative agency created by Congress or a state legislature to carry out a specific statute. Administrative bodies, while primarily executive in nature, may also have powers to exercise legislative or judicial authority. For example, the Civil Aeronautics Board not only issues regulations for air transportation but also adjudicates some disputes between airlines and their customers. Among the areas of concern covered by federal administrative agencies are taxation and revenue collections, civil rights, the environment, banks and banking, labor relations, veterans, railroads, and securities. Some of the federal administrative agencies with which law firms come into contact are the Commodity Futures Trading Commission, the Consumer Product Safety Commission, the Environmental Protection Agency, the Federal Deposit Insurance Corporation, the National Labor Relations Board, the Occupational Safety and Health Review Commission, the Internal Revenue Service, and the Federal Trade Commission.

The best single source of information in the field of federal administrative procedure is the *United States Government Manual*. The official handbook of the federal government, this manual provides comprehensive information on the agencies of the legislative, judicial, and executive branches of government as well as quasi-official agencies; international organizations in which the United States participates; and boards, committees, and commissions. The manual is published annually by the Office of the Federal Register, National Archives and Records Service, General Services Administration, and is available from the Superintendent of Documents, U.S. Government Printing Office, Washington, DC 20402.

State and local governments also have administrative agencies. They may be a part of an executive department of the state government or they may be independent entities. These agencies tend to function in areas not preempted by federal agencies, but they may also be found in fields subject to both federal and state regulation. State administrative agencies often have jurisdiction over these areas: unemployment and workers' compensation, taxation, education, motor vehicles, and health and safety. States generally publish a "blue book," a directory similar to the *United States Government Manual*, and it is helpful to have one of these available in the office. Examples of local administrative agencies include zoning boards and sewer commissions.

Administrative law is becoming an important legal specialty. As government agencies proliferate and their rules and regulations increase, it is a rare business client who is not affected by one or more agencies. It is important for the law office to keep abreast of developments taking place in administrative law.

**International and maritime law**    Other, less well-known types of public law are international law and maritime law.

International law is defined in Ballentine's as the "rules and principles which govern the relations and dealings of nations with each other." International law would thus include international conventions, both general and particular, which are expressly recognized by the world states.

Maritime law is defined in Black's as "that system of law which particularly relates to marine commerce and navigation, to business transacted at sea, . . . to ships and shipping, . . . [and] to the transportation of persons and property by sea . . . ." The Constitution of the United States has been judicially interpreted as having transferred maritime jurisprudence from the sovereignty of the states to that of the nation. Thus, any action brought under this body of public law will involve the federal government either indirectly or directly as a party.

**Civil and criminal law**    Cases that come before a court may generally be divided into two categories: civil and criminal. Black's defines civil law as "laws concerned with civil or private rights and remedies, as contrasted with criminal laws." Civil law is in essence the law of private rights. In civil law there is a conflict of interest between individuals or groups at least one of whom has a complaint against another. The complaint may be caused by the failure of a party to carry out an agreement or by a different kind of injury, called a tort, that does not involve a contractual relationship. When a civil case is brought, a private party seeks resolution of a personal rather than a public dispute. The civil law has several subcategories including real estate, domestic relations, partnership, tax, contracts, wills and trusts, probate, employment, personal injury, water, oil and gas, school, municipal, securities, commercial, banking, and labor.

Crimes are torts against society, and criminal law is "that law which for the purpose of preventing harm to society, (a) declares what conduct is criminal, and (b) prescribes the punishment to be imposed for such conduct" *(Black's Law Dictionary)*. In criminal law matters, the action is always brought in the name of the federal government, the state, or a political subdivision because the case is based on the alleged violation of the rights of *all* the people. The remedy sought in a criminal case is intended to punish the offender. The major categories of criminal law are homicide, burglary, larceny, fraud, rape, and assault.

**Substantive and adjective law**   Substantive law consists of the principal rules which a court will apply in considering the rights and obligations set forth in federal and state statutes, whereas adjective or procedural law states the procedural rules by which a person can secure his or her substantive rights. Black's defines adjective law as "the aggregate of rules of procedure or practice . . .; it means the rules according to which the substantive law is administered." Adjective law deals with *pleadings*, which are papers that pass between the parties; *practice*, which refers to the guides to the conduct of litigation; and *evidence*, the distillation of traditional doctrine governing the admissibility of evidence to achieve fairness while avoiding unnecessary expense or delay.

Although adjective law does not state the law, it quite often outlines the law in a statement accompanying the statement of the procedures which must be followed in applying the substantive law. The adjective law enables the attorney to decide whether a case should go to federal or state court. Adjective law will tell the attorney when a lawsuit must be started, what pleadings are required of all parties, and what kind of evidence can be presented at trial. It can be as important as the substantive law in determining the outcome of a case. A knowledge of adjective law is generally more useful to a legal secretary than a knowledge of substantive law. It is necessary that the legal secretary be aware of the procedures and pleadings involved in a civil case in order that deadlines be met and papers properly served and filed.

# 1.2

## THE AMERICAN JUDICIAL SYSTEM

Article III, Section 1 of the United States Constitution creates the federal judicial system. It says: "The judicial Power of the United States, shall be vested in one supreme Court, and in such inferior Courts as the Congress may from time to time ordain and establish." Sections 2 and 3 spell out the extent of the judicial power afforded the Supreme Court and the inferior federal courts. In turn, the constitutions of the various states have created state judicial systems, many of them similar to the United States judicial system but each one separate. The complexity of a state judicial system is normally in direct proportion to the population of the governmental unit. The judiciaries of many states with small populations are much less complex than the judiciaries of some large cities in the more populous states. Furthermore, some of the municipal judicial systems are nearly as autonomous within the state system as the state system is within the federal system.

## THE COURTS

The term *court* has several meanings. One meaning encompasses all the persons who are assembled for the administration of justice. These include judge or judges, clerk, marshal, bailiff, court reporter or public stenographer, jurors, and attorneys. Or court may refer to the hall, chamber, or place where court is being held. Frequently the judge or judges themselves are referred to as "the Court." The courthouse includes the offices occupied by many of the persons associated with the administration of justice.

The two principal functions of courts are settling controversies between parties and deciding the rules of law applicable in a particular case. In general, the judicial process as carried out by the courts consists of interpreting the laws and applying them justly to all cases arising in litigation. Most courts do not give advisory opinions. Exceptions exist, however, where the constitutions of some states permit the supreme courts of those states to render advisory opinions to the legislature or governor concerning the constitutionality of a statute. A detailed discussion of civil and criminal trial procedures appears in section 13.1 of Chapter 13.

## JURISDICTION

Jurisdiction may be explained as the authority of a court to hear a controversy or dispute. Affirmative answers to the following questions will determine that a court has jurisdiction over a particular case:

1. Has the court been vested by law with authority to decide this kind of case?
2. Does the court have authority over the parties in the case?
3. Has adequate notice been given to the parties, so that the court can make a valid judgment affecting them?
4. Has the court acquired jurisdiction over any property involved in the case?

Another way of testing the jurisdiction of the court over a matter is to determine whether it has *in personam* jurisdiction over the litigants (who may live in different geographical areas) or *in rem* jurisdiction over the subject matter (usually physical property such as real estate) in a controversy.

**Original and appellate jurisdiction**  Jurisdiction is either original or appellate. A court of original jurisdiction has the authority to receive the case when begun, to try the case, and to render a decision based on the law and facts presented. Appellate jurisdiction is set by statute or constitution. It is the authority to review, decide, or revise the action of a lower court.

The American judicial system at the state level and at the federal level is pyramidal and hierarchical. The courts at the top of the pyramid are supreme courts. Supreme courts are normally appellate courts, although they may have original jurisdiction in some matters. Below the supreme appellate courts are the courts of general jurisdiction. These courts have appellate jurisdiction and supervisory control over inferior courts except as laws provide otherwise, but they are also courts of original jurisdiction in certain areas prescribed by constitution or statute. Inferior courts are courts of limited jurisdiction whose decisions are subject to review and correction by higher courts.

**Concurrent and exclusive jurisdiction**    Jurisdiction is exclusive when only one court is empowered by law to hear the case in question. It is concurrent when the plaintiff has a choice of courts in which to initiate litigation.

**Diversity jurisdiction**    The federal courts have constitutional authority to try cases under diversity jurisdiction, which occurs when the litigants are resident in different states. Congress has added other stipulations, however—such as a minimum economic value involved in the dispute—before diversity cases may be decided in federal trial courts.

**Equity**    Most courts of general jurisdiction serve as both court of common law and court of equity. These courts frequently set different dockets and follow different procedures for cases in law and cases in equity. As combined law and equity courts they are able to award both money damages and equitable relief in the form of either injunction or specific performance. Some states, however—Arkansas, Delaware, Mississippi, New Jersey, and Tennessee—continue to maintain separate chancery courts or courts with chancery divisions that have general equity jurisdiction. The judges in these courts of equity are called chancellors.

**Courts of limited jurisdiction**    Inferior courts are courts of limited jurisdiction whose decisions are subject to review and correction by higher courts. Courts of limited jurisdiction are ordinarily created by statute, and their jurisdiction is limited to those matters set forth in the statute creating the court. Courts of limited jurisdiction may be called district courts, county courts, municipal courts, justice courts, county district courts, juvenile courts, or probate courts. Courts of limited jurisdiction may have exclusive jurisdiction where the amount of controversy does not exceed a fixed amount, perhaps $5,000. Courts of limited jurisdiction may also have jurisdiction over minor criminal matters, such as misdemeanors. A record may be kept in courts of limited jurisdiction. However, in small claims divisions of district courts and in justice of the peace courts, municipal courts, or magistrate's courts, no record is usually kept.

## THE FEDERAL COURT SYSTEM
The federal courts form a part of the United States judicial system, the jurisdiction of which is prescribed by Article III of the United States Constitution. The federal court system consists of a large number of district courts which are courts of general jurisdiction, twelve circuit courts of appeal, a Supreme Court, and a number of specialized courts.

**The Supreme Court of the United States**    The Supreme Court of the United States was created in accordance with Article III, Section 1 of the United States Constitution and was organized on February 2, 1790. The Supreme Court is comprised of the Chief Justice of the United States and a number of associate justices as Congress decides. Currently there are eight associate justices. The President of the United States has the power to nominate the justices, and appointments are made with the advice and consent of the Senate. The Supreme Court's term runs from October of each year until business is completed, usually about the end of June. The nine justices sit *en banc* (in full court). Six justices constitute a quorum, but certain cases can be acted upon by a single justice.

Article III, Section 2 of the United States Constitution defines the original and exclusive jurisdiction of the Supreme Court as (1) all controversies between states, and (2) all actions or proceedings against ambassadors or other public ministers of foreign states or their domestic servants, not inconsistent with the law of nations. The Court has original, but *not* exclusive, jurisdiction over (1) all actions or proceedings brought by ambassadors or other public ministers of foreign states or to which consuls or vice consuls of foreign states are parties; (2) all controversies between the United States and a state; and (3) all actions or proceedings by a state against the citizens of another state or against aliens.

The Court only occasionally hears cases in original jurisdiction, however; its chief function is as an appellate court. The Supreme Court may review cases from the U.S. courts of appeals either by writ of certiorari (a writ of a superior court to call up the records of an inferior court or quasi-judicial body) granted upon petition of any party to a civil or criminal case, before or after rendition of judgment or decree, or by appeal of a party relying on a state statute held by the court of appeals to be unconstitutional or illegal. A majority of its cases come on petition for certiorari from courts of appeals. The process of appeal precludes review by writ of certiorari by the appellant, and the review is limited to the federal questions presented.

The Supreme Court also has appellate jurisdiction over the final judgment of the highest court of a state in which a decision may be had if (1) there is a question as to the validity of a treaty or statute of the United States and the state court has decided against its validity or (2) the state court rendered a decision approving a state statute that is questioned as being unconstitutional or illegal. More than 40 percent of the Supreme Court's cases come from state supreme courts.

The Supreme Court of the United States normally reviews fewer than two hundred cases each year. By contrast, it refuses to review about two thousand cases each year: the majority of its decisions consist of denials of certiorari to review decisions of courts of appeal or state supreme courts.

The Supreme Court also possesses statutory power to prescribe rules of procedure to be followed in the lower courts of the United States. Studies are carried out and rules recommended by the Judicial Conference of the United States, the main policy-making group for the federal judiciary. The Supreme Court has set rules of procedure governing such matters as bankruptcy proceedings, copyright cases, appellate proceedings, civil law, and criminal law. These rules of procedure for the federal courts are published with the decisions of the Supreme Court in the *United States Reports* and also with the statutes of Congress in the *United States Code*.

**United States Courts of Appeal**   The courts of appeal were created by the act of March 3, 1891, to relieve the Supreme Court of considering all appeals for cases originally decided by the federal trial courts. By statute (28 U.S.C. 1291, 1292), they are empowered to review all final decisions and certain interlocutory decisions of federal district courts, although there are exceptions where direct review by the United States Supreme Court is provided. The courts of appeal are also empowered to review and enforce orders of many federal administrative bodies such as the National Labor Relations Board and the Federal Trade Commission and also to review appeals from the Tax Court of the United States. Decisions of the court of appeals are final, except as to discretionary review by or appeal to the Supreme Court. Each of the 50 states is assigned to one of the 11 judicial circuits, and there is an additional circuit for the District of Columbia. Each court of appeals usually hears cases in divisions consisting of a panel of three judges; however, it may sit *en banc* with all judges present. There are three to nine judges assigned to each U.S. Court of Appeals. Individual judges make decisions for the court only in procedural matters.

**United States District Courts**   The district courts are federal trial courts with general federal jurisdiction. There is at least one district court in each state while some larger states have as many as four. There are in all 89 federal district courts in the 50 states plus one in the District of Columbia and one in Puerto Rico. Each federal district

**Circuits of the United States Courts of Appeal**

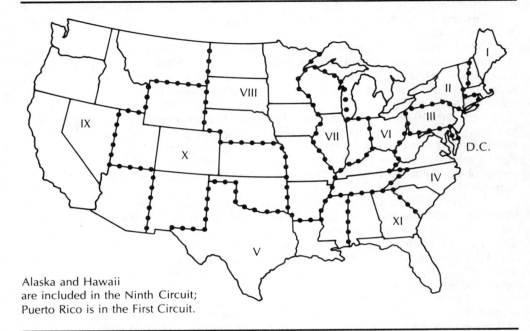

Alaska and Hawaii
are included in the Ninth Circuit;
Puerto Rico is in the First Circuit.

court may have from one to 25 or more judges. Normally only one judge hears a case, but in certain cases a three-judge panel is required.

Each district court is served by a clerk, a United States attorney, a United States marshal, and one or more United States magistrates, bankruptcy judges, probation officers, and court reporters. Magistrates are federal judicial officers who serve under the general supervision of the federal district, but who also have some responsibilities as defined in the Federal Magistrate Act of 1979.

The jurisdiction of the federal district courts is set forth in 28 U.S.C. 1331–1359, 1361. They possess only original jurisdiction. Among the cases tried are those involving crimes against the United States, cases involving diversity of citizenship—i.e., cases in which a citizen of one state brings a suit against a citizen of another state—admiralty and maritime cases, cases involving review and enforcement of orders of most federal administrative agencies, and civil cases arising under federal statutes, treaties, or the Constitution if the value of the controversy is in excess of $10,000. When the federal district court exercises diversity jurisdiction, it is not necessary for a federal question to be involved. In the diversity cases, the district court applies the law of the state in which the case arose.

The district courts have many administrative functions too, such as the naturalization of aliens and the approval of passport applications. Bankruptcy and parole cases form a large part of their work in addition to the regular civil and criminal cases.

**Special United States courts**   In addition to the courts discussed above, Congress has created from time to time special courts to deal with particular kinds of cases. Appeals from decisions of these courts may ultimately be reviewed by the Supreme Court. Among these courts are two created for the District of Columbia—the Superior Court and the District of Columbia Court of Appeals. Other courts include the Temporary Emergency Court of Appeals; the United States Court of Military Appeals, which is concerned exclusively with criminal law; and the Territorial Courts. The four major special courts—the United States Court of Claims, the United States Court of Customs and Patent Appeals, the United States Customs Court, and the United States Tax Court—are described here.

The United States Court of Claims was established in 1855. It has original jurisdiction to render judgment on claims against the United States. Examples are claims for compensations for the taking of property, claims arising under construction and supply contracts, claims by civilian and military personnel for back pay and retirement pay, and claims for the refund of federal income and excise taxes. The demonstrated purpose of the court was to relieve Congress of pressure to pass private bills to resolve claims. If the monetary amount of damages is small, claims may be settled by the federal executive departments involved; but large claims are filed either in the district courts or in the Court of Claims, which have concurrent jurisdiction. Judgments of the court are final and conclusive on both parties, subject to review by the Supreme Court on writ of certiorari.

The United States Court of Customs and Patent Appeals was created by Act of Congress in 1929 as successor to the United States Court of Customs Appeals. It consists of a chief judge and four associate judges, and it sits *en banc*. The jurisdiction of the court is nationwide, and among the appeals it hears are those from the United States Customs Court and the United States International Trade Commission. The judgments of the court are final and conclusive unless reviewed by the Supreme Court under writ of certiorari.

The United States Customs Court was created in 1926. Through subsequent legislation it was integrated into the federal court system and became a court of record. This court and the U.S. Court of Customs and Patent Appeals deal with questions of external revenue, while the United States Tax Court deals with questions of internal revenue. The U.S. Customs Court has exclusive jurisdiction of civil actions arising under the tariff laws, such as controversies over the appraised value of imported merchandise. The court has a chief judge and eight judges, not more than five of whom can belong to the same political party. The Chief Justice of the United States may temporarily designate and assign any of its judges as a federal district court judge. Ordinarily cases are tried before a single judge, although a three-judge panel may be used. Appeals are taken to the Court of Customs and Patent Appeals. The principal offices of the court are in New York City, but its nine judges are divided among three divisions which can conduct trials in ports other than New York.

The United States Tax Court is a court of record under Article I of the United States Constitution. The tax court tries and decides controversies involving deficiencies or overpayments in income, estate, gift, and personal holding company surtaxes in cases where deficiencies have been determined by the Commissioner of Internal Revenue. It hears taxpayers' claims against the Internal Revenue Service after the machinery of administrative adjudication within the Treasury Department has been exhausted. Other than in small tax cases, all decisions are subject to review by the United States Courts of Appeals and ultimately by the Supreme Court upon granting of a writ of certiorari. The court, which is located in Washington, D.C., has 16 divisions, one for each of its judges. Trials are public and are conducted by single judges in locations throughout the country.

## THE STATE COURT SYSTEMS

The judicial power of the states is limited by the United States Constitution, which states: "Full Faith and Credit shall be given in each State to the public Acts, Records, and judicial Proceedings of every other State" (Article IV, Section 1). It is further limited by the Fourteenth Amendment, Section 1, which states: "No State shall make or enforce any law which shall abridge the privileges or immunities of citizens of the

United States; nor shall any State deprive any person of life, liberty, or property, without due process of law; nor deny to any person within its jurisdiction the equal protection of the laws.''

Federal courts have exclusive jurisdiction in those areas provided by the United States Constitution—conflicts between states, conflicts between a state and the United States, petitions for federal regulatory agencies to enforce a decision, and prosecution of national criminal laws—and federal statutes and state courts cannot invade this jurisdiction. State courts, in turn, usually have exclusive jurisdiction over matters not held by the federal courts. Two areas which have remained exclusive to the states are probate and domestic relations. However, state courts may hold concurrent jurisdiction with federal courts in many other areas; there are many situations where claims may be litigated at the election of the plaintiff in either a federal or state court. If there is no overriding federal provision for cases involving diversity jurisdiction, federal and state forums are equally available. It is in the state courts, however, that most of the litigational problems that arise in the lives of most U.S. citizens are resolved. Conflicts resolved by state courts include those involving domestic relations, common crimes and misdemeanors, business relationships, morals offenses, personal injury and property damage, and aspects of business practice such as labor-management relations.

**State supreme courts**    The highest court in a state is usually called the Supreme Court, although in some states it is called the Court of Appeals (New York and Maryland), the Supreme Court of Appeals (West Virginia), or the Supreme Judicial Court (Maine and Massachusetts).

The supreme court in most states is given supervisory control over and appellate jurisdiction from all other courts in the state judicial system, limited only by the constitution and statutes. The supreme appellate court draws its authority from the state constitution. Appeals to the supreme court from lower state courts may be either *of right* or *on leave* granted by the court. The court rules and/or statutes will set forth the grounds on which either may be accomplished. In the few states that do not have an intermediate appellate court, appeals are made directly to the supreme appellate court. States with an intermediate appellate court usually require that an appeal from a court of original jurisdiction go to the intermediate court, but in very limited situations they may provide for direct appeal to the supreme appellate court. For example, in Illinois direct appeal to the state supreme court is possible in cases in which a circuit court imposes the death penalty. Ordinarily the state supreme court has very few areas of original jurisdiction. They are commonly limited to writs of mandamus, certiorari, habeas corpus, and the like.

**Intermediate appellate courts**    Thirty states have intermediate courts of appeal. In most cases the intermediate appellate court was created to lessen the caseload of the supreme appellate court. Intermediate appellate courts ordinarily have initial appellate jurisdiction over the final judgments of a state's superior court of general jurisdiction. Other courts may, by leave to appeal, reach the intermediate appellate court. The jurisdiction of the intermediate court of appeal may be established by statute, by rule of the supreme appellate court, or both. Intermediate courts of appeal may exercise original jurisdiction when it is required for the complete determination of a case on review and may issue certain writs when permitted by statute or court rule.

**Circuit courts**    Below the supreme and intermediate appellate courts in the state judicial hierarchy is the trial court of general jurisdiction. It may be called the circuit court, the superior court, the district court, the court of common pleas, or, in New York, the supreme court.

## American Federal Court System

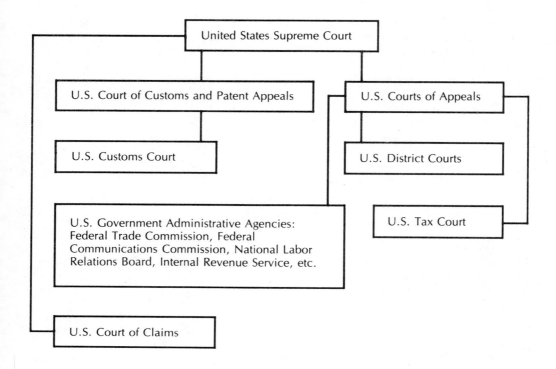

This court ordinarily has the authority to try both civil and criminal cases except where the constitution or a statute has limited that jurisdiction. Circuit courts are courts of record and are normally empowered to try cases arising under both equity and common law. The circuit court usually has appellate jurisdiction and supervisory control over inferior courts except as provided by law, and it ordinarily possesses the power to issue extraordinary writs. A basic rule to remember is that the circuit court has original jurisdiction in any matter unless that jurisdiction has been specifically placed in some other court by the state constitution or by statute. For example, the circuit court in Michigan has jurisdiction in such matters as divorce, injunctions, orders of mandamus, class actions, declaratory judgments, writs of habeas corpus, foreclosures of mortgages and land contracts, determinations of title to land, felonies, and serious misdemeanors. The circuit court can also hear appeals of cases from lower courts such as the district court, probate court, and municipal and county courts and from certain state agencies. It also exercises some control or supervision over the system of lower courts through appeals, error, and certiorari.

Circuit courts are geographically organized, with each circuit serving one or more counties. Each circuit may have one or more judges assigned to it, although each case is usually heard by a single judge.

State courts of general jurisdiction are courts of record. This means that their acts, decisions, and proceedings are documented in a written record that is maintained by the clerk of the court. Records of court decisions and the processes that led to those decisions are important. Without such records it is difficult to challenge a decision successfully in a higher court.

**American State Court Systems**

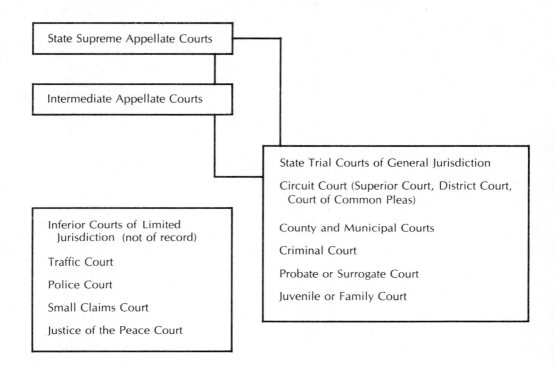

State Supreme Appellate Courts

Intermediate Appellate Courts

State Trial Courts of General Jurisdiction

Circuit Court (Superior Court, District Court, Court of Common Pleas)

County and Municipal Courts

Criminal Court

Probate or Surrogate Court

Juvenile or Family Court

Inferior Courts of Limited Jurisdiction (not of record)

Traffic Court

Police Court

Small Claims Court

Justice of the Peace Court

**County courts**   Sixteen states still have county courts. A county court is usually established on the basis of one for each county, but some states, to more effectively use the county court judges, have established multi-county districts. County courts may have exclusive jurisdiction over misdemeanor offenses and matters involving limited amounts of money. They may have concurrent jurisdiction with the circuit court in domestic relations cases. County courts in some states also act as probate courts, probating wills and handling matters involving juveniles. A few states have reversed the titles and jurisdictions so that the county courts are courts of general jurisdiction and the district courts possess limited jurisdiction. A number of district or county courts have established small claims divisions, which have very limited jurisdiction. In these divisions the parties represent themselves, the court is not of record, and there is no right of appeal. A call to the clerk of court in the courthouse nearest you or a review of the blue book published by your state will provide you with the correct information about the small claims court.

**Municipal courts**   Thirty-four states still have municipal courts. The jurisdiction of these courts may vary from major matters of the type usually handled by the circuit court to lesser matters such as traffic offenses, minor criminal matters, ordinance violations, and probable cause hearings. The jurisdiction of the municipal court will ordinarily determine whether it is a court of record, and that in turn determines whether and to what court an appeal may be taken. The territorial authority of the municipal court is ordinarily confined to the city or county where the court is located.

**Inferior courts of limited jurisdiction**   Courts of limited jurisdiction include probate or surrogate courts, family law courts, traffic courts, and a group of inferior courts variously designated as justice courts, justice of the peace courts, magistrate's courts, and police courts.

Twenty-one states have separate probate or surrogate courts. Probate courts are courts of limited jurisdiction. The jurisdiction is limited in subject matter but not by geographical or monetary restrictions. In some states probate courts may be organized into districts with a single court serving more than one county. The jurisdiction of the probate court is ordinarily limited to the settlement of estates, wills, and guardianship of minors and mental incompetents. In some states the probate courts also have jurisdiction over juvenile delinquents, dependents, and the adoption of children. Appeals from probate court are ordinarily taken to the state court of general jurisdiction.

Sixteen states have either juvenile or family law courts. Juvenile courts standing alone will ordinarily have exclusive original jurisdiction over all neglected, dependent, or delinquent children under a certain age. Family law courts will have exclusive jurisdiction over divorce, separation, annulment, support actions, suits involving temporary custody of children, and adoption. In some cases the functions of the juvenile and family law courts are combined, and the court has original jurisdiction over all of these matters.

Traffic courts are courts of limited jurisdiction geographically, monetarily, and with respect to the punishment which may be meted out. Jurisdiction is ordinarily limited to misdemeanors and traffic violations. While the traffic court is not a court of record, the right to appeal depends on the statute creating the court.

A few states have retained the police court. Jurisdiction is limited to misdemeanor offenses and to the conduct of preliminary examinations determining whether there is sufficient evidence to bind the case over to the court with jurisdiction for further proceeding. In some states the police court has jurisdiction to try civil cases within geographical and monetary limits.

## THE INTERNATIONAL COURT SYSTEM

Throughout the twentieth century, the leading nations of the world have sought a way to resolve international disputes. The ways in which this might be accomplished were discussed at the Hague Peace Conferences held in 1899 and 1907. Out of these conferences emerged the Permanent Court of International Arbitration, with headquarters at The Hague, The Netherlands. The court consisted of a panel of arbitrators nominated by the contracting parties. Each party might nominate to the panel persons of known competency in international law and of the highest moral reputation who would accept the duties of arbitrator. From this panel, the parties might choose a tribunal to resolve their case. However, there was no obligation on the parties to resort to arbitration. While there were a number of weaknesses in this arrangement of ad hoc tribunals, it did lead to the inclusion of an arbitration provision in a number of treaties and to resolution of a number of international disputes by arbitration. Many of the procedures developed through this court have continued to be used to the present day.

Another major step in the resolution of international disputes was the creation of the Permanent Court of International Justice in 1921. While not an organ of the League of Nations, it was the League's creation. Not all members of the League of Nations were a party to the statute creating the Court, however. During its existence the Court was called upon to decide 54 cases involving both decisions and advisory opinions. By the time it was abolished by the establishment of the World Court, the Court appeared to demonstrate that a permanent international judicial organ was feasible and helpful.

**The International Court of Justice**  The creation of the United Nations at the close of World War II resulted in the establishment of the International Court of Justice, or World Court. The International Court of Justice is the principal judicial organ of the United Nations—unlike the Permanent Court of International Justice, which was not a part of the League of Nations. The United Nations Charter provides that all members of the U.N. are parties to the statute creating the Court and that nonmembers may become parties on certain conditions. Each member of the United Nations must seek to comply with the decision of the Court if it is a party in any case, and failure of a party to comply permits the other party to have recourse to the Security Council. The General Assembly, the Security Council, and other organs and agencies of the United Nations are encouraged to seek advisory opinions from the Court, and member states of the U.N. are not precluded from seeking other tribunals to solve their differences.

Articles 34 through 39 of the statute creating the Court establish the proper jurisdiction. Only states, not individuals or other organizations, may be parties in cases before the World Court, although the Court may request information of public international organizations when such information is relevant to a matter before it. The Court is also obligated to advise a public international organization in writing when a constituent document of that organization is before it. The jurisdiction of the Court comprises all cases that parties refer to it and all matters provided for in the United Nations Charter or treaties or conventions in force. It further provides that states which are parties to the statute may recognize as compulsory the jurisdiction of the Court in the following legal matters: the interpretation of a treaty, a question of international law, the existence of a fact which if established would constitute a breach of an international obligation, and the nature or extent of reparation to be made for breach of an international obligation.

In making its decisions the Court is required to apply international conventions, international custom, the general principle of law applied by civilized nations, and judicial decisions and teachings of highly qualified publicists of various nations. The decision of the Court binds only the parties and the case at hand, while the judgment is final and without appeal. Questions are decided by a majority of the court, and dissenting judges may write a separate opinion. The court is a continuous, autonomous body composed of 15 judges elected by the U.N. General Assembly on recommendation of the Security Council. They sit at The Hague.

**Court of Justice of the European Communities**  This court both resolves disputes among member countries of the European Economic Community (the Common Market) and interprets treaties among them. Attorneys representing multinational corporations may have to appear before their body, which sits in Luxembourg.

# 1.3

## OFFICERS OF THE COURT AND OTHER LAW ENFORCEMENT OFFICIALS

### OFFICERS OF THE COURT
The officers of the court are persons assembled at the court to administer justice. They include the judge, who is the principal officer of the court, lawyers, a clerk of the court, sheriff, marshal, bailiff, and possibly a constable.

**Judges**   The judge may be elected or appointed. Judges in the federal judiciary are appointed for life by the President of the United States with the advice and consent of the Senate. Candidates for the federal judiciary are cleared through the office of the Deputy U.S. Attorney General, who receives reports of each candidate from the F.B.I. and the American Bar Association. The Senate Judiciary Committee then conducts hearings on the nomination and makes a recommendation to the full Senate.

There are five methods of selecting judges in the states. The leading method is selection by partisan election, often following nomination at party primaries or conventions. Slightly less common is the nonpartisan election. The remaining states use either elections by the legislature, gubernatorial appointments, or the Missouri Plan. The Missouri Plan, so called because of its origin, was designed to overcome the weaknesses of the elective system. It permits the governor to select a judge from a list of nominees recommended by a special commission but also requires the judge to be voted on in a public referendum after serving for a period of time. In those states where judges run for reelection, the initial appointment is usually for one of two periods: until the next general election or for the unexpired term of the office to which the judge was appointed. These elections may be conducted on a partisan or nonpartisan basis. Depending on the state, a judge may run on his or her record or against one or more opponents.

At trials and hearings the judge presides and rules on issues occurring during the trial. In jury cases, the judge presides over the selection of the jury and instructs the jury concerning the law of the case. The judge may also be called upon to rule on motions made before the start of the trial.

From the time the oath of office is taken, judges at all levels are bound to conduct themselves in an ethical manner and to adhere to a code of professional responsibility. A Code of Judicial Conduct was adopted by the American Bar Association in 1972. The table of contents of the code follows:

Canon 1   A Judge should uphold the integrity and independence of the judiciary.
Canon 2   A Judge should avoid impropriety and the appearance of impropriety in all his activities.
Canon 3   A Judge should perform the duties of his office impartially and diligently.
Canon 4   A Judge may engage in activities to improve the law, the legal system, and the administration of justice.
Canon 5   A Judge should regulate his extra-judicial activities to minimize the risk of conflict with his judicial duties.
Canon 6   A Judge should regularly file reports of compensation received for quasi-judicial and extra-judicial activities.
Canon 7   A Judge should refrain from political activity inappropriate to his judicial office.

State laws determine whether the court officers are referred to as judges or justices. In most states, as in the federal judiciary, the term *justice* is reserved for the members of the supreme appellate court. It is important for the legal secretary to know the correct terminology when preparing court orders and decrees for the court's approval.

**Administration of the courts**   The Chief Justice of the United States is the chief administrative officer of the federal judiciary. His title implies that he is not merely the Chief Justice of the Supreme Court, but the Chief Justice of the entire United States. Each federal court of appeals and district court has a chief judge. With the assistance of a circuit executive, the chief judge of a circuit administers most of the work of the court of appeals. The chief judge of the federal district court usually takes responsibility for most of the administration of that court. However, chief judges do not have authority over the decisions of cases made by their fellow judges. In deciding cases, the authority of chief judges is the same as that of any other judge.

Chief justices of the state supreme appellate courts, depending upon the language of the state constitution, may or may not be the chief judicial officers in the state. As chief justices, however, they do have influence over the administration of the entire court system through the supreme appellate court's superintending or rulemaking power. They are also responsible for the administration of the appellate courts.

Chief judges of intermediate appellate courts are responsible for the administration of those courts according to the constitution, statute, or court rule describing their responsibilities. Within the power given it, each court establishes rules to assist in the administration of the court.

**Attorneys**    Attorneys are also officers of the court. They are responsible for the preparation, management, and trial of their clients' cases. Like judges, they are held to a code of professional responsibility. The nine canons of the ABA's Code of Professional Responsibility are the following:

Canon 1    A lawyer should assist in maintaining the integrity and competence of the legal profession.

Canon 2    A lawyer should assist the legal profession in fulfilling its duty to make legal counsel available.

Canon 3    A lawyer should assist in preventing the unauthorized practice of law.

Canon 4    A lawyer should preserve the confidences and secrets of a client.

Canon 5    A lawyer should exercise independent professional judgment on behalf of a client.

Canon 6    A lawyer should represent a client competently.

Canon 7    A lawyer should represent a client zealously within the bounds of the law.

Canon 8    A lawyer should assist in improving the legal system.

Canon 9    A lawyer should avoid even the appearance of professional impropriety.

If a lawyer is found guilty of violating these ethical standards, he or she is subject to discipline including reprimand, fine, suspension, and even disbarment. A legal secretary should assist the lawyer in adhering to these canons.

**Other court personnel**    Other officers assigned to the court include the clerk and the sheriff. The clerk schedules trials and officially records all court business. The clerk also receives and files all court papers including summonses, complaints, answers, amendments, motions, and appearances and is responsible for the care of the jury. The sheriff, in addition to keeping the peace in the jurisdiction, serves summonses, complaints, and other court documents and carries out court orders.

Marshals in federal courts are appointed by the President of the United States, with the advice and consent of the Senate, to serve four-year terms. They are responsible for (1) serving as marshals of the federal district court and of the federal court of appeals when those courts are sitting in the district, (2) executing all writs, processes, and orders issued under the authority of the United States, including those of the courts, and (3) paying the salaries and expenses of the United States attorneys and their staffs, circuit judges, district judges, court clerks, and the marshals' own staffs. Marshals and their deputies may also exercise the same powers as sheriffs of the state in which they are located.

The bailiff is responsible for the protection of everyone in the courtroom and for maintaining dignity and decorum during court proceedings.

Courts of record also employ a court reporter, who records, usually on a stenotype machine, every word spoken during a trial. Additional court personnel may include law clerks and secretaries assigned to judges, a vast number of office workers in the office of the clerk of court, probation officers with their clerical staffs, and law clerks to the court reporters. In the federal district courts there are bankruptcy referees and receivers and trustees in bankruptcy with their staffs; there are also U.S. Commissioners, the federal equivalents of state magistrates and justices of the peace. The larger courts may also employ a number of messengers and librarians.

## LAW ENFORCEMENT AGENCIES

**The United States Department of Justice**    The United States Department of Justice, created in 1870, is headed by the U.S. Attorney General, who directs all the affairs and activities of the department. The Department of Justice conducts all Supreme Court suits in which the United States is involved; the Solicitor General usually argues special cases for the government in the Supreme Court, while members of his staff represent the government in other Supreme Court cases in which the United States is a litigant. The Justice Department also represents the government in legal matters generally, giving legal advice and opinions to the President and the heads of executive departments when requested.

The Attorney General supervises these activities and also directs the United States attorneys and U.S. marshals in the judicial districts around the country. (There is one United States district attorney and one United States marshal for every federal judicial district.) The Deputy Attorney General is primarily concerned with criminal law or investigative matters; he also directs the Executive Office of United States Attorneys. The Associate Attorney General supervises civil matters and matters relating to the internal administration of the department. The assistant attorney general in charge of the Office of Legal Counsel serves as legal adviser to the President and the heads of executive branch agencies.

Divisions within the Department of Justice are the Antitrust Division, the Civil Division, the Civil Rights Division, the Criminal Division, the Land and Natural Resources Division, and the Tax Division. The divisions may institute investigations or supervise or direct litigation in federal courts. Other bureaus and administrative units within the Department of Justice are the Federal Bureau of Investigation, Bureau of Prisons, United States Marshals Service, Immigration and Naturalization Service, Drug Enforcement Administration, Law Enforcement Assistance Administration, Board of Immigration Appeals, and Parole Commission.

**State law enforcement offices**    The state attorney general is the principal law enforcement officer in a state. The office brings actions in the name of the state when appropriate, serves as legal counsel to the legislative and executive branches, and issues opinions clarifying or interpreting statutes. The attorney general may also intervene in suits where it is felt the state's interest should be represented. The office, however, is much weaker than that of the United States Attorney General.

The office of the public defender is now active in many states. Public defenders provide legal counsel for people of limited means in both trial and appellate courts.

# 2

CHAPTER TWO

# EMPLOYMENT IN A LAW OFFICE

## CONTENTS

# 2.1

## THE LEGAL PROFESSION

Ever since members of civilized society began talking and writing to each other, there have been people performing the functions of lawyers. In essence, lawyers learn the rules of the society in which we live and seek to interpret them in the interests of fair and just treatment for their clients.

Law in the United States is basically an adaptation of the common law of England. As described in Chapter 1, our law may be divided into two major categories: written or statutory law and case or common law. Laws written by the various state legislatures and by the United States Congress, as well as ordinances passed by local authorities, constitute statutory law. Examples of this category are laws prohibiting criminal behavior and statutes concerning price-fixing, pollution control, immigration, and so forth. For example, driving on the highway without an operator's license is illegal only because a legislative body has made it so by writing a law.

Case or common law is the vast body of law based on precedents. Much of it concerns business matters, family matters, and disputes among various members of society. For example, a decision by a court settling a dispute between neighbors in 1890 would be a precedent for a case involving similar facts that might come before a court in the same state in 1980. The opinion written by a judge of the court in the earlier case would be persuasive, although not necessarily controlling, to the judge considering the case in 1980. How well the 1890 case controls, or is distinguished from, the 1980 case depends in large degree on the abilities of the lawyers on each side who urge the judge either to follow the precedent or to distinguish the present case from it.

In our complex business world, many honest differences arise between competitors or between suppliers and purchasers or between landlords and tenants. In the settlement of these differences, the businessman first consults counsel—i.e., a lawyer.

The lawyer, after gathering the facts, examines the applicable statutes and then reviews the cases to discover how similar disputes have been decided in the courts in the past. Upon concluding the research, the lawyer forms an opinion and advises the client accordingly. The client will ordinarily set out to close the matter in keeping with this advice.

## LAW SCHOOL

The study of statutory law and case law comprises the principal portion of the law school curriculum. As a general rule, law schools require full attendance for three academic years. Requirements for admission to law school usually include a baccalaureate degree from a recognized college. In other words, a prospective lawyer spends four years in college followed by three years in law school.

The three-year law school curriculum varies from school to school, but certain required courses are common to almost all. Such required courses are those in contracts, property, civil procedure, evidence, criminal law, and torts. In addition, the law student takes elective courses as a way to gain some understanding of or entry into a particular field of law. These subjects may include taxation, trusts, wills and estates, energy, and antitrust, environmental, labor, and family law.

Upon the successful completion of the three years of study, most schools now confer the J.D. (Juris Doctor, or Doctor of Jurisprudence) degree. The LL.B. (Bachelor of Laws) was formerly the standard degree conferred by law schools. When the J.D. came to be commonly conferred during the 1960s, many previously earned LL.B. degrees were retroactively changed to J.D.'s.

A few law schools do not require a baccalaureate degree for admission. Several of these schools will accept less than the three full years of day study, substituting evening study and some work experience. Prospective students must verify ahead of time whether completion of the courses at such a school will qualify them to take the state bar examination. The degree conferred by such schools is usually an LL.B. rather than a J.D.

It is possible to continue legal education beyond the J.D. degree. The master's degree (LL.M.) usually involves one year of additional study which combines course work and research beyond the J.D. The Doctorate of Juridical Sciences (S.J.D.) is a graduate academic research degree that involves advanced academic work, while the Master's in Comparative Law (M.C.L.) involves advanced work for foreign-educated lawyers.

## ADMISSION TO THE BAR

Most law graduates are interested in practicing law, and in order to do so they must be licensed. Admission to the bar is ordinarily governed by the supreme appellate courts of the individual states, and the procedure varies from state to state. In most cases, passing a written bar examination is required. The bar examination includes both a multistate portion, which is given nationally, and an examination prepared by the law examiners in the state where the examination is taken. The bar examination is intended to be a comprehensive inquiry into the applicant's legal education. It may include such subjects as real property; wills and trusts; contracts; constitutional law; criminal law and procedure; corporations, partnerships, and agency; evidence; creditors' rights; practice and procedure in trial and appellate courts at the state and federal levels; and equity, torts, and sales. The examinations are usually held twice a year, shortly after the law school academic year ends and again shortly after the end of the calendar year. Most persons taking bar examinations find it useful, after completing law school, to take special six- to eight-week courses designed to prepare them for the bar examinations. These courses are conducted in many cities and are also available for programmed home study.

In addition to successfully passing the bar examination, an applicant must satisfy the state bar committee on character and fitness as to his or her good moral character. Once the applicants have met the requirements, they appear in court to take the oath as a lawyer.

Admission to practice in one state does not carry with it authority to practice law in another state. Ordinarily it is necessary that a lawyer from one state take the bar examination for the other state before being permitted to practice in the second state although, depending on the length of time the lawyer has practiced in the first state, the second state may either waive the examination or require only a short professional examination rather than the full new-graduate examination. The lawyer who is considering practicing in another state must check these requirements.

In addition to the requirement of admission to the various state bars, there are special admission requirements to practice in the federal courts. The requirements for admission to practice in federal district courts and courts of appeal vary. To be admitted to the U.S. Supreme Court, an attorney must have practiced for three years in the highest court in his or her state and also be nominated by a member of the Supreme Court bar.

## CONTINUING LEGAL EDUCATION

After admission to the bar, lawyers often attend continuing education courses to maintain and sharpen their skills. A few states have adopted mandatory continuing legal education rules which require all members of the bar to attend a minimum number of hours of continuing legal education each year. Every state, through its state bar association, law school, or a combination of organizations, has continuing legal education courses available. Lawyers who have been certified as specialists usually are obligated to attend a fixed number of hours of continuing education courses annually.

Most law offices also encourage their secretaries, legal assistants, and other staff members to continue their educations, often at the firm's expense.

## THE PRACTICE OF LAW

The vast majority of lawyers in the 19th century, like the doctors, were general practitioners. The lawyer who hung out his shingle in 1890 was usually prepared to accept any legal problem that came his way. And almost without exception, lawyers were men. As with doctors, all this has changed. Today there are many, many women practicing law, and there are many, many specialists in the profession.

**Law specialties**   The complexity of the law requires many lawyers to focus on a single area of the law. In addition, the prospect of a malpractice action being brought for handling a matter beyond the competence of the lawyer has contributed to this movement. The profession of law today falls into several major specialties such as corporate, tax, antitrust, criminal, family, aviation, customs and immigration, real estate, probate, medical malpractice, personal injury, administrative, patent, and bankruptcy law. Fields that have emerged recently and that are expanding at a rapid pace are those in energy and environmental law. In addition, the number of public interest law firms has increased, and many lawyers work in legal aid societies, storefront law offices, and organizations such as the American Civil Liberties Union. Among the specialties practiced by these firms are housing, child welfare, mental health, and prison law.

The rapid expansion of the need for lawyers and of the need for legal specialists came about during the Great Depression of the 1930s. The impetus came from the legislation enacted during that decade that was aimed, in particular, at preventing another depression. The corporate securities market became carefully regulated, social security legislation was enacted, the National Labor Relations Board was established, and the entry of government into other fields required the ordinary citizen unsophisticated in matters of law to seek legal help. Enter the specialist lawyer.

Although little official sanction was given to the various specialties for many years, some bar associations have now recognized certain of them and formed sections to help practitioners keep current with developments in their fields. Today, some state bodies governing the practice of law have recognized particular specialties, have set out the requirements for certification, and have certified lawyers who meet the requirements and apply for certification. Among the certified specialties at the present are those in the fields of workers' compensation, family law, criminal law, and tax law. It is important to note that certification as a specialist in a field is not a prerequisite to practicing law in that field. Any lawyer admitted to the bar in a particular jurisdiction who feels qualified to handle a matter in a specialty field is free to do so; the certification is merely a recognition by the jurisdiction's governing body that the lawyer has met its requirements for specialization in the field.

**Bar associations**    As noted earlier, the practice of law in each state is regulated by the state supreme appellate court. To carry out this responsibility, many state supreme appellate courts have established boards and delegated to them the duty to set the requirements for admission to the bar and to certify persons for admission to the bar. In some states, this responsibility is carried out by a recognized state bar association. In such instances, all lawyers must belong to the bar association in order to practice law in that state. In states where this situation exists and the lawyer is automatically a dues-paying member of the bar association, the bar is referred to as an integrated or unified bar. Among the states having integrated bar associations are Florida, California, Texas, and Michigan. In those states where admission to the bar does not require dues-paying membership in the state bar association, membership in the state bar association is purely voluntary. In these latter instances, the vast majority of lawyers belong to the state bar association despite the fact that such membership is not required. In a few states both integrated and voluntary bar associations exist.

In addition to state bar associations, lawyers may belong to local bar associations. These associations are generally interested in the administration of justice in a city, county, or judicial district. The local bar associations are voluntary.

There are several national bar associations. The two largest are the American Bar Association and the Association of Trial Lawyers of America. Both associations are voluntary. The American Bar Association (ABA), with headquarters in Chicago and with membership throughout the fifty states, is the largest. Membership in the ABA does not carry with it the authority to practice law, but membership is a valuable means of keeping current with developments taking place in the law and in maintaining relations with fellow lawyers throughout the country. In addition to providing a number of services for its members, it serves as an umbrella for a number of groups which are interested in a single legal specialty. The Association of Trial Lawyers of America is of particular interest to trial lawyers throughout the nation. Both organizations offer continuing education programs for lawyers.

The ABA recommends rules for the ethical conduct of lawyers, rules which have been adopted and followed by many of the state bar associations and legislative bodies. The ABA and the state bar groups are vigilant in seeking to maintain high standards of professional conduct on the part of all lawyers in their respective jurisdictions. It is through these bodies that disciplinary proceedings may be carried out which result in the censure, suspension, or disbarment of lawyers who fail to meet the code of professional conduct.

**Directories**    One important source of information about lawyers and law firms is the Martindale-Hubbell Law Directory, published by Martindale-Hubbell, Inc., Summit,

New Jersey, and available in law libraries and many city public libraries. It tells the size of the lawyer's office, the educational background of the lawyer, and the areas of practice in which he or she feels competent. Other directories such as the ABA directory and your state bar directory are also important reference books.

## PROFESSIONAL LIABILITY

Lawyers, like other professionals, can be sued for professional malpractice. In recent years, lawyers and members of the general public have placed increasing emphasis on the lawyer's responsibility to represent clients properly and with due care. There is no question but that some lawyers are more skillful and aggressive than others, but the fact that one lawyer may not be as skillful as his or her adversary in a case is not a cause for legal action. On the other hand, the lawyer who, through gross negligence or criminal act, causes a client to be penalized may be charged with the financial responsibility to reimburse the client. The most common example of negligence is failure to meet a statutory deadline. This would include the failure to start an action before the statute of limitations ran out, the failure to file an answer or to move for a new trial in a timely manner, or the failure to file a tax return or secure an extension for filing. If a penalty and interest are assessed against the client because the lawyer failed to meet a deadline, the lawyer may be required to make good the sum so lost.

An example of criminality on the part of a lawyer is the diversion of clients' funds entrusted to the lawyer's safekeeping. If those funds are expended in the lawyer's personal interest, not only is the lawyer financially liable, but he or she may be subject to criminal prosecution and may be suspended or expelled from the profession.

**Preventing liability claims**   Many lawyers now carry professional liability (malpractice) insurance, often through a bar association-sponsored insurance company. As claims against lawyers increase and are sustained, the cost of this insurance increases. It is expensive and sometimes difficult to obtain. Many insurance companies, for instance, refuse to provide professional liability insurance to law firms until they are shown, among other things, proof of an efficient docket control system within the firm that prevents the missing of deadlines.

The lawyer's secretary is in a good position to help prevent instances that give rise to liability claims and that raise the cost of the lawyer's malpractice coverage. Among the many ways that the secretary can contribute to safeguarding the lawyer's and clients' interest are (1) by ensuring that the lawyer and all law office staff members maintain good client contact, (2) by ensuring that the law office has a good calendar and docket system and that important dates are called to the attention of the responsible person, (3) by continually working to improve the efficiency of the law office, and (4) by ensuring a sharp and complete separation between the lawyer's personal funds and the funds of clients. This is accomplished by the creation of a client trust account. In the small office where responsibility for handling funds devolves upon the secretary, top priority must be given to preserving the integrity of client funds. Client trust accounts are described in Chapter 7.

# 2.2

## THE LAW OFFICE

### GROWTH AND SPECIALIZATION OF LAW FIRMS

Law firms have changed a great deal since Abraham Lincoln practiced with one partner a century ago. There are still vast numbers of single practitioners. However, the tendency is toward ever-larger law firms and increasing specialization. Moving upward from the single practitioner, we find the small partnership or professional corporation with anywhere from two to a dozen lawyers. Then the middle-size firm, which ordinarily has from 13 to 40 lawyers, is followed by the large firm with up to about one hundred lawyers. Finally, there are the giant firms which may exceed three hundred lawyers.

The interesting point about these organizations is that, essentially, they all function in the same way. The client comes to the firm, whether it has one lawyer or 125, discusses a legal problem with a lawyer who will prosecute the matter and, under an agreed-upon basis, is billed for services performed. The basic services that a lawyer provides have changed little in the last century. They still include researching the law, providing information about the law, and giving advice to clients on the basis of the law; representing clients in litigation and in non-litigation matters such as negotiations with a third party; and preparing documents such as contracts and wills.

As a firm nears the 12-lawyer size, its lawyers have begun, in varying degrees, to specialize. The lawyers have begun to recognize, for example, that one or two of their number are better qualified and more interested in business matters, two or three prefer to go into the courtroom and try cases, one or two are drawn to settling domestic disputes, and one or two enjoy workers' compensation cases. The result is that while the firm engages in the general practice of law, individual members of the firm pursue their special interests. They help each other by developing expertise in a particular field and sharing their knowledge with their partners.

**Multiple offices**    As law firms grow, especially in the big cities, they find it highly desirable to establish and maintain multiple offices. In New York City, for example, a number of firms have their main office in the financial or Wall Street area with other offices several miles away in the uptown or Rockefeller Center area. Similarly, many firms with primary offices in New York or Chicago or San Francisco or Los Angeles find it helpful to their clients and productive of additional business to establish offices in the suburban areas of those cities. Additionally, those firms representing clients with interests closely connected with state or federal government often establish an office in the state capital or in Washington, D.C., so as to represent their clients before government agencies in those cities.

A major contributor to the proliferation of offices of large firms is the nature of their clients' business. As American business grows, it grows both nationally and internationally. There are corporations in the fields of automobile manufacturing, pharmaceuticals, and petroleum with interests on almost every continent and in over 30 or 40 nations. Since protection and prosecution of these interests requires the intervention of lawyers, the firms representing such corporations have found it necessary and desirable to establish national and foreign offices. As a result, we find law firms with main offices in major cities in the United States maintaining offices not only in other states but in London, Paris, Abu Dhabi, Brussels, Tokyo, Hong Kong, and elsewhere as their clients' needs dictate.

An even more recent phenomenon is the merger of law practices with established firms in other states in order to create national law firms. Although such mergers are far from common, they are increasing and contributing to the acceptance of the multi-office practice of law as a professional way of life.

## LAW OFFICE ORGANIZATION

Just as the structure and nature of business organizations have become more complex, so have the structure and nature of legal organizations, whether they be one-lawyer or one-hundred-lawyer firms.

The smallest law office, of course, is that of the sole practitioner. It is rare that a lawyer can engage profitably in such a practice, however, without at least one non-lawyer employee. The non-lawyer employee may fill many roles including secretary/typist, receptionist, telephone answering service, supply clerk, and librarian. As the volume of legal business grows and the single lawyer takes on additional lawyer help, the nonlegal functions increase and additional lay personnel may be employed to fill a variety of positions, but there is always a need for the legal secretary. Without the secretary, the lawyer is limited in ability to reduce thoughts to paper and to transmit written documents to courts, clients, and adversaries.

At the other extreme from the single-lawyer office is the very large firm. Before examining the structure of such organizations, however, we must understand how law firms function as businesses.

The majority of lawyers practice either as sole practitioners or in partnerships. A *partner* is one of the proprietors of a law firm. He or she owns a percentage of the firm's capital (leasehold, furniture, accounts receivable, and goodwill) and is liable for the firm's obligations. An *associate* is an employed lawyer. The associate owns no part of the firm, is not obligated for any of the firm's liabilities, and is paid a salary. In some instances, depending upon the firm's prosperity, the associate may also receive a bonus. In many firms there is a middle level between partner and associate—the *junior partner*. Some firms also employ lawyers as regular staff. Unlike associates, these lawyers are not in line to become partners of the firm.

Most states today allow lawyers to form professional corporations or professional associations (thus the abbreviation P.C. or P.A. in a firm's name). A professional corporation is composed of a group of professionals practicing not as individuals or in partnership but in corporate form. A corporation enjoys limited liability but is subject to certain state regulations.

In law firms embracing more than three or four lawyers, the support, or non-lawyer, personnel may start to outnumber the lawyers. In the smaller firms, those under about 25 lawyers, the person in charge of the support personnel may be one of the senior secretaries or the firm accountant or one of the paralegals. As firms increase to more than 25 lawyers, these responsibilities begin to require the exclusive attention of one individual. When the firm reaches this size, its structure usually will be firmly fixed more or less along the lines of the chart on page 28. Office structures will vary in detail, of course, and may be influenced by individual capabilities and personalities. Despite such differences, however, they will all encompass the areas depicted in the chart.

The key person in the chart is often called the Director of Administration. Up until about 1960, a lawyer in the firm usually did double duty, serving both as a practicing attorney and as the managing partner or lawyer-administrator. In the sixties, larger firms began to recognize that the assignment of administrative duties to a practicing lawyer was a waste of legal talent. They then turned to finding and employing business managers to run the business part of the organization.

The chart indicates that the four major areas in the administrative organization have to do with personnel, office services, finance, and computer services.

Personnel, both support and legal, are the heart of the firm. Usually the lawyers are not directed by the administrator but rather by a professional personnel committee consisting of partners or, in some instances, by a lawyer who has been designated as the managing or senior partner. Support personnel are under the authority of the chief administrator. Depending upon the size of the firm, the top administrator may employ a number of assistants. The qualifications of these assistants often depend upon the qualifications of the administrator. For example, if the administrator is an accountant, it is likely that the top assistant will be qualified in the personnel field. Conversely, if the administrator is qualified primarily in the personnel field, the assistant may be a specialist in accounting or finance.

**Personnel Organization in a Large Law Firm**

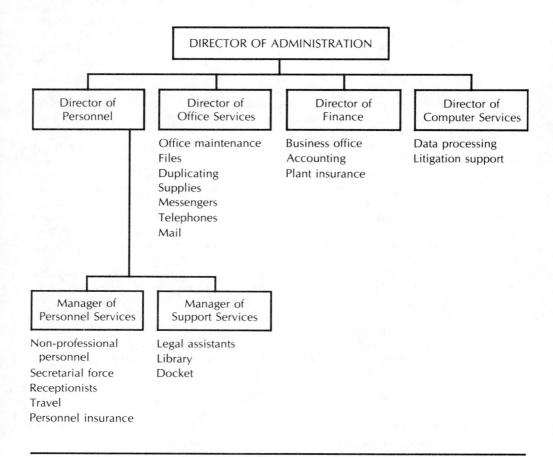

Large firms throughout the country now employ women in many of the key positions shown on the chart, including Director of Administration. This does not represent as much of a change as one might surmise since, for many years, law firms have employed women as their office managers and, as the scope of the job increased, elevated them to the position of top administrator.

Except for those positions listed within the finance and computer services departments, an ambitious and qualified legal secretary can fill any position named on the chart. A secretary should determine his or her qualifications to fill any of them and, if reassignment is desired, prepare for a particular job by study and training.

Assignments within the finance and computer services departments are quite different, since these areas require special education and training. Some legal secretaries with an interest or skills in finance have become qualified as accountants while carrying their secretarial assignments and have moved up to positions analogous to that of Director of Finance. There are instances of legal secretaries who have studied computer science and have become valuable to their firms in this area. This is the exception rather than the rule, however, since most legal secretaries prefer to remain aligned with the "people area" of a law practice, particularly lawyers, rather than becoming aligned with computers in the "things" area.

A final look at the chart is helpful. Observe that in the one-lawyer office, every function named in the chart, or an analogous function, is performed. Instead of a computer, you may have a calculator or an adding machine; instead of a section devoted to litigation support, you may be the person supplying such support as the lawyer requests. Normally, the secretary who is a jack-of-all-trades cannot be as efficient as a specialist, but is no less valuable.

## OFFICE DESIGN AND LAYOUT

**Making design decisions**  Designing, building, and furnishing a law office is a challenging and demanding experience. Naturally, the scope of the task depends on the size of the office planned. For a firm that numbers more than 25 lawyers, it is almost essential that an architect be employed. In such cases, a task force should be made up of three groups—the architect, the interior design team, and the ultimate user.

The architect is responsible for developing a space plan that makes maximum use of the space to be occupied and that provides each occupant with comfortable and adequate working quarters. The plan should take into account such key considerations as adequate lighting—not only for the lawyers, who spend a great deal of time studying documents, but for the secretarial and stenographic staff, who type and proofread documents. Adequate lighting, good air circulation, and good acoustics are the most important requirements for the space in which these people work.

The interior design group is responsible for making the space appealing and comfortable for the occupants. Wild colors or uncomfortable furniture, for example, can be deleterious to morale in the work environment and should be avoided. The impression that the office makes on clients must also be considered. A clean, comfortable reception area with a subdued color scheme and well-coordinated furnishings makes a positive impression on a client. Music and junk art are taboo.

The ultimate user, the lawyer, must be pleased with the result and for this reason should be consulted throughout the project. Lawyers usually know how their individual professional offices should be designed and furnished but, since they do not work in the secretarial area, advice on the design and furnishing of these spaces should be obtained from the secretaries. Many large firms place such importance on comfortable, attractive, and adequate secretarial work stations that, before giving approval to final plans, they insist that a mock-up of a typical secretarial work station be built, reviewed, and revised as appropriate by a team of the firm's secretaries. This practice has resulted in some invaluable suggestions being incorporated in the final design. Consequently, the secretary who is asked to comment on the design of a new work station or the revision of an old work station should not feel constrained to agree with the architect, the lawyer, or the interior designer but instead should offer constructive criticism aimed at improving the work area for all secretaries.

**Layout**  The layout of a law office depends almost entirely upon its size. A single practitioner's office may consist of only two rooms: the lawyer's private office and another room that serves as reception area, file room, and secretarial work area. If the reception room must serve also as a work area, care should be taken to separate waiting clients from the work area. This is important not only for the comfort of the clients but also for preventing visitors from viewing the work that is being done for other clients. Large firms may have separate rooms for the library, files, copying and duplicating equipment, word processing center, bookkeeping department, lounge, and the like. The private office of each lawyer may be attached to a private secretarial office.

Whether the firm is large or small, the attorney's office is always separate in order that the clients' affairs may be conducted in privacy. And whether the secretary has a private office or a work station, it must be easily accessible to the lawyer.

**Secretarial work stations**   A well-designed secretarial work station allows the secretary to reach all work areas without leaving her chair. There may be paper compartments above the drawers and pigeonholes to hold various items as needed. There should be shelves for books and binders, and storage compartments adequate for files. The entire area should be unenclosed, well lighted, and comfortable. Office policy will determine whether the work station may contain posters, children's art, plastic flowers, and the like. These decorations may distract the secretary and give clients the impression that their work is not being taken seriously.

Of course, in the modern office much of the typewritten work is accomplished in areas other than individual secretarial work stations—that is, in typing pools and word processing centers. Particular care must be taken in the design of these areas since many secretaries do not favor pool assignments. In order to attract good personnel to such assignments, the work space must be made particularly attractive. A big factor in the design of such spaces is the noise level. Noisy machines are sometimes segregated in enclosed spaces in order to prevent the transmission of sound in a wide area. Unfortunately, such separation, if carried to an extreme, will reduce the circulation of air and the availability of adequate light. The claustrophobic effect may bother some workers enough to reduce their efficiency. A better solution is to try to deaden the sound of typewriters and printers by the use of acoustical coverings and other means.

Lawyers, managers, and secretaries who are responsible for approving the design of multi-secretarial work areas should inspect work stations in other firms where similar types of equipment have been installed. Secretaries in such other firms will usually provide frank comments about their work areas, and a five-minute conversation may result in the savings of several thousands of dollars and assure better working conditions when new areas are built.

**The lawyer's private office**   Space planners and lawyers often provide too little space to support activities and more than enough space to individual lawyers' offices. Prior to about 1960, the status of a lawyer in a law firm was generally measured by length of tenure with the firm, reputation in the community, and size of the lawyer's private office. Successful lawyers near the top of their firms occupied offices measuring 15 by 20 feet or 20 by 20 feet, often located in the corner of the building. As rents escalated, this situation changed. Now it is not at all unusual to find all lawyers in a firm occupying offices of about equal size, ranging anywhere from 10 by 12 feet to 12 by 15 feet.

The reduction in size of lawyers' individual offices also results from the need of increased space for support activities—data processing, library, word processing, files, messenger services, reprographics, and the like. The staff providing these important services must have adequate space to operate efficiently. Here, again, input by the users should be obtained prior to approval and construction of any space for them.

## LAW OFFICE EQUIPMENT
**Typewriters**   A legal secretary requires a good electric typewriter. There are several excellent makes on the market as well as many so-called bargains. Machines in the latter category usually fail to provide good service or a high quality product after a relatively short period of time. On the other hand, a good self-correcting electric typewriter with a high-quality carbon ribbon is probably one of the best investments a lawyer can make for the office. The secretary should seek to have a voice in the selection of the make and model of the typewriter. The typeface should be uniform on all the office typewriters and should be chosen by the management of the firm, assisted by the secretarial supervisor. Pica type is preferred for legal work.

**Dictating equipment**  Many offices today have moved from person-to-person dictating and rely instead on dictating equipment. As in the case of typewriters, there are many good pieces of dictating equipment currently on the market. Before selecting a particular brand, the lawyer should determine which piece is best adapted to the needs of the firm and especially to the secretaries. This last concern is important because the fidelity of the playback will have a marked influence on the speed and accuracy of the secretary's transcription. Dictating equipment is discussed more fully in Chapter 8.

**Electronic equipment**  The emergence of electronic devices to assist secretarial production has caused a near-revolution in the legal secretaries' world. In addition to making it possible to do more work in less time, electronic word-processing equipment has split the traditional legal secretary's job in two. As explained in Chapter 15, many law offices now have administrative secretaries and word-processing secretaries.

The devices fall into three categories: stand-alone units, shared-logic units, and terminals tied to a minicomputer. Chapter 15 describes these machines and explains how each is used in law offices. The advanced automatic typewriter or text-editing machine commonly used by legal secretaries consists of a keyboard with a cathode-ray tube (CRT) display screen and a printer. The memory capacity of the unit permits it to retain, electronically coded and catalogued, thousands of words and documents. The operator can recall for display on the screen anything so retained by the unit's memory, revise it on the screen and, when the document is in final form, have it printed. Since much of a lawyer's work is repetitive—lease clauses, wills, contract provisions, etc.—a text-editing machine can save a great deal of lawyer and secretarial time.

As suggested above, in many offices that use electronic word-processing equipment the operators' duties are limited to operating the equipment. Whether the qualified legal secretary wants to become a word-processing specialist will depend almost entirely on the secretary's inclination and personal goals. While use of word-processing equipment clearly speeds the accomplishment of a task, it may diminish the valuable personal relationship between lawyer and secretary. If the secretary objects to working with word-processing equipment, such objection should be voiced at an early opportunity. In almost all cases, the individual lawyer or law firm will seek to accommodate the secretary's wishes. As in the case of office design, both the secretary and the firm benefit when the secretary is consulted and voices frank opinions about changes being made in the office.

# 2.3

## THE LEGAL SECRETARY

The well-organized lawyer will usually have a very clear concept of how the legal secretary should function. Much of this will depend on the lawyer's type of practice. For example, the litigator or trial lawyer often spends most of the working day in court. This means that the secretary will probably be expected either to arrive early in the morning so that, working together, they can plan what must be done in the office during the day; or to stay late in the day in order to plan how to process the work on the following day. At times and especially in some offices, this is not an either/or proposition, with the result that the secretary must arrive early and stay late. In such cases the secretary must try to organize the lawyer's work so that the hours it consumes can be reduced and overtime kept to a minimum.

## DUTIES OF A LEGAL SECRETARY

As noted in section 2.2, the secretary working in a single-lawyer office may do every-thing from taking dictation to brewing coffee. Depending on the size and nature of the office and the preferences of the attorney-employer, a legal secretary may be expected to perform the following tasks:

1. Typewriting correspondence
2. Writing routine business letters
3. Answering the telephone
4. Transferring calls to the attorney
5. Taking messages accurately
6. Placing telephone calls
7. Keeping a master telephone list
8. Filing and maintaining office records
9. Greeting clients and other callers
10. Making appointments and appointment reminders
11. Maintaining day books, diaries, and tickler files
12. Maintaining the court docket or suit register
13. Following court cases on court calendars
14. Serving as notary public
15. Maintaining financial records: bookkeeping, billing, banking, and collection for the firm
16. Keeping time sheets for the attorney
17. Transcribing, typewriting, and proofreading documents on electronic media
18. Taking live dictation and transcribing it
19. Preparing documents for clients (real estate, tax, wills, etc.)
20. Preparing documents for courts (probate, litigation)
21. Preparing copies of documents
22. Operating sophisticated telecommunications equipment
23. Using legal forms properly in preparing documents
24. Filing documents in the office of the clerk of the court
25. Preparing court documents for service to opposing parties
26. Handling incoming and outgoing mail
27. Ensuring that the suite is clean and orderly
28. Maintaining office and file security
29. Inventorying and ordering supplies
30. Handling the storage and circulation of library materials
31. Verifying citations
32. Doing library research
33. Making travel arrangements for the attorney
34. Arranging meetings and conferences for the attorney

As a firm expands with more lawyers, more space, and more support personnel, the secretary may drop many of the collateral assignments. The professional legal secretary's primary responsibilities are to be familiar with all aspects of the lawyer's professional work, including the needs of the lawyer's clients; to be able to take and transcribe dictation; and—an overriding requirement—to see that all legal deadlines are met.

**Office routine**   Almost immediately after being employed, especially in a well-structured law firm, the new secretary will be briefed by the head of the personnel department or someone else delegated the responsibility. The secretary will often be furnished a manual of information about the firm. The office or personnel manual should contain information about working hours, lunch periods, sick days, sick leave, vacations, major medical and life insurance, overtime procedures, banking facilities, how to answer the telephone, how and where to have copies made, and procedures for having work turned over to a typing pool or word-processing center. These are the topics that apply to all the office staff. In addition, the lawyer to whom the secretary is assigned should outline any routines or procedures peculiar to the assignment. If this is not done, the secretary should ask whether there are any special requirements. For example, does the lawyer wish to take all phone calls personally or is the secretary expected to screen incoming calls? Should the home telephone number of the lawyer be given to clients? If so, which clients? Lawyers are people and, like everyone else, they have their personal preferences and even idiosyncrasies. By identifying such requirements and learning to accommodate them, the secretary can contribute immeasurably to building a strong lawyer-secretary team and a pleasant working relationship.

## JOB QUALIFICATIONS

**Education**  The following indicates the educational background necessary for successfully performing legal secretarial duties.

**minimum**  high-school degree with courses successfully completed in business and general education (shorthand, transcription, typewriting, accounting, English, history, and government)

**average**  business college or two-year community or junior college degree, preferably an A.A. degree in Legal Secretarial Studies plus courses in economics, political science, and business law

**maximum**  bachelor's degree plus secretarial and business skills

**Dictation and typing skills**  The secretary is responsible for the appearance of the lawyer's end product, the legal document. Even if the content of a document is superb, the enthusiasm and degree of acceptance with which the document is received will depend to a large extent on how well the secretary has taken and transcribed the lawyer's dictation. Lawyers with years of experience quite often will state that fifty percent of their success in the practice is attributable to solid secretarial support, and a large part of that support is the production of accurate, attractive documents.

As education, training, equipment, and work spaces have improved, the speed and accuracy with which secretarial work is performed have advanced. At present, an acceptable typing speed is 60 to 70 words per minute, error-free. The norm for dictation speed is closer to 100 words per minute.

In recent years, there has been less emphasis placed on person-to-person dictation, partly as a result of advances in dictating equipment. The ability to transcribe machine dictation has become increasingly important. Many recently admitted lawyers have been trained to dictate to a machine and prefer to do so. The secretary should welcome the opportunity to build and maintain a skill in transcribing machine dictation in order to be more valuable to the firm. At the same time, the secretary should take advantage of opportunities to take dictation in shorthand. Only with practice can skills be kept at peak.

Levels of skill for dictation and transcription are indicated in the following list:

**typewriting**
80 wpm (words per minute) with a low frequency of errors for 10 minutes nonstop: GOOD
60–70 wpm with a low frequency of errors for 10 minutes nonstop: AVERAGE
40 wpm with fewer than 5 errors for 10 minutes nonstop: POOR

**stenography**  ability to take dictation live at 80–140 wpm
90–110 wpm: AVERAGE
120 wpm: GOOD
140 wpm in short spurts: DESIRABLE

**transcription from an electronic medium**
25 wpm transcribed and typed: EXCELLENT
16 wpm transcribed and typed: GOOD
 8 wpm transcribed and typed: POOR

**Other skills**   A prospective legal secretary will also find these additional skills useful when applying for a position:

1. **business machine operation**   Familiarity with and the ability to operate text-editing machines, electronic dictating/transcribing machines, adding machines, photocopy machines, conventional tape recorders, and telephone equipment.
2. **records management**   A good grasp of filing systems, both the alphabetic and the numeric methods, and how to set them up and use them.
3. **business math**   A strong background in bookkeeping, billing, banking, and collection procedures as well as tax recordkeeping.
4. **legal forms**   The ability to select and fill in legal forms with a minimum of attorney supervision.
5. **language arts**   A sound command of the English language—its grammar, syntax, and style including an understanding of the conventions of punctuation and capitalization peculiar to law. Familiarity with Latin phrases and locutions peculiar to the law. Excellent spelling ability.

## SPECIALIZED KNOWLEDGE

As firms grow and lawyers specialize, specialization among secretaries also takes place. During the first two or three years of a lawyer's time with the firm, the legal work assigned may cover several fields such as corporations, litigation, and tax. As the lawyer drives or drifts into a specialty, such as litigation, the secretary's work may become confined to that specialty. If this takes place, the secretary should try to become a specialist in that field. Some guidance will be furnished by the lawyer, but the best source of information in many firms is the secretary who has spent many years in the specialty. The relatively inexperienced legal secretary should seek out these experienced secretaries and discuss with them how best to become better prepared for the specialty.

Many firms have form books and reference books for each specialty. These books, usually loose-leaf binders, will provide many of the answers to the secretary's questions. If these books are not available, the secretary should learn whether a publication in the field is available and, if so, should have the lawyer or librarian obtain a copy. Apart from this, or as an adjunct to it, the secretary should begin to assemble a file of memoranda and forms for the particular discipline. Compiling and using such references is one way the secretary can advance in the firm.

Many secretaries are charged with the responsibility of keeping publications current by inserting sheets received on a regular basis from the publishers; they may also be charged with the responsibility of keeping an index of memoranda of law and cases for the lawyers for whom they work. These assignments are similar to some functions performed by the law librarian. The secretary who is interested in pursuing such a career is well advised to enroll in a course aimed at formal qualification as a law librarian.

## JOB TRAINING

**In-house training**   Many large firms seek to solve the secretarial problem by establishing in-house training programs. These firms employ secretarial trainees who possess only the basic dictation and typing skills. The in-house training through formal education and work assignments develops these skills, accelerating the rate at which one becomes a legal secretary. This method is probably one of the best ways to develop in the field.

**Courses of study**   In addition to in-house training, courses for legal secretaries are offered in many cities. These are offered by high school extension services, community colleges, and state universities. Some courses teach practical skills such as how to prepare legal documents; others introduce the student to particular areas of law such as real estate or criminal law. In addition, self-programmed guides like the Gregg Legal Typewriting Course may be purchased for home study.

**Secretarial associations**  The National Secretaries Association, located at 2440 Pershing Road, Suite 610 Crown Center, Kansas City, MO 64108, and the National Association of Legal Secretaries (NALS), headquartered at 3005 East Skelly Drive, Suite 120, Tulsa, OK 74105, also offer ways to continue or build upon earlier education. There are also a number of local associations or societies.

**Professional Legal Secretary**  The NALS offers a certification program which, when successfully completed, designates a person as a Professional Legal Secretary (PLS). The two-day examination is given in March and October of each year. Application to take the examination that leads to certification may be made after five years of experience as a legal secretary. Applicants prepare for the examination by studying the NALS's *Study Guide for the PLS Examination,* which is available from NALS headquarters at a nominal fee. The examination covers seven major subject areas: (1) written communication skills and knowledge, (2) human relations and ethics, (3) legal secretarial procedures, (4) legal secretarial accounting, (5) legal terminology, techniques, and procedures, (6) exercise of judgment, and (7) legal secretarial skills.

Whether a secretary joins a local or national secretarial group for educational purposes is, naturally, a personal decision. But it is pertinent to note that there are also certain side benefits of these affiliations such as social activities, making new friends, and being alerted to job opportunities in the area.

# 2.4

## THE LEGAL ASSISTANT

In the post-World War II era, there has been a marked development of the legal assistant or paralegal field as a career. This position is somewhat analogous to that of the medical assistant. There are many tasks formerly performed by doctors that are now performed by paramedics and medical assistants, leaving the doctor free to concentrate on complex problems requiring highly specialized skills. Assigned to the paramedics are those problems requiring specialized education of shorter duration and a different level from that required of the fully trained physician. In this respect, paralegals are like paramedics.

The duties of paralegals vary widely from office to office, and no nation-wide certification program has yet been established. In fact, many legal secretaries perform paralegal tasks without the recognition or salary. The National Association of Legal Assistants in Tulsa, Oklahoma, has adopted the following description of the legal assistant's work:

*Under the supervision of a lawyer,* the legal assistant shall apply knowledge of law and legal procedures in rendering direct assistance to lawyers, clients and courts; design, develop and modify procedures, techniques, services and processes; prepare and interpret legal documents; detail procedures for practicing in certain fields of law; research, select, assess, compile and use information from the law library and other references; and analyze and handle procedural problems that involve independent decisions.

The NALA manual further clarifies these duties by describing what the assistant may *not* do: "With the exception of *not accepting cases, not setting fees, not representing the client in court, nor giving legal advice to the client,* the legal assistant may perform any task delegated and *supervised by a lawyer*. The lawyer, of course, is and must be responsible to the client for the final work product."

Legal assistants were first extensively employed in the probate field. They were generally secretaries who had been working for lawyers in the wills and probate fields drawing wills, qualifying executors, preparing estate tax returns, and preparing accounts in estates. Lawyers and their secretaries in this specialty soon discovered that after working together for a while the secretary was often as qualified to carry out the administrative acts as was the lawyer. The estate tax return, for example, could be prepared initially by an experienced probate secretary with review by the lawyer, some possible discretionary revisions, and signature. When this task was assigned to the secretary, the lawyer time involved was reduced, as was the fee charged the client. Concurrently, the secretary's value to the firm was increased, and the compensation paid the secretary reflected this greater value. Finally, the firm profited since, as the time burden on the probate lawyer was reduced, the lawyer became available to handle additional matters.

Following the remarkable success of the probate paralegal movement, openings occurred in real estate, corporate, litigation, and antitrust law. In this last field, for example, much of the tedious, burdensome search through hundreds of thousands of documents can be accomplished at relatively low cost by paralegals, working with or without computers, compared with the very expensive conduct of such a search by qualified lawyers. These lawyers are also deprived of the opportunity to use their time and education more profitably in other matters. Other specialty practices that rely heavily on legal assistants are admiralty law, bankruptcy, criminal law, domestic relations, labor relations, oil and gas law, patent and trademark law, personal injury and medical malpractice, public utilities, tax law, and workers' compensation.

## LEGAL ASSISTANTS AND LEGAL SECRETARIES

Legal assistants having arrived on the scene in relatively recent times, their status vis-à-vis the lawyer and the legal secretary is not yet clearly defined. Obviously, they rank lower than the lawyer; but whether they enjoy a level superior to, or equal with, legal secretaries is not yet clear in most instances. The relationship between the legal assistant and the legal secretary should be close and cordial, since how well they mesh will determine how well they serve the lawyer for whom both of them work.

In recent years, many secretaries have become interested in pursuing careers as legal assistants. This interest may be pursued in various ways. One could simply ask to be assigned work projects within the firm that would allow one to achieve self-education as a paralegal. Or a secretary could attend academic courses. There are a number of paralegal training programs scattered throughout the country, most offered by universities and community colleges. Several of the programs have met the American Bar Association's standards and are approved by it. A current list of schools that offer these studies may be obtained by writing to the ABA headquarters in Chicago, Illinois. Many legal assistants are college graduates who have taken courses in specialized fields of law and also from among the following: office procedures, communications, behavioral sciences, and legal research techniques. Other useful courses include statistics, economics, industrial relations, management, insurance, and corporate finance.

A legal secretary who is interested in becoming a legal assistant should be cautioned, however. Competent and experienced legal secretaries are becoming a rare commodity, while competent and experienced paralegals or legal assistants are becoming more plentiful. As the need for good legal secretaries continues to increase and their numbers decrease, each one becomes more valuable. The same may not apply to paralegals since, although the fields in which they are employed may continue to increase, the number of competent persons in the various specialties may well increase at a greater rate. Employment as a paralegal may prove harder to find in the years to come than employment as an experienced legal secretary.

# 2.5

## EMPLOYMENT OPPORTUNITIES

A qualified legal secretary will find a wide choice of opportunities in the job market. Which path to follow is a matter of personal preference but, before one makes the decision, it is well to examine the major paths. The choices lie in the private sector (law firms and corporate legal departments) and in the public sector (courts and public governmental or quasi-governmental agencies).

### THE PRIVATE SECTOR

**Law firms**  Private law firms offer the widest variety of work and the greatest opportunity for the use of individual initiative. A legal secretary working for a sole practitioner or a small group of lawyers will find a myriad of tasks that may be undertaken or tactfully rejected. For example, a legal secretary who has some bookkeeping or accounting knowledge may become responsible for this area of the firm management if the firm has not employed someone in or out of the firm to do it. When such responsibilities are voluntarily assumed, the value of the legal secretary to the firm is enhanced and should be reflected in salary. A legal secretary may also be asked to take on menial tasks such as cleaning the conference room or waxing the furniture or mending the drapes. These tasks clearly do not constitute work for which a secretary is employed, and to allocate the valuable time of a qualified and well-paid legal secretary to them is a waste of money and talent. For this reason, secretaries ordinarily should not perform such tasks routinely but should bring to the attention of the employer the need to hire a person or a service to take care of them.

Many secretaries prefer the atmosphere of a large organization and contribute far more than when they work for one or two lawyers. Large firms may offer excellent training for the secretary with basic skills, permitting their development and the acquisition of additional skills such as those required in a litigation or probate practice. In the probate area, for example, it is not at all unusual for a legal secretary to reach a point of proficiency where a good portion—more than half—of the work associated with the estate is performed by the secretary and referred to the lawyer for minor revision and approval.

Legal secretaries relocating to a new city or initially coming on the job market should first look up the names and makeup of the firms in the area through use of a good law directory. Many local directories are published, but the most comprehensive and widely used directory is the *Martindale-Hubbell Law Directory* referred to in section 2.1. The biographical section, arranged by state and city, lists the major firms alphabetically and indicates their specialties. By learning the size of the office and the age level, educational background, and legal ability of the lawyers, the secretary can make a first judgment as to whether the firm should be considered as an employer.

**Corporate law departments**  Many corporations have law departments usually directed by a general counsel. Financial institutions such as banks and trust companies usually have large legal departments and ordinarily seek qualified legal secretaries.

Advantages of working for a corporate legal department are the well-defined work and the regular hours. This situation differs from that of the law firm where, at times, after-hour and weekend work may be required over a period of several weeks.

Another advantage of corporate legal work is the possibility of assignment to a particular field such as real estate with the opportunity to refine skills, establish a daily routine, and be free from numerous unwelcome shifts.

**Legal clinics**   A legal clinic is a law office that offers routine legal services at reasonable prices to people of low or moderate means. It does this by limiting its practice to certain routine matters that lend themselves to heavy reliance on paralegals and efficient systems for processing cases. Other features of the legal clinic are that it is usually located conveniently to its prospective clients—in a shopping district or mall or even next to the local courthouse—and that it frequently advertises in order to maintain a high-volume practice.

Although some clinics specialize in fields like bankruptcy or domestic relations, most of them offer a range of basic services needed by the ordinary citizen. Family law is their main service, followed in order by criminal law, wills, trusts and probate, landlord-tenant relations, real estate, consumer problems, bankruptcy, and personal injury cases.

Despite a high failure rate in the past few years, legal clinics have apparently become a permanent part of the legal scene. From only three clinics in 1974, the number had grown to more than one thousand at the end of 1980.

## THE PUBLIC SECTOR

The legal departments of towns, cities, and states offer employment to legal secretaries, as do numerous federal agencies. The courts and the public agencies associated with them have a constant need for qualified legal secretaries. One of the most demanding jobs is that of secretary to a judge whose court docket is extremely crowded. In the public prosecutor's office or the public defender's office, legal secretaries will be doing work similar to that performed in private law firms. The advantage of working in a public office is chiefly one of job security, since most of these positions are in civil service. After seniority is attained, the prospect of being terminated for reasons other than cause is very slim. On the other hand, the chances of rapid advancement tend to be limited since most civil service positions require time in grade at each step on the career ladder.

One should not overlook job opportunities with elected public officials. Many legislators, state and federal, prefer and demand hometown employees for jobs in the legislator's hometown or state capital or Washington, D.C. One should never be awed by these positions; any applicant who has the intelligence, skills, and personality to fit the job may be hired.

## JOBS OVERSEAS

A number of legal secretarial jobs exist overseas in government agencies such as the State Department or for U.S. corporations doing business in foreign countries. The large automobile manufacturing companies, for example, maintain a number of offices overseas, as do the major oil companies and a number of other business corporations. Many of these corporations pursue a policy whereby secretarial help in the foreign country is found in the country itself from among foreign nationals. Despite this practice, many corporations make necessary exceptions and arrange for work permits so that a competent legal secretary employed by the corporation in, let us say, its Chicago office may be assigned for a specified period of time to its branch office in Paris or London. Secretaries interested in such assignments should ascertain the location of the branch offices maintained by the parent corporation and should make known their desire for foreign assignment.

In the case of agencies of the United States government that maintain offices overseas, employment is easier since U.S. citizenship is usually a prerequisite. Legal secretaries who are interested in government assignments abroad may explore the opportunities available by directing a letter of inquiry to the government department involved, usually headquartered in Washington, D.C. For example, a letter of inquiry may be addressed to the Personnel Employment Office, Room 2815, Department of State, 22d and D Street, N.W., Washington, DC 20520, concerning the availability of jobs abroad under the cognizance of the State Department. Addresses of the employment offices of other departments in the federal government are listed in the *United States Government Manual,* which is published annually.

A great advantage when seeking employment abroad is a facility with the language of the country concerned. This is also an advantage to a secretary working in the United States, particularly in a large firm, since some of the correspondence received by the firm may be in a foreign language and require translation. Because of these factors, a legal secretary with facility in a foreign language should make every reasonable effort to maintain ability in that language at a peak, for one never knows when such skills will prove useful.

Generally, salaries abroad are competitive within the particular local market. They may be greater or less than salaries in the United States. Before accepting a job overseas, the secretary should ascertain the precise salary that will be paid in addition to general information concerning applicable taxes, cost of living, and other special factors which might affect the decision to take overseas employment. Another item to take into consideration is the opportunity for advancement overseas. As a general rule, employment overseas is for a particular job, and the opportunities for advancement at the foreign station are limited. However, outstanding performance in an overseas office may result in a transfer back to the United States at a substantially higher level than that enjoyed when the overseas assignment was made.

## APPLYING FOR A JOB

Although there is no such thing as complete job security, we are often told that there is security in knowing how to go about finding a job. The various ways in which you can obtain a position will differ according to (1) your educational background and the professional contacts you have made during your studies, (2) your past or current on-the-job experience, and (3) the nature of your geographical area. If, for example, you live in a small town or in the country where most of the inhabitants know each other, you will probably depend to a great extent on personal contacts with the local lawyers. On the other hand, if you live in a city or in a large suburb, you will undoubtedly rely more often on employment agencies and on advertisements in your search for the right position. Obviously, the competition for jobs is more acute in heavily populated areas than it is in rural areas. However, this feature is offset by the greater variety of legal office positions available in urban areas.

In seeking a position, it is always best to explore and evaluate every possible opportunity. Do not settle for the first offer that comes along unless you are absolutely sure that the job is right for you and that you are the right person for the job. Think of moving laterally as well as up the career ladder. Looking for a job in the right way takes time, energy, thoroughness, and organization. Visit places where you would like to work. For example, look at the roster of attorneys on the board in the lobby of an office building to see if, perhaps, you should investigate openings in some of these offices.

**Sources of employment information**    There are a number of sources of information available on legal secretarial positions. First, there is the classified section of the local newspaper, where positions will be listed under the heading of "Secretary" or "Legal Secretary." In addition to daily general-interest newspapers, a number of large metropolitan areas have daily newspapers devoted exclusively to the legal community. These also list positions in law offices.

These newspaper advertisements may be placed by employment agencies (discussed below) or directly by law offices. The ads may be blind or signed. A blind ad is one that lists and describes the job and sometimes the salary, and then gives a post office box to which you are supposed to send a letter of application, a résumé, and any other required material. A signed ad, on the other hand, gives not only the above information about the job but also the name, address, and possibly the telephone number of the prospective employer. (If you are answering a blind ad, be sure that your name and address are on the envelope, the letter, and the résumé.) If references are asked for, supply them. Be certain that your typewritten material is letter-perfect, as this is your initial chance to make a positive impression.

When responding to a signed ad requesting that you telephone the office for an appointment, make sure that you call only during the hours specified. Have your background material at hand so that you can respond concisely, coherently, and completely to all questions. You may be telephone-interviewed by another secretary, by an office manager, or by the lawyer, and your responses and your own questions ought to be tailored to the particular individual conducting the interview. For example, in talking with a lawyer, you should keep your responses and questions brief but inclusive so as to convey all necessary information but not waste the lawyer's valuable time. On the other hand, you can pursue important matters with the lawyer such as his or her personal expectations of the successful candidate—matters that you ordinarily would not bring up with a staff member. If the interviewer is an office manager or another secretary, you can discuss details of office routines.

Local legal secretarial associations may be helpful in locating job opportunities, but usually they are not the most appropriate for first-time job applicants. The association usually makes the vacancies known to its members, and the positions are filled before the newcomer is aware of them. Local bar associations and chambers of commerce are good contact points for general information about the job market for legal secretaries, but they do not ordinarily list particular jobs. The publications of large metropolitan bar associations, however, often list secretarial openings, and a few local bar associations run legal secretarial hiring services.

**Employment agencies** The source of employment information and assistance most often used by newcomers to the job market is the professional placement agency. Usually an employment agency places newspaper ads for its clients regarding job openings that they need to fill. The agency interviews and screens the candidates for the jobs and then refers the qualified candidates to the prospective employer. Depending on the job and the geographical location, the employment agency may charge you a fee for placing you in a position; or the fee may be charged entirely to your ultimate employer or split on a percentage basis between you and the employer. It is wise to investigate what you must pay the agency when it finds you a job.

Employment agencies are listed in the telephone Yellow Pages of the areas where they are located. If you are canvassing all of the opportunities and sources of information in a particular geographical location, you can make unsolicited inquiries about potential jobs by simply calling or writing to the agencies. If you write, be sure to include your résumé with your letter of inquiry so that the agency can act on it right away or call you later when any suitable openings come up.

Employment agencies, as noted earlier, advertise their listings in newspapers and in some legal periodicals. If you see an advertised job for which you are qualified, call the agency that placed the ad right away. Be sure to have on hand your résumé and references. This material is important because the initial screening will take place over the telephone. You will make a better impression with the account executive if you can supply all needed data quickly, crisply, and completely without delays or paper shuffling. Remember, the agency will want to interview you in person before recommending you or sending you to a prospective employer. You should be on time for the agency interview, and you should follow the guidelines for interview etiquette outlined on page 48. Take with you to the agency your résumé, your reference list, and any other requested materials. You will generally need two copies of the résumé and the reference list: one for the agency and another for the agency to send ahead to its client. Also be prepared to ask your high school and/or college to submit transcripts of your grades to the agency, if requested. This is *your* responsibility. (You may have to pay the schools a nominal fee for this service.)

Never forget that undoubtedly you are only one among many applicants being screened by the agency for a position. Therefore, be sure to show real interest in the job. Find out as much as you can about the tasks and responsibilities involved. Ask about the nature of the law practice. Find out the office hours and whether weekend work, night work, or other overtime is required. And most importantly—ask *exactly* what duties you will be expected to perform. Find out, if you can, whether any specialized skills (as machine dictation/transcription) are required. Ask whether the lawyer expects to train you further in specialized procedures during the course of the job. While the employment agency may not be able to give you all of the answers to these questions, you will have found out which questions to ask the employer later on, and you will also have demonstrated genuine interest in the job and a thorough knowledge of your field. After you have explored what the job entails, you can then discuss further with the agency the salary range and the benefits offered by the employer.

Apart from responding to advertisements, you should consider writing letters of application and enclosing résumés to particular firms or companies that you would like to work for, even though you are not aware of any vacancy in those organizations. Depending upon the size of the firm, the résumé should be addressed to the office manager, the personnel director, or the managing partner. If, when the résumé reaches the proper person in the firm, it discloses a job applicant who appears to be of top quality, the hiring official may well invite the applicant in for an interview and offer employment—even though a full vacancy does not then exist. A firm might do this to build up a reserve of legal secretarial talent.

**Telephoning a prospective employer's office**    When inquiring about a job that may be open or when responding to an employment ad by telephone, you must be polite and coherent. After all, one of a legal secretary's prime responsibilities is the easy handling of telephone calls. Thus, the members of the law office team will be evaluating your telephone performance from the beginning to the end of the conversation. If an applicant shows that he or she cannot converse with aplomb during an initial interview, it is obvious that the applicant may not be able to deal effectively with all of the many calls that come into or originate from a busy law office. Take into consideration the fact that clients can be demanding and often impatient. It is necessary, therefore, to project a smile in your voice and a relaxed, confident manner of self-assurance.

Be sure to prepare yourself before placing your call. If necessary, jot down any special questions you want to ask and any particular points you wish to make. Also, have your personal data information on hand by the telephone. If you are not placing the call yourself but are waiting for the lawyer to call you, keep these materials at hand, anyway. Since you can never know what kinds of questions will be asked, you must be ready for anything.

The following guidelines will help you make a positive impression on your telephone interviewer:

1. In your concern about the job, do not forget to say hello and good-bye.

2. Identify yourself at once and state your reason for calling.
3. Use the other person's name in the conversation and if for some reason it has not been mentioned, ask "To whom am I speaking, please?"
4. Give straightforward, complete, brief answers to all questions.
5. Ask the questions that *you* have, but keep in mind that there may be some questions that only the lawyer can answer.
6. Be polite and enthusiastic without becoming emotional.
7. If you have small children at home, do not try to call when they are in the room, making noise. Such a practice indicates that you aren't well organized. Make your call when they are outside or are napping.
8. If, for some reason, you discover during the conversation that you really are not qualified for the job or that you do not want to pursue the matter further, say so politely.
9. If the interviewer sounds rushed, ask if you can call at another time, or if the interviewer could call you back at his or her convenience.
10. It is usually pointless to discuss salary matters during an initial telephone conversation.

Sometimes the lawyer or office manager will return a phone call after reviewing your résumé and consulting your references. The following are suggestions for handling this type of telephone call:

1. If you are expecting a call or calls regarding employment, don't just answer the telephone with "Hello." Give your name.
2. Answer all questions politely and thoroughly. However, do not ramble: lawyers are too busy to waste time with irrelevant conversations.
3. Save most of your questions for the interview if the lawyer suggests a personal interview. You can, however, mention that you have some questions that cannot wait. That way, you will show your interest but not at the expense of the lawyer's valuable time. Also, jot down your questions for future reference.
4. Verify your appointment date, time of day, and location.
5. Let the caller terminate the conversation by saying good-bye first.

**The job application letter** A properly formatted and well-written letter of application will greatly assist in preselling you to a prospective employer. This type of letter is a concrete indication of your verbal and technical skills and of your general personality and intelligence.

You should typewrite the letter on plain bond paper. (*Do not* use social stationery or personalized letterhead.) Exotic typefaces should be avoided. Either the Block or the Modified Semi-block styling is appropriate. The letter ought not to exceed one page. Under no circumstances should you prepare and photocopy a form letter to be sent to numerous law offices. Such a procedure will create a most unfavorable first impression on those evaluating your application. The applicant lacking the time and the common courtesy to write a personal letter will most probably not receive careful consideration.

Before typewriting the letter, you should plan your approach in detail. An outline or a draft of the points to be made will assist you. If the letter is solicited (i.e., you are responding to an advertisement), you should mention in the first paragraph the specific position for which you are applying and the date and source of the advertisement. If the letter is unsolicited (i.e., you are applying on your own initiative), you should say as much in the first paragraph and indicate why you are interested in working for the particular practice. Next, you ought to focus on and develop your best assets. A concise statement of your technical skills (such as shorthand and typewriting rates) may be given along with mention of any more specialized skills (as operation of text-editing machines). Another sentence or even a paragraph expanding on some aspect of your education or on your previous employment experience not already developed fully in the résumé can be included in the letter. The tone throughout should be straightforward, yet modest and sincere. Of course, the material should be carefully proofread so that there will not be any grammatical or typographical errors. You should keep a copy of the letter for your records. (See the illustration of a sample job application letter that is found on page 45 of this section.)

**The résumé**   The lawyer, or the personnel director of a law firm or corporate legal office, may invite you to submit a résumé prior to setting up an interview. This permits the screening of applicants in order to ascertain in advance whether an interview would be profitable for both the applicant and the interviewer.

Because your résumé is the complete statement of your professional advancement and accomplishments to date, it is a key factor in achieving your employment objectives. Although books have been written on this subject, there are elements essential to all well-written résumés which can be set down here. These elements are: (1) personal identification: your full name, address, and telephone number (home and/or office) typewritten at the top of the résumé, (2) employment experience: each job that you have held listed chronologically from present to past, including the name and address of each firm or company, applicable employment dates, your job title and a *brief* job description if the responsibilities are not obvious from the title itself, and perhaps a concise summary of your special accomplishments in each position if space permits, (3) educational background: a list of the institutions that you have attended or from which you have graduated, starting with the highest level (as college) and concluding with high school, (4) special skills: a list of special skills that might prove a valuable asset to a prospective employer should you be hired, and (5) references: the sentence, "References will be provided on request," included at the end of the résumé. NOTE: If you have no previous employment experience, you can supplement your education category with a list of the business and secretarial courses that you have successfully completed, you can mention your typewriting and transcription rates, and you can list any academic or professional honors that you have been awarded. If you have completed any special free-lance secretarial projects (as the typing of manuscripts and theses), you can mention them under the heading "Special Projects" following the educational section.

It is desirable to include date and place of birth and whether male or female, married or divorced or single, but inclusion of these items is not usually required and may be omitted if desired.

The following data should *not* be given on the résumé itself: (1) names and addresses of references: references should be typewritten separately and should be provided by you at the interview or in an interview follow-up letter, (2) salary: it is best to discuss salary requirements and ranges during the interview itself, since you will not want to undersell yourself ahead of time or possibly price yourself out of a job market that you may be unfamiliar with, (3) your reasons, if any, for changing jobs: since wording can often be misunderstood without personal clarification, it is best to discuss this matter with the interviewer <u>and only if you are asked</u>, rather than committing yourself on paper, (4) your reasons for present unemployment, if applicable: this topic is also tricky and is therefore best dealt with in person or in a telephone conversation, since adequate explanations often require valuable page space that can be better used to highlight your assets, and (5) a photograph: a photo can work for or against you, depending on the subjectivity of the person evaluating your application; hence, it is best not to risk a premature negative reaction on the part of the employer before you have had a chance to present yourself in person.

Your résumé normally should not exceed one page. However, quality and comprehensiveness should not be sacrificed for brevity. A two-page résumé may be best for certain individuals. To achieve maximum brevity and at the same time attain comprehensiveness, you should plan the material and then write it out in draft form before typewriting it. All facts should be double-checked. Use plain, straightforward English devoid of technical jargon and superlatives. The material ought to be typewritten on plain standard bond paper. Margins should be balanced on all four sides.

Although there are many acceptable résumé formats, the simplest and cleanest treatment is to block all the material flush left. Entries should be single-spaced internally, with double- or triple-spacing between entries, depending on the page space available. Underscoring and capital letters may introduce main and secondary headings. Copies *must* be clean and legible; for this purpose, offset copies or photocopies are suggested. Avoid mimeographed copies and carbons. Your typewriter typeface must be sharp and clean. Avoid exotic typefaces (including italic). See the illustration of a sample résumé on page 46.

**References**   The references best suited for a future employer are those furnished by past employers. Most former employers will be happy to provide such references, but it is very important not to give a person's name as a reference to a prospective employer without first getting permission from that person. Almost invariably they will be happy to agree. If you have no prior work experience, the chief source for references is the instructors in the schools you have attended. In some cases these individuals will write blanket "To whom it may concern" letters of introduction and recommendation that you can take with you in sealed envelopes to prospective employers; in other cases they will write directly to each prospective employer; and in still other cases they will expect the prospective employer to telephone them for a recommendation. You should avoid using relatives as references since most employers feel that opinions obtained from relatives are not objective.

When you typewrite a list of references, follow the general format and style that you have used for your résumé. Do not change paper size or color and do not use a different type style. White bond paper is appropriate. Head the list REFERENCES. Single-space each entry and double- or triple-space between entries. Include the full name, address, and telephone number of each person who has consented to recommend you. Include at least one supervisor and/or attorney from each former place of employment. Include one former instructor if possible. You should not have unexplained gaps that will show up when the résumé and reference list are compared. Personal character references can be listed at the bottom of the sheet, if necessary. Give the employer the reference list when it is asked for but do not staple this list to your résumé.

**Tests**   Many law firms test the skills of applicants in one or more of the following areas: typing, dictation, spelling, vocabulary, grammar, proofreading, punctuation, and arithmetic. If a test is administered as part of the job application procedure, merely do your best and don't worry about the results. If the results are sufficiently bad, you are not ready for the job and should aim your search elsewhere. If the results are not top-notch but still acceptable, you may well be offered the job if your appearance, personality, and general qualifications suit the employer-attorney. In other words, relax and do your best.

**Employment application forms**   Many employers use application forms as a means of obtaining information about a prospective employee prior to an interview. You may be expected to fill out an application form for the personnel director. Be prepared. Write down the necessary information—details about past employment including company addresses, supervisors' names, dates, and salaries; details of your education, with dates; addresses and telephone numbers of references—and take it with you to the office.

**Letter of Application**

123 Smith Lane
Jonesville, ST 98765
June 1, 19--

Ms. Ann Stone
Director, Personnel
ABC Insurance
81 Albany Towers  Suite 12
Smithville, ST 12345

Dear Ms. Stone:

The ABC Insurance employment ad on page 48E of the May 30, 19--
issue of the <u>Sunday Republican</u> has attracted my immediate interest.
Because I believe that I am qualified for the secretarial position in
your Legal Department, I am sending you a copy of my résumé.

My shorthand rate is --- wpm; and my typewriting rate --- wpm.  I
am experienced in the use of machine dictation and transcription equipment, both cassette and belt.  I am also proficient in Spanish.

As you can see from the attached résumé, I am currently employed
as secretary to Helen P. Thornton, who is retiring from her law practice
at the end of July.  I believe that the experience gained in this position
would be useful in a corporate legal office.

I look forward to a personal interview at your convenience, if you
decide to follow up on this initial application.  ABC Insurance is indeed
a fine company -- one for which I know I would enjoy working.

Sincerely yours,

*Carol C. Mannington*

Carol C. Mannington

**Résumé**

R É S U M É

Katherine B. McQueen                          Date of Birth:    December 21, 1951
91 West Busch Garden Drive                     Place of Birth:   Los Angeles, California
South Pasadena, California 91784               Marital Status:   Single
                                               Health:           Excellent

EDUCATION:

2/78 - Present    Pasadena City College, Pasadena, California
                  Currently enrolled in paralegal courses

9/66 - 6/70       Lynwood High School, Lynwood, California
                  Top 10% of Class; Bank of America Award in Business

WORK EXPERIENCE:

9/77 - Present    Zechel, Armstrong & White (Law Firm)
                  Los Angeles, California
                  Legal Secretary -- Legal secretarial duties for corporate lawyer

9/72 - 9/77       Jones, Jones, Robinson & Burgin (Law Firm)
                  Los Angeles, California
                  Legal Secretary -- Initially legal secretarial trainee; then
                  assigned as legal secretary for litigation attorney

6/70 - 9/72       Security Pacific National Bank
                  Los Angeles, California
                  Secretary -- Secretarial duties for loan officer

4/70 - 6/70       Western Gear Corporation
                  Lynwood, California
                  Accounting Clerk -- Part-time while attending high school

SPECIAL SKILLS:   machine dictation/transcription
                  fluency in German

REFERENCES:       References will be provided on request.

## References

REFERENCES

Buckley White, Esq.
Zechel, Armstrong & White
783 West First Street
Los Angeles, CA 90031
213/880-1374

Gary Wayne Cole
Assistant Treasurer
Western Gear Corporation
7777 Avenue of the Stars
Lynwood, CA 96617
213/876-0543

Brian R. Burgin, Esq.
Jones, Jones, Robinson & Burgin
98543 Avenue 34, Suite 2
Los Angeles, CA 90506
213/999-1234

John L. Smithson
Assistant Vice President
Security Pacific National Bank
547 East Sunnyslope Drive
Los Angeles, CA 23145
213/690-6129

Personal reference

The Reverend Donald D. O'Leary
The Rectory
St. Mary's Church
6 North Street
Lynwood, CA 96618
213/876-1112

If you are given a form asking for information which you do not wish to provide, leave the pertinent space blank. If the matter of the blank space is raised later by the interviewer, you may say why the space was left blank or you may state that the question is not one that you wish to answer. Instances are becoming rare where such situations are raised by employment application forms.

**The job interview**    Once you reach the interview stage, you should prepare for it carefully. First impressions—whether created on the telephone, in writing, or in person—are *lasting* impressions.

You should dress carefully for your interview with the personnel manager or the lawyer. Clothing should be clean, pressed, and conservative. Exotic attire is definitely out of place. Be especially careful in cleaning your hands and manicuring your fingernails. If you are a woman, avoid excessive makeup. Dress simply and comfortably in a manner suitable for secretarial work. The dress need not be on the masculine side but should convey the image of a professional, skilled person. Men applying for secretarial positions are well advised to wear a suit, or slacks and jacket, with shirt and tie. It is possible that, after embarking on the job, it may not be necessary to wear a tie or jacket, but usually this outfit is best for the interview. Additionally, most businessmen like to see an applicant wearing shoes that are shined. A sloppy, unkempt appearance is often taken as an indicator of a sloppy worker.

Since the legal secretary is usually the first and last member of the law office team seen by clients and other visitors, it is essential that the secretary be a credit to the practice. Thus, impeccable manners are requisite. Since an applicant's manners will be carefully observed by an interviewer, the following are some of the most important points to remember:

1. **Punctuality**    Be on time for your interview. If you don't know exactly where the office is located, get directions beforehand. If the office is in a large city where traffic and parking are a problem, ask a staff member for the best driving or public transportation route and find out where you can park. This can be done when your appointment is being made. If you are still unsure of the directions, you can make a dry run in advance to make sure that you know the way. In any event, give yourself plenty of time to get there with minutes to spare. The longer you wait in the office, the more you can observe about the office routines.

2. **Arrival**    When you enter the office, identify yourself to the receptionist and state your business ("I'm here to see Mr. Yowell at 4:30 about a job"). Be cheerful and polite. If the weather is bad and you need to doff heavy outerwear, find out where to hang it up so that you won't be burdened with coat, scarf, mittens, hat, or the like during the interview.

3. **Waiting to see the lawyer**    If you have to wait for a while before seeing the lawyer or personnel manager, sit quietly and observe as much of the routines as possible without appearing nosy. This process may provide you with additional questions to ask later in the interview, and it will also give you a fairly accurate reading on the practice itself.

4. **Introductions**    When introduced to the lawyer or personnel manager, as well as to other staff members, smile, repeat their names ("How do you do, Mr. Lee," or "It's nice to meet you, Ms. Smith"), and appear enthusiastic but not gushy. The other extreme to avoid is appearing glum or sick (even if you *feel* that way!).

5. **Posture**    When sitting, do not sprawl. On the other hand, do not sit rigidly like a store mannequin. Try to relax and enjoy the experience.

6. **Smoking**    Many waiting rooms and private offices are now no-smoking areas. It is best not to smoke at all unless the interviewer asks if you would like to do so.

7. **Chewing gum**    Taboo!

During the interview, bear in mind not only that you are being interviewed but that you should be interviewing the prospective employer. In addition to answering questions fully and frankly, do not hesitate to ask questions that will help you determine whether you want the job if it is offered. While it is impossible to offer cut-and-dried guidelines to cover every eventuality in interviews, the following paragraphs give general suggestions that, if followed, will make your experience more positive.

1. **Eye contact** Look directly at the interviewer when you are speaking. Avoiding someone's eyes, especially when you are answering questions, can be interpreted as evasiveness. On the other hand, don't stare blankly at the interviewer.

2. **Speech mannerisms** Try to avoid those annoying verbal tics that many people use to cover up pauses or to give themselves time to think of what to say next. Some of the more irritating mannerisms are the use of "ah" or "uh" at the beginning or end of sentences; the use of "Like . . ." at the beginning of sentences; and the repetition of "you know" or "OK" throughout a conversation.

3. **Interview direction and the asking of questions** Don't try to lead the conversation since the lawyer undoubtedly will have decided what is to be asked and discussed. Follow the lawyer's lead. You can interject your own questions during appropriate lulls in the conversation, or you can save them for the end when you will probably be asked if you have any questions. However, feel free to ask intelligent questions about such matters as the nature of the practice. Another good question to ask the lawyer is his or her particular dislikes regarding routines. Many applicants fail to mention this (or the lawyer forgets to discuss it), and then the newly hired secretary inadvertently does things that the lawyer dislikes during the first weeks on the job. It is much better to find out what you are expected *not* to do as well as what you are expected to do right in the beginning.

4. **Your job description and on-the-job training** Be sure that you get a clear idea of just what you will be doing in the office. Understand the expected hours of work and any required overtime. Find out if the lawyer intends to give you any on-the-job training and, if so, what kind. During the interview, you should ascertain all the employee benefits available to you, and any orientation training necessary.

5. **Questions you can't answer** Many people are embarrassed when they discover during an interview that they don't know everything an interviewer expects them to know. If you are asked something that you cannot answer, say so honestly. Sometimes interviewers ask questions that they *know* you can't answer, just to see whether they will get an honest reaction.

6. **Weaknesses (if any) in your skills** If the lawyer mentions a required skill in which you know you are weak, admit it right away. Be prepared to say that you are willing to improve in that area, whether by programmed self-study, by taking a refresher course, or by learning on the job.

**Salary, fringe benefits, and insurance** The attorney-interviewer will tell you your base pay and will undoubtedly outline the fringe benefits. Feel free to bring up any one of these topics if the interviewer doesn't. Ascertain from the prospective employer the precise details of the position in question rather than relying on any information furnished by your employment agency. In many instances, the employment agency does not have the exact data, and you need to know the precise details of the job from the employer before accepting employment. It is bad practice to argue with a prospective employer about a salary that you feel is too low. You can ask about the employer's raise policy (for example, what is a standard raise and when are employees considered for them?). You can ask about staff promotions if the office is large enough to accommodate a large staff.

**Open salaries** Sometimes an employment ad that you are responding to will have stipulated that the salary is *open* (i.e., open to negotiation). If you have familiarized yourself beforehand with the usual and customary salary ranges for legal secretaries in your area, you ought to be able to discuss the issue intelligently with the lawyer. In cases like this, it is even more important to highlight your education, experience, and any specialized skills that you feel would place you as close as possible to the top range.

If you can see that the interview is about to end with the lawyer's still not having brought up the matter of salary, you might say, "Oh, by the way, Mr. _____, what do you feel is a reasonable salary based on your expectations and my qualifications?" Or you could say, "What will the starting salary be for this position?" Another way of wording your question could be, "May I ask what the salary will be?" You can also convey your knowledge of the usual and customary salary ranges in the particular geographical area by mentioning those ranges in round numbers. Example: "When I spoke recently with the bar association, it was suggested that the going salary for this type of position is currently _____." You should not be pushy or insistent, however. Just state the facts objectively.

**Professional liability insurance**    Determine during the interview whether or not you will be covered in the lawyer's professional liability insurance policy. This is very important, for as an agent of the lawyer, you too can be liable to litigation. (See section 2.1.)

**Introductions to other members of the office support staff**    If you are introduced to and are given time to talk with other staff members, be sure to use this time to your advantage by asking pertinent questions regarding their tasks and routines. In this way, you can get a valid idea of what it would be like to work for and/or with them. You can also find out how efficiently the office is managed.

**Office tour**    If your prospects look good or if you have been offered the job, try to get a brief tour of the office suite. Becoming generally familiar with the location of various rooms and equipment will ease your first day on the job. Another good idea is to borrow an extra copy of the procedures manual, if there is one, so that you can familiarize yourself with the actual management of the office prior to your first day on the job.

**The offer**    At the end of the interview, you may be offered a job on the spot or the employer may tell you that he or she will get back to you in a day or so, after all other applicants have been interviewed. If you would like a day or two to think about the offer, say so. However, you should set up a specific day and hour when you will call the employer back. Do not delay your return call more than one or two days.

If the employer indicates that you will be called regarding a possible offer, accept this decision politely. Try to get some idea of when you will be contacted so that you will be at home. You might also mention that you need to complete your own plans rather soon.

Be sure that you are thoroughly familiar with any job before you accept it. Once you accept a job offer, it is extremely ungracious to change your mind. And it is never a good idea to adopt the philosophy that you can always leave if the job isn't to your liking, since by so doing you may paint an image of yourself as a "job jumper" and find that personnel directors will avoid hiring you on this ground. Most personnel directors seek employees who not only have the skills, ability, and aptitude for the job offered but who are motivated or will become motivated for the organization and who will expect to stay with that organization as a lifetime career. While you may change your mind about making it a lifetime career after a year or more, you should consider long-term employment at the time you enter into the job.

**If you don't get the job**    If you are told that you are not quite qualified for the position, thank the lawyer for the candid evaluation and be sure to mention that the interview has been a pleasant as well as an informative experience. Say good-bye politely. Don't be needlessly discouraged: appreciate the honest evaluation, work to improve any indicated deficiencies, and keep on looking for the right position.

# 2.6

## SUCCESSFUL HUMAN RELATIONS

### THE LAWYER-SECRETARY TEAM

A lawyer and secretary working together are like a team of two musicians—like a violin soloist with piano accompanist. With practice, and by recognizing and accommodating to the strengths, weaknesses, and idiosyncrasies of each other, the musicians can give a performance of grace and beauty. Failure to make such an accommodation leads to a breakdown of harmony and results in discord. The same discord can occur between lawyer and secretary when the two fail to become attuned to each other.

In order to achieve harmony with the lawyer to whom you are assigned, try to learn exactly what he or she expects. For instance, how does the lawyer wish to be addressed? Is a formal *Mr. Smith* expected? If the lawyer is female, does she prefer *Miss, Mrs.,* or *Ms. Smith?* Don't trust to guesswork on this point but ask the question. Until you are sure of yourself, lean toward a formal relationship with the lawyer and stay there until it is clearly indicated that a more informal relationship is in order. The same principle applies to the manner in which you wish to be addressed. The best way to realize your wishes is by making them known at the very outset of the job.

Ascertain the work habits of the lawyer. Is he or she an early starter, a late worker, a workaholic? Is the lawyer methodical and well organized? Seek to come to an understanding of how your work schedule may be dovetailed with these traits so that maximum efficiency may be achieved. For example, if the lawyer is a late starter and works late, consider whether to have your working hours changed to accommodate such a trait and whether the change may be effected within the policies of the office. Ascertain such things as the following: how the lawyer wishes to have you answer the telephone, how to determine the clients' wishes, to which clients you may give the lawyer's home phone number, to which clients you are free to disclose where the lawyer is at a particular time, and the best time of day to schedule appointments. In other words, become an extension of the lawyer in all matters affecting the office—*except* the furnishing of legal advice. *Never* advise a client in the law; this is a commandment that must be observed at all times.

**How a secretary can increase a lawyer's billable time**   Perhaps the best way to begin to achieve success as a member of the lawyer-secretary team is by understanding how a lawyer earns fees. Fees make up the fund from which the lawyer pays the rent for the office, the myriad bills that represent operating costs, and the salaries of secretaries, paralegals, associates, file clerks, and messengers. After all of these are paid, what is left is the income of the lawyer or, if there is more than one, the income of the members of the firm, divided on the basis of some agreed formula.

In order to bill for fees, the lawyer keeps a record of time spent on a matter and bills the client at an appropriate rate. If the lawyer's billable time is valued at $50 per hour and ten hours are spent on the matter, the bill will be $500, absent some other understanding or special arrangement.

Assume the lawyer arrives at 9 a.m., takes an hour for lunch, and leaves at 5 p.m., thereby putting in seven office hours. If the time charge rate is $50 per hour and sixty minutes of each one of the seven hours is charged to a client and collected, the lawyer's production for that day will be $350. If, however, the lawyer spends half an hour looking for a file, another half hour waiting for the secretary to arrive in the morning, a quarter hour waiting while the secretary changes the typewriter ribbon and gets a notebook, half an hour waiting for the secretary to return from lunch, and three quarters of an hour correcting typed copy and then rereading it, the potential of seven chargeable hours is reduced by two and one-half hours to four and one-half hours, and the law office productivity for the day falls from $350 to $225. In a five-day week, this can result in a loss of $625 if each day follows the same pattern.

An understanding of this time charge system of billing indicates clearly how the secretary may best serve in a lawyer-secretary team—by doing everything possible to relieve the lawyer of all unnecessary detail and by maximizing the lawyer's charge-able time. In this way the lawyer's income goes up, the secretary's value is recognized, and the secretary's income goes up.

## THE OFFICE TEAM
In addition to being part of a lawyer-secretary team, the secretary is usually part of an office team. Since much of a secretary's working life is spent with an "office family," it is a good idea to contribute to making it a happy family. Be courteous with your fellow workers and helpful to them. Stay on a friendly but somewhat formal basis until such time as informality is clearly invited. Respect the privacy of others in the firm and try to prevent the formation of cliques that pit one group against another. Office politics waste time and impair morale. Finally, do more than your share of work whenever it is feasible. If you are not busy and your neighboring co-worker is swamped, lend a helping hand. The favor will be repaid and over a period of time will be recognized by office management and the members of your office family.

By following these precepts, the secretary can begin to demonstrate the qualities of leadership that are desirable in higher, supervisory positions. If your goal is to climb the office ladder, the fastest and best way to the top rung is by demonstrating outstanding ability and leadership starting at the bottom rung and continuing on each step up.

## RELATIONSHIPS WITH CLIENTS
The legal secretary is usually the first and last member of the office staff whom a client sees. The secretary contributes a great deal to the client's favorable impression of the office. The following guidelines will help you project a positive image of the law firm:

1. Be courteous to all clients and prospective clients on the telephone and in person. When clients enter the office, make them feel at home. It is always gracious to walk a new client to the lawyer's office and introduce him or her to the lawyer.
2. Get the client's name and get it right—both its spelling and its pronunciation. Make an effort to remember the name; use it in the conversation.
3. When clients try to discuss their affairs with you, be sympathetic but don't get overly involved. You may have to tactfully change the topic of conversation.
4. Never attempt to offer legal advice, even if the client tries to draw you into a conversation about it.
5. Make no comment if the client criticizes another attorney.
6. Make sure the client understands that you treat all matters with confidentiality. One way to do this is never to leave telephone messages for the client other than asking him or her to return the call.
7. Have on hand in the office a current edition of a respected book of social etiquette such as *The Amy Vanderbilt Complete Book of Etiquette: A Guide to Contemporary Living*, revised and expanded by Letitia Baldridge (New York: Doubleday, 1978).
8. Keep clients informed. Even if you have nothing to report, you may give the client a call to say that, while nothing new has developed, the attorney will let him or her know as soon as something does develop.
9. Avoid unnecessary delays in preparing a client's legal papers and correspondence.
10. Always be discreet.

# 2.7

## ETHICS

What takes place in a lawyer's office between the lawyer and the client is *always* confidential. Regardless of how important it is—and all matters are important to the client—neither the lawyer nor the secretary is at liberty to reveal or discuss it except as a necessary part of the lawyer's prosecution of the matter in behalf of the client. Conversations concerning client matters should not be indulged in the office, at home, in the elevators, in the rest rooms, over lunch at a restaurant—anywhere or at any time. Even the way you maintain your work area is important. You should never create the opportunity for an unauthorized person to read the papers on your desk.

### CODES OF ETHICS

The confidential nature of a lawyer's practice comes under the general heading of ethics. Confidentiality is but one of the tenets of the codes of ethics applicable to lawyers and legal secretaries. The aim of these codes is to ensure that lawyers and legal secretaries adhere to the highest standards of professional conduct. As one means to this end, the NALS has promulgated the following code of ethics:

Members of the National Association of Legal Secretaries (International) are bound by the objectives of this Association and the standards of conduct required of the legal profession. Every member shall:

Encourage respect for the law and the administration of justice;

Observe rules governing privileged communications and confidential information;

Promote and exemplify high standards of loyalty, cooperation, and courtesy;

Perform all duties of the profession with integrity and competence; and

Pursue a high order of professional attainment.

The legal profession, acting through the ABA, has adopted and promulgated a code of professional responsibility that sets forth in detail guideposts for the conduct of all members of the profession. The nine canons of this code are listed in section 1.3 of Chapter 1. Secretaries as well as attorneys are bound by these canons, and taking time to review the code is certainly worthwhile. The attorney has serious ethical responsibilities; if a secretary should undermine them, even unwittingly, it could result in harming a client, subjecting the lawyer to disciplinary action, or even ruining the lawyer's career by destroying his or her reputation.

By keeping the following precepts in mind at all times, a legal secretary can prevent such disasters:

1. All client matters are confidential, privileged information and may not be divulged to anyone.
2. All written office documents are confidential and may not be divulged without the attorney's permission.
3. Cases should not be commented on or discussed outside the office.
4. The Code of Professional Responsibility of the American Bar Association applies to secretaries as well as to lawyers.
5. The secretary must be absolutely loyal to the attorney-employer.
6. The secretary must at all times refrain from giving clients legal advice. Giving such advice could be construed as the illegal practice of law.

# 3

CHAPTER 3

# THE TELEPHONE

## CONTENTS

# 3.1

## INTRODUCTION

New technologies, greater transmission speeds, and new concepts in telecommunications are continually changing the procedures under which law offices operate. The practice of law is conducted in a competitive market, and a knowledge of the latest telecommunication services and their most efficient uses can result in important economies for a law office.

The newly competitive nature of the telephone industry has brought forth new products and new ideas that were unheard of a decade or two ago. In 1968, the Federal Communications Commission ended the prohibition against interconnecting privately owned telephone equipment to the Bell System. The Carterfone decision, as it is generally known, presently permits customer-owned telephone equipment—large PBXs, key systems, recording devices, data sets, and individual telephones—to be attached to the Bell network. Specialized common carriers, as the new companies are known, are also installing telecommunication networks via microwave and satellite in competition with the Bell System. These companies supply services for voice, data, and customized forms of telemetry requiring point-to-point transmission. While these new devices and services are appealing, economies must be weighed and overall service efficiency must be considered when a decision is made to interconnect one's own telephone equipment, to buy service from a specialized common carrier, or to lease from the Bell Telephone System.

The following section of this chapter discusses the office telephone as a tool for effective communication with clients and prospective clients. The last three sections explain some of the telecommunication systems, methods, and devices available to law offices.

# 3.2

## USING THE TELEPHONE PROPERLY

Telephones are an integral part of the successful law office. They not only provide instant communication but, when used properly, can enhance the professional reputation of the office. The correct use of the telephone can speed the delivery of legal services, build goodwill, and project the best possible image of your law firm. Knowing your equipment is important. Telephone company representatives are trained to provide their customers with information about the equipment and its use. Good telephone manners—tact, courtesy, and a genuine attempt to help the caller—are also important.

### RECEIVING CALLS

Keep a pen and pad always near the telephone. Try to answer at the end of the first ring. Complete any conversations in your office <u>before</u> you pick up the receiver to answer the call. Speak directly into the instrument, keeping the mouth from about one-half inch to one inch away, and do not begin to speak until the mouthpiece is in this position. All too often a caller hears only the last half of the firm's name. Put a smile into your voice whenever you speak on the telephone; callers like to hear an alert, pleasant, well-modulated, cordial, cheerful voice.

Identify your office (and yourself, if that is the office preference). Asking "Can I help you?" suggests a personal interest in the client's problems. But avoid saying illogical things like "Mr. Bonn's desk." And if you give your name, it isn't necessary to add "Speaking." Address the caller by name (Miss, Ms., Mrs., or Mr. Caller), and never call a woman "Madam," since many women today object to it.

If office practice requires the screening of calls say, "May I ask who's calling, please?" If you say instead, "May I tell him (or her) who's calling, please?" or "May I say who's calling?" you have indicated to the caller that the person he or she is trying to reach is there; such a situation might be embarrassing if the one being called chose *not* to take the call at that particular moment. If possible, obtain the reason for the call so you will be able to give the attorney the information if you transfer the call to the attorney.

Before transferring calls, be sure to tell the caller what you are going to do. You should also give the caller the proper number for returning the call in case the connection is broken during the transfer. Know exactly how to transfer calls or put calls on hold. If you leave the phone to obtain authorized information, get back to the caller before thirty seconds have elapsed. To the caller, thirty seconds will seem interminable. If it becomes clear that your task will take longer (and most tasks do), return to the phone and ask the caller if he or she cares to wait longer or if you may return the call later. The same courtesy should be extended if the caller is on hold for more than half a minute. Let him know that you haven't forgotten him.

When you take a message, beware of saying, "I'll have him call you." The proper words are something like "May I take a message for him?" or "I'll ask her to call you" or "I'll give her the message the moment she comes in." (After all, you really don't *have* a lawyer do things!) The next thing to do is *write down* the message; don't attempt to remember it. Telephone message forms are available from printing companies and stationery supply stores. One form is illustrated here. Note that it contains the following essential information: date, time of day, name and number of caller, message, name or initials of person taking the message, and whether the call is to be returned. Keep a carbon copy of each message in the appropriate legal file folder. Accurate recording of telephone calls is important in the law office for ensur-

**A Telephone Message Form**

```
          Date_____Sept. 22_____19--

                    9:30              A.M.
          Time_____XPXMX

    To_____Mr. Jones_____

           WHILE YOU WERE OUT

    M_____Dr. Bascom, Monroe, LA_____

                    URGENT
    _____
               505-234-5678
    Phone No._____

    ☒ Telephoned       ☐ Called to see you

           AND LEFT THIS MESSAGE
    Emergency surgery this a.m.; will not

    be able to appear today as witness in

    Yost case. Can testimony be postponed

    until tomorrow?
       ☒ Please call back    ☐ Will call again

              Signed_____DM_____

    FORM  3327   COLWELL CO., CHAMPAIGN, ILL.
```

Reprinted by permission of The Colwell Company.

ing that calls are returned, for billing the client, and for recording information that might be used in lawsuits.

As the illustration shows, each message should be dated and should contain the time that the message was received. Of course, telephone numbers and names should be recorded accurately. You should always indicate by initials or in some other manner that *you* took the message. It's a good idea to repeat a message—especially a complex one—to the caller to be sure it has been recorded correctly. If others are present when a message must be repeated to a caller, ask the *caller* to repeat the message to you in order to preserve confidentiality and ensure accuracy.

A listing or logging of calls similar to a register of incoming mail may also be helpful, especially if it includes an "action" column.

If it appears that a caller has dialed you by mistake, answer courteously and ask who he is trying to reach. If it is a wrong number you can say, "You've reached the wrong number, I believe."

Should the caller ask for someone who is already using another line of the telephone, you could say, "May I help you or would you care to speak with another attorney?" Of course, you would never say, "She hasn't come back from lunch yet" (and it's 3 p.m.) or "He's playing golf today," or "I don't know where he went," or "She isn't in," without elaboration. Telephone courtesy requires that you give correct information; however, it is important that you do not state facts that could lead to a misunderstanding and that you do not divulge information you are not authorized to give. Discretion is important. Be helpful but not too revealing. Learn to be courteously noncommittal.

Always end a call with "Goodbye," but be sure to <u>let the caller hang up first</u>. After the caller has hung up, replace your own receiver gently. If the caller persists in talking, you might have to say, "I'm sorry, but I have a call on another line," or "I'd like to talk longer, but I'm due at a meeting now," or "Excuse me, but Mr. Lawyer has just buzzed for me to take dictation."

You and the attorney should set up a priority list for his or her accepting calls. You might want to arrange a buzzer signal to let the attorney know of especially urgent phone calls that are waiting for his attention. Also, it should be established which calls you are authorized to handle and which calls must be handled exclusively by the attorney.

You may be asked to take dictation over the telephone. Because you have just one hand free (unless you have a hands-free telephone device), you may have to ask that some things be repeated. It is wise to read the entire dictation back to the dictator afterward. If you are asked to monitor a telephone conversation and to take notes on it, get the main points as you would do if you were taking notes at a lecture.

Some secretaries refuse to put a call through to their employers until the caller is ready to speak. If this happens to you, don't react stubbornly—perhaps the secretary is following orders. And perhaps your employer may, at some time, request that a call not be put through until you have made certain that the caller is already on the line; or, if the attorney is making a call, he or she may wish to make sure that the person being called is on the line first.

## RETURNING CALLS

The legal secretary and the attorney should work together in establishing priorities for certain types of messages and in devising a method for the timely return of telephone messages. A call placed to the attorney should be returned within the same day if possible. Some attorneys like to set aside a certain time each day just to return telephone calls. Sometimes you may have to tactfully remind the attorney to return a call; sometimes you may be asked to relay a message. A preplanned priority list for returning calls is especially useful when the lawyer has been away. Urgent matters should be at the top of the list, of course, but in general a judge's calls should be returned first, then attorneys' calls, then those of clients.

## PLACING CALLS

When you make calls for an attorney, always be sure that he or she is available before you actually place the call. Sometimes an attorney will ask you to make a call; then for some reason he or she will step out of the office for a minute or two. You don't want to be left holding the call with the person whom you have just dialed waiting impatiently on the other end of the line. Such a situation can be embarrassing for the secretary and the attorney: it needlessly wastes the time of the person being called and thus is irritating.

Having looked up the correct number in a directory (calls to the Directory Assistance Operator should be avoided unless absolutely necessary), you then dial the number. You should allow the telephone to ring at least six or seven times (the telephone company recommends that you let it ring as many as ten times if necessary). When the telephone is answered, identify yourself and state your business in a clear, coherent, polite way.

Many times the attorney will ask you to convey telephone messages yourself. Before placing such a call, you should first jot down what you want to say. Then place your telephone call, being sure to introduce yourself as Mr. or Ms. Lawyer's secretary.

**Frequently called numbers**    You will find that a list of frequently called numbers is extremely helpful. It is usually typed and attached to the pullout ledge of your desk. It may also be put on cards on a wheel or a rotary file, or it may be written on the pages of a flip-up index pad. The following example illustrates a skeleton file of frequently called numbers. Of course, such a file will vary with one's office requirements:

Accountants

Airlines

Attorneys regularly called

Bar associations

Bookbinder

Building manager or superintendent

Car rental agency

City offices

Committee members

Copying/duplicating service

County offices

Court clerks (municipal and circuit courts, court of appeals, state supreme court, U.S. District Court)

Court reporters

Emergency numbers (as ambulance, fire, or police)

Equipment repairmen

Family and friends

Federal offices

Hotels and motels used by attorney

Insurance agents

Investigators

Judges

Library information desk

Messenger service

Personal services (as bank, barber, club, stockbroker, doctor, etc.)

Post Office information

Process servers

Printing services

Railroads

Referral services

Register of Deeds

State offices

Stationer and office supply store

Tax offices

Time check (exact up-to-the-minute report)

Travel agency

Unlisted numbers

Weather information

Western Union

A private list of home phone numbers of the attorney, office employees, and important clients is also very helpful. This list should be considered confidential and should be kept out of sight. Your telephone lists should be kept up to date.

**Directories**    If your office is one in which long-distance calls are frequently made to certain cities, a file of out-of-town directories may be helpful. You may also find a street-address telephone directory valuable; this type of directory is available for large cities and may be rented from the telephone office.

Your city telephone directory contains much useful information in addition to the regular alphabetical listings. Learn to use the Yellow Pages. Look for the maps showing postal zones and telephone area codes. Some directories have perpetual calendars and a list of numbers to call for the correct time, for current weather information, and for postal rate information. Special instructions for making calls are contained in the front of each directory. Take time to familiarize yourself with the front pages of your directory. And remember that federal, state, county, and city offices are normally listed under "United States Government" or the name of the governmental unit. A helpful practice is to underline lightly, or to mark with a yellow felt-tip pen any number you look up, thus making it easier to find the next time you need it. Of value, too, is the current city directory for your locale. This book shows the addresses that have telephones, although telephone numbers are not included.

## TELEPHONE-RELATED PUBLIC RELATIONS SITUATIONS
Because of the fiduciary relationship between lawyer and client, you will often receive calls from insistent, upset, or irate clients or would-be clients. While these calls are not the most pleasant to handle, they can be taken care of in a tactful manner.

**The difficult client**    Once in a while an irritated client will call while the attorney is out of the office. Firmly and pleasantly tell the client that the attorney is not in but that you will transfer the message that the client called just as soon as the attorney returns—and then be sure to do so.

**Clients placing toll calls**    Clients frequently ask permission to place telephone calls. When these are toll calls, the thoughtful client immediately suggests payment, but many clients simply do not think about it. Ask permission to place the call for the client, then record time and charges. Keep a record of these calls and bill the client for them, unless special circumstances make it more diplomatic for the law firm to charge the call to overhead.

**Determining the purpose of the call**    When clients call for an appointment, the legal secretary is usually responsible for learning the reason for the appointment. Many callers are hesitant to reveal the reasons for their legal problems. Upon answering the call, introduce yourself and tell the caller that you are Mr. or Ms. Lawyer's secretary and that you will be pleased to set up an appointment. Inquire as to the date and time the caller would like the appointment. You should then suggest an appointment time. You now need to find out from the caller what he needs to see the lawyer about. You might say something like "Mr. Caller, so that Mrs. Lawyer will be ready for your appointment and be able to offer you some assistance, may I ask the nature of your problem? I do not need to have all the facts, just a short statement." Usually the caller will give you enough information that you can set up a firm appointment. If the requested attorney will be out of the office for an extended period, ask whether another attorney may help. Always be tactful and courteous.

**Legal advice and fee information**    Some callers will attempt to obtain legal advice or fee schedules over the telephone. Let the caller know that fees depend upon the services that the lawyer renders and that the lawyer is the *only* one who can discuss fees. Likewise, most lawyers do not give legal advice over the telephone. In both instances the client should make an appointment with the attorney, and the secretary is responsible for making the appointment.

**Establishing guidelines**    You and the attorney should work out a procedure to follow in the case of other telephone-related public relations situations such as when a reporter calls with respect to a headline case you are handling in the office; or when a caller insists upon seeing the attorney when he or she is seeing other clients or is busy briefing in the law library. To save you embarrassment should a client ask to see his or her file, the attorney should be specific as to which papers in the files that clients are allowed to see. The guidelines that you and the attorney agree upon will assist you in efficiently handling the telephone calls in the law office.

Another kind of telephone contact involves keeping the client informed as to the status of his case. Some law firms maintain a calendar for making periodic telephone calls to their clients to let them know how the case is progressing. The clients are thus assured that the attorney has not forgotten them.

## CONFIDENTIALITY
Canon 4 of the ABA's Code of Professional Responsibility provides that the lawyer should preserve the confidences and secrets of a client and act scrupulously in making decisions which may involve the disclosure of information obtained in the professional relationship. The canon also pertains to legal secretaries. The normal operation of a law office exposes confidential professional information to non-lawyer employees, particularly secretaries, and the lawyer is obligated to select and train employees carefully in order to preserve the confidentiality of the clients' affairs. You must be careful not to inadvertently expose any such information. For example, you should never leave a substantive telephone message for a client when the client is out (someone might then learn something of the client's personal matters) nor allow visitors in the reception area to hear you speaking about another client's affairs.

# 3.3

## TELECOMMUNICATIONS SYSTEMS

### TELEPHONE EQUIPMENT

A telephone has three parts: a transmitter, a receiver, and an electrical circuit that produces energy. This simple device has thousands of uses ranging from ordinary voice conversation to high-speed data transmission. Several types and styles of telephones are described here.

**Single line telephones**   The single line telephone is the familiar telephone set. It is available in many colors, sizes, and types—dial or pushbutton; desk, wall, Trimline, and so forth.

**Multi-button telephones**   The multi-button telephone offers 6, 10, 20, or 30 buttons; pressing a button transfers a call to a particular telephone within the office. Because various signals and intercommunications can be installed within these telephone sets, they are used by small law firms to answer, transfer, and screen calls.

**Hands-free telephones**   The hands-free telephone is commonly referred to as a *speakerphone*. Some hands-free telephone devices have individual receivers and transmitters, while others are an integral part of the telephone set. Hands-free devices are useful for conference calls or when the caller must perform other tasks such as examining files or taking notes while conversing.

**Automatic answering device**   Telephone answering and receiving devices answer incoming calls automatically with prerecorded messages. These recordings can tell the caller to leave a message, advise the caller where the person being called is or when he or she is expected back, or forward the call. They allow the office telephone to be covered 24 hours a day, every day.

**Automatic dialer**   The automatic dialer permits a repertoire of telephone numbers to be stored on magnetic tape or on prepunched plastic cards. It enables the caller to dial different numbers in succession or to dial the same number at intervals—all automatically.

**Radio paging**   Two types of radio paging equipment are available: *tone only* or *tone and voice*. The secretary dials the paging equipment to access tone-alert or voice-page pocket radio receivers that may be carried by the lawyer.

### TELEPHONE SYSTEMS

The wide variety of telephone systems on the market and their many special features provide an opportunity to select the system that suits your needs. Most of the systems are reliable, are easily maintained, and provide excellent service. The features of the available telephone systems are numerous and varied. Along with the standard Direct Inward Dialing (DID), Direct Outward Dialing (DOD), and station-to-station calling, a telephone system may include the following special features:

1. Local Automatic Message Accounting—a service providing a magnetic-tape record of all telephone calls except station-to-station calls; the tape may record the station calling, the number called, the time and length of the call, the trunk used, and the charges. This is an excellent tool to help control an office's toll costs.

2. Automatic Route Selection—a system that routes calls over the least expensive trunk (as tie line, WATS, or FX); or automatically steps the call up to the next most expensive route (Direct Distance Dialing) if all primary routes are busy.
3. Traffic Analysis—a system using trunk loading statistics to determine the number of facilities needed to handle a particular call load.
4. Call Transfer—the ability to transfer an established incoming or outgoing call to another party inside or outside the telephone system without the assistance of an attendant.
5. Add-On Conference—an option that permits the caller to add a third party to an ongoing conversation without outside assistance.
6. Call Forwarding—the ability to automatically reroute incoming telephone calls to another telephone number.
7. Camp On Busy—the ability of an operator to camp an incoming call on a telephone in use; a short tone may be sent over the busy line to advise that a call is waiting.
8. Call Pick-Up—the ability to answer an incoming call directed to another telephone.
9. Abbreviated Dialing—the ability to program one's telephone to use abbreviated numbers in lieu of full numbers to speed up outside dialing.
10. Automatic Call Back—a system that informs the caller that a certain office phone that was busy when a call was placed is now free. When the caller first finds that the line is busy, he dials a code and replaces the handset. As soon as the called station is idle, the caller's telephone rings and when it is picked up the called party's telephone will automatically ring.
11. Outgoing Trunk Queuing—if all outgoing trunks are busy, the system will remember the station being dialed and will call back as soon as a trunk is free.

## SPECIAL TELEPHONE EQUIPMENT SYSTEMS AND SERVICES

**Foreign Exchange Service**    Foreign Exchange (FX) provides the user with flat-rate service to other locations for outgoing or incoming calls. FX service can be purchased from the Bell System or from specialized common carriers at a 24-hour monthly rate.

**Answering services**    The Yellow Pages of your telephone directory contain advertisements for answering services. Most answering services respond 24 hours a day and will answer the telephone in the name you request. These firms offer services ranging from message relay to two-way radio dispatching or radio paging.

**Electronic transceivers**    These can be used for funds-transfer functions including check verification. The equipment features a telephone through which magnetically striped cards are passed and read. This information is then verified by a centralized computer. Another system uses the Touch-Tone pad on a regular telephone as the computer input device.

**Tie line service**    This is a point-to-point full-time leased service that permits engineering for either voice or data transmission. This service can be purchased on a 24-hour monthly basis and is available from the Bell System as well as from specialized common carriers.

**Telephone dictation service**    Centralized dictation systems have been installed by many law offices today. These systems may be accessed by telephone. When the access code is dialed, a recorder is activated. Following a prescribed procedure, the user dictates a document that is recorded on tape or on a magnetic disk and is ready for transcription. Playback, correction, stop, and operator assistance features are also available on these systems. The advantages of these systems are many: dictation can take place at any time of the day, centralized secretarial help may reduce an office's clerical staff, and the cost of centralized dictating equipment may be less than that of dictation equipment placed in individual offices.

**Facsimile transmission**   High-speed, digital facsimile transmission over regular telephone lines is generally available. Manufacturers now offer equipment capable of transmitting a page of copy in less than a minute's time. High-speed facsimile equipment is expensive but can often be justified by a reduction in telephone toll costs. Facsimile machines are used chiefly to send large volumes of information to a certain location, such as a branch office. At present, they are the most efficient means of transmitting already-prepared hard copy to remote places.

Most equipment is available in either a manual or an automatic mode, thus making it ideal for transmitting between two points after working hours. Documents can be stacked and transmitted automatically over tie lines or WATS facilities that are often idle in the late hours of the working day. Some manufacturers offer "store and forward" features which record documents on magnetic tape and transmit them on command. Automated facsimile devices can broadcast a single document to many locations or contact other minicomputers and request automatic transmission of documents from distant points.

**Data communication**   Data communication involves the transmittal of electric signals from one point to another at speeds of up to 250,000 bits per second. Data can be transmitted over ordinary telephone lines or via specialized point-to-point facilities. The Bell System has developed a Dataphone network for the exclusive use of transmitting data.

## SPECIALIZED COMMON CARRIERS
Specialized common carriers can also provide a wide range of telecommunication services. These companies specialize in voice and data transmission facilities and services similar to those offered by the Bell System. They transmit over private microwave and satellite transmission facilities to more than 100 metropolitan areas throughout the United States. The circuits offered by these carriers can interface with those of the local telephone company and can eliminate the need for two independent terminals in the office. These carriers serve selected segments of the communications market that need point-to-point transmission of voice or data and can offer a firm tailor-made communications services.

## CHOOSING THE RIGHT SYSTEM
Today's law offices have available a wide choice of telephone communications equipment, from the local telephone company and from common carriers and private interconnect companies. The telephone company usually supplies its services for an all-inclusive monthly charge while the private interconnect companies either sell or lease their equipment. As a legal secretary, you may be asked to help determine whether and what new telecommunication equipment may be required for purchase, lease, or rental. You may be asked to obtain quotations from available sources, and you may also be expected to analyze these bids to help the office reach a decision. Cost is not the only consideration; the system must meet the needs of the law firm. Inadequate equipment, poor design, and lack of maintenance could cost the firm more than any savings on the original purchase.

You and the attorney may wish to consult the *Communications Handbook for Attorneys: Telephone Systems and Facsimile*, edited by Paul S. Hoffman and Jerry W. Mills and published by the Section of Economics of Law Practice, American Bar Association, Chicago, Illinois (1978). This publication suggests that the following questions be considered when purchasing or leasing telephone communications equipment:

1. Will the rates increase?
2. Is leasing or purchase more practical?
3. What does the cost of the system cover?

4. How flexible is the system: can it be changed as the office expands?
5. What overhead costs are involved?
6. How much space will the equipment require?
7. What would it cost to move the system?
8. What special features does the system offer?
9. Will the source be able to install the system by the time the firm needs it?
10. Can the system be insured? If so, by whom?
11. Who will service the system? What will it cost?

Questions about maintenance are extremely important. Once you convert to private equipment, you cannot call the telephone company to make repairs. In considering service and maintenance you should ask the following questions, as suggested in the *Communications Handbook for Attorneys*:

1. Is maintenance included in the purchase or lease price?
2. Are all parts and labor covered?
3. If maintenance is not included in the purchase or lease price, how much will it cost?
4. Does the cost of a maintenance contract increase with time?
5. Who will perform the maintenance and repair work?
6. How financially stable is the company performing maintenance?
7. How long has the company been performing similar maintenance?
8. Can I talk to customers of the company performing maintenance?
9. How quickly will maintenance be provided?
10. How available are parts and supplies for this system?

Care should be taken in the choice of a private interconnect company; it must have a good reputation in both installation and maintenance. A written contract is usually drawn up; the attorney will look for paragraphs describing the system and covering such items as warranties, delivery and installation, maintenance, training, financial arrangements, and cancellation. When investigating private interconnect companies, the law firm should insist upon a system offering as much equipment and as many services as those offered by the local telephone company in order to fully compare the cost and maintenance of each system.

# 3.3

## TELEPHONE COMMUNICATIONS

### LOCAL CALLING
In most cities the telephone company uses the message unit to charge for local calls. This system charges a fixed fee for a predetermined number of calls; it differs from the system that was formerly in wide use, whereby a flat rate was charged for an unlimited number of local calls.

### LONG-DISTANCE CALLS
Long-distance calls are classified as *station-to-station, operator station-to-station,* and *person-to-person*. Charges are based on the time of day when the call is placed and the rate mileage. The Day Rate period is Monday through Friday from 8 a.m. to 5 p.m.; the Evening Rate (discounted from the Day Rate) is Sunday through Friday from 5 p.m. to 11 p.m., and the Night & Weekend Rate (considerably discounted from the Day Rate) is every night from 11 p.m. to 8 a.m. and all day Saturday and all day Sunday except for the hours 5 p.m. through 11 p.m. The rate is determined from the time zone of the caller, not the receiver.

## Time Zone Map

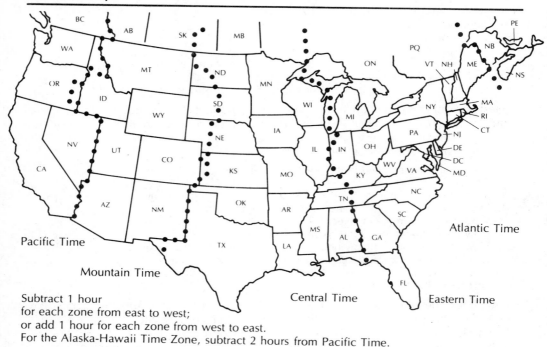

**Pacific Time**

**Mountain Time**

**Central Time**

**Eastern Time**

**Atlantic Time**

Subtract 1 hour
for each zone from east to west;
or add 1 hour for each zone from west to east.
For the Alaska-Hawaii Time Zone, subtract 2 hours from Pacific Time.

**Station-to-station calls (Direct-Distance Dialing)** This is the fastest and least expensive way to place telephone calls because the caller is willing to talk to anyone who answers. The charge is based on a one-minute minimum with an additional charge for each succeeding minute. Consult your directory to ascertain the times and rates for "station" calls. Be sure to check time zones before making long-distance calls to be sure you are within usual working hours. Check your directory to see if it is necessary in your area to dial 1 first to get into the long-distance mode.

**Operator station-to-station calls** These calls are either *credit card, collect,* or *bill-to-third-party* calls. Based on a three-minute minimum with an additional charge for each succeeding minute, these calls cost much more than station-to-station calls.

**Person-to-person calls** These calls are made when the caller wants to talk only to one specific person. The charge for these calls is based on a three-minute minimum plus an additional charge for each succeeding minute. This type of call is expensive and its use should be minimized.
  Person-to-person calls are made in one of two ways:

1. Dial the Operator and say, "This is a call to (name of *city* being called) at (number of telephone) to speak personally to (name of person)." If information is given in this order, the Operator can be starting the call while you are continuing to supply information.
2. Use direct-distance dialing (DDD), in which you dial 0 first followed by the area code and the telephone number; the Operator will answer, and while your call goes through the system, you give the Operator the name of the person to whom you want to speak. If you do not have the number you want to call, you obtain it by dialing the appropriate area code and 555-1212 anywhere in the United States. This is a Directory Assistance number, and there is usually no charge for this call.

**Conference calls**   Some telephone systems are capable of setting up conference calls with three to eight outside parties by means of the direct distance dialing network. The telephone company operator can also arrange a conference call as described below under "Operator-assisted long-distance calls," but the rate is expensive.

**Zero Express Dialing (ZED)**   ZED is commonly used for credit card calls, collect calls, or bill-to-third-party calls. The caller dials 0 followed by the complete telephone number. The operator comes on the line, requests your credit card number or other billing instructions, then connects the call. The call is charged as an operator-handled call.

**Wide Area Telephone Service (WATS)**   WATS is a reduced-rate, long-distance service for large users of telephone service. WATS is designated as *inward* or *outward*. Outward WATS will let you place as many calls as you wish, one after another, within the allotted time purchased. Two types may be purchased: the full business day (FBD) of 240 hours of service a month with additional use charged by the hour; or Measured Time (MT) providing 10 hours a month with additional use charged by the hour. The country is divided into bands by geographic areas that include Canada, Alaska, and Hawaii, and the service can be purchased for specific bands. Inward WATS permits you to receive an unlimited number of calls over a specific line by prefixing an 800 number to your inward WATS line number.

**Operator-assisted long-distance calls**   Long-distance calls may be made in a variety of ways:

1.  Appointment calls are made with the Operator. You ask to have a call placed at a certain time, which is done. The Operator then calls you when the person you have called is ready to converse.

2.  Collect calls follow the person-to-person routine. The first thing you say to the Operator is, "This is a collect call," and then you give your name. The operator will ask the person called if he wishes to accept the charges; if he declines, the call is not completed (unless you are willing to pay for it) and no charge is made.

3.  If your telephone system is not capable of setting up conference calls, they can be arranged. Ask for the Conference Operator and explain the setup that you want: the names, locations, and phone numbers of each person you want to reach and the time desired. All of the persons connected can talk with one another as if they were around a conference table. The Conference Operator can also arrange a *one-way* service whereby the caller can speak to listeners in up to 25 locations simultaneously.

4.  A credit card call permits a traveler to charge long-distance or toll calls from any telephone by means of a credit card which is issued by the telephone company. The call is placed through the Operator, with your first words being, "This is a credit card call. My card number is. . . . " If you want your call charged to another number, say first of all, "Please bill to (area code and telephone number to which the call is to be billed)" and follow with the usual long-distance information.

5.  Sequence calls are person-to-person calls handled by the Operator as rapidly as possible in the order you have indicated on the list that you have provided the Operator.

6.  Messenger calls are used when it is necessary to reach someone who does not have a phone. A messenger is dispatched by the Operator at the distant place to notify the person that there is a call for him.

**International dialing**   Generally, in order to place an overseas call you must call the local telephone operator and give the name of the city and country that you wish to call. You will then be connected with the overseas telephone operator who will place the call. The initial charge is for a three-minute minimum, and for each additional minute the charge is approximately one third of the three-minute rate. Rates are determined by the time the call originates and are categorized as *Day* and *Night/ Sunday*. The time period may vary for some countries, but the Day Rate most often extends from 5 a.m. to 5 p.m. and the Night Rate, from 5 p.m. to 5 a.m. Sunday rates apply all day Sunday.

Some areas throughout the United States have access to the International Direct Distance Dialing Service (IDDD). This expands your direct-dialing capability to over 74 countries overseas. IDDD is by far the simplest, fastest, and least expensive way to call abroad. If you work in an area which has access to IDDD, you can dial 011 + the country code + the city routing code + the local telephone number and be connected without operator assistance. IDDD can considerably reduce the cost of overseas telephone communication.

**Mobile calls**   Telephones may be installed in automobiles, trucks, aircraft, and ships. Calls are connected via land-line telephones through radio circuits. The mobile number is ordinarily listed in the telephone directory; otherwise, you can ask for the Mobile Service Operator.

**Keeping records of calls**   Most legal secretaries keep a record of all out-of-town and toll calls that have been made so that telephone charges can be checked against this list and costs can be allocated to the proper client files. If you are required to get the charges immediately after a call has been completed, you do so by asking the Operator <u>before</u> you say anything else when you place the call, as "Operator, please quote T and C on this call." (*T and C* means *time and charges.*)

## CONTROLLING TELEPHONE EXPENSES

The least expensive and most efficient way of calling is to do it yourself. Direct Distance Dialing (DDD) enables you to reach your party via the most direct route. Placing your own calls and answering your own telephone, rather than relying on another secretary or a receptionist to do it for you, saves time for others and money for the law firm.

Personal calls or nonbusiness-related calls can amount to 20 to 45 percent of a law firm's total daily telephone traffic. This cannot be eliminated entirely, but it can be curtailed. The best way to cut telephone costs is for management to make all personnel aware of the cost of telephone service. Traffic analyzers and equipment permitting automatic identification of outward dialing help to reduce communications expenses, especially if the telephone service comprises a mixture of trunks such as FX service, tie lines, WATS, and toll trunks. Such control systems can identify incoming and outgoing calls on magnetic tape and allocate telephone costs by extension number. Costs and methods of installation vary, so it is best to check with manufacturers before initiating one of these systems. Some advantages of the systems are that they (1) eliminate manual control of trunk calls, (2) reduce telephone abuse, (3) utilize trunk facilities to the utmost, (4) reduce billing errors, and (5) make management more cognizant of telephone costs, since individual station billing is used.

Some other hints for reducing telephone expenses are as follows:

1. Keep in mind that there is a three-hour time difference between the West Coast and the East Coast, and that a call placed after 5 p.m. on the East Coast will reach a West Coast office at lower rates.
2. When you have to call Europe, get up early. Place your call before 5 a.m. if possible. When it is 5 a.m. in the United States, it is 11 a.m. in much of Europe. Your call will also go through at a much cheaper rate. In addition, you should check time zones to make sure that the overseas party is likely to be in the office.
3. Review telephone equipment details (line 1 of your telephone bill) every month to make sure that all equipment is accounted for.

4. Review your toll statement and make an attempt to account for all calls listed. (When a toll call is made, it should be recorded immediately on a charge slip or in a small notebook so that the proper client may be charged.) In a small firm, you should pass the statement along to your attorney-employer for further scrutiny. For a large firm, the telephone company can provide a magnetic tape of monthly tolls so that you or the firm's administrator can analyze this information.
5. Report all service disruptions immediately to the telephone company.
6. When changes in service are requested, make sure that the work is done to your specification. Make sure that service terminations are carried out as required and that the billing coincides with the removal of the equipment.
7. Make sure you receive credit for service interruptions or misdialed numbers.
8. If your local telephone company charges for Directory Assistance, keep a supply of telephone directories for major metropolitan areas on hand so that you can look the numbers up yourself.
9. Telephone company personnel will perform usage studies and provide free training for lawyers and secretaries.
10. One individual within the firm should be responsible for ordering telecommunication equipment.

# 3.4

## TELEGRAPH COMMUNICATIONS

Sometimes a law office finds it necessary to send a brief, urgent message. Telegrams and Mailgrams are used to provide the speed, economy, and sense of urgency that are desired. Unlike telephone calls, they provide a written record of the message, and for this reason law offices frequently send telegrams to confirm legal transactions.

### DOMESTIC SYSTEMS AND SERVICES
A telegram may be delivered by messenger or by telephone. Messenger delivery, available in most places, is guaranteed within five hours, while phone delivery is guaranteed within two hours at any time of any day. A written copy of the telephone message can also be sent by mail.

**Telegram services**  A variety of services are available from Western Union, including Overnight Telegrams, which are priced lower than full-rate telegrams and which assure delivery by 2 p.m. the following day. Services for which extra charges are added include (1) delivery to an alternate address if the addressee is not at the specified location, (2) a confirmation copy of the message returned to the sender, and (3) a confirmation by telegram or Mailgram that the message was delivered.

**The telegram**  A telegram contains the date, an inside address, the message, and the name and firm of the sender. While telegrams are usually telephoned to Western Union, typed copies must be prepared for the firm's legal and financial records. After you have read the wire to the Western Union operator, ask to have it read back to you to make sure it is correct. If your office has a teletype machine with an optional printer, this last step may be omitted. Word count is very important in telegrams, because you are charged by the word. The following guidelines may help you send economical messages:

1. Only the address and signature are free.
2. Dictionary words are counted as one word.
3. Non-dictionary words longer than five letters are counted as two words or more.
4. Abbreviations of less than five letters are counted as one word.
5. Proper names are counted according to the way they are normally written.
6. Punctuation marks are not chargeable, but signs and symbols such as $, &, #, ' (for *feet*) and '' (for *inches*) are counted as part of a mixed group used in conjunction with other numbers and letters. Every five characters equals one word.

**Mailgram**   The Mailgram was developed jointly by Western Union and the U.S. Postal Service to speed written communications at a fraction of the cost of a telegram. A Mailgram can be prepared at one's teletype terminal or computer terminal or by facsimile machine; or it may be telephoned into one's local Western Union office. The message is transmitted via Western Union's microwave and satellite communication networks to a post office near the recipient's address. There it is typed and inserted into a distinctive blue and white envelope for delivery within the next day's mail.

## TELETYPEWRITER NETWORKS

New automated systems are competing with the conventional telegraph as the primary means of transmitting the written word. Private systems that use the direct-distance dialing network can be installed with high-speed teletypewriters or CRT (cathode-ray tube) devices. Store-and-forward minicomputers can store administrative traffic and forward information to other locations during non-prime time, thus enabling the user to take advantage of lower telephone rates. These systems can be built to accommodate AT&T and Western Union line circuits and can also access TWX and telex equipment.

Many law offices today have access to a teletypewriter, which is basically equipment that allows written communication with another office that is also equipped with a teletypewriter. The machines are connected by wire through automatic exchanges. Access to a teletypewriter provides direct-dial communication to more than 170,000 terminals in North America and many more worldwide.

**Telex and TWX**   Telex (*teleprinter* exchange) and TWX (teletypewriter exchange; pronounced *twix*) are two different but interconnected teletypewriter networks that can communicate with each other by means of a computer interface. The difference between the two lies mainly in speed: TWX is faster. There is also a difference in the method of charging, although both systems charge on the basis of distance and time used. Equipment can either be leased through Western Union or purchased from Western Union or another manufacturer. Many models of both systems are presently on the market.

With a teletypewriter, an office has the following advantages: (1) it can send a message at any hour of the day because messages can be received at an unattended terminal, (2) it will get an exact copy of every message sent and received, (3) it can easily send Mailgrams, telegrams, and cablegrams via telex or TWX. Special features of teletypewriters include an automatic identification, or *answerback*, which confirms that you have reached the desired recipient before the message is transmitted. To lower costs and ensure accuracy, the message can be recorded on punched paper tape within the machine. The punched tape is then used to transmit the message at maximum teletypewriter speed.

## INTERNATIONAL SYSTEMS

There are two basic ways of transmitting a message overseas, either by International Telegram, or cablegram, or by International Telex Service. The major international common carriers that can provide these services are the French Cable Company, ITT World Communications, RCA Global Communications, Western Union, and Western Union International.

**International telegrams (cablegrams)**    International telegrams can be sent by teletype or by the local Western Union office to almost any location in the world. Western Union will file the message with an international carrier of your choice, which will transmit the message overseas. It will then be delivered by the local telegraph company, post office, or government agency of the destination country. The two cablegram rates most commonly used are full rate service (International Telegram), which has a seven-word minimum, and letter rate (Letter Telegram), which has a 22-word minimum. International Telegrams are fast, but they are expensive and should be used sparingly. Most companies have registered cable addresses; use them. Specify the routing (i.e., the name of the international common carrier of your choice) and give delivery instructions, if desired.

**International telex**    Direct teletype connection can be made to more than 150 countries from any teleprinter that is connected directly to an international carrier. The message can be either directed by keyboard or prepared on punched paper tape and transmitted to your overseas correspondent. You can also have two-way written communication which provides you with instant confirmation and verification that your message has been received and understood. Most overseas teletypes are equipped with automatic answer-back features so that the printer you call is always ready to receive your message. Rates are much less than those for cablegrams, but they vary from country to country.

# 4

# THE MAIL

## CONTENTS

# 4.1

## INCOMING OFFICE MAIL

Efficient handling of incoming mail is one of the tasks expected of the legal secretary. The steps outlined in the following pages are applicable to mail processing in a small, medium-sized, or large law office.

### PRELIMINARY SORTING

In large corporations and large law firms the mail room personnel receive the mail directly from the carrier, or else a designated messenger picks it up from the post office. The mail is sorted in the mail room and then delivered to the various departments by mail room messengers. Within the individual departments one person is usually assigned the responsibility of sorting the mail for the lawyers and then delivering it to each lawyer's secretary. The mail will then be sorted for the lawyer in the same manner as it would be in a one-secretary law office. It saves time to sort the mail into stacks before it is opened. It may be sorted in these categories: telegrams, first class, second class (newspapers and magazines), third class (circulars, booklets, catalogs, and other printed materials), fourth class (domestic parcel post), priority mail (air parcel post), international mail, and interoffice memorandums.

### OPENING THE MAIL

Letters marked *personal* or *confidential* should not be opened by the secretary unless the lawyer has given permission to do so. If you open a letter unintentionally, simply mark the envelope "Opened by mistake," initial it, and reseal the envelope with tape. Before slitting open the envelope, tap the bottom edge to ensure that the contents are not at the top. This prevents damage to checks and other important enclosures. Be sure that everything is removed from the envelope; check enclosure notations on letters to be sure that nothing is missing. If an item has been omitted, make a notation of it on the letter. Follow the practice of your office as to whether or not to attach envelopes and enclosures to letters. Always check the letterhead and the envelope to be sure that you have the correct mailing address for the sender before throwing an envelope away.

## DATING THE MAIL

A hand or automatic date stamp is used to record the date and sometimes the time when the mail was received. The date and time received are often matters of critical importance in a law office. If a date stamp is not available, the secretary should write "Received" and the date and time on the letter. In some offices just the date in numerical form will suffice.

## SECONDARY SORTING

The next step is the secondary sorting of the mail for presentation to the lawyer. At this time the mail is arranged by priority so that the lawyer may handle the important mail first. Telegrams and Certified, Registered, or Special Delivery mail should be placed on top of the pile. A *system* of prioritizing mail is useful, whereby the lawyer determines that certain matters will automatically be marked urgent.

## READING THE MAIL

In some law offices the secretary reads the letters and underlines or marks with a yellow highlighter the important passages and dates for the lawyer. From this reading the secretary is able to secure dates and information about court cases and to enter them on the firm's calendar and court docket. Some secretaries make marginal notations on the letters to aid the attorney's reply, and some are authorized to draft replies.

## RECORDING THE MAIL

The final step in handling incoming mail in some law offices is making a record of it in a register or log. A sample mail register is illustrated below. All important mail is recorded in the register, but items such as advertisements are omitted. The following data are usually recorded in a mail register: the date and time of day received, the date of the letter itself, the writer, the addressee, a brief description (as of the subject or case), and the disposition of the letter. It is imperative that important communications dealing with court cases, such as dates for hearings and motions and deadlines for filing legal documents, be entered in the court docket and on the calendar of both the secretary and the lawyer.

**Mail Register or Log**

| Rec'd | Dated | Time | From | Addressed To | Description | Disposition | Date |
|-------|-------|------|------|--------------|-------------|-------------|------|
| 9/3/-- | 9/1/-- | 9 A.M. | A.B. COOK | LAWYER B. DAVIS | COLLECTION MATTER | LETTER TO CREDITOR | 9/3/-- |
| 9/3/-- | 8/31/-- | 9 A.M. | DON GREEN | LAWYER C. BROWN | WORKMEN'S COMP. | LETTER LABOR BOARD | 9/3/-- |
| 9/3/-- | 9/2/-- | 2 P.M. | OMEGA CORP. | LAWYER D. COLE | MINUTES - ANN-MTG. | PREPARED MINUTES | 9/4/-- |
| 9/4/-- | 9/3/-- | 9 A.M. | IRS | LAWYER G. FRANK | PENSION TRUST | LETTER - INFO | 9/4/-- |

## A Letter of Acknowledgment

**BILLINGSLEY AND NEVINS**
Attorneys-at-law
100 Ellory Boulevard
Masonville, ST 45678


September 26, 19--



Mr. Elton Jones
1234 Market Street
Marketville, ST 56789

Dear Mr. Jones:

Re: Jones v. Purcell

Since Mr. Brown is away from his office this week,
I am acknowledging your letter of September 22
concerning this case.  Your letter will be called
to Mr. Brown's attention as soon as he returns.

Sincerely yours,

*Melinda Hargrove*

Melinda Hargrove
Secretary to
Mr. Brown

## DELIVERING MAIL TO THE LAWYER

The mail, accompanied by the appropriate files, should be placed on the attorney's desk at the location designated by the attorney. Urgent mail should be delivered to the lawyer upon receipt together with its appropriate file. Checks received should be processed immediately, following the procedure established by your law office accounting system.

## HANDLING MAIL IN THE ABSENCE OF THE LAWYER

Lawyers are frequently out of town on business. In such instances it is a courtesy to the client for the legal secretary to acknowledge the correspondence, explaining that the lawyer is absent from the office but will be apprised of the correspondence upon his or her return. (See the sample letter on the opposite page.) There are instances, too, when you may be expected to write routine letters for the attorney, following guidelines previously established. Or you might draft a reply to make it easier for the lawyer to answer correspondence upon return. It is important in the law office that all mail be acknowledged promptly, and a standard practice for handling correspondence should be established in your office.

# 4.2

## OUTGOING OFFICE MAIL

In a corporate law office or a large law firm the secretary usually prepares outgoing mail and puts it in a mail tray. Messengers from the mail room pick it up periodically for weighing and applying the proper postage. If you work in a smaller office, you may have total responsibility for mailing. You may even have to go to the post office to send specially handled mail such as Certified Mail, Registered Mail, and Special Delivery items, although using an outside messenger service may be more efficient. The five common checking tasks in both a large and a small office are discussed in the following paragraphs.

## CHECKING ADDRESSES

The data in the inside address typed on the letter and that of the address on the envelope should be the same. To reduce the chance of error some firms use window envelopes so that the address is typed only once. If a window envelope is used, it is imperative that the inside address be complete: it should include the complete name, street address, city, state, and ZIP Code. (Lack of a ZIP Code can delay delivery a day or more.) The post office box and room number should also be included if applicable. If the letter is addressed to a post office box, the ZIP Code of the box number should be used and <u>not</u> that of the street address. The all-capitalized and unpunctuated two-letter state and provincial abbreviations listed on the following page are preferred by the post office.

Obtain a copy of the *U.S. Postal Service National ZIP Code & Post Office Directory*, available at your local post office for a nominal cost. Copies may also be purchased through the U.S. Government Printing Office in Washington, DC 20402. This directory is valuable for locating ZIP Codes that are omitted from return addresses on incoming mail. Local postal zones are also commonly shown on a map in the classified section of the telephone directory, and in many cities you can now dial a special telephone number to obtain ZIP Code information.

## Two-letter State Abbreviations for the United States and its Dependencies

| | | | | | |
|---|---|---|---|---|---|
| Alabama | AL | Kentucky | KY | Oklahoma | OK |
| Alaska | AK | Louisiana | LA | Oregon | OR |
| Arizona | AZ | Maine | ME | Pennsylvania | PA |
| Arkansas | AR | Maryland | MD | Puerto Rico | PR |
| California | CA | Massachusetts | MA | Rhode Island | RI |
| Canal Zone | CZ | Michigan | MI | South Carolina | SC |
| Colorado | CO | Minnesota | MN | South Dakota | SD |
| Connecticut | CT | Mississippi | MS | Tennessee | TN |
| Delaware | DE | Missouri | MO | Texas | TX |
| District of Columbia | DC | Montana | MT | Utah | UT |
| Florida | FL | Nebraska | NE | Vermont | VT |
| Georgia | GA | Nevada | NV | Virginia | VA |
| Guam | GU | New Hampshire | NH | Virgin Islands | VI |
| Hawaii | HI | New Jersey | NJ | Washington | WA |
| Idaho | ID | New Mexico | NM | West Virginia | WV |
| Illinois | IL | New York | NY | Wisconsin | WI |
| Indiana | IN | North Carolina | NC | Wyoming | WY |
| Iowa | IA | North Dakota | ND | | |
| Kansas | KS | Ohio | OH | | |

## Two-letter Abbreviations for Canadian Provinces

| | | | | | |
|---|---|---|---|---|---|
| Alberta | AB | Newfoundland | NF | Quebec | PQ |
| British Columbia | BC | Northwest Territories | NT | Saskatchewan | SK |
| Labrador | LB | Nova Scotia | NS | Yukon Territory | YT |
| Manitoba | MB | Ontario | ON | | |
| New Brunswick | NB | Prince Edward Island | PE | | |

## CHECKING MAILING NOTATIONS

Two types of notations may be typewritten on an envelope: (1) on-arrival reminders such as CONFIDENTIAL or PERSONAL and (2) mailing service reminders such as CERTIFIED MAIL or SPECIAL DELIVERY, all of which are typically typed entirely in capital letters. The secretary should ensure that every letter having an attention line, a special mailing notation, or an on-arrival notation also has the same notation or notations on its envelope.

On-arrival reminders or notations are typically typed four lines below the return address or nine lines below the top edge of the envelope, starting at *least* one-half inch in from the left edge of the envelope. On-arrival notations other than PERSONAL and CONFIDENTIAL (for example, Please Forward) are generally typed in capitals and lowercase letters and are underscored; however, their envelope placement is the same as any other on-arrival notation. Postal directions or special mailing notations are placed on the same line (line 9) as the on-arrival notations and are typed all in capital letters, one-half inch from the right edge of the envelope. Brochures which include pictures and detailed instructions on placement of envelope notations are available at no charge from your local post office. See also Chapter 10 for related envelope addressing instructions.

## CHECKING SIGNATURES

It is the secretary's responsibility to check all letters and legal instruments to see that they have been properly signed. If you are authorized to sign letters with the lawyer's signature, your initials must appear on them. A letter is an invalid document without a signature in ink.

## CHECKING ENCLOSURES

It is very important that you check carefully to see that all enclosures cited in the enclosure notation at the bottom of the letter are included with the letter. Some secretaries note enclosures by using visual reminders such as three hyphens or three periods typed in the left margin opposite each line in which mention is made of the item or items to be enclosed. In this way, the secretary is alerted to include the enclosures with the letter. It is frustrating for an addressee to receive a letter without an intended enclosure or to receive the wrong enclosure.

## CHECKING CARBON COPY NOTATIONS

The carbon copy notation (cc) indicates to whom additional copies of the letter should be sent. The secretary should check carefully to see that envelopes have been addressed to the individuals mentioned in regular (cc) and blind carbon copy (bcc) notations. The blind carbon copy notation usually appears *only* on the blind copies and the file copy, and these carbons should be checked for such notations. An extra carbon copy should always be made for filing.

## GENERAL POINTERS

**Sorting the mail**    Mail that must reach its destination the next day requires special separation and sorting from routine mailings. Special mail services that guarantee next-day delivery are discussed in section 4.3. So that one's office will receive faster service, the Postal Service suggests that the secretary or mailing department separate and presort mail as follows:

1. Separate the mail. Your mail can skip an entire sorting operation at the post office if you separate it into major categories such as *local, out-of-town, state,* or *precanceled.* The mail is usually bundled with an identifying label indicating the applicable category.
2. Use postage meters. Many law firms—both large and small—use postage meters (which are explained in more detail at the end of this section) to expedite the movement of mail. Five or more pieces of metered mail must be faced and bundled. The post office provides the needed printed bands. Large numbers of metered or permit mail may be placed in trays provided by the post office. Trayed mail should have addresses and postage faced in one direction to speed postal sorting and dispatching.
3. Presort your mail by ZIP Code. Large mailings are further expedited if sequenced by ZIP Code numbers with the lowest number first and the highest number last. Mail can be bundled by ZIP Code number if there are ten or more pieces destined for a single zone.

**When to mail**    The Postal Service suggests early mailings to alleviate the usual congestion at the close of the business day. If possible, mailings should be made throughout the day. One large mailing at the end of the business day is to be avoided.

## ZIP CODES

To handle the ever-increasing volume of mail, the Postal Service has automated mail handling by introducing optical character readers (OCRs) that can "read" a ZIP Code—a five-digit number which encodes the following information:

**the first digit**    designates one of ten national areas; each area is given a number (0–9)

**the first three digits**    designate a large city or sectional center; there are 552 sectional centers in the United States

**the last two digits**    designate a delivery area or post office within a sectional center

For example, the ZIP Code 06117 indicates the following:

**first digit 0**    one of the states in the Northeast

**first three digits 061**    the greater Hartford, Connecticut, area

**last two digits 17**    Bishops Corner Post Office in West Hartford, Connecticut

In 1981 the Postal Service was making plans to implement an additional 4-digit number in the ZIP Code to further narrow the delivery zone to a particular neighborhood. Large firms that address mail by computer may use without charge the "Zip-A-List," a magnetic computer tape providing ZIP Code listings. You can make application for the list through your main post office.

## FOLDING AND INSERTING LETTERS INTO ENVELOPES
The following diagrams depict the correct procedures for folding and inserting letters:

### Small Envelope

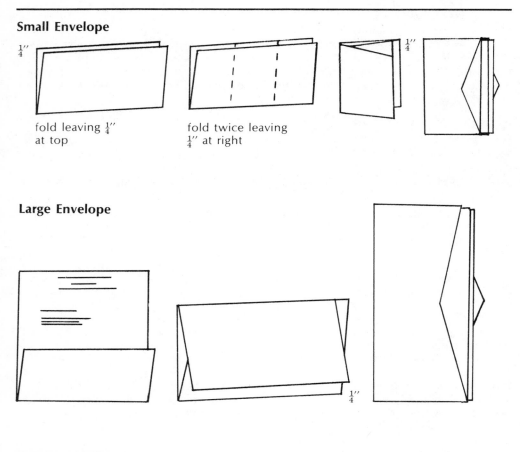

fold leaving ¼″
at top

fold twice leaving
¼″ at right

### Large Envelope

### Window Envelope

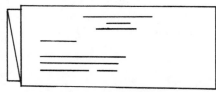

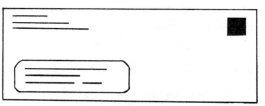

Some stationery has a fold line
indicating where to fold for
insertion in window envelopes.

Insert so that at least ¼″ is left between the
side and bottom edges of the address
and the window.

The following are some suggestions for sealing and stamping envelopes by hand:

1. Use a moist sponge or moistening device.
2. Never lick envelopes or stamps as this practice is both unsanitary and hazardous. You can be cut by the sharp edge of the envelope flap.
3. Moisten envelopes and stamps over a blotter. The blotter will absorb excess water.
4. A large quantity of envelopes can be moistened quickly by placing them one behind the other as follows and pressing down the flap of each envelope as it is moistened:

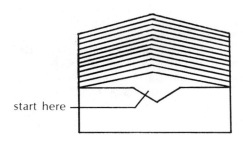

start here

## METERED MAIL

Mailing can be systematized by the use of modular mailing units. The number of machines employed in any modular system is relative to the size of the mailing operation. Mailing equipment that can be combined in modules to increase mailing efficiency includes postage meter machines, mailing scales, mail openers, folding and inserting machines, address printers, and embossing machines. A small mailing operation, on the other hand, might use only a postage meter machine, a mailing scale, and a mail opener.

Mail that bears an imprinted meter stamp is called *metered mail*. A postage meter is a useful convenience for many mailers. The postmark, date, and cancellation are imprinted by the meter directly onto the envelope or onto an adhesive strip that is then affixed to large envelopes or packages. The meter may also seal and stack envelopes. Meters are leased or rented from the manufacturer, and the mailer must obtain a meter permit from the post office. Payment for postage is made in a lump sum to the post office. The meter is then set for that amount of postage in advance. For a fee, a Postal Service representative will set the postage meter at one's office. Some of the advantages of metered mail are (1) accurate postage accounting that eliminates the theft of stamps, (2) speedier processing of mail in the office, (3) speedier processing of mail at the post office since envelopes do not have to be faced and stamps do not have to be canceled, (4) the option of using personalized meter ads, and (5) reduction in the number of trips to the post office.

# 4.3

## THE POSTAL SERVICE

### DETERMINING THE MAIL CLASSIFICATION

If the law office does not have a mail room, it is the secretary's responsibility to send the mail out efficiently and economically. Since postal rates change frequently, you will need to write or call the post office for a brochure of current rates as well as brochures for all of the various classes of mail, the special services, and the rates for each class or service. The brochures are offered at no charge and contain a wealth of information on the preparation of mail, wrapping instructions, weight, zones, and rates. Listed below are the most common types of mail used in the law office.

**First-class mail**   This category includes handwritten and typewritten messages, bills and statements of account, postcards and postal cards (postal cards are the ones printed by the Postal Service), canceled and uncanceled checks, and business reply mail. First-class mail is normally sealed and may not be opened for postal inspection. Within a local area, overnight delivery can ordinarily be expected. Your post office will designate what constitutes your local area. To qualify for overnight delivery, one must deposit letters by 5 p.m., or at a mail processing facility by 6 p.m.

Second-day delivery is standard for other points within 600 miles. Third-day delivery is standard for other points within the 48 contiguous states. It should be noted that mailable envelopes, cards, and self-mailers can be no smaller than $3\frac{1}{2} \times 5$ inches. First-class postage is required for cards exceeding $4\frac{1}{4} \times 6$ inches. Large envelopes or packages sent as first-class mail should be stamped FIRST CLASS to avoid confusion with third-class mail by postal employees.

**Second-class mail**   This category includes magazines and newspapers issued at least four times a year. A permit is required to mail material at the second-class rate. A mailer other than a publisher can mail individual, complete copies of a publication. The publication should be clearly marked SECOND CLASS.

**Third-class mail**   This category consists of circulars, booklets, catalogs, and other printed materials (as newsletters or corrected proof sheets with manuscript copy). Merchandise, farm and factory products, photographs, keys, and printed drawings may be sent third class. Some people refer to third-class mail as "advertising mail." This mail class is limited in weight to less than 16 ounces; should it exceed 16 ounces, it is classified as fourth-class mail or parcel post.

**Fourth-class mail (parcel post)**   This category consists mainly of domestic parcel post. Also included in it are special catalog mailings, special fourth-class mailings, and library mailings. It is mostly used to send packages or parcels weighing 16 ounces or more. Parcels mailed at, and addressed for delivery to, a first-class post office in the 48 contiguous states may not exceed 40 pounds in weight or 84 inches in combined length and girth. The parcel post regulations specify that all other parcels may not be more than 70 pounds or 100 inches in combined length and girth. Parcel post rates are based on the weight of the package and the delivery distance. The minimum weight is 16 ounces per parcel. Parcels under 16 ounces are mailed according to third-class, first-class, or priority regulations.

Overnight delivery to the destination post office can be expected within the local area if parcels are mailed by 5 p.m. at post offices or receiving platforms. Delivery to the addressee, however, may be delayed. Second-day service can be expected for distances up to 150 miles. Service time depends on the distance the parcel must travel; for example, service time may be as long as eight days for distances beyond 1,800 miles. An envelope may be taped to the outside of a parcel if first-class postage is attached to the envelope. Be sure to follow Postal Service recommendations in preparing packages for mailing. The use of string or masking tape, for instance, is discouraged.

**Priority mail or air parcel post**   This type of mail is given full airmail handling. All first-class mail exceeding 12 ounces is rated as priority mail. The maximum weight for priority mail is 70 pounds.

**International mail** This category includes letters, letter packages, printed matter, small packages of merchandise and samples, and parcel post destined for foreign countries. However, overseas military mail, i.e., APO (Army Post Office) and FPO (Fleet Post Office) mail, is *not* classified as international mail. Aerogrammes are a convenient form of prestamped stationery for international correspondence that folds into a self-enclosing envelope.

International mail consists of two categories: postal union mail and parcel post. Postal union mail is divided into two subcategories: LC mail (letters and cards) and AO mail (other articles). LC mail consists of letters, letter packages, aerogrammes, and postcards; on the other hand, AO mail comprises printed matter, matter for the blind, and small packets.

Postal union articles should be addressed legibly and completely. Roman letters and Arabic numerals should be used. The name of the post office and country of destination should appear entirely in capital letters. The sender should be sure to use the postal delivery zone number, if available. It is permissible to use a foreign-language address, provided that the names of the post office, province, and country are in English. The envelopes or wrappers of postal union mail should be endorsed ("Printed Matter," "Printed Matter—Catalogs," "Printed Matter—Books," "Letter," "Par Avion," or "Exprès") to show the mail classification.

Generally postal union articles except letters and letter packages must remain unsealed; however, the Postal Service requires that registered letters and registered letter packages be sealed. Neither insurance nor Certified Mail service is available for postal union mail. Special Delivery is available to most countries, though, and it is possible to obtain a return receipt. Mail going to most countries can be registered. There is daily airmail delivery to practically all countries.

All articles should be correctly prepaid in relation to weight in order to avoid delays. The proper postage should be affixed. If an article is returned for additional postage, the proper amount should then be affixed and the "Returned for postage" endorsement should be crossed out. To facilitate and encourage a prompt reply, a mailer can also send his correspondent international reply coupons that are used to prepay reply letters. Postal union mail is generally returned to the sender if delivery cannot be made.

Parcel post service is available to almost all countries. Prohibited articles include items that may damage the mail or cause injury to postal employees, such as matches and most live or dead creatures, and communications having the character of current correspondence (which means in effect that one cannot enclose a letter in a parcel post package). There are restrictions on firearms, on flammable liquids, and radioactive materials, and any country may prohibit or restrict various articles that it wishes to control. A customs declaration is required for parcel post packages mailed to other countries, and a dispatch note may be required by some countries.

For those law offices that conduct a great deal of international business it is suggested that a copy of Publication 42, *International Mail,* be obtained from the U.S. Government Printing Office, Superintendent of Documents, Washington, DC 20402. It gives further information on matters such as insurance and registration. The United States Postal Service also provides Publication 51, *International Postage Rates and Fees,* which may be obtained without charge from your post office.

In conjunction with the foregoing discussion of international mail, it should be mentioned that there are private companies licensed by the U.S. government that help importers prepare the customs documents required for imported packages and articles. Other services that may be included are export crating, reforwarding, delivery to and from airports and ocean ports, and bonded warehouse marking and distribution. These companies are called *customhouse brokers.* They offer savings on import/export charges, and they expedite delivery.

## SPECIAL SERVICES

Special services provided by the Postal Service include aerogrammes, Business Reply Mail, Certificates of Mailing, Certified Mail, Collect-on-Delivery, Controlpak, Express Mail, insured mail, Mailgram, money orders, passport applications, post office boxes, Registered Mail, Special Delivery, and Special Handling.

**Aerogrammes**    An economical means of communicating abroad is the combined letter and envelope called an aerogramme, described on page 79.

**Business Reply Mail**    To use the Business Reply service, make an application on Form 3614, obtained from the post office. There is no charge for the permit; however, the mailer must guarantee that he will pay the postage for replies. Postage may be collected when the reply is delivered; also, an advance deposit may be required under certain conditions. Business Reply Mail must be clearly identified on the envelope. In addition, the permit number, the post office issuing the permit, the words "No Postage Stamp Necessary if Mailed in the United States," and the words "Postage Will be Paid by Addressee" (or "Postage Will be Paid by" over the name and address of the person or firm) must appear on the envelope. Business Reply Mail is frequently used in law firms for sending statements to clients because it facilitates the prompt return of payments.

**Certificate of Mailing**    An original Certificate of Mailing for individual pieces of mail is issued for a fee. This service is used by a mailer to prove that an item was actually mailed, but it does not offer proof of delivery. The post office keeps no record of such certificates.

**Certified Mail**    This designation provides that a record of delivery be maintained by the addressee's post office. The carrier obtains a signature from the addressee on a receipt form which is kept by the post office for two years. There is a fee for this service. A retu n receipt will be provided the sender for an additional fee. Certified Mail is used almost daily by law firms in mailing copies of pleadings to opposing counsel, in filing papers in the courts, and in recording that certain other papers have been mailed. Certified Mail has the following advantages: (1) it provides the sender with a means of checking on the delivery of the letter, (2) it provides official evidence of mailing when a postmarked receipt is obtained, and (3) it gives a letter the appearance of importance and urgency. For these reasons it is frequently used by law firms and collection agencies.

**Collect-on-Delivery**    This is commonly referred to as C.O.D. Both the postage and the value of the contents of a parcel or letter are collected from the addressee. There is a maximum amount that can be collected. The fee charged for C.O.D. includes insurance against loss or damage and failure to receive payment. First-, third-, and fourth-class mail can be sent C.O.D., the regular postage being paid in addition to a C.O.D. fee. For an additional fee, the mailer of C.O.D. letters or parcels will be notified of nondelivery. First-class mail sent domestic C.O.D. may be registered at an additional charge.

**Controlpak**    To assure maximum security of credit cards and other valuable items, the Postal Service has developed Controlpak. The mailer addresses the envelopes, affixes first-class postage, sorts the mail by ZIP Code, and packages it in special Controlpak plastic bags which are heat-sealed against theft. The bag is then transported to the supervisor of the ZIP Code delivery unit from which distribution is made. It is opened under controlled conditions and the mail is delivered by carrier.

**Express Mail**    Express Mail is a fast, intercity delivery system linking most major metropolitan areas in the United States. It is used for the reliable delivery of urgent mail weighing up to 70 pounds. Overnight delivery of letters and parcels is guaranteed. A 95 percent reliability record of on-time delivery for Express Mail has been established.

Regular Express Mail service requires that your shipment be taken to a post office by 5 p.m. The post office supplies a special address label. The package will then be delivered to the addressee by 3 p.m. the following day, or it may be picked up at the post office as early as 10 a.m. the next business day. Rates include insurance, a receipt for shipment, and a record of delivery at the destination post office.

The Postal Service also offers Express Mail Same-Day Airport Service between many major airports. To use this service, you take the shipment to the airport mail processing facility, and the addressee picks it up on arrival at his airport. You can even arrange to have Express Mail shipments picked up at your office for an extra charge, but only on a regularly planned basis.

**Insured mail**    Third- and fourth-class mail can be insured against loss and damage up to $400. Items of greater value should be sent by Registered Mail. There are two kinds of insured service: unnumbered and numbered insured mail. A minimal fee is charged for unnumbered insured mail; delivery is by parcel post. With numbered insured mail, a receipt is given to the mailer at the point of origin, and a signature is required on delivery. There is an additional fee for this service. You may obtain a return receipt as proof of delivery for insured mail exceeding $15 in value.

**Mailgram**    The Mailgram is a special mail-via-satellite service offered jointly by the United States Postal Service and Western Union. These letter-telegrams are delivered the next business day by U.S. letter carriers to virtually any address within the 48 contiguous states. Small offices can use this service by supplying the Mailgram message to a Western Union office by telephone (toll-free) or in person. Rates are based on 100-word units in the message. Within larger firms, up to 50 common or variable-text messages can be typed directly from the company's teleprinter into the Western Union computer on a single connection. A basic fee is charged for each message, in addition to the telex/TWX usage charges. A business reply envelope can be incorporated in the Mailgram to ensure a quick response.

**Money orders**    Money can be sent through the mail by purchasing Postal Money Orders up to $400 that are redeemable at any post office. International Money Orders can be purchased for smaller amounts at large, i.e., first-class, post offices.

**Passport applications**    The Postal Service, working in conjunction with the United States Department of State, accepts applications for passports from those wishing to travel abroad.

**Post office boxes**    Boxes and drawers may be rented in post offices. These boxes and drawers facilitate the receiving of mail, since mail can be obtained at any time that the post office lobby is open. Having a post office box is of great assistance to the law firm since it not only affords the prompt receipt of mail but prevents its loss or temporary misdirection between post office and law office.

**Registered Mail**    Domestic first-class and priority mail may be registered to protect valuable items. This is the safest way to mail valuables. The fee for this service is based on the declared value of the mail, and the indemnity limit is $10,000. The customer is given a receipt at the time of mailing; therefore, Registered Mail cannot be dispatched from a regular collection box. The post office keeps a record of the mailing through the number it has been assigned. For an additional fee, a proof-of-delivery receipt will be returned to the mailer. Registered Mail is transported under lock and is kept separate from other mail.

**Special Delivery**   This designation virtually assures delivery on the day mail is received at the destination post office. As soon as the mail is received there, it is delivered by Special Delivery Messenger. Special Delivery mail must be addressed to a street address, not a post office box, or it cannot be specially delivered. An extra fee in addition to the regular postage is charged for this service, which may be used for all classes of mail.

**Special Handling**   This designation assures preferential, separate handling for third- and fourth-class mail and normally speeds its delivery between post offices. It does not ensure speedy delivery after arrival at the destination post office. There is an extra fee for Special Handling.

## ADDRESSING FOR AUTOMATION
To take full advantage of the post office's computerized sorting equipment, envelopes must be addressed properly for automation. All typescript should be clear and easy to read. The basic procedures in addressing envelopes are as follows:

1. Use rectangular envelopes no smaller than 3½ × 5 inches and no larger than 6⅛ × 11½ inches. There should be good color contrast between the paper and the type impressions.
2. The address should be single-spaced and blocked (straight left margin). The address must be at least 1 inch from the left edge of the envelope and at least ⅝ inch up from the bottom. There should be no print to the right or below the address.
3. Additional data (as the attention line, account number, or date) should be part of the blocked address; these data should be positioned above the second line from the bottom. Envelope addresses should be typed entirely in capital letters without punctuation marks. Use type fonts other than script, italic, or proportionally-spaced fonts. Do not type the address at a slant.
4. If mail is addressed to occupants of a multi-unit building, the unit number should appear after the street address on the same line.
5. The bottom line of the address should contain the city, state, and ZIP Code number.
6. A Post Office box number is typed on the line above the last to assure delivery to this point. (Use the ZIP Code for the box number, not the street address.) The box number precedes the station name.
7. At least ¼ inch should be left between the address and the sides and bottom edges of the opening on window envelopes.

```
C REEVES CORP
ATTN MR R C SMITH
186 PARK ST ROOM 960
HARTFORD CT 06106

C REEVES CORP
186 PARK ST
PO BOX 210 LINCOLN STA
HARTFORD CT 06106
```

One can save typing time and facilitate computerized sorting by using the two-letter state abbreviations and the abbreviations for street designators and for words that appear frequently in place names (for example, CTR for Center; ACAD for Academy). These abbreviations are listed in the *U.S. Postal Service National ZIP Code & Post Office Directory*.

In automated sorting a maximum of 22 strokes or positions is allowed on the last line of an envelope address. The Postal Service suggests the following maximum number of positions:

13 positions for the city (using the suggested abbreviations for cities that exceed 13 positions)
1 space between the city and state
2 positions for the state
1 space between the state and ZIP Code number
5 positions for the ZIP Code number

# 4.4

## OTHER DELIVERY METHODS

Shipments to and from law offices are often made by means other than the post office, and the legal secretary should be aware of these alternative methods of delivery. Shipments are made by air, rail, ship, bus, and truck. There are also delivery services, such as United Parcel Service, that use all of the above methods of delivery. You should check the Yellow Pages of your local telephone directory under "Delivery Service" for the names of other parcel delivery services in your area. Before preparing the package, be sure to find out what the carrier's regulations are concerning the wrapping and sealing of packages.

### EXPRESS SERVICE
**Air express**   Air express is a fast-growing industry. While it is expensive, it is the fastest means of shipping letters and parcels to the larger cities in the United States. Some air express companies will also send a courier to make a delivery for you overseas. This service, too, is expensive, but there are many occasions in a law office where quick delivery is essential and it is worthwhile to bear the extra cost.

**Bus express**   Most bus lines have a shipping service. This method of delivery is speedy and is especially suitable for delivery to small towns that are not served by airlines. Many items are insurable. The weight limit is 100 pounds per package, and the size of the package is limited to $24 \times 24 \times 45$ inches. There is an extra charge for pickup and delivery service.

**Railway express**   You may either telephone the railroad to have the package picked up or deliver the package to the railroad station for shipping.

### FREIGHT SERVICES
While the legal secretary will not use freight services to a great extent, it is desirable to know what services are available. Freight, although slower than express, is the most economical way to ship large quantities of material in bulky packages. The various types of freight are railroad, motor, air, and water freight.

### INTERNATIONAL SHIPMENTS
As the business dealings of corporations and their legal representatives increase internationally, there is a greater need for international deliveries. Shipments may be made by ship or by air. Since foreign shipments involve special forms and special packaging, it is advisable to contact international airlines and steamship companies

for instructions. They have personnel to assist with the preparation of the necessary forms and to furnish packing and shipping instructions.

## MESSENGER SERVICE

Many times in a one-secretary office the secretary will make trips to the court house when the lawyer is busy on other matters. Most large law offices, however, have their own messengers who make daily trips to the court house and to the office buildings in the downtown area and who also make special trips outside that area. Other law offices prefer to use some of the commercial messenger services available for a nominal fee. These messenger services are listed in the Yellow Pages of the telephone directory.

## ELECTRONIC MAIL

Electronic mail is a new term that generally refers to the process by which a message or document is electronically transmitted in visual, as opposed to auditory, form. Thus the telex, TWX, and facsimile machines described in Chapter 3, the intelligent communicating copiers described in Chapter 16, and the communicating text-editing machines described in Chapter 15 can all be considered as electronic mail systems. However, the term electronic mail is being used more specifically to refer to computer-based message systems that send digitally encoded documents directly from terminal to terminal and whose messages are displayed on a cathode-ray tube (CRT) terminal with the option of a printed hard copy.

Electronic mail has been used successfully in connection with text-editing machines to speed delivery of appellate opinions from a U.S. court of appeals. Law offices that communicate frequently with their branch offices, or with their corporate clients, have begun to take advantage of electronic mail. Through electronic mail systems, urgent correspondence and legal documents—briefs, contracts, closing documents—can be transmitted in a matter of seconds to most major cities around the world.

# 5

CHAPTER FIVE

# APPOINTMENTS AND REMINDER SYSTEMS

## CONTENTS

# 5.1

## INTRODUCTION:   Records and Reminders of Office Activities

One of the most important obligations of a legal secretary is the maintenance of a good docket control system. If you are new in the legal field, the phrase *docket control* may not mean a great deal to you. It is, however, essential to the success of a law firm. The word *docket* usually refers to a list of matters to be dealt with by an organization and often refers specifically to the agenda of a court. In a law office, docket control usually means a control system for the daily schedule—a reminder system which may be referred to variously as a tickler, calendar, come-up, or follow-up system. The law has very strict rules regarding its procedures, including specific time schedules for filing papers, making court appearances, and performing other actions involved in the practice of law. Some of these time periods are listed in section 5.2 of this chapter.

A poorly maintained docket control system may result in failure to file pleadings or to appear in court at the prescribed time, failure to file tax returns and related information on time, allowing a statute of limitations to expire without proper action, failure to answer interrogatories or to file motions, notices and other legal documents as required by law, and failure to file appeals and briefs on time. If a lawyer misses a statutory deadline, it can result in monetary damages to the client and the lawyer, loss of clients, and personal embarrassment.

Malpractice claims against lawyers are increasing, and as a result professional liability insurance premiums are very expensive. Agents are reluctant to write coverage if a law firm has a record of missed filing dates that have resulted in judgments against it. Explanation of the firm's tickler, reminder, or calendar system is required on most applications for liability coverage, and some insurance companies require an in-house physical inspection of the docket control procedure prior to writing coverage.

A docket control system does not have to be elaborate and expensive. It should not add work but rather function as a simple and efficient tool to help the lawyer dispose of matters on a timely basis. The reminder system should help prevent last-minute rushes to meet deadlines, requests to the court for extensions, tensions in the office, and the need to explain additional delays to the client.

All law offices should have copies of the rules of procedure for the courts and districts in which the lawyers practice. These are usually printed by the courts and are obtainable from the clerk of each court. In addition, you can prepare a reference book of your own by compiling a list, by courts, of all important documents that your office prepares and the time and place for filing them. Use a three-ring loose-leaf notebook. As statutes or rules change, new pages may be inserted, ensuring an up-to-date reference.

A good docket control system in an office of any size will require a legal secretary to calendar *all dates* that create deadlines, ensuring the timely disposition of cases and other matters. If you work in a firm that has a docket control clerk, you are responsible for routing information promptly to the docket clerk.

A good docket control system has four requirements:

1. The calendaring must be *immediate* and *automatic*. As soon as an appointment has been made over the telephone, it should be calendared. All incoming and outgoing mail and other documentation should be automatically checked for dates.

2. Every system should have a double or even a triple check. Lawyer and secretary can check each other with duplicate systems. A third person should be assigned to check each calendar in case both lawyer and secretary are absent at the same time. (For this reason, notations *must* be legible.) The docket clerk should have a backup to double-check the entire system. New employees should receive a thorough training session on the use of docket control.

3. The system should provide plenty of lead time to meet the requirements of the appointment. It may also require a series of reminders as a deadline approaches.

4. A follow-up check—a system of recording that a tax return was filed or interrogatories answered on a certain date, for example—needs to be made to ensure that the work has been done.

It is the secretary's responsibility, alone or together with a docket clerk, to keep the lawyer informed of calendared events. In many cases, even written reminders are insufficient. Do not hesitate to orally remind the lawyer of an appointment or a deadline even though normal calendaring procedures have been followed.

As you become familiar with the docket control system in your office, watch for ways to improve it and suggest them to the lawyer or office manager. No system is perfect, and few are immutable. As the law practice changes and as laws themselves are revised, your calendaring system may also change. When appointments are missed, study your system to find out what went wrong. Compare your system with others, always searching for improvements.

# 5.2

## CALENDAR SYSTEMS

### TYPES OF CALENDARS

There are any number of day books or diaries that can be purchased for recording daily appointments. The one-day-at-a-time desk calendar is useful for jotting down items that require little attention and do not have legal deadlines. Simple reminders for ordering supplies, calling repairmen, and other routine office matters do not rise to the magnitude of a place in the docket control system. Notations on this daily calendar of events can be reviewed and transferred later to a more permanent reminder system if they develop in importance. The secretary and the attorney may keep duplicate diaries, but the attorney's copy will not normally contain the routine office tasks that are noted in the secretary's copy.

**The double diary**    When a monthly calendar is used in conjunction with the day book, a double diary system is created. An 8½ × 11 month-at-a-glance calendar seems to be the most popular and practical for scheduling the lawyer's daily appointments and activities, since it allows you to look at an entire month before making appointments. Appointments, hearings, trial dates, directors' meetings, deposition dates, seminars, vacations—these and all other scheduled events should be noted on this calendar for the lawyer, with a duplicate at the secretary's desk. It is helpful to block out in advance any times that appointments *cannot* be made, such as holidays and conventions. It may also be helpful to make notations with a lead pencil in order that changes, which will be frequent, may be easily made. Making duplicate entries on the secretary's and the lawyer's calendars ensures that each acts as a check on the other and allows the secretary to add entries or rearrange appointments if the lawyer cannot meet the schedule.

The double diary system of daily and monthly calendars is simple and easy to use. It fits well with the docket control systems of large law firms, as the court matters can be referred to the docket control clerk, creating a triple check, while the personal reminders and appointments of the lawyer are retained on the diary.

**Pocket calendars**    To supplement this important monthly calendar the lawyer at all times will want to carry a pocket calendar or diary with pages for an entire year or more. Events scheduled on the desk calendar should be transferred regularly to the pocket calendar and vice versa. Many times when a lawyer is at the courthouse, in another office, or at lunch or happens to meet a client on the street, an oral appointment will be made. The pocket calendar is readily available for noting this event. If possible, the secretary should daily check the pocket calendar to transfer these appointments to the monthly calendars. Some lawyers are so involved in civic affairs, clubs, professional associations, and corporate directorships that two calendars are more practical than one. In these cases, one calendar should be kept for legal and business matters and the other for the many other activities that need to be scheduled but if missed will not have serious consequences.

**Wall calendars**    A large wall calendar is a helpful supplement, especially for the legal assistant. Filing dates, deposition dates, investigation times, pre-trial dates, and trial dates are recorded on the wall calendar and marked off when completed. Scheduled out-of-town trips to other courts will also be reflected here. This information often enables the scheduling of several matters that can be taken care of in one trip, saving travel time and client expense. By viewing this wall calendar a few minutes each week, the supervising lawyer can easily note the progress of each case or file.

## MAKING NOTATIONS ON CALENDARS
Diary notations should be made routinely from incoming and outgoing mail and immediately after phone calls are completed. Notices of trial settings, depositions, and all matters in litigation should be automatically calendared *before* copies of the relevant documents or correspondence are filed. Litigation items should be calendared several days prior to the event so that there is ample time for both the lawyer and the secretary to prepare the necessary documents.

## A Sample Checklist

CHECKLIST FOR REAL ESTATE TRANSACTIONS
(Attorney to check items needed in this file)

| | | Date | Initial When Done | Rec'd |
|---|---|---|---|---|
| X | Obtain Abstracts from _Mr. Jones/City Savings & Loan_ | 1/10 | gg | 1/15 |
| X | Order Abstract Supplement (before closing) | 1/15 | gg | 1/20 |
| X | Charge cost of abstracting to _Seller_ | | | |
| X | Order Tax Certificates | 1/15 | gg | 1/20 |
| X | List Certificates for gaps | 1/21 | gg | |
| X | Examine Abstracts | 1/25 | JB | |
| X | Prepare Title Opinion by _2/1/81_ _(Date)_ | 1/26 | JB | |
| _ | Order Title Policy from _____ _(Abstract Company)_ _(Amount)_ _____ _(Borrower)_ _(Lender)_ | | | |
| _ | Order Owner's Title Policy Commitment Letter | | | |
| _ | Order Mortgagee's Information Letter | | | |
| _ | Charge to _____ | | | |
| _ | Send Copy of Commitment & Mortgagee's Information to _____ | | | |
| X | Prepare Warranty Deed _Alvin B. Jones, a single man_ _(Grantor)_ _Charles B. Smith et ux, Donna E._ _(Grantee)_ | 2/10 | JB | |
| X | Prepare Real Estate Lien Note for $_50,000 to TN Bank_ | 2/10 | JB | |
| X | Prepare Deed of Trust _Paul Brown_, Trustee | 2/10 | JB | |
| _ | Prepare Truth in Lending Disclosure Statement | | | |
| _ | Prepare Affidavit in lieu of Truth in Lending Disclosure | | | |
| X | Prepare Closing Statement for _____ _(Seller)_ or _X_ _Buyer)_ | 2/14 | gg | |
| | _$55,000_ _2/15/81_ _(Amount)_ _(Date)_ | | | |
| X | Charge pro-rated taxes to _Seller_ | 2/14 | | |
| X | Charge recording costs to _Seller_ | 2/14 | | |
| X | Obtain Mortgage Balance from _City Savings & Loan_ | 2/13 | gg | 2/13 |
| _ | Prepare Letter re Transfer of Escrow Account to Buyer | | | |
| _ | Prepare _____ _(Affidavit/Releases/Etc)_ | | | |
| X | Secure _Release of Lien_ _(Corrective Instruments)_ From _Former Lienholder_ | | gg | 2/12 |
| X | Prepare Attorney's Statement for _Mr. & Mrs. Smith_ _(Client)_ $300 00 $10 75 _(Amount)_ _(Plus Expenses)_ | 2/14 | gg | |
| X | Record Executed Instruments (after closing) _Deed_ _Releases_ _Deed of Trust_ | 2/15 | gg | 2/18 |
| X | Supplement Abstract (after Closing picking up recorded instruments in Abstract) | 2/15 | gg | 2/18 |
| _ | Prepare Final Title Opinion (after Closing) | | | |
| _ | Send " " " to _____ | | | |

**Checklists**   Diary entries can be made from file folder checklists. A checklist for real estate transactions that is used by one law firm is illustrated here. These checklists, which itemize in chronological order the procedures and documents needed for each case, are usually kept attached to the inside of a file folder. The checklist will show the initials of the person responsible for a certain document as well as the time and date due. If your firm employs legal assistants, some of these duties should be calendared for the attention of the legal assistant, who will need to be provided with a duplicate calendar. After the work has been completed, the checklist in the file should indicate who did each part of the work and the date it was completed or filed. The reminders on the monthly desk calendars can then be marked off to show that this deadline has been met.

**Timetables**   Many state bar associations publish manuals that include deadlines and reminder dates for matters such as probate and appellate procedure. In addition, law offices may prepare their own timetables. The tables on the following pages list the important calendar dates incorporated in a docket control system for defense litigation and guardianship matters in one Texas law firm. These tables are included only as guides for preparing similar checklists. Other types of civil practice and other jurisdictions will require different information on the timetable. In connection with calendaring trials, note that a ten-week reminder allows time to obtain records or to send out interrogatories. A four-week reminder allows time to file amended pleadings, and a one-week reminder allows time to prepare issues and motions.

## A Sample Timetable for Defense Litigation

| Document/Action | Due date | Calendar dates |
|---|---|---|
| **Answer to petition** | Monday next following 20 days | 1 week before<br>2 working days before<br>1 day before |
| **Interrogatories (answered)** | 30 days from receipt | Allow time for contacting client for answers; preparing and having signed and sworn to; mailing, if out of town<br>Day due |
| **Interrogatories (objections to)** | 15 days from receipt | 1 week before<br>1 day before<br>Day due |
| **Request for admissions** | 10 days or within period designated in request | Calendar for sufficient time to prepare and file<br>Day due |
| **Notice of hearing** | Date stated therein | 1 week before<br>1 day before<br>Day of hearing |
| **Notice of deposition** | Date stated therein | 1 week before<br>1 day before<br>Day of deposition |
| **Trial settings** | Date stated in written notice from court | 10 weeks before<br>4 weeks before<br>1 week before<br>Day of trial |

## A Sample Timetable for Probate and Guardianship Matters

| Document/Action | Due date | Calendar dates |
|---|---|---|
| **Application to probate will (hearing)** | 10 days' notice by posting after application has been filed (determine date) | Thursday before Monday return date<br>Monday return date |
| **Preliminary estate tax return** | 2 months after date of death | 2 weeks before<br>1 week before<br>1 day before |
| **Inventory of estate** | 90 days after qualifying (determine date) | 2 weeks before<br>1 week before<br>1 day before |
| **Estate tax return** | 15 months after date of death | 3 months before<br>2 months before<br>1 month before<br>2 weeks before<br>1 week before<br>1 day before<br>Day due |

**Color symbols**   Different colored highlighter pens are ideal for calendared items that require a series of reminders before the scheduled event. For example, green could be used for month-before reminders, yellow for two-week reminders, blue for one-week, and red for day-before and day due. These color symbols should not be over-used but reserved for the most important deadlines. Some offices find that using only a red underscore for final dates is more effective.

**Calendaring financial items**   In offices where the legal secretary is also the book-keeper, the daily and monthly calendars are essential for scheduling financial matters. The lawyer may depend entirely on you to take care of deposits, accounts payable, quarterly tax reports, payroll, banking, and other financial matters relating to the day-to-day operation of the law office. If you are responsible for these activities and reports, you should schedule them wisely, calendaring all deadlines for your attention and planning ahead for them by comparing these tasks with your other calendar entries.

If your financial responsibilities are extensive, you may need to keep a separate bookkeeping calendar (such as the one illustrated on the opposite page) and compare it daily with your other calendars. Preparing complicated legal documents is far more important than routine bookkeeping duties, and when a crisis develops in the office (as they seem to do at certain times and on certain days), you will be able to produce a better legal document under less stress if you have already completed your financial tasks.

**Corporation calendars**   The secretary whose office is responsible for many corporate acts may need to keep a separate corporation calendar, supplemented by a tickler system such as that described in section 5.3. This calendar would remind the lawyer of such things as meetings of directors and stockholders, renewal and expiration dates of contracts and other documents, tax deadlines, annual stockholders' reports, and reports to state and federal authorities.

Secretary's Calendar for Bookkeeping Reminders

# July

| SUN | MON | TUE | WED | THU | FRI | SAT |
|---|---|---|---|---|---|---|
| | | | **1** Dominion Day (Canada)<br>Payroll taxes | **2** Gary Getess' last day. (Pay for one day to offset one sick pay) | **3**<br>HOLIDAY | **4** Independence Day |
| **5** | **6** Dr. Elkin's first day. Write check for petty cash | **7** Pay IBM KT 43430 Reports for Bd. directors meeting | **8** Start on bills for 10th Bd. directors meeting Pay IBM R54118 | **9** Due in payroll. Email 10th of month. Bills Salary advance Hospitalization | **10** Payroll deposit Mail vacation checks | **11** |
| **12** | **13** Set up ledger for contributions Petty cash | **14** Annual maint. contract or type writers due 1st. Update oil and new tax data | **15** Payroll taxes. Errored mail salary figures this report on use | **16** | **17** Deposit IRA or atty. for author-phone — employees form phone payroll forms ready | **18** |
| **19** | **20** Due new employees Petty cash IBM KF84869 | **21** Quarterly pay roll deposit due 31st FICA, etc. | **22** Corporate tax deposit due 31st. IBM M59632 | **23** Payroll Salary advance Hospitalization | **24** Payroll deposit Interest due on note # 53666 Mail vacation checks | **25** |
| **26** | **27** Compute unused sick leave for last 6 months Pricking for debit etc. for next month | **28** Printer — new checks needed Check amount on postage meter | **29** Pay IBM HU 42755 3R 93500 | **30** Ins. policy # 532 – Al. premium due | **31** Quarterly due today Make FUTA payment | |

**Time-keeping diaries**    Many lawyers prefer to use daily appointment calendars with hours broken into one-half or quarterly increments. This is a very good system for keeping track of time chargeable to clients. As secretary, you may be expected to construct a daily time sheet from the lawyer's daily calendar. If you are assigned to assist in keeping track of the lawyer's time, remember that accurate records are important and that every minute that cannot be charged to a client must be charged to overhead costs. Check the lawyer's diary for items noted there but not reflected on the time form to ensure that all chargeable time is actually charged to the client. Time sheets are discussed further in Chapter 7.

## PULL DATING

The daily calendar/dual diary system described in this section is only one of several calendaring systems. There are others that may be more effective for your office.

Many firms use a system of noting "pull dates" on each client's file folder. This date is decided on and penciled by the lawyer on the folder and on the lawyer's desk calendar. If the date is extremely important, a red pencil may be used. The file is then placed in the *out* basket, from which the secretary retrieves the file, calendars the pull date, and returns the file to storage. Each day the files with pull dates for that day are removed from the file cabinet and placed on the lawyer's desk for action. Files are never returned to storage without a new pull date being entered on them and calendared. If no action is necessary, the file is marked for monthly or quarterly review, depending on the nature of the matter. On these review dates the client can be advised of the status of the file.

Pull-date systems must be clearly defined. They are impractical if it becomes necessary for more than one lawyer to handle the file. However, the revolving system is simple, and a further advantage is that, by requiring the lawyer to review dormant files on a systematic basis, it may ensure that some client has not been overlooked simply because his or her file has been inactive for a long period. To make this a really foolproof system, a tickler card (see section 5.3) should also be made for the pull date noted on the file.

# 5.3

## PERPETUAL REMINDER SYSTEMS

Perpetual reminder systems function as adjuncts to the various types of calendars described in section 5.2. Perpetual calendaring is particularly adaptable to the word- and data-processing equipment that many law offices utilize, but it also works well in a manually controlled docket system.

### TICKLER FILES

The perpetual calendar system is described here in detail, using the term *tickler card* to describe any type of reminder placed in the system. Despite its name, a tickler is no laughing matter. It is so called because it tickles your memory to remind you of whatever subject needs attention. The perpetual calendar is designed to remind its users of recurring events and deadlines—annual meetings, tax deadlines, and the like—rather than day-to-day appointments. The day-to-day items, however, are not necessarily excluded, and tickler cards may be also prepared for them. Your law firm may want to have reminders for matters 20, 30, or even 100 years in the future. This can be accomplished with little effort and cost by using the tickler card perpetual calendar system.

**Setting up the perpetual calendar**    To set up a system you will need to start with the following inexpensive items, which can be purchased from any stationery supply store:

1.  A simple $3 \times 5 \times 12$ inch <u>card file box</u>.
2.  A $3 \times 5$ set of 12 <u>card guides</u>, marked January through December.
3.  A $3 \times 5$ set of <u>numerical guides</u> marked from 1 through 31. (Two sets make filing for the second month simpler but are not necessary.)
4.  A supply of $3 \times 5$ <u>blank index cards</u> to divide the file into years beyond the current year.
5.  A supply of $3 \times 5$ <u>tickler cards</u>. (These can be of various designs; see pages 95 and 96 for examples.)
6.  A <u>tray</u> or small box for receipt of tickler cards that will be filed in the system each day by the docket clerk.

You now have the necessary equipment for the perpetual calendar. The monthly and daily index cards will begin the system, and the first card in the tickler box will be the date that the system is started. Suppose that date is January 1 of the current year. The first guide card will be for the month of January, followed by guide cards for days 1 through 31, with cards for February through December following. If you have purchased more than one set of 31-day guides, they will follow the second month in the system, and so on. The last month, December, will be followed by blank index cards labeled for the immediately following year and each year thereafter up to ten years or more.

Now that the guide cards are in place, the tickler cards—the actual reminders— are ready for filing by day, month, and year. Ticklers for future years are simply filed behind the designated year, to be moved into monthly and daily sections when that 12-month period arrives.

**Using the tickler system**    The docket clerk or other designated person should be responsible for filing and distributing all ticklers. In a small office this duty could be assigned to the receptionist. The system should remain at a designated location, and the box for receiving tickler cards should be conveniently located. The tickler cards for each day will be removed and distributed to the responsible lawyer. A special holder in the lawyer's office should be determined, and the ticklers should always be placed there. The right location is critical. It should be conspicuous, and it should not allow the ticklers to become concealed by other material. This designated place should be reserved for ticklers only; other messages should be placed elsewhere. All members of the office staff should be made aware of the importance of adhering to these procedures. If the system takes hold, the lawyer will soon develop the habit of looking for a tickler to see what needs immediate attention.

The ticklers should be distributed to each lawyer before closing time every day or the first thing each morning. The afternoon of the day before is usually recommended in case there is a reminder for an early morning time that the lawyer might miss. Competent secretaries will study the working habits of their employers and decide on that basis the best time to distribute ticklers. On Friday ticklers should be pulled and distributed for Saturday, Sunday, and Monday. Ticklers for a holiday and the day following the holiday should be pulled the day before.

After the docket clerk has pulled the ticklers for the day, the date guide for that day is placed behind the last daily guide in the tickler box so that it may begin working forward again. For example, if you began your file in January 1981, on March 7 your tickler card box would read from the front as follows:

7–31 daily guides

April

1–31 daily guides (if 2 sets have been used)

May
1–6 daily guides (if 2 sets have been used)
June through December monthly guides
1982 (blank index card so marked)
January through March monthly guides
1983, 1984, etc. for as many years as are included in the system.

When the March 7 tickler cards have been pulled, the guide card for that date will be placed behind the May 6 index, and ticklers for May 7 will be filed behind the guide. As the reminders for the coming year move up, they are separated from the general year and month divisions and filed behind the appropriate month and day.

**Tickler cards**   Tickler cards are of many types and designs. They can be made in your office and designed to fit its needs. They can be purchased from suppliers in single pages or as carbon or NCR sets. Cards vary in the amount of information they are designed to contain. Color-coded cards can be assigned to specific deadline matters or, if the firm is very large, to departments within the firm. Colors can also be used to indicate the degree of urgency: perhaps orange for critical matters, white for personal reminders such as birthdays and anniversaries. If too many colors are used, however, a color-coded system might become too cumbersome. Tickler cards in carbon sets are extremely useful when a number of lawyers are receiving ticklers for the same file. Carbon sets are also useful in dual tickler systems—that is, when ticklers are filed alphabetically as well as chronologically. A dual system requires a second filing box and a set of A–Z card guides. The carbon tickler filed in the alphabet box is used as a check on the calendar system to confirm that the matter has been completed.

Tickler cards should be brief but contain enough information so that the lawyer receiving the tickler will know what case or client is referred to and exactly what is expected. Only one file or one client should be on a tickler. Individual ticklers should be prepared for each file even though there is only one lawyer in the office. The reason for this is that when the matter is completed or the appointment kept, that tickler is destroyed. If the matter is postponed or rescheduled, that tickler can be used again simply by changing the date and refiling in the tickler box. On the other hand, if more than one item is recorded on a tickler card, then complete new sets of cards would have to be prepared. Ticklers for the very distant future should be specific as to the action to be taken. These ticklers should contain additional information such as the location of closed files or where information might be located if files have been destroyed during the interim years. Tickler cards can be either typed or legibly written.

Tickler cards should be prepared for all recurring deadlines (monthly payments, retainer bills, annual accountings, annual corporate meetings, tax returns, bar association dues, etc.). Information for other ticklers will come from correspondence and matters in progress. It is useful to prepare a tickler for each piece of outgoing correspondence that requires a reply. Date it for an appropriate future time so that you can check to see if a follow-up letter is needed.

## PREPARING REMINDER SHEETS
A tickler system centralizes important data and due dates, providing a backup for the lawyers' and secretaries' daily and monthly calendars. This triple check is especially advantageous in large firms, where the docket clerk can use the filed tickler cards to prepare and distribute daily and weekly reminder sheets to all lawyers (see illustrations). These two reports can be expanded to include any type of information that would be helpful to the administration of a law office. They serve as a backup system

## Commercially Published Tickler Cards

CASE
STYLE _____

FILE
NO. _____

☐ Review Only  ☐ S/L

Action Required _____

_____

First Reminder  _____

Second Reminder  _____

Attorney Handling  _____

### LOCATOR COPY

Order from ROSEMONT FORMS, BOX 224, BRYN MAWR, PA. 19010        TICKLER (Form T-1)

**LPI  TICKLER RECORD**

© 1977 by Law Publications, Inc., 1180 South Beverly Drive, Los Angeles, CA 90035
(213) 553-9980. To re-order specify Form E-120.

Client/
Case _____  File No. _____

Event _____

_____

Date of Event  [ _____ ]

Reminder Date(s) _____  _____  _____

Attorney Responsible _____

Notes: _____

_____

_____

☐ Done

**REMINDER DATE**  Month _____  Day _____  Year _____

**DUE DATE**  Mo. _____ Day _____ Year _____ Time _____

**Client/Matter** _____  File No. _____

**To Lawyer(s)** _____

**Note(s)** _____

_____

**Statute of Limitations Date** _____

**Entered By** _____ **Date** _____

Completed ☐     Reschedule To _____

**IMPORTANT REMINDER/ASSIGNMENT**

© 1978 Safeguard Business Systems, Inc

**An Office-designed Tickler Form**

---

Date to be Reminded   **September 16, 19--**

**IMPORTANT REMINDER**

To:  **Name of Lawyer**

Re:  **CNA file**

   **M. Gomez v. W. Watters**

Message:  **Has plaintiff filed motion for new trial?  Due today.  Call clerk.**

---

to remind of matters that might be neglected. If, for example, the responsible lawyer and secretary should be absent from the office on the same date, other lawyers will be aware that some action has to be taken. A backup lawyer may be assigned to assist the docket clerk in these instances.

The docket clerk who has access to word- or data-processing equipment has numerous ways to provide lawyers and management with information. Not only can daily and weekly information sheets be prepared but, with a few software programs, reports can be sorted according to lawyer, court, field of law, corporate client, or any other category that the firm might wish to use. Reports produced from docket control information can be used to aid management in the distribution of work, especially where a number of new associates are being trained.

## LONG-RANGE TICKLERS

A tickler system for a will takes little additional time and is simple to maintain. At the time a will is executed, make a tickler for three to five years from the execution date. The tickler should state the testator's name, date of execution, and location of the will. A will tickler reminds the lawyer to contact the client to see if there have been changes during the elapsed time that might require a revision of the will. A tickler may also be made specifically to advise the lawyer when a minor named in the will becomes an adult.

Judgment files should also be included in the system. After a judgment has been properly recorded with the court clerk, it is in effect for the statutory period unless released. Ticklers should be prepared for one year before, three months before, and the month before the expiration date. The one-year reminder allows the lawyer time to review the judgment and ask the client whether the judgment should be renewed. Other matters that require long-range planning include trusts, renewals for leases, and guardianship matters.

There are still other ways of establishing tickler and docket control systems for the law office. Experimentation produces new and better systems all the time. Whether you are a legal secretary in a small office acting as docket clerk yourself, or whether you route information to central docket control in a large office, you are in large measure responsible for the lawyer's meeting deadlines. In both instances you should strive to develop a system that will remind the lawyer and avoid defaults, create a good image of the firm, expedite the work with as little stress as possible, improve client relations, and create harmony and a pleasant working relationship between the lawyer and the support staff.

## A Daily Docket Sheet

```
                    DOCKET DAILY INFORMATION SHEET

                           April 1, 19--


    Lawyer      Time            Matter


    MLE         8:30 a.m.       Committee meeting at Chamber office

    BJM         9:00 a.m.       Deposition of Bryce Hackett

    JDR         9:00 a.m.       Hearing on Blue custody - 16th Ct.

    HNM                         Answer to interrogatories due (Gomez v. Watters)

    CTA         12:00 noon      Lunch meeting - bank directors

    AMK         2:00 p.m.       Hearing in Dallas (Parker v. Witkowski)

    MM                          Vacation - return 4-16




    - - - - - - - - - - - - - - - - - - - - - - - - - - - - - - - - - -

    General Information:  Bar Association meeting third Friday, 19th.

    Personal income tax returns due April 15.

    All quarterly FICA and wage reports due by April 30.
```

# A Weekly Docket Sheet

DOCKET CONTROL WEEKLY REMINDER

July 1, 19--, through July 6, 19--

| Date | Day | Lawyer | Matter |
|------|-----|--------|--------|
| 7-1 | Monday | MEL | Trial (Doe v. Stetzen) |
| | | CCK | Probate hearing Tues. - Walker Estate |
| | | JJR | Depositions - Dr. Day at hospital |
| 7-2 | Tuesday | BTC | Waters real estate closing 2:30 |
| | | RRJ | Brown Estate tax return due 10-2 |
| | | CCK | Hearing 9:00 a.m. - Walker Estate |
| | | RBL | City Council 1:30 p.m., zoning |
| 7-3 | Wednesday | DWJ | Answers to Interrogatories due (Harris v. Monahan) |
| | | LVT | Airport hearing - Dallas |
| | | JTK | Vacation - Return July 10 |
| | | DWJ | Real estate seminar in Austin |
| 7-4 | Thursday | | HOLIDAY - OFFICE CLOSED |

# 5.4

## SCHEDULING APPOINTMENTS

In scheduling appointments, the legal secretary is faced with a number of problems that other business secretaries do not have to consider. The complexity of legal questions, the urgent nature of many cases, and erratic court dockets require flexible schedules. For example, a trial lawyer may be in court for weeks instead of just a few days. A tax lawyer must meet a tax return date to avoid the assessment of a penalty. A lawyer may be preparing a will for a terminally ill client. A real estate deal may fail if sales contracts are not immediately prepared and signed. These are a few of the reasons why a legal secretary must carefully assist the lawyer in timing and keeping appointments. The legal secretary should study the personal habits of the lawyer and make appointments accordingly. Some items to consider in scheduling appointments are these:

1.  Does the lawyer arrive early or late? Some people function best in the morning, some in the afternoon. Observe the lawyers in your firm for their best working time. Some lawyers like to set aside a period each day when they have no calls and no appointments; others like to set aside certain days to see clients.

2.  Always check the calendar and docket control report prior to making appointments.

3.  If the lawyer has a trial, limit other appointments to those of gravest importance. The trial has all the lawyer's attention.

4.  Avoid late afternoon appointments that might run past the office closing time.

5.  Keep Monday and Friday appointments as light as possible. Limit the appointments on the first day after vacation. The lawyer will need time to review matters that have accumulated during vacation.

6.  If an engagement is being made for a future date, check the calendar for holiday, Saturday, or Sunday dates. Calendar all court holidays; they often differ from those of other offices.

7.  If an appointment takes the lawyer outside the office, always call to confirm the appointment before the lawyer leaves the office.

8.  If the lawyer is going to be late for an appointment outside the office, always call to give the expected arrival time. This is especially important when litigated matters are involved.

9.  Scheduled appointments are always tentative until confirmed with the lawyer. Advise the caller of this procedure and say that you will confirm the time by telephone as soon as possible. When you set the initial appointment, get alternate dates or times that are convenient for the caller so that another date can be speedily selected if the lawyer has a conflict with the first suggested time.

10. Obtain as much information as possible from the caller when scheduling the appointment. This is especially essential when it involves a new client. The lawyer should tell you what information is required.

11. If your law firm employs legal assistants, one of them may need to be included in the appointment. Advise the assistant of the appointment. He or she may need to spend more time with the visitor than the lawyer does.

12. When an appointment is made with a client or a witness for a court appearance or deposition, always call the day before to remind them. It is good procedure to have the client come early to the office to meet with the lawyer so that they can go to court together.

13. Do not make appointments with salesmen until the appointments are approved by the lawyer. Large firms commonly assign one person in management to meet with all salesmen. The legal secretary in a small office probably has the authority to purchase supplies, but if new or costly equipment is being considered the secretary should gather as much information as possible and discuss it with the lawyer before making an appointment with the salesman.

## NEW CLIENT APPOINTMENTS
Setting appointments for new clients requires some special considerations that need not apply to all appointments.

1. Find out the nature of the client's problem in order to establish the time it may take. Explain to the client that you want the lawyer to have enough time to give the problem the attention it deserves. New client appointments generally take more time than average.
2. If you work for a large firm that has specialized areas of practice, explain this to a new client. Make the appointment with the lawyer whom the caller specifically requests; that lawyer may then refer the new client to another lawyer in the office if necessary.
3. Some law firms have standard policies regarding new client calls, and you must become familiar with these policies. For instance, when an appointment has been made with a new client, immediately check your client cross-index system (see page 111) to see if any names or information indicates a possible conflict of interest. If the information reveals a possible conflict, advise the lawyer.
4. Develop a system for remembering new clients and record pertinent information that might help you to recognize them. Using a file card or a loose-leaf notebook sheet, filed by name for each client, is recommended. (The information you record is only for your own use. Any information about personal features or mannerisms should be written in shorthand or a code understandable only to you.) Collect newspaper articles about the client's spouse, children, civic activities, or other information that would help in making light conversation.

## REFERRALS
There may be times when you cannot make an appointment because your office does not handle certain types of cases, such as criminal matters. On the advice of your employer, keep a list of referral telephone numbers available. If your city has a Lawyer Referral Service, you may give the caller its number when an appointment cannot be made with your firm. Legal Aid offices are also available in some cities for those who cannot afford private legal services.

## CLIENT RELATIONS
All appointments with clients are important and must be scheduled carefully. The legislatures and courts have recently concluded that lawyers sell a service and that they can be held liable for damages if misrepresentation adversely affects a client. A lawyer's actions are governed by strict rules of professional responsibility set by the ABA and the states in which lawyers have been licensed to practice; special grievance committees investigate complaints filed against lawyers. Missed appointments, lack of punctuality, and frequent rescheduling of appointments by the lawyer might result in the client's filing a complaint. Even though a complaint is groundless and is dismissed, no lawyer wants to suffer the embarrassment of responding to and appearing before a grievance committee for unintentional actions. A legal secretary should be alert to clients' reactions and attitudes. Criticism of the lawyer made by a client should be immediately and orally reported to the lawyer, because a good client relationship is essential to a successful law practice.

# 5.5

# HANDLING APPOINTMENT-RELATED SITUATIONS

Handling appointments competently and developing a good rapport with clients and other visitors is important, and the legal secretary should strive for this goal. You will be confronted daily with different and often difficult situations which require tact and diplomacy. You will be challenged to handle each with the professionalism required of your position, for your conduct in the office and your handling of each client affects the reputation of the lawyer.

## PREPARING FOR APPOINTMENTS

The legal secretary is often expected to serve as the office hostess. When a client arrives for an appointment, be friendly, pleasant, and professional. Immediately notify the lawyer that the client has arrived. The client should not ordinarily be kept waiting. If a delay is unavoidable, the legal secretary should explain the situation to the client, who will usually accept a reasonable explanation. The client may be offered a cup of coffee or a soft drink while waiting for the lawyer. Depending on the custom of your office, the legal assistant might be introduced at this time. Often the preliminary, routine information can be recorded by the legal assistant. Explain to the client that this procedure will enable the lawyer to spend more time on the legal problems involved. Finally, if the client and the lawyer have never met, it is an extra courtesy to go with the client to the lawyer's office and formally introduce them.

Before the client arrives, files and papers relative to the appointment should be ready. If the meeting is to be in a conference room instead of the lawyer's office, have that room reserved and ready for the meeting. A supply of pencils, legal pads, and new file and client information forms should be available so that information can be recorded during the first visit. Fee arrangement forms are very important and should be included. Be sure that all loose papers and files of other clients have been removed or covered so that they cannot be seen.

## SPECIAL PROBLEMS IN THE RECEPTION AREA

Some clients may be upset when they arrive for an appointment. They may want to discuss their problems with others in the reception area. If this happens, firmly but very politely try to guide the conversation to a lighter subject. Better yet, escort the client to an available conference room. Let the client feel that the problem deserves the utmost attention, yet that the details should be reserved for the lawyer. Never discuss the merits of the case with the client. Be certain that the client understands that you are concerned and sympathetic but that a legal secretary cannot give legal advice.

If a client arrives without an appointment, explain that the lawyer is unavailable, engaged in difficult briefing, preparing for a trial of a case, or whatever the reasonable explanation is. Offer to make an appointment at a time when the lawyer can give the client's problem the attention it deserves. If another lawyer is in the office, ask the client if seeing that lawyer might help. When a client sees that you are being truthful and genuinely helpful, other arrangements can usually be made agreeably.

A competent legal secretary will develop good judgment in screening callers. In this electronic age many clients prefer to transact business and legal matters by telephone. In some cases conference calls, speakerphones, telecopiers, and other electronic devices have almost eliminated personal office appointments, especially during the preliminary preparation of a case. Some clients may not be aware of these procedures and so cannot understand why "their lawyer" is always on the telephone and cannot hang up when they call or come in to discuss a matter. A legal secretary should be able to explain these electronic devices to the client. This is also an ideal time to refer the call to the legal assistant working with the lawyer on the case. The legal assistant may be able to take information or answer general questions, and the clients may find that they did not need to speak with the lawyer after all.

Appointments frequently run past the allotted time in a legal office. A problem turns out to be more complex than anticipated and cannot be resolved before the next client arrives. As legal secretary, you have to explain the situation to the client and, if the client cannot or will not wait, make every effort to reschedule the appointment as soon as possible at the client's convenience. In such a situation the lawyer might want to be advised that the second client has arrived and leave the first client for a few minutes to speak to the second. This courtesy assures the second client that his problem is as important as that of the client who is keeping him waiting.

Sometimes clients bring small children to the office, and the legal secretary must act as babysitter. A few small toys hidden in a desk drawer and brought out on these occasions may turn out to be the most important tools for that day's work.

A supply of tissues should be readily available. Someone recently widowed, for example, may be composed upon arrival for an appointment; but more often than not, when the deceased and the necessary legal matters must be discussed, composure evaporates. It is essential that a legal secretary be sensitive to the emotional needs of clients. Handle these situations smoothly and quietly, getting the client back to the business at hand as soon as possible.

The legal office receives visitors and callers from all walks of life and in a wide range of emotional states. The professional legal secretary must develop the skills and the confidence to handle any situation that might arise from contact with this great variety of people seeking legal assistance. Meeting this challenge is one of the rewards of being a legal secretary.

# 6

CHAPTER SIX

# LAW OFFICE RECORDS MANAGEMENT

## CONTENTS

# 6.1

## RECORDS MANAGEMENT: A Secretarial Overview

As ever-larger amounts of paper threaten to overwhelm today's offices, the need to control the flow of paper becomes more compelling. *Records management*—the systematic control over the creation, maintenance, retention, protection, and preservation of records—is the basic tool for handling the flow of paper. *Filing* may be defined more narrowly as the arrangement and storage of recorded information according to a simple and logical sequence so as to facilitate future retrieval. For a filing system to be effective, all required information must be located promptly: thus the use of *indexing*, which is a way of classifying items so that they can be retrieved when needed.

Virtually every action in a law office results in some form of documentation, from simple notes of telephone messages to important appeal briefs, and a good management system is indispensable for the proper storage and retrieval of these records. In a small law firm a secretary usually has control over every facet of records management. Primary tasks include opening files, filing incoming documents as well as documents generated in the office, keeping an index and cross-reference to the files, retrieving records, checking records to see that items are correctly placed, purging records at intervals, and destroying or transferring records to other storage areas at the proper time. In addition, the secretary may be asked to develop retention schedules that state when to dispose of records. Depending on the size of the firm, the secretary could also be responsible for personnel and accounting files as well as legal files.

The secretary in a large law firm usually works in conjunction with a records department that services the entire firm, and its records are housed in a central files facility. If the records department is set up to maintain control over all active cases, the secretary merely sees to it that all documents are correctly prepared and routed to the appropriate file by filling out a special filing form. When a document or file is requested by the attorney, the secretary calls the records department and gives it the information necessary for retrieval. The records management staff in this case will assume responsibility for the filing, while the secretary retains only those documents or copies of documents that the attorney wishes to keep at hand. Thus, even in large firms with central records departments, the legal secretary may be responsible for the short-term management of a large number of active files.

The secretary who has control over all the attorney's files is in a position to control the speed and accuracy of a document's retrieval. This is done by creating a primary index and cross-index system, by selecting suitable equipment and supplies, and by transferring or destroying records when appropriate. As a records manager, the secretary has three major duties: (1) ensuring that filing operations are systematized and uniform, (2) seeing that all information is easily located, and (3) carefully filing the documents. Although attorneys frequently help to design the records management system used in their offices, it is the secretary, file clerk, or central records department that normally assumes full responsibility for the daily maintenance of office files.

## CONFIDENTIALITY

You should assume that *all* of the documents law firms generate are confidential. The Code of Professional Responsibility of the American Bar Association requires that attorneys and all law firm employees treat all information regarding a client with the utmost confidentiality. In addition to the canons of the ABA Code, there are federal regulations governing the release of certain kinds of information. The Securities and Exchange Commission, for example, may penalize law firm employees found guilty of insider trading, i.e., using confidential information to personal advantage by buying or selling securities. Furthermore, private companies that hold government contracts to manufacture, distribute, or store classified government materials are required by the Department of Defense to assign special control numbers to all classified documents kept on the company's premises. When a law firm represents one of these companies, any papers regarding the classified information also require control numbers, and a legal secretary should be aware of the importance of properly handling these documents.

Special procedures for handling classified or extra-confidential material may be required. Documents marked with government terms such as LIMITED ACCESS should be stored in locked cabinets or a safe. The attorney may direct a secretary to mark documents with a stamp noting "Attorney-client privilege, Confidential." Special codes could be affixed to files that contain confidential documents, or these documents could be separated from the main set of files in locked cabinets or on premises with limited access. Another method of protecting confidential client files or classified government papers is to microfilm them and place them in a bank for safekeeping. Each law office sets its own standards for the security of such documents. Some offices may routinely lock most of their client files to prevent their easy removal. Locked files, however, are impractical for storing unclassified records that are frequently requested by attorneys.

Special procedures designed to ensure the confidentiality of client affairs may seem to prevent a filing system from reaching maximum efficiency. But in the law office, wherever efficiency conflicts with a client's trust, the latter always takes precedence.

## THE RECORDS MANUAL

The filing system selected by an office should be followed by everyone on the staff. Disparate systems will work only as long as files at one secretarial station are never commingled with files from another. Uniformity is achieved by creating standard procedures and policies and teaching them to the staff. This is where a records manual becomes necessary. The manual typically is planned and written by the firm's management in cooperation with secretaries and filing staff. All aspects of a firm's records operations should be included in the manual, from file creation to microfilm recording. A records manual should include the following information:

1. Statement of objectives
2. Description of the filing system and procedures
3. Description of filing equipment
4. List of items to be considered as records
5. List of terminology used to describe file contents
6. Retention schedules
7. Transfer and destruction requirements and procedures
8. Special procedures for extraordinary material
9. Facsimiles of all filing forms, retention slips, charge-out forms, etc., that the office uses.

The records manual, which may be incorporated into the firm's general office manual, helps new employees—both attorneys and support staff—learn the firm's records management system. For this reason, a manual is useful in law firms of every size. The manual should be durable and its contents clearly stated. Seminars may be held to introduce it to the staff and to answer questions about filing procedures and policies. Everything must be done to ensure that the manual is taken seriously. This is a necessity; effective records management requires the total cooperation of the law office staff. The manual should be periodically reviewed and revised. Suggestions as to the production and distribution of office manuals may be found in the discussion of word-processing manuals in section 15.2 of Chapter 15.

# 6.2

## TYPES OF LAW OFFICE FILES

Different kinds of records are maintained in every law office. The secretary must learn the categories in order to file documents accurately and retrieve them speedily. A new secretary should first review the manual, then survey existing files to become familiar with the subject areas of the law practice and the common types of documents. If no manual exists, the secretary may prepare a list or card index containing all the file subjects and the document types with the appropriate terminology. This index will provide the standard for classifying current and future documents.

When a new document is ready to be filed, the secretary must classify it. The categories most commonly used in law offices include client files, legal opinion and memoranda files, form files, office administration files, the attorney's personal files, miscellaneous correspondence files, and files for catalogs and bulletins. Additional, separate files may also be maintained for such subjects as client histories, legislative histories, time summaries, and collections.

### CLIENT CASES AND MATTERS

Client files are the most numerous and the most frequently handled in a law office. To make large numbers of client files more manageable, most firms keep separate cabinets for active and inactive files. Client files are generally grouped according to the name of the client, with each case or matter assigned a separate file. For example, a law firm representing the XYZ Corporation might have a dozen or more files for matters such as annual meetings, stock divestiture, or Federal Trade Commission matters—each of which is filed separately under the XYZ name. In many offices, client files are routinely divided into non-litigation and litigation matters, with the non-litigation matters sorted alphabetically by subject and litigation matters alphabetically by opposing party or by plaintiff. Non-litigation matters may be further divided into specific fields of law such as contracts, real estate, bankruptcy, and the like. If a client file includes a very large number of cases, they may be sorted according to the lawyer handling the case, with cases or matters further subdivided within the lawyer grouping.

A basic fact sheet, often called a "new matter" sheet, is usually prepared prior to the opening of a file and attached to the outside or to the inside front of each case/matter folder. This sheet prevents unnecessary searches through the file for certain data. It may include the client's address and telephone number, the name and address of the opposing party, a summary of the progress of the case with dates, how and when the client is to be billed, and other information such as a statute of limitations or the opposing attorney's name. Cross-indexes (see section 6.3) should be maintained for all client files.

**Contents of a client case/matter file**   Client files contain all the documents that relate to the client's affairs, categorized first according to the particular case or matter, then to subjects and document types. These categories are often separated by file dividers within the case/matter folder. The particular arrangement varies widely from office to office and is not nearly as important as the practice of arranging papers in the same order in every client file. Generally speaking, case/matter folders have two major divisions—correspondence and formal papers, with correspondence placed first—but if there is a large number of records, the following categories may be used with additional folders or folder dividers:

1. **Correspondence**   This file can be divided into correspondence with the client and correspondence with others concerning the matter. If the correspondence covers several years, it may be further subdivided chronologically. Because of the volume of letters written and received, it is often helpful to create these categories.

2. **Conference memoranda**   This file contains notes on attorney-client discussions made in meetings and in telephone conversations. It may also include telephone messages.

3. **Investigations**   Discovery material—i.e., case inquiries, examination of accident details, medical reports, character examinations, interviews with prospective witnesses, and other documents generated by exploratory, fact-finding work—is placed in this file. If investigations are extensive, the material should be subdivided.

4. **Legal research**   The research file includes copies of relevant cases, statutes, issues, rules, and regulations; printouts of computerized legal research; and other information pertinent to the legal aspects of a case.

5. **Memoranda of law**   Formal statements of law or other questions pertinent to a case should be maintained in a separate memorandum of law section. Because a legal memorandum prepared for one case may have value in another case, the different subjects covered by the memorandum should be listed in a cross-reference index. Memoranda of law are frequently removed from a client file when it becomes inactive and placed in a separately maintained memorandum file in the firm's library.

6. **Formal papers**   Significant documents such as wills, trusts, agreements, and copies of court pleadings are normally placed in a separate section for formal papers. If certain types of papers such as pleadings or motions are numerous, separate folders should be made for them, with attached checklists of their contents. It is especially important that original papers be protected from excessive handling.

7. **Billing**   The billing file is always separate. It contains recorded transactions concerning the attorney's billable progress on a case. It includes bills and invoices, receipts, time and work summaries, copies of checks, disbursement cards, telephone slips, and all other documents relevant to charging for the work performed in the client's behalf. The items in this file may be transferred to the accounting department if that is office policy, but having them in the client file is helpful to an attorney when a client requests information about the legal expenses involved in his case.

8. **Miscellaneous documents**   This category may include, among other things, the exhibits needed for litigation.

The eight categories listed above are among those frequently used in law offices to separate the materials within a client's case/matter folder. Categories will, however, vary a great deal. Firms that handle many personal injury cases, for instance, might routinely include a divider tabbed for medical bills, while a divorce action might include a category for the inventory of assets. Being familiar with the office manual and the different types of documents in the client files enables a secretary to devise standard classification terms for uniform filing and efficient retrieval.

## OTHER FILING CATEGORIES

In addition to their client case/matter files, most law firms use separate file cabinets or drawers for other categories of documents. The most common types are described here.

**Opinion files**   Copies of each important brief, court opinion, court decision, and law firm opinion generated in the course of handling a client matter may be placed in a separate filing cabinet. These documents are preserved because they might be needed as references in a similar case in the future. Making these documents accessible for future reference requires that subject cards and case title cards be made for them listing the particular points of law covered in each document, and that these cards be filed in a special card index.

An index card prepared from an appeal brief, as shown in the illustration, might contain the following information: subject of law, identification of case, name of document, and location of the document. In some cases, an index card may refer to several briefs in which the same question of law appears. If the documents are filed by case title, subject cards are prepared as cross-references to the case title; if filed by subject, case title cards are used as cross-references. The opinion files card index can be set up either alphabetically by subject or case title or numerically in accordance with a numbering system such as the West Publishing Company's key-number digest classification system (described in Chapter 18) or one of original design.

**An Index Card for the Opinions File**

```
     Issue:  Title VII Racial Discrimination

     [West Key-Number Digest Classification _____]

     Case:   Ray v. Home Corp.          (2d Cir. 1969)

     Document: Brief for Appellants filed

     Location and Accession Number:  File Cabinet 1,
                                     Shelf 2, Opinions
                                     File, 1 Tab A
```

**Memoranda of law files**    Each memorandum of law written by the firm should be maintained in a file for future reference. The secretary or records department must create a retrieval system for them. As in the case of opinion files, an index should be made to categorize the memoranda. Two file copies may be made of the original memorandum, one for the client file and one for the memoranda file. To avoid duplication, a single file copy could be placed in the client file with a cross-reference guide in the memoranda file that indicates the location of the document.

**Form files**    The form file stores standard documents that contain "boilerplate" language—i.e., paragraphs or whole pages that are used repeatedly and that therefore have permanent value. Examples of formal documents such as standard contracts, will paragraphs, bylaws, articles of incorporation, amendments, motions, and pleadings may be stored in this file. Using these standard documents as models for the preparation of similar documents saves time for both lawyer and secretary and results in a lower fee to the client. In addition to boilerplate, this file may also be used to store sample legal blanks—tax, court, government agency, and other forms—although a few copies of frequently used forms may also be kept at the attorney's or secretary's desk. A forms index should be maintained. For information on how to set up a form file, refer to Chapter 11.

**Client histories**    Many law firms keep separate files of documents relating to the history of a corporate client. Papers concerning a corporation's formation and financial background, annual reports and other company publications, and a history of all work performed for the client can be helpful. Information about individual clients, on the other hand, is ordinarily kept in the client's case/matter file.

**Legislative histories**    Although usually found on library shelves, materials relating to legislative histories (hearing reports, floor debates, bills, committee reports) may be placed in separate files, tabbed, and indexed. If a firm specializes to such an extent that certain laws are frequently researched, it may help the attorney if a secretary, legal assistant, or librarian assembles and maintains a ready-made file of all historical material pertaining to those laws.

**Office staff matters**    This file contains records regarding personnel and office maintenance, including interoffice memoranda, equipment purchase and repair records, and the like. Depending upon the size of the office, these files may be kept by the secretary or by the office administrator.

**Personal matters**    The personal files of an attorney might contain information about bar association activities, community affairs, and family financial matters as well as personal correspondence. This file is arranged alphabetically and needs no indexing.

**Reading files**    A special file is set up in some offices for the attorney's daily correspondence. A copy of every letter sent and received, arranged in chronological order and separated by year and month, is placed in this "chron" file so that the attorney may periodically review them. However, such a file requires extra copies of correspondence and is not necessary if a calendaring system such as that described in Chapter 5 has been set up with built-in ticklers.

**Time summaries**    Each attorney keeps daily records of his or her billable and nonbillable time. These should be collected and filed. Weekly, biweekly, or monthly time summaries may then be prepared for use by the firm's management.

**Collections**    When the number of commercial collections that a firm handles becomes significant, a separate collections file may be set up. A separate file is helpful because of the constant attention that must be paid to collections.

**Publications**    A file devoted to items such as suppliers' catalogs, brochures, and bulletins may be set up. However, to be useful, it must be strictly organized and periodically purged of outdated publications.

**Miscellaneous correspondence**    The letters in this file are arranged alphabetically by the name of the correspondent.

# 6.3

## TYPES OF FILING SYSTEMS

Record storage can be either centralized or decentralized. Centralized records are kept all together in a central filing facility that may be accessible to all members of the firm. Central files are common in large law offices. In a decentralized system, files are kept at individual departments or at individual secretarial work stations or in each attorney's office; there is no central records area. Many law offices depend on a combination of the two systems whereby active files are kept at the work station but transferred to a central facility when they become inactive.

### CENTRALIZED FILING

A central filing area consists of one or more rooms or organizational units placed in a central location and supervised as a single system. In a centralized system, the firm's records are retained in that location until the retention schedule or the responsible attorney directs their destruction or transfer to outside archives. Certain staff members are authorized to remove or refile records and other resource material. Large law offices generally maintain centralized systems in order to ensure prompt and convenient delivery of files to all users. In a centralized system, the legal secretary requests documents, photocopies of documents, or whole files for the attorney's use from the file department staff.

The staff of a central file department not only distributes and retrieves records but also creates and maintains indexes for the files. It often prepares form files and separate files for opinions, briefs, and memoranda of law. In some firms the central file staff will microfilm or microfiche documents, conduct document searches with the aid of reader-printers, store information from file indexes as a computer data base, and work on large litigation cases by collecting, sorting, and indexing documents.

The advantages of a centralized filing system are the following:

1. It locates files in a central area accessible to all staff.
2. It ensures uniform opening, maintenance, and closing procedures and permits supervision of files.
3. It makes optimum use of space.
4. It frees the secretary for other assignments.

The latter may be the major benefit of a centralized system. It is especially difficult and time-consuming for a secretary to maintain all of the files on a matter involving several attorneys and support staff members.

### DECENTRALIZED FILING

Small firms generally keep decentralized files because usually only one attorney works on a single case. In a decentralized system, the secretary has complete control over the files. Any requests for records are directed to the secretary rather than to a clerk in a central records area. Active files are maintained near the secretary's work station. A secretary's office or work station usually includes vertical or lateral file cabinets, while other means of storage—open shelves, electrically operated mobile units, microfilm, computer tape—are likely to be found in central records.

The advantages of a decentralized filing system are the following:

1. Files are close to the user and more quickly retrieved.
2. Familiarity with the files results in fewer misfiled documents.
3. Inactive and nonessential materials may be eliminated or transferred by the secretary, who is familiar with the contents of each file.

## COMBINATION SYSTEMS

While a decentralized filing system may afford rapid retrieval of a file, the failure to remove inactive files may result in a waste of secretarial work space. Many law firms have found that a combination of centralized and decentralized records management systems increases efficiency. In these cases, the secretary typically keeps all active files at the work station but, when a file is closed, sends it to the central facility. This procedure allows the attorney to control the active files. By checking with the attorney, the secretary can constantly monitor the amount of space needed for new files and arrange the transfer of less active files to the central location.

A major drawback of the combination system is the potential breakdown of communication between central file personnel and the secretary. However, a periodic review of the files by the file department under a "key date" system will prevent most problems.

The decision to adopt a centralized or decentralized filing system or a combination of the two depends on a number of factors. The size of the law firm, the volume of files it generates, the number of people who handle the documents, and the availability of time for a secretary to maintain an individual filing system will all affect this decision.

## ALPHABETIC FILING SYSTEMS

In alphabetically arranged files information can be retrieved directly, simply by going to the correct alphabetic sequence in the files. The office staff, however, must adhere to a strict alphabetic sequence, and all personnel must have a clear understanding of the indexing rules. A discussion of alphabetizing rules appears at the end of this section.

Client files in an alphabetic system are arranged by an individual client's surname and by a company's corporate name. In many instances, a client will have two or more cases or matters in the file. The file arrangement most commonly used by law firms contains the following sequence, each in alphabetic order: client name, case or matter names, and subjects. For example, the XYZ Corporation might have separate files for matters involving separate government agencies such as the Federal Trade Commission and Occupational Safety and Health Administration. A legal matter might be filed under the following guides:

Client name      XYZ CORPORATION
Case or matter   FTC
Subject          FLAMMABILITY STANDARDS

Files may also be broken down alphabetically within major categories of a client file such as litigation and non-litigation. In those files where a subject (such as a point of law or the name of a case) rather than a proper name is the unit of reference for filing, the subjects are filed alphabetically.

Alphabetic files make retrieval time short because information can be located directly without the use of a separate index. However, misspelled names and errors in alphabetizing can cause retrieval problems. A more serious problem with alphabetic files is the difficulty in planning for expansion; the secretary must leave enough space in the cabinets in the appropriate alphabetic sequences to accommodate the attorney's future client files.

## NUMERIC FILING SYSTEMS

A second filing system is the numeric. It is commonly used by firms which require records to be continually added for new clients and new matters. In a numeric filing system, each file is given a number and arranged sequentially. The first numbered file is for the first client; as new folders are required, new numbers are added in strict numeric sequence. The maintenance of numeric files is time-consuming because of the additional procedures needed. For example, an accession register which houses a record of the numbers assigned must be maintained. The register is a complete list of clients in numeric order beginning with 1; it may be in book or card form. It requires only three columns: (1) the numbers, (2) the clients' names, and (3) the dates of assignment. The purpose of the register is to prevent the same number being given to two different clients. It may also be used to record the date at which the file is transferred to inactive status.

In addition to the accession register, a cross-index must be maintained. The cards in the cross-index are arranged alphabetically by client name. Separate cross-reference cards are prepared under the matter name or adverse party name, each giving the file number. Consulting the index before locating the file takes extra time, but this disadvantage is generally thought to be offset by the advantages of the numeric system, which include the following: (1) papers may be refiled rapidly and accurately and the number of misfiles reduced, since people are less likely to file numbers out of sequence than names, (2) orderly expansion is possible through the use of additional numbers, (3) speedy retrieval is possible because it is unnecessary to search through several files labeled with the same surname in order to find the right full name, and (4) numbered labels give a client's files an extra measure of privacy. Moreover, in the case of files frequently referred to, once the number of the file is determined and noted by the secretary or attorney, the file can be requested or retrieved directly by number.

**Numbering systems** In a numeric filing system, clients are each given a master or key number. Each case or matter of the client is given a sub-number or number-letter combination. For example, a file for the XYZ Corporation/FTC might be given the code 4300–01NL (non-litigation), while XYZ Corporation/OSHA is given the number 4300–02L (litigation). Many coding variations are possible. Litigation and non-litigation cases can be assigned special numbers instead of identifying letters, or litigation case files can assume the court docket numbers. Many offices arrange files numerically according to the year the case was opened, along with a series number; thus 75–001 would be the first case opened in 1975. Some law offices reserve a series of numbers for certain types of cases; e.g., 1–200 for tax, 201–400 for real estate, and so forth. The numeric system for filing should be matched with the numeric system used by the accounting department of the firm. Other special considerations should be taken into account in the design of a numeric filing system. If the firm anticipates a transition to computers and word-processing machines, for instance, it should determine whether different departmental numbering schemes should be incorporated into a uniform system.

When it is time to transfer a file to inactive status or to place it in storage, it should be assigned a special inactive status or transfer number. Index cards for these files should be either so marked or else removed to a separate index card file for inactive cases.

## INDEXING SYSTEMS

Indexing systems are used to determine how a record is to be filed so that it can be found when needed. There are many different kinds of indexing systems. Whichever system your office chooses, the most important rule is to be consistent by treating each piece of information in the same manner. A respected and authoritative source for indexing rules is *Rules for Alphabetical Filing,* published by the Association of Records Managers and Administrators (ARMA). This publication and others on technical records management may be obtained by writing to ARMA, 4200 Somerset Drive, Suite 215, Prairie Village, KS 66208.

**Indexing individual names**    The following guidelines should be used to alphabetize individual client names:

1. Alphabetize the names of individuals by surname + given name + middle name or initial. Example: *Jones, Mary Ann.*

2. Arrange all cards and folders in alphabetical order letter by letter to the end of the surnames, then the given names and initials. For example, these names would be filed in the following order: *Morison, John A.; Morison, John Thomas; Morrison, John Andrew.*

3. Treat hyphened or compound names as one word. Example: *Fitzgerald, Marcia; Fitz Smith, Patrick; Foster-Brown, James; Fosteri, Arnold.*

4. During alphabetizing, disregard titles such as *Dr., Mrs., Captain* or *Senator.* However, these designations may be used to provide additional identifying information. Example: *Nyhus, Lloyd (Dr.); Smith, Walter (Senator).*

5. Disregard religious titles (such as *Reverend* and *Sister*) in filing. File the material according to the clients' last names. Example: *Raphael, Mary (Sister); Smith, John (Reverend).*

6. Alphabetize abbreviated prefixes such as *St.* according to the complete spelling *(Saint).* Example: *St. Peter, Joanne* is filed as if it were written *Saint Peter, Joanne.*

7. Disregard designations such as *Jr., Sr.,* or *2nd* in filing. Examples: *Smith, John T. (Sr.); Smith, John Thomas (Jr.).*

8. Consider the legal signature of a married woman in filing. Her husband's name may be cross-referenced if desired. Example: *Jones, Mary Ann (Mrs. John).*

9. File "nothing" before "something" if initials are used for a given name. For example, these names would be filed in the following order: *Peters, J.; Peters, J.G.; Peters, John.*

10. Arrange surnames having the prefixes *de, La,* and *Mac* just as they are spelled. For example, these names would be filed in the following order: *MacDougal, John; Mbasdeken, Joan; McDover, Mary.*

11. File as written those surnames in which it is impossible to determine the given name or middle name. Examples: *Chin Sing Hop, Osak Wong,* and *Hope Big Feather* should be filed in this order: *Chin Sing Hop; Hope Big Feather; Osak Wong.*

**Indexing name. of organizations or businesses**    When one is indexing the names of organizations or businesses, rules similar to the ones just described are observed. For example, in a company name composed of the full name of an individual, the name is inverted so that the surname appears first. For example, in the name *Ted Corvair, Inc., Corvair* is the first unit and *Ted* is second. When no complete name of an individual is used, the company name is indexed as it is ordinarily written. If the company name is *Corvair Construction Company,* the name appears on the file just as it is written here. Companies operating under two different names are indexed under the name that is used most often, and they are cross-referenced under the other name. When a compound word or a hyphenated name occurs, it is treated as one unit. The same is true of coined expressions. For instance, the *A-1 Manufacturing Company* would be filed under *A-1,* assuming that this expression is used when calling for records under that name. Compound geographical names are treated differently, however. The *Los Alamos Construction Company* would be filed under *Los* as the first unit, under *Alamos* as second unit, and under *Construction* as third unit, with *The* being ignored as is done with all prepositions, conjunctions, and articles. Punctuation within a name is ignored: *Smith's Grocery* would be filed under *Smiths.*

When indexing names that have compass points as essential elements (such as *Northwestern Life Insurance Company* or *North West Real Estate Company*), each directional word is filed separately: *North* as the first unit in both cases; *-western* and *West* as second units, respectively; and so forth. Single letters in names such as those used in radio or television stations are treated as separate units. *KXYZ* has four units and is filed at the beginning of the *K* section of the files. Names of companies containing numbers in figure form are filed in numerical order at the front of the entire file. If the numbers are spelled out, however, the written-out number is retained and is filed alphabetically. For example, *2015 Main Building* would be filed in the front of the complete files in the *2015* position, while *One Main Street* would be filed alphabetically under the *O's*. Names of foreign firms as well as titles included in them are filed as they are normally written unless elements of them are identifiable as surnames or as complete names, in which case they are treated like their English counterparts.

**Index cards**    Index cards are the keys to a filing system; they are essential to the normal retrieval of files in a numeric system, and they are useful for cross-reference in an alphabetic system. They reduce the chance of misplacing or losing documents, and they ensure expeditious retrieval. Index cards are usually filed alphabetically in card cabinets placed in a convenient location. The card should be designed to suit the individual law office. It should be structured as simply as possible. Any information that will expedite retrieval and make filing more efficient should be included on the card; any other information should be omitted.

The index card for a client matter in a numeric filing system may contain the following information: name of client, case/matter designation, file number and location, list of principal subjects, list of principal documents with dates, retention period, transfer and destruction dates, and other data needed for the office filing system. Examples are shown below. Even firms that use an alphabetic system will find a similar index card system useful for reviewing files without actually retrieving them and especially for noting retention dates.

**Client Matter Index Cards for a Numeric Filing System**

| Client | Smith, John M. | | | 100-02-L |
|---|---|---|---|---|
| Case/Matter | U.S. v. Smith -- Attempted Burglary | | | |
| Classification | | Location | Retain Until | |
| Docket File<br>Correspondence<br>--1970 | | Shelf 2<br>Shelf 2 | Case is<br>settled | |

Since the pleadings in this case will be of further use in drafting similar documents in the future, transfer the pleadings in the DOCKET FILE to the FORMS FILE when the case is completed.

| Client    Doe Corporation | File Number<br>401-01-NL |
|---|---|
| Case/Matter    FTC | Location<br>Cabinet 3 |
| Subject    Flammability Standards | |
| Contents/Document Type | |
| Client Correspondence (1960-70)<br>Formal Papers<br>FTC Investigation Report and<br>  DOE Corp. Submissions to FTC | |
| Retention Information    Transfer to Storage in 6/73 | |

If files are located in more than one area of the office, index cards may be color-coded to denote the different storage areas. Colors or other identifying data or symbols placed on an index card can also differentiate between active and inactive, litigation and non-litigation, and billable and non-billable cases.

**Cross-references**    If there is any chance that a file might be requested under a title other than the one under which it is filed, a cross-reference index card should be prepared for the alternate title, referring searchers to the proper location. Cross-reference cards should always be prepared for litigated cases in the name of both plaintiff and defendant and may also be made with names of opposing attorneys. Cross-referencing is also helpful when one cannot recall how to properly index the name of a government agency or court, or when a client company is referred to by an abbreviated form such as an acronym, or when a female client may be referred to by her husband's name instead of her own. A copy of a legal periodical article filed under its title may be cross-referenced under the subject or the periodical name to save time in searching for it.

In numeric filing systems, these cross-reference cards for alternate titles are simply placed in alphabetic order with the other cards in the card index. For firms using a strictly alphabetic filing system, a special cross-reference index box or loose-leaf notebook would be required. A cross-reference sheet for a client matter should contain the following information: client name, case/matter designation, attorney in charge, opening and closing date of file, file number, and adverse party if applicable. Cross-reference sheet and index card samples are shown in the illustrations.

## A Cross-reference Sheet

```
Client:   Domestic Fence Company

Case/Matter:  Incorporation

Partner-in-Charge:  Ralph Brown

Date Opened:  9/1/81

Date Closed:  _____

File Number:  122-01 NL

Adverse Party:   None

See following clients or titles:

        Association of Chain Link Fence Companies
        The "Chain Link" Report
        B & L Fencing, Inc.
        High Post Fence Companies
```

## A Cross-reference Index Card

```
Client:   Domestic Fence Company


See Also:   Association of Chain Link
              Fence Companies
            The "Chain Link" Report
            B & L Fencing, Inc.
            High Post Fence Companies
```

# 6.4

## FILING EQUIPMENT

In planning a filing area, a scaled drawing should be made that specifies the number and types of units necessary and that incorporates attention given to capacity and accessibility. Units should be strategically located to conserve as much floor space as possible. Equipment salesmen can help formulate the plans. The files in a centralized filing area—which may consist of several rooms—are generally taller and less attractive than those in a secretary's or attorney's office. Central file departments usually have a table for return of files and a desk for the clerk responsible for charging out files. (One should <u>never</u> remove material from a centralized filing area without following the proper charge-out procedures.) Cabinets in decentralized systems should be uniform in size and within close range of the secretary's work area. Facing cabinets should be placed sufficiently far apart to allow for full expansion of the drawers.

### CABINETS AND SHELVES

Files may be stored in vertical or lateral cabinets, on open shelves, or in automated retrieval systems. File cabinets are available in standard letter, legal, and card sizes.

**Vertical file cabinets**   The common vertical file cabinet can be two to five drawers in height but is normally four or five. If vertical file cabinets are selected, plenty of aisle space must be allowed so that the work area will be adequate for the operator when the drawers are fully extended. Each drawer should be labeled clearly to indicate its contents and should contain guides, i.e., heavy dividers that both separate and identify sections of the file. The guides should provide quick reference and adequate physical support for the folders. Hanging folders may be used; these differ from regular folders in that they are more expandable, they have several possible tab positions, and they can hold more records. The sides of hanging folders have hooks which enable the folders to rest on a frame inserted in the file drawer.

**Lateral file cabinets**   Lateral cabinets are similar to vertical units except that their length is against the wall and the drawers extend only about one foot toward the operator. The fronts of the folders face the left side of the drawers, the sides face the operator, and the folders are pulled out from the side, not the front. The back ledge of a lateral storage cabinet may be moved forward to accommodate letter-sized folders or back to accommodate legal-sized folders. Lateral cabinets can be from two to five drawers in height but are usually four or five. Retractable doors are optional. Lateral units are more accessible than vertical units, but at a sacrifice of some capacity.

**Open shelves**   Open-shelf storage and rail filing (folders hang from rails like clothes in a closet) offer quick and easy reference, since no drawers have to be opened. The shelves are adjustable and can be constructed on tracks for mobility. Open-shelf filing also makes it easier for the staff to shift files as client matters increase and client folders become bulkier. Open-shelf filing is more efficient than conventional drawer files, requires less floor space, and is less expensive. However, because the shelves are messy-looking and because files are more accessible to unauthorized persons, they are not used frequently in law offices. Optional doors may be purchased to enhance their appearance.

**Mobile units**   Carousel and swivel-type revolving filing units with double- or triple-bank capacity reduce filing space even further. Files are concentrated in a core of filing units that are usually placed on tracks or sliding panels. They may be manually or electrically operated. High-density, electrically powered, mobile filing and storage systems are normally found only in centralized filing facilities.

**Card cabinets** Vertical card cabinets holding one, two, or three rows of index cards are a necessary part of law office filing equipment. The quality of this equipment varies, but only metal cabinets with ball bearings and compressor blocks should be used. The most modern card cabinets are those in automatic retrieval units.

**Automated systems** An automated storage and retrieval system offers the advantages of optimum shelf-filing capacity, convenience, rapid retrieval, concentration of vast amounts of file material in a small amount of floor space, and superior control over records. Most automated units are made up of electronically driven, rotating carriers which present the operator with the desired tray after the correct button is pushed. Other filing machines can automatically sort and retrieve individual cards or files. These automated systems reduce the handling of cards and files and thus protect them against excessive wear. Card index storage and retrieval systems are especially adaptable to mechanized units. One type of automated system, for example, delivers the desired frame to an operator within seconds after keyboard commands are made. Automated storage and retrieval systems also handle microfilm and are adaptable to computer applications.

Mechanized filing operations are extremely expensive and thus are designed solely for users with a high daily volume of filing and a minimum amount of space. A cost analysis should be undertaken to determine whether the expense of a transition to any of these systems is justified. On the other hand, because of the increasing costs of office space and labor, many large firms may find mechanized units worth the expense.

**Selecting a filing system** The following considerations are important in the selection of filing equipment:

1. *Ratio of linear filing capacity to available floor space* (Linear filing capacity is determined by measuring the linear dimension perpendicular to the file material itself and multiplying that by the number of spaces provided. Available floor space is measured by multiplying the length of the equipment by its width; the product is usually stated in square feet.)
2. *Ratio of filing capacity to cost* (This ratio is determined by dividing the linear capacity of the equipment by its cost. The result is usually expressed in cost per linear filing inch.)
3. *Accessibility*
4. *Appearance*

The last consideration is extremely important if the files will be visible to clients and other visitors.

## FOLDERS, LABELS, AND GUIDES
**Folders** Plain file folders come in a variety of shapes and sizes. A straight-edged folder designed for use in a vertical cabinet for client files typically contains the file number and/or client case/matter name indexed on the top edge of the back flap, which is exposed a fraction of an inch. An end- or side-tabbed folder, with index information on the side edge, is designed for use in lateral file cabinets or on open shelves. Accordion or expandable file folders, sometimes secured with string, are used to hold a large number of documents. They may have tabs on either the top or the side. Although tabs often appear to facilitate filing, they soon become worn and tattered, so it is better to use straight-cut folders with rounded corners. Rounded corners retain their appearance better and are less likely to cause paper cuts. Legal files

are frequently kept in folders with two-pronged fasteners securely attaching the records, which must therefore be punched before filing. Folders may be purchased with several attached inserts, each with its own fastener, or with plain dividers.

Four types of materials are commonly used for constructing folders:

1. Manila—the most common and least expensive folder material. It is available with wax or Mylar coating for extra durability and it is available in multiple colors.
2. Kraft—heavier and darker in color than manila. It is quite durable and does not soil easily, but it is more expensive than manila and should be used only for folders subjected to much wear and tear.
3. Pressboard—expensive, heavy-duty, durable material. It is more suitable for guides than for folders.
4. Vinyl or other plastic—very durable, and thus suitable for holding certain papers of permanent value, but quite expensive. The texture is very smooth; hence, folders are slippery and do not stack well. Vinyl and other plastics are available in a variety of colors.

Law offices frequently use specially printed file folders for client matters so that information about the case may be filled in on the outside of the folder. This allows for quick perusal of the file's contents as well as a review of the history of a case. Printed folders with lines for fill-ins may be custom-printed or purchased from law office supply companies. Law office supply companies also provide preprinted envelopes for storing specific types of documents. Litigation filing envelopes, multipurpose docket envelopes, and docket envelopes designed for real estate or contract matters are examples. A trial folder is illustrated on page 118. Pre-numbered and color-coded folders are also commercially available.

**Labels**    All folders that are not preprinted should be marked with pressure-sensitive or self-adhesive labels that have been neatly and consistently typewritten. These labels or tabs may contain the file number, client name, the case or matter designation, the subject where applicable, and the lawyer's initials. Color-coded labels marked with letters or numbers provide an excellent identification system for files because one can easily determine if a file is placed out of sequence by noticing that the colors do not match. These labels, affixed to file folders in positions where they are highly visible, help prevent misfiling and reduce filing time. A color system may work in one of several ways. Colored labels denoting the first two or three letters of a surname or company name, for instance, may be placed on a folder. Alternatively, labels may be used to indicate each large grouping of files, or they may be used to denote successive years.

**Guides**    To expedite the filing and retrieving of records, guides should be placed throughout the files to separate the cards or folders into groups. With card files, one guide should be placed for every 25 cards.

When purchasing guides, the secretary should remember that durability and visibility are the most important considerations. The tab on each guide should project far enough beyond the folders to ensure complete visibility. With straight numeric files, new guides must be added constantly, but with alphabetic files, the guides are usually permanent. Guides should be made of pressboard or vinyl; pressboard is preferable for client records because heavy guides are needed to help support the records. Vinyl guides are very satisfactory for card files. Since guides are sold in sets based on the size of the files, potential growth within the office files must be considered when the guides are purchased.

OUT guides, special name guides, and permanent cross-reference guides should be used for efficient filing and retrieving. Guides may be color-coded to differentiate alphabetic and numeric sections or divisions. As a general rule, boldness in type or color is the best method of distinguishing file guide headings.

## A Pre-printed Trial Folder

The pre-printed trial folder form is oriented sideways on the page and contains the following labeled fields:

Name

Address

Business Phone — Home Phone

Forwarding Atty.

Name

Address

Business Phone — Home Phone

D/A

| COURT | COUNTY | INDEX NO. | CALENDAR NO. | PREFERENCE | STATEMENT OF READINESS FILED |
| --- | --- | --- | --- | --- | --- |

| DEFENDANT'S NAME | INS. CARRIER | ADDRESS | TEL. NO. | FILE NO. | ATTORNEY | ADDRESS | PHONE NO. |
| --- | --- | --- | --- | --- | --- | --- | --- |

| DATE | PART | JUDGE | PURPOSE | PLAINTIFF'S ATTORNEY | PLACE | DEFENDANT'S ATTORNEY | DEMAND | OFFER | COMMENTS |
| --- | --- | --- | --- | --- | --- | --- | --- | --- | --- |

| | | NAME OF JUDGE | | | |

| DISPOSITION: | DATE | DEFENDANT'S REPRESENTATIVE | PLAINTIFF'S REPRESENTATIVE | AMOUNTS |
| --- | --- | --- | --- | --- |
| SETTLEMENT ( ) | | | | |
| VERDICT ( ) | | | | |

S 582—Lit-A-Glance ™ trial folder: heavy duty.

© 1978 LIT-A-GLANCE ™ JULIUS BLUMBERG, INC. NYC 10013

Reprinted by permission of and available from Julius Blumberg, Inc., 62 White Street, New York, NY 10013

**Guide and Folder Arrangement for Cabinet Files**

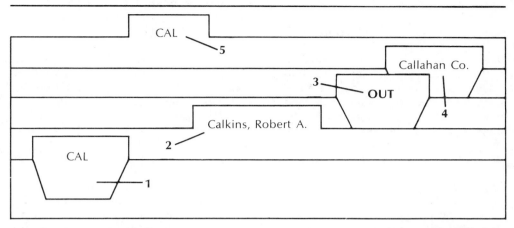

1. *Alphabetical Caption Guides*   The natural position for primary reading is at the left of the guiding area. These caption guides exhibit the basic breakdown of the material that has been filed.
2. *Individual Client Folders*   Records, documents, and correspondence regarding clients are kept here. Individual client folders are placed directly behind the alphabetical captions.
3. *Out Guides*   Out guides or substitution cards located at the right of the file control material that has been removed from the file. Their boldface lettering, large size, and distinctive position render them highly visible.
4. *Special Name Guides*   Guides can be inserted at the far right for very active cases. Special name guides carry the names of those entries that have more than one folder or that require special handling.
5. *Miscellaneous Folders*   These folders hold material not of sufficient quantity and activity to warrant use of an individual folder. Miscellaneous folders, if used, are placed at the end of each letter-caption category, and they bear the same caption identification as the alphabetical caption guides.

# 6.5

## PREPARING DOCUMENTS FOR THE FILES

Loose documents should be filed daily to prevent the confusion that can result from the continuous generation of paper in a law office. Daily organization of filing material will significantly reduce the number of misplaced documents and will greatly speed up retrieval time. The secretary should set aside an area at the work station for placing documents to be filed. Any necessary envelopes, folders, or office forms that make daily filing easier and more efficient should be used.

### OPENING A NEW CLIENT OR CASE FILE
**New matter information form**   The process of opening a file for a new client or for a new case should be uniform and systematic. The attorney's new business or new matter information form is designed to meet this need. The form records information that is usually obtained in preliminary client interviews. A representative form is shown on page 121. Forms may be purchased commercially or custom-designed. In

addition to the topics listed in the sample form, other topics such as information about statutes of limitation or estimates of costs may be included. In a large firm, the sheet may be filled out in three or more parts, with copies sent to the new-business partner, the accounting department, and the central files.

**New case file index**   The new matter information sheet should be used immediately by the secretary or file clerk to prepare a card for the client index. The most efficient practice is to use a multi-part new case file index. When information is typed on the form, it transfers to similar forms beneath. Each part of the index is filed under a different heading in a card index. The first card is filed alphabetically in the client case/matter section of the index; other cards may be made for cross-reference directives, for alphabetical insertion in indexes for adverse parties or responsible attorneys, or for chronological insertion in a separate retention review card index.

**Preparing a folder**   As noted in section 6.2, a separate file should be maintained for each case with the same client, listed alphabetically within that client's file. It is helpful to place on the outside of each case folder information similar to that listed on preprinted folders and envelopes. All developments in the case, including actions and their dates, should be noted on the outside of the folder or on the inside front cover. Labels and tabs should be typewritten and firmly secured to the folder. Only the most important classifications should be typed on labels, abbreviations used wherever possible. If lines run over, the runover lines should be indented a few spaces. The less information on a label, the greater the visual impact and the more easily a file can be located. Initial headings should be capitalized and not underlined. (Underlining clutters the label without making it more emphatic.)

## PREPARING DOCUMENTS FOR DAILY FILING

After the attorney has authorized material to be filed, the secretary should follow these procedures before filing the papers or sending them to the filing center:

1. Separate the material. If it is going into a client file, sort it first according to client, then case or matter, and then other classifications such as correspondence, memoranda, opinions, disbursements, etc.—whatever classifications are systematically used in the office.
2. Remove paper clips, staples, and other metal objects to eliminate excessive bulk and potential damage to documents.
3. Mend torn pages and smooth out wrinkles.
4. Check incoming documents to see that they are marked with the date received.
5. Check to be sure that all legal documents have been duly conformed (conforming of documents is detailed in Chapter 14).
6. See that all court papers bear the proper docket number and the dates on which they were filed with the clerk of court and served on opposing counsel.
7. Place any numerical file codes in an upper corner of the document.
8. If the procedure is required in the office, place the client's name, title of case, subject, or other codes on the document.
9. If filing slips are required, attach one to the document.
10. After checking to see that you have the correct folder, punch the document to fit the folder's fasteners. If it is too thick to be punched, place it in a similarly sized folder that has been punched at the top or side.
11. Place documents in the proper sections of the folder, with the most recent records always on top.
12. If there are documents that do not fit in the folder and must be placed in a special area for oversized documents, insert a cross-reference sheet that locates them.
13. Check to see whether a document needs to be cross-referenced. If it might be called for by a title other than the one it is filed under, make a cross-reference index card for it.

## New Matter Information Form

```
NEW MATTER INFORMATION SHEET


                                        Date opened____June 20, 19--_____

Client_____DOME SECURITIES HOUSE, INC._____   Client no.____5290_____

Matter_____Fraud Investigation_____   Matter no._____02_____

Address_____100 Wall Street, New York, NY_____

Services to be rendered__Representation of client in investigation_____

      of their trading and brokerage activities, particularly in margin accounts,

      by the New York Stock Exchange and the Securities & Exchange Commission.

Partner-in-Charge and Attorneys Assigned__Mr. Jones -- Partner-in-Charge___

_____Mr. Smith, Mrs. Hassett, and Mr. Camp -- Attorneys assigned to case__

Billing Partner for Client__Mr. Roosevelt_____for this Matter__Mr. Jones___

Adverse Party__not applicable_____

Adverse Party Representation__not applicable_____

Other Cross-References_____

_____

Field(s) of Specialty____Securities enforcement investigation, securities___

                         litigation_____

Type of Case/Section Assignment__Agency Investigation/Securities Section, Group I___

_____

Fee Arrangement_Time at hourly rate for partners and associates; all disbursements__

Billing Frequency        (1) Progress_____Quarterly_____
                         (2) Disbursements_____Monthly_____

Case Referred by____Mr. Wells of Wells and Brown_____

Check for Conflicts of Interest_Approved by Mr. Smith_____Date_June 20, 19--___

Entered into Master Client Index_By Clerk Foley_____Date_June 20, 19--___

Files to Be Set Up_____Correspondence, Billing File, Formal Papers_____

_____Client Documents (for investigation), Memoranda_____

Type of Files to Be Used_____Accordion_____

File Number Assigned_____5290-02-AL_____


      One copy each to New Business Partner, Accounting, and Central Files.
```

**A Multi-part Index Form for a New Case**

```
Client:  Baily Bank                Client No.:  723

Matter:  Acquisition of S Corporation    Matter No.:  01-NL

Subject:  Antitrust


Partner-in-Charge:  Mr. Oliver

Attorneys Assigned:  Mr. Jones, Ms. Kell

Billing Partner for Client:  Mr. Ogden


Adverse Party:  McCord Bank

Adverse Party Representation:  McCormick & Richards

Cross-Reference:  Bank Holding Company Act
                  ABD Bank
                  Jones, Ralph (Chairman of Baily Bank)

Case Referred By:  Mr. Smith
```

# 6.6

# RECORDS CONTROL: Retrieval, Retention, and Disposal

## CHARGE-OUT PROCEDURES

Law firm records must be easily retrieved and their location controlled. Many law firms consider this principle so important that they restrict removal of a file to the person responsible for records management. Removal of a record from the files should never be permitted until it has been properly charged out for a previously agreed-on length of time. A special form should be available for this purpose. An official requisition which includes the description of the record, the date of the record, the kind of record, and the signature of the person requesting it can often serve as a charge-out form. Whatever information is typed on labels and tabs should be included. The form can fit into a pocket on the OUT guide. If only one record is removed for charge-out, then an OUT guide or substitution card containing the same information about the record can replace the charged-out record in the file. If another request is made for that record, the secretary or the filing personnel will be able to tell the person requesting the material exactly where the record is and for what length of time it has been requisitioned. An OUT folder is preferred when an entire folder has been charged out; the OUT folder also serves as a receptacle for records that are to be stored while the original folder is charged out. However, OUT guides (with or without pockets) can be used for an entire folder.

An ON CALL guide could be placed in the same position as the OUT folder. The ON CALL guide directs the filing personnel to send related material on to the person listed on the ON CALL guide when the original folder is returned. Only when the material is returned can the OUT guide or folder be removed for reuse in a similar procedure. This records control procedure is absolutely essential. Examples of OUT folders, OUT guides, and ON CALL guides are found in the group of drawings on pages 124–125.

**Charge-out Form**

---

Name or Subject                                                    Date

Description of material charged out

Signature                                                          Dept.

---

## TRANSFER OF RECORDS

Continuous and systematic control over the retention, transfer, and disposal of records is necessary to manage limited, costly office space and to ensure the timely removal of inactive records. The law office has to create guidelines and schedules for the automatic and orderly disposition of files. Further, it has to describe those guidelines in a records manual that will be used by all attorneys and support staff. By policy, documents may be transferred or destroyed as soon as a case is settled or, more rarely, periodically at the attorney's discretion. Most firms use the availability of space as their main criterion for choosing between retaining, transferring, or destroying files. Active files are always retained in a limited amount of valuable filing space in a centralized or decentralized filing area. When this area becomes congested, files are transferred or destroyed. Some law firms remove inactive records to basement storage, while files that are permanently closed are sent to a low-cost storage facility outside the office. If closed files are stored in a commercial facility, a list of each file's contents should be kept in the office. For many law practices, microfilming may be a more feasible solution to the space problem. (Microfilming is discussed in more detail in section 6.7.)

A secretary or the records personnel are responsible for preparing material for transfer to inactive storage. Certain items, such as letters of transmittal and unimportant telephone messages, should be removed from client files before they are moved to inactive storage. If the file folder has cardboard dividers and inserts, the records should be transferred to a single two-pronged folder, preferably a used one. It will take less room in storage, and the divided file may be reused. Extensive legal memoranda with permanent value should be removed to a memorandum file and a notation made in the client file of their new location. Guides are not transferred since the folders which <u>are</u> transferred serve as the means for locating the material; also, guide support is not so necessary during transfer.

Transfer boxes, transfer forms, and instructions for labeling should be available from the inactive or central storage center. Transfer boxes are typically composed of paperboard and will accommodate either letter- or legal-size papers. Transfer forms indicate which records are scheduled to be moved, their codes, inclusive dates or

## Records Control Devices

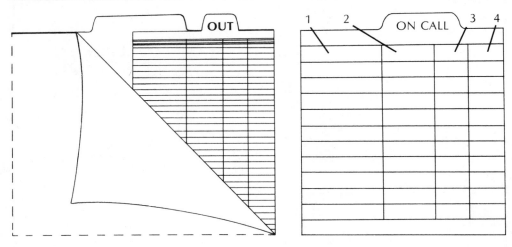

OUT Guide for Single Copy

ON CALL Guide
1. number, name, or subject
2. date of letter
3. needed by
4. date

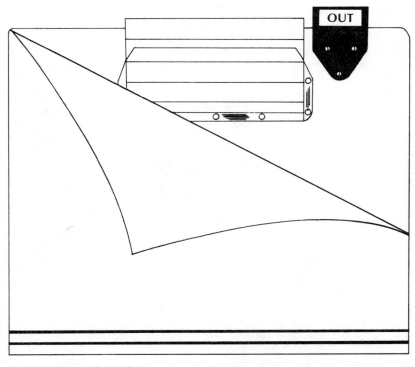

OUT Folder with Pocket

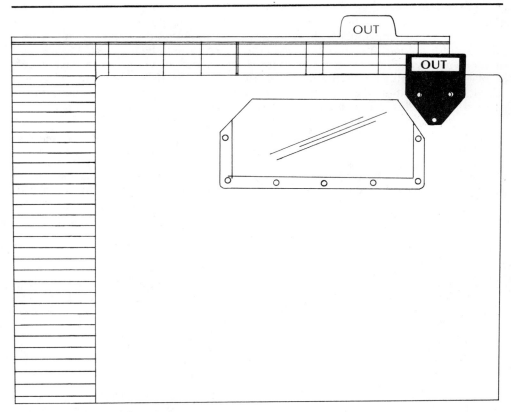

OUT Guide for an Entire Folder

series, and the length of time that the records are to be kept in the inactive area. The transfer boxes as well as the transfer forms should have labels and identification that conform to the requirements of the records administrator.

When records are transferred, a special transfer code is assigned to the file and so noted on all pertinent index cards. The new location of the file should also be noted on the index cards. Cards for inactive and transferred files should be separated from those for active files. A code designating the changed status of the file should also be attached to the file itself.

## RETENTION SCHEDULES

**Retention codes**    As an aid to records management personnel, each document or file should be marked with a code indicating a retention period such as six months, a year, five years, or longer. Letter codes such as P (Permanent), ACS (After Case Settled), OBS (Obsolete), USUP (Until Superseded), and AYE (At Year's End) are also effective. The best time to place a retention code on a file is when a matter is closed or a case settled.

**Devising a retention schedule**    Many firms use retention schedules that note when files are to be disposed of automatically, although most law offices retain closed client files in storage indefinitely. A retention schedule is a printed form that lists specific kinds of records—from machine repair records and purchase orders to formal legal instruments—and specifies how long each type of record should be kept. It also provides instructions for disposal—whether the papers are to be transferred to inactive or archival storage, destroyed, microfilmed, or placed in computer storage. Such timetables are commercially available, but many law firms design their own retention schedules to suit their legal specialties and office requirements. Some offices attach colored tabs to files to indicate that they may be destroyed in a certain year.

The following steps should be considered in devising a retention schedule:

1. Each document should be classified according to subject or type—will, income tax, OSHA, workers' compensation, and so forth—and its temporary or permanent value established. Permanent and original documents with long-term value such as contracts, promissory notes, releases, deeds, mortgages, and important correspondence should be retained indefinitely and transferred (or given to the client) only at the specific recommendation of the attorney. Wills and property transactions always have long-term reference value and require indefinite storage. Vital records such as the firm's financial records and personnel lists should be safeguarded for privacy and retained indefinitely.

2. Requests by clients that their documents be returned or retained for specific periods should be taken into account. A client's approval should always be obtained before disposing of his or her materials.

3. Legal requirements affect retention periods. These requirements include statutes of limitations, regulatory rulings, statutes controlling business practices and markets, contractual obligations to keep records for a certain time, pending litigation, tax audits, subpoenas, and other legal considerations that might suspend retention and transfer guidelines. The attorney will analyze these requirements and make the appropriate decisions.

4. If the law office keeps data on the frequency of use of documents, this information should be studied, including the number of requests during a fixed period, the source and purpose of the requests, and the age of the records requested.

A retention schedule that specifies time periods in years and months should be reviewed and approved by the firm's attorneys and then issued to all the staff. Periodic checks of the files must be made to determine when they are ready for disposal. For this purpose a separate key-date card index, arranged chronologically with disposal dates for each file noted on a card, is helpful.

**Final disposal of records**  A retention schedule describes the proper methods for disposal and destruction of records. Certain records may be microfilmed and stored in that form and the originals destroyed. Forms must be made out and signatures obtained to indicate that the records were microfilmed or destroyed and that proper authorization was obtained beforehand. The disposition of government classified material scheduled for destruction must comply with any government regulations. If the files are destroyed, the date of destruction (and the date of microfilming if it is applicable) is noted on the index cards for each file.

# 6.7

# MICROGRAPHICS AND COMPUTERS

## MICROFILM STORAGE SYSTEMS

Microfilm—a method for miniaturizing records on film—has become a useful medium for indefinitely storing legal documents and other file material such as financial records and library resources. The initial cost of a microfilm system is high, but savings accumulate over the course of a few years. The cost of microfilming a record is approximately equal to that of storing it in an inactive filing area for ten years.

Microfilm, as a general rule, should be considered when records that the firm wishes to retain but that are not charged out frequently expand to take up too much space. Microfilm has many advantages: (1) It is difficult to alter. (2) It offers protection against water and heat damage. (3) If maximum security is needed, microfilm can be stored easily in fireproof vaults. (4) Duplicate microfilm files can be maintained off the premises at little extra cost to guard against destruction of vital information. (5) Microfilm is adaptable to computer systems. (6) It can also be integrated with an automatic storage and retrieval system which can provide highly efficient automation and control when a substantial amount of microfilm is being handled. (7) Most important, it saves space and ultimately money. Microfilm may be stored in as little as two percent of the space needed to store equivalent hard-copy records, and the filing staff is freed from much of its sorting, retrieval, and filing duties.

The disadvantages of microfilm are that (1) a special viewer is required to read the microfilm, (2) microfilm records containing handwritten documents are hard to read, (3) it is difficult to update microfilmed client records, and (4) it is expensive to produce paper copies from the film.

Material is easily and speedily converted to microfilm by photographing hard copy of any size manually or automatically. When documents are in the form of papers that are generally of the same size and can be placed in a logical or sequential order, the process takes little time. Microfilm clerks prearrange the records, remove fasteners and, if necessary, attach records of unusual size to $8\frac{1}{2} \times 11$-inch sheets for automatic feeding.

**Types of microfilm**   The various forms in which microfilm may be used are roll film, a unit stored on an aperture card or cards with other identifying information keypunched on the card, strips of film and units mounted in transparent jackets, microfilm strip holders, and microfiche. Microfiche is basically strips of microimages cut into pieces and set in rows of 100 or more images on a card. Ultrafiche is like microfiche but with a greater number of smaller images on a card. Documents with high reference rates are best filmed on micro- and ultrafiche because search and retrieval time is much faster. Roll film is normally used for records that will be referred to infrequently. When information is sought more frequently, the roll film can be placed in a cartridge that enables one to load a reader without touching the film. An office usually begins with microfilm in reels, since it can be converted to the more expensive microfiche later if necessary.

**Filming office records**   The filming should be done in the office, either by a specially trained filing staff or by a commercial service with a portable camera. The law firm needs to institute written policies governing the microfilming procedure and adhere to them. For example, since file contents may be evidence in future litigation, the filming should be carefully regulated to ensure that the microfilm product is satisfactorily identified and that it is made by a process that completely and accurately reproduces the original on a durable medium. The standards of state and federal regulatory agencies regarding the acceptability of microfilm must be followed. Microfilming documents can also raise ethical problems regarding the disclosure of confidential client information. Consequently, the client's written permission should be sought before records are filmed, especially if filmed by an outside company.

## COMPUTER APPLICATIONS
**Computer Output Microfilm**   Another method of microfilming is called Computer Output Microfilm (COM), in which data stored in a computer are transferred directly to film instead of being printed out on paper. COM affords speedy retrieval of infor-

mation, considerable savings in computer time, easier distribution of information via film instead of printouts, accurate copy, a great savings of storage space, and elimination of paper-handling bottlenecks such as collating, bursting, and binding.

COM picks up data from magnetic tape and transfers it to a recorder by way of cathode-ray tubes which scan the data page by page. A camera records the pages onto microfilm at speeds of several thousand pages per hour. After recording is completed, the COM film is processed in the usual way and ends as roll film, microfiche, or aperture cards. If hard copies are needed, they can easily be duplicated.

**Litigation support**   The future of records management for the law office rests with computer applications. The computer has already advanced word processing, legal research, and accounting functions in law offices. Now the management of legal records is being improved by linking microfilm and computers, by using computers for indexing, and by storing file information in data banks. Computers also play a crucial role in litigation support, the process of preparing a case for trial. In complex and protracted litigation, documents collected can run into the millions. The gathering of data on such a large scale has resulted in the development of computer techniques to control it. Past procedures—using trial notebooks, tab locators, card indexes, and the like—have proved inadequate to handle discovery materials in many antitrust, product liability, class action, and labor discrimination cases.

A computer can categorize and give instant access to the vast numbers of documents that contain evidentiary material relevant to a case at considerable savings in time and cost over older methods. Entire documents may be stored, keyed, indexed, and cross-referenced in computers. Documents may be reviewed by either a full-text or index method. In the full-text method, the entire text of each document is coded into the computer. In the index method, only key words from documents are coded on a data base to assist a searcher to find a document.

The cost of a computer litigation support system is substantial, but expenses per document decrease as the number of documents increases. Small firms involved with document-heavy litigation usually share a computer system. In-house computer litigation support systems are usually found only where the amount of litigation work with excessive documentation justifies the cost.

# 7

# FINANCIAL MANAGEMENT IN THE LAW OFFICE

## CONTENTS

# 7.1

## INTRODUCTION

The role of secretaries in the accounting matters of law firms varies directly with the size of the firm. Medium-sized and large firms normally have a separate accounting department which handles all of the day-to-day accounting transactions. In small firms, where it is not economically possible to maintain such a staff, the accounting functions may be handled by a secretary, usually the secretary to a senior lawyer, or they may be divided among several secretaries within the firm. This chapter focuses on the accounting functions that are common to the law firm and highlights the procedures and systems that are utilized to perform these functions. While it is not intended as a textbook on accounting fundamentals, it does discuss some of these fundamentals in order to show how accounting relates to the rendering of professional legal services. The chapter describes the records that are normally kept and discusses some types of accounting systems, both manual and mechanical, that are available to law offices.

A legal secretary must understand at the outset that the practice of law is a business and that while the rendering of quality professional legal services is a lawyer's first concern, lawyers are also practicing law to earn a reasonable living. Accounting procedures must be managed so that the lawyer is paid fairly for the services rendered and so that adequate records are kept to satisfy the multitude of state and federal regulations which apply to all businesses.

# 7.2

## ACCOUNTING PROCEDURES

### FINANCIAL RECORDS

There are various terms used by accountants that need to be defined in order that one may understand how financial transactions occur and how accounting procedures provide a vehicle to record and account for these transactions. These terms, discussed below, are basic to most accounting situations.

**Chart of accounts** Every accounting transaction in the modern system of double-entry accounting involves a series of identifiable categories. Each of these categories, identified as *accounts,* is summarized in what is normally called the chart of accounts. The chart of accounts is divided into major categories: (1) assets, (2) liabilities, (3) capital, and (4) income and expense. Each major activity of the firm is categorized into one or more of these accounts.

1. *Assets* are those items that are owned by the law firm. They consist of classifications such as cash, accounts receivable, fixed assets, and advances to clients.
2. *Liabilities* consist of those items that are owed by the law firm. They consist primarily of loans that the law firm has taken for various expenditures which are being repaid to a lending institution, money held in trust for others, and other obligations payable to outside parties.
3. *Capital* represents the ownership interest by the partners or owners of the firm. In a partnership, it would normally be represented by the individual partners' capital; in a professional association or corporation, it would be represented by the equity of the stockholders.
4. *Income and expense* refers to the income of the firm (the fees which it collects for its services) and those expenses that occur as a result of the rendering of these services (salaries, rent, supplies, taxes, etc.).

Each of these items is categorized within the chart of accounts and posted to a ledger on a regular basis as the transactions which affect the accounts occur.

Separate accounts in the chart are usually given numerical designations. For example, the 100 numbers might be given to cash accounts, 200 to accounts receivable, 500 to income, and 600 and 700 to expenses. The extent to which the chart of accounts is organized will depend on the size of the firm, the number of different account classifications that are desired, and the information that the firm wishes to obtain for management controls. Some accounts are very broad and contain a multitude of transactions. Others are created in order to obtain financial information on specific activities. For example, "Continuing Legal Education" could be a specific expense category within the chart of accounts. The firm may decide that it wishes to divide this into two separate classifications, one dealing with those educational courses sponsored by the local bar association and one for courses sponsored by state or national bar associations. The account "Office Supplies and Services" may be divided into specific types of supplies and services such as copying paper, equipment rental, and typewriter repair. The key is to establish a chart of accounts that is flexible—one that can be expanded rapidly without affecting the overall numbering scheme. It should also be designed so that it can easily be converted to an automated system, should the firm decide to use a computerized accounting system in the future.

Setting up a chart of accounts is the first step in establishing an effective accounting system. There are many sources from which a chart of accounts may be obtained. A good one is published by the Economics of Law Practice section of the American

Bar Association. Any accounting firm or any company dealing in accounting systems for law firms can also provide a chart. The income and expenses section of a sample chart of accounts for a large law firm is illustrated on the following pages.

**Pages from a Chart of Accounts: Income and Expenses**

| Account Number | Description |
|---|---|
| | 4xx Gross Income |
| 400 | Net Fees Collected |
| 401 | Retainer Fees Received |
| 410 | Interest Income |
| 415 | Other Income |
| | 51x Compensation |
| 510 | Compensation—Associates |
| 512 | Compensation—Law Clerks |
| 513 | Compensation—Secretaries |
| 514 | Compensation—Non-Secretary—Legal |
| 515 | Compensation—Non-Secretary—Administrative |
| 516 | Overtime—Secretaries |
| 517 | Overtime—Non-Secretary—Legal |
| 518 | Overtime—Non-Secretary—Administrative |
| 519 | Compensation—Other |
| | 53x Payroll Taxes |
| 530 | FICA Taxes |
| 531 | Unemployment Insurance Taxes |
| 532 | Other Taxes |
| | 56x–58x Other Personnel Costs |
| 560 | Temporary Office Services |
| 561 | Hospitalization |
| 562 | Medical and Major Medical |
| 565 | Pension Plan |
| 570 | Other Employee Insurance |
| 580 | Other Personnel Costs |
| | 60x Depreciation and Amortization |
| 600 | Depreciation Control |
| 601 | Depreciation Expense—Office Furniture and Fixtures |
| 602 | Depreciation Expense—Office Equipment |
| 603 | Depreciation Expense—Library |
| 608 | Amortization Expense |
| | 61x–67x Other Occupancy Costs |
| 610 | Rent Expense |
| 620 | Records Storage |
| 630 | Moving Expenses |
| 640 | Alterations and Redecorations |
| 650 | Maintenance and Repairs—Furniture and Equipment |
| 660 | Minor Items of Furniture and Equipment |
| 670 | Parking |
| 675 | Other Occupancy Costs |

## 71x Professional Expenses

| | |
|---|---|
| 710 | Meetings—Professional Organizations |
| 711 | Continuing Legal Education—Bar Association |
| 712 | Continuing Legal Education—Other |
| 713 | Meetings—Bar Association |
| 715 | Dues and Fees—Professional Organizations |
| 718 | State and Federal Registration Fees |

## 72x Business and Community Activities

| | |
|---|---|
| 722 | Entertaining Clients |
| 724 | Club Dues and Assessments |
| 725 | Dues—Business and Community Associations |
| 726 | Meetings—Business and Community |

## 73x Recruiting Expenses

| | |
|---|---|
| 730 | Recruiting Expenses—Recruiters |
| 731 | Recruiting Expenses—Candidates |
| 733 | Ads and Agency Fees |
| 734 | Miscellaneous Recruiting Expenses |

## 74x General Staff Expenses

| | |
|---|---|
| 740 | Partners' Luncheons and Dinner Meetings |
| 742 | Firm Outings and Parties |
| 744 | Administrative Travel |
| 746 | Messenger Service |
| 747 | Messenger Service—Credits |
| 749 | Other Expenses Incurred by Staff |

## 75x Staff Reference Materials and Supplies

| | |
|---|---|
| 750 | CCH, P-H and Other Services |
| 751 | Library Books and Periodicals |
| 752 | Other Reference Material |
| 753 | Staff Supplies |
| 755 | Microfilm Reference Service |

## 76x Office Supplies and Services

| | |
|---|---|
| 760 | Office Supplies and Stationery |
| 761 | Reproduction—Supplies |
| 762 | Reproduction—Equipment Rental |
| 763 | Reproduction—Credits |
| 764 | Equipment Rental |
| 765 | Office Canteen Services |

## 77x Telephone and Telegraph

| | |
|---|---|
| 770 | Telephone, Telex and Cables |
| 771 | Telephone, Telex and Cables—Credits |
| 772 | Postage and Express |
| 773 | Postage and Express—Credits |

78x Other Operating Expenses

| | |
|---|---|
| 780 | Contributions |
| 781 | Insurance |
| 783 | Other Taxes—State and Local |
| 784 | Interest Expenses |
| 785 | Professional Fees |
| 788 | Sundry Expenses |
| 789 | Guaranteed Payments |

79x Outside Data Processing Services

| | |
|---|---|
| 790 | Timekeeping System |
| 791 | General Accounting |
| 796 | Other Data Processing Charges |

**General ledger**    The general ledger is the firm's main accounting document. It lists, in numerical sequence, each of the accounts from the firm's chart of accounts and provides columns for posting or recording the various financial transactions that take place in each account. The transactions are usually posted on a monthly basis from the summary journals which are described below. While the general ledger is susceptible to computerization, the transactions are posted manually in many law firms. The reason is that most accountants and bookkeepers are reluctant to entrust such a valuable financial document to a mechanized system; they would rather post it manually in order to retain control over it. However, it is relatively easy to adapt the general ledger to a mechanized system, and it should be done where appropriate.

**Cash receipts**    As the term implies, cash receipts are all the receipts in the form of cash or checks received by the law firm. Receipts normally include the payments on account by clients for professional services rendered and for expenses advanced, monies received on behalf of clients to be held in trust or be placed in escrow accounts, and miscellaneous cash receipts such as repayment of loans or advances by employees and vending machine receipts. The cash receipts are posted on a daily basis to a cash receipts journal, which has columns that identify the major classifications such as fees and expenses. The journal is then summarized daily; it provides the information for the bank deposit. Each month the journal is summarized and the individual column totals are posted to the corresponding accounts within the general ledger.

**Cash disbursements**    Cash disbursements are those items that are paid out or disbursed by the firm for expenses such as salaries and office supplies or disbursements made from the client trust funds in escrow account transactions. The source of information for the cash disbursements journal will be the various checkbooks. All checks are posted to a cash disbursements journal under the column corresponding to the nature of the disbursement. Those disbursements made regularly throughout the month are each given a separate column, with a general ledger column for those disbursements that are made infrequently. The cash disbursements journal is summarized monthly, and the individual column totals are posted to the specific accounts within the general ledger. By determining the cash receipts, cash disbursements, and prior cash balances, the accountant or bookkeeper can keep daily cash balances and maintain an effective program of cash management.

**Trial balance**    Once all of the entries have been posted to the general ledger from the cash disbursements book, the cash receipts book, and other journals, it is then necessary to prepare a trial balance. This is nothing more than a listing of all the accounts within the general ledger with their corresponding balances. The trial balance serves to assure that all entries have been posted in the proper amounts on the appropriate side of the ledger. It does not ensure that the entries have been posted to the correct accounts; however, because of the multitude of transactions that take place during the course of the month, preparing a trial balance assures that the books are in balance and provides a starting point from which other reviews are made before the preparation of financial statements.

## FINANCIAL STATEMENTS

The result of all the entries that record all the transactions during a certain period is the preparation of the financial statements from which management can determine the financial condition of the firm. In a law firm three financial statements should be prepared: (1) the balance sheet, (2) the income statement, and (3) the cash flow analysis.

**Balance sheet**   The balance sheet is a statement of financial position as of a given date, usually the end of the month. It lists in summary form the assets, liabilities, and capital accounts of the law firm. In many respects it can be used as a barometer of the net worth or value of a particular firm. This value is indicated by net assets, which are the total assets minus the liabilities or claims against the assets. If, in fact, a firm has a negative net worth—i.e., if its liabilities are greater than its assets—it is highly possible that the firm is in such a poor financial position that it may be on the verge of going out of business. A sample balance sheet appears below.

**A Sample Balance Sheet**

MARKHAM and SISITSKY
Balance Sheet
December 31, 19--

**Assets**

| | | |
|---|---|---|
| Cash | $50,000 | |
| Less: Funds Due Clients | 5,000 | $45,000 |
| Unbilled Advances to Clients | | 2,000 |
| Billed Advances to Clients | | 3,000 |
| Fixed Assets | | |
| Cost | $35,000 | |
| Acc. Deprec. | 5,000 | 30,000 |
| Total Assets | | $80,000 |

**Liabilities and Capital**

| | |
|---|---|
| Loan to Bank | 3,000 |
| Partners' Capital | 77,000 |
| Total Liabilities and Capital | $80,000 |

**Income statement**   The income statement or profit and loss statement recognizes the activity of the firm with respect to its income and expenses over a certain period of time, normally a calendar year. This statement is important to the law firm because it presents a net income or profit picture that can be compared to budgeted income amounts. Where possible, the income statement should contain a comparison with amounts for the previous year so that unusual fluctuations may be highlighted for review. The success of a law firm is often judged not only by its ability to generate profits in a given year but also by trends that indicate sustained profits over a period of several years. A sample income statement is shown on the next page.

## A Sample Income Statement

MARKHAM and SISITSKY
Income Statement
For the Period January 1–December 31, 19--

|  | Current Year | Prior Year |
|---|---|---|
| Fees Collected | $278,100 | $251,305 |
| Misc. Income | 900 | 740 |
| Total | $279,000 | $252,045 |
| | | |
| Expenses: | | |
| Compensation | $ 53,500 | $ 50,250 |
| Associates | 11,000 | 9,590 |
| Paralegals | 30,000 | 28,450 |
| Secretaries | 6,000 | 5,250 |
| Total | $100,500 | $ 93,540 |
| | | |
| Employee Insurance | 4,200 | 3,890 |
| Pension Plan | 5,000 | 4,260 |
| Payroll Taxes | 8,100 | 7,090 |
| Rent Expense | 8,500 | 7,600 |
| Maintenance and Repairs | 2,000 | 1,750 |
| Depreciation | 1,500 | 1,250 |
| Library | 6,000 | 4,950 |
| Telephone | 8,000 | 7,725 |
| Insurance | 7,000 | 6,420 |
| Taxes | 3,000 | 2,475 |
| Office Supplies | 12,000 | 10,460 |
| Meetings | 2,000 | 1,590 |
| Other Misc. | 1,000 | 960 |
| | | |
| Total Expenses | $168,800 | $153,960 |
| | | |
| Net Income | $110,200 | $ 98,085 |

**Cash flow analysis**   A cash flow analysis is perhaps the most important statement that can be prepared for a law firm although it is probably the least understood and most neglected. Many lawyers tend to view the firm's net income not only as an indicator of profitability but also as an indicator of cash flow. This view is incorrect because there are many transactions that affect cash balances but are not part of the income statement and therefore have no effect on profit. The most significant examples are the purchase of fixed assets such as office furniture and equipment and the repayment of debt obligations.

There are also transactions which, although part of the income statement, do not affect the cash balance. The most significant example of this is depreciation—listed as an expense in the income statement but without cash flow implications. Even though net income is reduced by the amount of the depreciation, the cash balance has not been affected.

The cash flow statement reflects the source and application of cash and provides information not directly provided in the income statement. The analysis is an important supplement to traditional financial statements. In addition to indicating current cash flow needs, it provides a basis for determining long-term cash requirements, specifically additions to the partners' capital or to the stock of a professional corporation. Projections of future cash needs can be made only through the careful preparation and examination of the cash flow analysis on a monthly basis. An example of cash flow analysis appears below.

**A Sample Cash Flow Analysis**

MARKHAM and SISITSKY
Cash Flow Analysis
For the Period January 1–December 31, 19--

| | |
|---|---|
| Balance Beginning of Year | $ 35,000 |
| | |
| Additions | |
| Net Income | $110,200 |
| Depreciation | 1,500 |
| Capital | 10,000 |
| | 121,700 |
| | |
| Deduction | |
| Partner Compensation | $100,700 |
| Fixed Asset Additions | 5,000 |
| Loan Repayment | 2,000 |
| | 107,700 |
| | |
| Other | |
| (Increase) Decrease in Other Assets | 4,000 ) |
| | |
| Balance End of Year | $ 45,000 |

# 7.3

# BANKING AND CASH TRANSACTIONS

The business activities of a law firm are so intertwined with banking that the secretary must be aware of how bank services are used by the firm. Secretaries in small to moderate-sized firms are often called on to perform such duties as writing checks, depositing funds, paying bills, handling petty cash transactions, and arranging travel finances.

## CHECKING ACCOUNTS

A checking account is opened at a commercial bank upon deposit of funds and the completion of bank forms listing the bank's rules and regulations. A signature card must be completed containing the signature(s) of anyone empowered to sign checks for the firm. The depositor is known as the *drawer*, the bank is the *drawee*, and the company or individual to whom a check is made out is the *payee*. A check made out to CASH can be cashed by anyone in possession of it.

**Deposit slips**   Funds deposited in the bank are accompanied by a deposit slip in duplicate listing the types and amounts of money being deposited. This money includes coins, bills, checks, and money orders. Interest coupons may be included, too. The duplicate is retained by the depositor.

**The checkbook**   A firm's checkbook usually contains three checks to a page, with prenumbered stubs attached by perforation to the prenumbered checks. Information about the check—date, payee, amount, and reason for the disbursement—is written on the stub prior to preparation of the check, thus assuring a permanent record of the payment. Checks may be typed, printed, or written in ink. The signature should be written or printed in facsimile. Erasures and deletions are not permitted. If an error is made, the word VOID should be written on both the stub and the check. In large firms, checks may be printed by computers which store information about the checks internally for quick reference. Checkwriters—machines that write check amounts so that they are difficult to change—may also be used to reduce the time it takes to write checks.

**Voucher checks**   Checks may be printed with attached stubs that contain information about the checks. The stubs (vouchers) are used by the payees for recording and reference purposes.

**Overdrafts**   Despite the best of intentions, or through an oversight, a firm's checks may occasionally be written for sums greater than the amount on deposit. As a customer service, the bank may honor the overdrawn check and ask the firm to deposit sufficient funds to cover it. On the other hand, it may refuse to honor the checks. Since the latter action can cause great embarrassment to the firm, overdrafts should be treated seriously, and good relations with the bank should be cultivated. Dishonored checks may be returned to a depositor with a bank notice indicating the reason for its return. The term NSF (Not Sufficient Funds) is usually written on the notice.

**Stop payments**   Should a depositor want to stop payment on an issued check, the bank must be notified immediately. However, the bank cannot stop the check if it has already been cleared. Stop payments are usually requested on stolen or lost checks and on those that contain errors.

**Check endorsements**   In order to negotiate a check, the payee must endorse it on its reverse side. When endorsed *in blank,* only the payee's name appears as the endorsement. This may be done by a payee who is a private individual, but it is a dangerous practice because the bearer of the endorsed check can cash it or negotiate it further. A *full* or *special* endorsement contains the name of the company or person to whom the check is being given, followed by the payee's signature, as: "Pay to the order of George Dean—Floyd S. Markham." Only the new payee can negotiate the check further. A *restrictive* endorsement indicates the condition of endorsement and limits the negotiability of the check, as: "For Deposit Only—Floyd S. Markham." The words *For Deposit Only* followed by the payee's signature mean that the check is to be deposited in the payee's bank account. It cannot be negotiated again.

## BANK STATEMENTS AND BANK RECONCILIATIONS

Depositors receive monthly statements from their banks which indicate the previous month's beginning balance, deposits made and checks paid during that month, other charges or additions, and the ending balance. Because it is likely that certain transactions have not been entered on both the bank's and the depositor's books by the last day of the month, their respective end-of-month balances will not coincide. A bank reconciliation statement must be prepared indicating the reasons for the disparity. The statement is prepared by the computer, an accountant, or a bookkeeper.

**Canceled checks** These are checks that have been paid by the bank and are returned in the envelope containing the bank statement. Many banks have developed computerized systems that eliminate the return of canceled checks, at no inconvenience to the depositor.

**Outstanding checks** If a depositor's check has not cleared the bank by the end of the previous month, it is considered outstanding. All outstanding checks must be considered when one is comparing the bank statement with the firm's books.

**Deposits-in-transit** Depositors may enter receipt amounts in their records which do not reach the bank as deposits by the last day of the previous month and are therefore not included on the bank statement. Such deposits are said to be late or in transit.

**Bank service charges and bank memos** Banks may charge depositors for services such as the collection of notes and stop payments. These charges are listed on the bank statements. In addition, deductions and additions indicated on bank statements are sometimes explained in debit and credit memos sent along with the statement to the bank customer.

## OTHER BANK SERVICES AND FEATURES

The secretary should be acquainted with the variety of services offered by banks. Such information is invaluable for use in assisting a busy lawyer. Bank officials are usually glad to explain how to take advantage of the bank's services.

**Cashier's check** A bank's customer who does not have a checking account may purchase a cashier's check from the bank by paying for the amount of the check plus a service charge. Also known as a *treasurer's check* or an *official check,* it is written by the bank on its own funds. The check is used in the same manner as an ordinary check, but the payee recognizes that the check is guaranteed.

**Bank draft** Similar in purpose to a cashier's check, a bank draft is a check written by a bank on funds it has in another bank. The customer pays for the amount of the draft plus a service charge.

**Personal money order** For customers requiring small sums, banks sell money orders similar to those sold by post offices. These bank money orders are negotiable and serve the same purpose as business or personal checks.

**Certified check** Should a payee require guaranteed payment, a bank will certify that a depositor's account contains sufficient funds to pay for the check. The amount is subtracted from the depositor's balance and the check is stamped "Certified."

**Certificate of deposit** Banks pay interest on short-term deposits (a minimum of 30 days) to customers who do not want cash to lie idle. The bank issues a promissory note to the depositor which can be negotiated to other parties or cashed at the end of the time period.

**Short-term checking account** A depositor can open a temporary checking account for a particular purpose. As soon as that purpose has been accomplished, the account is closed.

**Bank discounting**   If a company wants to secure cash for a draft or note it is holding, it may do so by discounting the instrument at a bank. After deducting interest, the bank gives the company the proceeds and collects on the instrument at the specified time.

**Foreign payments**   Firms doing business in foreign countries may send funds through banks in the form of cable money orders, bank drafts, and currency.

**Safe-deposit box**   For a fee, a firm or an individual may rent a safe-deposit box from a bank for the storage of valuable papers and other items. The amount of the fee is charged according to the size of the box.

### PETTY CASH FUND

Since it is impractical to pay small expenses by check, firms maintain petty cash funds for small items. Items such as taxi fare, postage, and small quantities of office supplies are often paid from the fund. To start the fund, a check is written and cashed. The cash is kept in a locked office drawer or box and is maintained by the person (frequently the secretary) designated to disburse the funds. The amount of the fund depends on the size of the office and the frequency of small payments. A disbursement from the fund is recorded on a petty cash receipt (written authorization) which indicates the date, receipt number, amount, and purpose of the expenditure. It also contains the signature of the person receiving the money. The receipts are kept in the petty cash box, so that at all times the total of cash and receipts equals the original amount. Where a bill has been received, it is attached to the petty cash receipt. When the fund is low, a check is cashed to restore the fund to its starting amount. The petty cash receipts are given to the accounting department for entry in the financial records.

**Petty Cash Receipt**

```
                    PETTY CASH RECEIPT

  Date __June 3, 19-- __                No. _25_

  Paid to _Lloyd Baron_
                                       ┌──────┬──────┐
  Reason _Car fare_                    │  4   │  20  │
                                       └──────┴──────┘
  Account charged _Travel Expenses_       Amount
  Received payment:
  _Lloyd Baron_
```

### TRAVEL FUNDS

The secretary must be certain that sufficient funds are available to the lawyer on foreign or domestic trips. Advance preparations involve visits to banks and offices to secure cash substitutes (or foreign money denominations if the trip involves leaving the country) and documents.

**Letter of credit**   This document is available from the firm's bank. It contains the name of the person who will be requesting the funds and the maximum amount that can be secured. This amount is deducted from the company's account with the bank. When the traveler needs funds in a foreign country, the letter of credit is presented to a designated bank and the amount received is listed on the document. A letter of credit usually involves a large amount of money.

**Traveler's checks**    For smaller amounts, traveler's checks can be purchased at banks, Western Union, American Express, and some travel agencies. They come in denominations of $10, $20, $50, and $100. The checks must be signed at the time of purchase by the person who will use them. The user's signature on the checks is required when they are cashed.

**Express money orders**    These may be purchased by a secretary and either given or sent to the traveler, who is designated as the payee. As with regular checks, the traveler may either cash the money orders or transfer them to other parties.

**Foreign currency**    Banks sell foreign money in $10 packages which may be used by the traveler as starter funds upon arrival in a foreign country.

# 7.4

## TRUST ACCOUNTS

Perhaps one of the most difficult and also potentially dangerous accounting functions performed in law firms is the handling of client trust funds—advances by clients for expenses, collections made for clients, and estates and trusts of which the firm is executor or trustee. These funds entrusted to the attorney by the client must be segregated and accounted for to avoid any semblance of impropriety on the part of the lawyer.

### SEPARATE TRUST ACCOUNTS
If you were to read any bar journal listing the disciplinary actions taken against lawyers, you would probably find that misappropriation of client funds, or failing to exercise proper care in accounting for them, is a major problem facing the legal profession, particularly the lawyers with smaller practices. The penalties for mishandling these funds range from private reprimand to revocation of license to possible imprisonment.

The handling of trust funds is delineated by the American Bar Association in Disciplinary Rule 9-102, which concerns preserving the identity of a client's funds and property. Basically it states that, with certain exceptions, "all funds of clients paid to a lawyer or law firm, other than advances for costs and expenses, shall be deposited in one or more identifiable bank accounts maintained in the state in which the law office is situated and no funds belonging to the lawyer or law firm shall be deposited therein." It also states that the lawyer must notify the client promptly of the receipt of his or her funds, maintain complete records of all the funds, and promptly pay or deliver to the client as requested the funds, securities, or other properties in the possession of the lawyer which the client is entitled to receive.

The rule against commingling was adopted to provide against the probability in some cases, the possibility in many cases, and the danger in all cases that such commingling of funds will result in a loss for clients. This section describes the various kinds of funds coming into a law firm's possession that are subject to the rules of rendering accountings to clients. Also discussed here are ways to account effectively for trust funds, and some auditing procedures that can prevent potential problems. Although this discussion concerns cash funds, the same rules apply to securities or other assets of the client.

**Trust accounts**    First of all, a separate bank account should be set up for all trust funds. This is a relatively simple procedure; one goes to the bank and has it set up a separate account under the firm's name with the notation "Trust Account" (as opposed to "Attorney's Account") as part of the account name. It is then necessary to have separate checks printed for that particular account and to authorize certain persons to sign the checks. The attorney may decide to set up separate accounts for separate types of transactions. For example, there may be one account set aside strictly for real estate transactions, one for collection matters, another for various types of closings such as loan financings, and perhaps yet another for those in which the firm is acting in a fiduciary capacity.

**Account ledger**    Next it will be necessary to set up an individual ledger account card for each client to record the transactions that occur. A sample escrow account ledger is illustrated below. This is a relatively simple form with columns for receipts, disbursements, and a balance. As receipts and disbursements occur they are posted to the ledger card, which is kept with copies of the check and other pertinent details of each transaction. Each month a trial balance should be taken of the individual ledger cards and reconciled with the bank statement. A trial balance is nothing more than a listing of all the trust accounts with a total that agrees with the bank reconciliation. This enables you to immediately determine the outstanding balance in each of the trust accounts and to answer questions clients might ask about their balances. These accounts should be reviewed periodically to make certain that, whenever there are balances after a transaction is completed, appropriate refunds are made.

ESCROW ACCOUNT LEDGER

Client Name: Frances K. More
Responsible Attorney: J. Sutter
Matter: Estate
Client Matter Code No.: EM–251

| DATE | Check No. or Description | DISBURSEMENTS | | RECEIPTS | | BALANCE | |
|------|------|------|------|------|------|------|------|
| 3/27/-- | S-54 | | | 3500 | 00 | 3500 | 00 |
| 3/29/-- | E-741 | 74 | 00 | | | | |
| " | E-742 | 250 | 00 | | | | |
| " | E-743 | 8 | 00 | | | 3168 | 00 |

**Interest-bearing accounts** When a large amount of money is held in trust, it is tempting to put it in a short-term interest-bearing account rather than in a regular checking account. The American Bar Association has ruled that a lawyer receiving money in his capacity as a lawyer, under circumstances that require him to account to another for such money, would be violating Canon 9 of the Code of Professional Responsibility should he place the money in an interest-bearing account and keep the interest for his or her own use unless specifically authorized to do so. The normal procedure is for the client to give written permission to have the money deposited in an interest-bearing account, normally in a savings account or as certificates of deposit, which are relatively free of risk. The client's tax identification number is obtained so that the interest earned inures to the client rather than to the lawyer. Records should be kept on a separate ledger card to show the disposition of the funds and the fact that they are kept in a separate interest-bearing account.

**Cash advances and retainers** Another problem deals with the proper handling of advances on behalf of clients—should advances be made from trust accounts or from the attorney's own funds? Obviously, funds cannot be disbursed for one client from the trust funds belonging to another. These cash advances must be made from the attorney's own funds.

Cash advances can create a serious cash drain on the law firm. All too often, clients have become accustomed to using a firm's funds to finance their transactions. In many cases, it is appropriate for the lawyer to ask for a retainer to cover anticipated expenses. This money is placed in the trust accounts; checks are disbursed and accounts controlled just as for other trust monies. If the balance gets low, the client should advance more funds. Retainers are now becoming more popular and have helped the cash flow problems of many firms. Retainers are also an answer to the fee collection problem because time expended can be applied against the retainer. If a client sends a check, part of which is for subsequent advances and the remainder for the fee, the amounts should be deposited into two separate accounts, the trust account and the regular account.

## COMMINGLING OF FUNDS WITHIN A TRUST ACCOUNT
The commingling problem must be examined not only as it pertains to setting up trust accounts separate from the regular disbursing accounts of the lawyer, but also with respect to the commingling of funds within the bank accounts themselves. There are two factors in this problem: one is the business risk involved in issuing checks on uncollected funds; the other is the ethics of paying out of the funds of one client for the account of another.

The ethical prohibition against commingling client funds with law firm funds was adopted primarily to prevent loss of a client's funds through their personal use by the attorney or through the claims of the attorney's creditors. In addition, the lawyer must always be able to promptly deliver the money to the client upon request. The lawyer cannot do this unless the funds of that client are actually in the account and can be drawn upon. It is unethical to put the funds of the other clients at risk or make them unavailable should one client demand all his escrow funds.

**Collected funds** Ethical codes do not address themselves to the mechanics of handling the cash flow of an account that contains the funds of many different clients. For example, there is no requirement that there actually be *collected* funds in the bank on which the check is drawn. Under Disciplinary Rule 9-102, therefore, you can conceivably draw a check against an escrow account even though the mechanical steps of depositing the funds to the account have not been completed. Furthermore, the code of ethics lists no requirements as to the types of banks or other financial institutions into which escrow funds should be deposited. It can be assumed, therefore, that failure of the depository is an acceptable risk. Consequently, a certified or a cashier's check, even when not yet deposited or classified as collected funds, should be valid, since the only risk of those funds is the solvency of the bank upon which the funds are drawn. Similarly, checks drawn on other institutions such as savings and loan associations and insurance companies would also be valid. The lawyer is apparently given latitude to exercise reasonable judgment as to the soundness of the depository and the soundness of the drawer's check.

## COLLECTIBILITY OF CHECKS

In addition to ethical considerations, there is the question of business risk in using trust funds. On the one hand, all checks may be presumed uncollectible until notification by the depository that the funds are available. On the other hand, all checks may be presumed to be good and be drawn against at once. Most law firms take the latter view, although the individual lawyer or business manager must make a subjective decision in each case.

In most cases, the firm takes no real risk of collection on cashier's checks on a local bank, on checks certified by local banks, on checks drawn on local banks by local savings and loan associations, and on checks drawn by similar lending institutions and by some law firms. Similarly, the firm normally takes no real risk of collection on cashier's or certified checks on certain reputable city banks. Your firm normally takes a minimal risk of collecting on checks drawn by major corporations.

**Time lags**   There is an additional consideration, however. Even if the risk of collection is assumed, the way in which the depository collects the funds will affect the timetable upon which checks may be drawn against the funds. The time lag involved in clearings through the banking system varies among different banks. Sometimes there is confusion between the terms *good* or *available funds* and *collected funds*. Good funds are available for use or investment but are not necessarily collected. Collected funds are those funds, represented by checks, that have physically been paid by the client's bank, i.e., matched against funds on deposit of the drawer. A check always provides good funds in no more than two days, but it can take as long as seven days to provide collected funds. The following guidelines may be used:

1.  Checks drawn on the depository become collected funds on the second day; these funds may be drawn upon without affecting the status of other client funds in the bank account. A certified check may also be drawn on these funds on the second day.

2.  Checks drawn on local banks other than the depository are collected funds on the third day after the check is deposited.

3.  Clearance of checks on out-of-town banks varies, depending on such things as distance, Federal Reserve districts, and the nature of the funds. Generally speaking, checks drawn on banks in your own Federal Reserve district but outside your immediate area will become collected in three days. It should be noted that using certified or cashier's checks may reduce the risk of collection but does not appreciably speed up the clearing process. As a practical matter, however, time can be saved because you do not have to await word from the depository that the check has cleared.

**Determining the collectibility of a check**   It is essential to designate a specific person or persons in the firm to make decisions on the acceptability of particular client checks as they are received.

For example, suppose that your office is involved in a $100,000 real estate transaction and you receive a check from a bank in New York. If this check is not certified, it will take at least three days for the check to clear and for the funds to become collected funds in, say, a Philadelphia bank. This means that if funds are disbursed from that account on the date the check is received, monies belonging to other clients in that escrow account are being used for this transaction. Should the check that you receive in connection with the closing not turn out to be collected, then another client's money has been improperly used since that client's funds cannot be made immediately available upon request.

However, as mentioned previously, there is also a prudent businessman's approach to the problem that involves making a subjective evaluation of each check. Your office could prepare a list of preferred corporations, lending institutions, lawyers, and other groups whose checks up to a certain amount will automatically be considered collected funds. Checks above that amount would have to be certified. It should not be embarrassing to ask a client to have a check certified; in fact, it is a normal business practice.

**Transfer of funds by wire**   There are certain methods now available to expedite and ensure the collectibility of funds. One of the most popular is the wire transfer system. There are two kinds of wire transfers. One is a Federal Reserve bank wire transfer—a transfer between banks through the Federal Reserve System. It uses a teletype or computer terminal to transmit money between accounts; the Federal Reserve System simply debits the sending bank and credits the receiving bank. The second type of wire transfer is the bank wire system, in which banks that are hooked up telephonically can debit or credit money to one another. Ironically, the bank wire system uses the Federal Reserve to make the various debits and credits. It is commonplace now to transfer funds by wire between banks in the same city. Wiring funds of less than $15,000 or so may be costly, but the convenience and security of wire transfer frequently justify its use. It removes the element of risk and, when large amounts of money are involved, provides the economic benefits of accelerated cash flow.

Wire transfer is one way of determining that there are collected funds in an account because a bank will not transfer money by wire unless it first makes sure that the funds are in the drawer's account. The easiest way to take advantage of wire transfer is to have various bank accounts at banks throughout the area and to call upon one person, normally the bank wire officer, to transfer funds when necessary. As an alternative, the firm's bank could be used and the client instructed to wire funds into this account. Wire transfer results in funds being immediately available for disbursement. It relieves the problems of collectibility and of having cash tied up for long periods of time.

**Cashier's and certified checks**   A *cashier's check*, as explained in section 7.3, is a check drawn by a bank on itself. The check does not represent collected funds, so it must go through the same process as regular checks to be collected and available for disbursement. A *certified check* is drawn by a bank after examination of the drawer's account to make sure that funds are available; the funds are subtracted from the drawer's account when the check is written. In most cases a bank will certify against a cashier's check if it knows the customer and against a bank if there is no chance that it will fail as a depository. Both certified checks and cashier's checks guarantee collectibility; the only risk is the failure of the depository.

**Trust funds in financial statements**   On the balance sheet of a financial statement client trust funds should be included as part of the firm's total cash balance; however, they are then deducted from that amount to reflect unrestricted cash balances, as illustrated in the sample balance sheet shown on page 134. The purpose of the balance sheet is to show accountability. Presenting escrow funds in this manner not only reflects accountability but also indicates the actual amount of free cash available for the firm's use.

## AUDITS

Bar associations studying the problems of trust funds have proposed that periodic audits be made of attorney trust accounts. An audit usually consists of nine basic steps:

1. Direct confirmation of the balance of the account or accounts is made with the bank. This is done with a standard confirmation form sent to the bank, signed, and returned directly to the auditor.
2. The reconciliation of the bank account(s) as of the date of the audit is examined and correlated with the confirmed account balances.
3. The auditor examines cancelled checks, determines whether the proper person signed the checks, and reviews endorsements for unusual items.
4. The auditor reviews cancelled checks that came in after the cutoff date in order to check the accuracy of the list of outstanding checks on the reconciliation.
5. On a spot-check basis, the auditor reviews the client files to see that the proper client accounts are being charged for disbursements.
6. The auditor may check to see if the amounts are being disbursed from collected funds.
7. Cash receipts are reviewed to ensure that all receipts were properly deposited and recorded to the proper client.
8. Trial balances of client accounts are examined and explanations obtained as to why certain accounts have long-term balances that have not been refunded.
9. The auditor reviews the internal control procedures concerning the receipt and disbursement of funds.

These procedures are a normal part of every audit performed by independent accountants. A legal secretary should be prepared to accept the auditing procedures and assist the auditors. Then the audit can be made in a way that meets the standards of the accounting profession as well as the ethical standards of the legal profession.

## SUMMARY

The following procedures for handling trust accounts should be instituted in your office to ensure that the lawyer's Code of Professional Responsibility is not violated.

1. Set up a bank account for all client trust funds separate from the account used for the firm's normal transactions. Use separate checks for the trust account and identify these checks on your books.
2. Keep separate ledger cards for each client, recording all receipts and disbursements and noting the balance.
3. Reconcile all escrow funds monthly, and make trial balances. Have a responsible individual within the firm periodically review the accounts to see that the transactions are proper and that funds are available to clients upon demand.
4. Establish procedures for disbursing funds that are not collected funds at the time of the transaction.
5. When feasible, use wire transfers and certified checks to speed up transactions and to avoid spending uncollected funds. This is particularly important in major transactions where funds are disbursed on the same day they are received.
6. Educate all lawyers and staff as to the proper procedures and the ethics of handling escrow accounts.

# 7.5

# PAYROLL

The secretary in a small law firm who is responsible for preparing the payroll must understand that, to an employee, few things are more sacred than one's paycheck.

Preparing accurate and timely payrolls that meet federal and state tax regulations necessitates a thorough understanding of the method by which payroll is computed, disbursed, accounted for, and coordinated with the various taxing authority regulations.

## COMPUTING AND RECORDING THE PAYROLL

**Payroll periods**    Traditionally, payroll periods are either biweekly, semimonthly, or monthly. Although there are still some law firms that pay on a weekly basis, you will find that semimonthly payment is probably the most popular for the non-partners or non-owners, with a monthly payment for the partners or owners of the firm. Payment is normally made on the 15th and last days of the month. If the pay period falls on a Saturday, Sunday, or holiday the payroll is distributed on the last working day before the normal paydate. Biweekly payrolls are prepared in some cases; however, when pay periods go past the last day of the month or past the last day of the year, certain accounting and administrative problems are encountered that do not occur when the firm is on a strict semimonthly or monthly pay schedule.

**Salary computation**    Most employees of a law firm are on an annual salary with their annual pay divided into 12 or 24 equal amounts, and this amount is the same each pay period unless there are circumstances—such as leaves of absence, sick pay, and overtime—which add to or subtract from the normal pay. Depending on the number of prescribed hours per week, most employees are paid their hourly rate up to 35 or 40 hours per week with an overtime rate of one and a half times the normal pay for all hours over the norm. The attorney will examine overtime pay regulations in your state or locality to make sure that you are adhering to them.

**Payroll forms and records**    There are three major forms associated with the preparation of the regular payroll:

1. *Payroll check* The check given to the employee is normally in two parts. The employee deposits or cashes the check portion and keeps the payroll stub as a record of gross wages, deductions, and net pay. Most stubs also contain the year-to-date information for these items.
2. *Employee's earnings card* This is a record of the total wages and deductions for each person in the firm over the course of a twelve-month period. It is an important record for preparing various tax returns. It contains the employee's name, address, social security number, number of exemptions claimed, date of birth, marital status, rate of pay, hours worked, earnings, deductions, net pay, check numbers, and year-to-date earnings.
3. *Payroll journal* The payroll journal is a listing of all the employees who are being paid in a specific pay period. It indicates gross pay, deductions, net pay amount, and the number of each check written for the net pay.

## PAYROLL TAXES

**Deductions**    The normal deductions from pay are Federal Withholding Taxes (FWT), state withholding tax, and FICA (Federal Insurance Contributions Act) tax, or social security. The social security amount—the percentage as well as the base on which this percentage is applied—varies from year to year. The actual deduction for an employee can be determined from FICA tax tables supplied by the government or purchased from stationers. The law also requires employers to match the taxes deducted from employees' pay by remitting a like amount. FWT refers to the income taxes which employers must withhold from their employees' salaries as the money is earned. The withheld funds are sent to the federal government periodically. The FWT deduction is based upon the employee's gross pay for the payroll period and the number of exemptions (dependents) claimed. Some states have their own income tax programs and require employers to deduct these taxes from salaries and wages. The Internal Revenue Service and state tax agencies publish booklets which list the deductions at various levels of pay.

If your firm is a partnership, the individual partners do not have federal, state, or social security deductions. Partners are treated differently from employees for tax purposes. They pay their taxes directly to the IRS on an estimated basis and do not have taxes withheld from their paychecks.

Other deductions may be made for U.S. Savings Bonds, health insurance, loans, pension funds, company stock purchase plans, and charitable contributions.

**Tax returns**   It is important to be familiar with the various tax returns that must be filed on a periodic basis with local, state, and federal taxing authorities. The following paragraphs describe the major federal tax forms that a legal secretary may be required to process for filing with the Internal Revenue Service.

**Federal Tax Deposit (Form 501)**   This form is filed at a commercial bank along with funds withheld for FICA and FWT whenever these amounts plus the employer's FICA contributions amount to more than $200 during a month. Tax regulations require that employers deposit withheld income tax and FICA taxes with an authorized commercial bank depository or a Federal Reserve bank.

**Federal Tax Deposit (Form 501)**

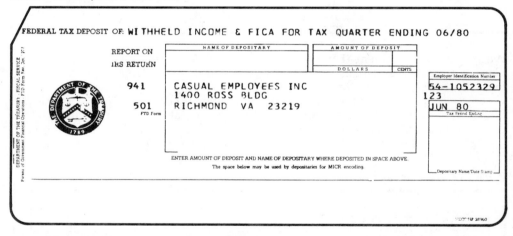

**Employer's Quarterly Federal Tax Return (Form 941)**   Amounts remitted with Forms 501 plus amounts not yet remitted are summarized on Form 941, which is filed during the month following the payroll quarter. The form also contains employees' names, social security numbers, taxable FICA wages, and FWT and FICA taxes deducted.

Whether your firm is required to make deposits depends on the amount of the liability at the end of each pay period or at the end of each quarter. The Internal Revenue Service in your area can provide information about filing the payments and the amount that must be deposited. The IRS is very strict on the timely preparation and submission of these returns. It is important that you understand the requirements and make your deposits on time.

**Reconciliation of Income Tax Withheld and Transmittal of Wage and Tax Statements (Form W-3)**   Income taxes withheld and listed on Forms 941 are summarized on Form W-3. The form is accompanied by copies of W-2 forms for all employees.

**Employee's Withholding Allowance Certificate (Form W-4)** The W-4 form is completed by individual employees to authorize the federal and state income tax deductions that are made from their pay. This form indicates whether the employee is married or single and how many dependents he or she claims; this information determines the amount of deductions from the check. W-4 forms should be kept in the individual employees' personnel files.

**Employee's Withholding Exemption Certificate (Form W-4)**

| Form **W-4** (Rev. October 1979) | Department of the Treasury—Internal Revenue Service **Employee's Withholding Allowance Certificate** | |
|---|---|---|
| Print your full name ▶ | Your social security number ▶ | |
| Address (including ZIP code) ▶ | | |
| **Marital status:** ☐ Single ☐ Married ☐ Married, but withhold at higher Single rate **Note:** *If married, but legally separated, or spouse is a nonresident alien, check the single block.* | | |

1 Total number of allowances you are claiming (from line F of the worksheet on page 2) . . . . . . . . .
2 Additional amount, if any, you want deducted from each pay (if your employer agrees) . . . . . . . . .    $
3 I claim exemption from withholding because (see instructions and check boxes below that apply):
  a ☐ Last year I did not owe any Federal income tax and had a right to a full refund of **ALL** income tax withheld, **AND**
  b ☐ This year I do not expect to owe any Federal income tax and expect to have a right to a full refund of **ALL** income tax withheld. If both

    **a** and **b** apply, enter "EXEMPT" here . . . . . . . . . . . . . . . . . . . . . . . . . . . . . . . . . ▶
  c If you entered "EXEMPT" on line 3b, are you a full-time student? . . . . . . . . . . . . . . . . . ☐ **Yes** ☐ **No**
Under the penalties of perjury, I certify that I am entitled to the number of withholding allowances claimed on this certificate, or if claiming exemption from withholding, that I am entitled to claim the exempt status.

Employee's signature ▶                        Date ▶        , 19
Employer's name and address (including ZIP code) **(FOR EMPLOYER'S USE ONLY)**        Employer identification number

**Wage and Tax Statement (Form W-2)** This statement is sent by employers to employees no later than January 31 of each year; it lists the previous year's gross pay, federal income taxes withheld, FICA taxes withheld, and total FICA wages paid. Where state income taxes are deducted, an additional copy is sent. The employee files a copy of the W-2 statement attached to the federal income tax form by April 15. It is important to remember that if an employee leaves your firm during the year a W-2 must be furnished within 30 days of the last payment of wages, not at the end of the calendar year.

**Wage and Tax Statement (Form W-2)**

| 1 Control number | ⧆⧆⧆⧆⧆ | | |
|---|---|---|---|
| 2 Employer's name, address, and ZIP code | | 3 Employer's identification number | 4 Employer's State number |
| | | 5 Stat. em- ☐ De- ☐ Pension ☐ Legal ☐ ployee ceased plan rep. | 942 ☐ Sub- ☐ Cor- ☐ Void ☐ emp. total rection |
| | | 6 | 7 Advance EIC payment |
| 8 Employee's social security number | 9 Federal income tax withheld | 10 Wages, tips, other compensation | 11 FICA tax withheld |
| 12 Employer's name, address, and ZIP code | | 13 FICA wages | 14 FICA tips |
| | | 16 Employer's use | |
| | | 17 State income tax | 18 State wages, tips, etc. | 19 Name of State |
| | | 20 Local income tax | 21 Local wages, tips, etc. | 22 Name of locality |

Form **W-2 Wage and Tax Statement 1980**   Copy B To be filed with employee's **FEDERAL** tax return   Department of the Treasury
This information is being furnished to the Internal Revenue Service.   Internal Revenue Service

**Unemployment tax**   The federal government and most states also impose an unemployment compensation tax on all earnings up to certain maximum amounts. The state unemployment compensation return is filed on a quarterly basis, normally by the last day of the month following the end of the quarter. Federal unemployment tax returns are filed annually; however, deposits are normally made quarterly and are credited against the final tax liability at the end of the year. The base upon which both the state and federal tax is computed changes periodically and varies from state to state. Therefore, you should obtain information locally about this tax at the time you are given the responsibility for the preparation of the payroll.

## METHODS OF PAYMENT
The two most popular ways of paying employees are by cash and by check, with the majority of firms paying by check. Recently, the concept of direct deposit—in which an employee's net pay is directly deposited into the employee's bank—has gained wide acceptance, and now most banks throughout the country offer this service. Direct deposit eliminates the need to prepare the check, sign it, control it, reconcile the bank statement, and concern yourself over lost checks. It also frees employees from having to go to the bank to make their deposits. There are many employees who do not like the concept of direct deposit, preferring the security of a check in hand; however, direct deposit is becoming more and more prevalent. You are encouraged, wherever possible, to suggest direct deposit to your firm.

# 7.6

## BILLING AND COLLECTIONS

It is important to bill clients on a current basis and to adequately follow up on accounts which become past due. Legal secretaries can be very helpful in this area. Once the attorney becomes confident of the secretary's skills, the entire billing and collection process can be turned over to the secretary. However, no matter how much financial responsibility a secretary is given, the determination of billing rates is always the attorney's decision, and the secretary is warned never to discuss fees with a client.

Time accounting is a key to the financial success of any law firm. Surveys have shown that those lawyers who keep close track of their time normally generate 30 to 40 percent more income than those who do not. However, timekeeping is of no value unless this time can eventually be converted into cash through the billing and collection process. In those firms which do keep time, lawyers are assigned billing rates which, when multiplied by the total hours expended, form the basis for the bill to the client.

In addition, the firm normally passes on to each client those disbursements or expenses that can be readily identified for that client. Disbursement cards are commercially available, frequently in carbon sets. They may be used to record client expenditures, both billable and non-billable, for work on a case. The card should list the name of the client and the case or matter, the corresponding docket number or reference number, the responsible attorney, the file number, the date, a description of the work done, and the amount of expenditure. Expenses that might be detailed on client disbursement cards include filing fees, toll calls, travel expenses, copying and printing charges, expert witness fees, local counsel expertise, and miscellaneous out-of-pocket expenditures.

**A Disbursement Card**

File No. _____          Amount _____

_____ 19___

EXPENSE VOUCHER

Client _____

For _____

Responsible Attorney _____

Check _____ Cash _____ Payment made by _____

## THE BILLING STATEMENT

The actual format of the bill will vary from firm to firm and from client to client within the firm. Clients normally wish to receive a bill which adequately describes (1) the work which was performed, (2) the period of time covered by the work, and (3) in some cases the individuals who performed it, with the hours, billing rates, and total value of each person's work listed. In the sample bill illustrated here, note that the statement includes these three items. In addition, the bill sets out in detail the out-of-pocket expenses which are appropriately passed on as client charges.

The advent of computerized timekeeping has assisted law firms in preparing bills. In many cases, information which is stored in the computer becomes the basis for the bill itself. Computerized systems can perform all steps in producing the bill, with the lawyer performing only a minor editing function before the bill eventually finds its way into the client's hand. A system of monthly billing can also be set up that incorporates the capabilities of advanced text-editing machines.

## COLLECTION

Once the bill has been rendered, it becomes an "account receivable" of the firm until the client makes payment and the receivable is converted into cash. Billings should be rendered as early as possible after the completion of the work or, if it is an ongoing matter, at frequent intervals—preferably every month. Bills that are sent promptly tend to be paid promptly. When the bill is submitted, it normally is posted to the client's accounts receivable ledger, as shown in the illustration on page 152. By examining this particular ledger, the lawyer is able to see at a glance when the bills were rendered, when they were paid, and the balance owing. By examining the entire group of client ledgers, the lawyer can take appropriate action to collect long-outstanding balances. This action may include first a friendly reminder, then perhaps a stronger letter and, in some cases, legal action. The latter course is taken only after all other means of collection have been exhausted.

## A Billing Statement

### MARKHAM AND SISITSKY

December 31, 19—
Ref. File No: 123456
Invoice No: 173

City Manufacturing Co.
24 South Street
Briarton, ST 34567

Fees for professional services rendered
for the period October 1—December 31, 19—
in connection with organization of Smith
Construction Company

| | | | |
|---|---|---|---|
| Sisitsky | - 20 hrs @ $80 | $ 1,600.00 | |
| Ritsler | - 10 hrs @ $75 | 750.00 | |
| Jones | - 30 hrs @ $50 | 1,500.00 | |
| | Total Fees | | $ 3,850.00 |

Disbursements:

| | | |
|---|---|---|
| Photocopy | $ 8.50 | |
| Travel | 162.25 | |
| Telephone | 3.25 | |
| Total Disbursements | | 174.00 |

| | |
|---|---|
| Total Fees and Disbursements | $ 4,024.00 |

**Client Account Receivable Ledger**

| DATE | ITEMS | FOLIO | ✓ | DEBITS | DATE | ITEMS | FOLIO | ✓ | CREDITS |
|------|-------|-------|---|--------|------|-------|-------|---|---------|
| 9-30 -- | # 143 | | | 6 35 20 | 10-18 -- | Receipt # 102 | | | 6 35 00 |
| 11-15 -- | # 158 | | | 1438 50 | 12-18 -- | Receipt # 158 | | | 1438 50 |
| 12-31 -- | # 173 | | | 4024 00 | | | | | |

SHEET NO._____
RATING
CREDIT LIMIT
TERMS

ACCOUNT NO. *123456*
NAME *City Manufacturing Co.*
ADDRESS *24 South St.*
*Briarton, ST 34567*

Collection of the firm's accounts receivable is the responsibility of the managing attorney. The legal secretary can assist in this effort by preparing a monthly list of unpaid accounts separated into "aging" categories: for example, accounts that have been outstanding for up to 90 days, from 90 to 180 days, from 180 days to a year, and over a year. The attorney can then focus on those accounts that have been outstanding for long periods of time and take whatever action is required to collect them. Another way that the secretary can help make collections more efficient is by making an extra copy of each bill and putting it in a separate file or notebook that is kept by the lawyer responsible for collection. When payment is received, this copy of the bill is destroyed.

Once the monies are received, the cash is deposited each day at the firm's designated bank. It is essential that the money belonging to the attorney be segregated from the money belonging to the client and deposited in the firm's escrow accounts. As monies are received, the amount is posted to the client ledger so that a continuing running balance of the client's account can be maintained.

# 7.7

## THE SYSTEMS APPROACH TO LAW FIRM ACCOUNTING

The precise nature of accounting, together with the need to record the numerous financial transactions that take place in a law office, establishes an ideal situation for the use of systems—procedures that create all of the necessary information in the least amount of time with the least amount of work. In many law firms, most of the accounting records are maintained on automated equipment—mechanical bookkeeping machines or sophisticated computer equipment. In smaller firms, however, manual systems are still very popular, and many companies have designed commercial systems to meet the needs of these firms. These systems permit the posting of several records at one time and efficiently generate the supporting documents so essential to financial transactions.

## ONE-WRITE SYSTEMS

The legal secretary in a small firm is normally involved in the following areas of law firm accounting, each of which is adaptable to a systems approach: (1) cash receipts, (2) cash disbursements, (3) escrow accounting (including both cash receipts and disbursements), (4) payroll, and (5) time accounting.

A complete system of law firm accounting will encompass these five areas. It will also allow the accountant, bookkeeper, or secretary to prepare systematically all the necessary documentation and to provide the data for posting to the general ledger and for preparing the financial statements. Most manual systems are described as *one-write systems* because, by writing only once, you can post and balance the several documents necessary in a financial transaction without having to write the same numbers on each document. Some of these systems are also called *pegboard systems* because the several forms are placed on pegs in a notebook or on a backing sheet in order to align the columns. If all of the major financial records can be posted at one time, the possibility of error in posting and balancing is reduced. There are several one-write systems on the market.

**Payroll**   In the discussion of payroll accounting in section 7.5 it was noted that the basic records necessary for payroll accounting are (1) the check which is given to the employee, (2) the earnings record which contains a chronological account of an employee's earnings, and (3) the payroll journal which serves as a summary of the total payroll written in any particular period. Illustrated on page 154 is a one-write system used for payroll. Note that the check, earnings record, and payroll journal are all posted at the same time when the check is prepared. This means that once the payroll journal is balanced the accountant can be satisfied that the check and the earnings card have been posted properly.

In most one-write systems the documents are attached to a board and aligned in such a way as to allow for the posting of various records in a single position. Note in the example that when the check and check stub are written the information will transfer itself, via carbon or chemically treated carbonless paper, onto the earnings card and the payroll journal. Since the forms are standard, the user is permitted a great amount of flexibility in determining if any additional copies should be made.

Each time a payroll check is written a different earnings card may be inserted between the check and the payroll journal. From information on the employee earnings card the annual W-2 is prepared, which the employee uses to file his or her annual tax return. The payroll journal permits a complete record of the payroll for any specific period. It is used to prepare the journal entries for posting to the general ledger.

**Cash disbursements, cash receipts, and escrow accounting**   The same one-write system used for payroll accounting can also be used to record disbursements. Again, it is simply a matter of writing the check, which transfers the information onto a ledger card that represents the account to which the amount is to be charged. A different kind of one-write system for recording disbursements involves writing the disbursement information on a self-adhering label which is later affixed to a client ledger or similar record of the costs of a case or matter. An example of a one-write check writing system is illustrated on page 155; an example of the label record system appears on page 156. In the system illustrated on page 155, the information is further transferred to the general cash disbursements journal.

The one-write system may also be used in a similar way to record cash receipts and client escrow fund transactions. It is also possible to prepare individual remittance advices with automatic receipts which can be used both for control purposes and for providing the client with a record of the payment.

## A One-write System for Payroll

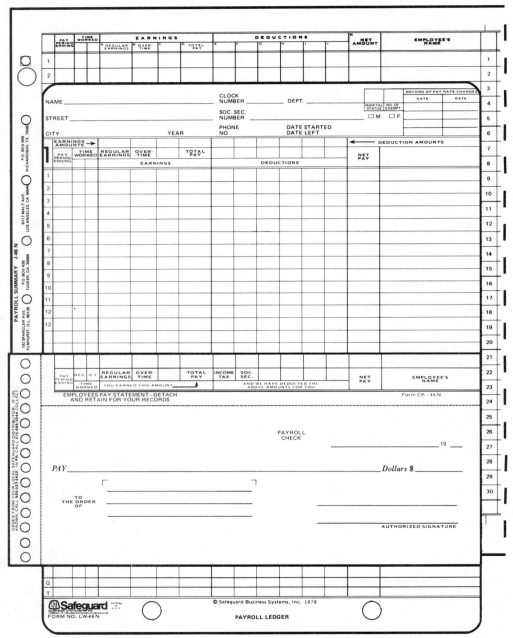

Reprinted by permission of Safeguard Business Systems.

The Systems Approach **155**

## A One-write Bookkeeping System

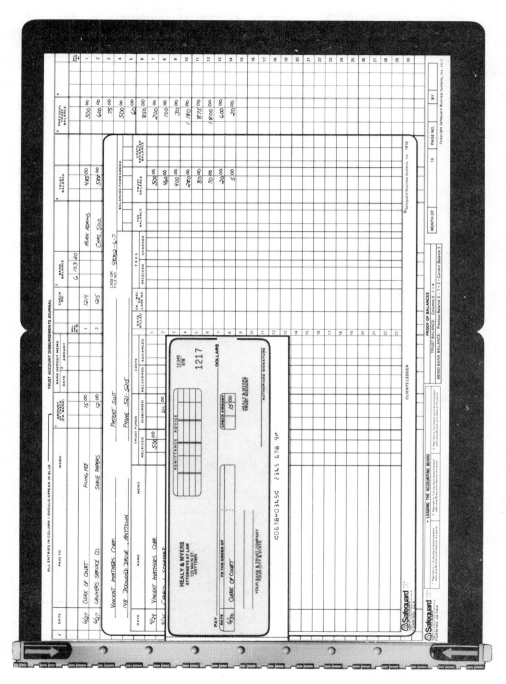

Reprinted by permission of Safeguard Business Systems.

## A One-write Bookkeeping System

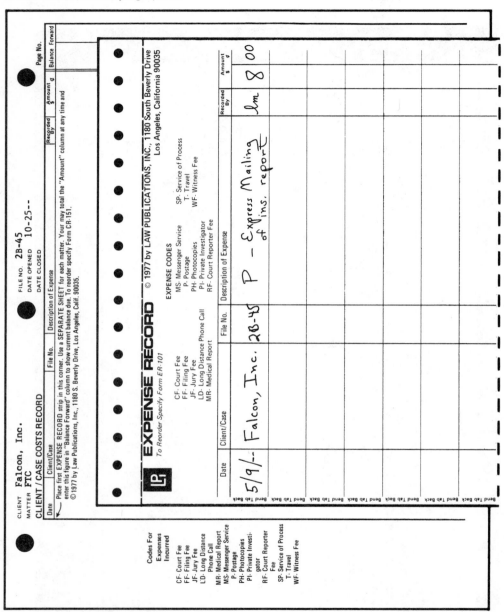

## A One-write System for Time Accounting

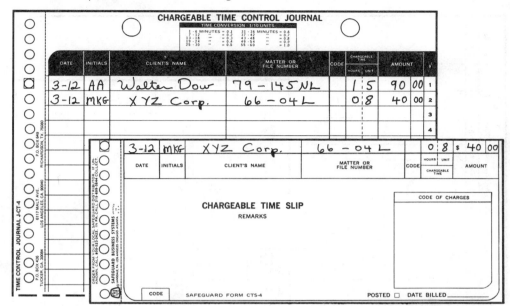

Reprinted by permission of Safeguard Business Systems.

**Time accounting**    One-write systems are also designed for time accounting. The above illustration shows a chargeable time control sheet as well as individual time slips which are posted by the lawyer. Carbon strips automatically transfer the writing onto a daily log of all recorded time. This is a very convenient method of keeping time. It not only creates individual time slips that can be filed and then summarized at billing time; it also permits the lawyer to describe the work performed with a code.

The normal procedure is for the time slips to be either filed in client case/matter folders and summarized at billing time or, in the case of larger files, posted to an individual client control ledger similar to the escrow account ledger illustrated on page 141. Such a client ledger provides a continuous record of all fees charged on a particular file.

Other commercially published timekeeping systems involve the use of self-adhesive labels that are filled out at the time work is done, then later peeled (or torn at the perforations) and affixed directly to the client's ledger. Samples of two of these systems are shown on the following pages.

The timekeeping system can further be expanded to record such things as the total fees received from each client and each lawyer's billable hours; such information is often required for management reports.

## SYSTEMATIZING THE LAW OFFICE

Every area of a law firm should be reviewed to determine whether it is susceptible to some type of systemization. The secretary in a small firm is in an excellent position to see where improvements in efficiency can be made and can suggest them to the attorney. Once an orderly manual system is in operation and working properly, it is then possible to examine whether the procedures should be mechanized through either a mechanical bookkeeping machine or a computer. For most law firms, a manual one-write system is sufficient. As a firm grows, however, with more lawyers and more clients, it will probably be more economically feasible to adopt a computerized system for timekeeping, bookkeeping, and accounting functions.

## A One-write System for Time Accounting

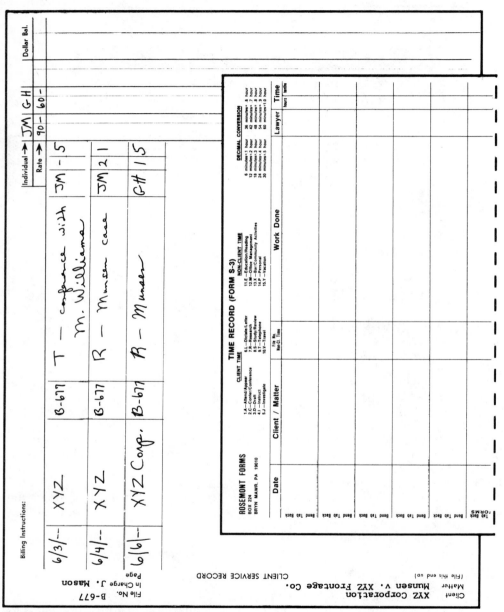

Reprinted by permission of Rosemont Forms.

## A One-write System for Time Accounting

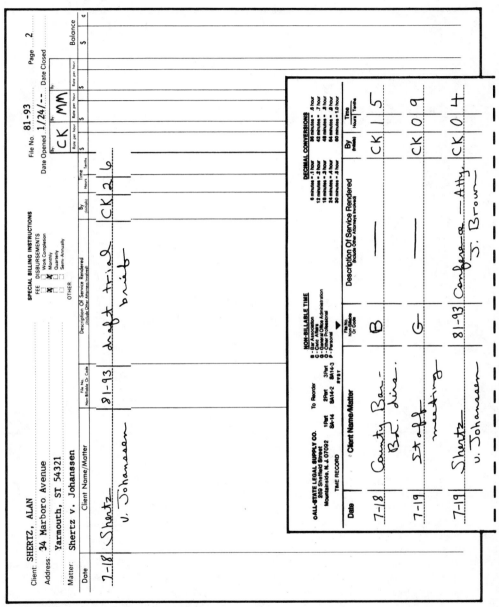

# 8

CHAPTER EIGHT

# DICTATION AND TRANSCRIPTION

## CONTENTS

# 8.1

## EQUIPMENT FOR MACHINE AND LIVE DICTATION

The proliferation of paper in the law office today has resulted in efforts by law firms to reduce the cost of dictation, transcription, and production of correspondence and documents. As the computer has saved money and increased efficiency in the handling of data, so text-editing machines have begun to permit the same economies in the processing of legal documents. The complexity of these documents, the volume of typed materials, the constant revision of hard copy, and the common reliance on boilerplate (frequently used standard phrases and paragraphs) have made sophisticated automatic typewriters increasingly valuable to the law office. A legal secretary or a transcription typist in the word-processing center, working at a typewriter with a memory and storage, can readily produce an error-free copy of a complicated legal document. These word-processing systems are detailed in Chapter 15, Text Editing in Law Offices.

A word-processing system is best utilized in combination with machine dictation and transcription. Studies have shown that a letter transcribed from machine dictation can be produced at 25 percent less than the cost of a similar letter dictated to a secretary taking shorthand. With a machine a lawyer can dictate two to three times faster; moreover, the secretary can transcribe twice as fast and more accurately from machine dictation than from pen-written shorthand notes.

## CHOOSING MACHINE DICTATION EQUIPMENT

Dictation equipment must be evaluated from both the dictator's and the transcriber's points of view. With any dictation equipment the quality of sound and convenience of the machine for both transcriber and dictator are important.

Choosing the proper combination of recording media and systems is becoming increasingly difficult because of the large selection of sophisticated equipment that is now available. There are many companies that make dictation equipment. However, there is little correlation between price and quality, so a careful review of the latest equipment should be made by the secretary with the aid of the employer. Attending business equipment shows is one way to keep up to date with the latest developments in machine dictation units. With the aid of the manufacturers' representatives, the secretary can appraise the equipment intelligently. Another good way to keep abreast is to request the loan of a machine as a prospective customer. This hands-on approach enables the user to properly evaluate the equipment.

Before your office contacts an equipment representative, you must determine what type of equipment will best fill the needs of the office. Machine dictation equipment generally falls into three categories: desktop, centralized, and portable.

**Desktop dictation machines**    For an office with a secretary assigned to each attorney and a moderate amount of dictation, desktop dictation and transcription machines are suitable. Desktop equipment may use any of the following recording media: magnetic belts, disks, reel-to-reel magnetic tape, and standard, mini-, and micro-cassettes. (Micro-cassettes are smaller than mini-cassettes.)

Most manufacturers offer several models, from basic to sophisticated. Some machines handle dictation and transcription tasks independently. With these systems, the lawyer has a desktop machine for dictating, and the secretary has a separate desktop transcription machine for transcribing the dictation. The cassette or other medium is removed from the dictating unit and inserted in the transcribing unit when the dictator has finished. Combination units, which combine recording and transcribing functions, are also available. The attorney plugs in a microphone to begin dictating; afterward the transcriber unplugs the microphone and attaches the foot pedal and headset. The unit can be moved from desk to desk or, if the unit is located on the secretary's desk, the attorney may use a microphone wired to the machine. The major drawback of a combination unit is that dictation and transcription cannot occur simultaneously.

The dictation machine used by the attorney should be equipped with a microphone/speaker and fast forward/rewind and volume/speed controls. More advanced models may be equipped with sonic search that enables the listener to quickly find the last word dictated after reviewing previously recorded material. Some models are capable of recording conferences or allowing private listening for confidential playback; some have a phone-in feature for remote dictation. To facilitate transcription, the unit at the secretary's desk should have features such as earphones, on/off foot or thumb controls, and an index slip system, as well as the same kind of speed, volume, and tone controls that are available on the dictation unit.

The decreasing cost of tape recorders used for entertainment purposes has led to experimentation with this equipment for office use. However, these recorders ordinarily lack the controls necessary for easy dictation and transcription. Furthermore, they are generally not built to withstand the constant starting and stopping required of dictation equipment.

**Central dictation systems**    In an office with many attorneys, paralegals, and support personnel, the volume of dictation may indicate the need for a dictation system with a central recorder and several extension microphones. Some central dictation systems consist of tanks with endless-loop recorders; others use a group of cassettes. Central systems receive input by private or public telephone from local or long-distance sources. A machine with an endless-loop system can accept input at the same time the secretary transcribes from it. However, even though dictation and transcription can occur simultaneously, only one dictator may input at a time into each tank. This tape loop system is frequently used by law firms because its recording capacity permits it to accept dictation during nights, weekends, and holidays.

With the earlier models of endless-loop machines, it was difficult to locate specific dictated materials. The lack of an indexing device in these early models also made transcription difficult because the transcriber did not know the length of a document. Central dictation systems are now available that overcome many of the disadvantages of earlier such systems. Some new models, for example, feature built-in electronic indexing. One recently introduced microprocessor-controlled system employs 24 standard cassettes that provide 18 hours of continuous dictation without the need to change cassettes, allowing many dictators to use the machine. For long-distance access, this system can be interfaced with PBX or Touch-Tone telephone systems. In a private wire dictation system, the unit is activated by lifting the telephone receiver. Automatically, the dictator receives voice instructions on how to operate the machine. The system's voice also informs the dictator when three minutes and again when only one minute of dictation time remain on the tape. At the end of the tape, the voice returns to request that the dictator wait until the cassette is changed. As a cassette is ejected, a hard-copy data input slip is printed out and ejected with the cassette. This slip identifies the author, date, time and length of input, time that the cassette was ejected, date transcription is due, and other pertinent information. With this system the supervisor is able to monitor the work flow, file input for easy storage and retrieval, increase productivity, and expedite transcription as necessary.

Central dictation systems are most compatible with word-processing centers. In these centers a team of word-processing operators transcribes documents soon after they are dictated. Using text-editing machines, they can quickly provide a finished product for the dictating attorney.

**Portable dictation units**   In addition to desktop and centralized equipment, portable dictation units are used increasingly by attorneys as supplemental dictation equipment. These units are lightweight and can be conveniently carried so that the attorney is able to dictate wherever and whenever necessary. The lawyer can dictate while working at home, in a plane or automobile, or in the office away from his or her desk. Portable units accommodate standard, mini-, and micro-cassettes. These media should be compatible with the secretary's transcribing unit; if they are not compatible, adapters may usually be acquired to enable the transcriber to play a mini- or micro-cassette on a standard cassette transcribing machine.

## SHORTHAND MACHINES

In many law offices, as well as in courtrooms, recording speeds of over 150 words per minute are necessary. Shorthand machines meet this requirement. Machine shorthand is especially useful in taking depositions, taking notes at conferences and meetings, and recording discussions. In the courtroom machine shorthand is employed to record proceedings verbatim.

The secretary or court reporter records notes on a 22-key, manually operated machine. Initial consonants are on the left side of the keyboard, final consonants on the right, and vowels at the bottom. Each light keyboard stroke prints a letter, syllable, word, or phrase phonetically on a line in English letters on a prefolded paper tape. This tape emerges in an A-frame configuration and folds into a tray behind the machine. Because the notes are machine-printed, there is never any distortion, whatever the writing speed. Machine shorthand notes are transcribed readily and quickly by the secretary and by others trained in reading notes and transcribing machine shorthand.

## MATERIALS NEEDED FOR LIVE DICTATION

Although most of the dictation in a law office today is by machine, there is a continuing need for live dictation. Having the following materials ready will expedite live dictation:

1. Use a stenographic notebook, preferably spiral bound with a stiff cover, which will lie flat and also stand alone during transcription.

2. Assemble a work folder or portfolio with a stationery pocket inside each cover. The stenographic notebook will fit easily into the right-hand pocket. The left-hand pocket is useful for reference copies of correspondence, reports, agendas, law blanks, or other items related to the day's dictation.

3. Place several pens, colored or black pencils, and a small ruler into the pocket of the folder beside the stenographic notebook. You may find a free-flowing, fine-point pen rather than a ball-point pen or pencil best for taking dictation, because it requires less pressure and thereby reduces fatigue. It is also easier on the eyes during transcription. Notes in ink are also more permanent. This is important in the law office, where a stenographic notebook is retained longer than in other offices.

4. Attach several paper clips at the side of the folder for use in flagging RUSH items.

5. Use several elastic bands around the top cover of the notebook to bind off transcribed notes. This facilitates finding the first available page for new dictation.

6. Tape a pocket-sized card calendar to the inside cover of the folder so you can quickly check the accuracy of a date.

7. If you take dictation from more than one attorney, use a separate notebook for each. In fact, for most efficient organization, you should have a portfolio arranged for each attorney. This will help to organize your work so that each lawyer's materials remain separate.

## Portfolio for Live Dictation

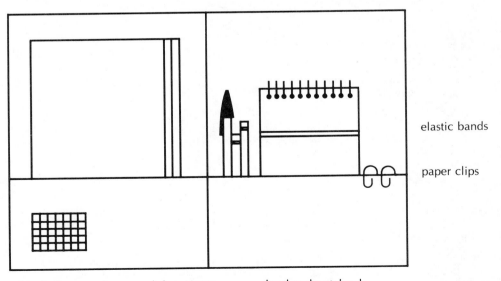

elastic bands

paper clips

related correspondence and documents            shorthand notebook

one-year calendar                                 pens and colored pencils

# 8.2

## INPUT: Dictation and Preparation for Transcription

Legal documents must be transcribed verbatim. If the wording is not exactly as the lawyer dictates, the meaning of a legal document or a letter may be changed, and the result may be unnecessary problems for the attorney and the client. Machine transcription reduces the possibility of error, since the secretary can replay the unclear passages. Most attorneys are comfortable with machine dictation, and an increasing amount of work in law offices is mechanically dictated. However, there are times when the lawyer who regularly uses a recording device may wish to dictate a short memo or even a long document directly to the secretary. Frequently, the secretary is also asked to take notes at a meeting. Some lawyers even prefer to dictate all of their material live.

### GIVING DICTATION

**Preparing to dictate**   To aid the secretary in producing transcribed material accurately and quickly, the dictator should take the preparatory steps listed here:

1. Plan ahead—dictation early in the day means quicker turnaround.
2. Let the word-processing center or legal secretary know immediately about any priority or rush work.
3. Organize your thoughts about any instructions that must be given. Briefly outline your dictation.
4. Review the correspondence to be answered or the material to be dictated. All pertinent facts, correspondence, and legal forms should be at hand <u>before</u> dictation begins. If you are answering correspondence, place a number on the letter. Then you may give only the number of the letter and the name of the addressee when dictating. (Be certain to hand the letters to the secretary with the media.)
5. For machine dictation, properly position the telephone or the microphone of the dictating machine; have extra input media (such as cassettes or belts) available.

**Instructing the transcriber**   The transcriber needs some special cues from the dictator in order to produce acceptable transcripts. If the dictator gives the transcriber all the necessary information, the transcriber is more likely to produce good work:

1. Identify yourself by name and title.
2. Indicate priority or rush work.
3. Give directions to erase <u>confidential</u> information immediately after transcribing, if desired.
4. Identify the nature of the dictation (such as a telegram, a letter, a brief, a will, a pleading, etc.). If a form is to be used, indicate the specific form and identify each portion of the dictation with a corresponding cue from the form.
5. Specify the number of copies needed.
6. Give any special instructions.

**Dictating**   The art of effective dictation involves the correct tone of voice, naturalness of expression, sufficient volume to project the message, moderate speed, and clear enunciation. Pay special attention to the following:

1. Pronounce complex medical and legal words carefully. Pronounce them slowly—syllable by syllable if necessary, or spell them out if they might be new to the transcriber.
2. Avoid mumbling or slurring words.
3. Dictate numbers slowly, numeral by numeral, e.g., "one, five, zero, eight" for 1508.
4. Dictate citations precisely.

5. Try to avoid distracting mannerisms. A tapping pencil, the squeak of a chair, or a chance remark can later confuse the transcriber.

6. Remember that the transcriber has to rely heavily on changes in pace or intonation to interpret the intended punctuation. Try to modulate your voice accordingly.

## USING THE STENOGRAPHIC NOTEBOOK

The legal secretary needs to devise a system for using the stenographic notebook. Individual methods will vary, but certain basic steps should be followed. Always keep the dictation supplies readily available so that you will be able to respond quickly to a request to take dictation. Paper clips, a triangularly folded notebook page corner, or colored pencil markings may be used to identify rush items that must be transcribed first.

**Planning space in the notebook**   Intelligent use of notebook space will enable you to add information with ease or to write in changes or instructions with care, either during or after dictation. Start each day's dictation on a new notebook page, writing the date at the bottom right edge of the page for easy reference. This enables you to retrace work quickly. Each item in a day's dictation series should bear an identifying number. Allow several blank lines before and after each identified dictation item. This will normally provide sufficient space for last-minute changes, insertions, and instructions. However, if the lawyer or legal assistant makes frequent or extensive revisions, it is advisable to record notes only in the left column of the shorthand notebook and to reserve the right column for major revisions.

If you take dictation from several attorneys and legal assistants, maintain a separate notebook for each one. Label each notebook cover with the name of the dictator and the date on which the notebook was started. When the notebook is filled, record the last date of dictation on the cover also. Completed notebooks may then be filed chronologically under the name of each dictator. It is important to check with the attorney as to how long a filled notebook should be kept; the time may vary from one year to many years, or forever, especially in law firms.

In the event that you omit a word in your notes or have reason to question the dictator, leave a conspicuous mark or an open space to remind you to ask the dictator about it when there is a convenient place to interrupt. Many dictators do not want their thoughts interrupted until the end of a document.

**Using law blanks**   Many legal documents are not typed in full. Law offices frequently use law blanks (standard printed forms with fill-in blanks) for documents such as acknowledgments, deeds, affidavits, mortgage leases, verifications, guardianships, summonses, subpoenas, petitions, powers of attorney, orders to show cause, writs, garnishments, injunctions, proxies, and standard contracts. When law blanks are used, it is advisable to have two copies available, one for the attorney and one for the secretary. Each blank space to be filled in is marked with an identifying number or letter on each of the duplicate copies. This makes it easy for the secretary to note where each section is to be inserted on the law blank. Refer to the illustration on page 186 for an example.

The use of law blanks is described further in Chapter 11.

**Coding the stenographic notebook**   Revisions in dictation are a part of the normal course of events in any stenographic recording session. The secretary should be familiar with the symbols that code these changes. Some examples of stenographic coding are the following:

Delete or remove a word or phrase.

Add a word or a short phrase.

Use at the beginning and at the end of a change or an instruction.

   Marks the first lengthy insert. (Each subsequent insert bears the letter b, c, and so on.)

Indicates a priority transcription item.

Strike out this section of the notes.

*stet*   Let it stand.

Shows a transposition; invert the order of the words.

Move this sentence or section to the new position indicated by the arrow.

Verify the accuracy.

Illustrations of some ways in which these stenographic codes may be useful are shown below.

## Examples of Changes in the Stenographic Notebook

### Addition:

THIS INDENTURE, made this 23rd day of August, 1981, by and between ROSE ROLLINS of 2141 Country Stream Drive, North Haven, Connecticut, and ERNEST PERRY of 41 Main Street, Essex, Connecticut, hereinafter referred to as "Landlord," and PARK INTERIORS, LIMITED, a corporation with offices at 321 Western Avenue, Hartford, Connecticut, referred to as "Tenant."

   Please add after the word *LIMITED*, a: *Connecticut*. Also, after *Hartford, Connecticut*, please add: *hereinafter*.

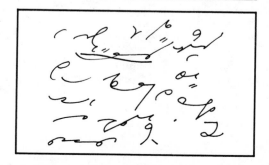

### Correction:

The Court of Appeals for the District of Columbia has limited the ability to challenge Internal Revenue Service rulings that allegedly give competitors an unfair economic advantage.

   Please change the word *limited* to *restricted*.

## Deletion:

And Furthermore, I, the said grantor, do by these presents bind myself and my heirs forever to warrant and defend the above granted and bargained premises to the said grantee, his heirs, successors, and assigns, against all claims and demands whatsoever, except as hereinbefore mentioned.

Please omit: *successors.*

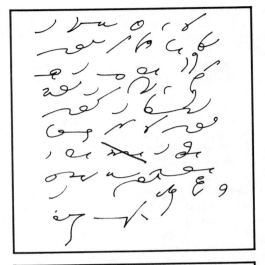

## Insertion:

An adverse party may require him to introduce any other part which ought in fairness to be considered with the part introduced, and any party may introduce any other parts.

At the beginning of that paragraph, please add the clause: *If only part of a deposition is offered in evidence by a party,*

## Restoration:

NOW, THEREFORE, in consideration of the sum of one dollar and other valuable considerations to each of the parties by the other in hand paid, receipt whereof is hereby acknowledged, it is hereby agreed that said partnership be and hereby is terminated as of the close of business on June 30, 1981.

Please delete: *and other valuable considerations.* On second thought, let it stand.

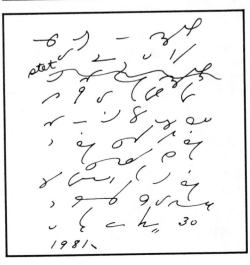

**Correcting errors in dictation**   Although most attorneys are well organized and able to dictate fluently, even the most disciplined dictator may occasionally make an error in grammar or sentence structure or mistakenly call the plaintiff the defendant. When an error becomes apparent during dictation, you should mark the location with a large question mark in colored pencil. Do not interfere with the dictator's trend of thought by interrupting. At the close of that document or letter, ask the attorney for clarification of the unclear passage.

You may encounter an error during transcription. With correspondence, it may be permissible for you to correct that error if you have standing permission to do so. In the case of an apparent error in a legal document, however, you must check with the attorney. What may seem like a correct solution to the secretary may in reality be an unwarranted change in the meaning of the document.

**High-speed dictation**   Although the average dictation rate is between 90 and 110 words per minute, reserve speed for fast spurts of dictation is helpful. A secretary may be called upon to take notes at a meeting with one or more clients and attorneys or at a staff meeting. In these cases, when word-for-word recording is not required, the reporting process is selective and good judgment is needed. There are other times, however, when verbatim transcription of high-speed dictation may be required, as when a secretary in a law office is called upon to take the testimony of a person under oath. The testimony is usually in question-and-answer form with counsel in attendance at the examination. Although this kind of dictation is usually taken by a court reporter working with a shorthand machine, a secretary with good shorthand skills and speed can also do it. You must take the testimony verbatim and transcribe it verbatim, even if it is grammatically incorrect. Should you fall behind in your notes, use a prearranged signal to request the attorney who is asking the questions to slow down so you can keep pace. It is vital that every word of the testimony be recorded exactly as spoken.

When taking a deposition, use a shorthand notebook to which you have added extra vertical lines. Each half of the page should have two vertical lines penciled lightly to give three columns. The examining attorney's questions are started at the left edge of the paper, just as you would ordinarily record your shorthand, and continue to the center line.

The second column—which begins to the right of the first vertical line—is for the start of the witness's answer. This line is also written to the center. Should the line run over, begin the runover line to the right of the first vertical line.

To the right of the second vertical line you would record any questions by the opposing counsel. Runover lines begin back at the right of the second vertical line.

Any actions that must be noted, such as identifying an exhibit, would be enclosed in brackets to differentiate them from testimony. These notations should be recorded in the opposing counsel's column.

The right half of the notebook is utilized in the same way. With this method of arranging shorthand notes, time is gained by not having to write "Question," "Answer," and "Opposing Attorney." This arrangement also makes it easier to read back your notes.

An illustration of a shorthand notebook page ruled for a deposition appears on the following page.

## REFERENCE AIDS
**Form file**   In any office it is customary for a secretary to have a loose-leaf notebook which contains copies of sample correspondence, office forms, and the like. This type of notebook is especially important in the law office. Just as the attorney has a form book to use as a guide for preparing documents, each secretary should have an

**Shorthand Notebook Ruled for Deposition**

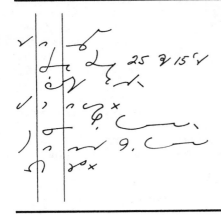

indexed binder containing samples of every type of legal document and correspondence that originates in the office. In the law firm with many departments the form file may contain only the forms used by the department, e.g., litigation. The samples provide an immediate reference and save the time it would take to refer to the files of a similar case. On each sample form you should note specific information as to number of copies, to whom copies are to be sent, mailing procedures, the court involved, etc. If you begin to work for a different law firm, you will have to make a new form file for the new office, since each law office has its own procedures. Form files are explained more fully in Chapter 11.

**Reference books**   Poor enunciation on the part of the dictator can lead to difficulty in transcription. The secretary should never guess about unclear words, especially legal and medical terms. Using the appropriate references can assist in clarifying unintelligible words. If references are not helpful, the secretary should ask the word-processing supervisor or the attorney for clarification.

   Just having access to reference books is not sufficient. The legal secretary must not only have the following essential reference books on hand but also know how to use them:

1.   the latest edition of at least one good general dictionary
2.   a standard law dictionary to clarify the exact legal meaning of a word or phrase
3.   *A Uniform System of Citation*, generally known as the *Bluebook*, for information on how to cite from various legal references
4.   a secretarial manual for general office reference
5.   a legal secretarial handbook for more specific law office reference
6.   a word division manual
7.   a thesaurus

In addition, an up-to-date, unabridged medical dictionary is essential for the law office involved in personal injury litigation. Specific reference books are listed in the Appendix of this handbook.

## TRANSCRIBING LEGAL TERMINOLOGY
Every profession uses terms with special meanings. This is especially true of the legal profession. A word—like *continuance*—may have one meaning in general usage and another in legal phraseology. Special compound words, unfamiliar foreign words and phrases, set phrases and clauses, and capitalized introductory words and phrases are

all a part of specialized legal terminology. It is important that the legal secretary try hard to learn new terms and their uses. Compiling a list of specialized legal terms and their meanings as you encounter them for the first time will help you become familiar with legal terminology. You should also develop your own brief shorthand outlines for these words and phrases which will permit you to commit them to paper very quickly.

An extensive list of foreign words and phrases with their corresponding Gregg shorthand outlines appears in section 8.7 of this chapter.

**Compound words** The language of legal documents is precise. Legal terminology includes many compound words which permit exact reference with minimal use of words. These compounds include words like *aforesaid* (said or named before or above), *hereinafter* (in the following part of this document), *herewith* (with this; enclosed with this), *therein* (in that place), and *the undersigned* (the person who signs his name at the end of a document). Always transcribe these words exactly as they are dictated. If you are not sure of their meaning or spelling, consult a dictionary.

**Introductory words and phrases** In legal documents visible recognition of introductory, closing, and special paragraphs is accomplished by typing the introductory words—such as IN WITNESS WHEREOF,—in all-capitalized letters. Examples are listed on pages 204–205 of Chapter 9.

**Sound-alike words** Many words are often confused by transcribers because they sound alike. In addition to the confusing word pairs in the general language, there are also legal and medical words that may be confused with similar terms. In taking and transcribing dictation you should be aware of these sound-alike words. You should be especially careful of those words which may have the same or similar shorthand outlines. A list of some of the terms that could confuse a transcriber follows:

**abjure**  to reject solemnly
**adjure**  to command

**abrogate**  to nullify
**obrogate**  to alter or repeal

**abstruse**  hard to understand
**obtuse**  not sharp

**accede**  to agree
**exceed**  to go beyond

**accent**  to emphasize
**ascent**  a mounting upward or upward slope
**assent**  to agree to something

**acceptor**  one that accepts an order or bill
**exceptor**  one who objects

**access**  right to enter
**excess**  intemperance

**addenda**  additional items
**agenda**  list of things to be done

**adjoin**  to be next to
**adjourn**  to suspend a session

**adjure**  see abjure

**adverse**  unfavorable
**averse**  disinclined

**advice**  counsel or information
**advise**  to give advice

**agenda**  see addenda

**alimentary**  relating to nourishment
**elementary**  simple or basic

**allegation**  positive assertion
**alligation**  binding together

**allocator**  person who allocates
**allocatur**  kind of writ

**amenable**  accountable
**amendable**  that can be amended

**antimony**  chemical element
**antinomy**  contradiction between laws

**aphasia**  loss of speech
**asphyxia**  suffocation
**astasia**  inability to stand

**appraise**  to set a value on
**apprise**  to give notice of
**apprize**  to appreciate or value

**approximate**  nearly correct or exact
**proximate**  very near or direct

**arraign**  to bring before a court
**arrange**  to come to an agreement

**asphyxia**  see aphasia

**assay**  to test for valuable content
**essay**  to try tentatively

astasia   see aphasia
atone   to make amends
attain   to reach or achieve
attorn   to agree to become tenant to a new owner or landlord

averse   see adverse

avert   to anticipate and ward off
overt   not concealed

bail   security given
bale   bundle of goods

bans   prohibitions
banns   announcement of a proposed marriage

biannual   *usu* twice a year; *sometimes* every two years
biennial   every two years

bloc   usually temporary combination
block   tract of land

born   produced by birth
borne   past participle of bear

breach   infraction of law
breech   the hind part of the body

by law,   according to law
bylaw, by-law   local or corporate rule

callous   hardened
callus   hard area on skin

cannon   artillery piece
canon   accepted principle or rule

capital   city that is the seat of government
capitol   building in which a state legislature meets
Capitol   building in which the U.S. Congress meets

carat   weight
caret   mark

carousal   drunken party
carrousel   merry-go-round, conveyor

carpus   wrist
corpus   body

carrousel   see carousal

casual   not planned
causal   being a cause

casually   by chance or accident
casualty   one injured or killed

causal   see casual

censer   vessel for incense
censor   to examine writings for improper content
censure   to express disapproval of

chalcosis   copper in body tissue
chalicosis   industrial lung disease

cite   to summon; to quote
sight   payable on presentation
site   piece of land

cliental   relating to clients
clientele   body of clients

collaborate   to work or act jointly
corroborate   to confirm

collision   action of colliding
collusion   secret agreement

coma   unconscious state
comma   punctuation mark

concurso   legal proceeding
concursus   religious doctrine

condemn   to censure; to pronounce sentence against
contemn   to scorn

consul   diplomatic official
council   administrative body
counsel   n legal representative
           vb to give advice

corespondent   joint respondent
correspondent   one who communicates

corpus   see carpus

correspondent   see corespondent

corroborate   see collaborate

council   see consul

counsel   see consul

courtesy   something allowed or accepted
curtesy   husband's right in dead wife's land
curtsy   slight bow

credible   worthy of being believed
creditable   worthy of praise

currant   fruit
current   n stream
           adj belonging to the present

curtesy   see courtesy

curtsy   see courtesy

cynosure   one that attracts
sinecure   easy job

decedent   deceased person
dissident   one who disagrees

decent   conforming to a standard
descent   passing of an estate by inheritance
dissent   difference in opinion

demean   to behave
demesne   landed property
domain   territory possessed and governed

demur   to protest
demure   shy

depositary   one who receives a deposit
depository   place where something is deposited

deprecate   to disapprove of
depreciate   to lower the worth of

deraign   to prove
derange   to disorder

**descent**   see decent
**desperate**   having lost hope
**disparate**   distinct
**diplomat**   one employed in diplomacy
**diplomate**   one certified as qualified
**disburse**   to pay out
**disperse**   to scatter
**discreetly**   in a discreet manner
**discretely**   separately
**disparate**   see desperate
**disperse**   see disburse
**disseminate**   to spread widely
**dissimilate**   to make or become dissimilar
**dissimulate**   to hide under a false
            appearance
**dissent**   see decent
**dissident**   see decedent
**dissimilate**   see disseminate
**dissimulate**   see disseminate
**domain**   see demean
**elementary**   see alimentary
**elicit**   to draw or bring out
**illicit**   not lawful
**eligible**   qualified to have
**illegible**   not readable
**elude**   to evade
**illude**   to deceive
**elusive**   hard to grasp
**illusive**   deceptive
**emanate**   to come out from a source
**eminent**   of higher status
**immanent**   inherent
**imminent**   menacingly near
**eminence**   high position
**immanence**   restriction to one domain
**imminence**   something imminent
**engross**   prepare a text; purchase in quantity
**in gross**   existing independently
**enumerable**   countable
**innumerable**   too many to count
**equable**   lacking variation
**equitable**   involving equity
**erasable**   removable by erasing
**irascible**   easily angered
**essay**   see assay
**exceed**   see accede
**exceptor**   see acceptor
**excess**   see access
**ex mora**   because of delay
**ex more**   according to custom
**extant**   currently existing
**extent**   size, degree, or measure

**forego**   to precede
**forgo**   to give up
**furlong**   one eighth of a mile
**furlough**   leave of absence
**gage**   security
**gauge**   measure
**gager**   giving of a gage
**gauger**   one that gauges
**gait**   manner of walking
**gate**   opening in a wall or fence
**gauge**   see gage
**gauger**   see gager
**hail**   to greet
**hale**   vb to compel to go
         adj healthy
**hangar**   shelter for aircraft
**hanger**   one that hangs
**hearsay**   rumor
**heresy**   dissent from a dominant theory
**humerus**   long bone of upper arm
**humorous**   funny
**illegible**   see eligible
**illicit**   see elicit
**illude**   see elude
**illusive**   see elusive
**immanence**   see eminence
**immanent**   see emanate
**imminence**   see eminence
**imminent**   see emanate
**immure**   to enclose within walls
**inure**   to accustom to something undesirable
**impassable**   not passable
**impassible**   unable to feel
**impracticable**   not feasible
**impractical**   not practical
**inapt**   not suitable
**inept**   unfit or foolish
**incite**   to urge on
**insight**   discernment
**incredibility**   unbelievableness
**incredulity**   disbelief
**incurable**   not curable
**incurrable**   that can be incurred
**indict**   to accuse formally
**indite**   to put in writing
**inept**   see inapt
**inequity**   lack of equity
**iniquity**   wickedness
**infirmation**   invalidation
**information**   knowledge received
**ingenious**   notably apt or clever
**ingenuous**   naively frank

**in gross**   see engross
**inherent**   being an essential part of
    something
**inherit**   to receive from an ancestor
**iniquity**   see inequity
**in jure**   according to law
**injure**   to do harm to
**innumerable**   see enumerable
**in re**   in the matter of
**in rem**   against a thing
**insight**   see incite
**interment**   burial
**internment**   confinement or impounding
**interpellate**   to question formally
**interpolate**   to insert words in a text
**interstate**   involving more than one state
**intestate**   leaving no valid will
**intrastate**   existing in a state
**inure**   see immure
**irascible**   see erasable
**larynx**   upper part of trachea containing the
    vocal cords
**pharynx**   space between the mouth and
    esophagus
**lean**   to rely for support
**lien**   legal claim upon property
**lesser**   smaller
**lessor**   grantor of a lease
**levee**   reception or embankment
**levy**   imposition or amount of a charge
**liable**   obligated by law or equity
**libel**   to make libelous statements
**lien**   see lean
**lumbar**   relating to vertebrae of the lower
    back
**lumber**   n timber ready for use
    vb to move clumsily
**malfeasance**   wrongful conduct
**misfeasance**   improper performance of a
    legal act
**nonfeasance**   failure to do what ought to be
    done
**mandatary**   one holding a mandate
**mandatory**   obligatory
**material**   adj having relevance or
    importance
    n that of which something is made
**matériel**   equipment and supplies
**mean**   n middle point
    adj stingy or malicious
    vb intend
**mesne**   middle or intervening
**mien**   appearance

**meat**   animal flesh used as food
**meet**   to come into contact with
**mete**   to allot
**meretricious**   falsely attractive
**meritorious**   deserving reward or honor
**meticulous**   extremely careful about details
**mesalliance**   a poor marriage
**misalliance**   an improper alliance
**mesne**   see mean
**meticulous**   see meretricious
**mien**   see mean
**mileage**   travel allowance
**millage**   rate in mills
**miner**   worker of a mine
**minor**   n one of less than legal age
    adj not important or serious
**misalliance**   see mesalliance
**misfeasance**   see malfeasance
**misogamy**   hatred of marriage
**misogyny**   hatred of women
**moot**   having no practical significance
**mute**   n a person unable to speak
    vb to tone down; to muffle the sound
**mucous**   relating to mucus
**mucus**   secretion from membranes
**mute**   see moot
**myatonia**   muscular flabbiness
**myotonia**   tonic muscular spasm
**naval**   relating to a navy
**navel**   umbellicus
**nonfeasance**   see malfeasance
**obliger**   one who obliges
**obligor**   one who writes a surety bond
**obrogate**   see abrogate
**obtuse**   see abstruse
**ordinance**   law, rule, or decree
**ordnance**   military supplies
**ordonnance**   compilation of laws
**overt**   see avert
**oyer**   hearing of a document read in open
    court
**oyez**   hear ye!—a call for silence in court
**packed**   filled to capacity
**pact**   an agreement or understanding
**parlay**   to bet again a stake and its winnings
**parley**   discussion of disputed points
**parol**   oral statement
**parole**   conditional release
**pedal**   relating to the foot or a pedal
**peddle**   to travel about and sell goods
**peer**   one of equal standing
**pier**   bridge support

**penal** relating to punishment
**penial** relating to the penis

**penance** act to show repentance
**pennants** flags or banners

**per annum** by or for each year
**per anum** by way of the anus

**peremptory** ending a right of action, debate, or delay
**preemptory** pre-emptive

**perpetrate** to be guilty of
**perpetuate** to make perpetual

**perquisite** a right or privilege
**prerequisite** a necessary preliminary

**persecute** to harass injuriously
**prosecute** to proceed against at law

**personality** distinctive personal quality
**personalty** personal property

**perspicacious** very discerning
**perspicuous** easily understood

**pharynx** see larynx

**pier** see peer

**placable** easily placated
**placeable** that can be placed

**plaintiff** the complaining party in litigation
**plaintive** expressive of sadness

**plantar** relating to the sole of the foot
**planter** plantation owner

**plat** plan of a piece of land
**plot** small piece of land

**practicable** feasible
**practical** skilled through practice

**precede** to go or come before
**proceed** to go to law

**precedence** priority
**precedents** previous examples to follow

**preemptory** see peremptory

**prerequisite** see perquisite

**prescribe** to assert a prescriptive right or title
**proscribe** to put outside the law

**presence** fact of being present
**presents** present legal instrument

**presentiment** premonition or prejudgment
**presentment** offering of something to be dealt with

**presents** see presence

**preview** advance view
**purview** part or scope of a statute

**principal** main body of an estate; chief person or matter
**principle** basic rule or assumption

**proceed** see precede

**pro rata** proportionately
**prorate** to divide proportionately

**proscribe** see prescribe

**prosecute** see persecute

**proximate** see approximate

**pubes** pubic hair or region
**pubis** pubic bone

**purpart** purparty
**purport** meaning

**purview** see preview

**reality** actualness
**realty** real property

**recession** ceding back
**recision** cancellation
**rescission** bringing to an end

**reclaim** to reform or better
**re-claim** to claim back

**recognizer** one that recognizes
**recognizor** one obligated under a recognizance

**recover** to obtain a right in court
**re-cover** to cover again

**reform** amend; amendment
**re-form** form again

**refuse** vb decline
**refuse** n waste

**release** to give up
**re-lease** to lease again

**relic** something remaining
**relict** widow

**rescission** see recession

**reserve** to keep back
**re-serve** to serve again

**resign** to relinquish
**re-sign** to sign again

**resume** to take up again
**résumé** summary

**revendicate** to recover something
**revindicate** to vindicate again

**saccharin** artificial sweetener
**saccharine** sugary

**settler** one who settles something or somewhere
**settlor** one who makes a settlement

**sight** see cite, site

**sinecure** see cynosure

**site** see cite, sight

**slough** side channel of a river
**slough** dead tissue separating from an ulcer

**specie** coined money
**species** class of individuals

**stationary** still
**stationery** writing material

**statue**   piece of sculpture
**stature**   natural height or achieved status
**statute**   law enacted by a legislature

**subordination**   placement in a lower rank
**subornation**   crime of procuring perjury

**tare**   weight allowance
**tear**   to pull apart by force

**tenere**   possess
**teneri**   clause in a bond

**tenor**   general character or sense
**tenure**   act or right of holding property

**therefor**   for that
**therefore**   for that reason

**tort**   wrongful act
**torte**   rich cake or pastry

**tortious**   involving tort
**tortuous**   lacking in straightforwardness
**torturous**   very painful or distressing

**trustee**   one entrusted with something
**trusty**   convict allowed special privileges

**tympanites**   swollen abdomen
**tympanitis**   ear inflammation

**venal**   open to bribery
**venial**   not grave

**veracity**   truthfulness
**voracity**   greediness

**waive**   to give up voluntarily
**wave**   to swing or shake

**waiver**   a waiving
**waver**   to be irresolute

**warrantee**   person to whom a warranty is
made
**warranty**   guarantee of integrity

**wave**   see waive

**waver**   see waiver

**wheal**   welt or raised patch on the skin
**wheel**   circular frame capable of turning

# 8.3

## OUTPUT: Transcription Systems

The product or output of the transcription process is the transcript, the written, printed, or typed copy. Superior transcription ability is expected of the legal secretary. A fast shorthand speed and a rapid typing rate must be joined with accuracy to yield quality documents that are free of errors. There are three basic kinds of transcription, paralleling the three major ways of taking dictation: (1) machine transcription by the legal secretary from belts, cassettes, disks, tapes, and other media, (2) transcription from machine shorthand notes, and (3) conventional transcription from the stenographic notebook.

The production of accurate, professional papers, both letters and legal documents, is the major goal of all transcribers, regardless of which method is used. It is also what determines the transcriber's net worth in many firms. An alert secretary combines knowledge, skill, and intellect to attain success in transcription.

### PRETRANSCRIPTION PREPARATIONS

Organization and planning play a major part in preparation for transcription. The work module should be arranged efficiently and the typeface and ribbon of the typewriter checked regularly.

**The work module organization**   Those items (the transcribing machine, the stenographic notebook, or machine shorthand notes) that are essential to specialized transcription ought to be assembled and arranged for easy use on the transcriber's desk. Standing the shorthand notebook in an upright position reduces glare. Reference books should be kept within easy reach. The basic kinds of stationery should be readily accessible in the stationery drawer: letterheads, forms, continuation sheets (plain bond), carbon paper (regular, film, or snap-out), envelopes, legal cap, numbered legal cap for court documents, and other items of this type. The secretary who does not have a self-correcting typewriter should place correction tools (tapes, liquids, or pencil erasers) beside the typewriter work station. The right-handed secretary will usually place erasing tools at the right side of the typewriter; the left-handed secretary will, as a rule, choose the left side.

**Chair adjustment**    Chair adjustment is important so that the transcriber can maintain a good, comfortable posture. Chairs with an adjustable backrest should fit the small of the back for maximum support. Correct chair and desk height definitely affect a typist's transcription production. For example, the slope of the typist's forearm should equal that of the typewriter keyboard. There should be less slope for electric machines.

**Typewriter condition**    The typewriter elements and the ribbon should always be in good condition. First, an inspection should be made to ensure a clean typeface. Daily brushing is vital to good typescript. Liquid cleaners may be used only on conventional manual or electric machines with type bars. You may use plastic cleaners and brushes on elements. Special fluid cleaners are available from the typewriter manufacturers; regular liquid cleaners are harmful to the components of an electric typewriter.

A ribbon check before transcription will indicate whether or not a new fabric ribbon is needed; changing the ribbon as necessary will ensure a uniform, dark typescript. Checking machines that use film ribbon will indicate whether a replacement ribbon will be required soon; having a spare cartridge or spool in advance will assure minimal interruption at the point when the ribbon change is needed.

**The copyholder**    When typing extensive copy, use a copyholder with an adjustable, line-spacing attachment to reduce the possibility of error. The right little finger depresses a lever which advances the copy guide. Using a copyholder is like using a ruler on the copy to keep your place, except that the copyholder is much easier to use and does not require you to remove your hand from the keyboard.

**Scanning your shorthand**    Before you begin to type a document, scan your notes for special instructions. Then read your notes, inserting punctuation and paragraphing where necessary. The lengthy sentences in legal documents and the frequent use of "that" clauses may make it difficult to comprehend a sentence. Be sure that you understand which are the subject and verb of each sentence. Again, remember that legal dictation must be transcribed exactly as dictated so as not to change the meaning of a document. Do not yield to the temptation to make corrections without authorization from the attorney. In transcribing notes from an interrogation, even grammatical errors must be transcribed faithfully.

## NUMBER OF COPIES

Before transcribing, find out how many copies of the document are required. The type of document will determine the number of copies it is necessary to type. A one-party client document such as a will, for example, requires a minimum of two copies: the signed and executed original, which is sent to the client for safekeeping, and a copy for the office file. A third copy should be given to the client for reference. A two-party client document such as a contract requires a minimum of three copies: one dated and executed copy for each party to the document and one for the office file. An extra reference copy may also be provided for the client. Multiparty documents require more copies: one executed copy for each party to the agreement and an office copy. If any parties to the agreement are represented by attorneys, each attorney should receive a conformed copy of the agreement.

Court documents require a minimum of three copies. The original is filed with the court, a conformed copy is sent to the opposing counsel, and a third copy is placed in the office file. Office policy dictates whether a fourth copy is sent to the client for his information.

The originator of the document will indicate the number of originals and copies necessary by saying, for example, "one and two," meaning one original and two copies. "Two and one" would mean one original; a second copy, called a *duplicate original,* that is signed and conformed and treated like an original; and one copy not signed but conformed. (For a discussion of the conforming of copies, see Chapter 14.)

Because photocopiers are now standard equipment in law offices, the attorney may agree that it is necessary to type only one original ribbon copy; multiple copies can then be made on the copy machine. With automatic typewriters, the multiple copies can be produced automatically.

## CORRECT FORMAT

The format required for legal correspondence is not as precise as that for legal documents. For detailed explanations of each refer to Chapter 10, Legal Correspondence Style; Chapter 12, Preparing and Typewriting Client Documents; and Chapter 13, Preparing and Typewriting Court Documents.

## ERASURES

Erasers should be clean so that they will not leave smudge marks. They can be cleaned by rubbing the soiled spot on a clean sheet of paper or fine sandpaper. When erasing, use quick, light strokes. To keep fragments from falling into the typewriter, move the carriage to the side. To prevent smudging the carbons, insert a steel eraser guard between the paper and the carbons. The use of an erasing shield, which can be purchased in any stationery store, will prevent you from erasing any letters surrounding the letters you intend to erase.

With the use of chalk-coated correction paper typographical errors can easily be corrected by backspacing to the error, inserting the correction paper, restriking the incorrect letter, removing the correction paper, and typing the correct letter. It is important to purchase this paper in colors to match your stationery. Special correction paper is also available for carbon copies.

Correction fluid also comes in a variety of colors, and the manufacturers will match any color of paper your office may use. Correction fluid should be painted on sparingly so as not to be obvious. Once the liquid has dried, you simply backspace and type in the correct letter or word.

When a document is being typed strictly for reproduction purposes, corrections may be made to block out sentences or whole paragraphs. This can be done by typing the correct information on a separate sheet of paper and affixing this sheet to its appropriate place.

## SELECTED TYPING TECHNIQUES

**Alignment**   The term *alignment* refers to the proper placement of characters (words, numbers, or symbols) within a text after the paper has been removed from the typewriter and reinserted.

**Procedure**

1.  Insert a sheet of paper into the typewriter.
2.  Type the alphabet without spacing between letters.
3.  Make a mental note of the spatial relationship of rulings on the alignment scale of the typewriter to the letters of the alphabet typed on the paper.
4.  Remove the paper from the typewriter.

5.  Reinsert the page to be corrected while maintaining the original paper-edge guide location. Straighten the paper if necessary.
6.  Roll the paper into the typewriter to the point of correction.
7.  Adjust the spatial relationship of the rulings on the alignment scale to the typed information surrounding the correction area (both horizontally and vertically) as noted in step 3. (When you are typing on a printed underline, as on a form, the typing should appear slightly above the line.)
8.  Type the correction.

**Specialized alignment**   The typing of degree symbols (32°), exponents ($A^2$), double underscores (__), and other specialties in formatting may require a temporary deviation from the original writing line. Most conventional typewriters are equipped with a mechanism which, when engaged, will assist the secretary in placing special characters and symbols by allowing temporary movement away from the established writing line. When the mechanism is disengaged, the original writing line location is found with a slight turning of the cylinder knob (right or left), thus creating perfect alignment of all typing on the page. Some automatic typewriters are equipped with a mechanical feature which allows for easy recording of technical typing and the automatic accurate indexing during playback for the accommodation of superior and subordinate numbers and symbols.

**Centering (horizontal)**   Horizontal centering of information can be accomplished in any specific area of a page—on the writing line, in a column, in a boxed area, or in other areas.

**Procedure**
1.  Position the printing point indicator at the center point of the area in which the centered information should appear.
2.  Backspace once for every two characters and spaces *within* the information to be centered.
3.  Start to type at the point where you have stopped backspacing.
4.  Repeat the process with each line you wish to center.

**Centering (vertical)**   Careful planning will result in the accurate vertical placement of the material to be typed.

**Procedure**
1.  Move the paper to the vertical center (i.e., on a standard 11-inch long paper, space down to Line 34).
2.  Roll the cylinder back once for each two lines of typewritten lines and blank lines.
3.  Start to type at the line where you have stopped rolling the paper back into the machine.

**Crowding characters**   The term *crowding* refers to the typing of a word, longer by one character, in a space previously occupied by an incorrectly typed word. This procedure is not appropriate for use with an automatic typewriter.

**Assumption**
*Desired information:* . . . at this convention.
*Typed in error:* . . . at the convention.
*Problem:* Crowd *this* into the space where *the* was typed.

**Procedure**
1. Remove *the* by erasing or other correction technique.
2. Position the typewriter where the *t* in *the* had been typed.
3. a. *Electric typewriter (typebar model)*
   Press against the left cylinder knob until the carriage moves back one half space; hold the

carriage in this position and at the same time type *t* in *this*. Repeat the half-backspace procedure for *h* and the remaining characters in the word.

b. *Electric typewriter (single-element type)*
Follow the procedure described in 3a above with the following exception: To move the carrier back one half space, place the edge of the index finger of the right hand against the right side of the carrier and manually push the carrier to the *left* the desired distance.

c. *Typewriter equipped with a half-backspace key*
Follow the directions provided by the typewriter manufacturer.

**Spreading characters**   The term *spreading* refers to the typing of a word, shorter by one character, in a space previously occupied by an incorrectly typed word. This procedure is not appropriate for use with an automatic typewriter.

#### Assumption
*Desired information:* . . . is being transferred to Denver.
*Typed in error:* . . . is being transferred to Detroit.
*Problem:* Spread *Denver* into the space where *Detroit* was typed.

#### Procedure
Follow the above procedure for *crowding* characters with the following exception: Position the typewriter at the point where the second letter of the incorrect word was typed.

## QUALITY STANDARDS
Production with emphasis solely on output is of little value if the product is unusable because of defects. Quantity standards must be accompanied by quality standards. Quality standards define the degree of accuracy and the minimal expected neatness of the completed transcription. These standards are set and defined by the attorney-employer, although the specific work environment (e.g., a single-lawyer office or a large transcription pool) helps to determine the standards. The following is a list of transcription quality standards useful in any legal office:

1. Type everything that is dictated. DO NOT assume responsibility for changing, rewording, deleting, or adding to any dictated material.
2. All words must be spelled correctly.
3. Do not hyphenate a proper name in legal documents. If possible, do not separate first and last names in legal documents.
4. Do not hyphenate the last word on a page in a legal document. (Some lawyers, however, insist that the last word on each page of an especially important document be divided in order to ensure continuity and prevent the unauthorized insertion or removal of pages.)
5. No typographical errors should appear on the final copy.
6. There should be no strikeover characters.
7. Squeezed characters are allowable if they are neatly executed.
8. Corrections are allowable if they are undetectable. However, NEVER correct proper names, dates, or sums of money in a legal document. A correction may jeopardize the legality of that document. Retype the page if necessary.
9. Use only the formats that the lawyer chooses for the various documents.
10. Style all abbreviations according to the dictionary designated by the attorney.

You should strive to transcribe all dictated material in a way that will match the quality standards outlined above. Section 11.2 of Chapter 11 provides further guidelines for the typing of fill-ins on a printed form, while Chapters 12 and 13 contain more detailed instructions for styling legal instruments and court documents.

Remember that the legal transcriber's goal is to produce a finished copy of a document the first time it is transcribed. Few offices can afford the luxury of having documents typed in rough draft form before a mailable copy is produced. If automatic text-editing machines are being used, of course, a rough draft may be quickly and easily edited to produce a high-quality copy.

## GENERAL POST-TRANSCRIPTION PROCEDURES

Regardless of the transcription method, the following procedures, if used by the legal secretary, will assure quality work:

1. Proofread the transcript and correct any previously undetected errors <u>before</u> removing the letter or document from the typewriter. Proofreading techniques are described below.
2. Compare the transcription of any data abstracted from another document with the original source.
3. If possible, enlist the aid of a proofreading assistant to help check statistical or technical data on a transcript. This is especially important in the case of a real estate description.
4. Draw a diagonal line through the shorthand notes as soon as that material has been transcribed.
5. Make certain that any enclosures are attached to the letter or document.
6. Present the letter or document to the attorney for signature.
7. If highly confidential material can be read from the carbon paper, destroy the carbon sheet.

**Proofreading techniques**    It is essential that names, addresses, dates, figures, and citations be exact in all legal correspondence and documents. An error in one of these items on a legal document can destroy its validity and even lead to litigation. Use the following proofreading techniques to ensure accuracy:

1. Documents should be examined to be sure the format is correct and the style consistent.
2. A guide, such as a ruler, line-advance mechanism, or even a finger, helps improve powers of concentration. A person reading copy for corrections cannot let the mind wander.
3. Initially, the text should be read for sense to detect missing or duplicated words, inappropriate sentence structure, and grammatical errors.
4. The second time through, attention can be devoted to spelling, punctuation, word division, capitalization, and the use of numbers. The majority of document errors fall into these categories. When in doubt, check a dictionary or reference manual.
5. Names, unfamiliar terms, and figures should be checked carefully, character by character, against the handwritten or dictated original document.
6. It is helpful during the second reading to try to read from right to left. This forces the proofreader to look at each word and letter.
7. The "buddy system," with one person reading the copy aloud and another following on a second copy, is not foolproof. An expert proofreader must be able to work independently. However, if a second person does help—as often occurs in proofreading real estate descriptions—the original material should be read silently by the transcriber while the newly typed copy is read aloud by another qualified person. Punctuation, abbreviations, and capital letters in technical material should be read aloud.

# 8.4

## MACHINE TRANSCRIPTION

*Machine transcription* is the identifying label usually given to the processing through typewriting of information located on discrete media such as belts, cassettes, disks, and tapes. The term *transcription* alone encompasses the typewriting of machine shorthand tape notes and stenographic notes as well. The manufacturers of transcribing machines provide helpful booklets with each new machine to assist the transcriber. If pertinent operating instructions are unavailable, the secretary should telephone the company's local representative for information and assistance.

## Triple-Form Typewriting Copy Guide

Baronial (half-sheet) stationery
Monarch (executive) stationery
Standard (full-sized) stationery

| | | |
|---|---|---|
| 1 | 1 | 1 |
| 2 | 2 | 2 |
| 3 | 3 | 3 |
| 4 | 4 | 4 |
| 5 | 5 | 5 |
| 6 | 6 | 6 |
| 7 | 7 | 7 |
| 8 | 8 | 8 |
| 9 | 9 | 9 |
| 10 | 10 | 10 |
| 11 | 11 | 11 |
| 12 | 12 | 12 |
| 13 | 13 | 13 |
| 14 | 14 | 14 |
| 15 | 15 | 15 |
| 16 | 16 | 16 |
| 17 | 17 | 17 |
| 18 | 18 | 18 |
| 19 | 19 | 19 |
| 20 | 20 | 20 |
| 21 | 21 | 21 |
| 22 | 22 | 22 |
| 23 | 23 | 23 |
| 24 | 24 | 24 |
| 25 | 25 | 25 |
| 26 | 26 | 26 |
| 27 | 27 | 27 |
| 28 | 28 | 28 |
| 29 | 29 | 29 |
| 30 | 30 | 30 |
| 31 | 31 | 31 |
| 32 | 32 | 32 |
| 33 | 33 | 33 |
| 34 | 34 | 34 |
| 35 | 35 | 35 |
| 36 | 36 | 36 |
| 37 | 37 | 37 |
| 38 | 38 | 38 |
| 39 | 39 | 39 |
| 40 | 40 | 40 |
| 41 | 41 | 41 |
| 42 | 42 | 42 |
| 43 | 43 | 43 |
| 44 | 44 | 44 |
| 45 | 45 | 45 |
| 46 | 46 | 46 |
| 47 | 47 | 47 |
| 48 | 48 | 48 |
| 49 | 49 | 49 |
| 50 | 50 | 50 |
| 51 | 51 | 51 |
| 52 | 52 | 52 |
| 53 | 53 | 53 |
| 54 | 54 | 54 |
| 55 | 55 | 55 |
| 56 | 56 | 56 |
| | 57 | 57 |
| | 58 | 58 |
| | 59 | 59 |
| | 60 | 60 |
| | 61 | 61 |
| | 62 | 62 |
| | 63 | 63 |
| | | 64 |
| | | 65 |
| | | 66 |

Baronial (half-sheet)

Monarch (executive)

Standard (full-sized sheet)

*Suggestions for Copy Guide Use:* A triple-form typewriting copy guide may easily be constructed on colored paper for ready identification. This vertical placement device can then be positioned behind the page or behind the carbon pack on which typewriting is to be done. The numbers on the copy guide should be exposed at the right-hand side. In this way, the typist may be guided as to the remaining lines on a page. A red pencil may be advantageously used to mark the copy guide at significant points such as the starting point of a date line, the place where the bottom margin is to begin, the length of an executive or half-page letter, and so on.

## Letter Placement Table
Three Sizes of Stationery

| Lines in Letter Body | Words in Letter Body | Starting Line for Inside Address* | Typewriter Marginal Stops Elite/Pica | Length in Inches of Typing Line |
|---|---|---|---|---|
| **Half-sheet Stationery:** Assume Letterhead takes 7 vertical lines. (Baronial—center No. 36 for Elite; No. 30 for Pica) | | | | |
| 9–10 | 60–66 | 17** | 15–60/10–50 | 4 |
| 11–12 | 67–73 | 16** | 15–60/10–50 | 4 |
| 13–14 | 74–80 | 15** | 15–60/10–50 | 4 |
| 15–16 | 81–87 | 14** | 15–60/10–50 | 4 |
| 17–18 | 88–94 | 13** | 15–60/10–50 | 4 |
| 19–20 | 95–100 | 12** | 15–60/10–50 | 4 |
| **Executive-size Stationery:** Assume Letterhead takes 8 lines. Monarch—center No. 44, Elite; No. 35, Pica) | | | | |
| 13–14 | 95–115 | 19** | 15–75/10–60 | 5 |
| 15–16 | 116–135 | 18** | 15–75/10–60 | 5 |
| 17–18 | 136–155 | 17** | 15–75/10–60 | 5 |
| 19–20 | 156–175 | 16** | 15–75/10–60 | 5 |
| **Full-size Stationery:** Assume Letterhead takes 9 lines. (Standard—center No. 50, Elite; No. 42, Pica) | | | | |
| 11–14 | 175–200 | 20** | 15–90/12–72 | 6 |
| 15–18 | 201–225 | 19** | 15–90/12–72 | 6 |
| 19–22 | 226–250 | 18** | 15–90/12–72 | 6 |
| 23–26 | 251–275 | 17** | 15–90/12–72 | 6 |
| 27–30 | 276–300*** | 16** | 15–90/12–72 | 6 |

*Begin to count at the very top edge of the stationery.
**The date should be typed three lines below the last line of the letterhead on all letters.
***Letters consisting of more than 300 words should be two-page letters.

## A MACHINE TRANSCRIPTION SIMULATION
The following steps outline some basic procedures for using the majority of transcribing machines found in modern offices. A simulation of the work flow of a machine transcriber is illustrated:

1. Place the recorded medium into the transcribing machine.
2. Connect the foot control to the unit. Position the control so it is comfortable for you. This control permits the operator to advance the dictation or back up for review. A hand control which serves the same purpose is available on some equipment.
3. Adjust the earpiece or headset so that it is comfortable. The headset chin band with sponge eartips screens out most outside sounds. The ear clip which fits on one ear permits the transcriber to listen for the telephone while transcribing.
4. Turn on the transcribing unit. Adjust the tone, volume, and speed controls.
5. Install the index strip that accompanies the medium in the holder. An index strip is a piece of paper with a numbered scale which indicates the length in minutes of the dictation and which contains instructions for the transcriber. Check below the horizontal line or numbers on the index slip for special instructions from the dictator. ALWAYS LISTEN TO ALL INSTRUCTIONS BEFORE BEGINNING TO TYPE. There may be instructions at the end of the medium that pertain to the first item of dictation, such as the need for an extra carbon copy or for changing or adding to a previous letter. Markings above the horizontal line or

number on the index slip indicate the end of each item of dictation. These markings help you estimate the length of an item. With practice you will be able to predict the length of a dictation. Each dictator's material will vary depending on the speed with which he or she speaks.

6. Move the index strip scanner (or pointer) to the first priority or rush item.
7. Depress the foot control or the thumb control to activate the machine for listening.
8. If you are typing a letter, estimate its length and determine the appropriate marginal settings. Refer to Chapters 12 and 13 for the correct marginal settings for legal instruments and court documents.
9. Set the typewriter margins, tabular stops, and correct vertical setting.
10. Insert the appropriate stationery, law blank, or legal cap.
11. Listen to the first transcription thought phrase.
12. Type only a *portion* of the first thought phrase.
13. Listen to the second thought phrase as the typewriting is completed on the first thought phrase. Refer to the following illustration for a sample of the listen/type procedure:

**An Illustration of the Listen/Type Transcription Process**

---

TYPExxxxxxxxxxxxxxxxxxTYPExxxxxxxxxxxxxxxxxTYPExxxxxxxxxxxxxxx
LISTEN))))))))))))))/LISTEN))))))))))))))/LISTEN))))))))))))))))))))
The term of this Lease shall be for three (3) years commencing

xxxxxxxxxxxxxxxxxxxxxTYPExxxxxxxxxxxxxxxxxxxxxxTYPExxxxxxxxxxx
LISTEN)))))))))))))/LISTEN))))))))))))))/LISTEN)))))))))))))))/
as provided in Paragraph 3 below, unless sooner terminated.

---

Your goal is to listen and remember as many words as you can, release the foot pedal, and type. With experience you can approach continuous typing while listening.

14. Continue the transcription process toward the goal of continuous typewriting as listening continues in spurts by thought phrases.

# 8.5

---

## TRANSCRIPTION SIMULATION: A Sample Dictation and Transcription

A simulation of dictation, instructions for the transcriber, and transcription is given in this section. The document being drawn is the one illustrated on pages 186–188. You will notice that in the sample the dictator has not given many instructions to the secretary. You will be expected to complete many routine parts by referring to the form book that you have compiled for your office.

**SIMULATION**
**Dictator's instructions**

This is attorney Andrew Howard please type a mortgage deed for Stephen that's S-T-E-P-H-E-N Marks M as in man A-R-K-S Mister Marks has an appointment to sign the deed on Monday of next week I am using a new form so I have included a copy with notations for your use of course I will expect you to add him his I am etcetera where appropriate as you have done on the previous form that we used I will need two and three the form is mortgage deed number one seventeen from Cleaveland Legal Blank Service Incorporated

**Interpretation of instructions**    The attorney has stated that he will need two and three. That means he will need two original signed and witnessed copies, one for Mr. Marks and one for Mr. Mattes, the grantee. The other three are reference copies, one for Mr. Marks, one for Mr. Mattes, and one for the office file. Since this is a new form for your office, you should make an extra copy for your own form file. Check the number to be sure that you have the correct law blank before you begin typing.

**Dictation A**    at number one add I Stephen Marks of the town of Waterford county of New London and state of Connecticut

**Interpretation of dictation**    You know from experience the special uses of capitalization in legal documents such as this mortgage deed. (Refer to Chapter 9.)

**Transcription A**    I, STEPHEN MARKS, of the Town of Waterford, County of New London, and State of Connecticut,

**Dictation B**    at number two add thirty three thousand four hundred thirty two dollars that's three three four three two received to my

**Interpretation of dictation**    Your experience has told you that important money amounts are typed in capital letters and repeated parenthetically in numerical form. (Refer to Chapter 9.)

**Transcription B**    THIRTY-THREE THOUSAND FOUR HUNDRED THIRTY-TWO and 00/100 DOLLARS ($33,432.00) received to my

**Dictation C**    at three add Richard that's R-I-C-H-A-R-D Mattes that's M as in man A-T-T-E-S of the town of West Hartford county of Hartford state of Connecticut

**Transcription C**    RICHARD MATTES of the Town of West Hartford, County of Hartford, State of Connecticut,

**Dictation D**    at number four add Richard Mattes his heirs and assigns forever certain pieces or parcels of land with the improvements thereon situated in the town of Waterford county of New London and state of Connecticut being lots numbers thirteen and fourteen that's one three and one four and the northerly seventy-five that would be seven five feet of lot number fifteen that's one five being that portion of lot number fifteen not previously conveyed by grantor to Howard Daly D-A-L-Y incorporated on a map entitled quote property of Harriet H-A-R-R-I-E-T Olsen O-L-S-E-N incorporated Waterford Connecticut September nineteen fifty-nine scale one inch equal sign two hundred two zero zero feet Ernest M Miller registered engineer West Haven Connecticut unquote which map is on file in the town clerk's office in said town of Waterford to which reference may be had paragraph said premises are more particularly bounded and described as follows to wit paragraph

**Transcription D**

RICHARD MATTES, his heirs and assigns forever, certain pieces or parcels of land with the improvements thereon, situated in the Town of Waterford, County of New London, and State of Connecticut, being Lots Nos. 13 and 14 and the northerly 75 feet of Lot No. 15, being that portion of Lot No. 15 not previously conveyed by Grantor to Howard Daly, Inc., on a map entitled "Property of Harriet Olsen, Inc., Waterford, Connecticut, September 1959 Scale 1 inch = 200 feet, Ernest M. Miller, Registered Engineer, West Haven, Connecticut," which map is on file in the Town Clerk's Office in said Town of Waterford, to which reference may be had.

Said premises are more particularly bounded and described as follows, to wit:

**Dictation E**

southerly by land now or formerly of Howard Daly incorporated eight three five feet more or less easterly by Cross road two seven five feet northerly by lot number twelve on the aforesaid map one zero four zero feet more or less northwesterly by land now or formerly of the estate of Milton Frances that's F-R-A-N-C-E-S one one zero feet more or less and southwesterly by land now or formerly of Foster and a stone wall three four zero feet more or less paragraph said premises are subject to building comma building line comma and zoning restrictions semicolon to easements as of record appear and drainage rights to the town of Waterford as of record appear semicolon and to the second installment of taxes on the list of October one nineteen seventy nine

**Transcription E**

SOUTHERLY: by land now or formerly of Howard Daly, Inc., 835 feet, more or less; EASTERLY: by Cross Road 275 feet; NORTHERLY: by Lot No. 12 on the aforesaid map, 1,040 more or less; NORTHWESTERLY: by land now or formerly of the Estate of Milton Frances, 110 feet, more or less; and SOUTHWESTERLY: by land now or formerly of Foster and a stone wall, 340 feet, more or less.

Said premises are subject to building, building line, and zoning restrictions; to easements as of record appear and drainage rights to the Town of Waterford as of record appear; and to the second installment of taxes on the list of October 1, 1979.

**Dictation F**

at five add Stephen Marks at six delete the line at seven add I Stephen Marks have

**Transcription F**

STEPHEN MARKS    I, STEPHEN MARKS, have

**Routine instructions**

Be sure to fill in all necessary blanks even though they have not been dictated. Proofread the land description carefully, having someone else help you if necessary. Because you are working with a law blank, it is necessary to proofread only the typed material that you have inserted.

## Law Blank Marked for Take-ins

MORTGAGE DEED            NO. 117                    Cleaveland Legal Blank Service, Inc.
East Hartford, Connecticut 06108

### To all People to whom these Presents shall come, Greeting:

KNOW YE, THAT ①

for the consideration of ②

received to          full satisfaction of ③

do     give, grant, bargain, sell and confirm unto the said ④

## Completed Mortgage Deed

MORTGAGE DEED     NO. 117

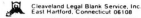
Cleaveland Legal Blank Service, Inc.
East Hartford, Connecticut 06108

# To all People to whom these Presents shall come, Greeting:

**KNOW YE, THAT** I, STEPHEN MARKS, of the Town of Waterford, County of New London, and State of Connecticut,

**for the consideration of** THIRTY-THREE THOUSAND FOUR HUNDRED THIRTY-TWO and 00/100 DOLLARS ($33,432.00)

**received to** my   **full satisfaction of** RICHARD MATTES of the Town of West Hartford, County of Hartford, State of Connecticut,

**do**   **give, grant, bargain, sell and confirm unto the said** RICHARD MATTES, his heirs and assigns forever, certain pieces or parcels of land with the improvements thereon, situated in the Town of Waterford, County of New London and State of Connecticut, being Lots Nos. 13 and 14 and the northerly 75 feet of Lot No. 15, being that portion of Lot No. 15 not previously conveyed by Grantor to Howard Daly, Inc., on a map entitled "Property of Harriet Olsen, Inc., Waterford, Connecticut, September 1959 Scale 1 inch = 200 feet, Ernest M. Miller, Registered Engineer, West Haven, Connecticut," which map is on file in the Town Clerk's Office in said Town of Waterford, to which reference may be had.

Said premises are more particularly bounded and described as follows, to wit:

SOUTHERLY:     by land now or formerly of Howard Daly, Inc., 835 feet, more or less;

EASTERLY:     by Cross Road, 275 feet;

NORTHERLY:     by Lot No. 12 on the aforesaid map, 1,040 feet, more or less;

NORTHWESTERLY:     by land now or formerly of the Estate of Milton Frances, 110 feet, more or less; and

SOUTHWESTERLY:     by land now or formerly of Foster and a stone wall, 340 feet, more or less.

Said premises are subject to building, building line, and zoning restrictions; to easements as of record appear and drainage rights to the Town of Waterford as of record appear; and to the second installment of taxes on the list of October 1, 1979.

## Law Blank Marked for Take-ins

To Have and to Hold  the above granted and bargained premises, with the appurtenances
thereof, unto          the said grantee                    heirs, successors, and assigns forever,
to          and their own proper use and behoof. And also,          the said grantor          do      for
        sel          ,            heirs, executors, administrators, and successors, covenant with the
said grantee  ,            heirs, successors, and assigns, that at and until the ensealing of these
presents,              well seized of the premises, as a good indefeasible estate in FEE SIMPLE;
and ha      good right to bargain and sell the same in manner and form as is above written and
that the same is free from all incumbrances whatsover, except as hereinbefore mentioned.

And Furthermore,      the said grantor      do      by these presents bind          sel
and              heirs forever to WARRANT AND DEFEND the above granted and bargained premises
to          the said grantee  ,          heirs, successors, and assigns, against all claims and demands whatsover, except as hereinbefore mentioned.

The Condition of this Deed is such, that whereas the said grantor ⑤
                                    justly indebted to the said grantee    in the sum of
                                                    Dollars as evidenced by
⑥ promissory note      for                                                Dollars
of even date herewith, payable to said grantee      or order

## Completed Mortgage Deed

To Have and to Hold  the above granted and bargained premises, with the appurtenances
thereof, unto him    the said grantee ,          his      heirs, successors, and assigns forever,
to  his and their own proper use and behoof. And also, I,  the said grantor ,          do      for
    my self          ,      my  heirs, executors, administrators, and successors, covenant with the
said grantee ,      his    heirs, successors, and assigns, that at and until the ensealing of these
presents,    I am      well seized of the premises, as a good indefeasible estate in FEE SIMPLE;
and ha ve  good right to bargain and sell the same in manner and form as is above written and
that the same is free from all incumbrances whatsover, except as hereinbefore mentioned.

And Furthermore, I, the said grantor ,      do      by these presents bind      my sel f
and      my   heirs forever to WARRANT AND DEFEND the above granted and bargained premises
to    him  the said-grantee  ,   his   heirs, successors, and assigns, against all claims and demands whatsover, except as hereinbefore mentioned.

The Condition of this Deed is such, that whereas the said grantor  STEPHEN MARKS
                            is  justly indebted to the said grantee    in the sum of
THIRTY-THREE THOUSAND FOUR HUNDRED THIRTY-TWO   Dollars as evidenced by  his
($33,432.00)
promissory note    for  said sum.                          x Dollars x x
xof xyxerx datexherxwithxpxayablxe txx xaixbxgrxxxtex xxx xx xxdxerx

Reprinted by permission of Cleaveland Legal Blank Service, Inc.

# 8.6

## THE USE OF THE SHORTHAND MACHINE

The secretary who knows how to use a shorthand machine can fill a special need for above-normal recording ability, when it arises.

### TAKING MACHINE SHORTHAND

Before a dictation session, adjust the inking of the machine shorthand ribbon so the notes will be readable. A few lines of sample notes should be written to ascertain whether or not a few drops of ink should be added to the top of the ink spool by means of the special ink applicator bottle. Be certain that a sufficient amount of paper tape is available in the machine for a given dictation session. Additional tape should be on hand. This tape is obtainable in 100 folds and 300 folds per package.

The shorthand machine may be set up on a separate table, a desk, or a pullout shelf of a desk. A sturdy, adjustable-height tripod is also available for the shorthand machine. In any situation, the height of the machine should allow the secretary to place curved fingers over the keyboard, keeping the wrists level in a position similar to the correct position at a typewriter. A comfortable, relaxed position is essential to prevent physical fatigue during extended periods of dictation or court testimony.

During pauses in dictation, the secretary may use the pencil from the top of the machine to cross out changed notes on the paper. Rush or priority items may be flagged for quick reference by pencil notation. Three machine asterisks at the beginning and end of notes indicate a complete unit of material to be transcribed. Special attention to the dictation when a pause is available will result in quicker, smoother, easier transcription.

### A Shorthand Machine Tape Transcription

```
STKPWHR
ST        A    U R
  T P          U      L
  T P H A   EU   P L
                    FRPBLGTS
        HR    EU   PB
            A          PB
          R O EU
STKPWHR
ST
      P H     EU            S
              O      R
    P  HR                   S
          R O EU
                  FRPBLGTS
  T                        S
        A    E
      P H     EU           S
          R O EU
STKPWHR
ST        A    U RPB
              O        B G
      P    A  EU        G S
      P
                  FRPBLGTS
              EU   P L
```

Q.  State your full name.

A.  Lynn Ann Roy.

Q.  Is it Miss or Mrs. Roy?

A.  It's Miss Roy.

Q.  State your occupation, please.

A.  I am a student.

## MACHINE SHORTHAND TRANSCRIPTION
Converting and interpreting machine shorthand English letter abbreviations and symbols into a readable typewritten format involves some new procedures and some that are similar to those of machine transcription.

**Machine shorthand transcription process** A description of the machine shorthand transcription process follows:

1. Remove the tape notes at the platen of the shorthand machine.
2. Place the tape into a transcription box so that only two lengths of notes are readily visible at a given time.
3. Scan the notes for priority or rush work.
4. Edit the notes to find corrections, deletions, additions, or other changes; mark these sections with a colored pencil for ready reference.
5. Estimate the number of actual words found in one fold of machine shorthand notes. Multiply this number by the number of prefolded sections in the recorded notes for a given document or letter. This will produce an estimated word count.
6. Strive for smooth continuous typewriting by reading a phrase ahead of the typewriting. (See the illustration of the listen/type process on page 183; substitute the word *read* for the word *listen* when studying this illustration.)

**Computer shorthand transcription** Computer transcription is available to qualified reporters for the production of depositions and transcripts. In one system the reporter's machine shorthand symbols are programmed into the computer to serve as a dictionary for transcribing that reporter's notes.

## POST-TRANSCRIPTION PROCEDURES FOR MACHINE SHORTHAND
To make it easier to identify transcribed machine shorthand notes, remove the completed tape from the transcription box, place an elastic band around the notes, and write the date on them. Transcribed tape notes may also be filed in long envelopes (4⅛" by 9½") for future reference. Identifying information written on the face of the envelope should include the date, the dictator, the file number, and any other pertinent data.

# 8.7

# SHORTHAND OUTLINES FOR FOREIGN WORDS AND PHRASES

| | |
|---:|:---|
| ab ante | |
| ab initio | |
| ab intestato | |
| actio civilis | |
| actio in personam | |
| actio in rem | |
| actio personalis | |
| ad captandum | |

| | |
|---|---|
| ad curiam | |
| ad damnum | |
| ad grave damnum | |
| ad hoc | |
| ad infinitum | |
| ad interim | |
| ad libitum | |
| ad litem | |
| ad locum | |
| ad rem | |
| ad respondendum | |
| ad valorem | |
| ad vitam | |
| a fortiori | |
| a gratia | |
| allegata et probata | |
| a mensa et thoro | |
| amicus curiae | |
| animo et acto | |
| animus furandi | |
| animus revocandi | |
| a posteriori | |
| a priori | |
| a quo | |
| assumpsit | |
| au contraire | |
| audita querela | |
| a vinculo matrimonii | |
| bon ami | |
| bona fide | |
| bona fides | |
| carte blanche | |
| capias | |

casus belli

causa mortis

causa prima

caveat emptor

caveat venditor

certiorari

cestui que trust

compos mentis

corpus

corpus delicti

corpus juris

cum testamento annexo

damnum absque injuria

de bene esse

de facto

de jure

del credere

de novo

duces tecum

et al.

et sequentia

et uxor

et vir

ex contractu

ex curia

ex delicto

ex officio

ex parte

ex post facto

ex statuto

fait accompli

femme sole

habeas corpus

| | |
|---|---|
| habendum | |
| ibidem | |
| id est (or) i.e. | |
| ignorantia juris non excusat | |
| in bonis | |
| in curia | |
| in delicto | |
| in esse | |
| in extenso | |
| in extremis | |
| in flagrante delicto | |
| infinitum | |
| in futuro | |
| in initio | |
| in judicio | |
| in jure | |
| in litem | |
| in loco | |
| in loco parentis | |
| in pari causa | |
| in personam | |
| in re | |
| in rem | |
| in toto | |
| ipso facto | |
| jurat | |
| lis pendens | |
| locus sigilli | |
| malo animo | |
| narratio | |
| nolo contendere | |
| non compos mentis | |
| non sequitur | |

non sui juris

obiter dictum

ore tenus

pendente lite

per capita

per se

persona non grata

per stirpes

praecipe

prima facie

pro forma

pro tempore

res

res gestae

res judicata

res nova

retraxit

sans recours

scilicet

seisin

sine die

status quo

sub rosa

sui generis

sui juris

ultra vires

venire

versus

vice versa

voir dire

writ of habeas corpus

# 9

CHAPTER NINE

# A GUIDE TO EFFECTIVE WRITING

CONTENTS

# 9.1

INTRODUCTION

The importance of cleanly typed correspondence is discussed in Chapter 10; the typing of legal documents is treated in Chapters 12 and 13. However, the mechanics of typing attractive-looking material is only one factor contributing to effective written communication. Other equally important elements are standard grammar, correct spelling, appropriate style, and sound presentation of ideas within logically constructed sentences and paragraphs. While the physical appearance and mechanical setup of the material will impress a reader at first glance, these other factors will create even more lasting impressions as the reader studies the material carefully and reflects on its content. If the grammar is substandard, if the spelling is incorrect, if the sentence structure is contorted, if the paragraph orientation is cloudy or irrational, and if the text is riddled with padding and clichés, one can reasonably anticipate negative reader reaction.

Although the writer or dictator bears the prime responsibility for his or her own grammar, diction, and usage, the secretary still should be competent enough in these areas to recognize basic grammatical and stylistic infelicities. Before typing questionable material, the secretary should research any doubtful points and then tactfully query the writer. The following sections have been prepared as a quick reference tool for just this sort of situation. Highly specialized questions may be answered by consulting a current book on English grammar (see the Appendix for a list of titles).

# 9.2

## ABBREVIATIONS

The occurrence of abbreviations in typed or printed material is directly related to the nature of the material itself. For example, technical literature (as in the fields of engineering and data processing) abounds in abbreviations, but formal literary writing features relatively few such terms. By the same token, the presence or absence of abbreviations in business writing depends on the nature of the business. A secretary in an electronics firm and one in a law office each will encounter widely different abbreviations. The use of abbreviations in a law office also depends on the documents being produced. A legal secretary may type numerous abbreviations for citations in an appeal brief while adhering at other times to the general rule not to use abbreviations in legal papers unless they are common and generally understood.

Abbreviation styling is, unfortunately, inconsistent and at the same time arbitrary. No rules can be set down to cover all possible variations, exceptions, and peculiarities. The styling of abbreviations—whether punctuated or unpunctuated, capitalized or lowercase, closed up or spaced—depends most often on the writer's preference or the policy of the office, court, or publication. It can be said, however, that some abbreviations (as *a.k.a., e.g., etc., f.o.b., i.e., No.,* and *viz.*) are backed by a strong punctuation tradition, and that others (as *GATT, LIFO, MIRV, PAYE,* and *SALT*) that are pronounced as solid words tend to be all capitalized and unpunctuated. Citations typed for briefs and for publication in law reviews follow fairly rigid patterns determined by federal and state courts and by style guides such as *A Uniform System of Citation.* Other styling problems can be alleviated by (1) consulting an adequate dictionary especially for capitalization guidance, (2) following the guidelines of one's own organization, and (3) consulting a legal dictionary for answers to highly specialized questions (see the Appendix for a list of titles).

Abbreviations are used (1) to avoid repetition of long words and phrases that may distract the reader, (2) to save space and time, (3) to reduce keystrokes and increase output, and (4) to reflect statistical data in limited space. When using an abbreviation that may be unfamiliar or confusing to the reader, one should give the full form first, followed by the abbreviation in parentheses, as

I shall address the American Bar Association (ABA) meeting in . . . .

followed in subsequent references by just the abbreviation, as

At this particular ABA meeting, I intend to . . . .

The following chart offers abbreviation guidelines listed alphabetically by key words in boldface type.

## ABBREVIATIONS

**1. a** or **an** before an abbreviation; *see* pages 243–244.

2. **A.D.** and **B.C.** are usually styled in printed matter as small punctuated unspaced capitals, but in typed material as punctuated unspaced capitals.

41 B.C.    A.D. 185 *also* 185 A.D.    fourth century A.D.
41 B.C.    A.D. 185 *also* 185 A.D.    fourth century A.D.

3. **Beginning a sentence with an abbreviation** should be avoided unless the abbreviation represents a courtesy title.

Page 22 contains . . . . *but not* P. 22 contains . . . .
*however*    Dr. Smith is here. *or* Doctor Smith is here.

4. **Capitalization** of abbreviations; *see* page 201.

5. **Case titles** In a running text the names of parties to a case are not abbreviated unless they can be identified by widely recognized initials such as *NAACP*. (Initials for government agencies or labor unions that are acceptable in other legal texts, however, are not allowed in briefs.) *United States* is typed in full when the federal government is a party to litigation. Abbreviations like *Co., Corp., Inc., Ltd., No.,* and *&* are used in case titles in the body of a text.

*United States* v. *Harriss*
*Kirk* v. *Standard Life & Accident Insurance Co.*

Case names appearing in footnotes follow standard abbreviations such as those listed in *A Uniform System of Citation* (the "Bluebook").

*Massman Const. Co.* v. *Lake Lotawana Ass'n*

Some parts of long case names may simply be omitted; consult a style guide such as the Bluebook or court rule books.

6. **Company names** are not abbreviated unless abbreviations comprise their official names;

Ginn and Company                          *but*    Copying Products Division/3M
The Bailey Banks and Biddle Company              Canon, U.S.A., Inc.

the words *Airlines, Associates, Consultants, Corporation, Fabricators, Manufacturing,* and *Railroad* should not be abbreviated when part of proper names.

Dictaphone Corporation      Eastern Airlines

7. **Compass points** are abbreviated when occurring after street names, and they can be unpunctuated. However, they are usually typed out in full when they form essential internal elements of street names.

2122 Fourteenth Street, NW      192 East 49th Street

8. **Contractions,** sometimes used instead of abbreviations, have no terminal punctuation.

sec'y *but also* secy.      ass'n *but also* assn.      dep't *but also* dept.

Certain contractions are frequently used in citations.

*aff'd      aff'g      rev'd*

9. **Dates** (as days and months) should not be abbreviated in running texts; months should not be abbreviated in general business-letter date lines but they may be abbreviated in government or military correspondence.

I expect to meet with you in Chicago on Monday, November 1.
*general business-letter date line* November 1, 19--
*military date line* 1 Nov --

10. **Division of an abbreviation** either at the end of a line or between pages should be avoided.

received an LL.D.   *but not*   received an LL.-
degree . . . .                          D. degree . . . .

11. **Geographical and topographical names** U.S. Postal Service abbreviations for states are all-capitalized and unpunctuated, as are the Postal Service abbreviations for streets and localities when used on envelopes addressed for automated mass handling.

*addressed for automated handling*   *regular address styling*
1234 SMITH BLVD                           1234 Smith Blvd. (*or* Boulevard)
SMITHVILLE, ST 56789                    Smithville, ST 56789

Ordinals are abbreviated in some street addresses.

147 East 31st Street    147 East 3d Avenue    147 East 3rd Avenue

Names of countries are typically abbreviated in tabular data, but are typed in full in running texts (exception: *U.S.S.R.*).

*in a table*   U.A.R. *or* UAR
*in a text*   The United Arab Republic and the U.S.S.R. announced the trade agreement.

*United States* is often abbreviated when it modifies names of federal agencies, courts, policies, or programs; when it is used as a noun, it is usually typed in full.

U.S. Department of Justice   *but*   The United States has offered to . . . .
U.S. foreign policy                      *United States* v. *Lee Wilson & Co.*

12. **Latin words and phrases** commonly used in general writing are often abbreviated, as are certain words and phrases typically used in bibliographical and legal citations.

ex rel.       sub nom.      ibid.
id.             ad loc.         et seq.

NOTE: Latin words like *et, sub, ex (ex parte),* and *re (in re)* are complete words and require no terminal punctuation.

13. **Latitude and longitude** are abbreviated in tabular data, but are typed in full in running texts.

*in a table*   lat. 10°20′N *or* lat. 10–20N
*in a text*   from 10° 20′ north latitude to 10° 30′ south latitude . . . .

14. **Laws and bylaws** when first mentioned are typed in full; however, subsequent references to them in a text may be abbreviated.

*first reference*   Article I, Section 1
*subsequent references*   Art. I, Sec. 1

15. **Measures and weights** may be abbreviated in figure + unit combinations; however, if the numeral is written out, the unit must also be written out.

15 cu ft *or* 15 cu. ft.   *but*   fifteen cubic feet

16. **Number** when part of a set unit (as a contract or index number), when used in tabular data, or when used in bibliographic references may be abbreviated to *No.* (sing.) or *Nos.* (plural).

Contract No. N-1234-76-57    Publ. Nos. 12 and 13
Policy No. 123-5-X              Index No. 7855

**17. Period** with abbreviations; *see* PERIOD, RULE 4, page 228.

**18. Personal names** should not be abbreviated; however, unspaced initials of famous persons are sometimes used in place of their full names.

George S. Patterson *not* Geo. S. Patterson
*but*
J.F.K. or JFK

Initials of a personal name are spaced.

J. F. Kennedy

**19. Plurals** of abbreviations may be formed by addition of -*s*

MPs; CLAs; CPAs

or by the addition of -*'s* especially if the abbreviation is internally punctuated or ends in a sibilant, except for a few such terms that are punctuated only with terminal periods, in which case the apostrophe is omitted

f.o.b.'s; PLS's; CLA's
*but*
Nos. 3 and 4; Arts. III and IV

or by repeating a letter of the abbreviation

p.→pp.    f.→ff.

or, in the case of weights and measures, by no suffixation.

1 sec→30 sec    1 ml→24 ml

**20. Possessives** of abbreviations are formed in the same way as those of nouns: the singular possessive is signaled by addition of -*'s*

*our CPA's report*

and the plural possessive, by addition of -*s'*.

*our CPAs' fees*

**21. Saint** may be abbreviated when used before the name of a saint or a city named for a saint; however, it may or may not be abbreviated when it forms part of a surname or the name of a disease.

St. Peter *or* Saint Peter; St. Louis
*but*
Ruth St. Denis; Augustus Saint-Gaudens; Saint Vitus' dance

**22. Scientific terms** In binomial nomenclature a genus name may be abbreviated after the first reference to it is typed out.

first reference    *Escherichia coli*    subsequent references    *E. coli*

**23. Time** When time is expressed in figures, the abbreviations that follow may be set in unspaced punctuated lowercase letters; if capitals or small capitals are used, one space should separate the letters (the writer's or organization's preference will dictate the style);

8:30 a.m. *or* 8:30 A. M. *or* 8:30 A. M.

standard measurements of time (as in tabular data) are expressed in figures and typically unpunctuated abbreviations.

10 sec; 18 min; 24 hr; 17 yr; 52 wk; 19 mo; 100 da

**24. Titles** The only titles that are invariably abbreviated are *Mr., Ms., Mrs.,* and *Messrs.* Other titles (except for *Doctor* which may be written out or abbreviated) are given in full form in business-letter salutations;

| | | |
|---|---|---|
| Ms. Lee A. Downs | *but* | Dear Professor Howe |
| Messrs. Lake, Mason, and Nambeth | | Dear General Howe |
| Dear Dr. Howe *or* Dear Doctor Howe | | Dear Private Howe |

but titles may be abbreviated in envelope address blocks and in inside addresses;

Dr. John P. Howe          GEN John P. Howe, USA
COL John P. Howe, USA     PVT John P. Howe, USA

also *Honorable* and *Reverend* when used with *The* are typed out, but if used without *The,* they may be abbreviated; *see also* pages 347–348; 350–351.

| | | |
|---|---|---|
| The Reverend Samuel I. O'Leary | *but* | Rev. Samuel I. O'Leary |
| The Honorable Samuel I. O'Leary | | Hon. Samuel I. O'Leary |

**25. Versus** is abbreviated as the lowercase Roman letter *v.* in legal contexts; it is either typed in full or abbreviated as lowercase Roman letters *vs.* in general contexts.

*in a legal context*   Smith v. Vermont
*in a general context*   honesty versus dishonesty *or* honesty vs. dishonesty

# 9.3

## CAPITALIZATION

Capitals are used for two broad purposes in English: They mark a beginning (as of a sentence) and they signal a proper noun or adjective. The following principles describe the most common uses of capital letters in legal documents as well as in general writing. These principles are alphabetically ordered under the following headings:

Abbreviations
Beginnings
Legal Document Terms
Proper Nouns, Pronouns, and Adjectives
    armed forces
    awards
    deity
    epithets
    geographical and topographical references
    governmental, judicial, and political bodies
    names of organizations
    names of persons
    numerical designations
    particles and prefixes
    personifications
    pronouns
    scientific terms
    time periods, zones, and divisions
    titles of persons
    titles of printed matter
    trademarks
    transport

When uncertain about the capitalization of a term not shown below, the secretary should consult a law dictionary, a general dictionary such as *Webster's New Collegiate Dictionary,* or the office style manual.

## CAPITALIZATION

### Abbreviations

1. Abbreviations are capitalized if the words they represent are proper nouns or adjectives; consult a dictionary when in doubt of styling.

   98 F for *Fahrenheit;* Nov. for *November;* NALA for *National Association of Legal Assistants*

2. Many abbreviations are capitalized when they represent single letters of words that are ordinarily lowercased; consult a dictionary for proper styling.

   OCR for *optical character recognition*   L.S. for *locus sigilli*
   TM for *trademark*   MSS for *manuscripts*
   *but*
   a.k.a. for *also known as*   d.b.a. for *doing business as*

3. Most acronyms are capitalized unless they have been assimilated into the language as parts of speech, and as such are lowercased; consult a dictionary when in doubt of styling.

   OPEC; MIRV; GATT
   *but*
   quasar; laser; radar; sonar; scuba

4. Abbreviations of government agencies, military units, and corporate names are usually capitalized.

   SEC; FBI; NLRB; USAF; JAG; RCA; ITT; GTE

5. Abbreviations of air force, army, coast guard, and navy ranks are all-capitalized; those of the marine corps are capitalized and lowercased; see FORMS OF ADDRESS, pages 336–342.

   BG John T. Down, USA   LCDR Mary I. Lee, USN   Col. S. J. Smith, USMC

6. Abbreviations of compass points are capitalized; punctuation styling depends on the writer's or organization's preference.

   lat. 10°20′N; 2233 Fourteenth Street, N.W. (*or* NW. *or* NW)

7. Abbreviations of academic degrees and professional ratings are all-capitalized or capitalized and lowercased, depending on the word; consult a dictionary when in doubt of styling.

   D.D.S.   M.B.A.
   P.E.   C.P.A.
   Ph.D.   Litt.D.
   LL.D.   Jur.D.

### Beginnings

8. The first word of a sentence, of a sentence fragment, or of a complete sentence enclosed in parentheses is capitalized;

The meeting was postponed.
Will you go?
Total chaos. Nothing works.
The meeting ended. (The results were not revealed.)

however, the first word of a parenthetical phrase or sentence enclosed by parentheses and occurring within another sentence is lowercased.

She studied economics under Dr. Heller (he wrote this text, you know) at the university.

**9.** The first word of a direct quotation is capitalized, but a split direct quotation tightly bound to the rest of a sentence is lowercased at the beginning of its continued segment or segments.

He said, "We must consider the publicity problems."

"The administration has denied the story," the paper reports, "and feels the media are irresponsible."

The first word of a quotation forming a complete sentence that is tightly bound to the main sentence is usually lowercased.

The paper goes on to say that "the President feels the media are irresponsible."

**10.** The first word of a direct question within a sentence or of a series of questions within a sentence may be capitalized.

That question is this: Exactly what procedures should your assistants themselves devise? How much initiative should they exercise? How much enterprise?

**11.** The first word following a colon may be lowercased or capitalized if it introduces a complete sentence; while the former is the more usual styling, the latter is common in formal writing, especially when the sentence introduced by the colon is fairly lengthy and distinctly separate from the preceding clause.

The advantage of this particular system is clear: it's inexpensive.

The situation is critical: This firm cannot hope to recoup the losses that were sustained this fiscal year.

**12.** The first words of run-in or blocked enumerations that form complete sentences are capitalized as are the first words of phrasal lists and enumerations blocked beneath running texts;

Do the following housekeeping tasks at the end of the day: 1. Clean your typewriter. 2. Clear your desktop of papers. 3. Cover office machines. 4. Straighten the contents of your desk drawers, cabinets, and bookcases.

This is the agenda:
    Call to order
    Roll call
    Minutes of the previous meeting
    Treasurer's report

however, phrasal enumerations run in with the introductory text are lowercased.

On the agenda will be (1) call to order, (2) roll call, (3) minutes of the previous meeting, (4) treasurer's report. . . .

**13.** The words *Whereas* and *Resolved* are capitalized in minutes and legislation and are often typed in solid capitals. The word *That* or an alternative word or expression which immediately follows either is frequently capitalized.

Whereas, Substantial benefits . . . .          Resolved, That . . . .
Whereas, The Executive Committee . . . .       RESOLVED, That . . . ; and be it
Resolved by the —, the — concurring, That . . . .   RESOLVED further, That . . . .

**14.** The first letter of the first word in an outline heading is capitalized.

    I. Date line
   II. Reference line
      A. First sheet
      B. Continuation sheet

**15.** The first letter of the first word in a salutation and a complimentary close is capitalized as is the first letter of each main word following SUBJECT, TO, *Re,* and *In re* headings (as in memorandums and subject lines).

Dear Bob; Gentlemen; My dear Dr. Smith; Very truly yours; Yours very truly
SUBJECT: Pension Plan; TO: All Department Heads; Re: Proposed Sale of Lot No. 512

**16.** The first word of a line of poetry is conventionally capitalized.

For swich lawe as a man yeveth another wight,
He sholde hymselven usen it, by right.
                         —Chaucer

## Legal Document Terms

NOTE: The following guidelines describe specialized capitalization practices in the typing of legal documents. Many of these practices are simply a matter of the individual lawyer's preference. What is important for the attorney and the secretary is to choose an acceptable style for each type of document the office produces, and to stick consistently to that style.

### Client Documents

**17.** Titles of client documents are usually capitalized by law offices. They are typed in solid capitals when they appear as headings on the documents. In the body of the document they are normally capitalized, sometimes with full capitals.

this Agreement; this Registration Statement; the foregoing Articles of Incorporation; draw up a Contract of Sale; this first Codicil of my Will

*but also* the following ARTICLES OF INCORPORATION; my LAST WILL AND TESTA-MENT; which are intended to constitute a GENERAL POWER OF ATTORNEY

*and also* revoke all former wills and codicils

**18.** Personal and corporate names appearing in the body of a client document are often typed in solid capitals.

JACOB J. JACOBSON, being sworn, says . . . .
THIS AGREEMENT is made . . . between THE SEZ CORPORATION . . . and MARCIA RODD . . . .

**19.** Terms that designate a person's function or capacity in a legal relationship are often capitalized in client documents.

the undersigned Incorporator; the Seller; the Buyer; my Executors; any Person; our names as Attesting Witnesses

*but also* my executor; the seller

Sometimes, when personal and corporate names are in solid capitals, their titles are similarly styled, especially at the point where they are first designated.

This Deed of Trust, Made . . . Between JACOB JACOBSON, herein called TRUSTOR, and THE SEZ CORPORATION, herein called TRUSTEE . . . .
I hereby nominate and appoint my husband, ROGER HARRISON WILSON, as EXECU-TOR . . . .

20. The numbered paragraphs of a will are frequently introduced by typed-out, solidly capitalized ordinals. Subsequent references to these paragraphs must also be
typed in solid capital letters.

FIRST: . . . .
SECOND: . . . .
Paragraph ''SECOND'' is hereby amended . . . .
. . . hereby amend paragraph FOURTH . . . .
*also* A new Paragraph shall be added to my said Will . . . .

## Court Documents

21. Titles of court documents are frequently capitalized. They are typed in solid capitals when they appear as headings on the documents themselves.

An Affidavit of Service must always be attached to the original Answer, which is filed in
Court.
. . . sign the Attorney's Affirmation that accompanies a Notice of Motion for Appeal.
. . . show cause why an Order should not be made . . . .
*but also* Defendant admits the allegations stated in paragraph 1 of the complaint.

22. The names of sections of court documents are sometimes capitalized.

. . . the Paragraph hereinafter named . . . .
*but also* Defendant admits the allegations stated in paragraph 1 of the complaint.

23. The personal or corporate names of parties to an action are typed in solid capitals
by most law offices. The terms that designate the parties' roles in the action are
capitalized by some offices, lowercased by others.

JACOB JACOBSON, the Defendant
*also* HANNAH JOHNSON, his attorney

24. Terms used to introduce and enumerate sections of pleadings (as a list of allegations) are capitalized; sometimes they are typed in solid capital letters.

*centered headings*
First Defense
ANSWER TO FIRST CAUSE OF ACTION

*headings that begin a paragraph*
As and for a First Cause of Action . . . .
FIRST COUNT: . . . .
AS AND FOR A FIRST CAUSE OF ACTION PLAINTIFF MARCIA RODD ALLEGES . . . .

25. In an Answer that refers to specific numbered paragraphs of a Complaint, the
terms should be capitalized or lowercased in the same way that they appear in
the Complaint.

paragraphs numbered ''THIRD'' and ''FOURTH''
Defendant admits the allegations contained in paragraphs 1 and 4 of the complaint.

## Introductory Words and Phrases

26. Words and phrases that conventionally introduce standard sections of legal documents are capitalized—usually in solid capitals—for visual emphasis.

IT IS HEREBY ORDERED . . . .
IT IS HEREBY CERTIFIED THAT: . . . .
FOR VALUE RECEIVED, . . . .
SIR: PLEASE TAKE NOTICE, that . . . .
PLEASE TAKE FURTHER NOTICE, that . . . .

KNOW ALL MEN BY THESE PRESENTS that . . . .
NOW, THEREFORE BE IT RESOLVED, that . . . .
RESOLVED FURTHER, that . . . .
THIS INSTRUMENT OF TRANSFER, dated . . . .
COMES NOW plaintiff, HANNAH JOHNSON, and complains . . . .
I, Horace Johnson, as Secretary of the Company, DO HEREBY CERTIFY that . . . .
SUBSCRIBED, SEALED, PUBLISHED and DECLARED by the Testatrix . . . .
THIS INDENTURE . . . BETWEEN . . . AND . . . WITNESSETH, that the grantor . . . ALL . . . TOGETHER with . . . TO HAVE AND TO HOLD . . . IN WITNESS WHEREOF . . . .

## Minutes

**27.** Corporate titles and the names of specific entities within a corporation are usually, but not always, capitalized in minutes.

the President, the Chairman, the Comptroller; the Board, the Company, Preference Stock, the Committee; incurred by the Board of Directors; the issuance of Common Stock; as described in the Corporate Bylaws; the Annual Meeting of the Corporation

*but also* the directors and shareholders of the corporation

## Numerals

**28.** Monetary units that are important to a document are capitalized; often they are typed in solid capitals.

the sum of Four Thousand Dollars ($4,000.00) to be paid . . . .
the sum of TEN THOUSAND DOLLARS ($10,000.00) to be paid . . . .

**29.** Other important figures are sometimes capitalized in their typed-out form.

within TEN (10) days . . . .

## "That" Clauses

**30.** When the word *that* introduces a dependent clause following a capitalized introductory word or phrase in a legal document, it is sometimes capitalized, especially when the clauses form a numbered series.

WE COMMAND YOU, That . . . .
JACOB J. JACOBSON, being sworn, says:
1. That . . . .
2. That . . . .
*more common*
ORDERED, that . . . ; and it is further
ORDERED, that . . . .
PLEASE TAKE NOTICE, that . . . .

**31.** *That* is frequently capitalized when it introduces the first of a series of clauses, but not in the succeeding clauses.

PLEASE TAKE NOTICE, That the defendant HARVEY JONES hereby appears in the above entitled action, and that HANNAH JOHNSON is retained as Attorney for the defendant therein . . . . also PLEASE TAKE NOTICE that . . . .
RESOLVED, That . . . . also RESOLVED, that . . . .

**32.** Sometimes *that* is typed in solid capitals as part of a solidly capitalized introductory phrase.

KNOW ALL MEN BY THESE PRESENTS, THAT . . . .
YOU ARE HEREBY NOTIFIED THAT a judgment by default . . . .

## Signature Lines

**33.** Personal and corporate names are often typed with solid capital letters in the signature lines of legal documents; sometimes the terms that describe the legal role of the signer are also solidly capitalized.

LMN LANDSCAPING, INC.

By _____          _____

        President          MARCIA RODD, Incorporator

                  _____

                  SELLER

**34.** ENTER, which closes a court order, is most often typed in solid capitals.

ENTER

_____

Hon. Justice L. A. Maddox

## Short Forms of Proper Nouns

**35.** A word or phrase that forms part of a proper name often retains its capitalization in legal documents when it is used instead of the full name; such a word or phrase is lowercased in general writing.

Osage Registry of Deeds . . . said Registry
the Controlled Substance Act of 1970 . . . the Act

## Proper Nouns, Pronouns, and Adjectives

### Armed Forces

**36.** Branches and units of the armed forces are capitalized as are short forms of full branch and unit designations.

United States Army *and* a contract with the Army
Corps of Engineers *and* a bridge built by the Engineers

### Awards

**37.** Awards and prizes are capitalized.

the Nobel Prize for Literature; Nobel Peace Prize; Nobel Prize winners; Academy Award; Oscar; Emmy

### Deity

**38.** Words designating the Deity are usually capitalized; *compare* RULE 75.

I'll be there next year, God willing.

### Epithets

**39.** Epithets used in place of names or titles are capitalized.

the Big Board
The Defense rests.
The White House has verified . . . .

## Geographical and Topographical References

**40.** Divisions of the earth's surface and names of distinct areas, regions, places, or districts are capitalized, as are adjectives and some derivative nouns and verbs; consult a dictionary when in doubt.

the Middle East; the Middle Eastern situation; Eastern Hemisphere; the Great Divide; Tropic of Cancer; Geneva; Texas; Vietnam; Vietnamization; Vietnamize; *but* sovietism *often* Sovietism; sovietize *often* Sovietize

**41.** Compass points are capitalized when they refer to a geographical region or when they are part of a street name, but are lowercased when they refer to simple direction.

out West; back East; down South; up North; the South; the Middle West; the West Coast; 157 East 92nd Street

*but* west of the Rockies; traveling east on I-84; the west coast of Florida; beginning at a point on the easterly side of Birch Road

**42.** Adjectives derived from compass points and nouns designating the inhabitants of some geographical regions are capitalized; when in doubt of the proper styling, consult a dictionary.

a Southern accent; a Western drawl; members of the Eastern Establishment; Northerners

**43.** Popular names of localities are capitalized.

the Corn Belt; the Gold Coast; the Loop; the Eastern Shore; City of Brotherly Love; Foggy Bottom; the Village

**44.** Topographical names are capitalized, as are generic terms (as *channel, lake, mountain*) that are essential elements of total names.

the English Channel; Lake Como; the Blue Ridge Mountains; Atlantic Ocean; Great Barrier Reef; Mississippi River; Bering Strait; Strait of Gilbraltar; Ohio Valley

**45.** Generic terms occurring before topographical names are capitalized except when *the* precedes them, in which case the generic term is lowercased.

Lakes Michigan and Superior; Mounts Whitney and Rainier
*but* the rivers Don and Volga; the river Thames

**46.** Plural generic terms occurring after multiple topographical names are lowercased, as are singular or plural generic terms that are used descriptively or alone.

the Himalaya and Andes mountains; the Don and Volga rivers; the valley of the Ohio; the Ohio River valley; the river valley; the valley

**47.** Words designating global, national, regional, or local political divisions are capitalized when they are essential elements of specific names. They are usually lowercased when they precede a proper name or stand alone; an exception is in legal documents, where they are often capitalized.

the British Empire *but* the empire; Oregon State *but* the state of Oregon; Bedford County *but* the county of Bedford; New York City *but* the city of New York; Ward 1 *but* fires in three wards

*in legal documents* the State of Oregon; the County of Bedford; the City of New York

**48.** Terms designating public places are capitalized when they are essential elements of specific names; however, they are lowercased when they occur after multiple names or stand alone.

Fifth Avenue; Brooklyn Bridge; Empire State Building; St. John's Church; the Dorset Hotel; Central Park; Washington Square; Bleecker Street; Ford Theater

*but* on the bridge; Fifth and Park avenues; the Dorset and the Drake hotels; St. John's and St. Mark's churches

**49.** Well-known short forms of place names are capitalized.

Fifth Avenue→the Avenue; Wall Street→the Street; New York Stock Exchange→the Exchange

## Governmental, Judicial, and Political Bodies

50. The terms *administration* and *government* are capitalized when they are applicable to a particular government in power.

    The Administration announced a new oil and gas program; the Ford Administration
    *but* White House parties vary from one administration to another.

51. The names of international courts are capitalized.

    the International Court of Arbitration

52. The U.S. Supreme Court and the short forms *Supreme Court* and *Court* referring to it are capitalized.

    the Supreme Court of the United States; the United States Supreme Court; the U.S. Supreme Court; the Supreme Court; the Court

53. Official and full names of higher courts are capitalized. Short forms of official court names are often capitalized in legal documents but lowercased in general writing.

    the United States Court of Appeals for the Second Circuit; the Michigan Court of Appeals; the Virginia Supreme Court; the Court of Queen's Bench
    *but* the federal courts; the court of appeals ruled that . . . ; the state supreme court

54. Names of city and county courts are usually lowercased; in legal documents, however, they are frequently capitalized.

    the Lawton municipal court; the Owensville night court; police court; the county court; juvenile court

55. The single designation *court* when specifically applicable to a judge or a presiding officer is capitalized.

    It is the opinion of this Court that . . . ; the Court found that . . . ; this Honorable Court

56. In general writing, the term *federal* is capitalized only when it is an essential element of a name or title, when it identifies a specific government, or often when it refers to a particular principle of government.

    the Federal Bureau of Investigation; efforts made by the Federal Government; the Federal principle of government
    *but* federal court; federal district court; federal agents; federal troops
    In legal writing, however, the term is often capitalized.
    the Federal estate tax

57. Full names of legislative, deliberative, executive, and administrative bodies are capitalized as are the easily recognizable short forms of these names; however, nonspecific noun and adjective references to them are usually lowercased.

    United Nations Security Council *and* the Security Council *but* the council
    United States Congress *and* the Congress *but* congressional elections
    the Maryland Senate *but* the state senate
    Department of State *and* the State Department *and* State *but* the department

58. The term *national* is capitalized when it precedes a capitalized word or when it forms a part of a specific name or title; however, it is lowercased when used as a descriptive word or as a noun.

    National Security Council
    *but* in the interests of national security; the screening of foreign nationals

**59.** The names of political parties and their adherents are capitalized, but the word *party* may or may not be capitalized, depending on the writer's or organization's preference.

Democrats; Republicans; Liberals; Tories; the Democratic party *or* the Democratic Party

## Names of Organizations

**60.** Names of firms, corporations, schools, organizations, and other such groups are capitalized.

GTE Telenet Communications Corporation; American Judicature Society; The University of Wisconsin

**61.** Common nouns used descriptively and occurring after two or more organization names are lowercased.

American and Allegheny airlines; the ITT and IBM corporations

**62.** The words *company* and *corporation* are capitalized when they refer to one's own organization even when the full organization name is omitted; however, they are lowercased when they refer to another organization.

It is contrary to the policies of our Company.
*but* He works for a company in Delaware; Give me the name of your company.

**63.** Words such as *group, division, department, office,* or *agency* that designate corporate and organizational units are capitalized when used with a specific name.

The ABA Section on Criminal Justice is in charge of the project.
*but* She is a member of that section.

## Names of Persons

**64.** The names of persons are capitalized.

John W. Jones, Jr.

**65.** Words designating peoples and their languages are capitalized.

Canadians; Turks; Swedish; Welsh; Iroquois; Ibo

**66.** Derivatives of proper names are capitalized when used in their primary sense; consult a dictionary when in doubt of styling.

Keynesian economics; Manhattanite; Orwellian society; Shepardize a case
*but* manila envelope; pasteurize; bohemian tastes

## Numerical Designations

**67.** Monetary units typed in full (as in legal documents and on checks) are capitalized.

Your fee is Two Thousand Dollars ($2,000.00), payable upon receipt of . . . .

**68.** Nouns introducing a set number (as on a policy) are usually capitalized.

Index No. 123; Policy 123-4-X; Flight 409; Regulation 15; Stock Certificate X12345; Form 2E; Catalog No. 65432

**69.** Nouns used with numbers or letters to designate major reference headings (as in a literary work) are capitalized; however, minor reference headings and subheadings are typically lowercased.

Book II; Volume V; Division 4; Article IV; Figure 8; Appendix III; Plate 16; Part 1
*but* footnote 14; page 101; line 8; note 10; paragraph 6.1; item 16; question 21

## Particles and Prefixes

**70.** Particles forming initial elements of surnames may or may not be capitalized, depending on the styling of the individual name; however, if a name with a lowercase initial particle begins a sentence, the particle is capitalized.

E. I. du Pont de Nemours; D'Albert; De Camp; de Tocqueville; Du Maurier; Von Braun; von Kleist; The discoveries of de Bary *but* De Bary's discoveries are . . . .

**71.** Elements of hyphened compounds are capitalized in running texts if they are proper nouns or adjectives; consult a dictionary when in doubt of styling.

East-West trade; U.S.-U.S.S.R. détente; Arab-Israeli relations; Tay-Sachs disease
*but* a nineteenth-century notion; . . . said the idea was un-American.

**72.** Prefixes occurring with proper nouns or adjectives are capitalized if they are essential elements of the compounds or if they begin headings or sentences; they are lowercased in other instances.

Afro-American customs; nationalism of the Pan-Slavic variety; Pro-Soviet sentiments were voiced.
*but* The pro-Soviet faction objected.

## Personification

**73.** Personifications are capitalized.

The Chair recognized the delegate from Delaware.

## Pronouns

**74.** The pronoun *I* is capitalized.

He and I will attend the meeting.

**75.** Pronouns referring to the Deity are capitalized; *compare* RULE 38.

They insist on referring to the Supreme Being as *It,* not *He.*

## Scientific Terms

**76.** Names of geological eras, periods, epochs, and strata and of prehistoric ages are capitalized, but the generic nouns which they modify are lowercased except when those generic nouns appear <u>before</u> the names of eras, periods, epochs, strata, or divisions, in which case they are capitalized.

Silurian period; Pleistocene epoch; Neolithic age
*but* Age of Reptiles

**77.** Names of planets, constellations, asteroids, stars, and groups of stars are capitalized, but *sun, earth,* and *moon* are lowercased unless they are listed with other astronomic names.

Venus; Big Dipper; Sirius; Pleiades
*but* sun; earth; moon; unmanned space probes to the Moon and to Mars

**78.** Meteorological phenomena are lowercased.

northern lights; aurora borealis

**79.** Genera in binomial nomenclature in zoology and botany are capitalized; however, species names are lowercased.

the rhesus monkey *(Macaca mulatta)*; opium poppy *(Papaver somniferum)*; the brown rat *(Rattus norvegicus)*; a bacterium *(Clostridium botulinum)* causing botulism

**80.** New Latin names of classes, families, and all groups above genera in zoology and botany are capitalized, but their derivative nouns and adjectives are lowercased.

Gastropoda *but* gastropod; Thallophyta *but* thallophyte

**81.** Proper names forming essential elements of terms designating diseases, syndromes, signs, tests, and symptoms are capitalized.

Parkinson's disease; syndrome of Weber; German measles; Rorschach test
*but* mumps; measles; herpes simplex

**82.** Proprietary (i.e., brand and trade) names of drugs and other chemicals are capitalized, but their generic names are lowercased.

tranquilized with Thorazine; sprayed with Sevin
*but* recommended chlorpromazine; used a carbaryl spray.

**83.** Proper names forming essential elements of scientific laws, theorems, and principles are capitalized; however, the descriptive nouns *law, theorem, theory,* and the like are lowercased.

Boyle's law; the Pythagorean theorem; Planck's constant; Einstein's theory of relativity; the second law of thermodynamics

## Time Periods, Zones, and Divisions
**84.** Names of the seasons are not capitalized unless personified.

The book will be published in the spring.
*but* the gentle touch of Spring

**85.** Days of the week, months of the year, holidays, and holy days are capitalized.

Tuesday; July; Independence Day; Good Friday; Passover

**86.** Historic periods are capitalized, but latter-day periods are often lowercased.

Christian Era; Golden Age of Greece; Roaring Twenties; Augustan Age
*often* nuclear age; the atomic age; space age

**87.** Numerical designations of historic time periods are capitalized when they are essential elements of proper names; otherwise, they are lowercased.

the Roaring Twenties
*but* the seventeenth century; the twenties

**88.** Historical events and appellations referring to particular time periods or events in time are capitalized.

the Reign of Terror; the Cultural Revolution; Prohibition; the Great Depression; the New Frontier; the Third Reich; the Fourth Republic

**89.** Time zones are capitalized when abbreviated, but lowercased when written out.

EST *but* eastern standard time

## Titles of Persons
**90.** Corporate titles are capitalized when referring to specific individuals; when used in general or plural contexts, they are lowercased.

Mr. John M. Jones, Vice-president *and* Mr. Carl T. Yowell, General Counsel
*but* The firm's administrator called me. All supervisors will be here.

**91.** Specific corporate and governmental titles may be capitalized when they stand alone or when they are used in place of particular individuals' names.

The Executive Committee approved the Treasurer's report.

The Secretary of State gave a news conference. The Secretary said . . . .

The Judge will respond to your request when she returns to chambers.

**92.** All titles preceding names are capitalized.

President Roosevelt; Archbishop Makarios; Queen Elizabeth; Dr. Doe; Professor Doe; The Honorable John M. Doe; The Very Reverend John M. Doe; Chief Justice Warren Burger

**93.** Words of family relationship preceding names are capitalized.

Aunt Laura *but* His aunt, Mrs. W. P. Jones, is the beneficiary.

## Titles of Printed Matter

**94.** Words in the titles of printed matter are capitalized except for internal conjunctions, prepositions (especially those having less than four letters), and articles;

*Writing and Communicating in Business; A Manual of Style;* an essay entitled ''Truth Instead of Falsity''; ''Getting Around in the Big Apple''

also verb segments (as *be* in *to be*) in infinitives, and particles (as *off* in *take off*) in two-word verbs are capitalized in titles.

*What Is to Be Done?; Go Down, Moses*

**95.** Major sections (as a preface, an introduction, or an index) of books, long articles, or reports are capitalized when they are specifically referred to within the same material.

The Introduction explains the scope of this book.

**96.** The first word following a colon in a title is capitalized.

*Legal Writing: The Strategy of Persuasion*

''Federal Regulation: Roads to Reform''

**97.** The *the* before a title of a newspaper, magazine, or journal is capitalized if considered an essential element of the title; otherwise, it is lowercased;

*The Wall Street Journal but* the New York *Times*

and descriptive nouns following publication titles are also lowercased.

*Legal Economics* magazine

**98.** Constitutional amendments are capitalized when referred to by title or number, but are lowercased when used as general terms.

I took the Fifth Amendment *but* states ratifying constitutional amendments

**99.** Formal titles of accords, pacts, plans, policies, treaties, legislation, constitutions, and similar documents are capitalized; the words *act* and *law* are capitalized only in the titles of bills that have become law.

The Geneva Accords; the Controlled Substance Act of 1970; the first Five Year Plan; New Economic Policy; Treaty of Versailles; the North Carolina Constitution

*but* gun-control legislation; various new economic policies; the state constitution; the Toxic Substances Control bill

**Trademarks**

**100.** Brand names, trademarks, and service marks are capitalized.

the IBM Selectric; Xerox; Wite-Out correction fluid; Air Express; Thermo-Fax; Laundromat; Touch-Tone

**Transport**

**101.** The names of ships, airplanes, and often spacecraft are capitalized.

M. V. *West Star;* Lindbergh's *Spirit of St. Louis; Apollo 13*

# 9.4

## ITALICIZATION

The following are usually italicized in print and underlined in typescript or manuscript:

1. **Bibliographical signals** (as *see also, infra, id., cf., contra*) are usually italicized in general writing as well as in legal citations.

   *Continued on p. 34; See* the *Glanton* case, *supra.*

2. **Case titles in legal citations,** both in full and shortened form, are italicized; however, when the person involved rather than the case itself is being discussed, the reference is typed in roman letters without underlining.

   *Jones* v. *Massachusetts;* the *Jones* case; *In re Jones; Smith et al.* v. *Jones; Jones*
   *but* the Jones trial and conviction; the XYZ antitrust suit

3. **Emphasis** may be obtained by italicizing a word in a running text.

   The typist should understand beforehand *exactly* how the writer wants the document styled.

4. **Foreign words and phrases** that have not been naturalized in English are italicized. There may be doubt as to whether a term has been naturalized; if the attorney has no preference, one should follow the guidance of a reputable dictionary with consistency.

   *aere perennius; sans peur et sans reproche; ich dien*
   *but* quid pro quo; enfant terrible; a priori; ex officio; ad hoc; bona fide; entente

   Italics are frequently used in legal documents to set off foreign words and phrases; however, there is a trend for law offices to write such terms in roman, especially in running texts of correspondence and similar material.

   *legal instrument*
   IT IS, THEREFORE, ADJUDGED, ORDERED, and DECREED that the complainant, John T. Keys, Jr., be and hereby is divorced *a vinculo matrimonii* from the defendant, Alice Royce Keys.

   *correspondence*
   I am pleased to send you a certified copy of the Decree A Vinculo Matrimonii entered in your husband's divorce suit on June 3, 19--, by the Honorable William A. Lyons, Jr.

   Latin phrases commonly used in legal writing (*e.g.,* duces tecum, sui generis, nolo contendere) are thought by many to have become so incorporated in the language that they should not be italicized.

5. **Letters** are often italicized when used as run-in enumerations, especially in printed matter, and when used to identify illustrations.

   . . . provided examples of *(a)* typing *(b)* transcribing *(c)* formatting *(d)* graphics . . . ; Figure *B*

6. **Names** of ships and airplanes and often spacecraft are italicized.

   M. V. *West Star;* Lindbergh's *Spirit of St. Louis; Apollo 13*

7. **New Latin scientific names** of genera, species, subspecies, and varieties (but not groups of higher rank such as phyla, classes, or orders or derivatives of any of these) in botanical and zoological names are italicized.

   a wild tobacco *(Nicotiana glauca);* the bacterium *Clostridium botulinum* causing botulism; the rhesus monkey *(Macaca mulatta);* the spirochete *Treponema pallidum*
   but
   The lion *(Felis leo)* belongs to the order Carnivora or the class Mammalia.
   nematodes; felid; a streptococcus; an amoeba

8. **Titles** of books, published theses, magazines, newspapers, plays, movies (but not radio or TV programs), works of art, and long musical compositions (but not symphonies) are italicized.

   T. S. Eliot's *The Waste Land; United States Code Annotated; Words and Phrases; The Wall Street Journal;* Shakespeare's *Othello;* the movie *Gone With the Wind;* Gainsborough's *Blue Boy;* Mozart's *Don Giovanni*

   NOTE 1: The geographic location of a newspaper is italicized only if the location is part of the actual masthead title.

   the [Helena, Montana] *Independent-Record;* the Helena *Independent-Record*

   NOTE 2: Plurals of such italicized titles have roman-type inflectional endings.

   . . . had two *Michigan Law Review*s under his arm.

   Chapter titles and titles of essays, short stories, short poems, and unpublished works are not italicized but are enclosed by quotation marks.

   CBS's "Sixty Minutes"; the Ninth Symphony; "Strangers in the Night"; Pushkin's "Queen of Spades"; Robert Frost's "Dust of Snow"; his unpublished dissertation "Problems in Cost Accounting Procedures"

   Titles of articles in periodicals and encyclopedias (but not the names of the periodicals) are frequently italicized when they appear in legal citations in briefs; when a brief refers to a periodical in the running text, however, the full name of the periodical is italicized.

   Turley, *A Wife's Right to Support Payments in Texas,* 16 So.Tex.L.J. 1 (1974)
   88 C.J.S. *Trial* § 192 (1955)

9. **Words, letters, and figures** when referred to as words, letters, or figures are italicized.

   The word *stationery* meaning "paper" is often misspelled.
   The *g* key on my typewriter sticks.

10. **Terms used between citations** that indicate the history of a case may be italicized.

    *Baity* v. *State,* 455 S.W.2d 305, *cert. denied* . . . .
    *United States* v. *Lee Wilson & Co.,* D.C. Ark. 1914, 214 F. 630, *affirmed* 227 F. 827

# 9.5

## NUMERALS

In modern business writing, most numerals—and especially exact numbers above *ten*—are expressed in figures. However, general usage allows all numbers below 100 to be styled as words, and the formal style of much legal writing encourages the spelling out of such numbers. If material is being prepared for publication (as in a professional journal), the writer and the typist should familiarize themselves with the particular style guidelines of the publication to which the manuscript will be submitted. The most important suggestion that can be offered is this: one should be consistent. For example, if one decides to use a figure in expressing a monetary unit, one should not use a written-out numerical designation in expressing a similar monetary unit within the same text. The office style manual may describe its policy on the styling of numbers in correspondence and in legal documents such as contracts of sale. Since usage is divided on some points, the following alphabetically arranged guidelines sometimes show alternative stylings.

### NUMERALS

1. **Ages** are expressed in figures.

   her 6-month-old son; the 11-day-old infant; a man 65 years old

2. **Beginning of a sentence** Numbers that begin a sentence are written out.

   Thirty-two attorneys attended the meeting.
   Fourteen judges heard 72 cases, 11 of which were appealed.

3. **Compounds** When two numbers comprise one item or unit, one of the numbers (usually the first) should be expressed in words, and the other (usually the second) should be expressed in figures; if, however, the second number is the shorter, it may be expressed in words instead.

   two 7-drawer files *but* 20 ten-drawer files

4. **Compounds adjacent to other figures** Two sets of figures (except for those in monetary units) should not be typed in direct succession in a text unless they comprise a series; *compare* MONETARY UNITS; SERIES

   By 1990, one hundred shares of stock will be . . . .
   *but not* By 1990, 100 shares of stock will be . . . .

5. **Date lines** Figures are used to express days and years in business-letter date lines; ordinals should not be used.

   January 1, 19-- *not* January 1st, 19--

6. **Enumerations** Run-in and vertical enumerations are often numbered.

   felt that she should (1) accept more responsibility, (2) increase her overall production, (3) maintain security precautions, (4) . . . .
   The secretary's responsibilities include:
   1. Taking dictation
   2. Transcribing dictated matter
   3. Typing correspondence
   4. Routing the mail

7. **Exact amounts** Exact amounts are usually expressed in figures unless they begin sentences, in which case they are expressed in words.

Of the 50 states, 49 ratified the amendment.
Forty-nine of the 50 states ratified the amendment.

8. **Figures** Figures are usually used to indicate policy, contract, docket, section, and page numbers; street, apartment, room, or suite numbers; sizes, weights, and measures; shares, mixed amounts, percentages, and mixed fractions.

Policy No. 123-X; page 3; p. 3; section 10; 123 Smith Blvd.; Room 7; Apt. 2; Suite 4; size 7; 9′ × 12′; 14,000 shares; 56.890; 90% or 90 percent; case 14; 17½

9. **Footnotes** Unspaced superscript numerals follow footnoted text material including its punctuation; superscript numerals followed by one space introduce the footnotes themselves.

. . . is a prime factor in successful management."[2]
[2] Ibid., p. 300.

10. **Four-digit numbers** A number of four or more digits has each set of three digits separated by a comma except in set combinations such as policy, contract, docket, check, street, room, or page numbers, which are unpunctuated.

15,000 keystrokes; assets of $12,500; a population of 1,500,000; 4,600 words
*but* check 34567; page 4589; the year 1980; Room 6000; Policy No. 3344

11. **Fractions** Common fractions are expressed in words in running texts. Fractions occurring with whole numbers in running texts are expressed either in words or in figures.

About three fourths of the budget has been used.
The book weighs three and one-half pounds. *or* The book weighs 3½ pounds.

NOTE: When some figure fractions in a text or table are not included on the keyboard, all fractions should be made up. Do not mix made-up and keyboard fractions.

1 1/2″ × 1 1/8″ *not* 1½″ × 1 1/8″

12. **Inclusive numbers** (as of dates or pages) should be expressed in full.

1977–1978 *not* 1977–78
pp. 140–149 *not* pp. 140–49

13. **Measures and weights** may be styled as figure + abbreviated unit combinations (as in tables); however, if the unit of measure or weight is typed out in full, the number is expressed in words.

15 cu ft *or* 15 cu.ft. *but* fifteen cubic feet

14. **Monetary units** Even-dollar amounts in all legal writing contain a decimal point plus two ciphers.

$5,000.00; $837.00

In general correspondence, monetary units containing both mixed and even-dollar amounts and typed in series should contain: decimal point + 2 ciphers for the even-dollar amounts. In addition, the $ should be repeated before each unit.

The price of the book rose from $7.95 in 1970 to $8.00 in 1971 and to $8.50 in 1972.
*but* The bids were $80, $100, and $300; $10–$20

Units of less than one dollar are usually typed in running texts as: figure + *cents* (or *¢*).

The pencil costs 15 cents. *or* The pencil costs 15¢.

---

**15. No.** or **#** should be avoided when a descriptive word appears before a figure, except for catalog, contract, or real estate lot numbers, which may be so labeled.

subdivision C-4; page 12
*but* Stock No. 1234; Land Lot No. 265

---

**16. Ordinals** are usually expressed in words in running texts; however, ordinals higher than *tenth* may be expressed in figure and abbreviation combinations unless they begin a sentence. They may also be expressed in figure and abbreviation combinations in some street addresses; *see also page* 285.

the twentieth century; the third time; the fifteenth applicant today *or* the 15th applicant today
Twelfth-grade students were dismissed early.
*but* 167 East 93rd (*or* 93d) Street

---

**17. Parenthetical figures** In legal documents, monetary units and other important numerals have traditionally been expressed in words followed by the Arabic numerals in parentheses. The trend today, however, is to avoid repetition by using only figures except when the numeral is legally significant, as in a bequest, a demand for judgment (but not a list of damages), a contractual amount to be paid (but not installment payments), and papers that transfer title.

SIX HUNDRED EIGHTY and 35/100 DOLLARS ($680.35) to be paid within TEN (10) days
the east forty (40) feet of Lot Seven (7) in Block Eleven (11) of . . . .
I give and bequeath . . . Seven Hundred Fifty Dollars ($750.00) to MILLICENT JONES . . . .
*but also* Lot No. 14 in Block No. 10

Receipt is hereby acknowledged by Landlord of the sum of $400.00 paid on account of the first month's rent; balance due $1600.00.

NOTE: The parenthetical figure <u>follows</u> the word *Dollars*.

Six Hundred Dollars ($600.00) *not* Six Hundred ($600.00) Dollars

---

**18. Percentages** are usually styled in running text as: figure + *percent,* but sometimes as figure + %, especially when decimals are involved. If a percentage begins a sentence, the number is written out, followed by *percent.*

. . . reported 55 percent of the research complete . . . .
. . . 48.5% of those interviewed. . . .
Fifty-five percent of the research is complete.

---

**19. Roman numerals** (as those used in outlines) should be aligned to the right for uniformity in the appearance of the typescript that follows the numerals. Horizontal strokes should not be added to the numerals I–X, since this multiplies the numbers by 1,000.

V.
VI.
VII.
VIII.
IX.
X.

20. **Round numbers** and approximations are usually expressed in words, although some writers prefer to express them in figures for added emphasis. Numbers over one million are often expressed in figures + words to save keystrokes and to facilitate the reader's interpretation; *compare* EXACT AMOUNTS.

> about thirty to fifty applicants *or for added emphasis* processed more than 3,000 citations
> a $10 million profit *or* a 10 million-dollar profit

21. **Series** Figures are usually used to express a series of numbers in a sentence if one of the numbers is greater than ten, is a mixed fraction, or contains a decimal fraction.

> We need 4 desks, 3 chairs, and 14 typewriters.
> They waited 3, 12, and 2½ hours, respectively.
> The percentage of deaths increased from 3.5% in 1970 to 5% in 1979.

22. **Short numbers** Numbers expressible in one or two short words may be written in words.

> . . . interviewed two new applicants.
> *but*
> . . . received 24 dozen job applications.

23. **Time** Time of day is expressed in words when it is followed by the contraction *o'clock* or when *o'clock* is understood; when time is followed by the abbreviations *a.m.* or *p.m.,* it is expressed in figures.

> He left for the day at four o'clock.
> He left for the day at four.
> We shall arrive at a quarter to ten.
> *but*
> He left for the day at 4:30 p.m.
> We shall arrive at 9:45 a.m.

The extra ciphers that follow even hours may be omitted; however, they are used for consistency when paired with non-even times.

> 10 a.m. to 2 p.m. *but* 10:00 a.m. to 2:30 p.m.

# 9.6

## PUNCTUATION

The English writing system uses punctuation marks to separate groups of words for meaning and emphasis; to convey an idea of the variations of pitch, volume, pauses, and intonation of speech; and to help avoid contextual ambiguity. Punctuation for the latter purpose is especially important in legal writing. The interpretation of a document or execution of a contract may depend upon its punctuation, and a misplaced comma has been known to result in extended litigation. Punctuation marks should be used sparingly: overpunctuating often needlessly complicates a passage and also increases keystrokes. English punctuation marks, together with general rules and examples of their use, follow in alphabetical order.

# ❾ APOSTROPHE

**1.** indicates the possessive case of singular and plural nouns and indefinite pronouns, as well as of surname and terminal title combinations

Senator Ceccacci's office; the attorney's client; the attorneys' clients; anyone's guess; everyone's questions; his father-in-law's car; their father-in-laws' cars; John Burns' *or* Burns's insurance policy; the Burnses' insurance policy; a witness' *or* witness's testimony; the two witnesses' testimony; John K. Walker Jr.'s house; the John K. Walker Jrs.' house

NOTE: The use of an apostrophe + *s* with words ending in /s/ or /z/ sounds usually depends on whether a pronounceable final syllable is thus formed: if the syllable is pronounced, the apostrophe + *s* is usually used; if no final pronounceable syllable is formed, the apostrophe is retained but an *s* is usually not appended to the word.

Mr. Gomez's store; Knox's products; the class's opinion
*but* Degas' paintings; Moses' laws; for righteousness' sake

**2.** indicates joint possession when appended to the last noun in a sequence

Kepler and Clark's law firm; Doyle Dane Bernbach's advertisement

**3.** indicates individual possession when appended to each noun in a sequence

Kepler's and Clark's respective clients; John's, Bill's, and Tim's boats; Benton & Bowles' and Doyle Dane Bernbach's advertisements

**4.** indicates possession when appended to the final element of a compound construction

Norfolk, Virginia's newest office supply store; XYZ Corporation's order

**5.** indicates understood possession

The book is at your bookseller's.

**6.** marks omissions in contractions

isn't; you're; o'clock; aff'g; ass'n; rev'd

**7.** marks omissions of numerals

the class of '67

**8.** often forms plurals of letters, figures, or words especially when they are referred to as letters, figures, or words

His *1*'s and *7*'s looked alike; She has trouble pronouncing her *the*'s; five YF-16's; the 1970's
*also* the 1970s *and also* two CPAs and four CLAs

**9.** is often used with *s* in expressions of time, measurement, and money but is not used with a plural noun used as a modifier

a dollar's worth; a year's subscription; ten cents' worth; six weeks' vacation; two years' probation
*but* earnings statement; systems analyst

**10.** is used with *s* before a gerund or gerund phrase

She objected to the editor's changing her material.

# ✳ ASTERISK

**1.** Three spaced asterisks are used in many law offices to denote an omission in the body of excerpted material. *See also* ELLIPSIS, p. 225.

The legislature seems to have abrogated this rule. * * * Such a procedure may be expected to conserve judicial resources.

**2.** Three spaced and centered asterisks indicate omission of one or more paragraphs of text.

* * *

# [ ] BRACKETS

**1.** set off extraneous data (as editorial comments especially within quoted material)

. . . said that "two [sic] witnesses are prepared to testify; namely, Jonathan D. Simpson, Marietta A. Lyons, and Kenneth Richardson."

The correspondence states that "this amount [$2,000,000.00] together with costs and expenses related to the litigation had been provided in 1979 as a charge to corporate operations for the years involved [1976 through 1978]."

**2.** function as parentheses within parentheses

Local regulation (City Ordinance 46 [§ 5]) prohibits it.

# ● COLON

**1.** introduces a clause or phrase that explains, restates, illustrates, or amplifies what has gone before

The sentence was poorly constructed: it lacked both unity and coherence.

Harrison T. Brown shall be awarded the complete custody and control of the infant children of the parties: John Thomas Brown and Anne Marie Brown shall be in the custody of the plaintiff, subject to reasonable rights of visitation by the defendant to see the children once a week.

**2.** directs attention to an appositive

He has only one grandchild: his daughter's son.

**3.** introduces a series

He has had trial experience on three judicial levels: county, state, and federal.

The plaintiffs allege:
1.
2. etc.

The Petitioners show to this Court:
1.
2. etc.

**4.** introduces lengthy quoted matter set off from a running text by blocked indentation but not by quotation marks

I quote from page 2 of the letter:

**5.** separates elements in set formulas such as those expressing ratios, time, volume and page references, biblical citations, and place and publisher

a ratio of 3:5; 8:30 a.m.; *Words and Phrases* 12:261; John 4:10; Springfield, MA: G. & C. Merriam Company

**6.** separates titles and subtitles (as of books)

*Natural Law: An Introduction to Legal Philosophy*

**7.** punctuates the salutation in a business letter featuring the mixed punctuation pattern

Gentlemen:    Dear Bob:    Dear Mr. Smith:

**8.** punctuates memorandum headings and some subject lines in business correspondence

TO:    THROUGH:    VIA:    SUBJECT:    REFERENCE:    In Re:

**9.** separates writer/dictator/typist initials in the identification lines of business letters

FCM:hg

**10.** separates carbon copy or blind carbon copy abbreviations from the initials or names of copy recipients in business letters

cc: RWP
 JES
bcc: MWK
 FCM

# **,** COMMA

**1.** separates main clauses joined by coordinating conjunctions (such as *and, but, for, nor, or,* and sometimes *so* and *yet*) and very short clauses not so joined

Directors are elected annually by shareholders, and corporate officers are appointed or elected by the directors to carry out their policies.
The defendant needed legal representation, so he asked for an attorney.
The witness knew, she was there, she saw it happen.

NOTE 1: Two brief and tightly connected clauses joined by a coordinating conjunction may be unpunctuated.
We have denied the charges and we have prepared our defense.

NOTE 2: Two predicates governed by a single subject and joined by a coordinating conjunction are usually unpunctuated.
The Court will take the matter under advisement and will announce its decision later.

**2.** sets off an adverbial clause that precedes a main clause

Because the defendant needed legal representation, he asked for an attorney.
Although the airport was shut down for an hour, I was still able to fly home that night.

**3.** sets off an introductory phrase (as a participial, infinitive, or prepositional phrase) that precedes a main clause

Having made that decision, he turned to other matters.
To understand this situation fully, you have to be familiar with the background.
On the following Monday, ten indictments were handed down.
IN WITNESS WHEREOF, . . . .

NOTE: If a phrase or a noun clause is the subject of the sentence, it is unpunctuated.

To have followed your plan would have been dishonest.
Whatever is worth doing is worth doing well.

**4.** sets off from the rest of a sentence interrupting transitional words and expressions (such as *on the contrary, on the other hand*), conjunctive adverbs (such as *consequently, furthermore, however*), and expressions that introduce an illustration or example (such as *namely, for example*)

The second charge against you is, on the other hand, much more serious.
It must be remembered, however, that the office closes at four o'clock.
I believe in ethics, i.e., professional ethics.

**5.** often sets off contrasting and opposing expressions within sentences

I note that he has changed his style, not his ethics.
The cost is not $65.00, but $56.65.
The procedure, not the law, has changed.

NOTE: When *and, or, either . . . or,* or *neither . . . nor* join items in a pair or in a series, the series is internally unpunctuated.

The cost is either $65.00 or $56.65.
He has changed neither his style nor his ethics nor his attitude.

**6.** separates words, phrases, or clauses in series joined at the end by a coordinating conjunction

The Will stipulates that his estate is to be divided equally among his wife, his sons, and his daughters.
We expect you to greet clients, take dictation, transcribe dictated material, and do research.
Ms. Smith, Mr. Inge, or Mrs. Williams will advise you.

NOTE: The final comma before the conjunction in a series is optional but is usually retained in legal and other formal writing in order to clarify meaning. The following sentence, for example, is ambiguous without the final comma.

Your duties will include greeting clients, taking dictation, transcribing dictated material and research.

**7.** separates coordinate adjectives and phrases modifying the same word (i.e., terms that share an equal relationship to the noun they modify); *see also* pages 235–236

thorough, careful pretrial preparation; expensive, completely handcrafted luggage

NOTE: Two or more tightly connected adjectives in series each of which modifies the same word or a whole phrase may not require punctuation; *see* page 236.

a new 90-story concrete and glass building; a civil antitrust complaint; three unfinished briefs

8. sets off from the rest of a sentence parenthetic elements (as nonrestrictive modifiers and nonrestrictive appositives)

This man, who is now being represented by a public defender, will appear in court tomorrow.
One of my associates, Mr. Ogden, delivered the opening arguments.
I, Morgan Harrison, as Secretary of the Company, do hereby certify that . . . .
Jacob J. Jacobson, being sworn, deposes and says . . . .

NOTE: The comma does not set off restrictive or essential modifiers or appositives required to give a sentence or a phrase meaning.

the late astronaut Gus Grissom
The defendant who was convicted yesterday will be sentenced next week.

9. introduces a run-in direct quotation, terminates a run-in direct quotation that is neither a question nor an exclamation, and encloses segments of a split quotation

Jim said, "I am leaving."
"I am leaving," Jim said.
"I am leaving," Jim said with determination, "even if you want me to stay."

10. sets off words in direct address, absolute phrases, and mild interjections

We would like to discuss the matter with you in person, Mr. Baker.
I fear the encounter, his temper being what it is.
Ah, that's my idea of a sensible man.
Your Honor, the Defense rests.

11. separates elements of bibliographical entries and legal citations

*United States* v. *O'Donnell,* Cal. 1938, 58 S.Ct. 708, 303 U.S. 501, 82 L.Ed. 980

12. may follow the introductory words and phrases conventionally used in legal documents

Please Take Notice, That . . . .
ORDERED, That . . . .
GREETING: Know Ye, that . . . .

13. separates a tag question from the rest of a sentence

It's been a fine convention, hasn't it?

14. indicates the omission of a word or words, and especially a word or words used earlier in a sentence

Common stocks are favored by some investors; bonds, by others.
Some attorneys hold LLBs; others, JDs.

15. is used to avoid ambiguity and also to emphasize a particular phrase

To Mary, Jane was someone special.
The more accessories on a car, the higher the price.

16. groups numerals into units of three in separating thousands, millions, etc.; it is generally not used with numbers of four or more digits in set combinations; *see also* NUMERALS, RULE 8

Smithville, pop. 100,000; $2,000.00; 7,206 miles away
*but* 3600 rpm; the year 1980; page 1411; 11274 Smith Street; Room 3000

**17.** punctuates the date line of a business letter, an informal letter, and the expression of dates in running texts

January 2, 19--
On January 2, 19--, this Court issued its opinion.
In June, 19--, [*or* In June 19--,] we met with them several times.

**18.** follows a personal-letter salutation

Dear Bob,

**19.** follows the complimentary close of a business letter or of an informal letter featuring the mixed punctuation pattern

Very truly yours,
Best regards,

**20.** separates names from corporate and professional titles in envelope address blocks, inside addresses, and signature blocks when the title appears on the same line as the name

Mr. John P. Dow, General Counsel          Very truly yours,
SWC Corporation
Smithville, ST 56789                      Lee H. Cobb, Editor
                                          General Reference Books

**21.** may separate elements within some official corporate names

Leedy Manufacturing Co., Inc.; Saxon Business Products, Inc.

**22.** punctuates an inverted name

Smith, John W.

**23.** separates a surname from a following academic, honorary, religious, governmental, or military title

John W. Smith, MD; John W. Smith, Esq.; The Reverend John W. Smith, SJ; General John W. Smith, USA

**24.** sets off geographical names (as that of a state or county from that of a city), items in dates, and addresses from the rest of a running text; also separates the name of a city and the name or abbreviation of a state (but not the ZIP Code) in an inside address

Shreveport, Louisiana, is the site of a large air base.
On December 9, 1971, the victim filed a complaint.
Mail your check to: XYZ Corporation, 1234 Smith Boulevard, Smithville, ST 56789.

■■■■■■ **DASH**

**1.** usually marks an abrupt change or break in the continuity of a sentence

The Grand Jury testimony—it is very sensitive testimony—has not yet been made public.

**2.** is sometimes used in place of other punctuation (as the comma) when special emphasis is required

Clean your desk—now!

Our arguments—and especially the one presented by our partner John Smith—impressed the jury.

**3.** introduces a summary statement that follows a series of words or phrases

*Self-destruction, suicide,* and *death by his own hand*—these are synonyms defined in *Words and Phrases* as "the voluntary destruction of one's self."

**4.** often precedes the attribution of a quotation

The next question was . . . how many administrative secretaries to a zone.
—Samuel T. Rose

**5.** may occur inside quotation marks if considered part of the quoted matter

"I'm just not going to—" and then he broke off very abruptly.

**6.** may be used with the exclamation point or the question mark

The faces of the crash victims—how bloody!—were shown on TV.
Your question—was it on our proposed merger?—just can't be answered.

● ● ●   **ELLIPSIS or SUSPENSION POINTS**   ● ● ● ●

**1.** indicates by three spaced periods the omission of one or more words within a quoted passage

"To crack down on these practices, laws are being urged . . . which would permit creditors either to repossess their goods or to sue for payment of the debt—but not both."
—Sylvia Porter

**2.** indicates by four spaced periods (the first of which represents a period) the omission of one or more sentences within a quoted passage or the omission of a word or words at the end of a sentence

"That things always collapse into the *status quo ante* three weeks after a drive is over, everybody knows and apparently expects. . . . And yet many managements fail to draw the obvious conclusion. . . ."
—Peter F. Drucker

**3.** indicates halting speech or an unfinished sentence in dialogue

"I'd like to . . . that is . . . if you don't mind. . . ." He faltered and then stopped speaking.

**4.** may be used as leaders (as in tables of contents) when spaced and extended for some length across a page

Issues Presented . . . . . . . . . . . . . . . . . . . . . . . . . . . . . . . . . . . . . . . . . . . . . . . . . . . . . Page  1
Statute and Regulations Considered . . . . . . . . . . . . . . . . . . . . . . . . . . . . . . . . . . . . . Page 10

NOTE: leaders should be in perfect alignment vertically and should end precisely at the same point.

● **EXCLAMATION POINT**

**1.** ends an emphatic phrase or sentence

Do this—now!

**2.** terminates an emphatic interjection

Encore!

## ■ HYPHEN

**1.** marks division at the end of a line concluding with a syllable of a word that is to be carried over to the next line; *see* page 233

es-           virol-
crow        ogy

NOTE: Many law offices recommend that no hyphens occur at the ends of lines in legal papers. An exception is the frequent practice of preventing alteration or insertion of new material in an important document by hyphenating the last word on a page and carrying it over to the top of the continuation sheet.

**2.** is used between some prefix and root combinations, such as prefix + proper name;

pro-Supreme Court; trans-Atlantic perspective

some prefixes ending with vowels + root;

re-ink *but* reissue

sometimes prefix + word beginning often with the same vowel;

co-opted *but* cooperate

stressed prefix + root word, especially when this combination is similar to a different word

re-treat a patient *but* retreat from an argument

**3.** is used in some compounds, especially those containing prepositions; consult a dictionary when in doubt of styling

president-elect; attorney-at-law; air-conditioned his house
*but* vice admiral; bought an air conditioner

**4.** is often used between elements of a compound modifier in attributive position in order to avoid ambiguity

a four-judge panel *but* a panel with four judges
a large-scale practice *but* practicing on a large scale

**5.** suspends the first part of a hyphened compound when joined with another hyphened compound in attributive position

an eight- to ten-hour day *but* a working day of eight to ten hours

**6.** is used in expressing written-out numbers between 21 and 99

forty-one; one hundred twenty-eight

NOTE: In some documents and proclamations, *and* is used after *hundred* in dates.

In the year one thousand nine hundred and sixty-three . . . .

**7.** is used between the numerator and the denominator in writing out fractions especially when they are used as modifiers; however, fractions used as nouns are usually styled as open compounds

a two-thirds majority of the stockholders
*but* used two thirds of the stationery

**8.** serves as an arbitrary equivalent of the phrase "(up) to and including" when used between numbers and dates

pages 40–98; the decade 1960–1970

**9.** is used in the compounding of two or more capitalized names but is not used when a single capitalized name is in attributive position

caught a New York-Chicago flight; U.S.-U.S.S.R. détente
*but* a New York garbage strike; Middle East exports

 **PARENTHESES**

**1.** set off parenthetic, supplementary, or explanatory material when the interruption is more marked than that usually indicated by commas and when the inclusion of such material does not essentially alter the meaning of the sentence; *see also* CAPITALIZATION, RULE 8

Labor-Management Relations (Taft-Hartley) Act
The chart (see Fig. 4) explains the situation.
We appreciate your nice remarks (especially your reference to our new assistant).

**2.** enclose Arabic numerals confirming a typed-out number in a general text or in a legal document

The purchasers agree that no later than ten (10) days prior to . . . .
The fee for your services is Two Thousand Dollars ($2,000.00), payable . . . .

**3.** may enclose numbers or letters separating and heading individual elements or items in a run-in series

We must set forth (1) our long-term goals, (2) our immediate objectives, and (3) the means at our disposal.

**4.** enclose abbreviations synonymous with typed-out forms and occurring after those forms, or may enclose the typed-out forms occurring after the abbreviations

a ruling by the Federal Communications Commission (FCC)
the manufacture and disposal of PVC (polyvinyl chloride)

**5.** indicate alternate terms and omissions (as in form letters)

Please sign the enclosed form(s) and return . . . .
On (date) we mailed you . . . .

**6.** have specialized uses in legal citations, where they enclose dates, editorial information about books and other publications, and the names of courts of jurisdiction and certain explanatory information in citations to cases

*Hoffa* v. *United States,* 385 U.S. 293, 87 S. Ct. 408 (1966)
N.D. Century Code, Tit. 49, Public Utilities, as amended (1971 Supp.)
PROSSER, HANDBOOK OF THE LAW OF TORTS (3d ed. 1963)
*Hawkins* v. *Cohen,* 408 S.W.2d 808 (Tex. Civ. App. — Houston 1966, writ ref'd n.r.e.)

7. are used as follows with other punctuation:

**a.** If the parenthetic expression is an independent sentence standing alone at the end of another sentence, its first word is capitalized and a period is typed <u>inside</u> the last parenthesis.

The discussion was held in the boardroom. (The results are still confidential.)

**b.** Parenthetic material within a sentence may be internally punctuated by a question mark, a period after an abbreviation only, an exclamation point, or a set of quotation marks.

Years ago, someone (who?) told me . . . .
The conference was held in Vancouver (that's in B.C.).
Sales this year have been better (knock on wood!), but . . . .
He was depressed ("I must resign") and refused to promise anything.

**c.** No punctuation mark should be placed directly before parenthetic material in a sentence; if a break is required, the punctuation should be placed <u>after</u> the final parenthesis.

I'll get back to you tomorrow (Monday), when I have more details.

## ● PERIOD

1. terminates sentences or sentence fragments that are neither interrogative nor exclamatory

Take dictation.  She took dictation.  She asked whether dictation was necessary.

2. often terminates polite requests especially in business correspondence

Will you please sign the enclosed releases and return them as soon as possible.

3. sometimes is used instead of a comma or semicolon to terminate long dependent clauses in legal documents, especially when the clauses appear as individual paragraphs

WHEREAS, the above entitled action was commenced on July 23, 19--, by service of the summons and complaint upon you.
WHEREAS, the time to appear and answer the summons and complaint herein has expired, and
WHEREAS, you have failed to appear and answer the summons and complaint herein within the time required by law.
YOU ARE HEREBY NOTIFIED THAT . . . .

4. punctuates some abbreviations, as

f.o.b., a.k.a., and Wis. 2d; *also*

**a.** courtesy titles and honorifics backed by a strong tradition of punctuation

Esq.; LL.B (*or* LLB); Mr.; Mrs.; Ms.; Dr.; Prof.; Rev.; Hon.; Jr.; Sr.; Ph.D.; Litt.D.

**b.** some abbreviations (as of measure) especially when absence of punctuation could cause misreading

98.6°F. *also* 98.6°F; p. 20; Paper, 521 ff.; 18 in.; No. 2 pencils; fig. 15

**c.** abbreviations of Latin words and phrases commonly used in texts

etc.; i.e.; e.g.; c. *or* ca. *or* circ.; q.v.; viz.

**d.** abbreviations of Latin phrases used in footnotes and citations

Ibid.; Op. cit.; Loc. cit.; Id.; sub nom.

**e.** compass points (NOTE: Punctuation styling varies.)

1400 Sixteenth Street, N.W. *or* 1400 Sixteenth Street, NW. *or* 1400 Sixteenth Street, NW

**f.** some geographical-name abbreviations (NOTE: Punctuation styling varies.)

U.S.-U.S.S.R. détente *or* US-USSR détente
*but not* U.S.-USSR détente *and not* US-U.S.S.R. détente

**g.** abbreviated elements of some official corporate names

Dowden, Hutchinson & Ross, Inc.

---

**5.** punctuates monetary units and decimal amounts

$435.35; 0.567; 16.6 feet

---

**6.** is used with an individual's initials

Mr. W. A. Morton

---

**7.** is used after Roman numerals in enumerations and outlines but not with Roman numerals used as part of a title

I. Objectives *but* John D. Harper III

---

**8.** is often used after Arabic numerals in enumerations whose numerals stand alone

Required skills are:
1. Shorthand
2. Typing
3. Transcription

---

# ? QUESTION MARK

**1.** terminates a direct question

Who witnessed the Will? "Who witnessed the Will?" he asked.

---

**2.** punctuates each element of an interrogative series that is neither numbered nor lettered; however, only one such mark punctuates a numbered or lettered interrogative series

Can you give us a reasonable forecast? back up your predictions? compare them with last-quarter earnings?

*but*

Can you (1) give us a reasonable forecast (2) back up your predictions (3) supply enough figures (4) compare them with last-quarter earnings?

---

**3.** indicates the writer's ignorance or uncertainty

John Jones, the President (?) of that company, said . . . .

---

# " " QUOTATION MARKS, DOUBLE

**1.** enclose direct quotations in conventional usage

The witness said, "I saw the accident."
"I saw the accident," he said.
"I saw the accident," he said, "and I heard the impact."
*but* He said that he saw the accident.

**2.** enclose fragments of quoted matter when reproduced exactly

The agreement makes it quite clear that he "will be paid only upon receipt of an acceptable manuscript."

**3.** enclose words or phrases borrowed from others, words used in a special way, and often a word of marked informality when it is introduced into formal writing

We will indeed cross-examine their "expert" witness.

If the stock is held by a small number of people, the corporation is referred to as "closed" or "privately held."

He was arrested for smuggling "smack."

**4.** enclose titles of legal documents introduced by the word *entitled* as well as titles of reports, catalogs, short poems, short stories, articles, lectures, chapters of books, songs, short musical compositions, and radio and TV programs; *compare* ITALICIZATION, RULE 9

the document entitled "Indenture of Trust"; the report "Paralegal Education in the Seventies"; the catalog "Office Copying Equipment"; Robert Frost's "Dust of Snow"; Pushkin's "Queen of Spades"; the article "Malpractice Claims Mount in Plastic Surgery"; the pamphlet "Office Etiquette for the Legal Secretary"; his lecture "Legal and Ethical Aspects of Human Organ Transplantation"; the chapter entitled "Torts"; "America the Beautiful"; Ravel's "Bolero"; NBC's "Today Show"

**5.** are used with other punctuation marks in the following ways:

**a.** the period and the comma fall <u>within</u> the quotation marks

Methamphetamine is sometimes called "speed."

His briefcase was described as "waterproof," but "moisture-resistant" would have been a better description.

**b.** the semicolon and the colon fall <u>outside</u> the quotation marks

He spoke of his "honesty"; however, he was later charged with perjury.

Three things caused this "accident": ignorance, negligence, and overconfidence.

**c.** the dash, question mark, and the exclamation point fall <u>within</u> the quotation marks when they refer to the quoted matter only; they fall <u>outside</u> when they refer to the whole sentence

The prosecutor asked, "What did you see?"
What is the meaning of the term "addict"?
The officer shouted, "Halt!"
Save us from his "mercy"!
"I just can't—" and then he stopped talking.
The chapter entitled "Malpractice Claims in the High-risk Specialties"—written by a noted attorney—is indeed informative.

**6.** are <u>not</u> used with quoted material comprising more than three typed lines and only one paragraph: such material is blocked and single-spaced internally but double-spaced top and bottom to set it off from the rest of the text

An article entitled "The Secretary in the Management Function" on page 9 of the December, 1975, issue of *The Secretary* makes this point:

> Good supervision comes from good planning before trying to meet goals, knowing the work and duties of each subordinate, carefully assigning the work, communicating both orally and through written facilities, and evaluating the work and correcting the deviations.

This, then, summarizes the major aspects of secretarial supervision.

7. are used with long quoted matter comprising more than three typed lines and more than one paragraph: double quotation marks are typed at the beginning of each paragraph and at the end of the final paragraph

We received the following comments from our attorney on Friday, August 4, 19—:

"The cases that you inquired about in your July 16 letter seek treble but unquantified damages and allege conspiracy among practically all domestic producers to fix and stabilize prices and freight charges for this product.

"In October, 19--, an administrative law judge of the Federal Trade Commission handed down an initial decision adverse to our Corporation and four other domestic producers in an FTC administrative proceeding initiated in 19—."

This background information, as well as other data, leads us to believe that . . . .

## ❛❜ QUOTATION MARKS, SINGLE

1. enclose a quotation within a quotation in conventional English

The witness said, "I distinctly heard him say, 'Don't be late,' and then I heard the door close."

2. are sometimes used in place of double quotation marks especially in British usage

The witness said, 'I distinctly heard him say, "Don't be late," and then I heard the door close.'

NOTE: When both single and double quotation marks occur at the end of a sentence, the period typically falls <u>within</u> both sets of marks.

The witness said, "I distinctly heard him say, 'Don't be late.' "

## ❜ SEMICOLON

1. links main clauses not joined by coordinating conjunctions

Make no terms; insist upon full restitution.
We have a copy of the document; you may keep the original.
The jury was unable to reach a verdict; the judge declared a mistrial.

2. links main clauses joined by conjunctive adverbs (as *consequently, furthermore, however, nevertheless*)

We are involved in similar litigation; however, we believe that our position is sound.

The jury was unable to reach a verdict; therefore, the judge declared a mistrial.

The appellant's argument and authorities do not clearly address the stated proposition; nevertheless, decided cases confirm the propriety of the trial court's holding.

3. separates phrases and clauses which themselves contain commas

Send copies to our offices in Portland, Maine; Springfield, Illinois; and Savannah, Georgia.

The assets in question include land, buildings, machinery, and office equipment; $259 million in cash and long-term investments; $340 million in accounts receivable; and $409 million in inventories.

**4.** may separate a series of clauses that are equally dependent on a main clause in a legal document; in such cases, the clauses (frequently "that" clauses) are sometimes capitalized and set in individual paragraphs

The complainant alleges: That . . . ;
That . . . ; and
That . . . .
Susan Sorenson, being sworn, did depose and say that . . . ;
That . . . ; that . . . ; and
That . . . .
WHEREAS it has become necessary . . . ; and
WHEREAS conditions are such as to warrant . . . ; and
WHEREAS, moreover, . . . ;
NOW, THEREFORE BE IT RESOLVED, that . . . ;
RESOLVED FURTHER, that . . . .

**5.** often occurs before phrases or abbreviations (as *for example, for instance, that is, that is to say, namely, e.g.,* or *i.e.*) that introduce expansions or series

In a smaller office, the secretary may have total responsibility for mailing; that is, the assumption of the duties of the mail room as well as preparatory responsibilities.

We discussed an important matter with Judge Smith; namely, the settlement of the Williams estate.

You must type the forms as attractively as possible; i.e., by aligning your typing with the printed margins, by typing slightly above the dotted lines, and by carefully spacing all the typewritten fill-ins.

**6.** connects string citations (a series of run-in citations)

*J. R. Watkins Company* v. *Hubbard,* 343 S.W.2d 189 (Mo. App. 1961); *In re Jackson's Will,* 291 S.W.2d 214 (Mo. App. 1956)

# / VIRGULE

**1.** separates alternatives

My wife and/or my attorney are authorized to sign the papers.

**2.** separates successive divisions (as months or years) of an extended period

the fiscal year 1975/76

**3.** often represents *per* in numeral + abbreviation combinations

9 ft/sec
20 km/hr
4000 bbl/da

**4.** often is an arbitrary punctuation mark within an abbreviation

L/C; C/D; d/b/a; a/k/a; a/o

**5.** serves as a dividing line between run-in lines of poetry in quotations

Say, sages, what's the charm on earth/Can turn death's dart aside?
                                                    —Robert Burns

# 9.7

## WORD DIVISION

Many law offices have a policy against dividing words at the end of a typewritten line in legal documents. In office correspondence, however, the policy is usually more flexible and words are divided as needed.

How to divide words at the end of a printed or typed line can be an object of concern. The very fact that widely used and respected dictionaries published by different houses indicate different points at which to divide many words is evidence enough that there is no absolute right or wrong and that for numerous words there are acceptable end-of-line division alternatives. The best policy to follow in individual instances is to consult an adequate dictionary whose main entries indicate points of division.

Common sense suggests some guidelines which will help to minimize the time spent consulting a dictionary. For instance, the division of a single letter at the beginning or end of a word should be avoided. On the one hand, in typed material a single letter hanging onto the end of a line with a hyphen may be dropped to the next line without leaving unsightly right-hand margins, and in printed material the space required for two characters (the letter and the hyphen) is, in most circumstances, easily filled. On the other hand, if there is room for a hyphen at the end of a line, there is room for the last letter of a word in its place. Thus, *abort, obey,* and *levy* should not be divided, for such divisions as

| a- | o- | lev- |
|---|---|---|
| bort | bey | y |

would detract from the appearance of the page.

Compounds containing one or more hyphens will cause a reader less trouble if divided after the hyphen. For the words *attorney-at-law, smoking-room,* and *vice-president* the divisions

| attorney- | attorney-at- | smoking- | vice- |
|---|---|---|---|
| at-law | law | room | president |

are less obtrusive than such divisions as

| attor- | smok- | vice-pres- |
|---|---|---|
| ney-at-law | ing-room | ident |

although there are no "rules" against the latter set of examples, and such divisions may occasionally prove necessary especially in narrow columns.

Similarly, closed compounds are best divided between component elements; thus, the divisions

| every- | speaker- | post- |
|---|---|---|
| one | phone | humous |

appear more natural and will cause the reader less trouble than

| ev- | speak- | posthu- |
|---|---|---|
| eryone | erphone | mous |

though divisions such as the ones above may be required in exceptional circumstances.

For words that are not compound, it is best to consult a dictionary or a guide to word division, and in order to maintain greatest consistency it is preferable always to consult the same source such as *Webster's New Collegiate Dictionary* or *Webster's Legal Speller.* Another general principle is to avoid end-of-line division altogether whenever possible, especially in successive lines.

There are, in addition, some specific instances in which one should avoid end-of-line division if at all possible. These are as follows:

1. The last word in a paragraph should not be divided.

2. The last word on a page (as of a business letter or a memorandum) should not be divided.

3. Items joined by *and/or* and the coordinating conjunction *and/or* itself should not be divided.

4. Proper names, courtesy titles, and following titles (as *Esq.*) should not be divided either on envelopes, in inside addresses, or in running texts:

| . . . to | *not* . . . to Mr. | *and not* to Mr. J. R. |
|---|---|---|
| Mr. J. R. Smith | J. R. Smith | Smith |

The one exception to this rule is the separation of long honorary titles from names especially in envelope address blocks and in inside addresses where space is often limited:

| The Honorable | *not*   The Honorable John |
|---|---|
| John R. Smith | R. Smith |

5. If dates must be divided (as in running texts), the division should occur only between the day and the year:

| . . . arrived on | *not* . . . arrived on Jan- |
|---|---|
| January 1, 19-- | uary 1, 19-- |
| . . . arrived on January 1, | *not* . . . arrived on January |
| 19-- | 1, 19-- |

6. Set units (as of time and measure) as well as single monetary units should not be divided:

| . . . at 10:00 a.m. | *not* . . . at 10:00 |
|---|---|
| | a.m. |
| . . . had a temperature of 98.6°F. | *not* . . . had a temperature of 98.6° |
| | F. |
| . . . a fee of $4,900.50. | *not* . . . a fee of $4,900.- |
| | 50. |

7. Abbreviations should not be divided:

| . . . received the M.B.A. | *not* . . . received the M.B.- |
|---|---|
| from Harvard. | A. from Harvard. |

8. Compound geographic designations (as city + state combinations) should not be divided:

| . . . to St. Paul, Minnesota. | *not* . . . to St. |
|---|---|
| | Paul, Minnesota. |

# 9.8

## COMPONENTS OF DISCOURSE

The word *discourse* is defined in *Webster's New Collegiate Dictionary* as "formal and orderly and usually extended expression of thought. . . ." Thus, no guide to effective communication can ignore the fundamental components of discourse: the word, the phrase, the clause, the sentence, and the paragraph. Each of these increasingly complex units contributes to the expression of a writer's points, ideas, and concepts.

The word, of course, is the simplest component of discourse. Words have been traditionally classified into eight parts of speech. This classification system is determined chiefly by a word's inflectional features, its general grammatical functions, and its positioning within a sentence. On the following pages, the parts of speech—the adjective, adverb, conjunction, interjection, noun, preposition, pronoun, and verb—are alphabetically listed and briefly discussed. Each part of speech is introduced by an applicable definition from *Webster's New Collegiate Dictionary*. The phrase, the clause, the sentence, and the paragraph are discussed later in this section.

## PARTS OF SPEECH

**Adjective**

²**adjective** *n* : a word belonging to one of the major form classes in any of numerous languages and typically serving as a modifier of a noun to denote a quality of the thing named, to indicate its quantity or extent, or to specify a thing as distinct from something else

Adjectives may occur in the following positions within sentences:

1. preceding the nouns they modify: the *black* hat; a *dark brown* coat
2. following the nouns they modify: an executive *par excellence;* I painted my room *blue.*
3. following the verb *to be* in predicate-adjective position: The hat is *black.* and following other linking (or "sense") verbs in predicate-adjective position: He seems *intelligent.* The food tastes *stale.* I feel *queasy.*
4. following some transitive verbs used in the passive voice: The room was painted *blue.* The passengers were found *dead* at the crash site.

Adjectives may describe something or represent a quality, kind, or condition (a *sick* man); they may point out or indicate something (*these* men); or they may convey the force of questions (*Whose* office is this?). Some adjectives (as *Puerto Rican, Hippocratic, Keynesian,* and others) are called "proper adjectives." They are derived from proper nouns, take their meanings from what characterizes the nouns, and are capitalized.

The following are general points of adjective usage:

**Absolute adjectives**    Some adjectives (as *prior, maximum, optimum, minimum, first,* and the like) ordinarily admit no comparison because they represent ultimate conditions. However, printed usage indicates that many writers do compare and qualify some of these words in order to show connotations and shades of meaning that they feel are less than absolute. The word *unique* is a case in point:

. . . we were fairly *unique* . . . .
—J. D. Salinger

. . . a rather *unique* concept . . . .
—E. Ohmer Milton

. . . the most *unique* human faculty
—Robert Plank

. . . some of the more *unique* and colorful customs . . . .
—Ernest Osborne

The more we study him, the less *unique* he seems . . . .
—James Joyce

While many examples may be found of qualification and/or comparison of *unique,* it is difficult to find printed evidence showing comparison of a word like *optimum.* When one is in doubt about the inflection of such an adjective, one should consult a dictionary.

**Coordinate adjectives**    Adjectives that share equal relationships to the nouns they modify are called coordinate adjectives and are separated from each other by commas:

a *concise, coherent, intelligent* opinion

However, in the following locution containing the set phrase *short story*

*a concise, coherent* short story

the adjectives *concise* and *coherent* are neither parallel nor equal in function or relationship with *short*, which is an essential element of the total compound *short story*. The test to use before inserting commas is to insert *and* between questionable adjectives, and then to decide whether the sentence still makes sense. Whereas *and* could fit between *coherent* and *intelligent* in the first example, it could not work between *coherent* and *short* in the second example.

**Adjective/noun agreement**    The number (singular or plural) of a demonstrative adjective *(this, that, these, those)* should agree with that of the noun it modifies:

these kinds of typewriters    *not*    these kind of typewriters
those sorts of jobs    *not*    those sort of jobs
this type of person    *not*    these type of people

**Double comparisons**    Double comparisons should be avoided since they are considered nonstandard:

the easiest *or* the most easy solution
*not* the most easiest solution

an easier *or* a more easy method
*not* a more easier method

**Incomplete or understood comparisons**    Some comparisons are left incomplete because the context clearly implies the comparison; hence, the expressions

Get *better* buys here!
We have *lower* prices.

These are commonly used especially in advertising. It should be understood, however, that the use of incomplete comparisons is often considered careless or illogical especially in formal writing.

---

**Adverb**

¹**ad•verb. . .** *n* **. . . :** a word belonging to one of the major form classes in any of numerous languages, typically serving as a modifier of a verb, an adjective, another adverb, a preposition, a phrase, a clause, or a sentence, and expressing some relation of manner or quality, place, time, degree, number, cause, opposition, affirmation, or denial

---

Adverbs may occur in the following positions within sentences:

1. before the subject: *Then* he announced his resignation.
2. after the subject: He *then* announced his resignation.
3. before the predicate: He praised the committee's work and *then* announced his resignation.
4. at the end of the predicate: He announced his resignation *then*.
5. in various other positions (as before adjectives or other adverbs): He also made an *equally* important announcement—that of his resignation. He adjourned the meeting *very* abruptly.

Adverbs answer the following questions: "when?" (Please reply *at once*), "how long?" (She wants to live here *forever*), "where?" (I work *there*), "in what direction?" (Move the lever *upward*), "how?" (The staff moved *expeditiously* on the project), and "how much?" or "to what degree?" (It is *rather* hot).

Adverbs modify verbs, adjectives, or other adverbs, as

He studied the brief *carefully*.
He gave the brief *very* careful study.
He studied the brief *very* carefully.

and may also serve as clause joiners or sentence connectors, as

*clause joiner:* You may share our car pool; *however,* we do insist that you be ready at 7:00 a.m.
*sentence connector:* He thoroughly enjoyed the symposium. *Indeed,* he was fascinated by the presentations.

In addition, adverbs may be essential elements of two-word verb collocations commonly having separate entry in dictionaries, such as

He looked *over* the figures.      The clerk took the file *away*.
He looked the figures *over*.      The clerk took *away* the file.

See also page 238 for a discussion of conjunctive adverbs, words like *however* in the example above that are adverbs functioning as conjunctions in sentences. The following paragraphs discuss general points of adverb usage.

**Placement within a sentence**     Adverbs are generally positioned as close as possible to the words they modify if such a position will not result in misinterpretation by the reader:

*unclear*
The project that he hoped his staff would support completely disappointed him.

Does the writer mean "complete staff support" or "complete disappointment"? Thus, the adverb may be moved to another position or the sentence may be recast, depending on intended meaning:

*clear*
The project that he hoped his staff would completely support had disappointed him.
*or*
He was completely disappointed in the project that he had hoped his staff would support.

**Emphasis**     Adverbs (such as *just* and *only*) are often used to emphasize certain other words. Thus, a writer should be aware of the various reader reactions that may result from the positioning of an adverb in a sentence:

*strong connotation of curtness:* He just nodded to me as he passed.
*emphasis on timing of the action:* He nodded to me just as he passed.

In some positions and contexts these adverbs can be ambiguous:

I will only tell it to you.

Does the writer mean that he will only tell it, not put it in writing, or does he mean that he will tell no one else? If the latter interpretation is intended, a slight shift of position would remove the uncertainty, as

I will tell it only to you.

**Adverbs vs. adjectives: examples of misuse**
**a.** Adverbs but not adjectives modify action verbs:

*not*   He answered very harsh.
*but*   He answered very harshly.

**b.** Complements referring to the subject of a sentence and occurring after linking verbs conventionally take adjectives but not adverbs:

*acceptable*    I feel bad.
            The letter sounded strong.
*questionable*    I feel badly.
                The letter sounded strongly.
*but acceptable*    He looks good these days.
                He looks well these days.

In the last two examples, either *good* or *well* is acceptable, because both words may be adjectives or adverbs, and here they are functioning as adjectives in the sense of "being healthy."

**c.** Adverbs but not adjectives modify adjectives and other adverbs:

*not*    She seemed dreadful tired.    *but*    She seemed dreadfully tired.

**Double negatives**    A combination of two negative adverbs (as *not* + *hardly, never, scarcely*) used to express a single negative idea is considered substandard:

*not*    We cannot see scarcely any reason why we should lease this copier.
*but*    We can see scarcely any reason why we should lease this copier.
    We can't ⎫
    cannot  ⎬  see any reason why we should lease this copier.
            ⎭

---

**Conjunction**

con•junc•tion . . . *n* . . . **4:** an uninflected linguistic form that joins together sentences, clauses, phrases, or words: CONNECTIVE

---

A comma is traditionally used <u>before</u> a coordinating conjunction linking coordinate clauses especially when these clauses are lengthy or when the writer desires to emphasize their distinctness from one another:

The victim is in serious condition, *and* she shows few signs of improvement.
Shall we consider this person's application, *or* shall we consider that one's?
We do not discriminate between men and women, *but* we do have high professional standards and qualifications that the successful applicant must meet.

In addition to the three main types of conjunctions listed and illustrated in the table on page 239, the English language has transitional adverbs and adverbial phrases called "conjunctive adverbs" that express relationships between two units of discourse (as two independent clauses, two complete sentences, or two or more paragraphs), and that function as conjunctions even though they are customarily classified as adverbs. The table on page 240 groups and illustrates conjunctive adverbs according to their functions.

Occurrence of a comma fault especially with conjunctive adverbs indicates that the writer has not realized that a comma alone will not suffice to join two sentences, and that a semicolon is required. The punctuation pattern with conjunctive adverbs is usually as follows:

clause + semicolon + conjunctive adverb + comma + clause

The following two sentences illustrate a typical comma fault and a rewrite that removes the error:

*comma fault*

The firm had flexible hours, however its employees were expected to abide by the hours they had selected for arrival and departure.

*rewrite*

The firm had flexible hours; however, its employees were expected to abide by the hours they had selected for arrival and departure.

## Three Major Types of Conjunctions and their Functions

| Type of Conjunction | Function | Example |
|---|---|---|
| **coordinating conjunctions** link words, phrases, dependent clauses, and complete sentences | *and* joins elements and sentences | He ordered pencils, pens, *and* erasers. |
| | *but, yet* exclude or contrast | He is a brilliant *but* arrogant man. |
| | *or, nor* offer alternatives | You can wait here *or* go. |
| | *for* offers reason or grounds | The report is poor, *for* its data are inaccurate. |
| | *so* offers a reason | Her diction is good, *so* every word is clear. |
| **subordinating conjunctions** introduce dependent clauses | *because, since* express cause | *Because* she is smart, she is doing well in her job. |
| | *although, if, unless* express condition | Don't call *unless* you have the information. |
| | *as, as though, however* express manner | He looks *as though* he is ill. We'll do it *however* you tell us to. |
| | *in order that, so that* express result | She routes the mail early *so that* they can read it. |
| | *after, before, once, since, till, until, when, whenever, while* express time | He kept meetings to a minimum *when* he was president. |
| | *where, wherever* express place or circumstance | I don't know *where* he has gone. He tries to help out *wherever* it is possible. |
| | *whether* expresses alternative conditions or possibilities | It was hard to decide *whether* I should go or stay. |
| | *that* introduces several kinds of subordinate clauses including those used as noun equivalents (as a subject or an object of a verb, or a predicate nominative) | Yesterday I learned *that* he has been sick for over a week. |
| **correlative conjunctions** work in pairs to link alternatives or equal elements | *either . . . or, neither . . . nor,* and *whether . . . or* link alternatives | *Either* you go *or* you stay. He had *neither* looks *nor* wit. |
| | *both . . . and* and *not only . . . but also* link equal elements | *Both* typist *and* writer should understand style. *Not only* was there inflation, *but* there was *also* unemployment. |

## Conjunctive Adverbs Grouped According to Meaning and Function

| Conjunctive Adverbs | Functions | Examples |
| --- | --- | --- |
| *also, besides, further-more, in addition, in fact, moreover, too* | express addition | This employee deserves a substantial raise; *furthermore,* she should be promoted. |
| *indeed, that is* [to say], *to be sure* | add emphasis | He is brilliant; *indeed,* he is a genius. |
| *anyway, however, nevertheless, on the contrary, on the one hand/on the other hand* | express contrast or discrimination | The major responsibility lies with the partners; *nevertheless,* associates should be competent in decision-making. |
| *e.g., for example, for instance, i.e., namely, that is* | introduce illustrations or elaborations | Losses were due to several negative factors; *namely,* inflation, competition, and restrictive government regulation. He is highly competitive—*i.e.,* he goes straight for a rival's jugular vein. |
| *accordingly, as a result, consequently, hence, therefore, thus, so* | express or introduce conclusions or results | Government overregulation in that country reached a prohibitive level in the last quarter. *Thus,* we are phasing out all of our operations there. |
| *first, second, further on, later, then, i ` conclusion, finally* | orient elements of discourse as to time or space | *First,* we can say that the account is long overdue; *second,* that we must consider consulting our attorneys if you do not meet your obligation. |

The following are general points of conjunction usage:

**Conjunctions as meaning clarifiers**   Properly used conjunctions ensure order and coherence in writing since they often serve to pinpoint shades of meaning, place special emphasis where required, and set general tone within sentences and paragraphs. Improperly used conjunctions may result in choppy, often cloudy writing, and in incoherent orientation of ideas. Therefore, the purpose of a conjunction is totally defeated if it creates ambiguities rather than makes things clear. The often misused conjunction-phrase *as well* is an example:

*ambiguous*
Jean typed the report *as well* as Joan. (Does the writer mean that both women typed the report together, or that both women typed the report equally well?

*clear*
Jean typed the report just *as well* as Joan did.
Jean and Joan typed the report equally well.
*or*
Both Jean and Joan typed the report.
Jean typed the report; so did Joan.
Jean typed the report, and so did Joan.

**Coordinating conjunctions: proper use**   These terms should link equal elements of discourse—e.g., adjectives with other adjectives, nouns with other nouns, participles with other participles, clauses with other equal-ranking clauses, and so on. Combining unequal elements may result in unbalanced sentences:

*unbalanced*
Having become disgusted *and* because he was tired, he left the meeting.

*balanced*
Because he was tired *and* disgusted, he left the meeting.
He left the meeting because he had become tired *and* disgusted.
Having become tired *and* disgusted, he left the meeting.

Coordinating conjunctions should not be used to string together excessively long series of elements, regardless of their equality.

*strung-out*
Sometimes there is an oversight even though your intentions are good and a firm might write checks for sums that are greater than the amount on deposit, so the bank might do the customer a service and honor the overdrawn checks and ask the firm to deposit sufficient funds to cover the check, but it may also refuse to honor the check.

*tightened*
Despite the best of intentions, or through an oversight, a firm's checks may sometimes be written for sums greater than the amount on deposit. As a customer service, the bank may honor the overdrawn check and ask the company to deposit sufficient funds to cover the check. On the other hand, it may refuse to honor the check.

Choice of just the right coordinating conjunction for a particular verbal situation is important: the right word will pinpoint the writer's intent and will highlight the most relevant idea or point of the sentence. The following three sentences exhibit increasingly stronger degrees of contrast through the use of different conjunctions:

*neutral*            He works hard *and* doesn't progress.
*more contrast*      He works hard *but* doesn't progress.
*stronger contrast*  He works hard, *yet* he doesn't progress.

The coordinating conjunction *and/or* linking two elements of a compound subject often poses a problem as to the number (singular or plural) of the verb that follows. A subject comprising singular nouns connected by *and/or* may be considered singular or plural, depending on the meaning of the sentence:

*singular*
All loss and/or damage *is* to be the responsibility of the sender. [one or the other and possibly both]

*plural*
John R. Jones and/or Robert B. Flint *are* hereby appointed as the executors of my estate. [both executors are to act, or either of them is to act if the other dies or is incapacitated]

**Subordinating conjunctions: proper use**    Subordinating conjunctions introduce dependent clauses and also deemphasize less important ideas in favor of more important ideas. Which clause is made independent and which clause is made subordinate has great influence in determining the effectiveness of a sentence. Notice how differently these two versions strike the reader:

> When the building burst into flames, we were just coming out of the door.
> Just as we were coming out of the door, the building burst into flames.

The writer must take care that the point he or she wishes to emphasize is in the independent clause and that the points of less importance are subordinated.

Faulty clause subordination can render a sentence impotent. Compare the following examples:

*faulty subordination*
Because the government of that country has nationalized our refineries, and since overregulation of prices had already become a critical problem, we decided to withdraw all our operations when the situation became intolerable.

*improved*
Since the country's government has overregulated prices and has nationalized our refineries, we have decided to withdraw our operations altogether.

**Correlative conjunctions: proper use**    These pairs of words also join equal elements of discourse. They should be placed as close as possible to the elements they join:

*misplaced (joining clause and noun phrase)*
*Not only* did he lose his wallet, *but* his briefcase too.

*repositioned (joining two clauses)*
*Not only* did he lose his wallet, *but* he lost his briefcase too.

*misplaced (joining clause and verb phrase)*
*Either* I must send a telex *or* make a long-distance call.

*repositioned (joining two verb phrases)*
I must *either* send a telex *or* make a long-distance call.

The negative counterpart of *either . . . or* is *neither . . . nor*. The conjunction *or* should not be substituted for *nor* because its substitution will destroy the negative parallelism. However, *or* may occur in combination with *no*. Examples:

He received *neither* a promotion *nor* a raise.

He received *no* promotion *or* raise.

---

**Interjection**
in•ter•jec•tion . . . *n* . . . **3 a :** an ejaculatory word (as *Wonderful*) or form of speech (as *ah*) **b :** a cry or inarticulate utterance (as *ouch*) expressing an emotion

---

Interjections exhibit no characteristic features or forms. As independent elements not having close grammatical connections with the rest of a sentence, interjections may often stand alone.

Interjections may be stressed or ejaculatory words, phrases, or even short sentences, as

Absurd! Quickly! Get out!

or they may be so-called "sound" words (such as those representing shouts, hisses, etc.):

Ouch! That hurts.
Shh! The meeting has begun.
Psst! Come over here.
Ah, that's my idea of a terrific deal.

---

**Noun**
noun . . . *n* . . . **1 :** a word that is the name of a subject of discourse (as a person, animal, plant, place, thing, substance, quality, idea, action, or state) and that in languages with grammatical number, case, and gender is inflected for number and case but has inherent gender **2:** a word except a pronoun used in a sentence as subject or object of a verb, as object of a preposition, as the predicate after a copula, or as a name in an absolute construction

---

Nouns exhibit these characteristic features: they are inflected for possession, they have number (singular, plural), they are often preceded by determiners (as *a, an, the; this, that, these, those; all, every,* and other such qualifiers; *one, two, three,* and other such numerical quantifiers; *his, her, their,* and other such pronominal adjectives), a few of them still have gender (as the masculine *host,* the feminine *hostess*), and many of them are formed by suffixation (as with the suffixes *-ance, -ist, -ness,* and *-tion*).

The only noun case indicated by inflection is the possessive, which is normally formed by addition of *-'s* (singular) or *-s'* (plural) to the base word. (See APOSTROPHE, page 219, for examples.)

Number is usually indicated by addition of *-s* or *-es* to the base word, although some nouns (as those of foreign origin) have irregular plurals:

*regular plurals*

| | |
|---|---|
| plaintiff→plaintiffs | excess→excesses |
| file→files | dish→dishes |
| essay→essays | buzz→buzzes |
| patriarch→patriarchs | branch→branches |

*irregular, variant, and zero plurals*

| | |
|---|---|
| inquiry→inquiries | subpoena duces tecum→subpoenas duces tecum |
| child→children | |
| foot→feet | father-in-law→fathers-in-law |
| phenomenon→phenomena | attorney general→attorneys general *or* attorney generals |
| index→indexes *or* indices | |
| testatrix→testatrices | res→res |
| memorandum→memorandums *or* memoranda | encephalitis→encephalitides |
| alga→algae | neurosis→neuroses |
| corpus delicti→corpora delicti | |

Plural patterns for names ending in *Jr.* and *Sr.* are:

| | |
|---|---|
| The John K. Walkers Jr. are here. | The John K. Walker Jrs. are here. |
| The John K. Walkers, Jr. are here. | The John K. Walker, Jrs. are here. |

When in doubt of a plural spelling, the secretary should consult a dictionary. Nouns may be used as follows in sentences:

1. as subjects: The *office* was quiet.
2. as direct objects: He locked the *office*.
3. as objects of prepositions: The file is in the *office*.
4. as indirect objects: He gave his *client* the papers.
5. as retained objects: His client was given the *papers*.
6. as predicate nominatives: Mr. Dow is the managing *partner*.
7. as subjective complements: Mr. Dow was named managing *partner*.
8. as objective complements: They made Mr. Dow managing *partner*.
9. as appositives: Mr. Dow, the managing *partner,* wrote that memorandum.
10. in direct address: *Mr. Dow,* may I present Mr. Lee?

**Compound nouns**   Since English is not a static and unchanging entity, it experiences continuous style fluctuations because of preferences of its users. The styling (open, closed, or hyphened) variations of noun and other compounds reflect changing usage. No rigid rules can be set down to cover every possible variation or combination, nor can an all-inclusive list of compounds be given here. The secretary should consult a dictionary when in doubt of the styling of a compound.

**Use of indefinite articles with nouns**   The use of *a* and *an* is not settled in all situations. Some words or abbreviations beginning with a vowel letter nevertheless have a consonant as the first <u>sound</u> (as *one, union,* or *US*). Conversely, the names of some consonants begin with a vowel sound (as *F, H, L, M, N, R, S,* and *X*).

**a**

---

**a.** Before a word (or abbreviation) beginning with a consonant <u>sound</u>, *a* is usually spoken and written: *a BA degree, a COD package, a hat, a human, a one, a union, a US senator.*
**b.** Before *h-* in an unstressed (unaccented) or lightly stressed (lightly accented) first syllable, *a* is more frequently written, although *an* is more usual in speech whether or not the *h-* is ac-

tually pronounced. Either one certainly may be considered acceptable in speech or writing: *a historian—an historian, a heroic attempt—an heroic attempt, a hilarious performance—an hilarious performance.*

**c.** Before a word beginning with a vowel <u>sound</u>, *a* is occasionally used in speech: *a hour, a inquiry, a obligation.* (In some parts of the United States this may be more common than in others.)

## an

**a.** Before a word beginning with a vowel <u>sound</u>, *an* is usually spoken and written: *an indenture, an FCC report, an hour, an honor, an MIT professor, an nth degree polynomial, an orthodontist, an Rh factor, an SPCA official, an unknown.*

**b.** Before *h-* in an unstressed or lightly stressed syllable, *an* is more usually spoken whether or not the *h-* is pronounced, while *a* is more frequently written. Either may be considered acceptable in speech or writing. (See the examples above at point b.)

**c.** Sometimes *an* is spoken and written before a word beginning with a vowel in its spelling even though the first <u>sound</u> is a consonant: *an European city, an unique occurrence, such an one.* This is less frequent today than in the past and it is more common in Britain than in the United States.

**d.** Occasionally *an* is used in speech and writing before a stressed syllable beginning with *h-* in which the *h-* is pronounced: *an huntress, an heritage.* This is regularly the practice of the King James Version of the Old Testament.

---

**Preposition**

**prep•o•si•tion** . . . *n* . . . : a linguistic form that combines with a noun, pronoun, or noun equivalent to form a phrase that typically has an adverbial, adjectival, or substantival relation to some other word.

---

Prepositions are identified chiefly by their positioning within sentences and by their grammatical functions. Prepositions may occur in the following positions:

1. before nouns or pronouns: *below* the desk; *beside* them
2. after adjectives: antagonistic *to;* insufficient *in;* symbolic *of*
3. after the verbal elements of idiomatically fixed verb + preposition combinations: take *for;* get *after;* come *across*

Prepositions may be simple, i.e., composed of only one element (as *of, on, out, from, near, against,* or *without*); or they may be compound, i.e., composed of more than one element (as *according to, by means of,* or *in spite of*). Prepositions are chiefly used to link nouns, pronouns, or noun equivalents to the rest of a sentence:

She expected resistance *on* his part.
He sat down *beside* her.

Prepositions may also be used to express the possessive:

one fourth *of* the employees; the top drawer *of* my desk

The following paragraphs discuss general points of preposition usage.

**Prepositions and conjunctions: confusion between the two**    The words *after, before, but, for,* and *since* may function as either prepositions or conjunctions. Their positions within sentences clarify whether they are conjunctions or prepositions:

*preposition*    I have nothing left *but* hope.   (*but* = "except for")
*conjunction*    I was a bit concerned *but* not panicky.   (*but* links 2 adjectives)

*preposition*    The device conserves fuel *for* residual heating.   (*for* + noun)
*conjunction*    The device conserves fuel, *for* it is battery-powered.   (*for* links 2 clauses)

**Implied or understood prepositions**    If two words combine idiomatically with the same preposition, that preposition need not be repeated after both of them:

We were antagonistic [to] and opposed *to* the whole idea.
*but*
We are interested *in* and anxious *for* raises.

**Prepositions terminating sentences**    There is no reason why a preposition cannot end a sentence, especially when it is an essential element of an idiomatically fixed verb phrase:

Her continual tardiness is only one of the things I put up *with*.
What does all this add up *to*?

**Use of *between* and *among***    The preposition *between* is ordinarily followed by words representing two persons or things:

*between* you and me; détente *between* the United States and the Soviet Union

and *among* is ordinarily followed by words representing more than two persons or things:

*among* the three of us; *among* various nations

However, *between* sometimes may express an interrelationship between more than two things when those things are being considered individually, not collectively:

. . . travels regularly *between* New York, Baltimore, and Washington.

---

**Pronoun**

**pro•noun** . . . *n* . . . **:** a word belonging to one of the major form classes in any of a great many languages that is used as a substitute for a noun or noun equivalent, takes noun constructions, and refers to persons or things named or understood in the context

---

Pronouns exhibit all or some of the following characteristic features: case (nominative, possessive, objective), number (singular, plural), person (first, second, third person), and gender (masculine, feminine, neuter). Pronouns may be grouped according to major types and functions, as shown in the table on the next page. The following paragraphs discuss points of pronoun usage.

**Personal pronouns**    A personal pronoun agrees in person, number, and gender with the word it refers to; however, the case of a pronoun is determined by its function within a sentence:

Everybody had *his* own office.
Everybody was given an office to *himself.*
Each employee was given an office to *himself.*
*You* and *I* thought the meeting was useful.
Just between *you* and *me,* the meeting was useful but far too lengthy.
My assistant and *I* attended the seminar.
The vice-president told my assistant and *me* to attend the seminar.

The nominative case (as in the locutions "It is I" and "This is she") after the verb *to be* is considered standard English and is preferred by strict grammarians; however, the objective case (as in the locution "It's me") also may be used without criticism especially in spoken English. However, when a personal pronoun occurs in a construction introduced by *than* or *as,* it should be in the nominative case:

He received a bigger bonus than *she* [did].
She has as much seniority as *I* [do].

The suffixes *-self* and *-selves* combine only with the possessive case of the first- and second-person pronouns *(myself, ourselves, yourself, yourselves)* and with the objective case of the third-person pronouns *(himself, herself, itself, themselves)*. Other combinations (as "hisself" and "theirselves") are considered nonstandard and should not be used.

## Types and Functions of Pronouns

| Type of Pronoun | Function | Examples |
|---|---|---|
| **personal pronouns** (such as *I, we, you, he, she, it, they*) | refer to beings and objects and reflect the person, number, and gender of those antecedents | Put the book on the table and close *it*. Put the baby in *his* crib and cover *him* up. |
| **reflexive pronouns** (such as *myself, ourselves, yourself, yourselves, himself, herself, itself, themselves*) | express reflexive action on the subject of a sentence or add extra emphasis to the subject | He hurt *himself*. They asked *themselves* if they were being honest. I *myself* am not afraid. |
| **indefinite pronouns** (*all, another, any, anybody, anyone, anything, both, each, each one, either, everybody, everyone, everything, few, many, much, neither, nobody, none, no one, one, other, several, some, somebody, someone, something*) | are indistinguishable by gender, are chiefly used as third-person references, and do not distinguish gender | *All* of the people are here. *All* of them are here. Has *anyone* arrived? *Somebody* has called. Does *everyone* have his paper? *Nobody* has answered. A *few* have offered their suggestions. |
| **reciprocal pronouns** | indicate interaction | They do not quarrel with *one another*. Be nice to *each other*. |
| **demonstrative pronouns** (*this, that, these, those*) | point things out | *This* is your seat. *That* is mine. *These* belong to her. *Those* are strong words. |
| **relative pronouns** (*who, whom, which, what, that, whose*) or combinations with *-ever* (as *whoever, whosesoever, whichever, whatever*) | introduce clauses acting as nouns or as modifiers | The trip *that* I just returned from was a great success. I'll do *what* you want. I'll do *whatever* you want. |
| **interrogative pronouns** (as *who, which, what, whoever, whichever, whatever*) | phrase direct questions | *Who* is there? *What* is his title? His title is *what*? *Whom* did the article pan? *Whatever* is the matter? |

When one uses the pronoun *I* with other pronouns or with other peoples' names, *I* should be last in the series:

Mrs. Smith and *I* were trained together.
The memorandum was directed to Ms. Montgomery and *me*.

Some offices prefer that writers use *we* and not *I* when speaking for their companies or firms in business correspondence. *I* is more often used when a writer is referring only to himself or herself. The following example illustrates use of both within one sentence:

*We* [i.e., the writer speaks for the firm] have examined the fabric samples that you sent to *me* [i.e., the samples were sent only to the writer] on June 1, but *we* [a group decision] feel that they are too colorful to be used in *our* reception room.

While the personal pronouns *it, you,* and *they* are often used as indefinite pronouns in spoken English, they can be vague or even redundant in some contexts and therefore should be avoided in precise writing:

| *vague* | *explicit* |
|---|---|
| *They* said at the seminar that the size of the average law firm would increase by 20%. (The question is: Who exactly is *they?*) | The lawyers on the panel at the seminar predicted a 20% increase in the size of the average law firm. |
| *redundant* | *lean* |
| In the graph *it* says that malpractice suits fell off by 50%. | The graph indicates a 50% drop in malpractice suits. |

Notwithstanding recent concern about sexism in language, forms of the personal pronoun *he* and the indefinite pronoun *one* are still the standard substitutes for antecedents whose genders are mixed or irrelevant:

Each employee should check *his* W-2 form.
Present the letter to the administrator for *his* approval.
If *one* really wants to succeed, *one* can.

**Indefinite pronouns: agreement**    Agreement in number between indefinite pronouns and verbs is sometimes a problem especially in contexts where the actual number of individuals represented by the pronoun is unclear. In some instances, there is also a conflict between written and spoken usage.

The following indefinite pronouns are clearly singular, and as such take singular verbs: *another, anything, each one, everything, much, nobody, no one, one, other, someone, something.*

Much *is* being done.
No one *wants* to go.

And these are clearly plural: *both, few, many, several.*

Several *were* called; few *were* chosen.

But the following may be either singular or plural, depending on whether they are used with mass or count nouns (a mass noun identifies something not ordinarily thought of in terms of numbered elements; a count noun identifies things that can be counted): *all, any, each, none, some.*

| *with mass noun* | *with plural count noun* |
|---|---|
| *All* of the *property is* entailed. | *All* of our *bases are* covered. |
| *None* of the *ink was* erasable. | *None* of the *clerks were* available. |

The following are singular in form, and as such logically take singular verbs; however, because of their plural connotations, informal speech has established the use of plural pronoun references to them: *anybody, anyone, everybody, everyone, somebody.*

*Everybody* roots for *their* own team.
I knew *everybody* by *their* first names.
Don't tell *anyone; they* might spread the rumor.

Even in more formal contexts, expressions such as

We called *everyone* by *their* first *names*.
*instead of*
We called *everyone* by *his* first *name*.

are being used increasingly as a result of attempts to avoid sexism in language. The question of number in pronoun phrases such as *each + of +* noun(s) or other pronoun(s), *none + of +* noun(s) or other pronoun(s), *either/neither + of +* noun(s) or other pronoun(s), and *some + of +* noun(s) or other pronoun(s), depends on the number of the headword. For example, when *either* means "one of two or more" or "any one of more than two," it is usually singular in construction and thus takes a singular verb. However, when *of* after *either* is followed by a plural, the verb that follows the whole phrase is often plural. This decision is really a matter of writer preference:

*Either* of the two pronunciations *is* standard.
*Either* of these pronunciations *is/are* standard.
*or*
*Either* of the two *is* satisfactory.
*Either* of them *is/are* satisfactory.

The word *none* involves similar variations:

*None* [i.e., *not any*] of them *were* updated.
*None* [i.e., *not any*] of those letters *are* urgent.
*but*
*None* [i.e., *not one*] of the systems *is* suitable for this office.
*None* [i.e., *not one*] *is* a faster typist than he.

**The indefinite pronoun *any* when used in comparisons**    The indefinite pronoun *any* is conventionally followed by *other(s)* or *else* when it forms part of a comparison of two individuals in the same class. Examples:

*not*    He is a better researcher than any in his field.
      (Is he a better researcher than all others including himself?)
*but*    He is a better researcher than any others in his field.
      He is a better researcher than anyone else in his field.
*not*    Boston is more interesting than any city in the U.S.
*but*    Boston is more interesting than any other city in the U.S.

**Demonstrative pronouns**    One problem involving demonstrative pronouns occurs when a demonstrative introduces a sentence referring to an idea or ideas contained in a previous sentence or sentences. One should be sure that the reference is definite and not cloudy:

*a cloudy sentence*
The heir's illness, the influence of a faith healer at court, massive military setbacks, general strikes, mass outbreaks of typhus, and failed crops contributed to the revolution. *This* influenced the course of history.
*The question is: What exactly influenced the course of history? All of these factors, some of them, or the last one mentioned?*

*an explicit sentence*
None of the participants in the incident kept records of what they said or did. *That* is quite unfortunate, and it should be a lesson to us.

When demonstrative pronouns are used with the words *kind, sort,* and *type + of +* nouns, they should agree in number with both nouns:

*not*    We want these kind of pencils.
*but*    We want *this kind* of *pencil.*    *or*    We want *these kinds* of *pencils.*

**Relative pronouns**   While a relative pronoun itself does not exhibit number, gender, or person, it does determine the number, gender, and person of the relative-clause elements that follow it because of its implicit agreement with its antecedent:

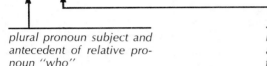

*Those who are ready to start their jobs should arrive at 8:00 a.m.*

| | |
|---|---|
| *plural pronoun subject and antecedent of relative pronoun "who"* | *relative pronoun refers to its antecedent "those" and affects number of following verb, pronoun, and noun* |

When the antecedent of a relative pronoun is doubtful (as when either of two nouns may be considered the antecedent), the number of the verb may vary according to the writer's preference. If a plural noun is closer to the verb, the writer may choose a plural verb. Examples:

He's one of those *executives* who *worry* a lot.   *or*   He's an *executive* who *worries* a lot.

The relative pronoun *who* typically refers to persons and some animals; *which,* to things and animals; and *that,* to both beings and things:

a man *who* sought success; a man *whom* we can trust; Seattle Slew, *who* won horse racing's Triple Crown

a book *which* sold well; a dog *which* barked loudly

a book *that* sold well; a dog *that* barked loudly; a man *that* we can trust

Relative pronouns can sometimes be omitted for the sake of brevity:

The man *whom* I was talking to is the judge.
*or*
The man I was talking to is the judge.

The relative pronoun *what* may be substituted for the longer and more awkward phrases "that which," "that of which," or "the thing which" in some sentences:

*stiff*    He was blamed for *that which* he could not have known.
*easier*    He was blamed for *what* he could not have known.

The problem of when to use *who* or *whom* has been blown out of proportion. The situation is very simple: standard written English makes a distinction between the nominative and objective cases of these pronouns when they are used as relatives or interrogatives, as

*nominative* case

*Who* is she?
*Who* does she think she is, anyway?
She thinks she is the one *who* ought to be promoted.
She's the one individual *who* I think should be promoted.
Give me a list of the ones *who* you think should be promoted.

*objective case*

*Whom* are you referring to?
To *whom* are you referring?
He's a man *whom* everyone should know.
He's a man with *whom* everyone should be acquainted.

In speech, however, case distinctions and boundaries often become blurred, with the result that spoken English favors *who* as a general substitute for all uses of *whom* except in set phrases as *"To whom* it may concern." *Who,* then, may be used not only as the subject of the clause it introduces, as

Let us select *who* we think will be the best candidate.

but *who* may be used also as the object of a verb in a clause that it introduces, as

See the manager, Mrs. Keats, *who* you should be able to find in her office.

or as an interrogative:

*Who* should we tell?

*Who* is rarely used as the object of a preposition in the clause that it introduces; however, as object of a preposition it is commonly used to introduce a question:

Presiding is a judge about *whom* (rarely *who*) I know nothing.
*Who* are you going to listen to?

The relative pronoun *whoever* follows the same principles as *who* in formal writing:

*nominative*   Tell *whoever* is going to research the case that . . . .
              He wants to help *whoever* needs it most.
*objective*    She makes friends with *whomever* she meets.

In speech, however, as with *who* and *whom,* case distinctions become blurred, and *whoever* is used without criticism in most sentences:

*Whoever* did she choose?

---

**verb** . . . *n* . . . **:** a word that characteristically is the grammatical center of a predicate and expresses an act, occurrence, or mode of being, that in various languages is inflected for agreement with the subject, for tense, for voice, for mood, or for aspect, and that typically has rather full descriptive meaning and characterizing quality but is sometimes nearly devoid of these esp. when used as an auxiliary or copula

**Verb**

---

Verbs exhibit the following characteristic features: inflection *(help, helps, helping, helped),* person (first, second, third person), number (singular, plural), tense (present, past, future), aspect (time relations other than the simple present, past, and future), voice (active, passive), mood (indicative, subjunctive, imperative), and suffixation (as by the typical suffixal markers *-ate, -en, -ify,* and *-ize).*

Regular verbs have four inflected forms signaled by the suffixes *-s* or *-es, -ed,* and *-ing.* The verb *help* as shown in the first sentence above is regular. Most irregular verbs have four or five forms, as *see, sees, seeing, saw,* and *seen;* and one, the verb *be,* has eight: *be, is, am, are, being, was, were,* and *been.* When one is uncertain about a particular inflected form, one should consult a dictionary that indicates not only the inflections of irregular verbs but also those inflections resulting in changes in base-word spelling, as

*blame; blamed; blaming*
*spy; spied; spying*
*picnic; picnicked; picnicking*

in addition to variant inflected forms, as

*counsel; counseled* or *counselled; counseling* or *counselling*
*diagram; diagramed* or *diagrammed; diagraming* or *diagramming*
*travel; traveled* or *travelled; traveling* or *travelling*

all of which may be found at their applicable entries in *Webster's New Collegiate Dictionary.*

There are, however, a few rules that will aid one in ascertaining the proper spelling patterns of certain verb forms. These are as follows:

1. Verbs ending in a silent *-e* generally retain the *-e* before consonant suffixes (as *-s*) but drop the *-e* before vowel suffixes (as *-ed* and *-ing*):

   *arrange; arranges; arranged; arranging*
   *hope; hopes; hoped; hoping*
   *require; requires; required; requiring*
   *shape; shapes; shaped; shaping*

   Other such verbs are: *agree, arrive, conceive, grieve, imagine,* and *value.*

   NOTE: A few verbs ending in a silent *-e* retain the *-e* even before vowel suffixes in order to avoid confusion with other words:

   *dye; dyes; dyed; dyeing* (vs. *dying*)
   *singe; singes; singed; singeing* (vs. *singing*)

2. Monosyllabic verbs ending in a single consonant preceded by a single vowel double the final consonant before vowel suffixes (as *-ed* and *-ing*):

   *brag; bragged; bragging*
   *grip; gripped; gripping*
   *pin; pinned; pinning*

3. Polysyllabic verbs ending in a single consonant preceded by a single vowel and having an accented last syllable double the final consonant before vowel suffixes (as *-ed* and *-ing*):

   *commit; committed; committing*
   *control; controlled; controlling*
   *occur; occurred; occurring*
   *omit; omitted; omitting*

   NOTE: The final consonant of such verbs is <u>not</u> doubled when

   a. two vowels occur before the final consonant, as

      *daub; daubed; daubing*
      *spoil; spoiled; spoiling*

   b. two consonants form the ending, as

      *help; helped; helping*
      *lurk; lurked; lurking*
      *peck; pecked; pecking*

4. Verbs ending in *-y* preceded by a consonant regularly change the *-y* to *-i* before all suffixes except those beginning with *-i* (as *-ing*):

   *carry; carried; carrying*
   *marry; married; marrying*
   *study; studied; studying*

   NOTE: If the final *-y* is preceded by a vowel, it remains unchanged in suffixation, as

   *delay; delayed; delaying*
   *enjoy; enjoyed; enjoying*
   *obey; obeyed; obeying*

5. Verbs ending in *-c* add a *-k* when a suffix beginning with *-e* or *-i* is appended, as

   *mimic; mimics; mimicked; mimicking*
   *panic; panics; panicked; panicking*
   *traffic; traffics; trafficked; trafficking*

   And words derived from this type of verb also add a *k* when such suffixes are added to them, as

   *panicky*
   *trafficker*

Verbs may be used transitively; that is, they may act upon direct objects, as

She *contributed* money.

or they may be used intransitively; that is, without direct objects to act upon, as

She *contributed* generously.

**Verbals**   A group of words derived from verbs and called *verbals* deserves added discussion. The members of this group—the gerund, the participle, and the infinitive—exhibit some but not all of the characteristic features of their parent verbs.

A gerund is an *-ing* verb form, but it functions mainly as a noun. It has both the active *(seeing)* and the passive *(being seen)* voices. In addition to voice, a gerund's verbal characteristics are as follows: it conveys the notion of a verb—i.e., action of some sort; it can take an object; and it can be modified by an adverb. Examples:

*Typing* tabular *data daily* is a boring task.

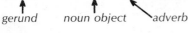

gerund      noun object      ʼadverb

He liked *driving cars fast.*

gerund      noun object      ʼadverb

Nouns and pronouns occurring before gerunds are expressed by the possessive:

She is trying to improve *her typing.*
We objected to *their telling* the story all over town.
We saw the *boy's whipping.* (i.e., the boy being whipped)
We expected the *senator's coming* (i.e., his arrival)

Participles, on the other hand, function as adjectives and may occur alone (a *broken* typewriter) or in phrases that modify other words (*Having broken the typewriter,* she gave up for the day). Participles have active and passive forms like gerunds. Examples:

*active-voice participial phrase modifying "he"*
*Having failed to pass the examination,* he was forced to repeat the course.

*passive-voice participial phrase modifying "he"*
*Having been failed* by his instructor, he was forced to repeat the course.

Participles, unlike gerunds, are not preceded by possessive nouns or pronouns:

We saw the *boy whipping* his dog. (i.e., we saw the boy doing the whipping)
We saw the *senator coming.* (i.e., we saw him arrive)

Infinitives may exhibit active *(to do)* and passive *(to be done)* voices and they may indicate aspect *(to be doing, to have done, to have been doing, to have been done).* Infinitives may take complements and may be modified by adverbs. In addition, they can function as nouns, adjectives, and adverbs in sentences. Examples:

*noun use*
*To be known* is *to be castigated.*
(subject)          (subjective complement)
He tried everything except *to bypass his superior.*
(object of preposition *except*)

*adjectival use*
They had found a way *to increase profits* greatly.
(modifies the noun *way*)

*adverbial use*
He was too furious *to speak.*
(modifies *furious*)

Although *to* is the characteristic marker of an infinitive, it is not always stated but may be understood:

He helped [to] complete the marketing report.

**Sequence of tenses**   If the main verb in a sentence is in the present tense, any other tense or compound verb form may follow it in subsequent clauses, as

| | |
|---|---|
| I *realize* that you *are leaving*. | I *realize* that you *will be leaving*. |
| I *realize* that you *left*. | I *realize* that you *will leave*. |
| I *realize* that you *were leaving*. | I *realize* that you *will have been leaving*. |
| I *realize* that you *have been leaving*. | I *realize* that you *can be leaving*. |
| I *realize* that you *had left*. | I *realize* that you *may be leaving*. |
| I *realize* that you *had been leaving*. | I *realize* that you *must be leaving*. |

If the main verb is in the past tense, that tense imposes time restrictions on any subsequent verbs in the sentence, thus excluding use of the present tense, as

| | |
|---|---|
| I *realized* that you *were leaving*. | I *realized* that you *would be leaving*. |
| I *realized* that you *left*. | I *realized* that you *could be leaving*. |
| I *realized* that you *had left*. | I *realized* that you *might be leaving*. |
| I *realized* that you *had been leaving*. | I *realized* that you *would leave*. |

If the main verb is in the future tense, it imposes time restrictions on subsequent verbs in the sentence, thus excluding the possibility of using the simple past tense, as

He *will see* you because he *is going* to the meeting too.
He *will see* you because he *will be going* to the meeting too.
He *will see* you because he *will go* to the meeting too.
He *will see* you because he *has been going* to the meetings too.
He *will see* you because he *will have been going* to the meetings too.

In general, most writers try to maintain an order of tenses throughout their sentences that is consistent with natural or real time, e.g., present tense = present-time matters, past tense = past matters, and future tense = matters that will take place in the future. However, there are two outstanding exceptions to these principles:

**a.** If one is discussing the contents of printed or published material, one conventionally uses the present tense, as

In *Duren* v. *State of Missouri,* the Court *argues* that . . . .
These interrogatories *give* all the information we need.
In his latest position paper on the Middle East, the Secretary of State *writes* that . . . .

**b.** If one wishes to add the connotation of immediacy to a particular sentence, one may use the present tense instead of the future, as

I *leave* for Tel Aviv tonight.

The sequence of tenses in sentences which express contrary-to-fact conditions is a special problem frequently encountered in writing. Careful writers avoid the use of "would have" in contrary-to-fact clauses such as those in the following examples, which show the sequence correctly maintained:

If he *were* on time, we *would leave* now.
If he *had been* (not *would have been*) on time, we *would have left* an hour ago.
If we *had been* (not *would have been*) more careful, we *wouldn't be* in this mess now.

**Subject-verb agreement**   Verbs agree in number and in person with their grammatical subjects. At times, however, the grammatical subject may be singular in form, but the thought it carries—i.e., the logical subject—may have plural connotations. Here are some general guidelines:

**a.** Plural and compound subjects take plural verbs even if the subject is inverted. Examples:

Both dogs and cats *were* tested for the virus.
Grouped under the heading "fine arts" *are* music, theater, and painting.

**b.** Compound subjects or plural subjects conveying a unitary idea take singular verbs in American English. Examples:

Kepler and Clark *is* a long-established law firm.
Five hundred dollars *is* a stiff fee.
*but* Twenty-five milligrams of pentazocine *were* administered.

**c.** Compound subjects expressing mathematical relationships may be either singular or plural. Examples:

One plus one *makes* (or *make*) two.
Six from eight *leaves* (or *leave*) two.

**d.** Singular subjects joined by *or* or *nor* take singular verbs; plural subjects so joined take plural verbs. Examples:

A PLS or CLA *is* eligible for the position.
Neither PLS's nor CLA's *are* eligible for the position.

If one subject is singular and the other plural, the verb usually agrees with the number of the subject that is closer to it. Examples:

Either the secretaries or the supervisor *has* to do the job.
Either the supervisor or the secretaries *have* to do the job.

**e.** Singular subjects introduced by *many a, such a, every, each,* or *no* take singular verbs, even when several such subjects are joined by *and:*

Many a graduating law student *has* gone to work for the government.
No supervisor and no secretary *is* excused from the staff meeting.
Every chair, table, and desk *has* to be accounted for.

**f.** The agreement of the verb with its grammatical subject ordinarily should not be skewed by an intervening phrase even if the phrase contains plural elements. Examples:

*One* of my reasons for resigning *involves* purely personal considerations.
The *president* of the company, as well as members of his staff, *has* arrived.
*He,* not any of the proxy voters, *has* to be present.

**g.** The verb *to be* agrees with its grammatical subject, and not with its complement:

His mania *was* fast cars and beautiful women.
Women in the work force *constitute* a new field of study.

In addition, the verb *to be* introduced by the word *there* must agree in number with the subject following it. Examples:

There *are* many complications here.
There *is* no reason to worry about him.

NOTE: For discussion of verb agreement with indefinite-pronoun subjects, see pages 247–248. For discussion of verb number as affected by a compound subject whose elements are joined by *and/or,* see page 241.

**Linking and *sense* verbs**   Linking verbs (as the various forms of *to be*) and the so-called "sense" verbs (as *feel, look, taste, smell,* as well as particular senses of *appear, become, continue, grow, prove, remain, seem, stand,* and *turn*) connect subjects with predicate nouns or adjectives. The latter group often cause confusion, in that adverbs are mistakenly used in place of adjectives after these verbs. Examples:

He *is* a vice-president.
He *became* vice-president.
The temperature *continues* cold.
The future *looks* prosperous.

I *feel* bad.
This perfume *smells* nice.
The meat *tastes* good.
He *remains* healthy.

**Split infinitives**   The writer who consciously avoids splitting infinitives regardless of resultant awkwardness or changes in meaning is as immature in his or her position as the writer who consciously splits all infinitives as a sort of rebellion against convention. Actually, the use of split infinitives is no rebellion at all, because this construction has long been employed by a wide variety of distinguished English writers. Indeed, the split infinitive can be a useful device for the writer who wishes to delineate a shade of meaning or direct special emphasis to a word or group of words—emphasis that cannot be achieved with an undivided infinitive construction. For example, in the locution

to *thoroughly* complete the interrogatories

the position of the adverb as close as possible to the verbal element of the whole infinitive phrase strengthens the effect of the adverb on the verbal element—a situation that is not necessarily true in the following reworded locutions:

to complete *thoroughly* the interrogatories
*thoroughly* to complete the interrogatories
to complete the interrogatories *thoroughly*

In other instances, the position of the adverb may actually modify or change the entire meaning, as

*original*
arrived at the office to *unexpectedly* find a new name on the door

*recast with new meanings*
arrived at the office *unexpectedly* to find a new name on the door

arrived at the office to find a new name on the door *unexpectedly*

The main point is this: If the writer wishes to stress the verbal element of an infinitive or wishes to express a thought that is more clearly and easily shown with to + adverb + infinitive, such split infinitives are acceptable. However, very long adverbial modifiers such as

He wanted to *completely and without mercy* defeat his adversary

are clumsy and should be avoided or recast, as

He wanted to defeat his adversary *completely and without mercy*.

**Dangling participles and infinitives**   Careful writers avoid danglers (as participles or infinitives occurring in a sentence without having a normally expected syntactic relation to the rest of the sentence) that may create confusion for the reader or seem ludicrous. Examples:

*dangling*   Walking through the door, her coat was caught.
*recast*   While walking through the door, she caught her coat.
Walking through the door, she caught her coat.
She caught her coat while walking through the door.
*dangling*   Having been told that he was incompetent and dishonest, the executive fired the man.
*recast*   Having told the man that he was incompetent and dishonest, the executive fired him.
Having been told by his superior that he was incompetent and dishonest, the man was fired.

Participial use should not be confused with prepositional use especially with words like *concerning, considering, providing, regarding, respecting, touching,* etc., as illustrated below:

*prepositional usage*
*Concerning* your complaint, we can tell you. . . .
*Considering* all the implications, you have made a dangerous decision.
*Touching* the matter at hand, we can say that. . . .

Having examined the eight parts of speech individually in order to pinpoint their respective characteristics and functions, we now view their performance in the broader environments of the phrase, the clause, and the sentence.

## PHRASES

A phrase is a brief expression that consists of two or more grammatically related words and that may contain either a noun or a finite verb (i.e., a verb that shows grammatical person and number) but not both, and that often functions as a particular part of speech within a clause or a sentence. The table below lists and describes seven basic types of phrases.

### Types of Phrases

| Type of Phrase | Description | Example |
|---|---|---|
| **noun phrase** | consists of a noun and its modifiers | *The concrete building* is huge. |
| **verb phrase** | consists of a finite verb and any other terms that modify it or that complete its meaning | She *will have arrived too late* for you to talk to her. |
| **gerund phrase** | is a nonfinite verbal phrase that functions as a noun | *Sitting on a patient's bed* is bad hospital etiquette. |
| **participial phrase** | is a nonfinite verbal phrase that functions as an adjective | *Listening all the time in great concentration,* he lined up his options. |
| **infinitive phrase** | is a nonfinite verbal phrase that may function as a noun, an adjective, or an adverb | *To do that* will be stupid. (noun)<br>This was a performance *to remember.* (adjective)<br>He struggled *to get free.* (adverb) |
| **prepositional phrase** | consists of a preposition and its object(s) and may function as a noun, an adjective, or an adverb | Here is the desk *with the extra file drawer.* (adjective)<br>He now walked *without a limp.* (adverb)<br>*Out of here* is where I'd like to be! (noun) |
| **absolute phrase** | is also called a nominative absolute, consists of a noun + a predicate form (as a participle), and acts independently within a sentence without modifying a particular element of the sentence | He stalked out, *his eyes staring straight ahead.* |

## CLAUSES

A clause is a group of words containing both a subject and a predicate and function-ing as an element of a compound or a complex sentence (see pages 258–263 for dis-cussion of sentences). The two general types of clauses are:

independent    It is hot, and I feel faint.
dependent      Because it is hot, I feel faint.

Like phrases, clauses can perform as particular parts of speech within a total sentence environment. The table below describes such performance.

Clauses that modify may also be described as restrictive or nonrestrictive. Whether a clause is restrictive or nonrestrictive has direct bearing on sentence punctuation.

Restrictive clauses are the so-called "bound" modifiers. They are absolutely es-sential to the meaning of the word or words they modify, they cannot be omitted without the meaning of the sentences being radically changed, and they are unpunc-tuated. Examples:

Women who aren't competitive should not aspire to high corporate office.

↑————┬————↑
no    restrictive    no
punctuation  clause  punctuation

In this example, the restrictive clause limits the classification of women and thus is essential to the total meaning of the sentence. If, on the other hand, the restrictive clause is omitted as shown below, the classification of women is now not limited at all, and the sentence conveys an entirely different notion:

Women should not aspire to high corporate office.

### Basic Types of Clauses with Part-of-speech Functions

| Type of Clause | Description | Example |
|---|---|---|
| **noun clause** | fills a noun slot in a sentence and thus can be a subject, an object, or a complement | Whoever is qualified should ap-ply. (subject)<br>I do not know what his field is. (object)<br>Route that journal to whichever department you wish. (object)<br>The trouble is that she has no am-bition. (complement) |
| **adjective clause** | modifies a noun or pronoun and typically follows the word it modifies | His administrative assistant, who was also a speech writer, was overworked.<br>I can't see the reason why you're uptight.<br>He is a man who will succeed.<br>Anybody who opts for a career like that is crazy. |
| **adverb clause** | modifies a verb, an adjective, or another adverb and typically fol-lows the word it modifies | They made a valiant effort, al-though the risks were great.<br>I'm certain that he is guilty.<br>We accomplished less than we did before. |

Nonrestrictive clauses are the so-called "free" modifiers. They are not inextricably bound to the word or words they modify but instead convey additional information about them. Nonrestrictive clauses may be omitted altogether without the meaning of the sentence being radically changed, and they are set off by commas; i.e., they are both preceded and followed by commas when they occur in mid-sentence. See the following examples:

Our guide, who wore a green beret, was an experienced traveler.

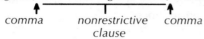

*comma*          *nonrestrictive*  *comma*
                      *clause*

Obviously, the guide's attire is not essential to his experience as a traveler. Removal of the nonrestrictive clause does not affect the meaning of the sentence:

Our guide was an experienced traveler.

The following paragraphs discuss basic points of clause usage.

**Elliptical clauses**    Some clause elements may be omitted if the context makes clear the understood elements:

I remember the first time [that] we met.
This typewriter is better than that [typewriter is].
When [she is] on the job, she is always competent and alert.

**Clause placement**    In order to achieve maximum clarity and to avoid the possibility that the reader will misinterpret what he reads, one should place a modifying clause as close as possible to the word or words it modifies. If intervening words cloud the overall meaning of the sentence, one must recast it. Examples:

*cloudy*    A memorandum is a piece of business writing, less formal than a letter, which serves as a means of interoffice communication.

*The question is: Does the letter or the memorandum serve as a means of interoffice communication?*

*recast*    A memorandum, less formal than a letter, is a means of interoffice communication.

**Tagged-on *which* clauses**    Tagging on a "which" clause that refers to the total idea of a sentence is a usage fault that should be avoided by writers who want to be precise. Examples:

| *tagged-on* | *recast* |
|---|---|
| The firm is expanding, which I personally think is a wise move. | The firm's decision to expand is a wise move in my opinion. |
| | *or* |
| | I believe that the firm's decision to expand is wise. |

**SENTENCES**

A sentence is a grammatically self-contained unit that consists of a word or a group of syntactically related words and that expresses a statement (declarative sentence), asks a question (interrogative sentence), expresses a request or command (imperative sentence), or expresses an exclamation (exclamatory sentence). A sentence typically contains both a subject and a predicate, begins with a capital letter, and ends with a punctuation mark. The table on the opposite page classifies the three main types of sentences by their grammatical structure and provides examples of each structural type.

## Sentences Classified by their Grammatical Structure

| Description | Example |
|---|---|
| **simple sentence** | |
| is a complete grammatical unit having one subject and one predicate, either or both of which may be compound | *Paper* is costly. *Bond* and *tissue* are costly. *Bond* and *tissue* are costly and *are* sometimes scarce. |
| **compound sentence** | |
| comprises two or more independent clauses | *I could arrange to arrive late, or I could simply send a proxy.* *This commute takes at least forty minutes by car, but we can make it in twenty by train.* *A few of the executives had Ph.D.'s, even more of them had B.A.'s, but the majority of them had both B.A.'s and M.B.A.'s.* |
| **complex sentence** | |
| combines one independent clause with one or more dependent clauses (dependent clauses are italicized in examples) | The committee meeting began *when the business manager and the secretarial staff supervisor walked in.* *Although the city council made some reforms,* the changes came so late *that they could not prevent these abuses.* |

**How to construct sentences**    The following paragraphs outline general guidelines for the construction of grammatically sound sentences.

One should maintain sentence coordination by use of connectives linking phrases and clauses of equal rank. Examples:

*faulty coordination with improper use of "and"*
I was sitting in on a meeting, and he stood up and started a long rambling discourse on a new word-processing system.

*recast with one clause subordinated*
I sat in on a meeting during which he stood up and rambled on about a new word-processing system.

*or—recast into two sentences*
I sat in on that meeting. He stood up and rambled on about a new word-processing system.

*faulty coordination with improper use of "and"*
This company employs a full-time research staff and was founded in 1945.

*recast with one clause subordinated*
This company, which employs a full-time research staff, was founded in 1945.

*or—recast with one clause reworded into a phrase*
Established in 1945, this company employs a full-time research staff.

One should also maintain parallel, balanced sentence elements in order to achieve good sentence structure. Examples illustrating this particular point are as follows:

*unparallel*
The report gives market statistics, but he does not list his sources for these figures.

*parallel*
The report gives market statistics, but it does not list the sources for these figures.

*unparallel*
We are glad to have you as our client, and please call us whenever you need help.

*parallel*
We are glad to have you as our client and we hope that you will call on us whenever you need help.
*or recast into two sentences*
We are glad to have you as our client. Please do call on us whenever you need help.

Loose linkages of sentence elements such as those caused by excessive use of *and* should be avoided by careful writers. Some examples of this type of faulty coordination are shown below:

*faulty coordination/excessive use of "and"*
This copier is the best on the market and it eliminates paper jamming and even recycles the toner and produces high quality copies that aren't expensive and that are copied on both sides of the paper.
*recast into three shorter, more effective sentences*
This copier is the best on the market. It prints on both sides of the paper, eliminates jamming, and even recycles the toner. It produces inexpensive but high quality copies.

In constructing one's sentences effectively, one should choose the conjunction that best expresses the intended meaning. Examples:

*not*
Overcrowding was a problem *and* we had to decentralize the files.
*but*
We had to decentralize the files *because* overcrowding was a problem.
Overcrowding was a problem, *so* we had to decentralize the files.
*or recast to*
Overcrowding forced us to decentralize the files.

Good writers avoid unnecessary grammatical shifts that interrupt the reader's train of thought and needlessly complicate the material. Some unnecessary grammatical shifts are shown below, and improvements are also illustrated:

*unnecessary shifts in verb voice*
Any information you *can give* us *will be* greatly *appreciated* and we *assure* you that discretion *will be exercised* in its use.
*rephrased* (note the italicized all-active verb voice)
We *will appreciate* any information that you *can give us*. We *assure* you that we *will use* it with discretion.

*unnecessary shifts in person*
*One* can use either erasers or correcting fluid to remove typographical errors; however, *you* should make certain that *your* corrections are clean.
*rephrased* (note that the italicized pronouns are consistent)
*One* can use either erasers or correcting fluid to eradicate errors; however, *one* should make certain that *one's* corrections are clean.
*or*
*You* can use either erasers or correcting fluid to eradicate errors; however, *you* should make certain that *your* corrections are clean.

*unnecessary shifts from phrase to clause*
Because of the lawyers' vacations and we are short-handed in the office, we cannot take any new clients now.
*rephrased*
Because of the lawyers' vacations and a shortage of office personnel, we cannot take any new clients now.
*or*
Because the lawyers are on vacation and the office staff is short-handed, we cannot take any new clients now.

Always keeping in mind the reader's reaction, the writer should strive for a rational ordering of sentence elements. Closely related elements, for example, should be placed as close together as possible for the sake of maximum clarity. Examples:

*not*
We would appreciate your sending us the instructions on copy editing by mail or cable.

*but*
We would appreciate your sending us by mail or by cable the copy-editing instructions.

*or*
We would appreciate your mailing or cabling us the copy-editing instructions.

*or*
We would appreciate it if you would mail or cable us the copy-editing instructions.

One should ensure that one's sentences form complete, independent grammatical units containing both a subject and a predicate, unless the material is dialogue or specialized copy where fragmentation may be used for particular reasons (as to reflect speech or to attract the reader's attention). Examples:

*poor*
During the last three years, our tax practice soared. While our real estate practice fell off.

*better*
During the last three years, our tax practice soared, but our real estate practice fell off.

*or, with different emphasis*
While our real estate practice fell off during the last three years, our tax practice soared.

**Sentence length**    Sentence length is directly related to the writer's purpose: there is no magic number of words that guarantees a good sentence. For example, a writer covering broad and yet complex topics in a long memorandum may choose concise, succinct sentences for the sake of clarity, impact, and fast dictation and reading. On the other hand, a writer wishing to elicit the reader's reflection upon what is being said in an appeal brief may employ longer, more involved sentences. Still another writer may juxtapose long and short sentences to emphasize an important point. The longer sentences may build up to a climactic and forceful short sentence.

Despite the "Plain English" movement that has begun to simplify the phrasing of insurance policies, contracts, and court forms, most legal documents employ long, complexly organized sentences. Yet their punctuation and their conventional phraseology serve to distinguish the parts of the sentence and make their relationship clear.

**Sentence strategy**    Stylistically, there are two basic types of sentences—the periodic and the cumulative or loose. The periodic sentence is structured so that its main idea or its thrust is suspended until the very end, thereby drawing the reader's eye and mind along to an emphatic conclusion:

*buildup* — While the Commission would wish to give licensees every encouragement to experiment on their own initiative with new and different means of providing access to their stations for the discussion of important public issues, it cannot justify the imposition of a specific right of access by government fiat. — *thrust*
—*Television/Radio Age*

The cumulative sentence, on the other hand, is structured so that its main thought or its thrust appears first, followed by other phrases or clauses expanding on or supporting it:

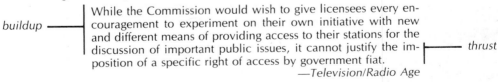

*main point* — A secretary needs to listen very carefully not only for the name of the caller but also for the purpose of the call so that she can handle it herself or accurately record the message for someone else to handle later. — *supporting phrase*

The final phrase in a cumulative sentence theoretically could be deleted without skewing or destroying the essential meaning of the total sentence. A cumulative sentence is therefore more loosely structured than a periodic sentence.

A writer may employ yet another strategy to focus the reader's attention on a problem or an issue. This device is the rhetorical question—a question that requires no specific response from the reader but often merely sets up the introduction of the writer's own views:

What can be done to correct the problem? Two things, to begin with: never discuss cases out of the office, and never allow a visitor to see the papers on your desk.

In some instances, a rhetorical question works as a topic sentence in a paragraph; in other instances, a whole series of rhetorical questions may spotlight pertinent issues for the reader's consideration.

A writer uses either coordination or subordination or a mixture of both to create different stylistic effects. As shown in the subsection on clauses, coordination links independent sentences and sentence elements by means of coordinating conjunctions, while subordination transforms elements into dependent structures by means of subordinating conjunctions. While coordination tends to promote rather loose sentence structure which can become a fault, subordination tends to tighten the structure and to focus attention on a main clause. Examples:

*coordination*
During the balance of 1981, this Company expects to issue $100,000,000 of long-term debt and equity securities *and* may guarantee up to $200,000,000 of new corporate bonds.
*subordination*
*While* this Company expects to issue $100,000,000 of long-term debt and equity securities during the balance of 1981, it may also guarantee up to $200,000,000 of new corporate bonds.

A reversal of customary or expected sentence order is yet another effective stylistic strategy, when used sparingly, because it injects a dash of freshness, unexpectedness, and originality into the prose. Examples:

*customary or expected order*
I find that these realities are indisputable: the economy has taken a drastic downturn, costs on all fronts have soared, and jobs are at a premium.
*reversal*
That the economy has taken a drastic downturn; that costs on all fronts have soared; that jobs are at a premium—these are the realities that I find indisputable.

Interrupting the normal flow of discourse by inserting comments is a strategy that some writers employ to call attention to an aside, to emphasize a word or phrase, to render special effects (as forcefulness), or to make the prose a little more informal. Since too many interrupting elements may distract the reader and disrupt his train of thought, they should be used with discretion. Examples:

*an aside*       His evidence, if reliable, could send our client to prison.
*emphasis*       Any contract for the commission of a civil wrong—even yours—is illegal.
*forcefulness*   This, your Honor, is Exhibit B.

While interruption breaks up the flow of discourse, parallelism and balance work together toward maintaining an even rhythmic flow of thoughts. Parallelism means a similarity in the grammatical construction of adjacent phrases and clauses that are equivalent, complementary, or antithetical in meaning. Examples:

These ecological problems are of crucial concern *to* scientists, *to* businessmen, *to* government officials, and *to* all citizens.

Our attorneys have argued *that* the trademark is ours, *that* our rights have been violated, and *that* appropriate compensation is required.

He was respected not only *for his intelligence* but also *for his integrity*.

Balance is the juxtaposition and equipoise of two or more syntactically parallel constructions (as phrases and clauses) that contain similar, contrasting, or opposing ideas, as shown in the following quotations:

To err is human; to forgive, divine.

—Alexander Pope

Ask not what your country can do for you—ask what you can do for your country.

—John F. Kennedy

And finally, a series can be an effective way to emphasize a thought and to establish a definite rhythmic prose pattern:

The thing that interested me . . . about New York . . . was the . . . contrast it showed between the dull and the shrewd, the strong and the weak, the rich and the poor, the wise and the ignorant.

—Theodore Dreiser

## PARAGRAPHS

The underlying structure of any written communication—be it a memorandum, a letter, or a brief—must be controlled by the writer if the material is to be clear, coherent, logical in orientation, and effective. Since good paragraphing is a means to this end, it is essential that the writer be facile when using techniques of paragraph development and transition between paragraphs. While the writer is responsible for the paragraphing system, the secretary still should be able to recognize various kinds of paragraphs and their functions as well as the potential problems that often arise in structuring a logical paragraph system. In this way, the secretary can assist the writer, especially by pointing out possible discrepancies that might result in misinterpretation by the reader or that might detract from the total effect of the communication.

A paragraph is a subdivision in writing that consists of one or more sentences, that deals with one or more ideas, or that quotes a speaker or a source. The first line of a paragraph is usually indented in reports, studies, articles, books, and legal documents. However, the first line of a paragraph in business letters and memorandums may or may not be indented, depending on the style being followed. See Chapter 10, section 10.6, for business-letter styling.

**Uses of paragraphs**     Paragraphs should not be considered as isolated entities that are self-contained and mechanically lined up without transitions or interrelationship of ideas. Rather, paragraphs should be viewed as components of larger groups or blocks that are tightly interlinked and that interact in the sequential development of a major idea or cluster of ideas.

Individual paragraphs and paragraph blocks are flexible: their length, internal structure, and purpose vary according to the writer's intention and his or her own style. For example, one writer may be able to express a point in a succinct, one-sentence paragraph, while another may require several sentences to make the same point. Writers' concepts of paragraphing also differ. For instance, some writers think of paragraphs as a means of dividing their material into logical segments with each unit developing one particular point in depth and in detail. Others view paragraphs as a means of emphasizing particular points or adding variety to long passages.

**Paragraph development and strategy**     Depending on the writer's intentions, paragraph development may take any of these directions:

1. The paragraph may move from the general to the specific.
2. The paragraph may move from the specific to the general.
3. The paragraph may exhibit an alternating order of comparison and contrast.
4. The paragraph may chronicle events in a set temporal order—e.g., from the beginning to the end, or from the end to the beginning.

5. The paragraph may describe something (as a group of objects) in a set spatial order—e.g., the items being described may be looked at from near-to-far, or vice versa.

6. The paragraph may follow a climactic sequence with the least important facts or examples described first followed by a buildup of tension leading to the most important facts or examples then followed by a gradual easing of tension. Other material can be so ordered for effectiveness; for example, facts or issues that are easy to comprehend or accept may be set forth first and followed by those that are more difficult to comprehend or accept. In this way the easier material makes the reader receptive and prepares him to comprehend or accept the more difficult points.

7. Anticlimactic order is also useful when the writer's intent is to persuade the reader. With this strategy, the writer sets forth the most persuasive arguments first so that the reader, having then been influenced in a positive way by that persuasion, moves along with the rest of the argument with a growing feeling of assent.

**Keys to effective paragraphing**   The following material outlines some ways of building effective paragraphs within a text.

A topic sentence—a key sentence to which the other sentences in the paragraph are related—may be placed either at the beginning or at the end of a paragraph. A lead-in topic sentence should present the main idea in the paragraph and should set the initial tone of the material that follows. A terminal topic sentence should be an analysis, a conclusion, or a summation of what has gone before it.

Single-sentence paragraphs can be used to achieve easy transition from a preceding to a subsequent paragraph (especially when those are long and complex), if it repeats an important word or phrase from the preceding paragraph, if it contains a pronoun reference to a key individual mentioned in a preceding paragraph, or if it is introduced by an appropriate conjunction or conjunctive adverb that tightly connects the paragraphs.

Since the very first paragraph sets initial tone, introduces the subject or topic under discussion, and leads into the main thrust of a communication, it should be worded so as to immediately attract the reader's attention and arouse interest. These openings can be effective:

**a.** a succinct statement of purpose or point of view
**b.** a concise definition (as of a problem)
**c.** a lucid statement of a key issue or fact

But these openings can blunt the rest of the material:

**a.** an apology for the material to be presented
**b.** a querulous complaint or a defensive posture
**c.** a rehash of ancient history (as a word-for-word recap of previous correspondence from the individual to whom one is writing)
**d.** a presentation of self-evident facts
**e.** a group of sentences rendered limp and meaningless because of clichés

The last paragraph ties together all of the ideas and points that have been set forth earlier and reemphasizes the main thrust of the communication. These can be effective endings:

**a.** a setting forth of the most important conclusion or conclusions drawn from the preceding discussion
**b.** a final analysis of the main problem or problems under discussion
**c.** a lucid summary of the individual points brought up earlier
**d.** a final, clear statement of opinion or position
**e.** concrete suggestions or solutions if applicable
**f.** specific questions asked of the reader if applicable

But the following endings can decrease the effectiveness of a communication:

**a.** apologies for a poor presentation
**b.** qualifying remarks that blunt or negate incisive points made earlier
**c.** insertion of minor details or afterthoughts
**d.** a meaningless closing couched in clichés

The following are tests of good paragraphs:

1. Does the paragraph have a clear purpose? Is its utility evident, or is it there just to fill up space?

2. Does the paragraph clarify rather than cloud the writer's ideas?

3. Is the paragraph adequately developed, or does it merely raise other questions that the writer does not attempt to answer? If a position is being taken, does the writer include supporting information and statistics that are essential to its defense?

4. Are the length and wording of all the paragraphs sufficiently varied, or does the writer employ the same types of locutions again and again?

5. Is the sentence structure coherent?

6. Is each paragraph unified? Do all the sentences really <u>belong</u> there; or does the writer digress into areas that would have been better covered in another paragraph or that could have been omitted altogether?

7. Are the paragraphs coherent so that one sentence leads clearly and logically to another? Is easy, clear transition among the paragraphs effected by a wise selection of transitional words and phrases which indicate idea relationships and signal the direction in which the author's prose is moving?

8. Does one paragraph simply restate in other terms what has been said before?

# 9.9

## TONE IN WRITING

The tone of a communication is usually set in the first paragraph and is ordinarily maintained throughout the subsequent paragraphs to the end. Of course, tone depends on a number of factors:

1. the underlying reason or reasons why something (as a memorandum or a letter) is being written in the first place
2. the personal attitude of the writer toward the reader and the subject matter
3. the content (as general vs. technical) of the material itself

Thus, a communication may be formal or informal, neutral or biased, friendly or critical, or it may reflect any number of other feelings and attitudes.

### THE IMPORTANCE OF TONE IN COMMUNICATIONS

The effect of the tone of a communication on its reader cannot be overemphasized. A letter, for example, may feature excellent layout, clean typewriting, attractive stationery, good sentence structure, correct spelling, and easy transition from one paragraph to another. It may contain complete, logically presented data. Yet, if the tone of the letter is needlessly abrupt or indeed rude, the effect of the material on the reader will be negative, of course. Reader responses should therefore be kept in mind at all times. Some principles relevant to tone in general office communications are outlined and discussed briefly in the following paragraphs.

A communication should be reader-oriented. When one is intent on setting forth one's own objectives, especially under pressure, one often unfortunately forgets the reader's point of view and possible responses. Compare the following two approaches:

*abrupt*
Our office is sponsoring a legal seminar on June 20 and 21, 19--. We will need your Mahogany Room conference suite with the following arrangements: . . . . Please reserve the suite and confirm this reservation at once.

*polite*
Would you please reserve your Mahogany Room conference suite for June 20 and 21, 19--. Our general manager, Mr. Harris, visited your hotel recently and was very impressed with its appearance and the high quality of your service. He told us that the Mahogany Room would be an ideal place to hold our legal seminar.

We shall need the following conference arrangements: . . . . An early confirmation of this reservation would be appreciated.

The writer should not assume *automatically* that the reader has the same degree of familiarity with the matter to be discussed as he has. He should consciously pitch his presentation at an appropriate level, neither writing down to experts nor writing over the heads of nonexperts.

Use of the personal pronoun *you* can personalize a communication and thus make the reader feel more involved in the discussion. Compare the following pairs of examples:

*impersonal*
Enclosed herewith is a copy of a Request to Dismiss without Prejudice, filed today with the Clerk of the Superior Court. It is the policy of this office to keep its clients informed of developments in their cases. Further inquiries may be made by telephone.

*personal*
The enclosed document is a copy of a Request to Dismiss without Prejudice, which we filed today with the Clerk of the Superior Court in connection with your case. We will continue to keep you informed of developments in the suit. Please call us if you have any questions.

In the same way, the personal pronouns *I* and *we* should not be consciously avoided in favor of passive or impersonal constructions that, when overused, can depersonalize a communication. Examples:

*impersonal*
Reference is made to your May 1 letter received by this office yesterday.
Enclosed is the requested material.
It is the understanding of this writer that the contract is in final negotiation stages.

*personal*
We are referring to your May 1 letter which we received yesterday.
We're enclosing the material you requested.
I understand that the contract is in final negotiation stages.

Common courtesy and tactfulness can be exercised without resort to obsequiousness. Considerate writers use polite expressions whenever possible.

# 9.10

## ACHIEVEMENT OF A MORE ORIGINAL WRITING STYLE

The language of legal documents is both precise and stylized. Locutions such as "for good and valuable consideration" and "know all men by these presents" have acquired specific legal meanings over the years, and lawyers hesitate to deviate from these established linguistic customs. In certain areas the Plain English movement has made headway in streamlining the language of contracts and insurance policies to make them clearer to the layman, and in a few areas the courts have begun to encourage less stylized, more natural expression in legal documents. In general, however, the conventional language of the law is well established and widely adhered to.

It is when the stylized language of legal documents is carried over into <u>non-legal</u> contexts such as interoffice communications and office correspondence that problems in communication can occur. In these instances, there is no legal reason to use phrases such as "herewith," "the undersigned," and "the aforesaid." In fact, such language can create a barrier between people instead of aiding communication between them. Clients, prospective clients, other attorneys, and judges do not expect a *breezy* tone in correspondence from a law firm—extreme informality can damage the dignified image that the firm tries to project. But a certain naturalness of expression helps to cement a friendly relationship between the sender and the recipient of a written communication.

To take one example, countless letters are sent out from law offices that begin, almost automatically, "Enclosed herewith please find . . . ." The phrase is a convenient opener, but it is stilted and impersonal. An opening such as "We are enclosing . . . ." or "Enclosed are . . . ." is not only more natural but also more likely to establish a rapport with the client or other recipient.

The effectiveness and overall output of communications can be markedly increased if one avoids the padding and clichés that can blunt what otherwise might be incisive writing. These expressions have become fixtures in the vocabularies of far too many writers. Some of the locutions (as "regret to advise you") are best avoided because they are stale. Others (as "aforesaid"), while common to legal documents, are stiff and awkward in general correspondence. Still others (as "beg to respond") have an antique ring. And then there are some expressions (as "forward on") that are redundant, and others (as "acknowledge receipt of") that are overlong.

Unfortunately, these verbal tics seem to occur most often in conspicuous areas of a text: either at the very beginning where initial tone is being set or at the very end where summations are being made, or at the beginnings and ends of individual sentences and paragraphs where particular ideas and points are being set forth. Needless to say, a busy reader can become quite annoyed when he or she must wade through superfluous or hackneyed expressions to get at the gist of a communication.

While this section does not presume to prescribe word choice, it does attempt to spotlight ways to shave away verbal fat so that the main ideas and points in a piece of writing will stand out. The following alphabetically ordered mini-glossary is a representative list of expressions better avoided by writers who seek more clarity, brevity, and originality in their business communications.

**abeyance**
**hold in abeyance**

| | |
|---|---|
| *stilted* | We are holding our final decision in abeyance. |
| *easier* | We are deferring ⎫ delaying ⎬ our final holding up ⎭ decision. |

**above**
While use of this word as a noun ("see the above"), an adjective ("the above figure shows"), and an adverb ("see above") is indeed acceptable, its overuse within one document can distract a reader. Alternative expressions are:

See the figure on page --.
See the figure at the top of the page.
This (that) figure shows . . . .
See the material illustrated earlier.

**above-mentioned**
is overlong and is often overworked within a single document.

| | |
|---|---|
| *longer* | The above-mentioned policy . . . . |
| *shorter* | This (That) policy . . . . |

**acknowledge receipt of**
requires 22 keystrokes, but the alternative expression *have received* is a 13-stroke synonym. Why not use the shorter of the two?

| | |
|---|---|
| *longer* | We acknowledge receipt of your check . . . . |
| *shorter* | We have ⎫ received your We've ⎬ check . . . . |

**advise**
has been overworked when meaning "to inform." Since "to inform" can be expressed by either of the shorter verbs *say* or *tell*, why not use one of them?

| | |
|---|---|
| *longer* | We regret to advise you that Mrs. Mercer is no longer with the firm. |
| *shorter* | We must tell you that Mrs. Mercer is no longer with the firm. |
| | We're sorry to say that Mrs. Mercer is no longer with the firm. |

### advised and informed
is redundant, since the two conjoined words simply repeat each other.

| | |
|---|---|
| *redundant* | He has been advised and informed of our position. |
| | We have advised and informed him of our position. |
| *lean* | He has been told of our position. |
| | We have told him of our position. |
| | He knows our position. |

### affix (one's) signature to
is padding, and can be reduced to *sign*.

| | |
|---|---|
| *padded* | Please affix your signature to the enclosed documents. |
| *lean* | Please sign these documents. |
| | Please sign the enclosed documents. |

### aforementioned/aforesaid
are commonly used in legal documents but sound verbose and pointlessly pompous in general contexts. The same idea may usually be conveyed by one of the demonstrative adjectives (*this, that, these, those*).

| | |
|---|---|
| *verbose* | The aforementioned company . . . . |
| *natural* | This (that) company . . . . *or* The company in question . . . . The company (we) mentioned earlier . . . . |
| *verbose* | . . . must reach a decision regarding the aforesaid dispute. |
| *natural* | . . . must make a decision about this (that) dispute. |

### and etc.
is redundant, because *etc.* is the abbreviation of the Latin *et cetera* meaning "and the rest." Omit the *and*.

| | |
|---|---|
| *not* | . . . carbon packs, onionskin, bond, and etc. |
| *but* | . . . carbon packs, onionskin, bond, etc. |

### as per
has been overworked when meaning "as," "in accordance with," and "following." It is a tired and formulaic way to begin a letter, paragraph, or sentence.

| | |
|---|---|
| *overworked* | As per your request of . . . . |
| | As per our telephone conversation of . . . . |
| | As per our agreement . . . . |
| *more natural* | As you requested . . . . |
| | According to your request . . . . |
| | In accordance with your request . . . . |
| | As a follow-up to our telephone conversation . . . . |
| | In accordance with our telephone conversation . . . . |
| | As we agreed . . . . |
| | In accordance with our agreement . . . . |
| | According to our agreement . . . . |

### as regards
can also be expressed by the terms *concerning* or *regarding*.

| | |
|---|---|
| *stiff* | As regards your complaint . . . . |
| *easier* | Concerning your complaint . . . . *or* Let's talk about your complaint. |

### as stated above
can be more naturally expressed as:
As we (I) have said . . . .

### assuring you that
is an outmoded participial-phrase ending to a business letter that should not be used.

| | |
|---|---|
| *outmoded* | Assuring you that your cooperation will be appreciated, I remain |
| | Sincerely yours |
| *current* | I will appreciate your cooperation. |
| | Sincerely yours |

### as to
has been as overworked as the phrase *as per*. Here are some alternatives for *as to*:
regarding   concerning   about   of

| | |
|---|---|
| *overworked* | As to your second question . . . . |

| | |
|---|---|
| *fresher* | Regarding your second question . . . . |
| | Coming to your second question . . . . |
| | Let's look at your second question. |
| *overworked* | We have no means of judging as to the wisdom of that decision. |
| *fresher* | We cannot (can't) judge the wisdom of that decision. |

—*compare* AS PER

### at about
is meaningless because *at* is explicit but *about* is indefinite. Thus, when conjoined, they cancel each other's meaning.

| | |
|---|---|
| *meaningless* | I'll get back to you at about 9:30 a.m. tomorrow. |
| *explicit* | I'll get back to you at 9:30 a.m. tomorrow. |
| | *or* |
| | I'll get back to you about 9:30 a.m. tomorrow. |

### at all times
may be shortened to *always*.

| | |
|---|---|
| *longer* | We shall be glad to meet with you at all times. |
| *shorter* | We'll always be glad to meet with you. |

### at an early date
is both long and vague. If the writer means "immediately," or "by (*date*)," he should say as much; if he means "when convenient," he should specify it.

### at once and by return mail
when conjoined are repetitious: either *at once* or *immediately* will suffice.

| | |
|---|---|
| *repetitive* | Please send us your check at once and by return mail. |
| *succinct* | Please send us your check at once (*or* immediately). |

—*see also* RETURN MAIL

### attached hereto/herewith
is quite impersonal and may be expressed in a more personal way as:
Attached is/are . . . .
We are attaching . . . .
We have attached . . . .
You'll see attached . . . .

—*compare* ENCLOSED HEREWITH

### at this point in time/at this time
may be shortened to
now
presently
at (the) present

### at this writing
may be shortened to *now*.

### at your earliest convenience
manages to convey nothing in 28 keystrokes; however, the alternative *as soon as you can* requires only 18 strokes and states the case explicitly. Still other expressions, as
now
immediately
by (*date*)
within (*number of days*)
may also be used, depending on context.

### basic fundamentals
is redundant. One of the following may be substituted:
the basics
the fundamentals

### beg
### beg to acknowledge
### beg to advise
### beg to state
and other such *beg* combinations sound antique. The following may be used instead:
We acknowledge . . . .
We've received . . . .
Thank you for . . . .
We're pleased to tell you . . . .
We can tell you that . . . .

### brought to our notice
is overlong and may be recast to:
We note . . . .
We notice . . . .
We see . . . .

### contents carefully noted
contributes little or no information and should be omitted.

| | |
|---|---|
| *not* | Yours of the 1st. received and contents carefully noted. |
| *but* | We've read carefully your June 1 letter. |
| | We've read your June 1 letter. |
| | The instructions in your June 1 letter have been followed. |
| | We've read your June 1 letter and have followed its instructions. |

**dated**

is unnecessary when used in locutions like "your letter dated June 1." The word may be omitted:

your June 1 letter
your letter of June 1

**deem** (it)

is a stiff way of saying *think* or *believe*.

*stiff*   We deem it advisable that you . . . .

*easier*   We think you ought to . . . .
We think it advisable that you . . . .

**demand and insist**

when conjoined are redundant; the use of just one of the following at a time will suffice: *demand* or *insist* or *require*.

**despite the fact that**

may be pared down to *although* or *though*.

**due to**
**due to the fact that**

are both stiff and may be reduced to: *because (of)* or *since*.

**duly**

is meaningless in expressions like

Your request has been duly forwarded.

and thus should be omitted:

Your request has been forwarded.
We've forwarded your request.

**earnest endeavor**

is cloying when used in this type of sentence:

It will be our earnest endeavor to . . . .
It should be replaced with more direct, straightforward phrasing:

We'll (*or* We shall *or* We will) try to . . . .

**enclosed herewith/enclosed please find**

are impersonal and stilted expressions better worded as:

We enclose . . . .
We are enclosing . . . .
We have enclosed . . . .
Enclosed is/are . . . .

—*compare* ATTACHED HERETO/HEREWITH

**endeavor**

is an eight-letter verb that can be replaced by the three-letter verb *try*, which is synonymous and not pompous.

*pompous and longer*
We shall endeavor to . . . .

*direct and shorter*
We'll (*or* We shall) try to . . . .
We'll make a real effort to . . . .
We'll do everything we can to . . . .
We'll do our best to . . . .

**esteemed**

is effusive when used in a sentence like

We welcome your esteemed favor of June 9.

and therefore should not be used. The sentence may be recast to:

Thank you for your June 9 letter.

**favor**

should never be used in the sense of a letter, a check, or other such item.

*not*   your favor of April 14
*but*   your April 14 letter

**for the purpose of**

may be more succinctly worded as *for*.

*padded*   . . . necessary for purposes of accounting.

*lean*   . . . necessary for accounting.

**forward on**

is redundant, since *forward* alone conveys the meaning adequately.

*redundant*   We have forwarded the lease on to the Register of Deeds.

*explicit*   We have forwarded the lease to the Register of Deeds.

**hand** (one) **herewith**

as in the locution

We are handing you herewith . . . .

is an inflated way of saying

We're (*or* We are) enclosing . . . .
Enclosed is/are . . . .

**have before me**

is superfluous. Obviously, the writer has previous correspondence at hand when responding to a letter.

*not*   I have before me your letter of June 1 . . . .

*but*   In reply
response   } to your June 1
answer   } letter . . . .

**hereto**

—*see* ATTACHED HERETO/HEREWITH

**herewith**
—*see* ATTACHED HERETO/HEREWITH
ENCLOSED HEREWITH/ENCLOSED PLEASE FIND

**hoping for the favor (*or* to hear)**
and other such participial-phrase endings for business letters are now outmoded and should be omitted. Instead of
Hoping for the favor of a reply,
I remain
one of these alternatives may be selected:
I (We) look forward to hearing from you.
I (We) look forward to your reply.
May I (we) hear from you soon?

**I am/I remain**
as in the expression
Looking forward to a speedy reply from you, I am (*or* remain)
should never be used as lead-ins to complimentary closes; instead, the writer might choose one of the following expressions:
I (We) look forward to your immediate reply.
I am (We are) looking forward to a reply from you soon.
May I (we) please have an immediate reply?
Will you please reply soon?

**immediately and at once**
when conjoined are redundant; however, each element of the expression may be used separately, as
May we hear from you immediately (*or* at once)?

**incumbent**
**it is incumbent upon** (one)
is more easily expressed as
I/we must . . . .
You must . . . .
He/she/they must . . . .

**in re**
should be avoided in the body of general correspondence, although it is often used in the subject line of a letter as well as in legal documents. Adequate substitutes are:
regarding
concerning
in regard to
about

| | |
|---|---|
| *stiff* | In re our telephone conversation of . . . . |
| *easier* | Concerning our telephone conversation of . . . . |

**institute the necessary inquiries**
is overlong and overformal, and may be reworded as follows:
We shall inquire . . . .
We'll find out . . . .
We are inquiring . . . .

**in the amount of**
is a long way to say *for*.

| | |
|---|---|
| *longer* | We are sending you a check in the amount of $50.95. |
| *shorter* | We are sending you a check for $50.95. |
| | We are sending you a $50.95 check. |

**in the course of**
may be more concisely expressed by *during* or *while*.

| | |
|---|---|
| *longer* | In the course of the negotiations . . . . |
| *shorter* | During the negotiations . . . . |
| | While we were negotiating . . . . |

**in the event that**
may be more concisely expressed by *if* or *in case*.

| | |
|---|---|
| *longer* | In the event that you cannot meet with me next week, we shall . . . . |
| *shorter* | If you cannot meet with me next week, we shall . . . . |

**in view of the fact that**
may be shortened to *because (of)* or *since*.

| | |
|---|---|
| *longer* | In view of the fact that he is now president of . . . . |
| | He was terminated in view of the fact that he had been negligent. |
| *shorter* | Since he is now president of . . . . |
| | He was terminated because of negligence. |

**it is incumbent upon**
—*see* INCUMBENT

**it is within** (one's) **power**
—*see* POWER

**meet with** (one's) **approval**
is a stiff phrase more easily expressed as:
is (are) acceptable
I (we) accept (*or* approve)

| | |
|---|---|
| *stiff* | If the plan meets with Mr. Doe's approval . . . . |
| *easier* | If the plan is acceptable to Mr. Doe . . . . |
| | If Mr. Doe accepts (*or* approves) the plan . . . . |

**note**
**we note that**
**you will note that**
often constitute padding and thus should be dropped.

| | |
|---|---|
| *padded* | We note that your prospectus states . . . . |
| | You will note that the amount in the fourth column . . . . |
| *lean* | Your prospectus states . . . . |
| | The amount in the fourth column . . . . |

Or, if a word of this type is required, a more natural substitute is *see*:
We see that you have paid the bill in full.

**oblige**
is archaic in the following locution:
Please reply to this letter and oblige.
The sentence should be recast to read:
Please reply to this letter immediately.

**of the opinion that**
is a stiff way of saying:
We think (*or* believe) that . . . .
Our opinion is that . . . .
Our position is that . . . .

**our Mr., Ms., Miss, Mrs.** + (surname)
is best omitted.

| | |
|---|---|
| *not* | Our Mr. Lee will meet with you next Tuesday. |
| *but* | Our legal assistant, Mr. Lee, will meet with you next Tuesday. |
| | Mr. Lee will meet with you next Tuesday. |

**party**
while idiomatic in legal documents, is nevertheless awkward in general business contexts when the meaning is "individual" or "person."

| | |
|---|---|
| *awkward* | We understand that you are the party who called earlier. |
| *smoother* | We understand that you are the person (*or* individual *or* one) who called earlier. |
| | We understand that you called earlier. |

**pending receipt of**
while used in legal documents is, in general contexts, a stiff way of saying "until we receive."

| | |
|---|---|
| *stiff* | We are holding the forms, pending receipt of your check. |
| *easier* | We'll process the forms as soon as we receive your check. |

**permit me to remain**
is outmoded and should not be used as part of the last sentence in a business letter.

**place an order for**
takes 18 keystrokes, but the verb *order* takes only 5 strokes. Why not use the shorter of the two?

**position**
**be in a position to**
The locutions
We are not in a position to
We are now in a position to
are unnecessarily long and may be recast to the shorter and more personal phrases
We cannot/can't
We are unable/aren't able
We can
We are now able

**power**
**it is** (not) **within** (one's) **power to**
is a lengthy way of saying
We can (*or* are able to)
We cannot/can't
We are unable to

| | |
|---|---|
| *longer* | It is not within our power to back such an expensive project. |
| | It is now within our power to help you. |
| *shorter* | We cannot back such an expensive project. |
| | We can help you now. |

**prior to**
is a stiff way to say *before*.

| | |
|---|---|
| *stiff* | Prior to receipt of your letter of July 1, we . . . . |
| *easier* | Before we received your July 1 letter, we . . . . |
| | Before receipt of your July 1 letter, we . . . . |
| | Before receiving your July 1 letter, we . . . . |

—*compare* SUBSEQUENT TO

**pursuant to**
is a stiff phrase that unfortunately occurs in the very beginnings of many follow-up letters and memorandums. It should be reworded to read:

In accordance with
According to
Following up (*or* As a follow-up to)

| *stiff* | Pursuant to our telephone conversation of June 1, let me say . . . . |
| *easier* | Following up our June 1 telephone conversation, I can say . . . . |

**reason is because**
is ungrammatical, because the noun *reason* + the verb *is* call for a following noun clause and not an adverbial clause introduced by *because*.

The reason is:        This is the reason.
The reason is that    Because (*or* since)

**receipt**
—*see* PENDING RECEIPT OF

**receipt is acknowledged**
is an unnecessarily impersonal passive construction more concisely expressed as

We received
We have received
We've received

**reduce to a minimum**
may be pared down to *minimize.*

**refer back to**
is a phrase in which *back* is redundant because the word element *re-* means "back."

| *redundant* | We must refer back to our closed files before we can answer your inquiry. |
| *lean* | We must refer to our closed files before we can answer your inquiry. |

**refuse and decline**
when conjoined are redundant; the use of one will suffice: *refuse* or *decline.*

| *redundant* | We must refuse and decline any further dealings with your company. |
| *lean* | We must refuse any further dealings . . . .
*or*
We must decline to have any further dealings . . . . |

—*compare* DEMAND AND INSIST

**reiterate again**
the adverb *again* is redundant, since the verb *reiterate* carries the total meaning by itself.

| *redundant* | Let me reiterate our policy again. |
| *succinct* | Let me reiterate restate repeat our policy.
May I reiterate restate repeat our policy?
*or*
Let me state our policy again.
May I state our policy again? |

**return mail**
**by return mail**
is a hackneyed and meaningless way of saying

immediately      at once
promptly         by (*explicit date*)

| *hackneyed* | Please send us your check by return mail. |
| *fresher* | Won't you mail (us) your check immediately?
Please send us your check at once.
We'd like to have your check by (*date*). |

**said**
is idiomatic in legal documents; however, it sounds stiff in general contexts.

| *stiff* | . . . a discussion of said matters. |
| *easier* | . . . a discussion of those (these) matters. |

**same**
is an awkward substitute for the pronoun *it* or *them,* or for the applicable noun.

| *awkward* | We have your check and we thank you for same.
Your July 2 inquiry has been received and same is being researched. |
| *easier* | Thank you for your check which arrived yesterday.
Your July 2 inquiry has been received and is being researched. |

**separate cover**
**under separate cover**
is a tired, overlong, vague phrase. If a specific mailing method (as SPECIAL DELIVERY) is not to be indicated, the adverb *separately* should be substituted.

*hackneyed*    We are mailing you our 1981 *Annual Report* under separate cover.

*fresher*    We're sending you separately our 1981 *Annual Report*.

## subsequent to
is longer than its synonyms *after* or *following*. Why not opt for fewer keystrokes?

*longer*    Subsequent to the interview, she . . . .

*shorter*    After the interview, she . . . .

—*compare* PRIOR TO

## take the liberty
is overlong and sounds somewhat obsequious.

*longer*    We are taking the liberty of consulting with a medical specialist.

*shorter*    We are consulting with a medical specialist.

## thanking you in advance
is an outmoded participial-phrase ending that should not be used in modern business letters. A writer who uses this phrase is also cavalier enough to presume that his request will be honored.

*not*    Thanking you in advance for your help, I am

Sincerely yours

*but*    Your help (*or* assistance) will be appreciated.

I'll appreciate your help.

Any help you may give me will be greatly appreciated.

I'll appreciate any help you may give.

If you can help me, I'll appreciate it.

I'll be grateful for your help.

Won't you help me?

## therefor/therein/thereon
are commonly used in legal documents, but sound stiff in general business contexts.

*stiff*    The order is enclosed herewith with payment therefor.

The safe is in a secure area with the blueprints kept therein.

Enclosed please find Forms X, Y, and Z; please affix your signature thereon.

*easier*    We're enclosing a check with our order.

The blueprints are kept in the safe which is located in a secure area.

Please sign Forms X, Y, and Z which we have enclosed.

## trusting you will
is an outmoded participial-phrase ending that should not be used in business letters. A writer who uses this phrase is also cavalier enough to presume that his request will be honored.

*not*    Trusting that you will inform me of your decision soon, I am

Sincerely yours

*but*    I hope that you'll give me your decision soon.

Will you please give me your decision soon?

Won't you give me your decision soon?

## under date of
is an awkward locution that should be omitted.

*not*    . . . your letter under date of December 31 . . . .

*but*    . . . your letter of December 31. . . .

. . . your December 31 letter . . . .

—*compare* DATED

## under separate cover
—*see* SEPARATE COVER

## (the) undersigned
while common in legal documents, is awkward and impersonal in other writings.

*awkward*    Please return these forms to the undersigned.

The undersigned believes that . . . .

*easier*    Please return these forms to me.

I believe that . . . .

## up to the present writing
is padding and should be omitted.

*padded*    Up to the present writing, we do not seem to have received . . . .

*lean*    We have not yet received . . . .

As of now we have not received . . . .

We still have not received . . . .

We haven't received . . . .

## valued
is redundant when used after the verb *appreciate* which carries the idea itself.

*redundant*    We appreciate your valued assistance.

*lean*    We appreciate your assistance.

Your assistance is, of course, appreciated.

# 10

CHAPTER TEN

# STYLE IN LEGAL CORRESPONDENCE

## CONTENTS

# 10.1

## THE LETTER AS AN IMAGE-MAKER

The word *style* as applied to letter writing encompasses format, grammar, stylistics, and word usage. All of these elements conjoin in a letter to produce a tangible reflection on paper not only of the writer's ability and knowledge and the typist's competence, but also of an office's total image. For example, an attorney may have spent considerable time and effort in building up the practice and in projecting a positive professional image; yet this image may be seriously eroded or negated altogether by carelessly prepared letters especially when produced over a long time span. On a smaller scale, a few letters of that kind may create such negative impressions on their recipients that they will have second thoughts about pursuing professional relationships with the writer. The letter, then, is actually representative of the attorney's professional stature, regardless of the size of the practice. And if there appears to be no pride in or concern for the quality of something as basic as one's correspondence, how then can there be concern for or pride in the quality of one's professional services?

An attorney may spend a great deal of time on correspondence, planning and thinking out the direction, tone, and content of his or her own letters as well as reading and acting on incoming letters. Secretaries spend even more of their time on correspondence. And time costs money. Therefore, if both writer and typist keep in mind the following simple aids to good letter production, the time and money involved will have been well spent:

1. Stationery should be of high-quality paper having excellent correcting or erasing properties.
2. Typing should be neat and accurate with any corrections or erasures rendered invisible.
3. The essential elements of a letter (such as the date line, inside address, message, and signature block) and any other included parts should conform in page placement and format with one of the generally acceptable business-letter stylings (as the Full Block Letter, the Modified Block Letter, the Modified Semi-block Letter, or the Indented Letter) illustrated in section 10.6.
4. The language of the letter should be clear, concise, grammatically correct, and devoid of padding and clichés.
5. The ideas in the message should be logically oriented, with the writer always keeping in mind the reader's reaction.
6. All statistical data should be accurate and complete.

Style in business and professional correspondence, like language itself, is not a static entity: it has changed over the years to meet the varying needs of its users, and it is continuing to change today. The Full Block Letter, for instance, which reduces typing time by eliminating all tab settings, has replaced the once-standard Indented Letter in many law offices. Open and mixed punctuation patterns have almost completely superseded the closed punctuation pattern. However, law firms have been slow to adopt the bare-bones look of the Simplified Letter, and the textual references in this book are therefore limited to the Full Block, Modified Block, Modified Semi-block, Indented, and Official Letter styles. A full-page facsimile of the Simplified Letter that illustrates all features of this modern letter style is found on pages 308–309.

# 10.2

## LETTER BALANCE AND LETTERHEAD DESIGN

It has often been said that an attractive letter should look like a symmetrically framed picture with even margins working as a frame for the typed lines that are balanced under the letterhead. But how many letters really <u>do</u> look like framed pictures? Planning ahead <u>before</u> starting to type is the real key to letter symmetry:

1. Estimate the approximate number of words in the letter or the general length of the message by checking the length of a dictated source or by looking over the writer's rough draft or one's shorthand notes.
2. Make mental notes of any long quotations, lists of citations, or anything that may require margin adjustments or a different typeface.
3. Set the left and right margin stops according to the estimated letter length: about one inch for very long letters (300 words or more, or at least two pages), about one and one-half inches for medium-length ones (about 100–300 words), and about two inches for very short ones (100 words or less).
4. Use a guide sheet that numbers each line in the margin (see page 181) as a bottom margin warning or lightly pencil a warning mark on the paper.
5. Continuation-sheet margins should match those of the first sheet, and at least three lines of the message should be carried over to the continuation sheet.

6. Letters should be single-spaced with double-spacing between paragraphs; very short letters may be double-spaced throughout.

Adjustments may be made by varying the number of spaces above and below the date line. The space between the identification initials and other notations may also be increased or decreased, especially when the signature is not blocked flush left.

## LETTERHEAD

The legal profession, more than almost all other businesses and professions, is conscious of its image. A law firm's desire to appear solidly reliable results in the use of stationery that is conservative, even distinguished-looking. Conservative colors are used—white to off-white, or perhaps a pale blue paper; black or occasionally blue ink—and the stationery is frequently engraved rather than printed. A few offices use letterhead engraved in old-fashioned script.

Letterhead designs vary with one's organization. Most law firm letterheads are positioned dead-center at the top of the page. Some are more elaborately balanced, with the names of the partners (and sometimes also of associates) listed additionally on the left side and telephone and telex numbers on the right. Some firms use two letterheads—one that includes the individual names of the attorneys, another with only the name and address of the firm. Less conventional variations in letterhead design may feature all data at the top left, all data spread out from the left to the right margin, or additional data printed in small letters at the bottom of the page.

Regardless of layout and design, a typical letterhead contains all or some of the following elements, with the asterisked items being essential:

  logo

\* full legal name of the firm, company, corporation, institution, or group

\* full street address

  suite, room, or building number, if needed—post office box number, if applicable

\* city, state, and ZIP Code

  Area Code and telephone number(s)

  other data (as telex or cable references, types of services offered, branch offices, or names of individuals associated with the practice)

The letter style used by an office should be taken into consideration in designing a letterhead. For example, a letterhead with a long list of names on the left side might be best balanced with the Modified Block Letter style, where the date and reference numbers appear on the right side of the page. Elaborate letterhead layouts require especially careful letter planning to avoid an unbalanced look.

**Personalized letterhead** Personalized or executive letterhead is widely used by high-level corporate officers and professionals. In the case of corporate executives, the standard company letterhead design may be supplemented with the name of the office ("Office of the General Counsel") or with the full name and title of the executive ("Gerald M. Jones, General Counsel") printed or engraved in small letters one or two lines beneath the letterhead at or near the left margin. Partners in law firms often select this style of letterhead for their personal communications. The full name of the partner is printed or engraved below and to the left of the letterhead, often on a better grade of paper than that of standard, printed office stationery.

Personalized letterhead on Executive or Monarch stationery is preferred by some attorneys. This stationery features a heading positioned at the top of the page that includes the lawyer's full name and full street address. Envelopes match the paper and must include the lawyer's name and return address. Executive and Monarch stationery is usually engraved and is smaller than standard letterhead, as shown in the table on page 278.

# 10.3

## ALL ABOUT PAPER

Paper and envelope size, quality, and basis weight vary according to application. The next table lists various paper and envelope sizes along with their uses.

Good-quality paper is an essential element in the production of attractive, effective letters. Paper with rag content is considerably more expensive than sulfite bonds. Nevertheless, most law firms prefer rag-content paper because it best conveys the professionalism of the firm. Since the cost of paper has been estimated at less than five percent of the total cost of the average professional letter, it is easy to understand why law firms consider high-quality paper to be worth the added expense. When one assesses paper quality, one should ask these questions:

1. Will the paper withstand corrections and erasures without pitting, buckling, or tearing?
2. Will the paper accept even and clear typed characters?
3. Will the paper permit smooth written signatures?
4. Will the paper perform well with carbons and in copying machines?
5. Will the paper withstand storage and repeated handling and will its color wear well over long time periods?
6. Is the color of the paper appropriate for a law office?
7. Will the paper fold easily without cracking or rippling?
8. Will the paper hold typeset letterhead without bleed-through?

An important characteristic of paper is its fiber direction or grain. When selecting paper, one should ensure that the grain will be parallel to the direction of the typewritten lines, thus providing a smooth surface for clear and even characters, an easy erasing or correcting surface, and a smooth fit of paper against the typewriter platen.

### Stationery and Envelope Sizes and Applications

| Stationery | Stationery Size | Application | Envelope | Envelope Size |
|---|---|---|---|---|
| Standard | 8½" × 11" <br> *also* <br> 8" × 10½" | general <br> business, legal, <br> or personal <br> correspondence | *commercial* <br> No. 6¾ <br> No. 9 <br> No. 10 | 3⅝" × 6½" <br> 3⅞" × 8⅞" <br> 4⅛" × 9½" |
| | | | *window* <br> No. 6¾ <br> No. 9 <br> No. 10 | 3⅝" × 6½" <br> 3⅞" × 8⅞" <br> 4⅛" × 9½" |
| Executive <br> or <br> Monarch | 7¼" × 10½" <br> or <br> 7½" × 10" | personal <br> correspondence <br> of professionals <br> and corporate <br> officers; <br> usually <br> personalized | *regular* <br> Executive <br> or <br> Monarch <br><br> *window* <br> Monarch | 3⅞" × 7½" <br><br><br><br><br> 3⅞" × 7½" |
| Half-sheet <br> or <br> Baronial | 5½" × 8½" | extremely <br> brief <br> notes | *regular* <br><br> Baronial | <br><br> 3⅝" × 6½" |

Every sheet of paper has what is called a felt side: this is the top side of the paper from which a watermark may be read, and it is on this side of the sheet that the letterhead should be printed or engraved.

The weight of the paper must be considered when ordering stationery supplies. Paper for standard, executive, and form letters as well as for half-sheets should be 24 or 20 basis weight. Basis weight, also called substance number, is the weight in pounds of a ream of paper cut to a basic size. Basis 24 is heaviest; stationery is also available in 20, 16, and 13 basis weights.

Continuation sheets, although blank, must match the letterhead sheet in color, basis weight, texture, size, and quality. Envelopes should match both the first and continuation sheets. Therefore, these materials should be ordered along with the letterhead to ensure a good match.

Letterhead and continuation sheets as well as envelopes should be stored in their boxes to prevent soiling. A small supply of these materials may be kept in the typist's stationery drawer, but they should be arranged carefully so as not to become damaged over time.

# 10.4

## GENERAL PUNCTUATION PATTERNS IN LEGAL CORRESPONDENCE

As with letterhead designs, the choice of general punctuation patterns in legal correspondence is usually determined by the office. However, it is important that specific punctuation patterns be selected for designated letter stylings, and that these patterns be adhered to for the sake of consistency and fast output. The most common pattern in law offices today is *mixed punctuation. Open punctuation,* which reflects the trend toward streamlining business correspondence, is only slowly gaining acceptance by attorneys. The older and more complex *closed punctuation*—requiring a terminal mark at the end of each element of a business letter—is sometimes used with the Indented Letter styling in law firms but is considered outmoded by other American business offices.

### MIXED PUNCTUATION PATTERN

1. The end of the date line is unpunctuated, although the comma between the day and year is retained.
2. The ends of the lines of the inside address are unpunctuated unless an abbreviation such as *P.C.* terminates a line, in which case the period after the abbreviation is retained.
3. The salutation is punctuated with a colon.
4. The complimentary close is punctuated with a comma.
5. The end(s) of the signature block line(s) are unpunctuated.
6. This pattern is used with either the Full Block, the Modified Block, or the Modified Semi-block Letter.

### OPEN PUNCTUATION PATTERN

1. The end of the date line is unpunctuated, although the comma between day and year is retained.
2. The ends of the lines of the inside address are unpunctuated, unless an abbreviation such as *P.C.* terminates a line, in which case the period after the abbreviation is retained.

3. The salutation if used is unpunctuated.
4. The complimentary close if used is unpunctuated.
5. The ends of the signature block lines are unpunctuated.
6. This pattern is always used with the Simplified Letter (see pages 308–309) and is often used with the Full Block Letter (see pages 300–301).

## CLOSED PUNCTUATION PATTERN

1. A period terminates the date line.
2. A comma terminates each line of the inside address except the last, which is ended by a period.
3. A colon punctuates the salutation.
4. A comma punctuates the complimentary close.
5. A comma terminates each line of the signature block except the last, which is terminated by a period.
6. This pattern is used chiefly with the Indented Letter.

**Closed Punctuation Pattern with the Indented Letter**

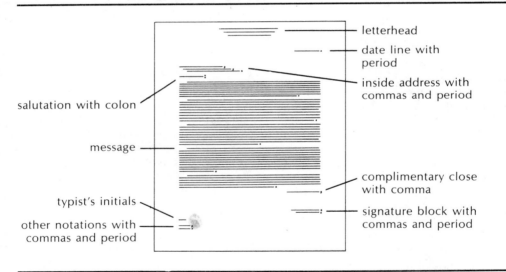

The above illustration depicts a fully closed punctuation pattern which is rarely used in the United States. The Indented Letter typed in a modern law office is likely to use a modified version of closed punctuation with fewer periods, such as that featured in the facsimile on pages 306–307.

# 10.5

## THE INDIVIDUAL PARTS OF A LETTER:
A Discussion of Each

The various elements of a letter are listed below in the order of their occurrence. While asterisked items are essential elements of any letter regardless of its general styling, those items that are unmarked may or may not be included, depending on general styling (as the Simplified Letter or the Full Block Letter) and on the nature of the letter itself (as general or confidential correspondence):

| | | |
|---|---|---|
| * date line | attention line | * signature block |
| reference line | salutation | identification initials |
| special mailing notations | subject line | enclosure notation |
| on-arrival notations | * message | carbon copy notation |
| * inside address | complimentary close | postscript |

## DATE LINE

The date line may be typed two to six lines below the last line of the printed letter-head; however, three-line spacing is recommended as a standard for most letters. Spacing may be expanded or contracted, depending on letter length, space available, letterhead design, and office policy. The date line consists of the month, the day, and the year (January 1, 19--), all on one line. Ordinals (as 1st, 2d, 24th) are never used. The use of an abbreviation or an Arabic numeral for the month is not permitted in date lines, although the day and the month may be reversed and the comma dropped in United States Government correspondence or in British correspondence, where this styling is common (1 January 19--).

The following page placements of date lines are all acceptable. The choice depends on the general letter styling or the letterhead layout; however, the date line should never overrun either right or left margins.

1. The date can be blocked flush with the left margin. This style is essential with the Full Block Letter.
2. The date can be blocked flush with the right margin so that the last digit of the date is aligned exactly with the margin. This style may be used with the Modified Block, Modified Semi-block, and Indented Letters. In order to align the date at the right margin, the typist moves the carriage to the right margin stop and then backspaces once for each keystroke and each space that will be required in the typed date. The typist can then set the tab stops when typing the first of several letters that will bear the same date.
3. The date line can be centered directly under the letterhead. This style may be used with the Modified Block and the Modified Semi-block Letters.
4. The date can be positioned about five spaces to the right of dead center. This style may be used with the Modified Block and the Modified Semi-block Letters.

## REFERENCE LINE

A reference line with file, correspondence, case, order, billing, or policy numbers is included in a letter when the addressee has specifically requested that correspondence on a subject contain a reference, or when it is needed for filing. It may be centered and typed one to four lines below the date, although some offices require that it be typed and single-spaced directly above or below the date to make it less conspicuous. With the Full Block Letter, the reference line should be aligned flush left, regardless of its position either above or below the date. With the Modified Block, Modified Semi-block, and Indented Letters, the reference line may be centered on the page or blocked under or above the date line wherever it has been typed.

| **reference line blocked left** | **reference line blocked right** |
|---|---|
| January 1, 19– | January 1, 19– |
| X-123-4 | X-123-4 |
| *or* | *or* |
| X-123-4 | X-123-4 |
| January 1, 19– | January 1, 19– |

**Reference Number Centered on Page Four Lines Beneath Date Line**

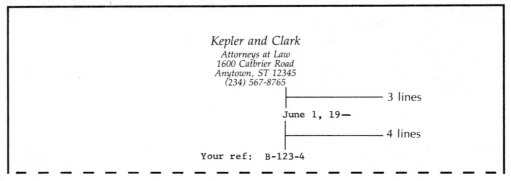

Some offices combine the reference line (which usually consists of numerals) with the *subject line* (which refers to the subject of the letter; see pages 287–289) by placing both textual and numerical information between the inside address and the salutation. Like the standard reference line, this information is blocked left in the Full Block Letter. In other letter styles, it may be centered or aligned with the date.

Re: Harrell v. Jones
Case No. X-123-4

Still another variation adopted by some firms that are unhappy with the way the reference number impairs the appearance of their letters is to place it beneath the identification line at the bottom of the page:

CRC/rw
X-123-4
Enclosure

Reference lines on the first sheet must be carried over to the heading of a continuation sheet or sheets. The styling of the date line and the reference line on a continuation sheet should match the one on the first page as closely as possible; for example, if the reference line appears on a line below the date on the first sheet, it should be so typed on the continuation sheet. The first setup below illustrates a continuation-sheet reference line as used with the Full Block Letter:

John B. Jones, Esq.
January 1, 19—
X-123-4
Page 2

The second example illustrates the positioning of a reference line on the continuation sheet of a Modified Block, a Modified Semi-block, or an Indented Letter:

John B. Jones, Esq.                                    —2—                                    January 1, 19—
                                                                                                                        X-123-4

See page 290 for continuation-sheet facsimiles.

## SPECIAL MAILING NOTATIONS

If a letter is to be sent by any method other than by regular mail, that fact is indicated on the letter itself and on the envelope (see pages 311–313 for details on envelope styling). The all-capitalized special mailing notation (as CERTIFIED MAIL or SPECIAL DELIVERY) in all letter stylings is aligned flush left about four lines below the line on which the date appears, and about two lines above the first line of the inside address. While some offices prefer that this notation appear on the original and on all copies, others prefer that the notation be typed only on the original.

**Special Mailing Notation in the Full Block Letter**

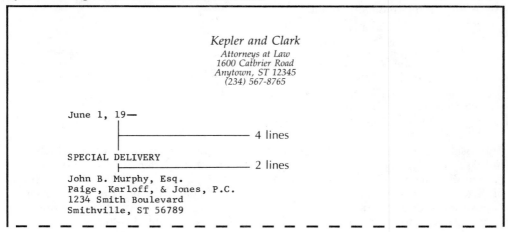

Vertical spacing (as between the date line and the special mailing notation) may vary with letter length; i.e., more space may be left for short or medium letter lengths.

## ON-ARRIVAL NOTATIONS

The on-arrival notations that may be included in the letter itself are PERSONAL and CONFIDENTIAL. The first indicates that the letter may be opened and read only by its addressee; the second, that the letter may be opened and read by its addressee and/or any other person or persons authorized to view such material. These all-capitalized notations are usually positioned four lines below the date line and usually two but not more than four lines above the first line of the inside address. They are blocked flush left in all letter stylings. If a special mailing notation has been used, the on-arrival notation is blocked one line beneath it. Spacing between the date line and the on-arrival notation may be increased to as much as six lines if the letter is extremely brief.

If either PERSONAL or CONFIDENTIAL appears in the letter, it must also appear on the envelope (see pages 311–313 for envelope styling).

**On-arrival Notation in a Modified Block Letter**

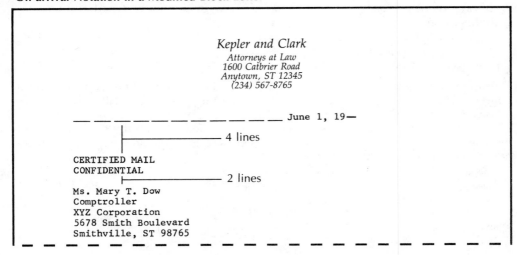

## INSIDE ADDRESS

An inside address typically includes:

1. *if letter is directed to a particular individual*
   addressee's courtesy title + full name
   addressee's business or professional title if required
   full name of addressee's affiliation
   full geographical address
2. *if letter is addressed to an organization in general*
   full name of the firm, company, or institution
   individual department name if required
   full geographical address

The inside address is placed about three to eight, but not more than 12 lines below the date. Its placement will depend on the length of the letter or the attorney's preference. It is always single-spaced internally. It is blocked flush with the left margin in all letter styles except the Indented. In an Indented Letter, the first line of the address is flush left, but each succeeding line is indented five spaces more than the line preceding it. Note the use of closed punctuation with the Indented Letter.

| **all block styles** | **Indented Letter** |
|---|---|
| Mr. Joseph R. Rowe | Mr. Joseph R. Rowe, |
| General Counsel | General Counsel, |
| XYZ Corporation | XYZ Corporation, |
| 1234 Smith Boulevard | 1234 Smith Boulevard, |
| Smithville, ST 56789 | Smithville, ST 56789. |

A courtesy title (as *Mr., Ms., Mrs., Miss, Dr.,* or *The Honorable*) should be typed before the addressee's full name, even if a business or professional title (as *Treasurer* or *Chief of Staff*) follows the surname. No courtesy title, however, should ever precede the name when *Esquire* or an abbreviation for a degree follows the name.

Before typing the addressee's full name, the secretary should, if possible, refer to the signature block of previous correspondence from that individual to ascertain the exact spelling and styling of the name. This information may also be obtained from printed executive letterhead. A business or professional title, if included, should also match the styling in previous correspondence or in official literature. If an individual holds several offices (as *Vice-president and General Manager*) within an organization, the title shown in the signature block of previous correspondence should be copied, or the title of the individual's highest office (in this case, *Vice-president*) may be selected. Business, professional, and judicial titles should not be abbreviated. If a title is so long that it might overrun the center of the page, it may be typed on two lines with the second line indented two spaces, as

The Honorable John P. Hemphill, Jr.
Judge of the United States District Court
   for the Western District of Arkansas

The addressee's title may be typed on the same line as the name, separated by a comma. Alternatively, the title may be typed on the second line either by itself or followed by a comma and the name of the organization. Care must be taken, however, to choose the style that will enhance and not detract from the total balance of the letter on the page. The following are acceptable inside-address stylings for business and professional titles:

| | |
|---|---|
| Mr. Arthur O. Brown | Ms. Ann B. Lowe, Director |
| Legal Staff Supervisor | Medical Records Division |
| Omicron, Inc. | North Bend Hospital |
| 1234 Peters Street | North Bend, XX 12345 |
| Jonesville, ZZ 23456 | |

Dr. Joyce A. Cavitt
Dean, School of Law
Stateville University
Stateville, ST 56789
*or*
Dr. Joyce A. Cavitt, Dean
School of Law
Stateville University
Stateville, ST 56789

If an individual addressee's name is unknown or irrelevant and the writer wishes to direct a letter to an organization in general or to a unit within that organization, the organization name is typed on line 1 of the inside address, followed on line 2 by the name of a specific department if required. The full address of the organization is then typed on subsequent lines, as

XYZ Corporation
Consumer Products Division
1234 Smith Boulevard
Smithville, ST 56789

The organization name should be styled exactly as it appears on the letterhead of previous correspondence, or as it appears in printed sources such as annual reports or business or professional directories. For example, is a firm's name *Roe and Doe* or *Roe & Doe? Roe, Doe, and Smith* or *Roe, Doe and Smith?* Is *Attorney-at-law* or *Attorney at Law* part of the name of a single practitioner's firm?

Street addresses should be typed in full and not abbreviated unless window envelopes are being used. Arabic numbers should be used for all building and house numbers except *one*, which should be typed out in letters, as

One Bayside Drive     *but*     1436 Freemont Avenue
                                6 Link Road

Arabic numerals should be used for all numbered street names above *twelve*, but numbered street names from *one* through *twelve* should be spelled out:

145 East 14th Street        167 West Second Avenue        One East Ninth Street

If a numbered street name over *twelve* follows a house number with no intervening word or words (as a compass direction), a spaced hyphen is inserted between the house number and the street-name number, as

2018 - 14th Street

An apartment, building, or suite number if required should follow the street address on the same line with two spaces or a comma separating the two:

62 Park Towers   Suite 9        62 Park Towers, Suite 9

Names of cities (except those following the pattern of *St. Louis* or *St. Paul*) should be typed out in full. The name of the city is followed by a comma and then by the name of the state and the ZIP Code. Names of states (except for the District of Columbia which is always styled *DC* or *D.C.*) may or may not be abbreviated: if a window envelope is being used, the all-capitalized, unpunctuated two-letter Postal Service abbreviation followed by <u>one space</u> and the ZIP Code must be used; on the other hand, if a regular envelope is being used, the name of the state may be typed out in full followed by one space and the ZIP Code, or the two-letter Postal Service abbreviation may be used. For the sake of fewer keystrokes and consistency, it is recommended that the Postal Service abbreviations be used throughout the material. See Chapter 4 for a complete list of these abbreviations. For the styling of Canadian addresses, see the discussion of envelope addresses on page 312.

An inside address should comprise no more than five typed lines. No line should overrun the center of the page. Lengthy organizational names, however, like lengthy business and professional titles, may be carried over to a second line and indented two spaces from the left margin.

## ATTENTION LINE

If the writer wishes to address a·letter to an organization in general but also to bring it to the attention of a particular individual at the same time, an attention line may be typed two lines below the last line of the inside address and two lines above the salutation. The attention line is usually blocked flush with the left margin. Some organizations prefer that the attention line be centered on the page; however, for the sake of fast output, it is generally recommended that the attention line be aligned with the left margin. It *must* be so aligned in the Full Block Letter. This line should be neither underlined nor entirely capitalized; only the first letters of the main elements are capitalized. Placement of a colon after the word *Attention* is optional unless the open punctuation pattern is being followed throughout the letter, in which case the colon should be omitted:

Attention: Mr. John P. Doe      *or*      Attention Mr. John P. Doe

The salutation appearing beneath the attention line should be "Gentlemen" even though the attention line routes the letter to a particular person. Such a letter is actually written to the organization; hence the collective-noun salutation.

**Attention Line in a Modified Block Letter with Mixed Punctuation**

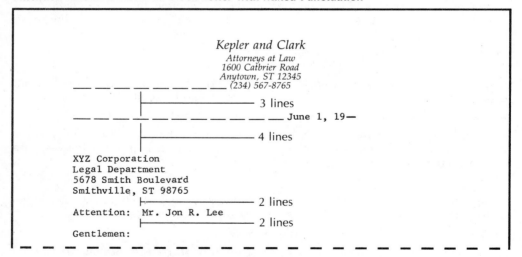

## SALUTATION

The salutation—used with all letter stylings except the Simplified—is typed flush with the left margin, two lines beneath the last line of the inside address or two lines below the attention line if there is one. Additional vertical lines of space may be added after the inside address of a short letter which is to be enclosed in a window envelope. The first letter of the first word of the salutation is capitalized, as are the first letters of the addressee's courtesy title and surname. If the mixed punctuation pattern is being followed in the letter, the salutation is followed by a colon; if open punctuation is being observed, the salutation is unpunctuated. The following are typical examples of various salutations, the last four of which are used in letters to high-level personages (as in the federal judiciary, the diplomatic corps, or the clergy):

| **most commonly used** | **reserved for high-level personages** |
|---|---|
| Gentlemen | My dear Justice Roberts |
| Dear Mr. (*or* Ms., Mrs., Miss, Dr., Professor) Smith | Your Excellency |
| | Excellency |
| Dear Bob | Right Reverend and dear Father |

The salutation "Dear Sir" is rarely used today except in form letters and in letters to high-level personages. Although the salutation "Dear Sirs" is now considered archaic in American business writing, it is still used in Great Britain.

With the advent of the women's rights movement and the ensuing national interest in equal rights and equal opportunity, some writers—both male and female—have discarded the conventional salutation "Gentlemen" and have coined what they feel are more neutral, non-sexist replacements for letters addressed to organizations whose officers may be both male and female. Among these coinages are *Gentlepeople, Gentlepersons, Dear People,* and *Dear Sir, Madam, or Ms.* Although a number of writers have used them, widespread general usage over a long time span has not yet been achieved and these expressions are therefore still not considered conventional. The most conventional way of addressing a male-female group is to write

Ladies and Gentlemen   *or*   Dear Sir or Madam

although the latter expression has become less popular in recent years since the use of *Madam* in a letter to an unmarried woman may offend her.

When a letter is addressed to an all-female organization, the following salutations may be used:

Ladies   *or*   Mesdames

The salutation for a married couple is styled as

Dear Mr. and Mrs. Hathaway
Dear Dr. and Mrs. Simpson

Salutations for letters addressed to two or more persons having the same or different surnames may be found in the Forms of Address section, page 345. Salutations in letters addressed to persons with specialized titles may also be found in the Forms of Address section, pages 315–344.

## SUBJECT LINE

A subject line gives the gist of the letter. It serves as an immediate point of reference for the reader as well as a convenient filing tool for the secretaries at both ends of the correspondence. It is especially useful in correspondence about legal matters and is a common feature on most letters sent out from law offices. In letters concerning litigation, the name of the case is usually the subject. The phrasing of the subject line is necessarily succinct and to the point: it should not generally be so long as to require more than one line. References to complex legal matters, however, may require as many as three lines. If continuation lines are needed, the typist should divide them into logical thought groups.

Re: Proposed Sale by C. T. Garcia
    Pursuant to Rule 144

The subject line is positioned two lines below the salutation. In a Full Block Letter, it is always flush left; in other letter styles, it is usually centered but sometimes flush right or aligned either with the date line or with the complimentary close. A growing number of law offices position the subject line two lines *above* the salutation instead of below. Whatever style the attorney prefers, that preference should be followed consistently in all office correspondence.

The subject line may be entirely capitalized and not underlined. As an alternative, only the initial letters of key words may be capitalized; in the latter case, every word in the line, including the heading, may be underlined. If underscoring is used and there are continuation lines, only the final continuation line is underscored. Continuation lines are aligned with the first word following the heading, not with the heading itself:

Re: Certificate of Sale Pursuant to Court Order
 for John Roe and Mary Schwarz Property

## Subject Line Centered in the Modified Semi-block Letter

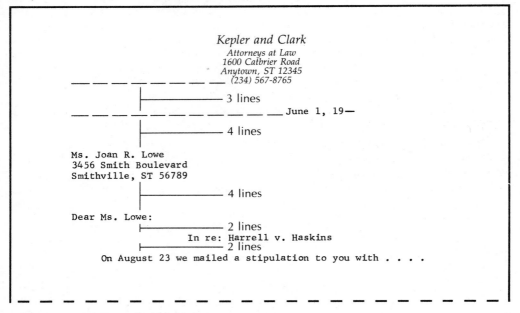

## Subject Line in a Short Full Block Letter

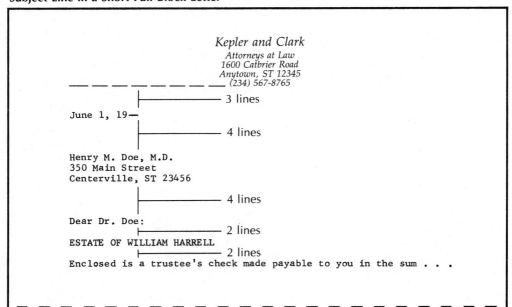

Law offices conventionally introduce the subject line with the word *Re* or the phrase *In re* or with no heading at all. Other types of business offices often use the heading *Subject*. *Re* and *In re* may or may not be followed by a colon, depending on the attorney's preference. Some alternative examples:

Re: Proposed Sale of Roe Property
In re Proposed Sale of Roe Property
PROPOSED SALE OF ROE PROPERTY

## MESSAGE

The body of the letter—the message—should begin about two lines below the salutation or two lines below the subject line if there is one.

Paragraphs are single-spaced internally. Double-spacing is used to separate paragraphs. If a letter is extremely brief, its paragraphs may be double-spaced throughout the letter. Paragraphs in such letters should be indented so that they will be readily identifiable to the reader.

Equal margins measuring one inch for long letters, about one and one-half inches for medium-length letters, and at least two inches for short letters should be kept. The first lines of indented paragraphs should begin five or ten spaces from the left margin. The five-space pattern is the most common in the Modified Semi-block Letter, but ten spaces are required in the Indented Letter. All other letter stylings feature flush-left paragraph alignment.

Long quotations should be indented and blocked five or ten spaces from the left and right margins with internal single-spacing and top-and-bottom double-spacing so that the material will be set off from the rest of the message. Long enumerations should also be indented: enumerations with items requiring more than one line apiece may require single-spacing within each item, followed by double-spacing between items. Tabular data should be centered on the page.

**Page Placement of a Long Quotation**          **Page Placement of an Enumeration**

double-spacing top and bottom and between items

internal single-spacing

double-spacing top and bottom

If a letter is long enough to require a continuation sheet or sheets, at least three message lines must be carried over to the next page. The complimentary close and/or typed signature block should never stand alone on a continuation sheet. The last word on a page should not be divided. Continuation-sheet margins should match those of the first sheet. At least six blank lines equaling one inch should be maintained at the top of the continuation sheet. The two most common continuation-sheet headings are described below.

**Continuation-sheet Heading: Full Block Letter**

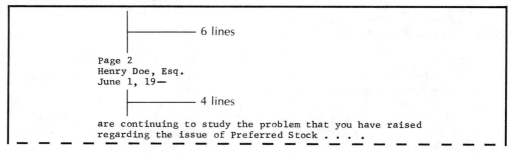

The format shown above is used with the Full Block Letter. It features a flush-left heading beginning with the page number, followed on the next line by the addressee's courtesy title and full name, and ending with the date on the third line. Some companies prefer that the page number appear as the last line of the continuation-sheet heading, especially if a reference number is included.

Another way to type the heading of a continuation sheet is to lay the material out across the page, six lines down from the top edge of the sheet. The addressee's name is typed flush with the left margin, the page number in Arabic numerals is centered on the same line and enclosed with spaced hyphens, and the date is aligned flush with the right margin—all on the same line. This format is often used with the Modified Block, the Modified Semi-block, and the Indented Letters.

**Continuation-sheet Heading: Modified Block, Modified Semi-block, and Indented Letters**

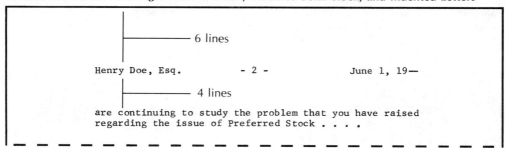

## COMPLIMENTARY CLOSE

There is no complimentary close in the Simplified Letter. However, a complimentary close is used with all other letter styles. The complimentary close is typed two lines below the last line of the message. Its alignment depends on the general letter styling being used:

1. With the Full Block Letter, the complimentary close is always aligned flush left.
2. With the Modified Block and the Modified Semi-block Letters, the complimentary close may be aligned directly under the date line (e.g., about five spaces to the right of dead center or flush with the right margin) or under some particular part of the printed letterhead that the attorney designates. It should never overrun the right margin.
3. With the Indented Letter, the complimentary close begins at or just to the right of dead center. It may begin a few spaces to the left of center to ensure that a long signature block does not overrun the right margin.

Only the first word of the complimentary close is capitalized. If the open punctuation pattern is being followed, the complimentary close is unpunctuated. If the mixed punctuation pattern is being followed, a comma terminates the complimentary close. The typist should always use the complimentary close that is dictated because the writer may have a special reason for the choice of phrasing. If the dictator does not specify a particular closing, the typist may wish to select the one that best reflects the general tone of the letter and the state of the writer-reader relationship. The following chart lists the most often used complimentary closes and also groups them according to general tone and degree of formality. For a complete list of complimentary closes for letters addressed to high-level officials and to persons with specialized titles, see Forms of Address, pages 315–344.

| General Tone & Degree of Formality | Complimentary Close |
| --- | --- |
| highly formal—usually used in diplomatic, governmental, or ecclesiastical correspondence to show respect and deference to a high-ranking addressee | Respectfully yours<br>Respectfully<br>Very respectfully |
| politely neutral—usually used in legal and general correspondence | Very truly yours<br>Yours very truly<br>Yours truly |
| friendly and less formal—usually used in legal and general correspondence | Most sincerely<br>Very sincerely<br>Very sincerely yours<br>Sincerely yours<br>Yours sincerely<br>Sincerely |
| more friendly and informal—often used when writer and reader are on a first-name basis but also often used in general and legal correspondence | Most cordially<br>Yours cordially<br>Cordially yours<br>Cordially |
| most friendly and informal—usually used when writer and reader are on a first-name basis | As ever<br>Best wishes<br>Best regards<br>Kindest regards<br>Kindest personal regards<br>Regards |
| British | Yours faithfully<br>Yours sincerely |

## SIGNATURE BLOCK

The first line of the signature block indicates responsibility for the letter. Either the name of the dictator or the name of the firm, company, or institution may appear on the first line of the signature block. In the former case, the dictator's name is typed at least four lines below the complimentary close; in the latter, the firm name is typed two lines below the complimentary close and the dictator's name at least four lines below the firm name.

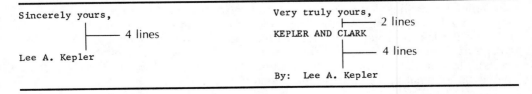

It is also common for firms of attorneys and certain other professional groups to sign correspondence manually with the firm's name, especially when the letters give opinions about legal matters.

---

`Very truly yours,`

*Kepler and Clark*

`KEPLER AND CLARK`

---

Letters signed—by typewriter or hand—with the name of the organization should be written in the plural *we*. The secretary will be guided by the dictator's wishes in styling the signature.

With the Full Block Letter, the signature block is aligned flush left. With the Modified Block and Modified Semi-block Letters, the signature block begins with the name of the writer or the firm typed below the complimentary close (e.g., about five spaces to the right of center, or flush with the right margin) or under a particular part of the printed letterhead. The first letter of each line in the signature block is aligned directly below the first letter in the complimentary close, unless this alignment will result in an overrunning of the right margin, in which case the signature block may be centered under the complimentary close.

---

`          Very truly yours,`

`FITZ, JOHNSON, JACOBSON & BERNSTEIN, P.A.`

*Alicia Jacobson*

`          Alicia Jacobson`

---

Only the first letter of each element of the writer's name is capitalized, and only the first letter of each major element of the writer's official position and/or department name is capitalized if they are included. The title and department name may be omitted if they appear in the printed letterhead:

John D. Russell, Director          *if title and department name*
Legislative Council Service       *are needed for identification*

*or*
John D. Russell                    *if department name is already*
Director                           *printed on the letterhead*

*or*
John D. Russell                    *if both title and department*
                                   *name appear on printed letterhead*

The signature block in the Indented Letter also begins at least four lines below the complimentary close when it begins with the name of the dictator and two lines below when the firm's name is signed. The first line of the signature is indented either three spaces or five spaces from the first letter of the complimentary close, and each succeeding line is indented a further three or five spaces. In order to prevent overrunning the right margin, the complimentary close and signature block may begin a few spaces to the left of center. Only the first letter of each of the major elements of the writer's name, title (if used), and department name (if used) are capitalized. Unless one is following the completely closed punctuation pattern illustrated on page 280, there is no terminal punctuation in the signature lines.

Very truly yours,

 (Ms.) Sarah L. Talbott, Director
  Department of Legal Affairs

Very truly yours,

 (Ms.) Sarah L. Talbott
  Assistant Attorney General

There are several ways in which an attorney may sign the name of the law office. The name of the firm must, however, be spelled and punctuated exactly as it appears on the printed letterhead. The most common style is for the firm's name to be typed all in capitals (or all in capitals except for the word *and*), with the dictating attorney signing his or her name below—with or without the heading *By, By:* or *by.* (The heading *By* is designed chiefly for letter writers who are not officials in a company; it is therefore particularly useful for lawyers who have no business title.) If the dictator's full name is printed on the letterhead, it is not necessary for it to be typed below the signature. Examples:

## Some Common Stylings for Law Firm or Company Signatures

KEPLER AND CLARK

By *Lee A. Kepler*
Lee A. Kepler

KEPLER and CLARK

*Lee A. Kepler*

Lee A. Kepler
Attorney at Law

KEPLER AND CLARK

*Lee A. Kepler*

KEPLER AND CLARK

*Lee A. Kepler*

By:  Lee A. Kepler

XYZ CORPORATION

*Marian Doe*
Marian Doe, General Counsel

OFFICE OF THE PUBLIC DEFENDER

*Roy M. Dow*

Roy M. Dow
Assistant to Mr. Smith

*Attorney at Law* or *Attorney-at-law* (and rarely *Esq.*) may follow the dictator's typewritten name but not the handwritten signature. The terms *Partner* and *Associate* are never used in the signature.

 Most law offices omit the office name in the signature, since it is always prominent in the printed letterhead, and have the letter signed directly by the writer or dictator.

## Some Common Stylings for Personal Signatures

Very truly yours,

*Lee A. Kepler*

Lee A. Kepler

Very truly yours,

*Lee A. Kepler*

Lee A. Kepler
Attorney at Law

Very truly yours,

*Lee A. Kepler*

Very truly yours,

*Lee A. Kepler*

Lee A. Kepler, Attorney-at-law

Two variations from the signature stylings discussed on the preceding page are frequently encountered. The dictator's signature in a Modified Block or Modified Semiblock Letter may be centered to set it off from the firm's signature.

---

FITZ, JOHNSON, JACOBSON & BERNSTEIN, P.A.

By     *John V. Fitz*
            John V. Fitz

---

In addition, personal names may be typed all in capitals to set them off in a complicated signature block:

---

Very truly yours,

JOHN RODD
District Attorney

By     *Marcia Johnson*
          MARCIA JOHNSON
          Assistant District Attorney

---

Regardless of page placement and letter styling, the dictator's signature if typed should be spelled and punctuated exactly like the written signature. The only title that may precede a signature is *Miss, Mrs.,* or *Ms.,* and if one of these appears in the handwritten signature (as when a typed signature is omitted), it must be enclosed with parentheses. There is a marked trend for a woman to omit the courtesy title altogether, but if her name might be confused with a man's name (as Marion, Leslie, Lee), it is courteous to use one of these titles to avoid embarrassment for the recipient who must address a return letter.

---

**Signature Stylings for Unmarried Women**

Sincerely yours,       Sincerely yours,       Sincerely yours,

*Joan Dunn*        *Joan Dunn*        *Joan Dunn*

Joan Dunn         (Ms.) Joan Dunn      (Miss) Joan Dunn
City Attorney       City Attorney        City Attorney

**Signature Stylings for Women who Consider their Marital Status Irrelevant**

Sincerely yours,               Sincerely yours,

*Joan Dunn*               *Joan Dunn*

(Ms.) Joan Dunn          Joan Dunn
City Attorney             City Attorney

**Signature Stylings for Married Women Using Given Name + Maiden Name Initial + Husband's Surname**

Sincerely yours,               Sincerely yours,

*Joan M. Dunn*             *Joan M. Dunn*

(Mrs.) Joan M. Dunn       (Ms.) Joan M. Dunn
City Attorney             City Attorney

**Signature Styling for Married Woman Using her Husband's Full Name**

Sincerely yours,

*Joan Dunn*

Mrs. Robert A. Dunn
City Attorney

---

A widow may use either her first name and her maiden name initial and her late husband's surname with the courtesy title *Mrs.* or *Ms.* enclosed in parentheses, or she may use her husband's full name with *Mrs.*, as

Sincerely yours,                              Sincerely yours,

*Joan M. Dunn*                                *Joan Dunn*

(Mrs.) Joan M. Dunn                           Mrs. Robert A. Dunn
*or* (Ms.)

A divorcee may use her maiden name if it has been legally regained, along with the courtesy title *Ms.* or *Miss* enclosed by parentheses or she may omit the title:

Sincerely yours,                              Sincerely yours,

*Joan M. Dunn*                                *Joan M. Dunn*

(Ms.) Joan M. Dunn                            Joan M. Dunn
*or* (Miss)

or she may use her maiden name and her former husband's surname with *Mrs.*:

Sincerely yours,

*Joan Dunn*

Mrs. Matthews Dunn

If the secretary signs a letter for the dictator or writer, the dictator's name is followed by the typist's initials immediately below and to the right of the surname, or centered under the full name, as

*Peter S. Weiss* ck                          *Peter S. Weiss* ck

If the secretary signs a letter in her own name for someone else, that individual's courtesy title and surname only are typed directly below, as

Sincerely yours,          Sincerely yours,          Sincerely yours,

*Janet A. Smith*          *Seymour T. Barnes*        *Lee L. Linden*

(Miss) Janet A. Smith     Seymour T. Barnes          Lee L. Linden
Assistant to Mr. Wood     Secretary to Senator Ross  Secretary to Ms. Key

## IDENTIFICATION INITIALS

The initials of the typist and sometimes those of the writer are placed two lines below the last line of the signature block and are aligned flush left in all letter stylings. There is a marked trend towards complete omission of the writer's initials if the name is already typed in the signature block or if it appears in the printed letterhead. Most offices prefer that three capitalized initials be used for the writer's name and two lowercase initials be used for the typist's. Many organizations indicate the typist's initials only on carbons for record-keeping purposes, and they do not show the dictator's initials unless another individual signs the letter. These are common stylings:

| | | | | |
|---|---|---|---|---|
| FCM/HL | FCM:HL | hol | FCM:hl | Franklin C. Mason:HL |
| FM/hl | FCM:HOL | hl | FCM:hol | Franklin C. Mason |
| | | | fcm:hol | HL |

A letter dictated by one person (as an administrative secretary), typed by another (as a corresponding secretary), and signed by yet another person (as the writer) may show (1) the writer/signer's initials entirely in capitals followed by a colon and (2) the dictator's initials entirely in capitals followed by a colon and (3) the transcriber/typist's initials in lowercase, as AWM:COC:ls

## ENCLOSURE NOTATION

If a letter is to be accompanied by an enclosure or enclosures, one of the following expressions should be aligned flush left and typed one to two lines beneath the identification initials, if there are any, or one to two lines beneath the last line of the signature block, if there is no identification line:

Enclosure    *or if more than one*    Enclosures (3)
*or*
enc.    *or*    encl.    *or if more than one*    3 encs.    *or*    Enc. 3

If the enclosures are of special importance, each of them should be numerically listed and briefly described with single-spacing between each item:

Enclosures:    1. Copy of Promissory Note, executed
               2. Copy of Deed of Trust, executed
               3. Copy of title policy

The following type of notation then may be typed in the top right corner of each page of each of the enclosures:

Enclosure (1) to <u>recipient's name</u> letter No. 1–234/X,
dated January 1, 19--, page 2 of 8
(if enclosure has more than one page)

If the enclosure is bound, a single notation attached to its cover sheet will suffice.

## CARBON COPY NOTATION

A carbon copy notation showing the distribution of courtesy copies to other individuals should be aligned flush left and typed two lines below the signature block if there are no other notations or initials, or two lines below any other notations. If space is very tight, the carbon copy notation may be single-spaced below the above-mentioned items. The most common stylings are:

cc    cc:    Copy to    Copies to

This notation may appear on the original and all copies or only on the copies.

    Multiple recipients of copies should be listed alphabetically. Sometimes only their initials are shown, as

cc:WPB
  TLC
  CNR

or the individuals' names may be shown, especially if the writer feels that such information can be useful to the addressee:

cc:  William L. Carton, Esq.    *or*    cc:  Ms. Lee Jamieson
     45 Park Towers, Suite 1         Copy to Mr. John K. Long
     Smithville, ST 56789         Copies to Mr. Houghton
                                Mr. Ott
     Dr. Daniel I. Maginnis                Mr. Smythe
     1300 Dover Drive
     Jonesville, ZZ 12345

If the recipient of the copy is to receive an enclosure or enclosures as well, that individual's full name and address as well as a description of each enclosure and the total number of enclosed items should be shown in the carbon copy notation:

cc:  Ms. Barbra S. Lee (2 copies, Landlord-Tenant Agreement)
     123 Jones Street
     Smithville, ST 56789
     Ms. Sara T. Tufts
     Ms. Laura E. Yowell

If the writer wishes that copies of the letter be distributed without this list being shown on the original, the blind carbon copy notation   bcc   *or*   bcc:   followed by an alphabetical list of the recipients' initials or names may be typed on the carbons in the same page position as a regular carbon copy notation. The *bcc* notation may also appear in the upper left-hand corner of the carbon copies.

**Page Placement of Identification and Enclosure Notations in a Modified Block Letter**

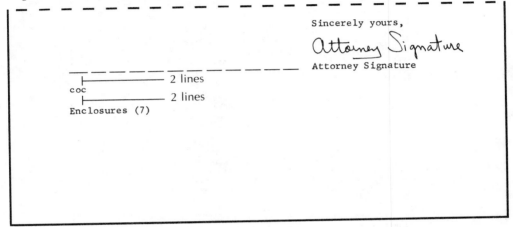

## POSTSCRIPT

A postscript is aligned flush left and is typed two to four lines (depending on space available) below the last notation. If the letter's paragraphs are strict-block, the postscript reflects this format. If the paragraphs within the letter are indented, the first line of the postscript is also indented. All postscripts are single-spaced. Their margins conform with those maintained in the letters themselves. The writer should initial a postscript. While it is not incorrect to head a postscript with the initials *P.S.* (for an initial postscript) and *P.P.S.* (for subsequent ones), these headings are redundant and require extra keystrokes; therefore, it is recommended that they be omitted.

# 10.6

## ESSENTIAL LETTER STYLES FOR LEGAL CORRESPONDENCE

### LETTER FACSIMILES

The following pages contain full-page letter facsimiles of the formats most often used in law offices: the Full Block Letter, the Modified Block Letter, the Modified Semiblock Letter, and the Indented Letter. A facsimile of the Simplified Letter is also included. In addition, the section contains facsimiles of the Official Letter Styling on executive letterhead, the Official Letter Styling on plain bond, and the Half-sheet. Each facsimile contains a detailed description of letter format and styling.

# The Official Letter Styling with Printed Executive Letterhead

*Office of the General Counsel*

**XYZ CORPORATION**
1234 Smith Boulevard
Smithville, ST 56789

February 1, 19--

Dear Ms. Peterson:

This is a facsimile of the Official Letter Styling often used for personal letters written by an executive or a professional, or for letters typed on personalized company stationery. The paper size is either Executive or Monarch. The latter is illustrated here.

The Official Letter Styling is characterized by the page placement of the inside address: It is typed flush left, two to five lines below the last line of the signature block or below the written signature.

The typist's initials if included are typed two lines below the last line of the inside address. An enclosure notation if needed appears two lines below the typist's initials, or two lines below the last line of the inside address. These notations are also flush left.

A typed signature block is not needed on personalized Executive or Monarch stationery; however, if the writer's signature is either difficult to decipher or if it might be unfamiliar to the addressee, it may be typed four lines below the complimentary close.

Open punctuation and blocked paragraphs may also be used in this letter.

Sincerely,

*Attorney Signature*

Ms. Martha Peterson
490 Jones Street
Smithville, ST 56789

## The Official Letter Styling with Plain Executive Letterhead

4400 Ambler Boulevard
Smithville, ST 56789
January 1, 19—

Dear Bob

This is a facsimile of a letter typed on plain
Executive or Monarch stationery. The basic
format is the same as that of the Official Letter Styling. The block paragraphs and the open
punctuation pattern are illustrated here.

The heading which includes the writer's full
address and the date may be positioned six lines
from the top edge of the page and flush with the
right margin as shown here. Approximately six
vertical lines may be placed after the date line
down to the salutation.

The complimentary close is typed two lines below the last line of the message. The inside
address is flush left, two to five lines below
the last line of the signature block or below
the written signature.

Typist's initials, if included, should be positioned two lines beneath the last line of the
inside address. An enclosure notation or any
other notation if required should be typed two
lines below the typist's initials or two lines
below the last line of the inside address if
there are no initials.

Sincerely

*Attorney Signature*

Mr. Robert Y. Owens
123 East Second Avenue
Jonesville, ST 45678

## The Full Block Letter

---

*John A. Terry*
*Attorney-at-law*

*57 Center Building*
*Centerville, ST 34567*
*(303) 333-8888*

February 1, 19—
X-123-4

XYZ Corporation
Legal Department
1234 Smith Boulevard
Smithville, ST 56789

Attention Mr. John Doe

Gentlemen

RE:   FULL BLOCK LETTER

This is a facsimile of the Full Block Letter, whose structural
parts are flush left.  It may feature either the open or the mixed
punctuation pattern:  The open pattern is shown here.

The date line is typed two to six lines below the last letterhead
line.  Here it is placed three lines below the letterhead.  Reference numbers if required are single-spaced and blocked either above
or below the date line.

Placement of the inside address varies by letter length.  Here, it
is typed four lines below the date line.  If window envelopes are
used, the all-capitalized, unpunctuated Postal Service state abbreviations should be employed.  One space intervenes between the
state abbreviation and the ZIP Code.  If regular envelopes are to
be used, state names may be typed out in full or abbreviated, depending on office preference.  An attention line if required is
typed two lines below the last inside-address line.

The salutation is typed two lines below the attention line or two
to four lines below the last inside-address line.  The salutation
is "Gentlemen" if the letter is addressed to an organization, even
if there is an attention line directing the letter to a particular
individual within that organization.  If the letter is addressed
to an individual whose name is one line 1 of the inside address,
the salutation is "Dear Mr. (or Ms. or Mrs. or Miss) + surname" or
"Dear + first name" depending on the writer/reader relationship.
A subject line, typically all in capitals, may be typed two lines
below the salutation.  The subject line is optional.

The first message line is typed two lines below the salutation, or
two lines below the subject line if there is one.  The message is

XYZ Corporation
Legal Department
February 1, 19—
X-123-4


single-spaced internally and double-spaced between paragraphs.
At least three message lines must be carried over to a continuation sheet:  At no time should the complimentary close and the
signature block stand alone.  The last word on a sheet should not
be divided.  The continuation-sheet heading is typed six lines
from the top edge of the page.  Reference numbers if used on the
first sheet must be included in the continuation-sheet headings.
The message begins four lines below the last line of the heading.

The complimentary close is typed two lines below the last message
line, followed by at least four blank lines for the written signature, followed by the writer's name in capitals and lowercase.
The writer's title and/or name of his department may be included
in the typed signature block, if they do not appear in the printed
letterhead.

Identification initials may comprise only the typist's initials if
the same person dictated and signed the letter.  These initials
are typed two lines below the last signature-block line.  The enclosure notation if used is typed one line below the identification line.  The carbon copy notation if needed is placed one or
two lines below any other notations, depending on available space.

Sincerely yours

*Attorney Signature*
Attorney Signature
Title if Applicable

coc
Enclosures (2)

cc Mr. Howard T. Jansen

## The Modified Block Letter

Frank O. Perez
David S. Milbank
Marcia T. Ritsler

**THE LAW OFFICES OF PEREZ & MILBANK**
99 Main Street
Centerville, ST 34567

Area Code 303
Telephone 444-4567

February 1, 19—

REGISTERED MAIL
PERSONAL

Mr. John Z. Taller
General Counsel
XYZ Corporation
1234 Smith Boulevard
Smithville, ST 56789

Dear Mr. Taller:

In re:  Modified Block Letter

This is a facsimile of the Modified Block Letter.  It differs from the Full Block Letter chiefly in the page placement of its date line, its complimentary close, and its signature block that are aligned at center, toward the right margin, or at the right margin. Either the open or the mixed punctuation pattern may be used:  The mixed pattern is illustrated here.

While the date line may be positioned from two to six lines below the last line of the letterhead, its standard position is three lines below the letterhead, as shown above.  In this facsimile, the date line is typed five spaces to the right of dead-center.  If a reference number is required, it is blocked and single-spaced on a line above or below the date.

Special mailing notations and on-arrival notations such as the two shown above are all-capitalized, aligned flush left, and blocked together two lines above the first line of the inside address.  If used singly, either of these notations appears two lines above the inside address.

The first line of the inside address is typed about four lines below the date line.  This spacination can be expanded or contracted according to the letter length.  The inside address, the salutation, and all paragraphs of the message are aligned flush left.  The salutation, typed two to four lines below the last line of the inside address, is worded as it would be in the Full Block Letter.  A subject line if used is typed two lines below the salutation and is either blocked flush left or centered on the page.  It may be capitalized and lower cased as shown here, or it may be fully capitalized.  Underscoring the subject line is also acceptable, but in this case, only the first letter of each word would be capitalized.

Mr. Taller                    - 2 -                    February 1, 19—

The message begins two lines below the salutation or the subject
line if there is one.  Paragraphs are single-spaced internally and
double-spaced between each other; however, in very short letters,
the paragraphs may be double-spaced internally and triple-spaced
between each other.

Continuation sheets should contain at least three message lines.
The last word on a sheet should not be divided.  The continuation-
sheet heading may be blocked flush left as in the Block Letter or
it may be laid out across the top of the page as shown above.  This
heading begins six lines from the top edge of the page, and the
message is continued four lines beneath it.

The complimentary close is typed two lines below the last line of
the message.  While the complimentary close may be aligned under
some portion of the letterhead, directly under the date line, or
even flush with but not overrunning the right margin, it is often
typed five spaces to the right of dead-center as shown here.

The signature line is typed in capitals and lowercase at least four
lines below the complimentary close.  The writer's business title
and department name may be included if they do not already appear
in the printed letterhead.  All elements of the signature block
must be aligned with each other and with the complimentary close.

Identification initials need include only those of the typist, providing that the writer and the signer are the same person.  These
initials appear two lines below the last line of the signature
block.  An enclosure notation is typed one line below the identification line, and the carbon copy notation if required appears
one or two lines below any other notations, depending on space
available.

                              Very truly yours,

                              *Attorney Signature*
                              Attorney Signature
                              Title if Applicable

coc
Enclosures (5)

cc Mr. Doe
   Mr. Franklin
   Mr. Mason
   Ms. Watson

## The Modified Semi-block Letter

---

FITZ, JOHNSON, JACOBSON & BERNSTEIN, P.A.
*3000 Beltline Road*
*Centerville, ST 34567*
*Telephone 303-333-4567*


                                        February 1, 19—


Carroll D. Thompson, Esq.
Thompson, Barnes & Gagnon
P.O. Box 594
Smithville, ST 56789

Dear Mr. Thompson:

                    MODIFIED SEMI-BLOCK LETTER

        This is a facsimile of the Modified Semi-block Let-
ter.  It features a date line aligned either slightly to
the right of dead-center or flush right (as shown above).
Its inside address and salutation are aligned flush left,
while the paragraphs of the message are indented five to
ten spaces.  Its complimentary close and signature block
are aligned under the date, either slightly to the right
of dead-center, or flush right.  Identification initials,
enclosure notations, and carbon copy notations are aligned
flush left.

        A special mailing notation or an on-arrival notation
if required would have been typed flush left and two lines
above the first line of the inside address.  A reference
number if needed would have been blocked with the date,
one line above or below it.  The page placement of these
elements parallels their positioning in the Modified Block
Letter.  An attention line if required is aligned flush
left, two lines below the last line of the inside address.
A subject line may be typed in all-capitals two lines below the salutation and is typically centered on the page.

        The paragraphs are single-spaced internally and
double-spaced between each other unless the letter is extremely short, in which case the paragraphs may be double-
spaced internally and triple-spaced between each other.
Continuation sheets should contain at least three message
lines, and the last word on a sheet should never be divided.  The heading for a continuation sheet begins at
least six lines from the top edge of the page, and follows the format shown in this letter.

Mr. Thompson          - 2 -          February 1, 19—


    The complimentary close is typed at two lines below
the last line of the message.  The signature line, four
lines below the complimentary close, is aligned with it
if possible, or centered under it if the name and title
will be long.  In this case, it is better to align both
date and complimentary close about five spaces to the
right of dead-center to ensure enough room for the signature block which should never overrun the right margin.
The writer's name, business title and department name
(if not already printed on the stationery), are typed in
capitals and lowercase.

    Although open punctuation may be followed, the mixed
punctuation pattern is quite common with the Modified
Semi-block Letter, and it is the latter that is shown
here.

                        Sincerely yours,

                        Attorney Signature
                        Title if Needed


coc

Enclosures:  2

cc:  Dr. Bennett P. Oakley
     Addison Engineering Associates
     91011 Jones Street
     Smithville, ST 56789


    A postscript if needed is typically positioned two
to four lines below the last notation.  In the Modified
Semi-block Letter, the postscript is indented five to ten
spaces to agree with message paragraphs.  It is not necessary to head the postscript with the abbreviation P.S.
The postscript should be initialed by the writer.

## The Indented Letter

**MARKHAM AND SISITSKY**
Law Offices
129 Main Street
Centertown, ST 87654
222-333-4444

June 1, 19—

    Mrs. Alice Patterson,
        Thompson, Barnes & Gagnon,
            Post Office Box 594,
                Smithville, State 56789

Dear Mrs. Patterson:

Re:  Indented Letter

      This is a facsimile of the Indented Letter, rarely used in the United States outside of conservative law firms. Its main feature is the indentation not only of the paragraphs but also of the inside address and the signature block. Each line of the inside address is indented five spaces more than the preceding line. Paragraphs are indented ten spaces, so that the third line of the address aligns with the first word of each paragraph. The signature lines are also indented—the first line five spaces to the right of the complimentary close and additional signature lines, if any, five more spaces each. Some offices, to avoid overrunning the right margin, indent only three spaces in the signature block, and others block the first line of the signature with the complimentary close.

      Indented Letters traditionally follow the closed punctuation pattern. However, this facsimile is typical in that it deviates from the closed pattern in some respects: the terminal periods following the date line, the inside address, and the signature line are omitted. Otherwise, closed punctuation is followed here: a comma terminates each line of the inside address except the last, and each line of the signature block except the last. As an alternative, mixed punctuation may be followed throughout the letter.

Mrs. Patterson                - 2 -              June 1, 19—

    In other respects the Indented Letter is similar to the
Modified Semi-block Letter.  The date line may be aligned to end
with the right margin or may begin slightly to the right of
center.  If a subject line is used, it is usually centered.  The
complimentary close may begin slightly to the left of center, if
necessary, to make room for a lengthy signature.

    Special mailing notations and on-arrival notations if
used are typed flush left, as are the salutation, identification
initials, and other special notations.  A reference number would
be blocked either above or below the date line.

    In the inside address of this facsimile, the name of
the state is spelled in full, a conservative feature that rein-
forces the conservatism of the Indented Letter.  The postal abbreviation, however, is also correct.

                Very truly yours,

                *Attorney Signature*

                Attorney Signature,
                  Title if Needed

coc
Enclosures:  2

# The Simplified Letter

**OFFICE OF THE CITY ATTORNEY**
33 City Center
Centerville, ST 34567
303-444-5678

February 1, 19—

Ms. Sarah H. Smith
Director, Environmental Affairs
XYZ Corporation
1234 Smith Boulevard
Smithville, ST 56789

SIMPLIFIED LETTER

Ms. Smith, this is the Simplified Letter recommended by the Administrative Management Society. Its main features—block format, open punctuation, and fewer internal parts—reduce the number of keystrokes and typewriter adjustments your secretary must make, thus cutting costs, saving time, and increasing overall letter output.

The date line is typed six lines below the last letterhead line. The inside address, also flush left, appears three lines below the date line. Since the placement of the inside address is designed for window envelopes, it is suggested that the all-capitalized, unpunctuated Postal Service state abbreviation be typed after the city name, followed by one space and the ZIP Code.

The traditional salutation has been dropped and replaced by an unheaded, all-capitalized subject line typed flush left, three lines beneath the last inside-address line. The subject line summarizes the message.

The first message line begins three lines below the subject line. The first sentence serves as a greeting to the reader. The addressee's name should appear in the first paragraph, preferably in the first sentence as shown above. Inclusion of the name adds a personal touch. All paragraphs are blocked flush left, single-spaced internally, and double-spaced between each other. Tabular data and numbered lists are also blocked flush left but are set off from the rest of the message by double-spacing. Long quotations and unnumbered lists should be indented five to ten spaces from the left and right margins and set off from the rest of the message by top and bottom double-spacing.

Ms. Smith
Page 2
February 1, 19—


If a continuation sheet is required, at least three message lines
must be carried over.  Continuation-sheet format and margins match
those of the first sheet.  At least six blank lines are left from
the top edge of the page to the first line of the heading which is
blocked flush left, single-spaced internally, and typically composed of the addressee's courtesy title and name, the page number,
and the applicable date.  The rest of the message begins four lines
beneath the last heading line.

There is no complimentary close in the Simplified Letter, although
closing sentences such as "You have my best wishes," and "My best
regards are yours" may end the message.  The writer's name (and
business title if needed) is aligned flush left and typed all in
capitals at least five lines below the last message line.  Although
the Administrative Management Society uses a spaced hyphen between
the writer's surname and his business title, some companies prefer
a comma.  The writer's department name may be typed flush left all
in capitals, one line below the signature line.

The identification initials, flush left and two lines below the
last line of the signature block, comprise the typist's initials
only.  An enclosure notation may be typed one line below the identification initials and aligned flush left.  Carbon copy notations
may be typed one or two lines below the last notation, depending
on available space.  If only the signature block and/or typist's
initials appear before it, the carbon copy notation is typed two
lines below.

*Attorney Signature*
ATTORNEY SIGNATURE - TITLE OF POSITION

coc
Enclosures (12)

cc Dr. Alice L. Barnes

## The Half-Sheet

### THE LAW OFFICES OF
#### PEREZ & MILBANK
99 Main Street
Centerville, ST 34567

January 1, 19—

Mr. Ken T. Row
123 Key Place
Smithville, ST 56789

Dear Mr. Row:

    This is a facsimile of the half
sheet which is used for the briefest
of notes—those containing one or
two sentences or two very short paragraphs.

    The Block, Modified Block, or
Modified Semi-block Letters may be
used, and open or mixed punctuation
may be followed.

Sincerely yours,

*Attorney Signature*

## ENVELOPES

The following information may appear on any envelope regardless of its size. Asterisked items are essential and those that are unmarked are optional, depending on the requirements of the particular letter:

*1. The addressee's full name and full geographical address typed approximately in the vertical and horizontal center

2. Special mailing notation or notations typed below the stamp

3. On-arrival notation or notations typed about nine lines below the top left

*4. Sender's full name and geographical address printed or typed in the upper left corner.

The typeface should be block style. The Postal Service does not recommend unusual or italic typefaces. The typewriter keys should be clean.

The address block on a regular envelope should encompass no more than 1½" × 3¾" of space. There should be ⅝" of space from the bottom line of the address block to the bottom edge of the envelope. The entire area from the right and left bottom margins of the address block to the right and left bottom edges of the envelope as well as the area under the center of the address block to the bottom center edge of the envelope should be free of print. With regular envelopes, most address blocks are begun about five spaces to the left of horizontal center to admit room for potentially long lines. The address block should be single spaced.

If a window envelope is being used, all address data must appear within the window space, and at least ¼" margins must be maintained between the address and the right, left, top, and bottom edges of the window space.

Address-block data on a regular envelope should match the spelling and styling of the inside address. The U.S. Postal Service now recommends block styling for all envelope addresses. If a law firm that uses the Indented Letter follows the postal recommendation, the blocked address style on its envelopes will not match the indented style of the inside address on its letters. Nevertheless, most law offices that use the Indented Letter have chosen to adopt the recommended block styling for envelope addresses. Address-block elements are positioned as follows:

### first line

If the addressee is an individual, that person's courtesy title + full name are typed on the first line.

If an individual addressee's business title is included in the inside address, it may be typed either on the first line of the address block with a comma separating it from the addressee's name, or it may be typed alone on the next line, depending on length of title and name.

*Examples:*
Mr. Lee O. Idlewild, President
*or*
Mr. Lee O. Idlewild
President

If the addressee is an organization, its full name is typed on the first line.

If a particular department within an organization is specified, it is typed on a line under the name of the organization.

XYZ Corporation
Consumer Affairs Department

### next line

The full street address should be typed out (although it is acceptable to abbreviate such designations as *Street, Avenue, Boulevard,* etc.).

Room, suite, apartment, and building numbers are typed immediately following the last element of the street address and are positioned on the same line with it.

## last line

The last line of the address block contains the city, state, and the ZIP Code number. Only one space intervenes between the last letter of the state abbreviation and the first digit of the ZIP Code; the ZIP Code should never be on a line by itself. The ZIP Code is mandatory, as are all-capitalized, unpunctuated, two-letter Postal Service abbreviations. It is correct, however, to spell the name of a state in full on the letter while using the Postal Service abbreviation on the envelope.

*Examples:*
Mr. John P. Smith
4523 Kendall Place, Apt. 8B
Smithville, ST 56789
*or*
Mr. John P. Smith
4523 Kendall Pl., Apt. 8B
Smithville, ST 56789

When typing a foreign address, the secretary should refer first to the return address on the envelope of previous correspondence to ascertain the correct ordering of the essential elements of the address block. Letterhead of previous correspondence may also be checked if an envelope is not available. If neither of these sources is available, the material should be typed as it appears in the inside address of the dictated letter. The following guidelines may be of assistance:

1. All foreign addresses should be typed in English or in English characters: if an address must be in foreign characters (as Russian), an English translation should be interlined in the address block.
2. Foreign courtesy titles may be substituted for the English; however, it is unnecessary.
3. The name of the country should be typed in all-capital letters. Canadian addresses always carry the name CANADA, even though the name of the province is also given.
4. When applicable, foreign postal district numbers should be included.

Canadian addresses should adhere to the form requested by the Canada Post for quickest delivery through its automated handling system. As shown in the examples below, the name of the city, fully capitalized, is followed by the name of the province, spelled in full, on one line; the Postal Code follows on a separate line. For mail originating in the United States, CANADA is added on a final line. (Note that capitalization and punctuation differ slightly in French-language addresses.)

Mr. F. F. MacManus
Fitzgibbons and Brown
5678 Main Street
HALIFAX, Nova Scotia
B3J 2N9
CANADA

Les Entreprises Optima Ltée
6789, rue Principale
OTTAWA (Ontario)
K1A 0B3
CANADA

The Canadian Postal Code consists always of letter-numeral-letter, space, numeral-letter-numeral. Failure to include the correct code number may result in considerable delay in the delivery of mail. When space is limited, the Postal Code may be typed on the same line with the province. In this case, it must be separated from the name of the province by at least two character spaces. The two-letter provincial and territorial abbreviations listed in Chapter 4 may also be used when space is limited.

OTTAWA, Ontario K1A 0B3     *or*     OTTAWA, ON K1A 0B3

On-arrival notations such as PERSONAL or CONFIDENTIAL must be typed entirely in capital letters, about nine lines below the left top edge of the envelope. Any other on-arrival instructions such as Hold for Arrival or Please Forward may be typed in capitals and lowercase, underlined, and positioned about nine lines from the top edge of the envelope.

    If an attention line is used in the letter itself, it too must appear on the envelope.

Attention lines are typed in capitals and lowercase. They may be placed directly above the next-to-last line, as

XYZ Corporation
Legal Affairs Department
Attention Mr. E. R. Bailey
1234 Smith Boulevard
Smithville, ST 56789

---

**Facsimile of a Commercial Envelope Showing On-arrival and Special Mailing Notations**

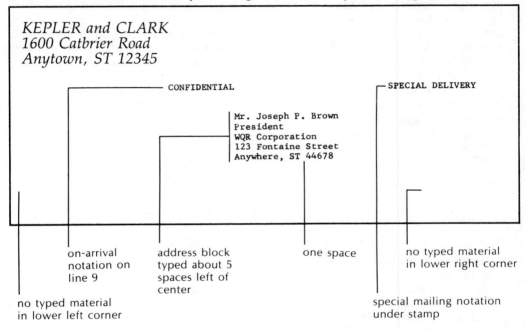

---

A special mailing notation (as CERTIFIED, REGISTERED MAIL, or SPECIAL DELIVERY) is typed entirely in capitals just below the stamp or about nine lines from the right top edge of the envelope. It should not overrun a ½" margin.

The printed return address (as of a law firm) may be supplemented by the name of the writer typed in at the top. The return address on a plain envelope should be styled as

Stephen P. Lemke
123 Ann Street
Jonesville, XX 12345

with at least two blank lines between the return address and the left and top edges of the envelope.

See page 278 for a chart showing stationery and envelope sizes and applications. See Chapter 4 for detailed treatment of mailing procedures, including a table of the Postal Service's two-letter state abbreviations and illustrations of how to fold letters correctly for insertion into envelopes.

# 10.7

## FORMS OF ADDRESS

It has already been emphasized that the initial impression created by a letter is vital to the letter's ultimate effectiveness. It follows that proper use of the conventional forms of address is essential, especially since these forms appear in conspicuous areas of the letter: on the envelope, in the inside address, and in the salutation.

### FORMS OF ADDRESS CHART

The following pages contain a chart of alphabetically grouped and listed forms of address for individuals whose offices, ranks, or professions warrant special courtesy titles, salutations, and complimentary closes. The chart also indicates in its last column how these individuals should be addressed orally (as in an introduction or in a conversation) and how they should be referred to in a written text (such as in a letter, a report, or an article).

The main categories covered in the chart are listed below in the order of their appearance:

Clerical and Religious Orders
College and University Faculty and Officials
Consular Officers
Diplomats
Foreign Heads of State
Government Officials
Military Ranks
Miscellaneous Courtesy, Business, and Professional Titles
United Nations Officials

Titles of special interest to legal secretaries include the following:

**Federal government officials**
U.S. Attorney General   page 324
U.S. District Attorney   page 326
federal judge   page 326
U.S. Supreme Court Justices   page 329
**Local government officials**
city attorney   page 331
county clerk   page 331
judge   page 331
**State government officials**
state attorney/attorney general   page 332
clerk of court   page 332
judge   page 333
secretary of state   page 334
supreme court justices   pages 335–336

A special chart headed "Multiple Addressees" immediately follows the Forms of Address Chart.

When two or more stylings are shown in the Forms of Address Chart, it should be understood by the reader that the most formal styling appears first. It should also be understood that male and female addressees (as in the clergy and in the armed forces) are addressed alike unless stated otherwise. An acute space problem within this chart has precluded mention of both male and female addressees in every single instance. The fact that female addressees are not shown throughout the material in no way suggests that women may not hold these positions or ranks.

| Addressee | Form of Address | Salutation | Complimentary Close | (1) Oral Reference (2) Written Reference |
|---|---|---|---|---|
| CLERICAL AND RELIGIOUS ORDERS | | | | |
| **abbot** | The Right Reverend John R. Smith, O.S.B. Abbot of ---- | Right Reverend and dear Father Dear Father Abbot Dear Father | Respectfully yours Sincerely yours | (1) Father Abbot (2) Father Smith |
| **apostolic delegate** | His Excellency, The Most Reverend John R. Smith Archbishop of ---- The Apostolic Delegate *or* The Apostolic Delegation | Your Excellency My dear Archbishop  Gentlemen | Respectfully yours Respectfully  Sincerely yours | (1) Your Excellency (2) the Apostolic Delegate  (1 *and* 2) the Apostolic Delegation |
| **archbishop** | The Most Reverend Archbishop of ---- *or* The Most Reverend John R. Smith Archbishop of ---- | Your Excellency  Your Excellency Dear Archbishop Smith | Respectfully yours  Respectfully yours Sincerely yours | (1) Your excellency (2) the Archbishop of ----  (1) Archbishop Smith (2) Archbishop Smith |
| **archdeacon** | The Venerable The Archdeacon of ---- *or* The Venerable John R. Smith | Venerable Sir  Venerable Sir My dear Archdeacon | Respectfully yours  Respectfully yours Sincerely yours | (1) Archdeacon Smith (2) the Archdeacon of ----  (1 *and* 2) Archdeacon (or if having doctorate Dr.) Smith |
| **bishop, Catholic** | The Most Reverend John R. Smith Bishop of ---- | Your Excellency Dear Bishop Smith | Respectfully yours Sincerely yours | (1 *and* 2) Bishop Smith |

| Addressee | Form of Address | Salutation | Complimentary Close | (1) Oral Reference<br>(2) Written Reference |
|---|---|---|---|---|
| **bishop, Episcopal Presiding** | The Most Reverend John R. Smith Presiding Bishop | Most Reverend Sir<br>Dear Bishop<br>Dear Bishop Smith | Respectfully yours<br><br>Sincerely yours | *(1 and 2)* Bishop Smith |
| **bishop, Episcopal** | The Right Reverend The Bishop of ----<br>*or*<br>The Right Reverend John R. Smith Bishop of ---- | Right Reverend Sir<br><br><br>Right Reverend Sir<br>Dear Bishop Smith | Respectfully yours<br><br><br>Respectfully yours<br>Sincerely yours | *(1)* Bishop Smith<br>*(2)* the Episcopal Bishop of ---- |
| **bishop, Methodist** | The Reverend John R. Smith Methodist Bishop | Reverend Sir<br>Dear Bishop Smith | Respectfully yours<br>Sincerely yours | *(1 and 2)* Bishop Smith |
| **brotherhood, member of** | Brother John, S.J. | Dear Brother John | Respectfully yours<br>Sincerely yours | *(1)* Brother John<br>*(2)* Brother John, S.J. |
| **brotherhood, superior of** | Brother John, S.J., Superior | Dear Brother John | Respectfully yours<br>Sincerely yours | *(1)* Brother John<br>*(2)* Brother John, S.J., Superior of ---- |
| **canon** | The Reverend John R. Smith Canon of ---- Cathedral | Dear Canon Smith | Respectfully yours<br>Sincerely yours | *(1 and 2)* Canon Smith |
| **cardinal** | His Eminence John Cardinal Smith Archbishop of ----<br>*or*<br>His Eminence Cardinal Smith Archbishop of ---- | Your Eminence<br>My dear Cardinal Smith<br>Dear Cardinal Smith | Respectfully yours<br><br>Sincerely yours | *(1)* Your Eminence or Cardinal Smith<br>*(2)* His Eminence Cardinal Smith or Cardinal Smith |

**chaplain, college or university**—see COLLEGE AND UNIVERSITY FACULTY AND OFFICIALS

| | | | |
|---|---|---|---|
| **clergyman, Protestant** (excluding Episcopal) | The Reverend John R. Smith *or if having doctorate* | Dear Mr. Smith | Respectfully yours Sincerely yours | (1) Mr. Smith (2) The Reverend Mr. Smith or The Reverend John R. Smith or Mr. Smith |
| | The Reverend Dr. John R. Smith | Dear Dr. Smith | Respectfully yours Sincerely yours | (1) Dr. Smith (2) The Reverend Dr. Smith or Dr. Smith |
| **dean** (of a cathedral) | The Very Reverend John R. Smith ---- Cathedral *or* Dean John R. Smith ---- Cathedral | Very Reverend Sir Dear Dean Smith<br><br>Very Reverend Sir Dear Dean Smith | Respectfully yours Sincerely yours<br><br>Respectfully yours Sincerely yours | (1 and 2) Dean (*or if having doctorate Dr.*) Smith |
| **moderator, Presbyterian** | The Moderator of ---- *or* The Reverend John R. Smith *or if having doctorate* Dr. John R. Smith | Reverend Sir My dear Sir Dear Mr. Moderator My dear Mr. Smith<br><br>My dear Dr. Smith | Respectfully yours Sincerely yours Respectfully yours Sincerely yours<br><br>Respectfully yours Sincerely yours | (1 and 2) the Moderator of ----<br>(1 and 2) Mr. Smith<br><br>(1 and 2) Dr. Smith |
| **monsignor domestic prelate** | The Right Reverend Monsignor John R. Smith *or* The Rt. Rev. Msgr. John R. Smith | Right Reverend and dear Monsignor Smith<br><br>Dear Monsignor Smith | Respectfully yours<br><br>Sincerely yours | (1 and 2) Monsignor Smith |
| **papal chamberlain** | The Very Reverend Monsignor John R. Smith *or* The Very Rev. Msgr. John R. Smith | Very Reverend and dear Monsignor Smith<br><br>Dear Monsignor Smith | Respectfully yours<br><br>Sincerely yours | (1 and 2) Monsignor Smith |

| Addressee | Form of Address | Salutation | Complimentary Close | (1) Oral Reference<br>(2) Written Reference |
|---|---|---|---|---|
| **patriarch** (of an Eastern Orthodox Church) | His Beatitude the Patriarch of ---- | Most Reverend Lord | Respectfully yours | (1) Your Beatitude<br>(2) John R. Smith, the Patriarch of ---- or The Patriarch |
| **pope** | His Holiness the Pope<br>or<br>His Holiness Pope ---- | Your Holiness<br>Most Holy Father | Respectfully yours | (1) Your Holiness<br>(2) His Holiness the Pope or His Holiness, Pope ---- or The Pope |
| **president, Mormon** | The President<br>Church of Jesus Christ of Latter-Day Saints | My dear President<br>Dear President Smith | Respectfully yours<br>Sincerely yours | (1 and 2) Mr. Smith |
| **priest, Catholic** | The Reverend John R. Smith<br>or if having doctorate<br>The Reverend Dr. John R. Smith | Dear Father Smith<br><br>Dear Father Smith | Respectfully yours<br>Sincerely yours<br>Respectfully yours<br>Sincerely yours | (1 and 2) Father Smith<br><br>(1 and 2) Father Smith |
| **priest, Episcopal** | The Reverend John R. Smith<br>or if having doctorate<br>The Reverend Dr. John R. Smith | Dear Mr. Smith<br>Dear Father Smith<br>Dear Dr. Smith<br>Dear Father Smith | Respectfully yours<br>Sincerely yours<br>Respectfully yours<br>Sincerely yours | (1 and 2) Mr. (or Father) Smith<br>(1 and 2) Dr. (or Father) Smith |
| **priest/president**—see COLLEGE AND UNIVERSITY FACULTY AND OFFICIALS (of a college or university) | | | | |
| **rabbi** | Rabbi John R. Smith<br>or if having doctorate<br>Rabbi John R. Smith, D.D. | Dear Rabbi Smith<br>Dear Dr. Smith | Respectfully yours<br>Sincerely yours | (1 and 2) Rabbi Smith<br>(1 and 2) Dr. (or Rabbi) Smith |

| | Envelope and inside address | Salutation | Complimentary close | Informal |
|---|---|---|---|---|
| **sisterhood, member of** | Sister Mary Angelica, S.C. | Dear Sister / Dear Sister Mary Angelica | Respectfully yours / Sincerely yours | (1 and 2) Sister Mary Angelica |
| **sisterhood, superior of** | The Reverend Mother Superior, S.C. | Reverend Mother / Dear Reverend Mother | Respectfully yours / Sincerely yours | (1) Reverend Mother / (2) The Reverend Mother Superior or The Reverend Mother |

## COLLEGE AND UNIVERSITY FACULTY AND OFFICIALS

| | Envelope and inside address | Salutation | Complimentary close | Informal |
|---|---|---|---|---|
| **chancellor** (of a university) | Dr. John } R. Smith / Amelia } Chancellor | Sir   Madam / Dear Dr. Smith | Very truly yours / Sincerely yours | (1) Dr. Smith / (2) Dr. Smith or John } R. Smith, Amelia } Chancellor of ---- University |
| **chaplain** (of a college or university) | The Reverend John } R. Smith / Amelia } Chaplain | Dear Chaplain Smith / Dear Mr. } Miss } Smith Mrs. } / Dear Father Smith | Respectfully / Sincerely yours | (1 and 2) Chaplain Smith or Mr., Miss, Mrs. Smith or Father Smith |
| **dean** (of a college or university) | Dean John } R. Smith Amelia } / or / Dr. John } R. Smith Amelia } Dean | Sir   Madam / Dear Dr. Smith / Dear Dean Smith | Very truly yours / Sincerely yours | (1) Dean or Dr. Smith / (2) Dean or Dr. Smith or Dr. Smith, Dean of ---- |
| **instructor** | Mr., Dr. John R. Smith / Ms., Miss, Mrs., Dr. } Amelia R. Smith / Instructor | Dear Mr., Dr. Smith / Dear Ms., Miss, Mrs., Dr. Smith | Very truly yours / Sincerely yours | (1 and 2) Mr., Ms., Miss, Mrs., Dr. Smith |

| Addressee | Form of Address | Salutation | Complimentary Close | (1) **Oral Reference** (2) **Written Reference** |
|---|---|---|---|---|
| **president** | Dr. John ⎫ R. Smith Amelia ⎭ President *or* President John ⎫ R. Smith Amelia ⎭ | Sir    Madam Dear Dr. Smith<br><br>Dear President Smith | Very truly yours Sincerely yours<br><br>Very truly yours Sincerely yours | (1) Dr. Smith (2) Dr. Smith or Dr. Smith, the President of ---- |
| **president/priest** | The Very Reverend John R. Smith, S.J. President | Sir Dear Father Smith | Respectfully yours Sincerely yours | (1) Father Smith (2) Father Smith, President of ---- |
| **professor, assistant or associate** | Mr., Dr. John R. Smith Ms., Mrs., Miss, Dr. Amelia R. Smith Assistant/Associate Professor of ---- | Dear Mr., Dr. Smith Dear Ms., Mrs., Miss, Dr. Smith *or* Dear Professor Smith | Very truly yours Sincerely yours | (1) Mr., Ms., Mrs., Miss, Dr. Smith (2) Professor Smith |
| **professor, full** | Professor John ⎫ R. Smith Amelia ⎭ *or* Dr. John ⎫ R. Smith Amelia ⎭ Professor of ---- | Dear Professor Smith Dear Dr. Smith | Very truly yours Sincerely yours | (1 and 2) Professor or Dr. Smith |
| CONSULAR OFFICERS | | | | |
| **consulate, American** | The American Consulate (foreign city, country) or if in Central or South America The Consulate of the United States of America (foreign city, country) | Gentlemen<br><br>Gentlemen | Very truly yours<br><br>Very truly yours | (1) ---- (2) the American Consulate in ----<br><br>(1) ---- (2) the United States Consulate in ---- |

| | Envelope and Letter Address | Salutation | Complimentary Close | Informal Reference |
|---|---|---|---|---|
| **consuls, American** (covers all consular grades such as Consul General, Consul, Vice-Consul and Consular Agent) | The American Consul (foreign city, country) *or if in Central or South America* The Consul of the United States of America (foreign city, country) *or if individual name is known* John } R. Smith, Esq. Amelia } American Consul *or if in Central or South America* Consul of the United States of America | Sir Madam Dear Mr. Ms. Mrs. Miss } Smith | Respectfully yours Very truly yours | (1) ---- (2) the American Consul in ---- (1) ---- (2) the United States Consul in ---- (1) Mr., Ms., Mrs., Miss Smith (2) the American or United States Consul in ---- |

NOTE: Since these officers are frequently transferred it is advisable to address letters to the office and not to the individual.

| | Envelope and Letter Address | Salutation | Complimentary Close | Informal Reference |
|---|---|---|---|---|
| **consulate, foreign** | The ---- Consulate *or* The Consulate of ---- (U.S. city, state, ZIP) | Gentlemen | Very truly yours | (1) ---- (2) the ---- Consulate or the Consulate of ---- |
| **consuls, foreign** (covers all consular grades) | The ---- Consul *or* The Consul of ---- (U.S. city, state, ZIP) *or if individual name is known* The Honorable John } R. Smith Amelia } ---- Consul *or* Consul of ---- (U.S. city, state, ZIP) | Sir Madame Dear Mr. Ms. Mrs. Miss } Smith | Respectfully yours Sincerely yours Respectfully yours Sincerely yours | (1) ---- (2) the ---- Consul in (city) or the Consul of ---- in (city) (1) Mr., Ms., Mrs., Miss Smith or Mr., Ms., Mrs., Miss Smith, the ---- Consul (2) Mr., Ms., Mrs., Miss Smith, the ---- Consul in (city) |

NOTE: Since these officers are frequently transferred it is advisable to address letters to the office and not to the individual.

| Addressee | Form of Address | Salutation | Complimentary Close | (1) Oral Reference (2) Written Reference |
|---|---|---|---|---|
| **DIPLOMATS** | | | | |
| **ambassador, American** | The Honorable John } R. Smith Amelia } American Ambassador or if in Central or South America The Ambassador of the United States of America | Sir Madam<br><br>Dear Mr. } Ambassador Madam } | Very truly yours<br><br>Sincerely yours | (1) Mr., Madam Ambassador or Mr., Ms., Mrs., Miss Smith<br>(2) the American Ambassador or the Ambassador of the United States or the United States Ambassador or Mr., Ms., Mrs., Miss Smith, the American Ambassador or the Ambassador |
| **ambassador, foreign** | His } Excellency Her } John } R. Smith Amelia } Ambassador of --- or if from Great Britain His Excellency The Right Honorable John R. Smith British Ambassador | Excellency<br><br>Dear Mr. } Ambassador Madame } <br><br>Excellency<br><br>Dear Mr. Ambassador | Respectfully yours<br><br>Sincerely yours<br><br>Respectfully yours<br><br>Sincerely yours | (1) Mr., Madame Ambassador<br>(2) the Ambassador of --- or the Ambassador or Mr., Ms., Mrs., Miss Smith<br><br>(1) Mr. Ambassador<br>(2) the British Ambassador or The Honorable Mr. Smith, the British Ambassador |
| **chargé d'affaires ad interim, American** | John } R. Smith, Esq. Amelia } American Chargé d'Affaires ad Interim or if in Central or South America United States Chargé d'Affaires ad Interim | Sir Madam<br><br>Dear Mr. Ms. } Smith Mrs. Miss } | Very truly yours<br><br>Sincerely yours | (1) Mr., Ms., Mrs., Miss Smith<br>(2) the American Chargé d'Affaires in --- or the United States Chargé d'Affaires in --- or Mr., Ms., Mrs., Miss Smith |

| | Address on envelope | Salutation | Complimentary close | In conversation or writing |
|---|---|---|---|---|
| **chargé d'affaires ad interim, foreign** | Mr. / Ms. / Mrs. / Miss } John / Amelia } R. Smith <br> Chargé d'Affaires ad Interim of ---- | Sir    Madame <br><br> Dear Mr. / Ms. / Mrs. / Miss } Smith | Respectfully yours <br><br> Sincerely yours | (1) Mr., Ms., Mrs., Miss Smith <br> (2) the ---- Chargé d'Affaires or Mr., Ms., Mrs., Miss Smith |
| **chargé d'affaires (de missi), foreign** | Mr. / Ms. / Mrs. / Miss } John / Amelia } R. Smith <br> Chargé d'Affaires of ---- | Sir    Madame <br><br> Dear Mr. / Ms. / Mrs. / Miss } Smith | Respectfully yours <br><br> Sincerely yours | (1) Mr., Ms., Mrs., Miss Smith <br> (2) the ---- Chargé d'Affaires or Mr., Ms., Mrs., Miss Smith |
| **minister, American** | The Honorable <br> John / Amelia } R. Smith <br> American Minister <br> or if in Central or South America <br> Minister of the United States of America | Sir    Madam <br><br> Dear Mr. / Madam } Minister | Very truly yours <br><br> Sincerely yours | (1) Mr., Madam Minister or Mr., Ms., Mrs., Miss Smith <br> (2) the American (or the United States) Minister, Mr., Ms., Mrs., Miss Smith or the Minister or Mr., Ms., Mrs., Miss Smith |
| **minister, foreign** | The Honorable <br> John / Amelia } R. Smith <br> Minister of ---- | Sir    Madame <br><br> Dear Mr. / Madame } Minister | Respectfully yours <br><br> Sincerely yours | (1) Mr., Madame Minister or Mr., Ms., Mrs., Miss Smith <br> (2) the Minister of ---- or the Minister or Mr., Ms., Mrs., Miss Smith |

| Addressee | Form of Address | Salutation | Complimentary Close | (1) **Oral Reference** (2) **Written Reference** |
|---|---|---|---|---|
| FOREIGN HEADS OF STATE: A BRIEF SAMPLING | | | | |
| **premier** | His ⎫ Excellency Her ⎭ John ⎫ R. Smith Amelia ⎭ Premier of ---- | Excellency Dear Mr. ⎫ Madame ⎭ Premier | Respectfully yours Sincerely yours | (1) Your Excellency or Mr., Ms., Mrs., Miss Smith (2) the Premier of ---- or the Premier or Mr., Ms., Mrs., Miss Smith |
| **president of a republic** | His ⎫ Excellency Her ⎭ John ⎫ R. Smith Amelia ⎭ President of ---- | Excellency Dear Mr. ⎫ Madame ⎭ President | Respectfully yours Sincerely yours | (1) Your Excellency (2) President Smith or Mr., Ms., Mrs., Miss Smith |
| **prime minister** | His ⎫ Excellency Her ⎭ John ⎫ R. Smith Amelia ⎭ | Excellency Dear Mr. ⎫ Madame ⎭ Prime Minister | Respectfully yours Sincerely yours | (1) Mr., Madame Prime Minister or Mr., Ms., Mrs., Miss Smith (2) the Prime Minister of ---- or the Prime Minister or Mr., Ms., Mrs., Miss Smith |
| GOVERNMENT OFFICIALS—*FEDERAL* | | | | |
| **attorney general** | The Honorable John R. Smith The Attorney General | Sir Dear Mr. Attorney General | Very truly yours Sincerely yours | (1) Mr. Attorney General or Attorney General Smith or Mr. Smith (2) the Attorney General, Mr. Smith or the Attorney General or Mr. Smith |

| | Envelope and Inside Address | Salutation | Complimentary Close | Informal Introduction or Reference |
|---|---|---|---|---|
| **cabinet officer(s) addressed as "Secretary"** | The Honorable<br>The Secretary of ----<br>or<br>The Honorable<br>John ⎱ R. Smith<br>Amelia ⎰<br>Secretary of ----<br>or<br>The Secretary of ---- | Sir    Madam<br><br>Sir    Madam<br>Dear Mr. ⎱<br>Madam ⎰ Secretary<br>Sir    Madam | Very truly yours<br><br>Very truly yours<br>Sincerely yours | (1) Mr., Madam Secretary or Secretary Smith or Mr., Ms., Mrs., Miss, Dr. Smith<br>(2) the Secretary of ----, John ⎱ R. Smith or Amelia ⎰ the Secretary or Mr., Ms., Mrs., Miss, Dr. Smith |
| **cabinet officer, former** | The Honorable<br>John ⎱ R. Smith<br>Amelia ⎰ | Dear Mr. ⎱<br>Ms. ⎬ Smith<br>Mrs. ⎪<br>Miss ⎰ | Very truly yours<br>Sincerely yours | (1 and 2) Mr., Ms., Mrs., Miss Smith |
| **chairman of a (sub) committee, U.S. Congress** (stylings shown apply to House of Representatives & Senate) | The Honorable<br>John ⎱ R. Smith<br>Amelia ⎰<br>Chairman<br>Committee on ----<br>United States Senate | Dear Mr. ⎱ Chairman<br>Madam ⎰<br>Dear Senator Smith | Very truly yours<br><br>Sincerely yours | (1) Mr., Madam Chairman or Senator Smith or Senator<br>(2) (title) Smith, the Chairman of the ---- Committee on ---- or the Chairman or Senator Smith |
| **chief justice**—see SUPREME COURT, FEDERAL; STATE | | | | |
| **commissioner** | if appointed<br>The Honorable<br>John ⎱ R. Smith<br>Amelia ⎰<br>Commissioner<br>if career<br>Mr. ⎱ John<br>Ms. ⎬ Amelia ⎱ R. Smith<br>Mrs. ⎪<br>Miss ⎰<br>Commissioner | Dear Mr. ⎱ Commissioner<br>Madam ⎰<br>Dear Mr. ⎱<br>Ms. ⎬ Smith<br>Mrs. ⎪<br>Miss ⎰<br><br>Dear Mr. ⎱<br>Ms. ⎬ Smith<br>Mrs. ⎪<br>Miss ⎰ | Very truly yours<br><br>Sincerely yours<br><br>Very truly yours<br>Sincerely yours | (1) Mr., Ms., Mrs., Miss Smith<br>(2) Mr., Ms., Mrs., Miss Smith, the Commissioner or the Commissioner of ----<br>(1) Mr., Ms., Mrs., Miss Smith<br>(2) Mr., Ms., Mrs., Miss Smith or the Commissioner of ---- |

| Addressee | Form of Address | Salutation | Complimentary Close | (1) Oral Reference<br>(2) Written Reference |
|---|---|---|---|---|
| **congressman**—SEE REPRESENTATIVE, U.S. CONGRESS | | | | |
| **director**<br>(as of an independent federal agency) | The Honorable<br>John ⎱<br>Amelia ⎰ R. Smith<br>Director<br>---- Agency | Dear Mr.<br>Ms.<br>Mrs.<br>Miss ⎬ Smith | Very truly yours<br>Sincerely yours | (1) Mr., Mr., Ms., Mrs., Miss Smith<br>(2) John ⎱<br>Amelia ⎰ R. Smith<br>Director of ---- Agency or The Honorable Mr., Ms., Mrs., Miss Smith |
| **district attorney** | The Honorable<br>John ⎱<br>Amelia ⎰ R. Smith<br>District Attorney | Dear Mr.<br>Ms.<br>Mrs.<br>Miss ⎬ Smith | Very truly yours<br>Sincerely yours | (1) Mr., Ms., Mrs., Miss Smith<br>(2) District Attorney Smith or the District Attorney or Mr., Ms., Mrs., Miss Smith |
| **federal judge** | The Honorable<br>John ⎱<br>Amelia ⎰ R. Smith<br>Judge of the United States District Court for the ---- District of ---- | Sir   Madam<br>My dear Judge Smith<br>Dear Judge Smith | Very truly yours<br>Very sincerely yours | (1) Judge Smith<br>(2) the Judge or Judge Smith |
| **justice**—SEE SUPREME COURT, FEDERAL; STATE | | | | |
| **librarian of congress** | The Honorable<br>John R. Smith<br>Librarian of Congress | Sir<br>Dear Mr. Smith | Very truly yours<br>Sincerely yours | (1) Mr. Smith<br>(2) the Librarian of Congress or the Librarian or The Honorable Mr. Smith or Mr. Smith |

| | Envelope and inside address | Salutation | Complimentary close | Informal address |
|---|---|---|---|---|
| **postmaster general** | The Honorable John R. Smith The Postmaster General | Sir Dear Mr. Postmaster General | Very truly yours Sincerely yours | (1) Mr. Postmaster General or Postmaster General Smith or Mr. Smith (2) the Postmaster General, Mr. Smith or the Postmaster General or Mr. Smith |
| **president-elect of the United States** | The Honorable John R. Smith President-elect of the United States (local address) | Dear Sir Dear Mr. Smith | Very truly yours Sincerely yours | (1) Mr. Smith (2) the President-elect or President-elect Smith or Mr. Smith |
| **president of the United States** | The President The White House or The Honorable John R. Smith President of the United States The White House | Mr. President My dear Mr. President Dear Mr. President Mr. President My dear Mr. President Dear Mr. President | Respectfully yours Very respectfully yours Respectfully yours Very respectfully yours | (1) Mr. President (2) The President or President Smith or The Chief Executive or Mr. Smith |
| **president of the United States** (former) | The Honorable John R. Smith (local address) | Sir Dear Mr. Smith | Respectfully yours Very truly yours Sincerely yours | (1) Mr. Smith (2) former President Smith or Mr. Smith |
| **press secretary to the President of the United States** | Mr. John R. Smith Press Secretary to the President The White House | Dear Mr. Smith | Very truly yours Sincerely yours | (1) Mr. Smith (2) the President's Press Secretary, John Smith or Presidential Press Secretary John Smith or White House Press Secretary John Smith or Mr. Smith |

| Addressee | Form of Address | Salutation | Complimentary Close | (1) Oral Reference / (2) Written Reference |
|---|---|---|---|---|
| **representative, United States Congress** | The Honorable John / Amelia } R. Smith United States House of Representatives | Dear Sir Dear Madam  Dear Representative Smith  Dear Mr. / Ms. / Mrs. / Miss } Smith | Very truly yours  Sincerely yours | (1) Mr., Ms., Mrs., Miss Smith  (2) John / Amelia } R. Smith U.S. Representative from ——— or Congressman, Congressperson, Congresswoman ——— Smith |
| **representative, United States Congress** (former) | The Honorable John / Amelia } R. Smith (local address) | Dear Mr. / Ms. / Mrs. / Miss } Smith | Very truly yours Sincerely yours | (1 and 2) Mr., Ms., Mrs., Miss Smith |
| **senator, United States Senate** | The Honorable John / Amelia } R. Smith United States Senate | Sir  Madam Dear Senator Smith | Very truly yours Sincerely yours | (1) Senator Smith or Senator  (2) Senator Smith or the Senator from ——— or the Senator |
| **senator-elect** | The Honorable John / Amelia } R. Smith Senator-elect (local address) | Dear Mr. / Ms. / Mrs. / Miss } Smith | Very truly yours Sincerely yours | (1) Mr., Ms., Mrs., Miss Smith  (2) Senator-elect Smith or Mr., Ms., Mrs, Miss Smith |
| **senator** (former) | The Honorable John / Amelia } R. Smith (local address) | Dear Senator Smith | Very truly yours Sincerely yours | (1) Senator Smith or Senator or Mr., Ms., Mrs., Miss Smith  (2) Senator Smith or former Senator Smith |

| | Address | Salutation | Complimentary close | Formal reference / In speaking |
|---|---|---|---|---|
| **speaker,**<br>**United States House of**<br>**Representatives** | The Honorable<br>The Speaker of the House<br>of Representatives<br>*or*<br>The Honorable<br>Speaker of the House of<br>Representatives<br>*or*<br>The Honorable<br>John R. Smith<br>Speaker of the House of<br>Representatives | Sir<br><br><br>Sir<br><br><br>Sir<br>Dear Mr. Speaker<br>Dear Mr. Smith | Very truly yours<br><br><br>Very truly yours<br><br><br>Very truly yours<br>Sincerely yours | (1) Mr. Speaker or Mr. Smith<br>(2) the Speaker, Mr. Smith or Speaker of the House John R. Smith or John R. Smith, Speaker of the House or the Speaker or Mr. Smith |
| **speaker,**<br>**United States House of**<br>**Representatives**<br>(former) | The Honorable<br>John R. Smith<br>(local address) | Sir<br>Dear Mr. Smith | Very truly yours<br>Sincerely yours | (1) Mr. Smith<br>(2) Mr. Smith or John R. Smith, former Speaker of the House |
| **supreme court,**<br>**associate justice** | Mr. Justice Smith<br>The Supreme Court<br>of the United States | Sir or Mr. Justice<br><br>My dear Mr. Justice<br>Dear Mr. Justice<br>Dear Mr. Justice Smith | Very truly yours<br><br>Sincerely yours | (1) Mr. Justice Smith or Justice Smith<br>(2) Mr. Justice Smith or John R. Smith, an associate Supreme Court justice or John R. Smith, an associate justice of the Supreme Court |
| **supreme court,**<br>**chief justice** | The Chief Justice<br>of the United States<br>The Supreme Court<br>of the United States<br>*or*<br>The Chief Justice<br>The Supreme Court | Sir<br><br>My dear Mr. Chief Justice<br>Dear Mr. Chief Justice<br><br>Sir<br>My dear Mr. Chief Justice<br>Dear Mr. Chief Justice | Respectfully<br><br>Very truly yours<br><br><br>Respectfully<br><br>Very truly yours | (1) Mr. Chief Justice<br>(2) the Chief Justice or Chief Justice John R. Smith or John R. Smith, Chief Justice of the U.S. Supreme Court |

| Addressee | Form of Address | Salutation | Complimentary Close | (1) Oral Reference<br>(2) Written Reference |
|---|---|---|---|---|
| **supreme court, retired justice** | The Honorable<br>John R. Smith<br>(local address) | Sir<br><br>Dear Justice Smith | Very truly yours<br><br>Sincerely yours | (1) Mr. Justice Smith or Justice Smith<br>(2) Mr. Justice Smith or retired Supreme Court Justice John R. Smith |
| **special assistant to the President of the United States** | Mr. ⎱<br>Ms. ⎰ John ⎱<br>Mrs. ⎰ Amelia ⎰ R. Smith<br>Miss | Dear Mr. ⎱<br>Ms. ⎰ Smith<br>Mrs. ⎰<br>Miss ⎰ | Very truly yours<br>Sincerely yours | (1 and 2) Mr., Ms., Mrs., Miss Smith |
| **territorial delegate** | The Honorable<br>John ⎱ R. Smith<br>Amelia ⎰<br>Delegate of ----<br>House of Representatives | Dear Mr. ⎱<br>Ms. ⎰ Smith<br>Mrs. ⎰<br>Miss ⎰ | Very truly yours<br>Sincerely yours | (1) Mr., Ms., Mrs., Miss Smith<br>(2) Mr., Ms., Mrs., Miss Smith, Territorial Delegate of ---- |
| **undersecretary of a department** | The Honorable<br>John ⎱ R. Smith<br>Amelia ⎰<br>Undersecretary of ---- | Dear Mr. ⎱<br>Ms. ⎰ Smith<br>Mrs. ⎰<br>Miss ⎰ | Very truly yours<br>Sincerely yours | (1) Mr., Ms., Mrs., Miss Smith<br>(2) Mr., Ms., Mrs., Miss Smith or ---- Smith, Undersecretary of ---- or the Undersecretary of ----, ---- Smith |
| **vice president of the United States** | The Vice President<br>of the United States<br>United States Senate<br>or<br>The Honorable<br>John R. Smith<br>Vice President<br>of the United States<br>Washington, DC ZIP | Sir<br><br>My dear Mr. Vice President<br>Sir<br>My dear Mr. Vice President<br>Dear Mr. Vice President | Respectfully<br><br>Very truly yours<br><br>Respectfully<br>Very truly yours | (1) Mr. Vice President or Mr. Smith<br>(2) the Vice President or the Vice President, Mr. Smith or Vice President Smith or John Smith, Vice President of the United States |

## GOVERNMENT OFFICIALS—LOCAL

| | | | |
|---|---|---|---|
| **alderman** | The Honorable<br>John ⎱ R. Smith<br>Amelia ⎰<br>Alderman | Dear Mr. ⎱<br>Ms. ⎰ Smith<br>Mrs.<br>Miss | Very truly yours |
| | | Dear Alderman Smith | Sincerely yours |
| | *or*<br>Alderman John ⎱ R. Smith<br>Amelia ⎰ | Dear Alderman Smith | Very truly yours |
| | | Dear Mr. ⎱<br>Ms. ⎰ Smith<br>Mrs.<br>Miss | Sincerely yours |
| | | | (1 *and* 2) Mr., Ms., Mrs.,<br>Miss Smith |
| **city attorney**<br>(includes city counsel,<br>corporation counsel) | The Honorable<br>John ⎱ R. Smith<br>Amelia ⎰ | Dear Mr. ⎱<br>Ms. ⎰ Smith<br>Miss Mrs. | Very truly yours<br>Sincerely yours |
| | | | (1 *and* 2) Mr., Ms., Mrs.,<br>Miss Smith |
| **councilman**—see ALDERMAN | | | |
| **county clerk** | The Honorable<br>John ⎱ R. Smith<br>Amelia ⎰<br>Clerk of ---- County | Dear Mr. ⎱<br>Ms. ⎰ Smith<br>Mrs.<br>Miss | Very truly yours<br>Sincerely yours |
| | | | (1 *and* 2) Mr., Ms., Mrs.,<br>Miss Smith |
| **county treasurer**—see COUNTY CLERK | | | |
| **judge** | The Honorable<br>John ⎱ R. Smith<br>Amelia ⎰<br>Judge of the ----<br>Court of ---- | Dear Judge Smith | Very truly yours<br>Sincerely yours |
| | | | (1 *and* 2) Judge Smith |
| **mayor** | The Honorable<br>John ⎱ R. Smith<br>Amelia ⎰<br>Mayor of ---- | Sir Madam<br>Dear Mayor Smith | Very truly yours<br>Sincerely yours |
| | | | (1) Mayor Smith<br>(2) Mayor Smith *or* the<br>Mayor *or* ---- Smith,<br>Mayor of ---- |

| Addressee | Form of Address | Salutation | Complimentary Close | (1) **Oral Reference** (2) **Written Reference** |
|---|---|---|---|---|
| **selectman**—see ALDERMAN | | | | |
| GOVERNMENT OFFICIALS—*STATE* | | | | |
| **assemblyman**—see REPRESENTATIVE, STATE | | | | |
| **attorney** (as commonwealth's attorney, state's attorney) | The Honorable John } R. Smith Amelia } (*title*) | Dear Mr. Ms. } Smith Mrs. Miss | Very truly yours Sincerely yours | (1 and 2) Mr., Ms., Mrs., Miss Smith |
| **attorney general** | The Honorable John } R. Smith Amelia } Attorney General of the State of ---- | Sir    Madam Dear Mr. } Attorney Madam } General | Very truly yours Sincerely yours | (1) Mr., Ms., Mrs., Miss Smith or Attorney General Smith (2) the Attorney General, Mr., Ms., Mrs., Miss Smith or the state Attorney General |
| **clerk of a court** | John } R. Smith, Esq. Amelia } Clerk of the Court of ---- | Dear Mr. Ms. } Smith Mrs. Miss | Very truly yours Sincerely yours | (1 and 2) Mr., Ms., Mrs., Miss Smith |
| **delegate**—see REPRESENTATIVE, STATE | | | | |
| **governor** | The Honorable The Governor of ---- *or* The Honorable John } R. Smith Amelia } Governor of ---- or in some states | Sir    Madam Sir    Madam Dear Governor Smith | Respectfully yours Very sincerely yours Respectfully yours Very sincerely yours | (1) Governor Smith or Governor (2) Governor Smith or the Governor or the Governor of ---- (only used outside his or her state) |

| | Address on Letter | Salutation | Complimentary Close | Informal Reference |
|---|---|---|---|---|
| **governor** (continued) | His ⎱ Excellency, the<br>Her ⎰ Governor of ---- | Sir   Madam<br>Dear Governor Smith | Respectfully yours<br>Very sincerely yours | (1 and 2) same<br>as above |
| **governor**<br>(acting) | The Honorable<br>John ⎱ R. Smith<br>Amelia ⎰<br>Acting Governor of ---- | Sir   Madam<br>Dear Mr.<br>Ms. ⎱ Smith<br>Mrs. ⎰<br>Miss | Respectfully yours<br>Very sincerely yours | (1 and 2) Mr., Ms., Mrs.,<br>Miss Smith |
| **governor-elect** | The Honorable<br>John ⎱ R. Smith<br>Amelia ⎰<br>Governor-elect of ---- | Dear Mr.<br>Ms. ⎱ Smith<br>Mrs. ⎰<br>Miss | Very truly yours<br>Sincerely yours | (1) Mr., Ms., Mrs., Miss<br>Smith<br>(2) Mr., Ms., Mrs., Miss<br>Smith, the Governor-elect |
| **governor**<br>(former) | The Honorable<br>John ⎱ R. Smith<br>Amelia ⎰ | Dear Mr.<br>Ms. ⎱ Smith<br>Mrs. ⎰<br>Miss | Very truly yours<br>Sincerely yours | (1) Mr., Ms., Mrs., Miss<br>Smith<br>(2) John ⎱ R. Smith,<br>Amelia ⎰<br>former Governor of ---- |
| **judge,**<br>**state court** | The Honorable<br>John ⎱ R. Smith<br>Amelia ⎰<br>Judge of the ---- Court | Dear Judge Smith | Very truly yours<br>Sincerely yours | (1 and 2) Judge Smith |

**judge/justice,**
**state supreme court**—see SUPREME COURT, STATE

| Addressee | Form of Address | Salutation | Complimentary Close | (1) Oral Reference (2) Written Reference |
|---|---|---|---|---|
| **lieutenant governor** | The Honorable<br>The Lieutenant Governor<br>of ----<br>or<br>The Honorable<br>John } R. Smith<br>Amelia<br>Lieutenant Governor<br>of ---- | Sir   Madam<br><br>Sir   Madam<br><br>Dear Mr.<br>Ms. } Smith<br>Mrs.<br>Miss | Respectfully yours<br><br>Respectfully yours<br><br>Sincerely yours | (1) Mr., Ms., Mrs., Miss Smith<br>(2) Lieutenant Governor Smith or the Lieutenant Governor or ---- Smith, Lieutenant Governor of ---- (only used outside his or her state) or the Lieutenant Governor of ---- (only used outside his or her state) |
| **representative, state** (includes assemblyman, delegate) | The Honorable<br>John } R. Smith<br>Amelia<br>House of Representatives<br>(or The State Assembly<br>or The House of<br>Delegates) | Sir   Madam<br><br>Dear Mr.<br>Ms. } Smith<br>Mrs.<br>Miss | Very truly yours<br><br>Sincerely yours | (1) Mr., Ms., Mrs., Miss Smith<br>(2) Mr., Ms., Mrs., Miss Smith or ---- Smith, the state Representative (or Assemblyman or Delegate) from ---- |
| **secretary of state** | The Honorable<br>The Secretary of State<br>of ----<br>or<br>The Honorable<br>John } R. Smith<br>Amelia<br>Secretary of State<br>of ---- | Sir   Madam<br><br>Sir   Madam<br>Dear Mr. }<br>Madam } Secretary | Very truly yours<br><br>Very truly yours<br>Sincerely yours | (1) Mr., Ms., Mrs., Miss Smith<br>(2) Mr., Ms., Mrs., Miss Smith or ---- Smith, Secretary of State of ---- |

| | | | | |
|---|---|---|---|---|
| **senate, state, president of** | The Honorable<br>John }<br>Amelia } R. Smith<br>President of the Senate<br>of the State (or<br>Commonwealth) of ---- | Sir   Madam<br>Dear Mr.<br>Ms.<br>Mrs. } Smith<br>Miss<br>Senator | Very truly yours<br><br>Sincerely yours | (1 and 2) Senator, Mr.,<br>Ms., Mrs., Miss Smith |
| **senator, state** | The Honorable<br>John }<br>Amelia } R. Smith<br>The Senate of ---- | Sir   Madam<br>Dear Senator Smith | Very truly yours<br>Sincerely yours | (1) Senator Smith or<br>Senator<br>(2) Senator Smith or<br>---- Smith, the state<br>Senator from ---- |
| **speaker, state assembly, house of delegates, or house of representatives** | The Honorable<br>John }<br>Amelia } R. Smith<br>Speaker of ---- | Sir   Madam<br>Dear Mr.<br>Ms.<br>Mrs. } Smith<br>Miss | Very truly yours<br>Sincerely yours | (1) Mr., Ms., Mrs., Miss<br>Smith<br>(2) the Speaker of the<br>---- or ---- Smith,<br>Speaker of the ---- |
| **supreme court, state, associate justice** | The Honorable<br>John }<br>Amelia } R. Smith<br>Associate Justice of the<br>Supreme Court of ---- | Sir   Madam<br>Dear Justice Smith | Very truly yours<br>Sincerely yours | (1) Mr., Madam Justice<br>Smith or Judge' Smith<br>(2) Mr., Madam Justice<br>Smith or Judge Smith<br>or ---- Smith, associate<br>justice of the ----<br>Supreme Court |
| **supreme court, state, chief justice** | The Honorable<br>John }<br>Amelia } R. Smith<br>Chief Justice of the<br>Supreme Court of ---- | Sir   Madam<br>Dear Mr.<br>Madam } Chief Justice | Very truly yours<br>Sincerely yours | (1) Mr., Madam Chief<br>Justice or Chief Justice<br>Smith or Judge Smith<br>(2) Chief Justice Smith<br>or ---- Smith, Chief<br>Justice of the ----<br>Supreme Court |

| Addressee | Form of Address | Salutation | Complimentary Close | (1) Oral Reference<br>(2) Written Reference |
|---|---|---|---|---|
| **supreme court, state, presiding justice** | The Honorable<br>John } R. Smith<br>Amelia<br>Presiding Justice<br>—— Division<br>Supreme Court of —— | Sir  Madam<br>Dear Mr. } Justice<br>Madam | Very truly yours<br>Sincerely yours | (1) Mr., Madam Justice Smith *or* Judge Smith<br>(2) Mr., Madam Justice Smith *or* Judge Smith *or* —— Smith, Presiding Justice of —— |

MILITARY RANKS—A TYPICAL BUT NOT EXHAUSTIVE LIST: TITLES APPLY TO BOTH MALE AND FEMALE MEMBERS OF THE ARMED FORCES—BOTH FULL TITLES AND ABBREVIATIONS SHOWN

| Addressee | Form of Address | Salutation | Complimentary Close | (1) Oral Reference<br>(2) Written Reference |
|---|---|---|---|---|
| **admiral**<br>(coast guard or navy) | Admiral *or* ADM<br>John R. Smith, USN | Dear Admiral Smith | Very truly yours<br>Sincerely yours | (1 *and* 2) Admiral Smith |
| **rear admiral** | Rear Admiral *or* RADM<br>John R. Smith, USCG | Dear Admiral Smith | Very truly yours<br>Sincerely yours | (1 *and* 2) Admiral Smith |
| **vice admiral** | Vice Admiral *or* VADM<br>John R. Smith, USN | Dear Admiral Smith | Very truly yours<br>Sincerely yours | (1 *and* 2) Admiral Smith |
| **airman**<br>*as*<br>**airman basic**<br>**airman**<br>**airman first class** | AB<br>AMN } John R. Smith,<br>A1C } USAF | Dear Airman Smith<br>Dear Airman Smith<br>Dear Airman Smith | Sincerely yours<br>Sincerely yours<br>Sincerely yours | (1 *and* 2) Airman Smith<br>(1 *and* 2) Airman Smith<br>(1 *and* 2) Airman Smith |
| **brigadier general**—*see* GENERAL | | | | |
| **cadet**<br>U.S. Air Force Academy<br>U.S. Military Academy | Cadet John } R. Smith<br>Amelia<br>Cadet John } R. Smith<br>Amelia | Dear Cadet Smith<br>Dear Cadet Smith | Sincerely yours<br>Sincerely yours | (1 *and* 2) Cadet Smith<br>(1 *and* 2) Cadet Smith |

| | | | | |
|---|---|---|---|---|
| **captain** | | | | |
| air force | Captain or CPT John R. Smith, USAF | Dear Captain Smith | Sincerely yours | (1 and 2) Captain Smith |
| army | Captain or CPT John R. Smith, USA | Dear Captain Smith | Sincerely yours | (1 and 2) Captain Smith |
| coast guard | Captain or CAPT John R. Smith, USCG | Dear Captain Smith | Sincerely yours | (1 and 2) Captain Smith |
| marine corps | Captain or Capt. John R. Smith, USMC | Dear Captain Smith | Sincerely yours | (1 and 2) Captain Smith |
| navy | Captain or CAPT John R. Smith, USN | Dear Captain Smith | Sincerely yours | (1 and 2) Captain Smith |
| **colonel** (air force, army) | Colonel or COL John R. Smith, USAF (or USA) | Dear Colonel Smith | Sincerely yours | (1 and 2) Colonel Smith |
| (marine corps) | Colonel or Col. John R. Smith, USMC | Dear Colonel Smith | Sincerely yours | (1 and 2) Colonel Smith |
| **commander** (coast guard or navy) | Commander or CDR John R. Smith, USCG (or USN) | Dear Commander Smith | Sincerely yours | (1 and 2) Commander Smith |
| **corporal** (army) | Corporal or CPL John R. Smith, USA | Dear Corporal Smith | Sincerely yours | (1 and 2) Corporal Smith |
| **lance corporal** (marine corps) | Lance Corporal or L/Cpl. John R. Smith, USMC | Dear Corporal Smith | Sincerely yours | (1 and 2) Corporal Smith |
| **ensign** (coast guard, navy) | Ensign or ENS John R. Smith, USN (or USCG) | Dear Mr. Smith *or if female* Dear Ensign Smith | Sincerely yours | (1) Mr. Smith; Ensign Smith (*if female*) (2) Ensign Smith |
| **first lieutenant** (air force, army) | First Lieutenant or 1LT John R. Smith, USAF | Dear Lieutenant Smith | Sincerely yours | (1 and 2) Lieutenant Smith |
| (marine corps) | First Lieutenant or 1st. Lt. John R. Smith, USMC | Dear Lieutenant Smith | Sincerely yours | (1 and 2) Lieutenant Smith |

| Addressee | Form of Address | Salutation | Complimentary Close | (1) Oral Reference (2) Written Reference |
|---|---|---|---|---|
| **general** (air force, army) | General or GEN John R. Smith, USAF (or USA) | Dear General Smith | Very truly yours Sincerely yours | (1 and 2) General Smith |
| (marine corps) | General or Gen. John R. Smith, USMC | Dear General Smith | Very truly yours Sincerely yours | (1 and 2) General Smith |
| **brigadier general** (air force, army) | Brigadier General or BG John R. Smith, USAF (or USA) | Dear General Smith | Very truly yours Sincerely yours | (1 and 2) General Smith |
| (marine corps) | Brigadier General or Brig. Gen. John R. Smith, USMC | Dear General Smith | Very truly yours Sincerely yours | (1 and 2) General Smith |
| **lieutenant general** (air force, army) | Lieutenant General or LTG John R. Smith, USAF (or USA) | Dear General Smith | Very truly yours Sincerely yours | (1 and 2) General Smith |
| (marine corps) | Lieutenant General or Lt. Gen. John R. Smith, USMC | Dear General Smith | Very truly yours Sincerely yours | (1 and 2) General Smith |
| **major general** (air force, army) | Major General or MG John R. Smith, USAF (or USA) | Dear General Smith | Very truly yours Sincerely yours | (1 and 2) General Smith |
| (marine corps) | Major General or Maj. Gen. John R. Smith, USMC | Dear General Smith | Very truly yours Sincerely yours | (1 and 2) General Smith |
| **lieutenant** (coast guard, navy) | Lieutenant or LT John R. Smith, USCG (or USN) | Dear Mr. Smith or if female Dear Lieutenant Smith | Sincerely yours | (1) Mr. Smith; Lieutenant Smith (if female) (2) Lieutenant Smith |

| | | | | |
|---|---|---|---|---|
| **lieutenant colonel** (air force, army) | Lieutenant Colonel or LTC John R. Smith, USAF (or USA) | Dear Colonel Smith | Sincerely yours | (1) Colonel Smith (2) Lieutenant Colonel Smith |
| (marine corps) | Lieutenant Colonel or Lt. Col. John R. Smith, USMC | Dear Colonel Smith | Sincerely yours | (1) Colonel Smith (2) Lieutenant Colonel Smith |
| **lieutenant commander** (coast guard, navy) | Lieutenant Commander or LCDR John R. Smith, USCG (or USN) | Dear Commander Smith | Sincerely yours | (1) Commander Smith (2) Lieutenant Commander Smith |
| **lieutenant, first**—see FIRST LIEUTENANT | | | | |
| **lieutenant general**—see GENERAL | | | | |
| **lieutenant junior grade** (coast guard, navy) | Lieutenant (j.g.) or LTJG John R. Smith, USCG (or USN) | Dear Mr. Smith or if female Dear Lieutenant Smith | Sincerely yours | (1) Mr. Smith; Lieutenant Smith (if female) (2) Lieutenant (j.g.) Smith |
| **lieutenant, second**—see SECOND LIEUTENANT | | | | |
| **major** (air force, army) | Major or MAJ John R. Smith, USAF (or USA) | Dear Major Smith | Sincerely yours | (1 and 2) Major Smith |
| (marine corps) | Major or Maj. John R. Smith, USMC | Dear Major Smith | Sincerely yours | (1 and 2) Major Smith |
| **major general**—see GENERAL | | | | |
| **midshipman** (Coast Guard and Naval Academies) | Midshipman John / Amelia } R. Smith | Dear Midshipman Smith | Sincerely yours | (1 and 2) Midshipman Smith |

| Addressee | Form of Address | Salutation | Complimentary Close | (1) Oral Reference (2) Written Reference |
|---|---|---|---|---|
| **petty officer and chief petty officer ranks** (coast guard, navy) | Petty Officer or PO John R. Smith, USN (or USCG) Chief Petty Officer or CPO John R. Smith, USN (or USCG) | Dear Mr. Smith Dear Mr. Smith | Sincerely yours | (1) Mr. Smith (2) Mr. Smith or Petty Officer Smith (1) Mr. Smith or Chief Smith or Chief Petty Officer Smith |
| **private** (army) | Private or PVT John R. Smith, USA | Dear Private Smith | Sincerely yours | (1 and 2) Private Smith |
| (marine corps) | Private or Pvt. John R. Smith, USMC | Dear Private Smith | Sincerely yours | (1 and 2) Private Smith |
| **private first class** (army) | Private First Class or PFC John R. Smith, USA | Dear Private Smith | Sincerely yours | (1 and 2) Private Smith |
| **seaman** (coast guard, navy) | Seaman or SMN John R. Smith, USCG (or USN) | Dear Seaman Smith | Sincerely yours | (1 and 2) Seaman Smith |
| **seaman first class** | Seaman First Class or S1C John R. Smith, USCG (or USN) | Dear Seaman Smith | Sincerely yours | (1 and 2) Seaman Smith |
| **second lieutenant** (air force, army) | Second Lieutenant or 2LT John R. Smith, USAF (or USA) | Dear Lieutenant Smith | Sincerely yours | (1 and 2) Lieutenant Smith |
| (marine corps) | Second Lieutenant or 2nd. Lt. John R. Smith, USMC | Dear Lieutenant Smith | Sincerely yours | (1 and 2) Lieutenant Smith |

**sergeant** (a cross section of sergeant ranks)

| | Envelope and inside address | Salutation | Complimentary close | Speaking to and introduction |
|---|---|---|---|---|
| **first sergeant** (army) | First Sergeant or 1SG John R. Smith, USA | Dear Sergeant Smith | Sincerely yours | (1 and 2) Sergeant Smith |
| (marine corps) | First Sergeant or 1st. Sgt. John R. Smith, USMC | Dear Sergeant Smith | Sincerely yours | (1 and 2) Sergeant Smith |
| **gunnery sergeant** (marine corps) | Gunnery Sergeant or Gy. Sgt. John R. Smith, USMC | Dear Sergeant Smith | Sincerely yours | (1 and 2) Sergeant Smith |
| **master sergeant** (air force) | Master Sergeant or MSGT John R. Smith, USAF | Dear Sergeant Smith | Sincerely yours | (1 and 2) Sergeant Smith |
| (army) | Master Sergeant or MSG John R. Smith, USA | Dear Sergeant Smith | Sincerely yours | (1 and 2) Sergeant Smith |
| **senior master sergeant** (air force) | Senior Master Sergeant or SMSGT John R. Smith, USAF | Dear Sergeant Smith | Sincerely yours | (1 and 2) Sergeant Smith |
| **sergeant** (army, air force) | Sergeant or SGT John R. Smith, USA (or USAF) | Dear Sergeant Smith | Sincerely yours | (1 and 2) Sergeant Smith |
| **sergeant major** (army) | Sergeant Major or SGM John R. Smith, USA | Dear Sergeant Major Smith | Sincerely yours | (1 and 2) Sergeant Major Smith |
| (marine corps) | Sergeant Major or Sgt. Maj. John R. Smith, USMC | Dear Sergeant Major Smith | Sincerely yours | (1 and 2) Sergeant Major Smith |
| **staff sergeant** (air force) | Staff Sergeant or SSGT John R. Smith, USAF | Dear Sergeant Smith | Sincerely yours | (1 and 2) Sergeant Smith |
| (army) | Staff Sergeant or SSG John R. Smith, USA | Dear Sergeant Smith | Sincerely yours | (1 and 2) Sergeant Smith |
| **technical sergeant** (air force) | Technical Sergeant or TSGT John R. Smith, USAF | Dear Sergeant Smith | Sincerely yours | (1 and 2) Sergeant Smith |

| Addressee | Form of Address | Salutation | Complimentary Close | (1) Oral Reference (2) Written Reference |
|---|---|---|---|---|
| **specialist** (army) as specialist fourth class | Specialist Fourth Class or S4 John R. Smith, USA | Dear Specialist Smith | Sincerely yours | (1 and 2) Specialist Smith |
| **warrant officer** (army) as warrant officer W1 | Warrant Officer W1 or WO1 John R. Smith, USA | Dear Mr. Smith | Sincerely yours | (1) Mr. Smith (2) Mr. Smith or Warrant Officer Smith |
| **chief warrant officer** (army) as chief warrant officer W4 | Chief Warrant Officer W4 or CWO4 John R. Smith, USA | Dear Mr. Smith | Sincerely yours | (1) Mr. Smith (2) Mr. Smith or Chief Warrant Officer Smith |
| **other ranks not listed** | full title + full name + comma + abbreviation of branch of service | Dear + rank + surname | Sincerely yours | (1 and 2) rank + surname |

MISCELLANEOUS PROFESSIONAL TITLES

| Addressee | Form of Address | Salutation | Complimentary Close | (1) Oral Reference (2) Written Reference |
|---|---|---|---|---|
| **attorney** | Mr. / Ms. / Mrs. / Miss { John / Amelia } R. Smith Attorney-at-Law or { John / Amelia } R. Smith, Esq. | Dear Mr. / Ms. / Mrs. / Miss } Smith | Very truly yours | (1) Mr., Ms., Mrs., Miss Smith (2) Mr., Ms., Mrs., Miss Smith or Attorney (or Atty.) Smith |
| **dentist** | { John / Amelia } R. Smith, D.D.S. or Dr. { John / Amelia } R. Smith | Dear Dr. Smith | Very truly yours Sincerely yours | (1 and 2) Dr. Smith |

| | Address | Salutation | Complimentary close | Informal |
|---|---|---|---|---|
| **physician** | John } R. Smith, M.D. / Amelia } *or* / Dr. John } R. Smith / Amelia } | Dear Dr. Smith | Very truly yours / Sincerely yours | (*1 and 2*) Dr. Smith |
| **veterinarian** | John } R. Smith, D.V.M. / Amelia } *or* / Dr. John } R. Smith / Amelia } | Dear Dr. Smith | Very truly yours / Sincerely yours | (*1 and 2*) Dr. Smith |

## UNITED NATIONS OFFICIALS

| | Address | Salutation | Complimentary close | Informal |
|---|---|---|---|---|
| **representative, American** (with ambassadorial rank) | The Honorable / John } R. Smith / Amelia } / United States / Permanent / Representative to the / United Nations / (address) | Sir    Madam / My dear Mr. } Madam } Ambassador / Dear Mr. } Madam } Ambassador | Respectfully / Sincerely yours | (1) Mr., Madam Ambassador or Mr., Ms., Mrs., Miss Smith / (2) Mr., Ms., Mrs., Miss Smith or the United States Representative to the United Nations or UN Representative ---- Smith |
| **representative foreign** (with ambassadorial rank) | His } Excellency / Her } / John } R. Smith / Amelia } / Representative of ---- / to the United Nations / (address) | Excellency / My dear Mr. } Madame } Ambassador / Dear Mr. } Madame } Ambassador | Respectfully / Sincerely yours | (1) Mr., Madame Ambassador or Mr., Ms., Mrs., Miss Smith / (2) Mr., Ms., Mrs., Miss Smith or the Representative of ---- to the United Nations or UN Representative ---- Smith |

| Addressee | Form of Address | Salutation | Complimentary Close | (1) Oral Reference (2) Written Reference |
|---|---|---|---|---|
| **secretary-general** | His Excellency John R. Smith Secretary-General of the United Nations (address) | Excellency<br><br>My dear Mr. Secretary-General<br>Dear Mr. Secretary-General | Respectfully<br><br>Sincerely yours | (1) Mr. Smith or Sir<br>(2) the Secretary-General of the United Nations or UN Secretary-General Smith or The Secretary-General or Mr. Smith |
| **undersecretary** | The Honorable John } R. Smith Amelia Undersecretary of the United Nations (address) | Sir    Madam<br>       Madame<br><br>My dear Mr.<br>Ms. } Smith<br>Mrs.<br>Miss<br><br>Dear Mr.<br>Ms. } Smith<br>Mrs.<br>Miss | Very truly yours<br><br><br>Sincerely yours<br><br><br>Sincerely yours | (1) Mr., Ms., Mrs., Miss Smith<br>(2) Mr., Ms., Mrs., Miss Smith or the Under-secretary of the United Nations or UN Under-secretary ––– Smith |

## Multiple Addressees

| Inside Address Styling | Salutation Styling |
| --- | --- |

**two or more men with same surname**

| | |
| --- | --- |
| Mr. Arthur W. Jones | Gentlemen |
| Mr. John H. Jones | |
| *or* | *or* |
| Messrs. A. W. and J. H. Jones | |
| *or* | Dear Messrs. Jones |
| The Messrs. Jones | |

**two or more men with different surnames**

| | |
| --- | --- |
| Mr. Angus D. Langley | Gentlemen *or* Dear  Mr. Langley and |
| Mr. Lionel P. Overton | Mr. Overton |
| *or* | |
| Messrs. A. D. Langley and | Dear Messrs. Langley and Overton |
| L. P. Overton | |
| *or* | |
| Messrs. Langley and Overton | |

**two or more married women with same surname**

| | |
| --- | --- |
| Mrs. Arthur W. Jones | Mesdames |
| Mrs. John H. Jones | |
| *or* | *or* |
| Mesdames A. W. and J. H. Jones | |
| *or* | Dear Mesdames Jones |
| The Mesdames Jones | |

**two or more unmarried women with same surname**

| | |
| --- | --- |
| Miss Alice H. Danvers | Ladies |
| Miss Margaret T. Danvers | |
| *or* | *or* |
| Misses Alice and Margaret Danvers | |
| *or* | Dear Misses Danvers |
| The Misses Danvers | |

**two or more women with same surname but whose marital status is unknown or irrelevant**

| | |
| --- | --- |
| Ms. Alice H. Danvers | Dear Ms. Alice and Margaret Danvers |
| Ms. Margaret T. Danvers | |

**two or more married women with different surnames**

| | |
| --- | --- |
| Mrs. Allen Y. Dow | Dear Mrs. Dow and Mrs. Frank |
| Mrs. Lawrence R. Frank | |
| *or* | *or* |
| Mesdames Dow and Frank | Mesdames *or* Dear Mesdames Dow |
| | and Frank |

**two or more unmarried women with different surnames**

| | |
| --- | --- |
| Miss Elizabeth Dudley | Ladies *or* Dear Miss Dudley and |
| Miss Ann Raymond | Miss Raymond |
| *or* | *or* |
| Misses E. Dudley and A. Raymond | Dear Misses Dudley and Raymond |

**two or more women with different surnames but whose marital status is unknown or irrelevant**

| | |
| --- | --- |
| Ms. Barbara Lee | Dear Ms. Lee and Ms. Key |
| Ms. Helen Key | |

## SPECIAL TITLES, DESIGNATIONS, AND ABBREVIATIONS: A GUIDE TO USAGE

**Doctor**    If *Doctor* or its abbreviation *Dr.* is used before a person's name, academic degrees (as *D.D.S., D.V.M., M.D.,* or *Ph.D.*) are not included after the surname. The title *Doctor* may be typed out in full or abbreviated in a salutation, but it is usually abbreviated in an envelope address block and in an inside address in order to save space. When *Doctor* appears in a salutation, it must be used in conjunction with the addressee's surname:

Dear Doctor Smith *or* Dear Dr. Smith *not* Dear Doctor

If a woman holds a doctorate, her title should be used in business-related correspondence even if her husband's name is also included in the letter:

Dr. Ann R. Smith and
  Mr. James O. Smith
Dear Dr. Smith and Mr. Smith

If both husband and wife are doctors, one of the following patterns may be followed:

| | |
|---|---|
| Dr. Ann R. Smith and<br>  Dr. James O. Smith | Drs. Ann R. and James O. Smith |
| | Ann R. Smith, M.D. |
| The Drs. Smith | James O. Smith, M.D. |
| The Doctors Smith | |
| *more formal*<br>My dear Doctors Smith | *informal*<br>Dear Drs. Smith<br>Dear Doctors Smith |

Address patterns for two or more doctors associated in a joint practice are:

| | |
|---|---|
| Drs. Francis X. Sullivan and<br>  Philip K. Ross | Francis X. Sullivan, M.D.<br>Philip K. Ross, M.D. |
| *more formal*<br>My dear Drs. Sullivan and Ross | *informal*<br>Dear Drs. Sullivan and Ross<br>Dear Doctors Sullivan and Ross<br>Dear Dr. Sullivan and Dr. Ross<br>Dear Doctor Sullivan and Doctor Ross |

**Esquire**    The abbreviation *Esq.* for *Esquire* is used in the United States after the surnames of professional persons such as attorneys, architects, consuls, clerks of the courts, and justices of the peace (but never in conjunction with *The Honorable*). In addition, a few law offices address their clients as *Esquire*. In Great Britain, *Esq.* is generally used after the surnames of people who have distinguished themselves in professional, diplomatic, or social circles. For example, when addressing a letter to a high corporate officer of a British firm, one should include *Esq.* after his surname, both on the envelope and in the inside address. Under no circumstances should *Esq.* appear in a salutation. This rule applies to both American and British correspondence. If a courtesy title such as *Dr., Hon., Miss, Mr., Mrs.,* or *Ms.* is used before the addressee's name, *Esq.* is omitted. The plural of *Esq.* is *Esqs.* and is used with the surnames of multiple addressees.

    *Esquire* or *Esq.* is frequently used in the United States after the surname of a woman lawyer, although the practice has not yet gained acceptance in all law offices or among all state bar associations. Always consult the writer's or dictator's wishes in this instance. A safe alternative is to write *Attorney-at-law* after the lawyer's surname.

*Examples:*

| | |
|---|---|
| Carolyn B. West, Esq.<br>American Consul | Dear Ms. West |
| | |
| Samuel A. Sebert, Esq.<br>Norman D. Langfitt, Esq.<br>*or*<br>Sebert and Langfitt, Esqs.<br>*or*<br>Messrs. Sebert and Langfitt<br>Attorneys-at-law | Gentlemen<br>Dear Mr. Sebert and Mr. Langfitt<br>Dear Messrs. Sebert and Langfitt |
| | |
| Simpson, Tyler, and Williams, Esqs.<br>*or*<br>Scott A. Simpson, Esq.<br>Annabelle W. Tyler, Esq.<br>David I. Williams, Esq. | Dear Ms. Tyler and Messrs. Simpson<br>   and Williams |
| | |
| *British*<br>Jonathan A. Lyons, Esq.<br>President | Dear Mr. Lyons |

**Honorable**    In the United States, *The Honorable* or its abbreviated form *Hon.* is used as a title of distinction (but not rank) and is accorded elected or appointed (but not career) government officials such as judges, justices, congressmen, and cabinet officers. Neither the full form nor the abbreviation is ever used by its recipient in written signatures, letterhead, business or visiting cards, or in typed signature blocks. While it may be used in an envelope address block and in an inside address of a letter addressed to him or her, it is <u>never</u> used in a salutation. *The Honorable* should never appear before a surname standing alone: there must always be an intervening first name, an initial or initials, or a courtesy title:

The Honorable John R. Smith
The Honorable J. R. Smith
The Honorable J. Robert Smith
The Honorable Mr. Smith
The Honorable Dr. Smith

If *The Honorable* is used with a full name, a courtesy title should not be added. *The Honorable* may also precede a woman's name:

The Honorable Jane R. Smith
The Honorable Mrs. Smith

However, if the woman's full name is given, a courtesy title should not be added. When an official and his wife are being addressed, his full name should be typed out, as

| | |
|---|---|
| The Honorable John R. Smith<br>   and Mrs. Smith | *or*   The Honorable and Mrs. John R. Smith<br>Dear Mr. and Mrs. Smith |

The stylings "Hon. and Mrs. Smith" and "The Honorable and Mrs. Smith" should <u>never</u> be used. If, however, the official's full name is unknown, the styling is:

The Honorable Mr. Smith and Mrs. Smith

If a married woman holds the title and her husband does not, her name appears first on business-related correspondence addressed to both persons. However, if the couple is being addressed socially, the woman's title may be dropped unless she has retained her maiden name for use in personal as well as business correspondence:

*business correspondence*

The Honorable Harriet M. Johnson
and Mr. Johnson

Dear Mrs. (*or* Governor, etc.)
Johnson and Mr. Johnson

*social correspondence*

Mr. and Mrs. Robert Y. Johnson

Dear Mr. and Mrs. Johnson

**if maiden name retained:**

*business correspondence*

The Honorable Harriet A. Mathieson
and Mr. Robert Y. Johnson

Dear Ms. Mathieson
and Mr. Johnson

*social correspondence*

Ms. Harriet A. Mathieson
Mr. Roger Y. Johnson

Dear Ms. Mathieson
and Mr. Johnson

If space is limited, *The Honorable* may be typed on the first line of an address block, with the recipient's name on the next line:

The Honorable
John R. Smith
and Mrs. Smith

When *The Honorable* occurs in a running text or in a list of names in such a text, the *T* in *The* is then lowercased:

. . . a speech by the Honorable Charles H. Patterson, the American Consul in Athens . . .

In informal writing such as newspaper articles, the plural forms *the Honorables* or *Hons.* may be used before a list of persons accorded the distinction. However, in official or formal writing either *the Honorable Messrs.* placed before the entire list of surnames or *the Honorable* or *Hon.* repeated before each full name in the list may be used:

**formal**      . . . was supported in the motion by the Honorable Messrs. Clarke, Goodfellow, Thomas, and Harrington.

. . . met with the Honorable Albert Y. Langley and the Honorable Frances P. Kelley.

**informal**      . . . interviewed the Hons. Jacob Y. Stathis, Samuel P. Kenton, William L. Williamson, and Gloria O. Yarnell—all United States Senators.

**Jr.** and **Sr.**      The designations *Jr.* and *Sr.* may or may not be preceded by a comma, depending on office policy or writer preference; however, one styling should be selected and adhered to for the sake of uniformity:

John K. Walker Jr.      *or*      John K. Walker, Jr.

*Jr.* and *Sr.* may be used in conjunction with courtesy titles and with academic degree abbreviations or with professional rating abbreviations, as

Mr. John K. Walker[,] Jr.
Dr. John K. Walker[,] Jr.
General John K. Walker[,] Jr.
The Honorable John K. Walker[,] Jr.

Hon. John K. Walker[,] Jr.
John K. Walker[,] Jr., Esq.
John K. Walker[,] Jr., M.D.

**Madam** and **Madame**      The title *Madam* should be used only in salutations of highly impersonal or high-level governmental and diplomatic correspondence, unless the writer is certain that the addressee is married. The French form *Madame* is recommended for salutations in correspondence addressed to *foreign* diplomats and heads of state. See Forms of Address Chart for examples.

**Mesdames**   The plural form of *Madam, Madame,* or *Mrs.* is *Mesdames,* which may be used before the names of two or more married women associated together in a professional partnership or in a business. It may appear with their names on an envelope and in an inside address, and it may appear with their names or standing alone in a salutation:

| | |
|---|---|
| Mesdames T. V. Meade and P. A. Tate | Dear Mesdames Meade and Tate |
| Mesdames Meade and Tate | Mesdames |
| | |
| Mesdames V. T. and A. P. Stevens | Dear Mesdames Stevens |
| The Mesdames Stevens | Mesdames |

See also the Multiple Addressees Chart, page 345.

**Messrs.**   The plural abbreviation of *Mr.* is *Messrs.* It is used before the surnames of two or more men associated in a professional partnership or in a business. *Messrs.* may appear on an envelope, in an inside address, and in a salutation when used in conjunction with the surnames of the addressees; however, this abbreviation should never stand alone. Examples:

| | |
|---|---|
| Messrs. Archlake, Smythe, and Dabney | Dear Messrs. Archlake, Smythe, and Dabney |
| Attorneys-at-law | Gentlemen |
| | |
| Messrs. K. Y. and P. B. Overton | Dear Messrs. Overton |
| Architects | Gentlemen |

*Messrs.* should never be used before a compound corporate name formed from two surnames such as *Lord & Taylor* or *Woodward & Lothrup,* or from a corporate name like *H. L. Jones and Sons.* For correct use of *Messrs.* + *The Honorable* or + *The Reverend,* see pages 348 and 351, respectively.

**Misses**   The plural form of *Miss* is *Misses,* and it may be used before the names of two or more unmarried women who are being addressed together. It may appear on an envelope, in an inside address, and in a salutation. Like *Messrs., Misses* should never stand alone but must occur in conjunction with a name or names. Examples:

| | |
|---|---|
| Misses Hay and Middleton | Dear Misses Hay and Middleton |
| Misses D. L. Hay and H. K. Middleton | Ladies |
| | |
| Misses Tara and Julia Smith | Dear Misses Smith |
| The Misses Smith | Ladies |

For a complete set of examples in this category, see the Multiple Addressees Chart, page 345.

**Professor**   If used with a surname, *Professor* should be typed out in full; however, if used with a given name and initial or a set of initials as well as a surname, it may be abbreviated to *Prof.* It is, therefore, usually abbreviated in envelope address blocks and in inside addresses, but typed out in salutations. *Professor* should not stand alone in a salutation. Examples:

| | |
|---|---|
| Prof. Florence C. Marlowe | Dear Professor Marlowe |
| Department of English | Dear Dr. Marlowe |
| *or* | Dear Miss Marlowe |
| Professor Florence C. Marlowe | Mrs. Marlowe |
| Department of English | Ms. Marlowe |
| | *but not* |
| | Dear Professor |

When addressing a letter to a professor and his wife, the title is usually written out in full unless the name is unusually long:

| | |
|---|---|
| Professor and Mrs. Lee Dow | Dear Professor and Mrs. Dow |
| Prof. and Mrs. Henry Talbott-Smythe | Dear Professor and Mrs. Talbott-Smythe |

Letters addressed to couples of whom the wife is the professor and the husband is not may follow one of these patterns:

| | |
|---|---|
| Professor Diana Goode and Mr. Goode | *business correspondence* |
| Mr. and Mrs. Lawrence F. Goode | *business or social correspondence* |
| Professor Diana Falls<br>Mr. Lawrence F. Goode | *if wife has retained maiden name* |
| Dear Professor Goode and Mr. Goode | *business correspondence* |
| Dear Mr. and Mrs. Goode | *business or social correspondence* |
| Dear Professor (*or* Ms.) Falls and Mr. Goode | *wife having retained her maiden name* |

When addressing two or more professors—male or female, whether having the same or different surnames—type *Professors* and not "Profs."

| | |
|---|---|
| Professors A. L. Smith and C. L. Doe | Dear Professors Smith and Doe<br>Dear Drs. Smith and Doe<br>Dear Mr. Smith and Mr. Doe<br>Dear Messrs. Smith and Doe<br>Gentlemen |
| Professors B. K. Johns and S. T. Yarrell | Dear Professors Johns and Yarrell<br>Dear Drs. Johns and Yarrell<br>Dear Ms. Johns and Mr. Yarrell |
| Professors G. A. and F. K. Cornett<br>The Professors Cornett | *acceptable for any combination*<br>Dear Professors Cornett<br>Dear Drs. Cornett<br>*if males*<br>Gentlemen<br>*if females*<br>Ladies *or* Mesdames<br>*if married*<br>Dear Mr. and Mrs. Cornett<br>Dear Professors Cornett<br>Dear Drs. Cornett |

**Reverend**   In formal or official writing, *The* should precede *Reverend;* however, *The Reverend* is often abbreviated to *The Rev.* or just *Rev.* especially in unofficial or informal writing, and particularly in business correspondence where the problem of space on envelopes and in inside addresses is a factor. The typed-out full form *The Reverend* must be used in conjunction with the clergyman's full name:

The Reverend Philip D. Asquith
The Reverend Dr. Philip D. Asquith
The Reverend P. D. Asquith

*The Reverend* may appear with just a surname only if another courtesy title intervenes:

The Reverend Mr. Asquith
The Reverend Professor Asquith
The Reverend Dr. Asquith

*The Reverend, The Rev.,* or *Rev.* should not be used in the salutation, although any one of these titles may be used on the envelope and in the inside address. In salutations, the following titles are acceptable for clergymen: *Mr.* (or *Ms., Miss, Mrs.*), *Father, Chaplain,* or *Dr.* See the Forms of Address Chart under the section entitled "Clerical and Religious Orders" for examples. The only exceptions to this rule are salutations in letters addressed to high prelates of a church (as bishops, monsignors, etc.). See the Forms of Address Chart. When addressing a letter to a clergyman and his wife, the typist should follow one of these stylings:

| | |
|---|---|
| The Rev. and Mrs. P.D. Asquith | *but never* |
| The Rev. and Mrs. Philip D. Asquith | Rev. and Mrs. Asquith |
| The Reverend and Mrs. P. D. Asquith | |
| The Reverend and Mrs. Philip D. Asquith | |

Two clergymen having the same or different surnames should not be addressed in letters as "The Reverends" or "The Revs." or "Revs." They may, however, be addressed as *The Reverend* (or *The Rev.*) *Messrs.* or *The Reverend* (or *The Rev.*) *Drs.,* or the titles *The Reverend, The Rev.,* or *Rev.* may be repeated before each clergyman's name; as

| | |
|---|---|
| The Reverend Messrs. S. J. and D. V. Smith | The Rev. S. J. Smith and |
| The Rev. Messrs. S. J. and D. V. Smith | The Rev. D. V. Smith |
| The Reverend Messrs. Smith | Rev. S. J. Smith and |
| The Rev. Messrs. Smith | Rev. D. V. Smith |

with "Gentlemen" being the correct salutation. When writing to two or more clergymen having different surnames, the following patterns are acceptable:

| | |
|---|---|
| The Reverend Messrs. P. A. Francis and F. L. Beale | Gentlemen |
| The Rev. Messrs. P. A. Francis and F. L. Beale | Dear Mr. Francis and Mr. Beale |
| | Dear Father Francis and Father Beale |
| The Rev. P. A. Francis | |
| The Rev. F. L. Beale | |

In formal texts, "The Reverends," "The Revs.," and "Revs." are not acceptable as collective titles (as in lists of names). *The Reverend* (or *Rev.*) *Messrs.* (or *Drs.* or *Professors)* may be used, or *The Reverend* or *The Rev.* or *Rev.* may be repeated before each clergyman's name. If the term *clergymen* or the expression *the clergy* is mentioned in introducing the list, a single title *the Reverend* or *the Rev.* may be added before the list to serve all of the names. While it is true that "the Revs." is often seen in newspapers and in catalogs, this expression is still not recommended for formal, official writing. Examples:

. . . were the Reverend Messrs. Jones, Smith and Bennett, as well as . . . .
Among the clergymen present were the Reverend John G. Jones, Mr. Smith, and Dr. Doe.
Prayers were offered by the Rev. J. G. Jones, Rev. Mr. Smith, and Rev. Dr. Doe.

**Second, Third**  These designations after surnames may be styled as Roman numerals (I, III, IV) or as ordinals (2nd/2d, 3rd/3d, 4th). Such a designation may or may not be separated from a surname by a comma, depending on office policy or writer preference:

Mr. Jason T. Johnson III (*or* 3rd *or* 3d)
Mr. Jason T. Johnson, III (*or* 3rd *or* 3d)

**Professional designations**  The following illustrates the proper order of occurrence of initials representing academic degrees, religious orders, and professional ratings that may appear after a name and that are separated from each other by commas:

| | | |
|---|---|---|
| religious orders (as *S.J.*) | academic degrees (as *Ph.D.*) | professional ratings (as *C.P.A.*) |
| theological degrees (as *D.D.*) | honorary degrees (as *Litt.D.*) | |

Such initials are not often used in addresses, and two or more sets of initials appear even more rarely. Only when the initials represent achievements in different fields that are relevant to one's profession should more than one set be used. When initials follow a name, the courtesy title (*Mr., Mrs., Ms., Miss, Dr.*) is always omitted.

Nancy Robinson, P.L.S.

Mary R. Lopez, C.P.A.

John R. Doe, M.D., Ph.D.
Chief of Staff
Smithville Hospital

John R. Doe, J.D., C.M.C.

The Rev. John R. Doe, S.J., D.D., LL.D.
Chaplain, Smithville College

# 10.8

## MEMORANDUM FORMAT

The interoffice memorandum or memo is a means of informal communication within a firm or organization. Its special arrangement replaces the salutation, complimentary close, and written signature of the letter with identifying headings.

Although a memorandum may be typed on a plain sheet of paper, it is usually typed on special prepared forms, which are most often full sheets. The forms may be in pads or in special carbon packs to facilitate preparation and distribution of carbon copies. Some carbon packs have the file copy printed on a sheet of colored paper. Space is provided for the message which is typically informal in style and routine in content. Since many companies design their own interoffice memorandum forms, the variety of sizes, styles, and arrangements is great. Generally, the format is simple and comprises two major parts: (1) the *heading* consisting of the printed guide words *To, From, Date,* and *Subject,* and (2) the *body* or *message.*

### THE MAIN PARTS OF A MEMORANDUM
**The heading**    Although the heading usually contains only the guide words shown just above, other guide words such as *Telephone Extension* or *Department* may be added. The *To* line identifies the individual(s) or group(s) intended to receive the memorandum. It includes the addressee's name (courtesy titles such as *Mr., Ms., Mrs., Miss,* and *Dr.* are optional; they are more likely to be used when addressing a person of higher rank), job title (optional), and department (especially in large organizations). Several names may be listed after *To* if the memorandum is being sent to several people. A check is placed after the name of each person on his or her copy to facilitate handling. Multiple distribution may also be achieved by listing several names in a carbon copy notation at the bottom of the memorandum and then checking each name off. The *From* line indicates the name of the writer. A courtesy title is generally not used, but the writer's job title or department may be included. Some forms feature guide words for job titles and department designations. The *Date* line contains the full date, which should not be abbreviated or appear in all-numerical form. The *Subject* line pinpoints the gist of the memorandum and serves to orient its recipients before they begin to read. It is usually one line in length and should be as brief as possible. Since this line is often used for filing purposes, it must be accurate.

The guide words are usually followed by a colon. The typist begins insertions two spaces after the colon. The guide words are often but not always aligned at the right on a printed form to make typing easier for the secretary:

|  | | |
|---|---|---|
| TO: | | TO: |
| FROM: | *or* | FROM: |
| SUBJECT: | | SUBJECT: |

**Interoffice Memorandum Typed on a Plain Sheet of Paper**

```
        TO:       Alison Paige
                  Secretarial Services

        FROM:     Maria Rodriguez
                  Personnel Department

        DATE:     November 21, 19—

        SUBJECT:  Format for Interoffice Memorandums on Plain Paper


                  Leave top and side margins of at least one inch when
        typing memorandums on plain paper.  Align all guide words at the
        left margin.  For easier typing, use a ten-space tab stop to
        align the fill-in data.

                  Leave two or three blank lines after the subject line.
        Indent all paragraphs of the message by ten spaces or use the
        blocked paragraph style illustrated in the printed memorandum
        facsimile.

                  Type the writer's initials two spaces beneath the last
        line of the last paragraph and position them slightly to the
        right of dead center.

                                   M. R.

        coc

        cc Wesley Torrence
           Annette Roberts
```

Since the guide word or words and the insertions must align horizontally, the variable line spacer or the ratchet release lever on the typewriter is used:

*Incorrect*   FROM:            *Correct*   FROM:   Thomas Kingsford
                   Thomas Kingsford

**The body or message**   The body or message of the memorandum is separated from the subject line by two or three blank lines. It may be typed in block style (with no indentations for paragraphs), it is usually single-spaced (with double-spacing between paragraphs), and it normally has one-inch side margins. It is also appropriate to double-space short memorandums. The tone or degree of formality of a memorandum message varies with the level of management it will reach, with the subject being discussed, and with the reader-writer relationship. The basic organization of the message usually follows one or the other of these patterns: *direct*—where the main idea is presented first and followed by explanations or facts, and *indirect*—where the explanations and facts are given first and the main idea is set forth last.

Although there is no formal closing to a memorandum form, the writer's initials are usually typed at the end. Some writers prefer to initial or sign a memorandum. The typist's initials as well as enclosure and carbon copy notations also appear at the bottom in the same position as those in a regular letter.

Since the memorandum form is an informal communication tool, it is common for the respondent to pen a reply directly on the form. One form in use even states, "SAVE TIME: If convenient, handwrite reply to sender on this same sheet."

**Interoffice Memorandum Typed on a Printed Form**

---

# MARKHAM AND SISITSKY

## MEMORANDUM

**To:**    Cynthia A. Barnes                **Date:** May 20, 19—
           William P. Cook
           Joan T. Davis

**From:**   Roger N. Taylor
**Subject:** Interoffice Memorandum Format

If the printed words To, From, and Subject are aligned to the right, leave two blank spaces after the colons and then proceed to typewrite the fill-in data. If, however, the guide words are aligned to the left as shown here, block the fill-ins so that they will be vertically aligned with the body of the memorandum. Set a tab stop two spaces after the guide word Date and then type the fill-in which should not be abbreviated. Thus, if the writer's initials are to be typed at the end of the message, the first letter of the typed date and the first letter of the initials will be vertically aligned later on.

All fill-ins should be horizontally aligned with their guide words. Horizontal alignment is accomplished by use of the variable line spacer or the ratchet release lever on the typewriter.

If the memorandum is confidential, type the word confidential in the center of the page about three lines below the top edge of the sheet or about two lines below the printed heading Memorandum. This designation may be typed all in capital letters or in underscored capital and lower case letters.

Maintain side margins of at least one inch. Leave three blank lines between the subject line and the first message line. Block all paragraphs flush left. Single-space the paragraphs internally; double-space between paragraphs.

Type the writer's initials two lines below the last message line and align them with the date.

                                        R. T.

coc

# 11

# USING LEGAL FORMS

## CONTENTS

# 11.1

## LAW BLANKS AND OTHER PRINTED FORMS

Law blanks—printed legal forms on which part of the pertinent information has already been supplied—and other printed forms are often used in the law office for routine business transactions and for certain kinds of court proceedings. Printed forms offer many advantages. They are accurate, complete, reliable, and clearly and economically worded. They eliminate lengthy dictation, transcription, and proofreading sessions since only a limited amount of information is required to fill in the blank spaces. An experienced legal secretary can often complete these forms with limited instruction from the attorney by obtaining facts from the case file.

Printed forms that comply with local regulations and conventions are often prepared and distributed for specific jurisdictions. Since most business operations are controlled by state or local regulations, locally printed forms are generally used for business transactions when they meet all the legal requirements of the transaction. There are many types of law blanks and printed forms available; some are quite specialized.

### IDENTIFICATION OF FORMS

Before using a form, it is important to check both its title and its identification number (the printer's catalog number). Many forms—such as subpoena and subpoena duces tecum, warranty deed and corporation warranty deed—are similar and easily confused. In addition to checking the title and identification number, you should check the form for currency and proper jurisdiction. The identification number, printed in small type in a corner, often includes the date of the latest printing or revision. Check to be sure that all copies of a form have the same identification number if you are typing carbon copies. If the titles of two law blanks are the same but their identification numbers differ, the contents of the forms may not be identical.

## SOURCES OF FORMS

**Court forms**   The use of court forms saves time for the court, the clerk's office, and your office. Court papers that are completely typed must be proofread and checked in full, whereas only the filled-in portions of printed forms need to be checked by the attorney, the legal secretary, and court personnel. Printed court forms may be obtained, usually free of charge, from the office of the clerk of court. Widely used court forms include divorce forms, jury instructions, probate forms, subpoenas, summonses, and affidavits of service.

**Commercial forms**   Law form printers publish catalogs listing the titles and identification numbers of forms they print. Hundreds of different types of law blanks may be obtained by mail and at stationery and office supply stores. Agreements, bankruptcy forms, powers of attorney, contract forms, bills of sale, promissory notes, deeds, and rental forms are commonly purchased in this way. Some are sold as pads in lots of from 25 to 100. Sometimes the firm's name and address may be printed on the stock forms.

Special business forms are also supplied, free of charge, by banks, insurance companies, and title and abstract companies. Legal forms supplied by title and abstract companies—companies that search changes in ownership of real property by examining official records—include deeds, mortgages, and notes secured by deeds of trust.

**Government forms**   Government forms are usually supplied free of charge by agencies of the federal, state, and local governments. State tax forms may be obtained from the state division responsible for collection of taxes; the Internal Revenue Service supplies forms for federal taxes. State and local police departments and courts supply accident report forms. Federal agencies such as the Social Security Administration (SSA), Securities and Exchange Commission (SEC), Small Business Administration (SBA), and Veterans Administration (VA) supply forms frequently used in law offices.

## INTEROFFICE FORMS

Interoffice forms are designed to transmit information or instructions only to other persons within the organization or to be transcribed to other business records. Examples of printed interoffice forms include office memorandums, telephone message slips, charge-out forms for files or library material, time tickets, procedural checklists, expense account forms, new client information sheets, petty cash forms, and disbursement slips. Interoffice forms are frequently used among the attorneys, staff, and agents of a law firm because they convey information quickly, simplify tasks, and reduce mistakes.

A printed interoffice form should be used whenever information is too complicated or too important to be left to word of mouth or memory. Examples are work instructions, policy statements, requests for information, and reminders for future action. Printed forms should also be used when the communication includes repetitive elements. The repetitive elements should be printed, with blanks left for the variable information. The forms should be practical and simple, the purpose being to eliminate or minimize clerical work.

**Customized interoffice forms**   Stationery and office supply stores offer a wide variety of interoffice forms, but many firms prefer to design their own. The task to be performed should be analyzed and the form carefully designed to direct the user from the beginning of the job to the end. Deliberate planning can save time and assure better results. Care must be taken to make the form complete and efficient.

The following guidelines will help you design forms for your office.

1.  The paper on which forms will be printed should be chosen carefully; whether the form will be typewritten or written in pen or pencil, whether carbon copies are to be prepared, and how often the paper will be handled should be considered.

2.  The size and weight of the paper should be standardized as much as possible.

3.  The use of colored forms will aid in routing and filing if the colors have useful meaning.

4.  If forms are not prepared by a commercial printer but are typed on an office machine, they should be prepared with the same style and size of type that will be used to complete them. This is especially important if the form will be sent out of the office.

5.  Formatting the design on an automatic typewriter will speed revisions and also allow you to make variations in the form whenever required.

You should ask a printer to advise you concerning type arrangement, spacing, and paper characteristics. If possible, place all printing orders with one company to ensure receiving good service. Interoffice forms may also be duplicated on office reprographic equipment (see Chapter 16).

Two types of interoffice forms that are commonly designed for an individual firm to meet its specific needs are time sheets and new client/matter information sheets. Time sheets, such as those illustrated on pages 157–159, generally provide space to describe the lawyer's services, the time intervals, the name of the client, and the matter. New client/matter sheets may provide space for the client's name, address, and telephone number; the name of the person who recommended the law firm to the client; a brief description of the new matter; the names and addresses of other parties and the names and addresses of their attorneys; a description of the retainer or billing arrangement; documents received; tickler, file, and accounting instructions; the name of the responsible partner; and miscellaneous remarks. An example of a new client/matter information sheet appears on page 121.

In addition to creating interoffice forms, many law firms develop their own forms for contracts and other common legal instruments. The design and the use of such customized forms are discussed in sections 11.3 and 11.4 of this chapter.

## MAINTENANCE OF FORMS

A well-planned forms inventory control system can save trips to the courthouse to pick up forms, prevent delays in delivery from the stationery store or the printer, and reduce the number of forms that become outdated and must be discarded.

The legal secretary may be responsible for maintaining an adequate supply of forms and reordering them when necessary. Installing a forms inventory control system will ensure that forms are available when needed and will eliminate the extra cost of special orders and rapid deliveries. Such a system may be as simple as keeping a list of the forms your office uses, including the title and identification number, the source of each form, the price, the quantity last ordered, and the date last ordered.

The following procedures will help you control your inventory of forms:

1.  Store all printed forms together in a forms cabinet where they will be accessible to all users. This will make it easy to determine when the forms need to be reordered.

2.  Ask staff members to keep only a few copies of each form at their desks in order not to tie up a large inventory of forms that may become outdated.

3.  Order forms in large quantities to take advantage of lower prices, but only when you are certain that the form will not be revised soon.

As suggested in Chapter 6, forms should be segregated from other filed material, assigned file numbers, and arranged according to general categories such as court forms, tax forms, real estate transactions, wills, trusts, personal property transactions, corporations, and miscellaneous. Each general category may be broken down by file number into subcategories. For example, real estate transactions may be further divided into deeds, mortgages and related documents, leases, documents related to the sale of real estate, and miscellaneous.

Forms are normally stored in legal-size files. The subject categories should be indicated on dividers with colored tabs. Each file folder in a particular category may be tabbed with the same color. Color coding in the file drawer aids in locating and refiling the desired folder.

An index of forms available within the office should be maintained in a loose-leaf notebook. The secretary may keep the notebook, or it may be kept near the file cabinet with a copy at each secretary's desk. The first page of the notebook should list the forms by subject, providing an index. Succeeding pages should give the file number and a brief description of each form. It is important to add and retype pages as your supply of forms changes. In some instances, the year of publication should be included as a part of the description of the form. This is essential for United States government forms and certain court forms. The individual forms should be described exactly and specifically in order that each form will be clearly distinguished from every other form. It is desirable to include the name of the publisher, particularly when different mortgage and note forms are supplied by various banks, insurance companies, and mortgage companies. When forms fall into two or more classifications, place them in one category with cross-references in the other categories.

Forms <u>must</u> be kept up to date. When adding newly ordered forms to the form file, you should compare the identification numbers of the new and the old forms. If the identification numbers are different, destroy the old forms and use only the new. If you are not sure that a form is up to date, you may telephone the office to which the form will be sent, give the number of the form, and ask if it is current. Forms supplied by government agencies are frequently revised. Tax forms present a particular problem inasmuch as their useful life is often only one year.

# 11.2

## TYPING FILL-INS ON A PRINTED FORM

### DICTATION

The attorney may dictate the information to be typed on the legal form. When information is dictated, the attorney and the legal secretary should have before them identical copies of the form. The secretary should look at the form during dictation but write the fill-ins in a notebook or on machine shorthand tape. It is important to code the information to indicate the proper blank. One method of coding, illustrated in section 8.5 of Chapter 8, is to pencil a 1 on the blank line of the form and a 1 preceding the shorthand notes to be transcribed in that space. A pencilled 2 on the next blank of the form and a 2 preceding the associated shorthand notes mean that the information should be transcribed in the identically coded space.

If you are taking notes in manual shorthand, it is wise to leave a few unwritten lines in the notebook between the items. A machine shorthand operator should also leave a blank space between items in order to distinguish them. Most of the dictation will consist of phrases rather than sentences, and leaving spaces between pieces of information will clearly indicate the beginning and end of the phrase to be transcribed on the blank.

Sometimes a blank space on a form is not to be filled in with any information. The attorney should indicate this, and you should note it with a special symbol.

## TYPING THE FORM

The following guidelines will help you produce an accurate, legible, and attractive document:

1. Margins for inserts of typed material should match the margins of the lines printed on the form. An exception is land descriptions; see guideline 8 below.

2. If there are no ruled or dotted lines below the blank spaces, the typed line should be perfectly aligned with the printed line.

3. If the fill-ins must be made on ruled or dotted lines, the bases of the typewritten characters should appear slightly above those lines. (The tails of the letters *g, j, p, q,* and *y* will rest on the ruled or dotted line.) A small bit of white space between the typed words and the underlining increases legibility.

4. The law blank should be inserted into the typewriter so that fill-ins do not appear slanted upward or downward.

5. Care must be taken to fill in <u>all</u> of the small blanks, many of which call for only one or two letters. In most law blanks these are not underlined but are indicated by a small space. Many of these spaces call for letters to complete words which describe the person or persons signing the document. For example, a printed lease might include the following: "And the lessee    hereby covenant    with the lessor    and    heirs . . . ." If there is only one lessee, *s* is added to *covenant* and, if there is only one lessor, *his* (or *her*) is filled in before *heirs*. If there is more than one lessee, *s* is added to *lessee* and, if there is more than one lessor, *their* is filled in before *heirs*. The dictator will normally not bother with these details but expect the secretary to take care of them.

6. If phrases or words are to be deleted, type *x*'s over them, as shown in the illustration. Occasionally, a substitute word must be typed in above the *x*'d portion.

7. When a large space is deliberately left blank, two or three hyphens, centered on the space, should be typed to indicate to the reader that dictator and typist have not simply forgotten to fill in this space with information.

8. Quotations, including land descriptions, are usually indented and single-spaced.

9. A signature should be typed all in capitals and placed a single space below the signature line.

10. It is important to check to see if the form is continued on the back of the paper. Two-sided forms may also cause problems when you are typing carbon copies; you must make sure that the original is typed as an original on both sides, not an original on the front and a carbon copy on the back.

11. The dollar sign should not be used if the word *Dollars* is printed at the end of the space provided for inserting a sum of money. It may be used, however, with figures within parentheses.

12. Monetary units which are typed in full on legal documents are generally capitalized. Type the sum in words, then in figures within parentheses. All words except conjunctions should be capitalized; figures less than one dollar need not be spelled out. Example: Two Thousand and 10/100 Dollars ($2,000.10) payable upon receipt. Some attorneys prefer that the words used to type dollar amounts be typed all in capital letters. Example: TWO THOUSAND and 10/100 DOLLARS ($2,000.10) payable upon receipt.

13. Spaced hyphens may be used to fill any remaining space following the monetary units.

14. When a contract specifies a quantity, type it in both words and figures: ten thousand (10,000) gallons of gasoline. Type both words and figures when describing an important period of time: forty-five (45) days.

---

with mortgage covenants to secure the payment of   Twenty-eight Thousand Five

Hundred and no/100 - - - - - - - - - - - - - - - - - - - - - - - Dollars

($28,500.00) - - - - - - - - - - - - - - - - - - - - - - - - - - -

in   ten (10)      years with   twelve (12) - - - - - - per cent interest, per annum

payable  monthly

---

Additional guidelines are listed in the discussion of wholly typewritten client documents in section 12.2 of Chapter 12.

**Z-marks**  Sometimes a legal form will provide more space than is needed to complete it. In order to prevent the addition of unauthorized information, you should draw a Z-mark to fill the space. Use dark ink, preferably black, to draw Z-marks. The top line of the Z should begin at the end of the last line of typing and should extend to the right margin. The bottom line of the Z should begin at the left margin, approximately a single horizontal space above the first line of printing following the unfilled blank space, and should continue to the right margin. Drawing a diagonal line joining the opposite ends of the horizontal lines will form a Z, as shown in the illustration on page 371. Draw the Z-mark on all copies of the form.

**The endorsement**  Typewritten legal documents are usually bound in a separate cover called a legal back, which is described in section 12.2 of Chapter 12. The information typed on the legal back is called the endorsement. The endorsement generally includes a brief description of the enclosed document and the names of the parties. When a form is used, a panel for the endorsement is often printed on the last page of the form, making it unnecessary for the typist to use a legal back.

**Property descriptions**  In the absence of other instructions, the legal secretary should observe the following style in preparing descriptions of real property for use in deeds and other real estate instruments:

1. Indent a property description five or ten spaces from each margin; use single spacing, with double spacing between paragraphs.

2. Do not abbreviate words like Street, Avenue, Road, Terrace, or Boulevard.

3. Use initial capitals for words which name compass points such as North, Northeast, East, Southeast, and South. Do not capitalize descriptive words such as northwesterly, northeasterly, and southerly.

4. Capitalize the terms Quarter, Township, Section, Metes and Bounds, Lot and Block, and the name or number of a prime meridian. A Township is a six-mile square divided by parallel lines into 36 one-mile squares, or *sections*. Each section is divided into half sections, quarter sections, etc. Metes and Bounds describe boundaries by distances and di-

rections between natural and artificial landmarks such as streams, trees, and stakes. Lot and Block descriptions designate land which has been surveyed and divided into parcels.

5.  Write courses as follows: "South nineteen (19) degrees, thirty-one (31) minutes, forty (40) seconds West."

6.  Type distances as follows: "One hundred twenty-five and thirty-six one hundredths (125.36) feet" or "One hundred twenty-five and 36/100 (125.36) feet."

Although it is preferred practice not to use figures, symbols, and abbreviations, many law offices use them because space is limited on a printed form. A description where space is limited might be written "East 19° 32' 54" South, 50 ft." rather than "East nineteen (19) degrees, thirty-two (32) minutes, fifty-four (54) seconds South, fifty (50) feet." If the number of degrees is less than ten and the number is not spelled out, it should be preceded by a zero: "South 04°" or "South 04 degrees." In law offices where many real estate papers are typed, a special key is placed on the typewriter that has the symbol for degrees. If the law office typewriter is not specially equipped with such a key, you can type the symbol by turning the platen back half a space and striking the small o.

Sometimes several courses and distances are given in succession, introduced by a phrase such as "the following several courses and distances." Type each of the courses and distances separately, indented and single-spaced, separated from one another by double spacing. End each course and distance with a semicolon except for the last course and distance, which should be followed by a period.

In some instances the street address is added in order to clarify the property description. The attorney should let you know if a street address is to be used.

**Preparing copies**   Before typing, the secretary should determine the number of copies which are required. Usually each person signing a document receives a copy, and one copy is retained for the office. In the case of a real estate contract to be held in escrow, the original is executed and deposited in escrow, the buyer and the seller each receive a copy, and another copy is retained for the office. Although the number of copies varies with the form, you should always retain at least one copy for the office files.

In most instances an original is prepared on the typewriter and copies made on the photocopy machine. When a photocopier is not available and the forms are printed on paper too stiff to use carbons, you may type each copy individually. If you do this, however, you must mark COPY on all the duplicates.

When carbon copies are made, the forms must be properly aligned so that the information typed on a space in the original falls on the same space on the carbon copies. Two common procedures that ensure proper alignment—the desk assembly method and the machine assembly method—are described in section 16.1 of Chapter 16. After the carbon pack has been assembled and inserted in the typewriter, and before you type, it is a good idea to check to be sure that the glossy side of the carbon is facing the page on which you wish to type the information. This is especially important when typing on multi-page forms.

## ADDENDA OR RIDERS

There are instances where too little space is provided on a legal form for the information that must be supplied. When this occurs, it will be necessary to staple to the law blank an addendum, also known as a rider. The rider should be single-spaced on paper of the same size as the law blank. The following information should be typewritten as a single-spaced heading that starts about four spaces from the top: (1) the term *rider* or *addendum,* (2) the name of the document, (3) the parties to the document, and (4) the date of the document.

## Rider to a Legal Blank

```
                    BEGINNING at a point on the easterly side of Ridge Avenue,
        which point is located 46 feet on a course of South 04 degrees 46'
        35" West from the point of intersection of the southerly side of the
        Northeast corner of the premises herein intended to be described:
        running thence South 86 degrees 13' 26" East and part of the way
        through a wall 100 feet to a point in the westerly line of lands now
        or formerly of Mennley; thence along the westerly line of lands now
        or formerly of Mennley, South 06 degrees 46' 45" West 36 feet to a

                                              (see Rider attached)
```

```
                    RIDER to Mortgage dated the 15th day of August, 19—, by
        and between JEFFREY STEVENS and ANDREA STEVENS, husband and wife,
        Mortgagors, and THE NICKEL SAVINGS AND LOAN ASSOCIATION, Mortgagee.

        point in the westerly line of lands now or formerly of Jackson
        Corporation; thence along the northerly line of lands now or
        formerly of Jackson Corporation, North 78 degrees 23' 34" West 100
        feet to the easterly side of Bridge Avenue; thence along the
        easterly side of Bridge Avenue, North 04 degrees 12' 45" East 46
        feet to the point or place of beginning.

                    TOGETHER with all fixtures and articles of personal
        property attached to or used in connection with said premises.
```

## PROOFREADING

Accurate proofreading is extremely important in a law office where inaccurate words or numbers may nullify or alter a legal document. The secretary must carefully proofread all forms to be sure that every blank space on the form is filled in either with information or with a series of hyphens to indicate that the line is purposely left unfilled. The secretary must also ensure that information is placed on the correct blank lines, that carbon copies are exact copies of the original, that names are spelled correctly, that dates and figures are right, and that typing is accurate.

It is essential to check a land description carefully for accuracy and completeness. The land description must be a perfect copy with all errors acceptably corrected. An error in a description of land is a serious matter that can result in a lawsuit. It is easy to make an error in copying that is not evident from merely reading the description. For example, the land description in the illustration on page 370 contains five examples of the phrase "turning an interior angle." It would be easy to omit the phrase once and difficult to realize the omission in reading the description, but the omission would inaccurately describe the land to be conveyed by the deed. Because of the importance of accuracy in a land description, it is a good idea to use both proofreading methods described on page 180: the typist should first carefully proofread the description, word for word, from right to left, then read it aloud to another person from the original copy while the second person follows the typed copy.

If there is a plat or diagram available showing the location of the parcel described, the legal secretary can use it to check the accuracy and completeness of the description. To compare a Government Survey description with the map designation, read the parts of the description in reverse order; begin with the township and range and read back to the designated plat.

# 11.3

## FORM PARAGRAPHS

Much of the language in legal instruments is repetitive. Whether the legal secretary works with printed forms or transcribes individually dictated documents, it is helpful to have a backlog of form paragraphs readily available. Form paragraphs include specific clauses that can either be used without change or provide a starting point for a draft. In either case, ready access to such material will result in a reduction of effort and time. Many attorneys combine form paragraphs and specially dictated paragraphs to draw up instruments such as wills, leases, complaints, answers, motions, and notices that tend to follow a standard pattern. The attorney can select the appropriate form paragraphs and add the special dictation required.

**A form paragraph notebook**   A book of form paragraphs may be developed for the office. Such a book provides convenient access to paragraphs and clauses for examination or for removal and copying, permits continuous improvement of basic forms so that they may be used with confidence, eliminates searching through old files, provides a single source for the style that everyone in the office can use, and frees attorneys and secretaries from dependence on memory.

To set up a form paragraph notebook, you and the attorney need to develop a master form of each paragraph and clause used frequently in your law office. Keep refining the form with revisions, additions, optional clauses, and variations. Each form paragraph or clause should use words economically and clearly, have as few blanks to be filled in as possible, and lend itself to easy amending.

Model paragraphs or clauses should be typed one to a page and filed in a loose-leaf binder. Clauses suitable for inclusion in a pending contract, for example, may easily be removed from the binder, reproduced on a photocopier, and forwarded to the person preparing or typing the document. This one-to-a-page method of organization facilitates the preparation of tailor-made documents. Since each paragraph is typed on a separate page, it is a simple matter to organize paragraphs in a desired sequence.

When a group of form paragraphs typically follows a certain sequence, it is best to file the forms in the sequence used. When the document consists of many parts, as in a lease or a negligence complaint, it may be desirable to establish a divider for each document and a tab for each clause. Binders should be indexed according to the various types of law and should contain a table of contents. Subdivisions should be indexed by specific paragraph or clause titles or by a general classification such as Wills. Subdivisions should also be tabbed for easy reference. There may be a Miscellaneous subdivision in each binder, provided that the number of form paragraphs in it is not allowed to grow too large.

**Typing from form paragraphs**   Suppose that you are to type a lease using a form paragraph book. First, you would assemble the separate sheets. The first page of the lease may require typing the date, the names and addresses of the parties, a description of the leased property, and the terms of the lease. The second page may vary according to whether the property is vacant or occupied and whether it is an entire building or part of a building, a store or an apartment. You would choose pages from the paragraph form book which are relevant to the lease being prepared. The last sheet of the lease may consist of standard lease clauses and signature lines, followed by individual or corporate acknowledgment forms.

If a form paragraph book with one paragraph to a page is not available, you may be instructed to copy certain paragraphs from an old document into the new document. In this case, care must be taken to copy only the specified paragraphs. If the paragraphs are to be numbered, the paragraph numbers in the old document may have to be changed to match the sequence in the new document. You must also make necessary minor revisions such as changing *defendants* to *defendant,* or *he* to *she* or *they,* with perhaps a corresponding change in verb form. The new document must be proofread carefully for content, for typing and spelling accuracy, and for completeness.

# 11.4

## ASSEMBLING A FORM FILE

A form file is a collection of sample completed law blanks. The purpose of the form file is to preserve the results of past work so that it can be retrieved for instant use by attorneys and secretaries. Used properly, such a file can save time and money, produce better work, reduce dependence on memory, and eliminate duplication of effort. The legal secretary uses the sample forms as patterns when typing legal forms. The sample forms are usually accompanied by supplementary information such as the number of copies required, the date due, and a description of documents or fees that must accompany the form. Given information found in the case file and a specimen form to refer to, the experienced secretary can complete many printed law blanks independently.

### COLLECTING THE FORMS
To develop a form file, you need to save one copy of each new law blank prepared in the office and place it in a binder without classification. Keep a table of contents in the front of the binder which numbers and briefly describes each document. Occasionally the table of contents must be retyped as the stock of forms changes.

As the form collection grows and some classification appears necessary, the forms may be transferred to separate binders for particular fields of law such as family law, tax law, real estate, trusts, probate, and corporations, with lists in front of each binder describing the separately numbered forms.

When you are ready for a more sophisticated form file and a more detailed classification within a particular area of law becomes desirable, then you may develop a systematic outline of the different forms that go into a particular binder and place the forms behind corresponding dividers. Additional information, such as the number of copies to prepare, their distribution, whether they should be carbon copies or photocopies, and information about filing, recording, enclosures, and fees may be placed with the form on a separate sheet of paper.

### CUSTOMIZED LEGAL FORMS
Many attorneys have found that commercially printed legal forms do not always suit the particular needs of their law firms; they design their own legal forms. If clients give your law firm a certain item of business regularly, the time spent in preparing a form which can be used more than once will result in an important economy. A customized form has many advantages. The attorney can use it as a rough draft without first dictating a draft and having it typed. Because unnecessary paragraphs are omitted from the customized form, it can be proofread more rapidly than standard longer forms. Errors are reduced, and the time and effort of both attorney and secretary are reduced.

**Making copies of customized forms**  Legal forms require a higher quality of reproduction than the interoffice forms described in section 11.1. A commercial printer may be used to reproduce your office-designed forms, or they may be duplicated on the word processing equipment in the office. In some instances the form may be duplicated on the copy machine, filled in, and treated as an original. Documents duplicated and used as originals in some law firms include notices to quit or pay rent, small claims actions, litigation forms for suits on account, replevins and suits reducing notes to judgment, and letters to government agencies. Forms which may be handled in this fashion will vary among the states.

When the nature of the document—a will, for example—demands that it be typed as an original, a customized form may still be used to prepare a rough draft. Many attorneys begin to construct a file of customized forms by duplicating the appropriate page of a form book such as a lawyer's form manual. They prepare a form in rough draft from the duplicated page and edit the rough draft. The secretary types the draft in final form on letter-size paper, single spaced. This serves as the master form. The master form, with a number of duplicates, should be filed in an indexed file folder. When a document is to be filled in, the secretary should remove one of the duplicate copies and type information in the blanks provided. This typed copy becomes the original for a legal matter. The master copy is never filled in and is used only as the form which is photocopied to produce duplicates. Duplicates should be added as the supply diminishes.

**Designing a customized legal form**  When the decision to design a master form for the file is being made, the precise purpose of the form should be determined. The form should accomplish its task simply and efficiently, and unnecessary additions or complexities should be avoided. Forms should have as few blanks as possible so that they can be quickly completed. Abbreviations should be avoided, and the title of the form should be clearly visible at the top of the page. Many offices prepare separate forms for male and female clients and for single and joint clients to avoid having to fill in so many variables. For example, one version of a probate form may be designed using the words *executrix, she,* and *her,* while another version is printed with the words *executor, he,* and *his.* It takes time to prepare such forms, but they reduce the time spent in preparing subsequent documents.

The sample form should be prepared on a typewriter which uses the same size and style of type as the machine which will be used when filling out the actual form. Both horizontal and vertical spacing should be considered.

In addition to the master form that is kept clean for photocopying, it is helpful to make a second specimen form on which you may describe the information to be typed and the maximum number of characters that can be used in each blank. On this form you may also wish to note additional data such as filing instructions, number of copies required, and accompanying documents.

## LETTER FORM BOOK
A form book of correspondence may be developed to save office time and allow the legal secretary to type letters with a greater degree of independence. A great deal of correspondence in the law firm is routine. There may not be a need to have such letters dictated separately when the office is equipped with a letter form book which includes a set of standard, well-written letters.

The first step to take in assembling a letter form book is to determine what types of letters are sent most frequently and therefore should be included. There are several ways to collect this information: (1) make and save an extra copy of all outgoing letters for a period of three to six months, (2) make a copy of each letter in the open files, then sort by subject matter, (3) examine the open files and summarize the letters

## A Form Letter Used in a Foreclosure Action

```
 1
 2
 3
 4
 5
 6        PRE-FORECLOSURE NOTICE
 7
 8
 9
10
11
12
13
14
15        __(Date)__
16
17
18
19        __(Name)_____
20        __(Address)_____
21        _____
22
23
24
25       Dear M_____:
26
27                      Re: Foreclosure proceedings
28
29       (Name of holder of mortgage), holders for the mortgage on your
30       (business/residence) property, (have/has) given us the notes
31       and mortgage for foreclosure.
32
33       Foreclosure, as you no doubt realize, means that the whole amount
34       of the mortgage will become due and payable.  It may further im-
35       pose on you the need to pay attorneys' fees and the costs of
36       foreclosure.  The records placed in our hands indicate that you
37       have omitted payment on the last (number of months overdue)
38       monthly installments.  You are therefore delinquent in the
39       amount of $_____.
40
41       We have been instructed to commence proceedings for foreclosure
42       at once, but we feel that you should have one more opportunity
43       to clear these delinquent payments.  If you have not made satis-
44       factory arrangements to pay these overdue amounts before
45       (deadline date), we shall start foreclosure proceedings without
46       further notice to you.
47
48       Yours very truly,
49
50       MARKHAM and SISITSKY
51
52
53
54       (Attorney's name)__
55
56
57
58
59
60
61
62
63
64
```

in these files by subject matter, and (4) list from memory the subject matter of letters most frequently sent. After you have determined what types of letters are sent most frequently, choose the letters to be used in the form letter book. It is better to include too many form letters than not enough.

Place letters on similar subjects together. Choose the best parts of each to use in the form letter and draft a composite form letter. Try to plan each form letter so that it can be used for more than one situation.

Number the paragraphs or the lines in the form letter and use the numbers for identifying sections to be changed or locations for inserting variable information. Underline blank spaces where variable information will be inserted, and indicate in parentheses, as (name of insurance company), what goes in the blank. Include special information such as margin settings and signature and enclosure instructions, as shown on the form letter illustrated here.

Assemble the form letter book, arranging the letters in some order, perhaps by subject area such as domestic, personal injury, or criminal cases. Clear plastic covers will protect the form letters. Prepare a table of contents for the front of the book.

# 11.5

## SYSTEMS FOR THE LAW OFFICE

Law offices are increasingly adopting the management practices followed in other businesses to ensure the most efficient use of time. Systems analysis—the study of methods of organizing work to produce a high-quality product with the least time and effort—was initially used in law offices as a financial management tool. Later it was recognized that systems work equally well with the substantive areas of a law practice such as personal injury, probate, and the like. According to the American Bar Association, the productivity of a legal secretary or legal assistant may increase by as much as 10 to 15 percent through the use of office systems. Furthermore, the resulting team effort usually results in higher quality work.

An extremely useful guide for the attorney and the legal secretary who are considering the establishment of a system for handling their professional work is the American Bar Association's 1975 publication, How to Create-A-System for the Law Office, edited by Roberta Cooper Ramo. With the ABA system, each step of each transaction is documented in a loose-leaf binder containing the following checklists and forms:

1. Variable forms for all written documents, including legal documents, letters, and statements
2. Standard law forms where applicable
3. Questionnaires and other information-gathering devices
4. Checklists which record each step to be taken in a legal transaction and when and by whom it is to be taken
5. A master list of significant dates and deadlines
6. Lists of pertinent statutes and regulations
7. Instructions and practical hints

The creation of customized forms to expedite legal transactions is a basic step in any law office system. A customized form can even be used to prepare something as personal as a will. The standard opening paragraphs, for instance, may be programmed on media for a text-editing machine in different versions; the attorney chooses the version appropriate for the situation of the testator, depending on the testator's marital status and whether he has children. Such a system is adaptable to a secretary working with a regular typewriter. The lawyer tells the secretary which situation (A, B, C, etc.) applies, and the secretary types the variables from a numbered list that the lawyer provides.

It takes time and care to produce a form like this—one that is applicable to several different situations without requiring a great many variables to be inserted. In a busy law office, however, such a form will probably prove its worth in a very short while.

# 11.6

## PRINTED FORMS COMMONLY USED IN THE LAW OFFICE

Printed forms are used for legal documents that have many repetitive elements. On the other hand, when the circumstances are unique, documents are wholly typed. Papers that are to be filed with a court or a recorder of deeds are usually printed forms, however, and a typical law office prepares many of these.

### LEGAL FORMS PUBLISHED AS BOOKS

In addition to the single law blanks described in section 11.1, lawyers frequently rely on practice manuals and form books to prepare pleadings and legal instruments. A practice manual illustrates the proper forms of pleadings within a particular state. The attorney may refer to the practice manual when dictating, or the experienced secretary may prepare a draft pleading from it without dictation. Practice manuals include complete documents and clauses which may be substituted for portions of a document when appropriate. Legal form books are used in much the same way as practice manuals. They contain samples of instruments and documents, often for all states. Some books contain forms for only one legal field such as corporate law, but others contain models for many legal fields and describe deeds, mortgages, and wills suitable for each state.

The American Law Institute-American Bar Association (ALI-ABA) Committee on Continuing Professional Education has published form and procedure books for law firms in many jurisdictions. Other well-known form books are *American Jurisprudence Forms, Second, Jones Legal Forms Annotated, Nichols Cyclopedia of Legal Forms Annotated,* and *Current Legal Forms.* (For details of publication, refer to the Appendix of this book.) These books are published for attorneys. However, the experienced secretary who can work with little supervision may also need to refer to one of these legal form books.

If the legal secretary is faced with the problem of typing a legal form and is uncertain as to the type of information called for, the 20-volume *American Jurisprudence Forms, Second,* may offer help. It provides model legal forms covering the whole spectrum of law, it includes forms used in every jurisdiction in the United States, and it notes important variations. For example, Chapter 7, Sections 1:1–18:8, describes and provides models of acknowledgments for use in various states, the District of Columbia, and Puerto Rico. The secretary may refer to the state and choose the relevant acknowledgment, such as "individual" or "of corporation or joint stock association." The model form will describe the type of information which is required.

## COMMONLY USED LAW BLANKS
The following pages describe and illustrate many of the commonly used law blanks and give further suggestions on how to add fill-ins. For more information about the purpose of these legal documents, refer to Chapters 12 and 13.

**Real estate transactions**    Printed forms are nearly always used for transactions involving the transfer of title to real estate. Printed forms in this category are warranty deeds, quitclaim deeds, real estate mortgages, closing statements, and leases.

**Deeds**    A deed is a written instrument by which legal title to real estate is transferred. The requirements of deeds differ in the various states, but most deeds include the names of the parties, the operative words of conveyance, and descriptions of the consideration, the property, and the encumbrances, if any. The parties to the transfer of title are referred to as the *grantor* (or seller) and the *grantee* (or purchaser). The statutes of most states require that a deed be in writing and signed by the grantor, that the deed contain words expressing the grantor's intention to transfer title, that the description of the real property be specific and identify it unmistakably, and that the deed be witnessed and acknowledged.

A *warranty deed* is one by which the grantor conveys all his interest in the real estate and guarantees that he has a good title to convey. The warranty deed may also be known as an indenture deed or a deed poll, depending upon the statute of the state in which the deed is executed. The indenture deed is executed between two or more parties and begins with the phrase "This Indenture Made." The deed poll is made by one person and begins with "Know All Men by These Presents." If there are encumbrances, such as taxes, these should be typed immediately after the property description. The habendum clause (To Have and To Hold) names the grantee and defines the extent of his or her ownership.

A *quitclaim deed* is one by which the grantor conveys whatever interest he or she may have in the property with no guarantee of title.

**Personal names used in deeds**    In typing warranty deeds where individuals are involved, the marital status of the grantor or grantors is inserted whenever their names appear in the body of the document as well as in the acknowledgment. Examples: PRISCILLA COTE, divorced and not remarried; PRISCILLA COTE, a spinster; PRISCILLA COTE, a widow, WALTER COTE, a bachelor; WALTER COTE, divorced and not remarried; WALTER COTE and PRISCILLA COTE, husband and wife; WALTER COTE and PRISCILLA COTE, his wife. Usually the social designation—as "Michael Noto and Mrs. Michael Noto, his wife"—is not used. However, if it is customary in your geographic area to include *Mrs.* with the name, you should follow the preferred form. (The form "Mr. and Mrs. Michael Noto" is never used.) Sometimes an indication of how title is to be held must also be added after the names of the grantees: "Charles Vincent and Patricia Vincent, his wife, as joint tenants and not as tenants in common." An example of a warranty deed appears on page 370.

**Property descriptions**    As explained in section 11.2, the legal description of property should be indented and single spaced. You may discover that the space provided on the law blank is too small for the dictated material. When this occurs it is necessary to type the additional dictated material on a separate piece of paper and attach it to the form as a rider, as illustrated on page 362.

The best source for a correct legal description is a title paper. As you copy a land description from a title paper or other source, it is advisable to lay a ruler under each line. Move the ruler down the page as each line is copied. This will prevent skipping and recopying lines.

## Warranty Deed

MASSACHUSETTS WARRANTY DEED INDIVIDUAL (LONG FORM) 872

PATRICK JAMES RUSSELL

of the City of Springfield, Hampden          County, Massachusetts

*being unmarried,* for consideration paid, and in full consideration of Twenty Thousand Dollars
($20,000.00) - - - - - - - - - - - - - - - - - - - - - - - - - - - - - - - - - - *
grants to THORNTON S. KELLY and MAUREEN KELLY, his wife, as joint tenants and not     *
as tenants in common

of the City of Springfield, Hampden County, Massachusetts,     with **warranty covenants**

the land in the City and County of Providence, Rhode Island:

[Description and encumbrances, if any]

That certain tract or parcel of land with all the buildings and improvements thereon, located between Proctor Street and Ramsey Street, Providence, Rhode Island, as shown as Parcel 2 on an unrecorded plan entitled
"Subdivision of Land belonging to Seth Goddard Estate, Providence, R.I.
Scale: 1" = 10', Jan. 1978, Survey by P.H. Guilding, Inc.," bounded and
described as follows:

BEGINNING at a point on the northerly line of Proctor Street, said point
being a R.R. spike set at the southwesterly corner of land now or formerly
belonging to Frederick and Marian Thomassian and the southeasterly corner
of the parcel herein described.  Said point being ninety and 20/100
(90.20) feet easterly from the easterly line of Plain Street; thence southwesterly along said Proctor Street thirty-eight and 08/100 (38.08) feet to
a point; thence turning an interior angle of 88° 14' 43" and running northerly bounded westerly by remaining land of Grantors ninety-five and 61/100
(95.61) feet to a point; thence turning an interior angle of 90° and running
easterly bounded northerly by said remaining land of Grantors eleven and
36/100 (11.36) feet to a point; thence turning an interior angle of 270°
and running northerly bounded westerly by said remaining land of Grantors
thirty-nine and 65/100 (39.65) feet to a point set on the southerly line
of Ramsey Street; thence turning an interior angle of 101° 25' 44" and
running northeasterly along said Ramsey street twenty-three and 53/100
(23.53) feet to a drill hole set at the northeasterly corner of the lot
herein described; thence turning an interior angle of 80° 04' 18" and running southerly bounded easterly in part by land now or formerly of Adele
and Henry Gordon and in part by said Thomassian land one hundred thirty-
eight and 81/100 (138.81) feet to the point and place of beginning.  The
last described course forms an interior angle of 90° 15' 16" with the intersection of the first described course.  The area of this parcel is
4,494.0 square feet.

**Witness** ...... my ............ hand and seal this ...... fourth ........ day of ........ August ............ 19—

............................................................      ............................................................ (L.S.)
                                            PATRICK JAMES RUSSELL

............................................................

............................................................      ............................................................

## Quitclaim Deed

𝕿𝖍𝖎𝖘 𝕯𝖊𝖊𝖉, *made the* 4th *day of* August 19—,

𝕭𝖊𝖙𝖜𝖊𝖊𝖓 JANE SYLVIA CARROLL

*residing or located at* 831 South Jamestown Boulevard *in the* City *of* Bridgeton *in the County of* Cumberland *and State of* New Jersey *herein designated as the Grantors,*

𝕬𝖓𝖉 JOHN McLAUGHLIN and PAULA McLAUGHLIN, his wife,

*residing or located at* 1140 North Cheyenne Street *in the* City *of* Tulsa *in the County of* Tulsa *and State of* Oklahoma *herein designated as the Grantees;*

𝖂𝖎𝖙𝖓𝖊𝖘𝖘𝖊𝖙𝖍, *that the Grantors, for and in consideration of* Sixty-five Thousand Five Hundred and 00/100 Dollars ($65,500.00) - - - - - - - - - - - - - - - - - -

*lawful money of the United States of America, to the Grantors in hand well and truly paid by the Grantees, at or before the sealing and delivery of these presents, the receipt whereof is hereby acknowledged, and the Grantors being therewith fully satisfied, do by these presents remise, release and forever Quitclaim unto the Grantees forever,*.

𝕬𝖑𝖑 that tract or parcel *of land and premises, situate, lying and being in the* City *of* Bridgeton *in the* County of Cumberland *and State of New Jersey, more particularly described herein.*

Tax Map Reference

*(NJS 46: 15 - 2.1) Municipality of:* Bridgeton    *Account No.* X-123
*Block No.* 560    *Lot No.* 09
☐ *No property tax identification number is available on date of this deed. (Check box if applicable.)*

That certain tract or parcel of land, with its buildings and improvements thereon, located in the City of Bridgeton, County of Cumberland, State of New Jersey, bounded and described as follows:

BEGINNING at a point on the easterly side of Banner Street, sixty (60) feet wide, distant one hundred eighty-seven and 43/100 (187.43) feet southerly from the corner formed by the intersection of the easterly side of Banner Street and the southerly side of Dickerson Street, as said street is shown and laid down on the final topographical map of the City of Bridgeton, for the county of Cumberland; running thence easterly at right angles to Banner Street, one hundred seventy-five (175) feet; thence southerly parallel with Banner Street, forty-five (45) feet; thence westerly, again at right angles to Banner Street, and part of the distance through a party wall, one hundred seventy-five (175) feet to the easterly side of Banner Street; thence northerly forty-five (45) feet to the point or place of beginning. Said premises being known as and by the street number 113 Banner Street.

**Mortgages**   A mortgage is a pledge or security of property for the payment of a debt. Mortgages are executed when an individual or business wishes to borrow money on real estate or personal property. Real estate mortgages occur when the owner borrows money on his property and gives the lender a mortgage. Real estate mortgages are called *mortgages* when the conveyance is to the lender and are called *trust deeds* when the conveyance is to a trustee. A real mortgage must be in writing by virtue of the Statute of Frauds. In many states the form of the mortgage is similar to that of a deed, the major differences being the addition of a defeasance clause (which states that the mortgage shall cease when the obligation is performed), a description of the obligation secured, and sometimes a covenant to perform the obligation.

The mortgage is executed by the persons who are the owners of the property. If John Parks and his wife, Sally Parks, own a home and use it as security to obtain a loan from a bank, John and Sally Parks are the mortgagors; the bank is the mortgagee.

Printed mortgage forms similar to that illustrated on page 373 are used extensively in the law office. Law blanks for the ordinary mortgage and deed of trust usually can be completed without dictation from the lawyer. The lawyer may, however, dictate special clauses as needed.

**Contracts**   A contract is a promise for the breach of which the law offers a remedy or the performance of which the law regards as a duty. A contract may relate to the performance of personal services, the transfer of ownership of property, or a combination of both of these. Because of the unique circumstances of most contractual agreements, contracts are generally typed in full. However, in some instances standardized forms may be used. Two standard contract forms—an apartment lease and a building contract form—are shown on the following pages.

The person who makes the promise is the promisor; the person to whom the promise is made is the promisee. These persons are often referred to as the "party of the first part" and "party of the second part." Distinctive names are given to the parties, depending upon the type of contract. In a lease agreement they may be called landlord and tenant, or lessor and lessee. In a sales contract they are referred to as the vendor and vendee. In an insurance contract they are called the insurer and the insured. A party to a contract may be an individual, a corporation, or a government.

Some states require a seal to be placed on important contracts such as those conveying real estate. A contract under seal is executed by affixing a seal to the instrument. The word "Seal" or the initials "L.S." following the signature are usually accepted by today's courts as being the equivalent of a seal.

**Incorporation**   Standardized forms printed in each state are widely used by lawyers involved in setting up corporations. A corporation is an artificial legal being created by government grant. It is formed by obtaining approval of a certificate of incorporation, articles of incorporation, or a charter from the state government. The persons who apply for the charter are called incorporators. When a corporation has been created by a particular state, it is called a domestic corporation with respect to that state. Corporations doing business within that state, but formed in other states, are called foreign corporations.

Ownership in a corporation is evinced by shares of stock. Certificates of stock are issued as evidence of the shareholder's ownership of stock. The ABA Model Business Corporation Act requires that the stock certificate include the state of incorporation; the name of the person to whom the certificate is issued; the number and class of shares represented and the designation of the series, if any; par value or a statement that there is no par value; and, if there is more than one class of stock, the rights and restrictions of each class or a statement that this information will be furnished upon request.

## Mortgage

MASSACHUSETTS REAL ESTATE MORTGAGE INDIVIDUAL (SHORT FORM) 891

JOHN F. SULLIVAN

of the Town of Lowell, Middlesex                              County, Massachusetts,

*being unmarried* for consideration paid, grants to  THE BAY STATE SAVINGS BANK                    *

                   of the City of Springfield, Hampden County,

Commonwealth of Massachusetts,

with **mortgage covenants** to secure the payment of

Thirty-eight Thousand Two Hundred Fifty and 00/100 - - - - - - - - - - - - Dollars
($38,250.00) - - - - - - - - - - - - - - - - - - - - - - - - - - - - - - -

in ten (10) - - - - - years with eleven (11) - - - - - - - - - per cent interest, per annum
payable monthly
as provided in promissory note of even date,
the land in the City and County of Providence, Rhode Island

[Description and encumbrances, if any]

That lot of land with the buildings and improvements thereon, situated
on the northerly side of Barnard Street and on the southeasterly side
of Paine Street in the City of Providence and State of Rhode Island,
laid out and delineated as lot No. 13 (thirteen) on that plat entitled,
"PLAT NO. 1 of House Lots Belonging To Bennett Land Company Surveyed
and platted February, 1903 by W.H.G. Temple" and recorded in the Office
of the Recorder of Deeds in said Providence in Plat Book 26 at page 50
and on Plat Card 882. Said lot is further bounded and described as
follows:

BEGINNING at the southwesterly corner of said lot at the point in said
Barnard Street and at the southeasterly corner of land now or lately
of Clara Newton, said point being one hundred four (104) feet more or
less easterly from the southeasterly line of said Paine Street as
measured along the northerly line of said Barnard Street; thence northerly
bounding westerly on said Newton land eighty and 52/100 (80.52) feet to
said Paine Street; thence northeasterly bounding northwesterly on said
Paine Street fifty-one and 55/100 (51.55) feet to land now or lately of
Bella Ronstadt; thence southerly bounding easterly on the last named
land one hundred twelve and 20/100 (112.20) feet to said Barnard Street
and thence westerly bounding southerly on said Barnard Street forty (40)
feet to the place of beginning. Containing 3892 square feet of land
more or less.

This mortgage is upon the statutory condition,

for any breach of which the mortgagee shall have the statutory power of sale.

**Witness**....my......hand and seal this..twenty-fifth..................day of September.........19—

..................................................................    ..................................................(SEAL)......
                                 JOHN F. SULLIVAN

..................................................................    ..................................................................

..................................................................    ..................................................................

### The Commonwealth of Massachusetts

        ss.                                                          19

Then personally appeared the above named  JOHN F. SULLIVAN, unmarried,

and acknowledged the foregoing instrument to be his    free act and deed,
before me,

..................................................................
                  Notary Public — XXXXXXXXXXXX

           My Commission Expires.................June 30.................19 —

(*Individual — Joint Tenants — Tenants in Common.)

## Building Contract

H&W INC. FORM 199

THIS IS A LEGALLY BINDING CONTRACT. IF NOT UNDERSTOOD, SEEK COMPETENT ADVICE.

BUILDING CONTRACT LABOR – MATERIAL 199

**Building Contract** *made this* fourth *day of*

August *one thousand nine hundred and* --

*by and between* HUGH S. JONES *of* Chester, Pennsylvania

*and* VINCENT L. GIRARD *of* Hadley, Massachusetts,

*builder.*

*The said* VINCENT L. GIRARD *agrees with the said*

HUGH S. JONES *to make, erect, build and finish in a*

*good, substantial, and workmanlike manner,* a dwelling-house

*upon* his land

*situate* in Springfield, Massachusetts, at Lot 43, on that plat entitled "Plat No. 1 of House Lots Belonging to Brewster Land Co." and recorded in Springfield in Plat Book 26 at page 50;

*said* dwelling-house *to be built of good and*

*substantial materials and in accordance with the drafts, plans, explanations, or specifications,*

*furnished or to be furnished to said* VINCENT L. GIRARD

*by* HUGH S. JONES *; said to be finished complete*

*on or before the* first *day of* July, 19--.

*And the said* HUGH S. JONES *agrees to pay for*

*the same to the said* VINCENT L. GIRARD *the sum of*

Ninety-five Thousand and no/100 ($95,000.00) - - - - *dollars, as follows:*

Not later than the tenth day of each calendar month, owner will make a partial payment to builder on the basis of a duly certified and approved estimate of the work performed during the preceding calendar month under this contract; but to insure the proper/performance of this contract, the party of the first part will retain ten percent of each estimate until final completion and acceptance of all work covered by this contract.

*Security against mechanics' or other liens is to be furnished by said* VINCENT L. GIRARD

*prior to* first *payment by said*

HUGH S. JONES.

*And for the performance of all and every the articles and agreements above mentioned*

*the said* HUGH S. JONES *and* VINCENT L. GIRARD

*do hereby bind themselves, their heirs,*

*executors, and administrators, each to the other, in the penal sum of* One Hundred and no/100

*dollars, firmly by these presents.* ($100.00)

**In witness whereof,** *we the said* HUGH S. JONES and VINCENT L. GIRARD

*hereto and to*

*another instrument of like tenor, set our hands and seals the day and year first above written.*

*Executed and delivered in presence of*

.................................................... HUGH S. JONES

.................................................... VINCENT L. GIRARD

## Lease

APARTMENT LEASE 217
PERPETUATING RENTAL CLAUSE, FURNISHED HEAT, AIR CONDITIONING, UTILITIES, ETC.

𝕿𝖍𝖎𝖘 𝕴𝖓𝖉𝖊𝖓𝖙𝖚𝖗𝖊, made this  fourth                            day of  August
in the year one thousand nine hundred and  --              between  NATHAN DALE, party

of the first part, and ROBERT PAQUIN, party

of the second part, Witnesseth:—

𝕿𝖍𝖆𝖙 the said party of the first part doth hereby demise and lease unto the said party of the second part
the SUITE OF ROOMS on the  first  floor numbered  101    in the building numbered 23 on
Catalina Street, in the City of Springfield, County of Hampden, Commonwealth of
Massachusetts,

𝕿𝖔 𝖍𝖆𝖛𝖊 𝖆𝖓𝖉 𝖙𝖔 𝖍𝖔𝖑𝖉    the above described premises for the term of  one year

beginning with the  first                  day of  September          A. D. 19 -- and this lease
shall continue in full force and effect thereafter from year to year, until one of the parties shall on or before
the     first        day of     August          in any year, give to the other party written
notice of h is  intention to terminate this lease, on the  first              day of the following
month, in which case the lease hereby created shall terminate in accordance with such notice.

𝖄𝖎𝖊𝖑𝖉𝖎𝖓𝖌 𝖆𝖓𝖉 𝕻𝖆𝖞𝖎𝖓𝖌    (except only in case of fire or other casualty as hereinafter mentioned)
as rent, the sum of Four Thousand Eight Hundred and no/100 ($4,800.00) - - - - Dollars yearly,
by equal monthly  payments of   Four Hundred and no/100 ($400.00) - - - - - - - - Dollars
at the beginning of each and every    month        hereafter during said term, and at that rate for such
further time as the said lessee  ~~or any other person or persons claiming under~~          shall hold the
said premises or any part thereof; the first payment thereof to be made on the  first
day of  September        now next ensuing.

And the lessor  hereby covenant s with the lessee  that  he     shall peaceably hold and enjoy the
said premises; and that except in case of accident, or except during necessary repairs, the lessor  will, during
said term supply said suite with hot and cold water for ordinary household purposes, and furnish heat, air
conditioning and all utilities except telephone, to the various rooms in said suite where radiators or registers
are provided by the lessor   , except in the case where coal, oil or gas can not be obtained due to conditions
over which said lessor  has no control.

And the lessee  hereby covenant s with the lessor  and   his      heirs, successors, and assigns that
he      and   his   executors and administrators will pay the said rent in manner aforesaid; that they
will not assign this lease nor underlet the whole or any part of the leased premises without the written consent
of the lessor   ; that they will not make or suffer any unlawful, improper, noisy or otherwise offensive use
thereof, nor any use whatsoever other than as and for a private residence; that they will not drive any nails or
screws in, or otherwise mar, deface or alter the plastering, woodwork, or any other part of the leased premises;
that they will allow the lessor   and   his   heirs, successors and assigns, and their agents, at all seasonable
times to enter upon said premises, and examine the condition thereof, and make necessary repairs, and show
the said premises to others, and at any time within three months next before the expiration of said term affix to
any suitable part of said premises a notice of letting or selling and keep the same so affixed without hindrance
or molestation, and remove placards, signs, awnings and wires not approved and affixed as herein provided;
that they will conform to such reasonable regulations as may from time to time be established by the lessor   , or
by  his    heirs, successors or assigns, for the general convenience and comfort of the tenants and the

## Stock Certificate

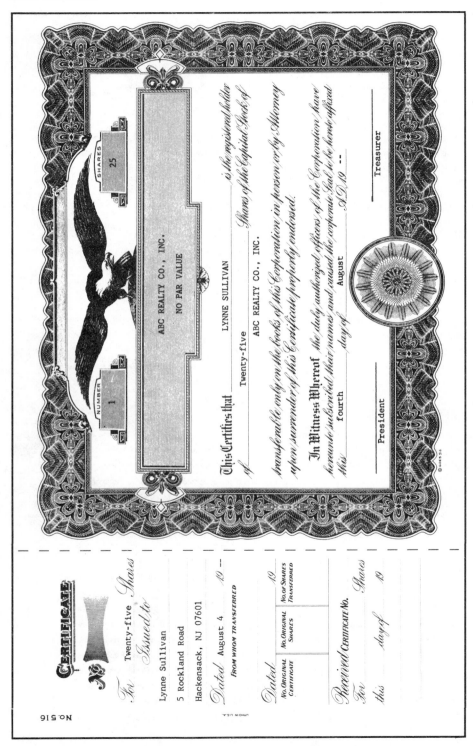

The section on corporations in Chapter 12 shows a sample corporate charter typewritten on a standard form. A common type of stock certificate that you might be required to prepare is illustrated here. Among the other kinds of corporate forms you might prepare are bylaws, notices of meeting, waivers of notice of meeting, proxies, and certificates of dissolution. Corporate kits are commercially available which contain many of the forms necessary for creating and maintaining a corporation.

**Probate**    The probate court assists in settling the estate of a decedent. Through letters testamentary or letters of administration it allows for a personal representative—either an executor or an administrator—to be appointed to administer the decedent's estate. A petition must be filed with the probate court giving the details of the decedent's death, stating that the decedent lived within the county or that the decedent's property is within the county, and reciting facts to justify the appointment. After taking possession of the estate, the executor or administrator pays outstanding debts, administers real estate, determines the proper distributees, and then applies to the court to be discharged from office.

Probating a will in court is a lengthy process that involves the preparation of numerous forms. The probate court in your area will supply you with the necessary forms. One of these forms—a complaint or petition for probate of will and letters testamentary—is illustrated on page 379.

**Matrimonial and family actions**    Family law is concerned with divorce, separation, paternity, custody, support, and child care; and court-provided forms are usually available for handling matrimonial actions such as actions for a separation, an annulment or dissolution of a marriage, a divorce, a declaration of the validity or nullity of a foreign judgment of divorce, and a declaration of the validity or nullity of a marriage. A petition for divorce is illustrated on page 380.

**Other court documents**    There are many other court documents: judgments, decrees, and verdicts; depositions, examinations, and inquisitions; and writs, warrants, and pleadings, to name a few. Many are available in preprinted form. Subpoenas, summonses, and affidavits are nearly always printed forms. An affidavit of service, commonly printed on the back of a form, certifies the service of a writ, notice, or summons.

**Certificate of acknowledgment**    An acknowledgment is the act by which a person who has signed an instrument goes before an authorized officer, such as a notary public, and affirms or declares that he or she executed the instrument. The notary public signs the certificate of acknowledgment or the acknowledgment clause.

An acknowledgment is necessary when the instrument concerns real property, such as a deed, mortgage, or lease. The completed certificate of acknowledgment allows the instrument to be recorded or filed and also authorizes it to be given in evidence. The law of the state where the instrument will be recorded is the law which governs. Although the necessity for and the requirements of an acknowledgment differ among states, all acknowledgments have certain basic elements:

1.  *Venue*    The venue contains the name of the state, territory, county, country, or other political subdivision in which the acknowledgment is made. In Kentucky, Massachusetts, Pennsylvania, and Virginia the venue recites the name of the commonwealth instead of the state; in Louisiana, the venue recites the parish instead of the county. The venue should be typewritten, bracketed, and followed with the initials *ss*. The initials may be in capital or lowercase letters and are followed by a period. There is a common notion that *ss.* is an abbreviation for the Latin term *scilicet,* meaning "to wit"; however, the origins of *ss.* are in doubt. Some law offices place a colon after the *ss.,* but most do not.

2. *Date*   An acknowledgment always recites the date on which it is made. When typing the certificate of acknowledgment, the secretary should leave blank spaces for the date and also for the name of the month if the instrument is being prepared near the end of the month. Although a client is expected to sign and acknowledge an instrument on the 30th of June, it might not be signed until the first day of July. The date of the acknowledgment does not have to be the same as the date of the instrument, but the date of an acknowledgment must never precede the date shown on the instrument.

3. *Names of participants*   The name of the person making the acknowledgment must appear in the certificate. Type the name in solid capitals. If the person making the acknowledgment is making it in a capacity other than that of an individual, the capacity is stated but not in solid caps. When a person makes an acknowledgment as secretary of a corporation, the designation is written "GLADYS NEUWIRTH, secretary of O'Keeffe, Inc." The person who makes the acknowledgment does not sign the certificate; the signature is that of the officer taking the acknowledgment. If necessary, type the title of the officer taking the acknowledgment under the signature line; some law blanks do not require this step since they are printed with the words "Notary Public" under the signature line.

   Many states require that an acknowledgment taken by a notary public show the date of the expiration of his or her commission. On acknowledgments to be used in those states, type "My Commission Expires [date of expiration]" two spaces below the signature. Sometimes an inked rubber stamp is used instead.

4. *Seal*   In many cases the certificate of acknowledgment must also show the notary's seal, especially if the instrument is acknowledged outside the state or if the acknowledgment is to be recorded.

**Affidavit**   An affidavit is a written statement of facts confirmed by the oath or affirmation of the party making it before a notary public. The individual who makes the affidavit is called the affiant or deponent. The affiant swears to the truth of the document; the notary public administers the oath. An affidavit for a court case recites the venue, which is the state and county in which the affidavit is signed. The venue is followed by the name of the affiant, the statement that the affiant appeared before the notary public and swore under oath to the truth of the information in the document, and the statement of the relevant facts. This is followed by the signature of the affiant.

The notary public also signs and seals the document; this section and the statement that the document was signed in the notary's presence and sworn to under oath is called the *jurat*. The form for the jurat varies among states; generally a recital of the official character following the signature is sufficient. If the affidavit is to be used in a state other than the one in which it is executed, a certificate by a state or court official authenticating the officer's identity, signature, and authority to act is necessary. This form is usually called a *certificate* of *authentication*.

An acknowledgment should not be confused with an affidavit. An acknowledgment simply states that the person whose signature is on the attached document affirms that he or she executed that document. An affidavit, which is also sworn to or affirmed before an authorized officer, declares that the person signing the instrument attests to the truth of the statements contained in the instrument. An affidavit is a complete instrument, while an acknowledgment is a part of another instrument.

## LEGAL FORMS AND THE SECRETARY

Law blanks and other printed forms are widely used because they streamline legal transactions between law firms, businesses, courts, and government agencies. They save time for those who prepare the form and for those who receive it. The typing of forms for legal transactions can be a relatively simple task when the attorney has given you a precise list of fill-in words and phrases for the blanks on the form. But the secretary who wishes to grow in the job will make efforts to understand each form by asking the attorney questions, looking up terms in a law dictionary, and assembling a form file—and will thus be able to work with a greater degree of independence.

## Petition for Probate

Docket No.................................................................

Filed.........................................................19.........

and Microfilmed in the Surrogate's Office of Atlantic County
at Mays Landing, N. J.

........................................................................

SURROGATE

Atty. ᴏғ ᴘʀᴏxᴇ̆ss. Jane Doyle .....................................

Address:.............1702 Main Street, Room 602.........

City and State:......Atlantic City, NJ 08401..............

Telephone...............000-0000.......................................

# Atlantic County Surrogate's Court

In the Matter of the Estate of

Martin Cuthbertson

)

**COMPLAINT FOR PROBATE OF WILL
AND LETTERS TESTAMENTARY**

DECEASED

1. MAE C. ROBERTS                                      residing at

   23 Catalpa Terrace, Atlantic City, New Jersey

   respectfully show that:  On     December 2,            19 -- ,
   MARTIN CUTHBERTSON                                 died leaving a will

   dated: August 4, 19--          , wherein plaintiff   w as    appointed

   execut rix.

2. The said decedent was domiciled at:   15 Maynard Terrace, Atlantic City, New
   Jersey.

3. The said decedent left surviving as heirs at law and next of kin:

| NAME | AGE | KIN | P.O. ADDRESS |
|------|-----|-----|--------------|
| June Cuthbertson | 59 | wife | 15 Maynard Terrace<br>Atlantic City, NJ 08401 |
| Michael Cuthbertson | 29 | son | 250 Clinton Street<br>Flint, MI 48507 |

4. There are no other heirs or next of kin known to the plaintiff and all of the persons named are
   of full age, except as noted.

5. The decedent had not married, nor were any children born to or adopted by the decedent since the
   execution of said will.

   WHEREFORE, the plaintiff  demands judgment:

   A. Admitting to probate the last will   and testament           of  the
      above named decedent.

   B. Directing that Letters Testamentary be granted to plaintiff.

DATED:..December 29, 19--.........................

........................................................................
                                        Plaintiff

**Petition for Divorce**

## State of Rhode Island and Providence Plantations.

### Providence, sc.

*To the Honorable Family Court, next to be holden at Providence, within the County of Providence, on the first Monday of*       June       *A. D. 19--*

**Respectfully Represents,** MARIAN STINSON BROWNE

*of* Providence    *in the County of* Providence    *that* s *he resides in said County, and has been a domiciled inhabitant of said State and has resided therein for more than two years next before the preferring of this petition and is now a domiciled inhabitant of said State; that*   s *he was married to*   THOMAS RAY BROWNE,

*her present* husband,       *on the* twenty-fifth      *day of* September      *A. D. 19-- , and hath ever since on* her *part demeaned* her *self as a faithful* wife      *and performed all the obligations of the marriage covenant; but that the said* THOMAS RAY BROWNE      *hath violated the same in this;* *that* ~~he hath~~ there are irreconcilable differences which have caused the irremediable breakdown of the marriage.

*Wherefore your petitioner prays that a decree of this Court may be made divorcing* her *from the bond of Marriage, and from the said*   THOMAS RAY BROWNE.

*Subscribed and sworn to before me at*    Providence      *in the County of* Providence      *in said State of Rhode Island and Providence Plantations, this*   thirteenth    *day of* May      *A. D. 19-----*

...............................................................

~~Notary Public~~
*Justice of the Peace.*

Reprinted by permission of E. L. Freeman Company.

## Subpoena with Proof of Service

*Attorney(s):* Cowell and Nordstrom
*Office Address & Tel. No.:* 4002 Sixteenth Street
Oceanside, NJ   000-0000
*Attorney(s) for* the Plaintiffs

DAVID MARGOLIS and
ANDREA MARGOLIS

*Plaintiff(s)*

*vs.*

CITY MANUFACTURING COMPANY

*Defendant(s)*

IN THE COUNTY COURT
WITHIN AND FOR THE
COUNTY OF CAPE MAY

*DOCKET NO.*   56-789X

*CIVIL ACTION*

## Subpoena
*AD TESTIFICANDUM*

𝕿𝖍𝖊 𝕾𝖙𝖆𝖙𝖊 𝖔𝖋 𝕹𝖊𝖜 𝕵𝖊𝖗𝖘𝖊𝖞, 𝖙𝖔:    THOMAS GREEN

𝔜𝔬𝔲 𝔞𝔯𝔢 𝔥𝔢𝔯𝔢𝔟𝔶 𝔠𝔬𝔪𝔪𝔞𝔫𝔡𝔢𝔡 *to attend and give testimony before the above named Court at*
Cape May Court House, Cape May, New Jersey,
*on* Tues *day,* October 4            *, 19 -- , at* 10:30 *o'clock*   A *. M., on the part of*
the plaintiffs
*in the above entitled action.*

*Failure to appear according to the command of this Subpoena will subject you to a penalty, damages in a Civil Suit and punishment for contempt of Court.*

*Dated:*   September 1,    19 -- .

..................................................................

*Attorney   for* the Plaintiffs

.......................................................................
*Clerk*

### PROOF OF SERVICE

*On*   September 2,    19 -- , *I, the undersigned, being over the age of 18, served the within Subpoena by delivering a copy thereof to the person named therein, at* 3:02 West Main
Street, Ocean Gate, New Jersey
*and by tendering*
*to such person the attendance fee of $* 25.00    *and mileage of $*15.00    *as allowed by law.*

*I certify that the foregoing statements made by me are true. I am aware that if any of the foregoing statements made by me are wilfully false, I am subject to punishment.*

*Dated:*   September 2,    19 --

.......................................................................

*Address for Service:*

## Subpoena Duces Tecum

---

FORM 494 - SUMMONS WITH OFFICERS RETURN
DUCES TECUM REVISED DEC. 1971

HOBBS & WARREN, INC PUBLISHERS
BOSTON, MASS.

### The Commonwealth of Massachusetts

Hampden ............................................................ *ss.*

### To ..............................................................................

.................................................................................

JOHN GREENE

..................................................................................................... *greeting.*

**You are hereby commanded**, *in the name of The Commonwealth of Massachusetts, to appear*
*before the* ............ District ....................... *Court* ................................................
*holden at* ...... Springfield .... *within and for the county of* ... Hampden ......................
*on the* ......... first ................................ *day of* ... June ........................................ *at*
................. two ................ *o'clock in the* .. after .. *noon, and from day to day thereafter, until the action*
*hereinafter named is heard by said Court, to give evidence of what you know relating to an action*
*of* ........ damages ............... *then and there to be heard and tried between* ...........................
........................................................................................ THOMAS BROWNE ................................................. *Plaintiff* , *and*
................................................... DAVID LINDEN .................................................... *Defendant* , *and*
*you are further required to bring with you* .. financial records of GREENE'S, INC., ........
together with all copies, drafts and vouchers relating to said financial
records that can or may afford any information or evidence in said cause.

..................................................................................................................

..................................................................................................................

..................................................................................................................

..................................................................................................................

..................................................................................................................

     **Hereof fail not**, *as you will answer your default under the pains and penalties in the law*
*in that behalf made and provided.*
     **Dated at** ... Springfield ................... *the* ........ twentieth ........... *day of* .. May ........
A. D. 19 --

.............................................................
Notary Public ~~Justice of the Peace~~

---

Reprinted by permission of Hobbs & Warren, Inc.

## Affidavit and Request for Entry of Judgment

B-203 (1/74)

**STATE OF
RHODE ISLAND
AND
PROVIDENCE PLANTATIONS**

**Affidavit And Request For Entry
Of Judgment**

Providence ........................................... **sc.** ....................... District ............... Court

THOMAS BROWNE ........................................................
**Plaintiff**

**vs**                          C.A. 00-000 ....................................................

DAVID GREEN ........................................................
**Defendant**

I, THOMAS BROWNE ......................, of the City of Providence ..............., County of
Providence ......................, State of Rhode Island, upon oath depose and say as follows:

1. That the defendant has failed to plead or otherwise defend as provided by the rules of this Court.

2. That the defendant was not at the time of the commencement of this action nor is the defendant now in the Military Service of the United States as defined in the Soldiers' and Sailors' Civil Relief Act of 1940; nor is the defendant an infant or an incompetent.

3. That the defendant presently resides at 23 Bryant Road ....................................................
in the City of Providence ......................, Rhode Island.

4. That this cause was commenced to recover the sum of $900.00 plus interest from 1/1/-- ...............
to 12/31/-- in the amount of $90.00 ......................, totalling $990.00 ...............

5. That the defendant has no setoffs or counterclaims against this account and, in my opinion, there is no defense to this claim or cause of action.

.......................................................

Sworn to before me this fourth day of March ...........................

A.D. ~~19X~~ 19--

.......................................................
**Notary Public**

Wherefor the Plaintiff, by his ...................... Attorney, moves that judgment be entered by default in the above-entiled cause pursuant to RCP 55 and that the garnishee be charged to the full extent of the sum of money reported by the garnishee's affidavit.

.......................................................
**Attorney for Plaintiff**

Default entered

.......................................................

## Summons

*Attorney(s):* Cowell and Nordstrom
*Office Address & Tel. No.:* 4002 Sixteenth Street
Oceanside, NJ   000-0000
*Attorney(s) for Plaintiff*

ROGER L. BROWN

*Plaintiff*

*vs.*

TERESA TATE BROWN

*Defendant*

*SUPERIOR COURT OF NEW JERSEY*

*CHANCERY DIVISION*

MERCER   *COUNTY*

*DOCKET NO.* 123-456

*CIVIL ACTION*

**Summons**

MATRIMONIAL

**The State of New Jersey, to the Above Named Defendant:**

YOU ARE HEREBY SUMMONED in a Civil Action in the Superior Court of New Jersey, instituted by the above named plaintiff and required to serve upon the attorney(s) for the plaintiff, whose name and office address appears above, either (1) an answer to the annexed complaint, or (2) a written appearance in accordance with R. 4:79-3, within - - - 20 days after the service of the summons and complaint upon you, exclusive of the day of service. If you fail to answer, or fail to file a written appearance in accordance with R. 4:79-3, judgment by default may be rendered against you for the relief demanded in the complaint. You shall promptly file your answer or your written appearance and proof of service thereof in duplicate with the Clerk of the Superior Court, P. O. Box 1300, Trenton, New Jersey 08625, in accordance with the rules of civil practice and procedure.

If you are unable to obtain an attorney you may communicate with the New Jersey State Bar Association by calling toll free 800-792-8315. You may also contact the Lawyer Referral Service of the County in which you reside, by calling   000-0000   . If you cannot afford an attorney, you may communicate with the Legal Services office of the County in which you reside, by calling **000-0000.**

*Dated:*   **March 7**   , 19 - - .

*Clerk of the Superior Court*

*Defendant's age:* 25   *Residence:* 416 Newbery Court
Trenton, NJ 08608

*Occupation:* Teacher
Whittier School
Trenton, NJ 08608

33—N. J. SUMMONS SUPERIOR COURT          D G R V   T          COPYRIGHT© 1980 BY ALL-STATE LEGAL SUPPLY CO.
  (MATRIMONIAL - Revised Sept. 8, 1980)                              269 SHEFFIELD STREET, MOUNTAINSIDE, N.J. 07092

Reprinted by permission of All-State Legal Supply Co.

## Individual Acknowledgment

1—N. J. ACKNOWLEDGMENT, IND.    G R V   T

ALL-STATE LEGAL SUPPLY CO.
269 SHEFFIELD STREET, MOUNTAINSIDE, N.J. 07092

**State of New Jersey,**

**County of** Cape May } **ss.:**

**Be it Remembered**, *that on this* 5th *day of* October 19 -- *, before me,*
*the subscriber,* NANCY HOLLOWELL, a Notary Public,
*personally appeared* WALTER R. BAINES and DOLORES L. BAINS, his wife,

*who, I am satisfied,* are *the person*s *named in and who executed the within Instrument,*
*and thereupon* they *acknowledged that* they *signed, sealed and delivered the same as*
their *act and deed, for the uses and purposes therein expressed.*

-------------------------------------------------

*Prepared by:*

Reprinted by permission of All-State Legal Supply Co.

## Corporate Acknowledgment

**The Commonwealth of Massachusetts**

HAMPDEN    ss.    August 4, 19 --

Then personally appeared the above named  DENISE BURLOW, Secretary,
and acknowledged the foregoing instrument to be the free act and deed of YANKEE PRODUCTS, INC.

before me,

-------------------------------------------------
Notary Public — ~~JACKSON HODGES~~

My commission expires    June 30  19 --

Reprinted by permission of Hobbs & Warren, Inc.

## Affidavit

FORM 196   HOBBS & WARREN, INC. PUBLISHERS

### The Commonwealth of Massachusetts

HAMPDEN      } ss      On this ____fourth____ day of ____August____ A. D. 19--

before me, FRANCES DOLAN,                    a Notary Public, duly commissioned

and qualified for the Commonwealth of Massachusetts personally appeared

LEON CARPENTER _____

who, being duly sworn, declared that the annexed statement, by him

subscribed is true to the best of   his knowledge and belief.

In testimony whereof, I have hereunto set my hand and

affixed my seal of office, the day and year above written.

-------------------------------------------
                                        Notary Public

Reprinted by permission of Hobbs & Warren, Inc.

## Certificate of Authentication

### State of Rhode Island and Providence Plantations

DISTRICT COURT

____Sixth____ DIVISION

PROVIDENCE, SC.                    ____August 4,____ A. D. 19 --

I, ____JOHN CIANCI____, Deputy Clerk of the ____6th____ Division,
Rhode Island District Court, the same being a Court of Record and
having by law a seal,

DO HEREBY CERTIFY, that _____BETTE GRANDE_____
whose name is subscribed to the annexed certificate was at the time of signing said certificate a NOTARY PUBLIC
in and for said State of Rhode Island _____
duly appointed and qualified, and authorized to administer oaths and take depositions and to take the acknowledgment or proof of deeds or conveyances of lands, tenements or hereditaments lying in said State and which deed
or conveyances are to be recorded in said State; that I am well acquainted with the handwriting of said_____
_____BETTE GRANDE_____
and verily believe that the signature to the said Certificate, purporting to be ⊗⊗⊗ hers is genuine; that the laws of said
State do not require the use of a seal by a notary and no copy of a notary's seal is on file or required to be on file in
this office.

In attestation whereof, I hereunto subscribe my name, and
affix the seal of said Court, the day and year above written

_____Deputy Clerk.

S-169  (11-73)

# 12

# PREPARING AND TYPEWRITING CLIENT DOCUMENTS

## CONTENTS

# 12.1

## THE PREPARATION OF CLIENT DOCUMENTS:
A Secretarial Overview

The legal secretary is responsible for the careful preparation of a vast array of legal documents. Many of these involve filling in blanks on a printed form, as described in Chapter 11. Others must be individually prepared for processing by the courts, as explained in Chapter 13. A great many legal documents, however, are prepared for a single client to formalize an agreement or other legal action. These are referred to as *client documents*. Another name for formal documents that are not court papers is *legal instruments*. Although the attorney is responsible for the content of all documents, their preparation and their final appearance are the responsibility of the legal secretary.

### LEGAL CAP
Legal cap is a type of paper conventionally used for client documents and court papers. It is available in either standard legal size (8½ by 13 or 14 inches) or letter size (8½ by 11 inches). The longer paper allows you to include more information per page, so that fewer pages are used. On the other hand, letter-size legal cap is easily interfiled with correspondence, and its use reduces the need for legal-size file cabinets. The current trend is to use the shorter paper for many documents; however,

lengthy documents still necessitate the longer paper. The decision concerning the size of legal cap to use will be made by the attorney and will be based on the customs in your locality.

Legal cap paper in both sizes is available in good quality erasable bond and is found in three styles: ruled and numbered, ruled and unnumbered, and plain (un-ruled and unnumbered). Ruled paper uses vertical lines to set off a wide margin on the left and a narrow one on the right. Legal cap with numbers along the left margin is used in some states. The documents chosen to illustrate legal instruments in this chapter are typewritten on ruled and unnumbered legal cap, while the court documents shown in Chapter 13 are typewritten on ruled and numbered legal cap. Instructions for aligning the typewritten line with the numbers are given on page 438.

Paper of basis weight 16 is normally used for originals and 13-basis weight paper for carbon copies. However, a higher quality paper of basis weight 20 is frequently used for wills.

### Size and Type of Paper Commonly Used for Client Documents

| Document | Law Blank | 8½ × 11 | 8½ × 13 | 8½ × 11 3-hole paper |
|---|---|---|---|---|
| Affidavits | | X | | |
| Agreements/Contracts | X | X | | |
| Corporate Documents (to be placed in the corporate minute book) | | | | |
|   Bylaws | X | | | X |
|   Certificate of Dissolution | X | | | |
|   Certificate of Incorporation | X | | | |
|   Minutes | | | | X |
|   Notices of Meetings | | | | X |
|   Proxies | X | | | X |
|   Waivers of Notice | X | | | X |
| Leases | X | X | | |
| Powers of Attorney | X | X | | |
| Promissory Notes | | X | | |
| Wills/Codicils | | | X | |

This table should serve merely as a guide. Usage differs from office to office. You should always abide by the wishes of the attorney in matters of this nature.

## ROUGH DRAFTS

It is often necessary to type a rough draft of a complex legal document so that the attorney can review it and make any necessary alterations. The words ROUGH DRAFT should be typed across the top of the page so that the draft will not be mistaken for the final document. The rough draft should be double- or triple-spaced. One copy is usually sufficient. After the draft has been checked and the final document typed, the draft should be presented to the attorney with the final copy so that the attorney can compare it with the original if desired.

## MAKING COPIES

The number of copies needed for each document depends on the nature of the document, the number of parties involved, and office policies. As explained in Chapter 8, documents such as wills or powers of attorney which are prepared for the sole use of the client require an executed (signed) original and at least one copy. The original and frequently a reference copy are given to the client. Another copy is retained by the attorney as an office file copy.

Documents such as contracts or agreements which are prepared for use by the client and a second party require an executed original and at least three copies, one of which is a duplicate original (i.e., a carbon copy typed on the same weight of paper as the original and dated and executed). The original and frequently one copy are given to the client—the original for safekeeping and the copy for reference. The duplicate original is given to the second party to the contract. Another carbon copy, usually on onionskin, is kept for the office files. Additional copies may be required for the second party's attorney and for real estate brokers if they are involved. When documents involve several individuals, each party requires an executed copy of the document (a duplicate original), and each attorney may also require a copy. One is always retained as an office file copy.

The text-editing machines described in Chapter 15 are capable of producing several identical "original" documents in a short time. This capability is especially convenient when duplicate originals are required.

## CORRECTIONS AND INSERTIONS

In section 8.3 of Chapter 8 there is a general discussion of transcription procedures with suggestions on proofreading techniques and the handling of erasures. Legal documents must be proofread with extreme care; the proofreader must be certain that format and styling are correct, that typographical errors are pinpointed and corrected on all copies, and that page and paragraph numbers are in sequence. The spelling of names must be absolutely right, and figures must also be exact.

**Insertions**   You must make certain that there are no omissions. If you should discover an omission, you may sometimes insert missing words by the use of a diagonal as illustrated below. This may be done only on occasion, and never in connection with important names, dates, or figures. Any insertion should be included on all copies of the document. If you notice that more than one insertion is necessary in the document, or if the insertion is lengthy, it would be wise to retype the page.

```
are hereby directed, authorized and empowered to execute,
                                    such
acknowledge and deliver/documents, instruments and papers and to
```

When the document is executed, the insertion should be initialed in the margin by all signers. This procedure indicates that the insertion was made with the signers' full knowledge and approval. When copies are being conformed, it is important that these initials are included on all copies.

## POST-TRANSCRIPTION DUTIES

**Collating**   After the document has been prepared and carefully proofread, it must be collated, or arranged in order. All originals should be assembled in page sequence, all first carbons should be assembled in page sequence, and so forth. You must double-check to make certain that all pages are numbered and in proper sequence.

**Conforming**   After the document has been properly executed, it will be your responsibility to see that _all_ copies are conformed to the original; i.e., that they match the original in every way. Do this by marking on each copy all information that appears on the original but not on the copies: signatures, initials in the margin, insertions, seals, dates, etc. Some attorneys allow instruments to be conformed in pen; others prefer that it be done on the typewriter. Many offices make photocopies of the completed document rather than conforming carbon copies.

If you will be conforming on the typewriter, you can insert pages without removing any staples by using the procedure described on page 502 of Chapter 14. Section 14.1 of that chapter also tells how to conform signatures and seals.

**Witnessing documents**    You will frequently be requested to witness the documents that you prepare. You should witness the signature <u>only</u> if you see the person execute the document in your presence. It is unwise to verify a signature if you did not witness its execution. If others are witnessing the signature, you should help the attorney ensure that those witnesses also saw the person execute the document.

**Notarizing documents**    As a service to clients, the secretary often serves as a notary public. Section 14.1 of Chapter 14 tells how to obtain the commission of notary public and describes the notary's duties.

# 12.2

## STYLING CLIENT DOCUMENTS

This section offers guidelines for the typewriting of client documents in general. The procedure in your office may differ in some details. Specific documents that are frequently typewritten in full (as opposed to legal blanks and other printed forms) are discussed in the following sections of this chapter.

### MARGINS
When the paper is ruled, the margins are predetermined; when unruled, they should be approximately 1¼ to 1½ inches on the left and 1 inch on the right. The left margin may be reduced if space is at a premium or if the paper is not to be bound or stapled at the left side. The margins should be set exactly the same for each page of a particular legal document. Begin typing about two spaces inside the left ruled line, and <u>never</u> extend your typing onto or over the right ruled line. Set your right margin adequately to keep hyphenated words at a minimum. (See the guidelines for word division later in this section.)

Typewritten legal documents are normally stapled at the top and inserted in legal backing; for this reason it is essential that you start all typing at least ten spaces (about 1½ inches) down from the top of the page. A margin of about one inch should appear across the bottom. A light pencil mark two inches from the bottom will warn that you are nearing the bottom of the page and allow you to plan to insert a new sheet of paper if necessary. This will prevent typing too close to the bottom of the page. Some offices use ruled legal cap with broken rules near the bottom to indicate the end of the page. Another way to anticipate the bottom margin is to use a copy guide like the triple-form typewriting copy guide illustrated on page 181. A similar guide can be constructed for use with letter-size and legal-size paper.

It is practical to establish a predetermined number of lines for all legal documents typed in your office. The number most often used is 32 double-spaced lines for legal-size pages and 24 lines for letter-size pages.

### HEADINGS
All legal documents contain an identifying heading or title. The heading starts ten spaces from the top of the paper and is typed in all-capital letters, underlined, and centered.

**Heading for a Client Document**

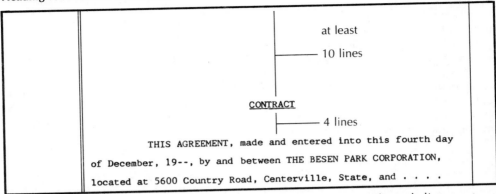

Lengthy headings are usually typed on more than one line, with each line centered but only the last line underscored.

WAIVER OF NOTICE OF MEETING
OF BOARD OF DIRECTORS

WAIVER OF NOTICE
OF MEETING OF
BOARD OF DIRECTORS

A brief title may be expanded, if desired, by spacing between the characters: either LEASE or L E A S E.

**Subheadings** Subheadings, if they are used, are typed in lowercase letters with the first letter of each significant word capitalized. Articles (*a, an,* and *the*), conjunctions (*and, or*), and short prepositions (*to, by, of,* etc.) are not capitalized unless they are the first word in the subheading. The subheading starts two spaces below the heading and is centered and underlined. Neither headings nor subheadings have terminal punctuation.

TITLE OR HEADING
Subtitle Heading

**SPACING**

Four lines of space should appear between the heading or subheading of the document and the opening paragraph so that the heading will be prominent. Typewritten legal documents are double-spaced to allow for easy reading and for any insertion that may be necessary when the document is executed. Property descriptions and long quotations, however, are usually single-spaced and indented on both the right and left sides to set them off from the main text of the document.

**Spacing for a Property Description**

```
        from the Landlords, the following described premises:

                ALL that certain one-story brick dwelling,
                with attached garage, situate and known as
                210 Clover Drive, Suffern, New York,

        for a term of two (2) years, to commence on the 1st day of

        February, 19--, and to terminate on the 31st day of January, . . .
```

Triple spacing is frequently used between numbered paragraphs or between paragraphs with side headings.

The typewriting of many legal documents requires careful planning. Signature lines and attestation clauses, for example, must appear together on the last page along with at least two lines of the text of the document. Furthermore, the document should be attractive; the secretary's attempts to crowd extra lines onto a page should not be too obvious. You can adjust the spacing by (1) increasing or decreasing top and bottom margins, (2) increasing or decreasing side margins unless you are using ruled legal cap, (3) where possible, carrying over the last word of a paragraph to make a new line, (4) triple spacing between paragraphs, or (5) increasing or decreasing the space before a signature line.

## PARAGRAPHS

To allow paragraphs to be easily located and identified, you should indent each paragraph ten spaces from the left margin. Block styles are not acceptable in legal documents.

The paragraphs of legal documents are often identified by number. When the paragraphs require numbers, the numbering may be handled in any of the following ways, depending on the document and the attorney's preference:

| | | | | |
|---|---|---|---|---|
| 1. | I: | FIRST: | Item I: | Article I: |
| 2. | II: | SECOND: | Item II: | Article II: |
| 3. | III: | THIRD: | Item III: | Article III: |

The enumeration should be typed ten spaces from the left margin, at the normal beginning of the paragraph; the text of the paragraph begins two spaces after the period or colon. Frequently a legal document makes reference to earlier paragraphs in the same document. Subsequent references to a paragraph should be styled exactly as that paragraph is numbered. For example, if the paragraphs are numbered *First, Second*, etc., a subsequent reference might read, " . . . subject to the provision of Paragraph "Sixth" above . . . ."

To ensure continuity between pages of a document, you should try to carry over one or two lines of a paragraph to a new page instead of ending the paragraph on the last line of a page.

## PAGINATION

Pages must be numbered to ensure continuity. Whether to number the first page is the choice of the typist; however, numbers <u>must</u> appear on all ensuing pages. The page number should appear approximately three spaced lines below the last typewritten line and should be centered on the page. Arabic numerals are generally used. Any of the following styles is acceptable:

Page 2                              - 2 -                              Page 2 of 4

Many attorneys recommend enclosing the page number with hyphens or parentheses to prevent alteration after the document has been executed. Whichever pagination style your office prefers, it should be followed consistently on all documents produced by the office.

**Inserted pages**   As a general rule, additional pages should not be inserted in a legal document after it has been typed in final form. If additional pages are necessary, however, and if the attorney approves, the pages should be initialed by the signer(s) or by the notary public to verify that they approved the insertion. (Be sure to carry these initials to the copies when you conform them.) If the pages have already been numbered, you should identify the additional pages with the number of the preceding page plus a lowercase letter, as Page 10-a.

## CAPITALIZATION

Client documents adhere to special styling conventions, one of which is a tendency to capitalize many terms that are not capitalized in general English. For instance, in addition to following the general rules for capitalization, you may be expected to capitalize terms like *Village, Town, City, County,* and *State* when they appear in phrases like *Town of Monsey, County of Rockland, State of New York.* You may also be expected to capitalize the descriptive terms that identify parties such as Executor, Administratrix, Party of the First Part, Landlord, Secretary, and so forth (as in "incurred by the Board of Directors" or "the undersigned Incorporator"). Also frequently capitalized in legal documents are textual references to the document itself, as "this first Codicil to my Will" or "this Agreement." Some attorneys, however, prefer to fully capitalize such terms (as in "the following ARTICLES OF INCORPORATION"), while an increasing number of attorneys prefer to use lowercase letters. The use of capital letters in legal documents is thoroughly discussed in section 9.3 of Chapter 9.

**Names**　Proper names that appear in legal documents are generally typed in full capital letters for easy identification and recognition.

PAUL SHARFIN and MYRA SHARFIN, husband and wife
THE BESEN REALTY CORPORATION, a California corporation

As emphasized in Chapter 11, the first and last name of each party should be used. You should <u>not</u> consolidate the name of a couple by typing PAUL and MYRA SHARFIN, husband and wife, and especially not MR. and MRS. PAUL SHARFIN.

**Introductory phrases**　Words or phrases that traditionally introduce certain paragraphs of legal instruments are typewritten in all-capital letters. In this way the conventional parts of a document can be quickly located and identified. For instance, a property description traditionally begins, "ALL . . . ." A testimonium clause is identified by the opener, IN WITNESS WHEREOF, . . . ." A list of typical examples appears on pages 204–205 of Chapter 9.

## NUMBERS

Amounts of money should be capitalized in legal instruments and should be written in both words and figures, with the figures in parentheses. In legal documents both dollars and cents are expressed, even when there is an even dollar amount, for clarity and exactness:

TWELVE THOUSAND FIVE HUNDRED and 00/100 DOLLARS ($12,500.00) to be paid . . . .
*or*
Twelve Thousand Five Hundred and 00/100 Dollars ($12,500.00) to be paid . . . .

There should be no evidence of any erasures in the sums, especially in the figures, because a question may later arise as to whether the amount was altered before or after the document was executed.

　Important numbers other than those representing sums of money are also written in both words and figures, with the figures in parentheses. These words are not usually capitalized unless they begin a sentence.

twelve (12) months
twenty-five (25) copies

The following numbers do *not* have to be spelled out: paragraph numbers, page numbers, telephone numbers, policy numbers, invoice numbers, house or street numbers, ZIP codes, and the like. In these cases only the numerals are used:

Policy No. 20456 7780
Lot No. 84

## ABBREVIATIONS
With the exception of citation forms and commonly used abbreviations such as etc., Esq., Jr., et al., i.e., No., St. (for Saint), a.m., p.m., and so forth, abbreviations should be avoided in legal documents. Legal writing must be precise, and abbreviations are avoided because of the chance that they might be misinterpreted.

## DATES
Dates on legal documents are written as cardinal numbers unless they are preceded by the word *the,* in which case ordinals are used:

| cardinal numbers | ordinal numbers |
|---|---|
| February 9 | the 9th of February, 19-- |
| February 9, 19-- | February the 9th |

The ordinal form of the date is frequently spelled out on the date line of a signature block: the twenty-fourth of August, 19--. Months are always spelled in full.

## PUNCTUATION
In legal documents sentences may vary in length from one line to one page. If the proper punctuation is not supplied, the sentence could be misleading or misinterpreted. The purpose of punctuation is to help transmit a message clearly and accurately by dividing it into parts and showing the relationship between the parts. For reasons of clarity, therefore, a greater than normal number of commas, semicolons, and colons are often used to separate the segments of long sentences. Frequently, a period is used to separate the major parts of a document even though the part does not form a complete sentence. For an example of this common usage, see the document illustrated on page 406.

Many attorneys will dictate this unique legal punctuation to an inexperienced secretary. If not, you can often detect the marks of punctuation if you listen carefully to pauses in the dictator's voice while he or she is dictating.

Many attorneys disapprove of the optional final comma in series consisting of set legal phrases such as the following:

we give, devise(,) and bequeath
signed, sealed(,) and delivered
for and in the name, place(,) and stead of the undersigned
all the rest, residue(,) and remainder

You should find out if your employer objects to the optional comma and punctuate all series accordingly.

## WORD DIVISION
Dividing words at the end of a line should be avoided whenever possible in legal documents. If you must divide a word, refer to Chapter 9 for directions, keeping in mind the following guidelines:

1. Consult a good dictionary for a proper point of division.
2. Try not to have more than one hyphenated word on a page.
3. Never hyphenate a proper name, a number, an amount of money, or a contraction.
4. Never divide the last word on a page and carry the remainder of the word to the next page unless directed so by the attorney. (Some lawyers require that the last word on every page of an important document be carried over to the next page to ensure continuity.)
5. Never divide the last word in a paragraph.
6. If you are unable to complete a date on a given line, break it only before the year:

    September 16,    *not*    September
19--                        16, 19--

## THE TESTIMONIUM CLAUSE

The testimonium clause is the concluding paragraph of many documents. It serves as a transition to the signature lines. In it the parties state that their signatures (and seals or corporate seals) to the document are attached. The testimonium clause is not numbered, and it usually begins, "IN WITNESS WHEREOF, . . ." or "IN TESTIMONY WHEREOF, . . . ."

IN WITNESS WHEREOF, the parties hereto have set their hands on the day and in the year first above written.

*or*

IN TESTIMONY WHEREOF, the parties hereto have set their hands and seals on this fourth day of September, 19--.

## SIGNATURE LINES

Lines are usually typed for signatures to client documents—a separate line for each signer. Signature lines are typed slightly to the right of the center of the page and continue to the right margin. Below each line appears the name of the signer, centered and typewritten exactly as it is to be signed but fully capitalized. The style of the signature must agree with the name of the party as it appears in the document. Instead of the party's name, some attorneys prefer to indicate the capacity in which the person is signing, as Seller or Purchaser—the terms used in the text of the document. (In these cases only the initial letter of the term is capitalized.) Four or five spaces should be allowed between the signature line and the line above it to accommodate large signatures.

_____

Seller

_____

Purchaser

**Married woman's signature**  A married woman may sign her name in a variety of ways in correspondence, as illustrated in Chapter 10, but in legal documents she has the option of signing her legal name in one of the following ways:

1. First name, maiden name, married name: MARIE McPHERSON BROWN
2. First name, middle name or initial, married name: MARIE SHERYL BROWN    *or*
    MARIE S. BROWN

**Seals**  When a document concludes with the phrase "hand and seal" in the testimonium clause, the letters L.S. (for the Latin phrase *locus sigilli,* meaning "the place of the seal") or the word SEAL should follow the signature line. L.S. or SEAL sometimes appears in parentheses. The practice of sealing an instrument can be traced to the days when one would imprint on the instrument the seal from one's ring after it had been pressed into hot wax. Today an individual's signature serves as the seal, and many attorneys have dispensed with the *L.S.*

L.S.

_____

MARC ALLEN, President

L.S.

_____

ERIC LAURENCE, Landlord

Seals *are* used, however, when an officer is executing a document on behalf of a corporation. The officer impresses the corporate seal upon the document, usually just to the left of the signature.

**Corporate signatures** Corporate signatures require that you type first the name of the corporation in solid capitals, and below it a signature line frequently preceded by the word *By:* to indicate that an officer will sign for the corporation. The corporate officer's title is typed immediately below the signature line, centered and capitalized. If the signer is a member of a partnership rather than an officer of a corporation, the signature line is typed as for a corporate signature but the title is omitted.

The secretary of the corporation is frequently required to attest to the fact that the imprinted seal is the actual seal of the corporation. When a corporate seal is to be attested (the testimonium clause will indicate if it is to be attested), the word ATTEST is typed on the left side of the page and below the signature line, as shown here. The corporate secretary signs above the word *Secretary.*

XYZ CORPORATION

[corporate seal]                    By _____

Vice-President

ATTEST:

Secretary

**Spacing** A signature line should never appear alone on the final page of the document. At least one line (preferably two and, in the case of single-spaced lines, three) from the preceding paragraph (preferably from the body of the document rather than from a testimonium clause) should be carried over. This prevents the unauthorized substitution or inclusion of additional pages.

Furthermore, the signatures should be all on one page unless there are a great number of signatures. If spacing should present a problem, you may wish to follow the suggestions for adjusting space that are listed on page 392. As an alternative, you may prefer to use a Z-mark (illustrated in section 11.2 of Chapter 11) on the next-to-last page of the document so that the last lines of the text, the testimonium clause, and all the signatures fall on the final page.

## ATTESTATION CLAUSE

Many client documents require that signatures be witnessed. In these cases, an attestation clause precedes the signatures of the attesting witnesses. The attestation clause may be lengthy and detailed, as in the will illustrated on pages 425–427, or it may consist of the simple phrase, "In the presence of." A common form of the clause is the following: "Signed, sealed, and delivered in the presence of."

An attestation clause is normally typed on the left side of the page, directly opposite the signatures of the parties on the right side. Below the attestation clause, a line is typed for each witness's signature. If the two parties to an agreement are not able to sign the document at the same time, separate attestation clauses and separate witness's signatory lines must be typed opposite the signature lines for the two parties.

**Attestation clause of a will** In a will, the attestation clause is arranged differently. It is begun at least four lines below the signature of the testator and may be typed from margin to margin, although it is more often indented on the left side or on both sides. Since the attestation clause of a will is often lengthy, it is usually single-spaced. It declares that the witnesses signed in the presence of the testator and of each other and that the testator requested them to witness the will; the clause may also include details such as the number of pages in the will.

The secretary must type lines for the addresses as well as the signatures of the witnesses, since the witnesses may have to be located when the will is ready for probate. Two common forms of signature lines for witnesses are illustrated here: one for a will and one for a typical two-party client document.

> The foregoing instrument, consisting of four (4) pages, including this page signed by the witnesses, was on the date hereof signed by the said MARTIN PETER CUTHBERTSON and declared by him to be his last will and testament, and at his request, and in his presence, and in the presence of each other, we have subscribed our names as witnesses to the said will.
>
> _____ Address_____
>
> _____
>
> _____ Address_____
>
> _____

> In the Presence of:
>
> _____    _____ SEAL
>                               CHARLES H. McCORMICK
>
> _____    _____ SEAL
>                               NANCY K. PATTERSON

All signatures on a will should appear on the same page. The ideal arrangement is for at least the last two lines of the text of the will, the testimonium clause, the testator's signature, the attestation clause, and the signatures of all witnesses to be all on one page. If it is impossible for the signatures to be all on one page, an alternative is to type at least one line of the attestation clause on the signature page, with the remainder of the clause on the last page with the witnesses' signatures.

## ACKNOWLEDGMENT

Certain documents must be subscribed to in the presence of a notary public before they can be recorded or filed. They must bear a certificate of acknowledgment that is annexed to the document. An acknowledgment is a formal declaration in which a notary public or other authorized individual affirms that the signature is genuine and that the person signing the document did so as his or her own act. The acknowledgment may be either single- or double-spaced, and it must contain the following: (1) a statement of venue, (2) the date, (3) the purpose of the acknowledgment, and (4) the signature and frequently the seal and the expiration date of the commission of the notary public. Each of these parts is described in the paragraphs below.

Acknowledgment forms vary from state to state. The two acknowledgments illustrated on these pages—one an individual acknowledgment, one a corporate acknowledgment—are only two of many possible forms. Two other forms are shown in Chapter 11. Since you will be typing many certificates of acknowledgment, you will need to have the appropriate samples in your form file. It is important to remember that the form of the acknowledgment is determined by the state where the instrument is to be recorded, not by the state in which the instrument or the acknowledgment was prepared. If your office is involved in interstate legal work, it would be wise to include acknowledgment forms from other states in your form file. Or you may refer to one of the form books listed in the Appendix to this book.

## An Individual Acknowledgment

```
STATE OF NEW YORK)
                         ss.:
COUNTY OF ORANGE )


        BE IT REMEMBERED, that on this 2d day of December,
19--, before me, the subscriber, a Notary Public of the State of
New York, personally appeared HARRY C. FORBES who, I am satisfied,
is the person named in and who executed the within Instrument,
and thereupon he acknowledged that he signed, sealed and
delivered the same as his act and deed, for the uses and purposes
therein expressed.

        (seal)                    _____
                                          Notary Public

My Commission expires January 5, 19--.
```

**Venue**   The venue shows the political subdivision in which the instrument was executed. It is typed in two double-spaced lines, as follows:

STATE OF KANSAS      )

                   :   ss.

COUNTY OF WILSON)

The venue is typed at the upper left margin of the acknowledgment. It is fully capitalized and bracketed with closing parentheses (or a combination of closing parentheses and colons) at the point of the longer line. The venue is followed in the center by the initials ss. or SS. (sometimes followed by a colon—ss.:), which is thought by some to be an abbreviation for the Latin term *scilicet,* meaning "to wit" or "namely," but which may have had other origins. When typing an acknowledgment, leave three lines of space between the venue and the body of the acknowledgment.

**Date**   The acknowledgment gives the date on which the signer makes the acknowledgment to the notary public, <u>not</u> the date on which he or she signed the document. The date may appear at the beginning of the acknowledgment, as shown in the illustrations, or it may appear as a separate paragraph at the end in a form similar to the following:

IN WITNESS WHEREOF, I have herewith set my hand and affixed my official seal this 30th day of October, 19--.

**Purpose**   The body of the acknowledgment is a report of the declaration of the person making the acknowledgment. This person's name is always included and is typed in solid capital letters. If he or she is acting in the capacity of a representative of an organization, the title must also be given, with initial capitalization only, as follows: JOHN K. MUMFORD, Vice President of XYZ Corporation.

**A Corporate Acknowledgment**

```
STATE OF FLORIDA)
                        SS.
COUNTY OF DADE   )

        BE IT REMEMBERED, that on this 10th day of October,
19--, before me, the subscriber, a notary public of the State of
Florida, personally appeared HELEN V. TANABE who, being by me
duly sworn on her oath, deposes and makes proof to my
satisfaction, that she is the Secretary of Southern Confections
Company, the Corporation named in the within Instrument; that
MARTIN LUSBY is the President of said Corporation; that the
execution, as well as the making, of this Instrument has been
duly authorized by a proper resolution of the Board of Directors
of the said Corporation; that deponent well knows the corporate
seal of said Corporation; and that the seal affixed to said
Instrument is the proper corporate seal and was thereto affixed
and said Instrument signed and delivered by said MARTIN LUSBY,
President, as and for the voluntary act and deed of said
Corporation, in presence of the deponent, who thereupon
subscribed her name thereto as attesting witness.


    (notarial seal)          _____
                                        Notary Public
                             My commission expires        19  .
```

**Notary public information**    The notary public or other official who takes the acknowledgment signs the certificate. The person making the acknowledgment does not sign it. A ruled line for the signature is typed four spaces below the last line of text, and the officer's title (usually *Notary Public*) is centered and typed just below the signature line. In some states the typing of the notary's name is also required. If your state is one which requires that an acknowledgment include the date on which the notary's commission expires, type the phrase "My commission expires 19    ," two spaces below the signature. Or, if you are notarizing the document yourself, you may use a rubber stamp to that effect. Many states require a notary's seal to be affixed to acknowledgments, and all states require the seal when the acknowledgment is made in one state but recorded in another.

For further discussion of the duties of a notary public and the use of the notary's seal, refer to section 14.1 of Chapter 14.

## LEGAL BACKS

In order to protect and identify typewritten legal documents, you will be expected to staple them into heavyweight covers. The covers are generally blue in color and therefore sometimes referred to as blue backs, although they come in an assortment of colors. The legal back is usually 9 by 15 inches in size for legal-size paper and 9 by 13 inches for letter-size paper.

All legal backs bear a typewritten endorsement, or a brief description of the document within. When the back is properly folded, the endorsement appears on the front of the cover. The endorsement should include (1) the names of the parties involved, usually typed at the top, (2) the title of the document (all-capitalized and frequently set off by rules), (3) the name and address of the law office that prepared the document, usually typed at the bottom, and (4) in some instances the date of the document. All typing should be completed prior to inserting the document, and each endorsement should be individually prepared, since the legal back is too thick for carbon paper to be effective.

Many legal backs are printed with guidelines to mark where you should type the endorsement. Law firms may also order backs that are printed with the firm's name and address. Some covers, however, are plain. If there are no printed panels to use as a typing guide, you may have to fold the cover before typing the endorsement in order to determine the proper panel on which to type. Fold the cover as shown in the illustration and use the creases as a typing guide:

1. Fold the cover one inch down from the top.
2. Bring the bottom up to the crease made by the first fold and crease again.
3. Repeat, bringing the new bottom fold up to the first fold, and crease again.
4. Turn the cover vertically to find the front panel on which the endorsement will be typed (the open edges of the cover should be on the right side).

You may wish to make a light pencil mark to indicate where to begin typing.

Once endorsed, the legal back should be refolded down one inch from the top and the document inserted under the flap. To secure the document, place two staples approximately one-half inch from the top. The back is then refolded, with the document folded to match the creases in the legal back.

If the document has been prepared on letter-size paper, you will fold the back in thirds as you would a letter.

Law blanks and some court papers have endorsements printed on the last page; therefore, no legal backs are necessary when preparing law blanks. All copies of a typewritten client document are backed with the exception of the office file copy, which will have one staple affixed diagonally in the upper left corner so as not to interfere with the two-pronged fastener in the file.

## How to Fold a Legal Back

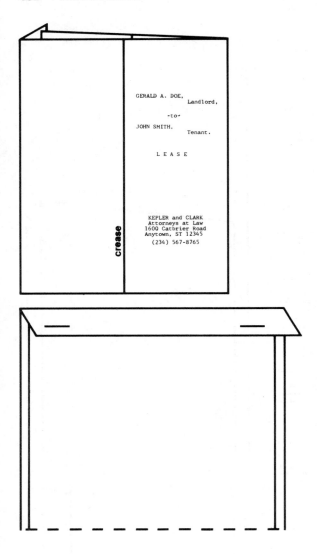

GERALD A. DOE,
Landlord,

-to-

JOHN SMITH,
Tenant.

L E A S E

KEPLER and CLARK
Attorneys at Law
1600 Catbrier Road
Anytown, ST 12345

(234) 567-8765

crease

# 12.3

## CONTRACTS AND AGREEMENTS

A contract is a legally enforceable agreement, binding between two or more competent parties and based upon sufficient legal consideration, to do or refrain from doing something. Once the contract has been validated by signing, all concerned parties are legally bound to perform all the obligations described in the contract. If there is a breach of the contract, the aggrieved party may seek compensatory damages in a court of law. In order to be enforceable, a contract must involve the following elements: (1) competent parties, (2) an agreement which is legal, (3) sufficient consideration, and (4) absence of duress, fraud, or misrepresentation.

## TERMS COMMONLY USED IN CONTRACTS

It is helpful in preparing contracts for the secretary to understand certain terms. Some terms frequently used in contracts have meanings different from their commonly understood meanings. *Consideration,* for example, is the inducement to a contract; that is, the reason or material cause (as money, goods, or services) that induces a person to enter into a contractual arrangement. *Competent* parties are those persons who are legally qualified to execute a contract, and *infants,* or minors, are those persons who have not reached the legal age of maturity, which in most states is 21 years. The secretary who takes the job seriously will look up unfamiliar words in a law dictionary as they are encountered.

**Types of contracts** The attorney may use the following terms to describe various types of contracts:

Executed contract—One in which the terms have been performed by both or all contracting parties.

Executory contract—One in which the terms, or some of them, are yet to be performed. A contract can be executed by one party and executory on the part of another.

Implied contract—One in which the contract terms are understood without having been expressed in writing.

Express contract—One in which the terms are expressed by written or oral agreement.

Bilateral contract—One in which mutual promises are exchanged by all concerned parties.

Unilateral contract—One in which one party promises to do something in exchange for which the other party makes no promises.

**Assignment of contract** In certain situations, persons who were not parties to the original contract may incur obligations or duties under the contract. For example, a person may assign his or her obligations to a third person who was not a party to the original agreement. Statutes vary in this regard, and some states require that assignments be written. Duties of a personal nature, or duties that would place an unfair burden or risk upon the third party, are usually not transferrable.

## TYPING THE CONTRACT

A contract must contain the following information, usually in this order:

1. date
2. names of the parties
3. purpose of the contract
4. duties and responsibilities of each party

5. consideration for the contract
6. duration
7. signatures of all parties
8. witnesses or notarization, if applicable

Law blanks are available for many contracts; however, because of the diversity of agreements, it is often necessary to prepare a completely typewritten contract. An original or duplicate original must be typed for each signatory to the agreement.

**A sample contract** The employment contract shown on pages 406–407 illustrates many of the styling guidelines for client documents that are detailed in section 12.2. The heading (EMPLOYMENT CONTRACT) states the nature of the agreement. THIS AGREEMENT is a standard way of introducing the body of a contract. Note that the date is written at the very beginning of the contract and that the month is not abbreviated. The names of the parties to the agreement appear in the first paragraph, fully capitalized, and the addresses are not abbreviated. Terms that denote the capacity in which the parties appear (Employer, Employee) are initially capitalized. The first time these identifying terms are used, they are enclosed in quotation marks (hereinafter referred to as the "Employer"); in later references, however, the quotation marks are dropped.

The second paragraph illustrates the practice (not always followed) of capitalizing all references to the document itself (the Agreement). Note that this paragraph does not form a complete sentence; however, since it is a standard contract clause, it is typed as a paragraph and punctuated as if it were a complete sentence.

In the third paragraph the duties of the parties are listed. Each duty is punctuated as if it were a complete sentence. Important numbers—one (1) year; ten (10) miles—are spelled out first and then repeated in numerals, for clarity.

The consideration is detailed in the fourth paragraph. Amounts of money in contracts are always spelled out and capitalized (in this case fully capitalized) and repeated with the figures in parentheses. Note that the only abbreviations used in the body of the contract occur here: they are the commonly understood *a.m.* and *p.m.*

In the testimonium clause, the phrase "hands and seals" alerts the secretary to the need to add *L.S.* to the signature lines. Both a business organization signature and an individual signature are illustrated. Witnessing and notarization are not usually required for this type of simple contract.

# 12.4

## LEASES

A lease is a multi-party contract governing the arrangements for the rental of real or personal property. As a formal written instrument, it should follow all the styling guides discussed in section 12.2. Short-term leases tend to conform to standard patterns and are generally prepared on forms. Long-term leases are generally typewritten in full.

### TERMINOLOGY

Parties to a lease are referred to by a variety of interchangeable terms: The landlord may be termed *lessor, owner,* or *party of the first part.* The tenant may be termed *lessee, renter,* or *party of the second part.* The terms and provisions of the lease are often referred to as *covenants* and the property as *the demised property.* The lease itself may be called an *indenture.*

You will encounter many types of leases. A lease for *tenancy for a stated period,* for example, may have a duration of six months, two years, or whatever the negotiated terms are. The lease terminates without notice at the end of the indicated tenancy period. Or a lease may be for *tenancy from period to period;* that is, it may be negotiated to run a specified calendar year and to continue from year to year thereafter until sufficient termination notice has been given by either party. When there is no predetermined termination period, a lease is for *tenancy at will. Tenancy at sufferance* occurs when the tenant does not vacate the premises at the time of termination. In such cases the landlord may elect to allow the tenant to remain in occupancy of the premises or may evict him.

### PREPARING A LEASE

The lawyer will dictate standard lease clauses from a form book or ask you to arrange clauses from your own form file. The secretary should become familiar with these standard clauses so that when the lawyer says, for example, to insert the usual liability clause, it may be done quickly and without supervision. On the other hand, some lease clauses may have to be prepared from a rough draft because they encompass a number of unique circumstances. Clauses in a lease are generally numbered or otherwise headed so that they can be easily located.

**Copies**    A minimum of three copies must be prepared: The original will be given to the client, who is usually the landlord. A duplicate original is given to the tenant, and one conformed copy is kept for the office file. If a real estate broker and a second attorney are involved in the transaction, additional copies will probably be necessary for them.

**Format**    As indicated in section 12.2, the title is typed ten spaces down from the top, centered, underlined, and fully capitalized.

LEASE   *or*   L E A S E

The introductory paragraph conventionally begins with one of the following phrases: THIS LEASE, THIS AGREEMENT, THIS LEASE AGREEMENT, or THIS INDENTURE. It further gives the date and the name and address of each landlord and tenant. In this paragraph only, the words *landlord* and *tenant* are placed in quotation marks.

The next paragraph is usually marked with the heading WITNESSETH:, which introduces the paragraphs that detail the terms of the lease. In the lease illustrated on pages 408–409, this paragraph describes the property or item to be rented and declares the terms of the lease. (There may be several WHEREAS clauses, but only the first is introduced by WITNESSETH:.) The conditions of the lease are clearly enumerated in the succeeding paragraphs.

The testimonium clause concludes the text, gives the date of execution, and provides a transition to the signatures. In the facsimile lease shown here, the date has been left blank. You may wish to do this whenever you are not sure what day the parties will actually sign the lease. If you type the lease toward the end of the month, you should leave a blank space for the month as well as the day.

A lease must be signed by both parties to the agreement—the lessor and the lessee. If the tenant is a corporation, the proper officers must sign their individual names. If the tenant is a partnership, it is advisable to have all the partners sign the lease. A lease is normally witnessed and sealed, although some states do not require it. The parties should sign the two or more originals plus the broker's copy. Witnesses' signatures should appear on the same page as the parties' signatures.

In most states a lease for tenancy of more than a year must be acknowledged, notarized, and then recorded by the lessee. Short-term leases such as those for typical apartment rentals are not normally acknowledged and recorded. However, any lease may be formally recorded if it is considered important enough.

All copies must be conformed, and all but the file copy will be placed in a legal back.

**Contents of a lease**    The lease defines the rights and responsibilities of both tenant and landlord. Many provisions are standard, such as the following:

the date of signing
the names and addresses of landlord and tenant
the location of the unit to be rented
the duration of the lease
the amount of rent and when it is due
provisions for termination of the lease

Other common provisions are optional:

extra charges that may be incurred, as those for utilities, parking, or recreational facilities
the amount of security
provisions for subletting
rules for pets
a list of furnishings provided
military or transfer clause

# A Typewritten Contract

<u>EMPLOYMENT CONTRACT</u>

THIS AGREEMENT, made and entered into this 15th day
of August, 19—, by and between THOMAS JAMES ASSOCIATES, a
New York Corporation, having its principal place of business
at 79 Blazer Way, Spring Valley, New York, hereinafter referred
to as the "Employer," and ARLENE KARP, residing at 560 Requa Road,
Pomona, New York, hereinafter referred to as the "Employee."
The parties herein bind themselves, their heirs, designees and
legatees to the contract.

That consideration herein of the Agreement, being
mutual agreements, covenants, warranties and ONE and 00/100
DOLLAR ($1.00) and other good and valuable consideration given
between the parties hereto.

That the Employee agrees that, if there is any
termination of the Employer/Employee relationship between
herself and THOMAS JAMES ASSOCIATES, the Employee will not cause,
by any direct or indirect act, any interference with the
Employer's business, the same being in electrical supplies.
That the Employee further warrants, guarantees and covenants
that, if the Employee's employment is terminated or if the
Employee refuses further employment with the Employer, she shall
not engage in a similar business and/or activity for a period
of one (1) year after the said termination and will not further
engage in a said related business and/or field within a radius
of ten (10) miles from THOMAS JAMES ASSOCIATES. It being
understood that THOMAS JAMES ASSOCIATES presently draws customers

-1-

from said radius, and the Employer and Employee agreeing that the Employee shall not in any way interfere with the orderly business of the Employer, if and when the Employee terminates the said employment with the Employer.

As a further consideration, the Employer agrees to pay on a weekly basis commencing the 1st day of September, 19—, and terminating the 31st day of August, 19—, the salary of FOUR HUNDRED FIFTY and 00/100 DOLLARS ($450.00), and thereafter the salary and terms of employment shall be renegotiated. The Employee shall be employed as a salesman. Said employment shall be on a six-day basis (exclusive of Sundays) from 9 a.m. to 6 p.m. daily.

IN WITNESS WHEREOF, the parties hereto have hereunto set their hands and seals on the date and in the year first above written.

THOMAS JAMES ASSOCIATES


By _____ L.S.
         THOMAS JAMES, President


_____ L.S.
         ARLENE KARP, Employee

## A Typewritten Lease

LEASE

THIS LEASE AGREEMENT, made this        day of September, 19--,
between PAUL KRAFT and ANN KRAFT, husband and wife, residing at
4 Connelly Court, Suffern, New York, hereinafter referred to as the
"Landlords," and MICHAEL SCHWARTZ and LYNNE SCHWARTZ, husband and
wife, residing at One Greenway Terrace, Monroe, New York, hereinafter
referred to as the "Tenants."

WITNESSETH: WHEREAS, the Landlords do  hereby lease to the
Tenants, and the Tenants do hereby rent from the Landlords, the
following described premises:

> ALL that certain one-story brick dwelling, with
> attached garage, situate and known as 210 Clover
> Drive, Suffern, New York,

for a term of two (2) years, to commence on the 1st day of February,
19--, and to terminate on the 31st day of January, 19--, to be used
and occupied only and for no other purpose than the personal use
of said Tenants.

UPON THE FOLLOWING CONDITIONS AND COVENANTS:

FIRST: The Tenants covenant and agree to pay to the
Landlords, as rent for and during the term thereof, the sum of
FOUR THOUSAND and 00/100 DOLLARS ($4,000.00) in the following manner:
A monthly rental of ONE HUNDRED SIXTY-SIX and 66/100 DOLLARS $166.66),
payable in advance on the 1st day of each and every month during the
term of this Lease.

SECOND: The Tenants shall pay when due, all charges for
water, gas and electricity used by the Tenants.

-1-

THIRD:  The Tenants agree that if any rent shall be due or unpaid for a period in excess of sixty (60) days, or if default shall be made in any of the covenants herein contained, it shall be lawful for the Landlord to enter the premises and to remove all persons therefrom.

FOURTH:  At the expiration of the term or the termination of the Lease, the Tenants will quit and surrender the premises hereby demised, in as good a state and condition as reasonable use and wear thereof will permit, damages by the elements excepted.

FIFTH:  The Landlord covenants that the Tenants, on paying the rent as herein specified, in the amounts, at the time, and in the manner aforesaid, and performing the covenants thereof, shall and may peaceably and quietly have, hold and enjoy the said premises for the term aforesaid.

IN WITNESS WHEREOF, the said parties have hereunto set their hands and seals on the      day of          19--.

_____ (L.S.)<br>
PAUL KRAFT, Landlord<br>
<br>
_____ (L.S.)<br>
ANN KRAFT, Landlord<br>
<br>
_____ (L.S.)<br>
MICHAEL SCHWARTZ, Tenant<br>
<br>
_____ (L.S.)<br>
LYNNE SCHWARTZ, Tenant

Witnesses:

_____

_____

-2-

# 12.5

## CORPORATE DOCUMENTS

There are three major types of business ownership in our economic system: the sole proprietorship, the partnership, and the corporation. In a sole or single proprietorship, the owner controls the creation and operation of the business. A partnership is the voluntary joining of two or more people who pool their skills and resources; each partner is legally responsible for the total liabilities of the business. A corporation is a legal entity created under specific state laws and having powers and liabilities granted under state statutes.

### INCORPORATION PROCEDURES

The regulations that govern the incorporation of a business are specific to each state, and they are often complex. Lawyers with a large number of corporate clients may have their secretaries handle certain procedural requirements. The next paragraphs summarize the steps that a legal secretary may take toward creating a corporation.

**Selection of a corporate name**   States have strict rules governing the choice of a corporate name. Inasmuch as the selected name may already be in use in your state or may be too similar to another name, you must send a letter to the secretary of state, or to the officer in your state designated for such purpose, asking if a specific name is available. To save time in the event that the name is not available, you may list more than one choice; the state officer will notify you which ones are available. Once the names have been checked, the incorporators will make their final choice. To reserve the name, you will then write a letter to notify the secretary of state of the selection. In many states you must include a check for a fee to reserve the chosen name for a certain period of time.

**Certificate of incorporation**   Once the name has been reserved, a certificate of incorporation (also known as *articles of incorporation* or a *charter*) must be prepared. State laws determine the format and content of the certificate. The certificate is frequently prepared on a printed form and in quadruplicate. It generally includes (1) the name of the corporation, (2) its principal place(s) of business, (3) the purpose for which it is organized, (4) the laws and/or authority under which it is formed, (5) its powers, (6) the amount of capital stock and the number of shares to be issued, (7) the names of the incorporators, and (8) the names of the directors. The precise items that must be included on the certificate are stated in the law governing incorporation in a state.

Whether you are preparing a printed form like the one in the illustration or typing the document in full, you should first refer to your form file for certificates to use as models. Several copies of the certificate are required: one for the secretary of state, one for corporate headquarters, one for the minute book, and one for the office files. In addition, extra copies may be needed in some states to accompany an application to sell securities; some states require copies to be filed in each county where the corporation owns real estate; copies will also have to be filed in all the states in which the corporation does business. You will probably need to type the document twice— once as a formal certificate of incorporation on letter-size, high-quality bond or legal cap with the required number of copies, and again on three-hole minute paper for insertion in the corporation's minute book. (The minute book is a three-ring binder that contains minutes of shareholders' and directors' meetings, a copy of the incorporation procedures and the bylaws, and frequently also a stock register.)

When preparing a fully typewritten certificate of incorporation, follow the guidelines for client documents that are outlined in section 12.2. Use pica type and a good ribbon. The document may be headed in the following fashion:

CERTIFICATE OF INCORPORATION

OF

<u>XYZ CORPORATION</u>

Initial capitals are generally (but not always) used in reference to the corporation, its officers, and its documents (this Corporation; the Board of Directors; the foregoing Bylaws).

The signatures on a certificate of incorporation are those of the incorporators. Most states require the signatures to be sealed. Many states require an acknowledgment. If an acknowledgment is needed, type it on <u>all</u> executed copies of the document, and <u>type it in the form required by the state which governs the corporation, even though the venue of the acknowledgment may recite a different state.</u> Ask the attorney if it will be necessary for you to prepare an authentication. (Certificates of authentication are described in Chapter 14 and illustrated on page 386.)

After the certificate has been executed and properly acknowledged, the original and the required number of copies are forwarded to the secretary of state or other authorized official for filing, together with a letter of transmittal and the appropriate fee. (Fees vary from state to state.) Some states require a certain number of ribbon copies, some require duplicate and triplicate originals, and some accept conformed carbon copies with the original. The secretary of state or other state officer will file the original, certify the copies, and return the certified copies to your office. The certified copies will be marked to show that the original has been approved and properly filed with the public official. One certified copy should be filed in the corporation's minute book; the others will be filed according to the regulations of the state: for example, certified copies may need to be filed with the county in which the corporation is conducting business. An uncertified copy is retained for the attorney's file. It should be conformed, however, with the date of certification.

**Stocks**  A stock certificate is that piece of paper which the stockholder receives as written evidence of ownership of a certain number of shares in the corporation. A sample stock certificate is illustrated on page 376.

If the company issues only one type of stock, it will be common stock. Common stock has no fixed rate of return; however, the owner can participate fully in the ownership of the corporation by exercising the right to vote. Holders of preferred stock receive a fixed rate of return and have a prior claim to dividends or to any assets upon the dissolution of the corporation. Stocks are issued as either par value or no-par value; the choice is based upon rules of incorporation. Par value is the price assigned to the stock when issued. If the shares have no-par value, or no assigned value, that fact is usually indicated on the stock certificate.

## CORPORATE BYLAWS

Bylaws contain the rules and regulations under which the corporation determines that it will operate. They identify the type of stock certificates to be issued, the number of officers and directors, the responsibilities of the officers and directors, the method of electing and removing the officers, the time and place of the meetings of the directors and stockholders, and the method by which the bylaws can be amended. Preprinted, self-explanatory forms are available for this purpose, but corporate bylaws are frequently typewritten in full on letter-size paper that can be inserted in the minute book. Double spacing is generally used, but the bylaws may also be single-spaced (as shown in the example on pages 414–415), with double spacing between paragraphs, especially when there is a very large number of short paragraphs.

## Certificate of Incorporation Typewritten on a Printed Form

359—N J. CERTIFICATE OF INCORPORATION          A D G                 COPYRIGHT© 1969  ALL-STATE LEGAL SUPPLY CO.
  (One or more Incorporators)                                           269 SHEFFIELD STREET, MOUNTAINSIDE, N.J. 07092

# Certificate of Incorporation
## of

ABC REALTY CO., INC.

**This is to certify that,** *there is hereby organized a corporation under and by virtue of N.J.S. 14A:1-1 et seq., the "New Jersey Business Corporation Act."*

14A:2-7 (1) (a)  *1.  The name of the corporation is* ABC REALTY CO., INC.

14A:2-7 (1) (g)  *2.  The address (and zip code) of this corporation's initial registered office is*
235 Vanderbilt Street, Hackensack, New Jersey 07601

*and the name of this corporation's initial registered agent at such address is*
JANICE TEISCH.

14A:2-7 (1) (b)  *3.  The purposes for which this corporation is organized are:*

*To engage in any activity within the purposes for which corporations may be organized under the "New Jersey Business Corporation Act." N.J.S. 14A:1-1 et seq.*

To provide a sales/marketing service to the people of the State of New Jersey, specifically those located in Bergen County, with the intention of making a profit.

To borrow money, to make and issue promissory notes, bills of exchange, bonds, debentures, obligations, and evidences of indebtedness of all kinds, whether secured by mortgage, pledge or otherwise, without limit as to amount, and to execute the same by mortgage, pledge or otherwise.

To carry on any other business which may, in the discretion of the directors seem advantageous and capable of being carried on, or calculated directly or indirectly to enhance the value of the corporation's property or rights.

The corporation shall have the power to conduct its business in all its branches, have one or more offices, and ultimately to hold, purchase, mortgage or convey real and personal property in any state or territory of the United States.

14A:2-7 (1) (c)  *4.  The aggregate number of shares which the corporation shall have authority to issue is*
one hundred (100) shares.

All or any part of said shares of common stock, with or without nominal par value, may be issued by the corporation from time to time, and for such consideration as may be determined and fixed by the board of directors, as provided by law.

14A:2-7 (1) (h) 5. *The first Board of Directors of this corporation shall consist of* four (4) *Director(s) and the name and address of each person who is to serve as such Director is:*

| Name | Address | Zip Code |
|------|---------|----------|
| JANICE TEISCH | 235 Vanderbilt Street, Hackensack, NJ | 07601 |
| MORTON TEISCH | 235 Vanderbilt Street, Hackensack, NJ | 07601 |
| LYNNE SULLIVAN | 5 Rockland Road, Hackensack, NJ | 07601 |
| GARY SULLIVAN | 5 Rockland Road, Hackensack, NJ | 07601 |

14A:2-7 (1) (i) 6. *The name and address of each incorporator is:*

| Name | Address | Zip Code |
|------|---------|----------|
| JANICE TEISCH | 235 Vanderbilt Street, Hackensack, NJ | 07601 |
| MORTON TEISCH | 235 Vanderbilt Street, Hackensack, NJ | 07601 |
| LYNNE SULLIVAN | 5 Rockland Road, Hackensack, NJ | 07601 |
| GARY SULLIVAN | 5 Rockland Road, Hackensack, NJ | 07601 |

7. The period of existence of this corporation is unlimited.

**In Witness Whereof.** *each individual incorporator, each being over the age of eighteen years, has signed this Certificate; or if the incorporator be a corporation, has caused this Certificate to be signed by its authorized officers, this            day of                      19 - -*

................ JANICE TEISCH ................          ................ LYNNE SULLIVAN ................

................ MORTON TEISCH ................          ................ GARY SULLIVAN ................

Reprinted by permission of All-State Legal Supply Co.

## A Set of Corporate Bylaws

```
                        BY-LAWS
                          OF
                  ABC REALTY CO., INC.

                Adopted:  June 21, 19--


ARTICLE I:  Officers

        1.  Registered Office and Agent:  The registered
office of the Corporation in the State of New Jersey is at
235 Vanderbilt Street, Hackensack, New Jersey.  The registered
agent of the Corporation at such office is JANICE TEISCH.

        2.  Principal Place of Business:  The principal place
of business of the Corporation is 235 Vanderbilt Street, Hackensack,
New Jersey.

        3.  Other Places of Business:  Branch or subordinate
places of business or offices may be established at any time by
the Board at any place or places where the Corporation is qualified
to do business.

ARTICLE II:  Shareholders

        1.  Annual Meeting:  The annual meeting of shareholders
shall be held upon not less than ten or more than sixty days'
written notice of the time, place and purpose of the meeting at
9 a.m. on the fifth day of the month of June, of each year, or
at such other time as shall be specified in the notice of meeting,
in order to elect directors and transact such other business as
shall come before the meeting.  If the date is a Sunday or legal
holiday, the meeting shall be held at the same hour on the next
succeeding business day.

        2.  Special Meetings:  A special meeting of shareholders
may be called for any purpose by the president or the Board.  A
special meeting shall be held upon not less than ten or more than
sixty days' written notice of the time, place, and purpose of the
meeting.

        3.  Action Without Meeting:  The shareholders may act
without a meeting if, prior or subsequent to such action, each
shareholder who would have been entitled to vote upon such action
shall consent in writing to such action.  Such written consent or
consents shall be filed in the minute book.

        4.  Quorum:  The presence at a meeting in person or by
proxy of the holders of shares entitled to cast four of the votes
shall constitute a quorum.

ARTICLE III:  Board of Directors

        1.  Number and Term of Office:  The Board shall consist
of four members.  Each director shall be elected by the shareholders
at each annual meeting and shall hold office until the next annual


                          -1-
```

meeting of shareholders and until that director's successor shall have been elected and qualified.

2. <u>Regular Meeting</u>: A regular meeting of the Board shall be held without notice immediately following and at the same place as the annual stockholders' meeting for the purposes of electing officers and conducting such other business as may come before the meeting. The Board, by resolution, may provide for additional regular meetings which may be held without notice, except to members not present at the time of the adoption of the resolution.

3. <u>Special Meetings</u>: A special meeting of the Board may be called at any time by the president or by directors for any purpose. Such meeting shall be held upon thirty days' notice if given orally (either by telephone or in person) or by telegraph, or by thirty days' notice if given by depositing the notice in the United States mails, postage prepaid. Such notice shall specify the time and place of the meeting.

4. <u>Action Without Meeting</u>: The Board may act without a meeting if, prior or subsequent to such action, each member of the Board shall consent in writing to such action. Such written consent or consents shall be filed in the minute book.

5. <u>Quorum</u>: Four members of the entire Board shall constitute a quorum for the transaction of business.

6. <u>Vacancies in Board of Directors</u>: Any vacancy in the Board may be filled by the affirmative vote of a majority of the remaining directors, even though less than a quorum of the Board, or by a sole remaining director.

ARTICLE IV: Waivers of Notice

Any notice required by these by-laws, by the certificate of incorporation, or by the New Jersey Business Corporation Act may be waived in writing by any person entitled to notice. The waiver may be executed either before or after the event with respect to which notice is waived. Each director or shareholder attending a meeting without protesting, prior to its conclusion, the lack of proper notice shall be deemed conclusively to have waived notice of the meeting.

ARTICLE V: Officers

1. <u>Election</u>: At its regular meeting following the annual meeting of shareholders, the Board shall elect a president, a treasurer, a secretary, and it may elect such other officers, including one or more vice presidents, as it shall deem necessary. One person may hold two or more offices.

2. <u>Duties and Authority of President</u>: The president shall be chief executive officer of the Corporation. Subject . . . .

The preparation of bylaws is fairly routine; the lawyer may note certain paragraphs that you can copy from a form book but dictate others in detail. The state incorporation law to a large extent determines the content of the bylaws, but the format is variable. You will probably want to refer to an existing set of bylaws for the format customary in your state.

Bylaws differ from other client documents in that they are divided into articles (major divisions) and sections (subdivisions). As shown in the facsimile, articles are customarily identified by the all-capitalized heading ARTICLE followed by a Roman numeral. Article headings may be flush left as shown or centered on the line, and they are usually on a line by themselves. Section headings, on the other hand, customarily use Arabic numerals, are initially capitalized and underlined, and appear at the beginning of the paragraphs they introduce. These prominently marked headings make it easy to locate particular parts of a lengthy document.

## CORPORATE MEETINGS

State laws provide that written notice of meetings must be given to the directors and stockholders of a corporation. The notice must contain the time and place of the meeting and the matters and issues that will be discussed. In instances where the interested parties are in close contact, they may elect to sign a waiver of notice of meeting, which must be attached to the minutes of the meeting of the corporation.

The secretary routinely prepares these notices or waivers of notice before each meeting. The law office may use commercial or custom-designed forms or the secretary may type the notices in full. Facsimiles of a fully typewritten waiver of notice of meeting and a proxy are shown here. For illustrations of notice of meeting and proxy forms, refer to section 17.2 of Chapter 17. Another document that the secretary may prepare in connection with corporate meetings is a formal certificate that authenticates either a resolution made at a meeting or the minutes themselves. See Chapter 17 for a discussion of the secretary's role in taking minutes at a corporate meeting.

# 12.6

## AFFIDAVITS, POWERS OF ATTORNEY, AND PROMISSORY NOTES

There are a number of relatively brief client documents that the secretary may be expected to prepare—sometimes on printed forms, sometimes on legal cap. The preparation of affidavits is a typical secretarial responsibility. Powers of attorney and promissory notes are examples of other types of short, typewritten client documents.

### AFFIDAVITS

An affidavit is a written statement of fact designed to help prove that fact. It must be sworn to in the presence of a notary public or a bonded public officer qualified to administer such oaths. The officer verifies only the validity of the signature, not the contents of the statement. The person who makes the affidavit is called the "affiant" or "deponent." Affidavits and acknowledgments are sometimes confused by inexperienced secretaries. An affidavit is a sworn statement that asserts the truth or validity of the statements contained in it; it is signed by the deponent as well as by the person giving the oath. An acknowledgment, on the other hand, verifies only the signature on a document and is signed by a notary public. An acknowledgment is an appendage to another document; an affidavit is a separate legal instrument.

## A Typewritten Waiver of Notice of Meeting

WAIVER OF NOTICE OF MEETING OF BOARD
OF DIRECTORS

        THE UNDERSIGNED, each being a Director of ABC
REALTY CO., INC., waive all notice required by the Corporation's
by-laws and laws of the State of New Jersey, of the time and
place of a meeting of the Board, and fix September 22, 19--,
as the date, 9:30 a.m. as the time, and 235 Vanderbilt Street,
Hackensack, New Jersey, as the place of such meeting.

Dated:

                                    _____
                                            JANICE TEISCH

                                    _____
                                            MORTON TEISCH

                                    _____
                                            LYNNE SULLIVAN

                                    _____
                                            GARY SULLIVAN

## A Typewritten Proxy

PROXY

    THE UNDERSIGNED, holder of twenty-five (25) shares
of stock of ABC REALTY CO., INC., a New Jersey Corporation,
hereby appoints GARY SULLIVAN, with the power of substitution,
to vote for and on behalf of the undersigned at a meeting of
shareholders to be held at 9:00 a.m. on the 3rd day of May,
19--, and at any adjournment thereof, for the following purpose:
The transaction of such business as may properly come before
the meeting.

Dated:  _____
                                 LYNNE SULLIVAN

## Certificate Authenticating a Resolution or Minutes

I HEREBY CERTIFY that I am the duly elected and qualified
Secretary of ACE CORPORATION, an Ohio corporation, with
offices in the City of Cleveland, Ohio, and the keeper of the
records and corporate seal of said corporation; that the
following is a true and correct copy of a Resolution (or
Minutes) duly adopted at a meeting of the Board of Directors
thereof, held in accordance with its bylaws, at its offices
at Cleveland, Ohio, on the 15th day of September, 19--, and
that the same are now in full force:

(Here insert a copy of the Resolution or Minutes or a note
that it is attached.)

I HEREBY FURTHER CERTIFY that on the 15th day of September,
19--, JOHN CARTER was President of said Corporation and GILBERT
SMITH was Secretary of said Corporation and that they continue
to hold said offices at the present time.

IN WITNESS WHEREOF, I have hereunto affixed my name as Secretary
and have caused the corporate seal of said corporation to be
hereto affixed this 16th day of September, 19--.

    (corporate seal)      _____
                                               Secretary

Affidavits are as varied as the situations that can arise, and they encompass both court and noncourt situations. Affidavits may be prepared to verify that something was mailed, to affirm citizenship, to assert a person's age, and to support motions, to name only a few situations. This section explains how to set up an affidavit in a form acceptable in most jurisdictions. You should always check with the attorney, however, to determine the details of the form used in your office.

**Heading**   The title AFFIDAVIT may head the document, or a more specific heading may be desired. If the affidavit is being used in litigation, the name of the case may appear as a subheading.

AFFIDAVIT    AFFIDAVIT OF MAILING    AFFIDAVIT OF RESIDENCY

**Venue**   The venue, which is typed four spaces down from the heading, denotes the state and county in which the affidavit will be executed. The venue starts at the left margin, is double-spaced, and is usually bracketed with a row of closing parentheses. A venue is illustrated on the opposite page.

**Opening statement**   Three spaces down from the venue, the deponent is named and said to have made an oath. The deponent's name is typed in all-capital letters:

I, ROBERT O'MALLEY, being duly sworn, according to law, depose and say:

The example above is written in the first person. Affidavits may also be written in the third person ("ROBERT O'MALLEY, being duly sworn, deposes and says:").

**The oath**   The body of the affidavit is an enumeration of facts. If more than one fact is included, they are listed in numbered paragraphs. Arabic numerals are sufficient for this purpose.

**Signature line**   Whether the affidavit is written in the first person or the third person, the deponent must execute the document in the presence of a notary public. The signature line and the deponent's name are typed according to the instructions in section 12.2 of this chapter.

**Jurat**   The jurat is a certification at the conclusion of the affidavit that indicates when, before whom, and where the affidavit is to be notarized. The jurat is usually single-spaced on the left side of the page, three spaces below the deponent's signature. It should not extend more than halfway across the page. One common form of the jurat is shown below.

Sworn and subscribed to before
me this          day of May, 19--

_____
          Notary Public

It is wise not to type the date of the jurat until immediately after the deponent has signed the affidavit. Willfully falsifying an affidavit in any way is an act of perjury.

## POWERS OF ATTORNEY

A power of attorney is a written legal document in which the principal (a person, partnership, or corporation) appoints an agent (a person, partnership, or corporation) and gives that agent the authority and power to act in his, her, or its behalf.

Most legal rights or powers that a person possesses may be transferred to another. Authority may be given to borrow money, collect debts, prosecute a lawsuit, or manage, sell, or lease real estate. Acts of a personal nature, however, such as the making of a will or the taking of an oath, may not be performed by an agent. When one person empowers another to represent him or her at a corporate stockholders' meeting, this authority is commonly known as a proxy, or authority for a limited purpose. Authority may be granted for a limited purpose, a limited period of time, an unlimited purpose, or an unlimited period of time.

**Format**    Law blanks for powers of attorney are available; however, some legal offices prefer the document to be completely typewritten. In the latter case, the styling referred to in section 12.2 would apply. The title (POWER OF ATTORNEY) is centered at least ten spaces down from the top, all-capitalized, and underlined. The initial paragraph traditionally begins with the following phrase:

KNOW ALL MEN BY THESE PRESENTS:

A signature line is prepared for the principal only. Since the power of attorney is a one-party client document, the agent does not need to sign it. Typewritten powers of attorney are placed in legal backs. The agent or attorney-in-fact receives the original. One conformed copy is given to the principal and one is kept in the office files. The file copy should contain a note as to the location of the original.

If the powers granted concern the conveyance of real estate, the formalities associated with the writing of a deed may apply: that is, the power of attorney may have to be witnessed, acknowledged, and recorded. Otherwise, the document may not require witnessing and acknowledgment.

**Using a power of attorney**    If an agent executes a legal instrument on behalf of the principal, the acknowledgment on that document may read as follows:

```
STATE OF NEW YORK )
                        ss.:
COUNTY OF ROCKLAND)


        On this second day of March, 19--, before me personally

appeared ERIC LAURENCE, known to me to be the person whose name

is subscribed as the attorney in fact for MARC ALLEN, and

acknowledged that he executed the same as the act of his principal

for the purposes contained therein.

        IN WITNESS WHEREOF, I have hereunto set my hand and

official seal on the day and in the year first above written.



        (seal)              _____
                            Notary Public
                            My Commission expires      19--.
```

## PROMISSORY NOTES

A promissory note is a written commitment to pay a specified sum at a specified time, or on demand, to a specified person or that person's agent. One example is a bond. A bond is a commitment by a government agency or corporation to pay a certain sum of money to a certain party on a certain day—the maturity date. Promissory notes are not rigid in format, but they must contain the following information:

current date
date of payment
names of parties involved
sum of money involved
rate of interest, if any
place of payment, if any

The parties may choose to have the note notarized or witnessed.

### A Typewritten Promissory Note

April 20, 19--

On demand, I, MARVIN L. SEARS, promise to pay to ELSIE HERSCH the sum of FIVE THOUSAND and 00/100 DOLLARS ($5,000.00), with interest thereon at the rate of twelve percent (12%) per annum.

Should default be made in the payment of said principal and interest when due, and a lawsuit be commenced, I agree to pay such additional sums as the court may adjudge reasonable.

_____
MARVIN L. SEARS

# 12.7

# WILLS AND CODICILS

A last will and testament, more commonly known as a will, is a one-party document in which the testator (the maker of the will) arranges for the disposition of property owned at the time of his or her death. Typing a will in its final form is a challenge to the legal secretary not only because the client expects an attractive document but also because of the demands of absolute accuracy. A will must be able to meet the challenges of probate.

A will is usually thought of as a formal legal document, one which has been properly typewritten and properly executed and witnessed. There are, however, two additional categories of wills: a holographic will—completely handwritten by the testator—and a nuncupative will—an oral will which the testator declares before witnesses just before his death and which is later committed to writing. A nuncupative will is difficult to prove in a court of law. The laws differ in the various states regarding the validity of holographic and nuncupative wills.

Wills, like other legal instruments, use a number of specialized terms. When these are unfamiliar, the secretary should look them up in a law dictionary. Certain nouns used in wills, codicils, and probate documents have masculine and feminine forms: the maker of a will is known as a *testator* if male, *testatrix* if female. Similarly, the person named by the testator/testatrix to carry out the provisions of the will is called either the *executor* or the *executrix*. The person appointed by the court via letters of administration to administer the estate of the deceased person may be an *administrator* or an *administratrix*.

## FORMAT

Although printed forms are occasionally used for simple wills, most wills are fully typewritten, and extra pains are taken to make the document attractive. A will should be typed according to the rules described in section 12.2. It should be prepared on either plain white paper or legal cap, depending on the preference of the office. The paper should be of the highest quality. Legal-size (8½ by 13 inches) paper is normally used.

A minimum of three copies is required: an original and two carbon copies. The original should be stored in a secure place. (Many testators prefer to have the attorney store the will in a safe-deposit box designated for that purpose.) One conformed copy will be given to the testator, and one conformed copy will be kept as an office file copy. If the testator desires, additional copies may be made for each heir. Upon the testator's death the courts may require several copies for probate proceedings, but these copies are generally made at that time.

At one time no erasures were permitted in a will; however, with the newer erasable paper, this prohibition is not always strictly adhered to, provided the erasure is not in a critical word such as a name or an amount of money. You should follow the attorney's preference regarding erasures.

In order to prevent the insertion or removal of pages at a later date, many attorneys do not allow a paragraph to start a page. In such cases, a portion of the preceding paragraph may be carried to the next page by placing a Z-mark near the bottom of the page to fill the vacant space.

However, since a Z-mark detracts from the appearance of the page, you may wish instead to adjust the spacing of the will according to the suggestions on page 392. Paragraphs are numbered consecutively with the use of one of the following styles of headings: FIRST:, ARTICLE I:, ITEM I:, or I.

The original and one carbon copy are affixed to a legal backing. White or a pastel color is considered appropriate to back a will. After the will has been executed, it is placed in a specially marked envelope and stored for safekeeping.

## PARTS OF A WILL

The title of a will should be single-spaced, centered, all-capitalized, underlined, and set in a style similar to the following:

THE LAST WILL AND TESTAMENT OF

MAX LORENZ

LAST WILL AND TESTAMENT
OF
MAX LORENZ

A list of standard will clauses appears below:

1. **Introductory clause**   This clause is not numbered. It names the testator, gives his address, and revokes all prior wills and codicils.
2. **Debt clause**   This is usually the first of the numbered paragraphs. It directs the executor to pay all the just debts and funeral expenses as soon as possible after the death occurs.
3. **Distribution clause**   This set of paragraphs expresses the testator's intentions for the distribution of his personal and real property.
4. **Trust clause**   This clause designates property to be held in trust of an individual or institution for a specific purpose.
5. **Guardianship clause**   If the testator is responsible for minor children, this clause names a competent adult who would assume responsibility for the minors.
6. **Residuary clause**   This clause disposes of all property for which specific disposition has not been made.
7. **One-dollar clause**   This clause is inserted in certain wills where the testator feels that someone who has been omitted may contest the will. The testator gives a named person an insignificant amount to indicate that the person was not overlooked.
8. **Testimonium clause**   This clause is not numbered. It is the concluding clause in which the date and signature appear, and it usually begins with the all-capitalized phrase IN WITNESS WHEREOF, . . . .
9. **Attestation clause**   This clause verifies that the witnesses viewed the execution of the will in the presence of the testator and each other. It starts approximately six lines below the signature of the testator. If space is at a premium, it may be single-spaced. It may also be typed only on the left side of the page. At least the first line of the attestation clause should appear on the page containing the testator's signature. All witnesses' signatures must appear on the same page, and their addresses should be included so that they may be located if necessary when the will is probated.

It is imperative that the will be typed neatly and accurately. It should be very carefully proofread and all names, addresses, and amounts double-checked.

Once the will has been typed and properly backed, an appointment should be made for its execution. The appropriate number of witnesses (some states require two, others three) must be present, and all parties should execute the will using the same pen. In many instances both the attorney and the secretary will serve as witnesses. A witness must be 21 years of age and not mentioned in the will. The testator and the witnesses must remain together until the will has been witnessed by all concerned. It is the responsibility of the legal secretary to conform all copies of the will to the original.

## CODICIL

Once a will has been executed, it may be revoked or amended at any time. If the amendment is minor, a codicil may be prepared as an alternative to rewriting the will. The same care should be taken for the preparation of the codicil as was taken for the preparation of the will. The format and terminology are the same for the codicil as for the will.

Specific reference should be made to the original will that is being modified. In the codicil illustrated on pages 428–429, for example, the date of the original will is mentioned in the introductory clause. Also, the paragraphs of the will that are revoked are referred to specifically by number, and the numbers are styled exactly as they appeared in the original will: "We revoke Items III and IV of our said last Will . . . ." The testator should ratify and confirm the unchanged parts of the will, and the codicil should be executed in the same manner as the will.

## A Sample Will

LAST WILL AND TESTAMENT

OF

MAX LORENZ

I, MAX LORENZ, residing at 2 Maxwell Court, San
Francisco, California, being of sound and disposing mind and
memory and intending to dispose of all my property by this Will,
do make, publish and declare the following as and for my Last
Will and Testament, hereby revoking any and all other wills or
codicils by me heretofore made.

ITEM I: I direct my Executrix to pay all of my
funeral expenses, all enforceable debts, and all succession,
legacy, inheritance, death, transfer, or estate taxes, including
any interest and penalties thereon imposed by any law, upon
property passing under this Will or otherwise, testamentary or
non-testamentary, out of my residuary estate, as an expense of
administration without any apportionment thereof or reimbursement
from any beneficiary.

ITEM II: All the rest, residue and remainder of the
property, real and personal, of every kind and description,
wheresoever situate, which I may own or have the right to dispose
of at the time of my decease, I give, devise and bequeath to my
wife, ETHEL LORENZ, absolutely and in fee simple.

ITEM III: In the event that my wife, ETHEL LORENZ,
shall not survive me, or is considered under the law as not

-1-

having survived me, then all the interest in and share of my
estate hereinbefore devised and bequeathed to my said wife, shall,
by way of substitution, pass to and vest in my children, HARRY
LORENZ and MARILYN LORENZ, and any other children who may
survive me, equally share and share alike.

ITEM IV:  In the event that any of my children shall
have predeceased me leaving issue surviving them, then such

issue shall collectively take the share which their deceased
parent would have taken if living.

In the event that any of my children shall predecease
me without leaving issue surviving them, then I direct that their
share shall pass in equal shares to the survivors or to any one
lone survivor.

ITEM V:  The provisions made in this Will, unless
otherwise specifically provided, are intended to and shall
include and relate to all children of mine, whether natural born
or adopted, and shall include any now living or hereafter born
either before or after my decease.

ITEM VI:  I make, nominate and appoint my wife, ETHEL
LORENZ, to be the Executrix of this, my Last Will and Testament,
hereby authorizing and empowering my said Executrix to compound,
compromise, settle and adjust all claims and demands in favor
of or against my estate; to make distribution in cash or in kind;
and to sell, at private or public sale, at such prices, and upon
such terms of credit or otherwise, as she may deem best, the
whole or any part of my real or personal property, and to
execute, acknowledge and deliver deeds or other proper
instruments of conveyances thereof to the purchaser or purchasers.
No purchaser from my Executrix need see to the application of
the purchase money order to or for the purpose of the trust, but

the receipt of my Executrix shall be a complete discharge
therefor.  I request that no bond be required of my Executrix.

      IN WITNESS WHEREOF, I have hereunto set my hand and
seal on this     day of          19XX.

                                                  _____ L.S.
                                                        MAX LORENZ

      On the above written date, the said MAX LORENZ
declared to us, the undersigned, that the foregoing instrument
is his Last Will and Testament, and he requested us to act as
witnesses to the same and to his signature thereon, and he
thereupon signed said Will in our presence, we being present
at the same time, and we at his request and in his presence, and
in the presence of each other, do hereunto subscribe our names
as witnesses, and we, each of us, declare that we believe this
Testator to be of sound mind and memory.

_____residing at_____

                                       _____

_____residing at_____

                                       _____

_____residing at_____

                                       _____

## A Sample Codicil

CODICIL TO LAST WILL AND TESTAMENT

OF

BENJAMIN SWARTZ and RAYE SWARTZ

WE, BENJAMIN SWARTZ and RAYE SWARTZ, residing at 14 Wharf Street, Columbus, Ohio, being of sound mind and disposing memory and not under any restraint, having made our Last Will and Testament on the 9th day of April, 19--, do now make, publish and declare this as and for a Codicil to our said Last Will and Testament as follows:

We revoke Items III and IV of our said Last Will and Testament and substitute therefor the following Items III and IV as if originally written in our said Last Will and Testament, as follows:

ITEM III: All the rest, residue and remainder of our property, both real and personal, of every kind and description, wheresoever situate, which we may own or have the right to dispose of at the time of our decease, we give, devise and bequeath to our nephews MARC ALLEN and ERIC LAURENCE, or the survivor, equally share and share alike.

ITEM IV: In the event that neither of our nephews shall survive us, then we direct that our estate shall pass as set forth in Item IV of our Last Will and Testament dated the 9th day of April, 19--.

Page 1 of 2

        In all other respects we hereby ratify and confirm our said Last Will and Testament.

        IN WITNESS WHEREOF, we have hereunto set our hands and seals on this     day of        19—.

_____ L.S.
BENJAMIN SWARTZ

_____ L.S.
RAYE SWARTZ

        Signed, sealed, published and declared by the Testators, BENJAMIN SWARTZ and RAYE SWARTZ, as and for a Codicil to their Last Will and Testament, in our presence, who, at their request, and in their presence, and in the presence of each other, have hereunto subscribed our names as witnesses at the time and place aforesaid.

_____residing at _____

_____residing at _____

_____residing at _____

_____

Page 2 of 2

# 13

CHAPTER THIRTEEN

# PREPARING AND TYPEWRITING COURT DOCUMENTS

## CONTENTS

# 13.1

## AN OVERVIEW OF COURT PROCEDURES

Legal secretaries prepare a great variety of legal papers. These documents may be divided into two categories: (1) papers for the use of the parties who sign them, such as wills, deeds, and contracts, which are referred to as client documents or legal instruments, and (2) papers for the use of the court, such as complaints, petitions, motions, orders, and judgments, which are referred to as court documents. Client documents are the topic of Chapter 12. Court documents are discussed in this chapter.

### STANDARDIZATION OF LEGAL PROCEDURES

Legal procedures vary from state to state and from court to court. This lack of uniformity has led legislatures and bar associations to try to reduce the number of disparities among various jurisdictions by standardizing court procedures, legal terminology, and legal forms. Standardizing legal procedures is of great value to the courts and the legal profession in the efficient administration of justice. A major objective of standardization is to enable attorneys to prepare documents that will be technically correct and clearly understood with no possibility of misinterpretation. Standardization will also improve the efficient handling of cases in court.

In an effort to simplify common law pleading, Congress in 1938 adopted a set of rules known as the *Federal Rules of Civil Procedure*. These rules set out each step in a civil proceeding, including the method of preparing required documents in all federal courts. Since then, the majority of the states have adopted similar rules. Consequently, the rules of procedure in the state courts are to a certain extent now uniform. New York and California are among the larger states that have not adopted the Federal Rules of Civil Procedure.

At another level, many legal secretaries' associations, often with the full support of judges and attorneys, have sponsored studies designed to standardize the wording and format of legal papers. In some states a handbook for legal secretaries is published that incorporates the rules and forms used by the courts in that state. A list of titles may be found in the Appendix to this handbook.

Many law firms have developed law office style manuals designed to guide lawyers in standardizing the form, content, arrangement, and style of the documents produced by the firm. Law firms that wish to embark on such a project may be interested in obtaining the publication *Create-A-System for the Law Office Style Manual,* prepared by Leo Eisenstatt and issued by the Section of Economics of Law Practice of the American Bar Association.

## TYPES OF COURT ACTION

The courts have responsibility in three general areas—criminal, civil, and equity law. In most jurisdictions, the same courts try cases in all three areas. In a few jurisdictions, however—such as Tennessee, Mississippi, and Arkansas—special courts known as chancery courts hear equity cases, and some states—Texas and Oklahoma, for instance—have separate courts for civil and criminal cases. Under the Federal Rules of Civil Procedure, there is no longer a distinction between law and equity in the preparation of pleadings in civil law cases.

**Criminal actions**  An individual or a group breaking a law designed to protect society from harm has committed a crime. Because the public has suffered as a result of the crime, the people of the state or of the United States bring the action; they are represented in court by a public official who may be known as a *district attorney,* a *public prosecutor,* or a *United States attorney.* The jurisdiction of each court determines the types of crimes that are to be prosecuted there. Generally, courts of limited jurisdiction hear lesser crimes, or misdemeanors, while courts of general jurisdiction try the more serious crimes, or felonies.

**Civil actions**  A civil case may arise when the actions of an individual or a group cause harm to another, who then goes to court seeking compensation for that harm. The injured party, called the *plaintiff* or *complainant,* asks the court to grant damages in the form of a payment of money. In some jurisdictions, if either party in the case requests it, a jury may hear the trial. If neither party requests a jury, the judge renders judgment after hearing both sides. In civil actions the party who brings the action must present a *preponderance of evidence* or the action will fail.

**Equity actions**  In most jurisdictions equity actions are encompassed within civil actions, although a few states provide separate courts of equity. In equity cases the party who brings suit is called the *petitioner* or *complainant.* The petitioner asks the Court to order the opposing party, usually known as the *respondent,* to perform or to cease from performing a specific act. Equity will be sought when relief is not available to the petitioner through money damages. No jury can be requested in equity matters; the judge alone makes the decision. Technically, the decision of the judge in a case in equity is a *decree* instead of a judgment; in practice, however, the words are commonly interchanged.

## STEPS IN CRIMINAL PROCEDURE

**Arrest**  An individual may file an informal complaint with a law enforcement officer, after which a judge signs a warrant, which is written authority for a law enforcement officer to make an arrest. The officer may also make an arrest without a warrant if there is probable cause to do so.

**Bail**    Bail is a deposit of money that helps to guarantee that an accused person will appear for trial at the time and date specified. When the accused has been taken into custody, the Court may set bail and release the accused person. If he or she does not appear, bail is forfeited. If the accused can reasonably be expected to appear when ordered, the Court may release the accused on his or her own recognizance (that is, without bail), depending on local rules and the seriousness of the crime.

**Preliminary hearing**    A preliminary hearing is held to determine whether there is probable cause for holding the accused for trial. A preliminary hearing may also be held to fix bail.

**Arraignment**    The next step in a criminal procedure is an arraignment. Arraigning an accused person has three purposes: (1) to establish the identity of the accused, (2) to inform the accused of the charges, and (3) to allow the Court to hear the *plea* of the accused—that is, the answer to the charge, or a declaration of guilt or innocence.

**Trial**    If the trial is to be held before a jury, it is selected and sworn. A trial jury typically consists of 12 citizens who listen to the facts and present their decision, the verdict. In criminal actions a unanimous vote of the jurors is usually necessary. In a jury trial the judge rules on points of law, and the jury decides questions of fact.

After the jury has been sworn in, the trial usually follows this sequence: (1) opening statement by the prosecutor, (2) opening statement by the defendant's lawyer (this may be delayed, however, until the beginning of step 4), (3) presentation of evidence by the prosecutor, (4) presentation of evidence by the defendant's lawyer, (5) closing argument by the prosecutor, (6) closing argument by the defendant's lawyer, and (7) the judge's *charge* to the jury.

The judge charges the jury, instructing them regarding the law that relates to the case, and provides guidance in reaching a verdict. The judge prepares the instructions, but prior to the trial each attorney prepares and submits to the judge a set of requested jury instructions. In this way, each attorney can make sure that the judge does not overlook any point that the attorney considers important.

**Verdict**    The jury retires to a private room and considers the case. A vote of the jury is taken to arrive at a decision. If the defendant is found guilty, the Court has the authority to impose sentence, although in some jurisdictions the jury will determine the sentence. The sentence is based on specific findings of fact and conclusions of law. The verdict is signed by the judge and recorded so that it may be included in the transcript of the case. If the accused is found guilty, the case may be appealed. An *appeal* is a proceeding by which the decision of a lower court is reviewed by a higher court.

## STEPS IN CIVIL PROCEDURE
Civil procedure consists of four fairly well-defined phases: (1) pleadings, (2) discovery, (3) trial and judgment, and (4) conclusion of litigation.

**Phase 1: Pleadings**    The general term *pleadings* refers to the series of written claims and defenses that form the first phase of a lawsuit. During this phase the attorneys prepare and file various documents to initiate the action and narrow the issues. Section 13.3, Pleading Procedure, discusses the secretary's role in the preparation of pleadings. In this section pleadings are briefly described as steps in a civil proceeding.

**Complaint**    As the first step in a civil lawsuit, the plaintiff's attorney files a *complaint,* which may also be known as a *petition* or a *declaration,* against the defendant.

Where courts of equity exist, the first pleading in an equity action is called a *bill of complaint* or a *bill in equity*. The complaint states the specific kind and amount of damages suffered by the plaintiff and the acts of the defendant alleged to have caused those damages.

**Summons**    The defendant must be given positive notice that a complaint has been filed and that a response to the complaint must be made. This notice is called a *summons*, and in most states it must be served with a copy of the complaint. Once the action has been initiated by filing and serving the complaint and summons, it cannot be terminated unless specified legal steps are taken.

**Appearance**    Taking the correct legal steps to respond to a complaint or summons within the specified time limit is known as making an *appearance*.

**Objections**    Rules of court procedure require that a complaint be clear, definite, and complete and that it be prepared in accordance with the law and the rules of the court. When the defense believes that the complaint is not in accordance with court rules or the law, the attorney may object to it by means of various documents such as a *demurrer*, a *motion to strike*, a *motion to quash*, or a *motion to make complaint more definite and certain*. These documents, and others, attempt to invalidate the complaint on the grounds that it is not legally supported. As these documents are based on points of law, most courts require a supporting document to be prepared and attached. This document may be a brief, a legal memorandum, or a memorandum of points and authorities.

**Answer**    The next step in a civil action is the preparation of an *answer*, in which the defendant responds to the allegations in the complaint. Court rules in many jurisdictions permit the answer to contain a *counterclaim* against the plaintiff. This counterclaim arises out of the subject of the complaint; it is not merely an answer to the charge but a separate charge against the plaintiff. Though it could be the subject of a separate lawsuit, it is often more conveniently included in the answer.

**Cross-complaint or Cross-claim**    If the defendant believes that another party is responsible, the attorney will respond to the complaint with an *answer and cross-claim* or *cross-complaint*. The cross-claim or cross-complaint may be filed and served as a document separate from the answer, or it may be combined with the answer into one document.

**Phase 2: Discovery**    When the initial pleading stage of litigation is concluded, the attorneys will attempt to locate all witnesses and uncover all evidence while learning as much as possible about the issues. This process is known as discovery.

Numerous discovery devices are available, and the attorney must decide which devices to use and when. The legal secretary will be primarily involved in arranging for depositions of parties and witnesses and for preparing necessary notices, motions, written interrogatories, and other documents that may be specifically related to discovery. Some of these discovery devices are discussed below.

**Interrogatories**    Information may be obtained by means of a written set of questions in a court document, usually entitled *interrogatories*, that require written answers. Testimony may also be taken by asking witnesses oral questions. This discovery activity is known as taking a *deposition* or using *oral interrogatories*. The manner in which the questioning can be conducted is precisely determined by the rules governing procedure in civil cases.

**Subpoena**    When witnesses will be required to give testimony in court, they must receive official notice that they are to appear. This notice is called a *subpoena*. Some states require that witnesses who are to give depositions be subpoenaed. If an attorney knows that a witness may refer to certain documents or other evidence in the testimony—either in court or in a deposition—or if the attorney wants certain items admitted as evidence, a document called a *subpoena duces tecum* ("under penalty you shall bring with you") is required. This document tells a person to appear at a specified time and place with those particular exhibits (documents, photographs, or other items) related to the suit.

**Other discovery devices**    The attorney may petition the Court for the right to inspect evidence or documents and also for the right to order a physical or mental examination of a party.

**Pretrial conference**    After all preliminary work has been completed and the case has been set for trial, the attorneys of record may meet informally with the judge to discuss the issues involved in the lawsuit. These conferences are not required in all states. At a pretrial conference the attorneys discuss the issues, the allegations, and the facts involved in the case. As the issues are discussed, information is exchanged; and sometimes evidence is produced that results in a request to dismiss the litigation without trial. Sometimes certain aspects of the case can be settled by *stipulation,* or agreement, between the attorneys with the approval of the judge. Because trials are expensive in terms of time, emotion, and money, both parties may reevaluate the situation and decide to settle out of court.

**Conclusion of litigation without trial**    Many lawsuits never go to court. Sometimes the reason is personal, having to do with the attitude of the parties. On the other hand, a high percentage of lawsuits are terminated before trial for legal reasons. Sometimes evidence is uncovered that is so significant that a judge may decide a trial is not required. Sometimes one of the parties or the attorney deliberately does not respond within the time specified. At other times the parties mutually agree to terminate the suit. Whatever the reason for concluding a case without trial, the attorneys of record must prepare, file, and serve certain documents in order to bring the case to a conclusion.

**Summary judgment**    The defendant's attorney may uncover positive evidence that proves the allegations in the complaint to be unfounded. Instead of or in addition to filing an answer, the attorney may file a document requesting a summary judgment for the defendant. The document filed requires a supporting document that sets forth precisely the evidence refuting the allegation in the complaint. After reviewing these documents, the judge decides either for or against the motion.

**Discontinuance**    For a variety of reasons, a lawsuit may be discontinued. To obtain a discontinuance, the lawyer must file and serve appropriate documents that set forth the reason for stopping the action. Discontinuance may be voluntary or involuntary. When the parties agree to settle out of court, *voluntary abatement* occurs. If the plaintiff fails to meet certain legal requirements, the law requires that an action be discontinued. In this case, the Court mandates the discontinuance, which is sometimes referred to as *involuntary dismissal.*

**Statute of limitations and dismissal**    The statute of limitations in each state precisely prescribes the time allowed a potential party to commence a lawsuit. If a party fails to meet these statutory deadlines, the lawsuit must be terminated.

**Motion to dismiss for failure to prosecute**    After a complaint has been issued, if a plaintiff's attorney fails to cause a date to be set for an action to come for trial, the defendant's attorney may file a motion to dismiss the action for failure to prosecute. This motion is accompanied by a supporting document that states significant dates and claims that the plaintiff did not take the steps necessary to bring the matter to court for trial.

**Dismissal with and without prejudice**    Dismissal may be filed with prejudice or without prejudice. The plaintiff may file for dismissal without prejudice at any time before the commencement of the trial. In this case, the plaintiff has the option of filing suit against the same defendant on the same matter at a later date. However, if the action is terminated *after* the trial has begun, it is by dismissal with prejudice, which prevents the plaintiff from filing at a later date on the same matter.

**Release**   When a case is dismissed as the result of a settlement out of court, the party who is to make restitution usually will not do so unless given a properly executed agreement most often called *release* or *release of all claims*. In this document, the person who receives the settlement agrees never again to bring suit for additional costs on the matter in dispute.

**Phase 3: Trial and judgment**   If a case cannot be settled by mutual agreement and if there are no grounds for dismissal or default, the case must go to trial for a decision on the merits. Rules have been developed which carefully prescribe the procedures to be followed for setting the matter for trial, conducting the trial, and entering the judgment of the Court.

**Trial**   When either attorney feels that the case is ready for trial, the clerk of the court is notified through the filing of a *note of issue, a memorandum setting for trial,* or a *notice of trial*. The calendar clerk places the trial on the calendar, meaning that it is added to the list of cases that are going to be tried. The clerk notifies the parties to the action when and where the trial will be held. For the customary sequence of a trial, refer to the preceding section on steps in a criminal proceeding. In civil cases the plaintiff's attorney rather than a prosecutor argues the case, and in most jurisdictions the plaintiff's attorney is permitted a rebuttal immediately following the defense lawyer's final argument.

**Judgment**   When there is no jury, the judge hears the case, applies the law, and issues a judgment in favor of one party or the other based on the facts and the merits of the case. When a case is heard before a jury, the jury decides in favor of one of the parties on the basis of the facts presented and sets the amount of damages. In civil cases the judgment or decree is issued in favor of the party judged to have the preponderance of evidence. The party in whose favor judgment is made is the *prevailing party*.

**Phase 4: Conclusion of litigation**   After the Court hands down a judgment, the losing party has several options: (1) to perform satisfaction, thereby taking the final step in litigation; (2) to fail to perform satisfaction, in which case the prevailing party may have to take measures to obtain what is owed; or (3) to appeal the case to a higher court. If the losing party chooses to appeal, no payment is made to the prevailing party. The attorney for the losing party must make the appeal within the time limit prescribed by law or lose the right to appeal.

**Satisfaction**   The judgment is a court order requiring the losing party to provide satisfaction in some manner to the prevailing party. Satisfaction may take several forms: the losing party may be required to pay court costs and monetary damages to the prevailing party, to perform a specified action requested by the other party, or to stop a certain action to which the other party objects. Once satisfaction has been made, the Court must be given a document indicating that the judgment has been satisfactorily carried out.

In settling court costs the prevailing party must submit for the Court's approval a statement of all recoverable expenses incurred in the course of litigation. The appropriate motion is filed and served on opposing counsel. The opposing party may object to the costs indicated and file a motion to that effect. The Court will rule on both motions. If the Court allows all costs, the order signed by the judge is filed, and conformed copies are served on opposing counsel.

When the prevailing party has been paid all money owed, both damages and costs, the prevailing attorney files a document stating the amount of money received and declaring that full satisfaction of claims has been made. It also shows that judgment was entered into the official records. The document must be signed by the prevailing party, filed, and served on opposing counsel.

**Writ of execution**    If the required satisfaction is not performed, the prevailing party may petition the Court for a writ of execution. A *writ* is a form of court order, and a writ of execution is a court order that commands the losing party to perform as adjudged.

**Writ of attachment**    If the losing party still fails to pay damages as ordered by the Court in a writ of execution, it may become necessary to obtain a writ of attachment to attach wages, personal property, or real property to obtain the money to settle the judgment.

# 13.2

## GUIDELINES FOR THE PREPARATION OF COURT DOCUMENTS

### COURT SPECIFICATIONS
The rules of each court specify with great precision how documents are to be prepared: the size and kind of paper to be used, the size of type, the styling of the heading or caption, and other details of format. One general reference book cannot prescribe for legal secretaries throughout the country the correct format for documents in all courts. Rules vary from court to court, city to city, county to county, and state to state. Also, the rules of state courts differ from those of the federal courts.

As a result of these differences in requirements, every law office must obtain from the clerk of each court before which the attorney practices the publications setting forth the rules of that court. When preparing court documents, the legal secretary must follow meticulously the rules of the court with which papers are to be filed.

The attorney and legal secretary must also be aware of changes in legal specifications and in court requirements as they occur from time to time. As such changes are published, either officially or commercially, the secretary must file the information for use when needed. Regular contact with the office of the clerk of the court will help to ensure that all new information has been received. Legal secretaries' organizations keep up-to-date in all these matters and frequently are instrumental in preparing summaries or consolidations of changes that have occurred during a certain period. State legal secretarial manuals are usually revised annually to bring the requirements up-to-date.

**Law blanks**    Printed forms, known as law blanks or legal blanks, are available for many court documents. All the standardized portions of the document are printed so that the secretary needs only to fill in blanks with the information pertinent to the particular case. Some jurisdictions require the use of law blanks when they are available; others make it optional. Some jurisdictions provide law blanks for nearly every court document required. Obviously, using law blanks requires less typing for the secretary and contributes greatly to standardization. The use of these printed forms is discussed in Chapter 11.

**Statutes of limitations**    The law is specific about the time within which a party must act in any given legal situation. In order to minimize problems regarding time limitations, you should always prepare court documents as soon as possible after you have the information needed to prepare them. Often both attorney and secretary are involved with many different legal cases simultaneously. The office docket calendar is used to keep the attorney as well as the secretary informed of the dates that documents must be filed. If you are responsible for docket control in your office, you must keep the calendar completely up-to-date and determine the priority for each separate part of the work that must be done.

**Making copies of court documents**   Most court documents require a minimum of three copies: (1) the original to be filed with the court, (2) a copy to be delivered to counsel for each opposing party, and (3) an office file copy.

In many instances additional copies are necessary. For example, the court may require the original *and* one copy, sometimes copies are required for both plaintiff and defendant as well as their attorneys, and occasionally a copy must be supplied to every individual or organization mentioned in the document. Even when copies for clients are not required, it is good practice to send clients a copy of every document produced on their behalf. In addition, many secretaries like to keep a copy of each document in a personal file for future reference. If it is the first time you have typed a particular document, you will definitely need an extra copy for your own form file. It is important to determine the maximum number of copies that will be required before beginning to type.

Some offices require that all copies be carbon copies. However, since photocopy machines are now available that reproduce documents with nearly the same quality as the original, many courts now accept photocopies for their files. And even if the court requires the original ribbon copy for filing, the copies for clients, opposing counsel, and office files may usually be made on the photocopier. Additionally, with the availability of modern word-processing equipment, it is possible to produce more than one "original" once the document has been originally typed and recorded on a storage medium. In these cases, you should type COPY across the top of all duplicates that are not treated as an original.

**Paper**   Court documents are usually typed on paper specified by the court. Legal cap—also referred to as *pleading paper* or *legal-ruled paper*—is most commonly used. This paper may have ruled margins and numbered lines or it may have only numbered lines or only ruled margins. The facsimiles that illustrate this chapter are typed on legal cap that is both ruled and numbered. Some jurisdictions permit documents to be completely typed on plain bond paper. Many courts require legal cap measuring 8½ by 13 or 14 inches for all completely typed court documents. However, the current trend is toward using 8½ by 11-inch paper for both printed law blanks and legal cap. At least three factors contribute to this trend: (1) the use of standard-size filing equipment and a standardized frame size for microfilming, (2) the use of word-processing and photocopy equipment built to handle standard-size paper, and (3) the tendency for legal blanks to be printed on 8½ by 11-inch paper. In each factor mentioned, probably economy is the major consideration, though ease of handling and storage is undoubtedly a close second.

**Type style**   Most courts require that documents be typed in pica type, which provides ten characters to the linear inch and six lines to the vertical inch. Pica type is easier to read than the smaller elite type, which provides 12 characters to the linear inch. Most law offices use electric typewriters equipped with pica type and a carbon ribbon. Electric typewriters are preferred because of their speed, their efficiency, and the excellent appearance of the finished product.

## GUIDELINES FOR TYPING COURT PAPERS
The following guidelines suggest the most commonly used practices in the typing of court documents. You should always consult the attorney, the office style manual, or the court rule book for the formats that are customary or required in your area.

**Margins**   When court papers are to be bound into a backing sheet or into an office folder, the top margin of every page must be at least 1½ inches deep to allow room for the fasteners; it is common for the top margin to be 2 inches deep. If the pages are not to be bound and numbered legal cap is used, the first line begins opposite the number one. When ruled legal cap is used, side margins are usually set one or two spaces inside the ruling. Typing <u>never</u> extends beyond the ruled lines. If unruled paper is used, the left margin is usually not less than 1¼ inch (it should be more if the paper is to be bound on the left side) and the right margin is at least one-half inch, preferably about one inch. The bottom margin should be at least one-half inch and preferably one inch.

**Typing on numbered legal cap**   Numbered lines are designed to allow the quick location of a typewritten line. It is therefore important to align your typing with the numbers as closely as possible. You should begin the first line of every paragraph even with a number. When leaving extra space (such as triple-spacing between sections), instead of the triple space used on unnumbered paper, use two double spaces so that the first line of a new paragraph will begin on a numbered line. You should type the first line of the caption even with a number, but the other parts of the caption may come between lines. This will make it possible to plan the bottom line of the caption so that the first paragraph of the document can begin on a numbered line without extra space being left.

The body of a court document is double-spaced. Even land descriptions and quotations are usually double-spaced, although some courts allow these to be single-spaced. If single-spaced copy is used, the same principle applies as in double-spaced copy: Begin the first line of each paragraph opposite a number. You can always accomplish this by using either a triple space or two double spaces.

In no case should any copy be typed below the final numbered line of a page.

Frequently it is expedient to leave one or more numbered lines blank at the bottom of a page, as when you carry the first line of a new paragraph to the new page, or when it is necessary to carry over two or three lines of a document to appear above the signature on the last page. Another situation in which lines may be left blank is when only one line of single-spaced copy remains to be carried over. (At least two lines and preferably three lines of single-spaced copy should be carried over to the next page.) When lines are left blank at the bottom of a page, some method of indicating that this was intentional should be used to prevent possible unauthorized additions to the document after it is typed. When several lines are left open, a Z-ruling may be used, as illustrated on page 450. If only one or two lines are left, a method often used is to type three or more diagonals or asterisks at each margin of each blank numbered line, as shown in the illustration below.

```
22

23

24

25   in the manner provided by law; and that all other necessary and

26   proper audits be made in the premises.

27   * * *                                              * * *

28   * * *                                              * * *

                              -4-
```

**Pagination**   Page numbers are typed one-half inch from the bottom of the page, centered or at the right margin. Pages should be numbered consecutively. Customs and requirements differ on whether the first page is numbered. Some court rules require numbering page 1; others do not. In the absence of a specific rule, it is recommended that the first page be numbered in all court documents except those that consist of one page only. It is also recommended that the page number be enclosed with hyphens, periods, or parentheses to prevent it from being changed after the document has been typed.

**Paragraphs**   The numbering of paragraphs should follow court rules or custom. Three styles are commonly used: (1) Arabic numerals, (2) Roman numerals, and (3) spelled-out ordinal numbers, as First, Second, Third, etc. Sometimes the paragraph number, regardless of style, is centered on a separate line between the paragraphs, as shown on pages 446–450. At other times the number appears at the indention point of each paragraph.

Paragraphs are usually indented ten spaces, and a tab stop should be set at that point. Paragraphs are never blocked in court documents. Land descriptions, which may be single-spaced, should be indented five spaces to the right of the left margin and may or may not also be indented five spaces within the right margin. Paragraphs within quoted material are indented a further five spaces from the left margin. Frequently a section of a court document will make reference to an earlier section of the same document. In these cases, you must be careful to refer to the paragraph exactly as it is identified in the document. For example, in the complaint illustrated on page 449, reference is made to "Paragraphs I–III" of the First Cause of Action on a previous page of the complaint.

**Capitalized introductory locutions**   Certain words and phrases in legal documents are often typed in full capital letters. These include the heading or the first word or phrase of a paragraph, especially opening or closing paragraphs, and the names of documents, individuals, or firms. The use of capitals in this manner is usually not specified in court rules, and customs differ. When in doubt, you should follow the custom in your local jurisdiction as shown in file copies of similar documents or obtain the preference of the attorney for whom you work. A few examples of all-capitalized introductory words and phrases that appear frequently in court documents are listed below:

COMES NOW (first paragraph of a complaint)
WHEREFORE (last paragraph of a document)
PLEASE TAKE NOTICE (beginning of a notice)
IT IS HEREBY ORDERED, ADJUDGED, AND DECREED (an order of the court)
IT IS HEREBY STIPULATED (beginning of a stipulation)

## BASIC ELEMENTS OF A COURT DOCUMENT

**Law firm identification**   Every court document bears the name, address, and telephone number of the law firm that prepares it. The firm may have this information printed on the paper, usually at either the upper or lower left margin. In some states, however, even when it is printed the information must also be typed on the document. In some states it is typed below the firm's name in the signature block. In other states it is typed on the first page of the document, usually starting about two inches from the top of the page. In all cases this information is single-spaced. When paper with numbered lines is used, the attorney's name or the name of the law firm generally starts at line 1. The firm's telephone number is usually typed below the address. Below that, generally on line 5, is a line stating whom the attorney represents, as "Attorneys for the Cross-Complainant."

**Caption** All court documents are identified at the top by captions. The format for captions varies from one jurisdiction to another, as suggested in the sample captions on the following pages. The information in a caption is specified by court rules, but in most jurisdictions each office is free to choose its own styling. Before typing a caption for a particular court, you should check with the attorney or the office form files to ascertain the form required by the court or preferred by your office. Study the preferred form and make notes as to tab settings, underlining, punctuation, capitalization, and the spacing between each item. It is helpful to memorize this information so that captions on all documents prepared for that court may be typed quickly.

The content of a caption is largely the same for all courts:

1. Venue and jurisdiction of the court
2. Title of the action (names of the parties)
3. Index number of the case (the number assigned by the clerk of court)
4. Nature of the document and character of the action (title of the document)

## A Sampling of Captions Used in Court Documents

```
 1          IN THE CIRCUIT COURT OF _____ COUNTY, ALABAMA

 2                                      )

 3    RALPH BENNETT,                    )

 4                      PLAINTIFF       )

 5        VS.                           )        No._____

 6    CROCKETT, INC.,                   )
 7    A FLORIDA CORPORATION,
      AND DOE ONE AND DOE TWO,          )

 8                      DEFENDANTS      )

 9                              ANSWER

10

11
```

```
 1             IN THE DISTRICT COURT IN AND FOR

 2                  THE COUNTY OF _____

 3                   STATE OF COLORADO

 4                 Civil Action No. _____

 5    RALPH BENNETT,              )
                                  )
 6               Plaintiff,       )
                                  )
 7        vs.                     )        AMENDED ANSWER
                                  )
 8    CROCKETT, INC., a Florida   )
      corporation and DOE ONE     )
 9    and DOE TWO,                )
                                  )
10               Defendants.      )

11
```

1                NO. _____

2     IN THE SUPREME COURT OF THE STATE OF HAWAII

3              MARCH TERM 19__

4

5  RALPH BENNETT,               )

6       Plaintiff-Appellee,  ) CIVIL NO. _____

                        )

7     vs.                ) APPEAL FROM JUDGMENT FILED
                        ) JANUARY 10, 19__

8  CROCKETT, INC., a Florida  ) FIRST CIRCUIT COURT
  corporation, and DOE ONE   )

9  and DOE TWO,          )

                        )

10      Defendants-Appellants.  )

11

---

1  RALPH BENNETT              : NUMBER_____, DIVISION____

2                      : ____JUDICIAL DISTRICT COURT

3  VERSUS                : PARISH OF _____

                      :

4  CROCKETT, INC., AND     : STATE OF LOUISIANA
  DOE ONE and DOE TWO     :

5  :::::::::::::::::::::::::::::::::::::::::::::::::::::::::::::::

6

7

8

9

10

---

1  STATE OF MAINE             SUPERIOR COURT
  LINCOLN, SS.       CIVIL DOCKET NO. _____

2

3  RALPH BENNETT, Petitioner   )

                     )

4        vs.           )      PETITION

                     )

5  CROCKETT, INC., a Florida  )
  corporation, and DOE ONE   )

6  and DOE TWO, Respondents   )

7

8

9

10

```
1        IN THE DISTRICT COURT OF _____ COUNTY, NEBRASKA

2

3   RALPH BENNETT                    )    DOCKET _____    PG _____
                                     )
4                 Plaintiff,         )
                                     )
5   vs.                              )         NOTICE OF APPEAL
                                     )
6   CROCKETT, INC., a Florida        )
    corporation, and DOE ONE         )
7   and DOE TWO,                     )
                                     )
8                 Defendants.        )

9

10
```

```
1   SUPREME COURT OF THE STATE OF NEW YORK
    COUNTY OF _____
2   _____

3   RALPH BENNETT,                   )    Index Number: _____
                                     )
4                 Plaintiff,         )
                                     )
5        -against-                   )    ANSWER
                                     )
6   CROCKETT, INC., and              )
    "JOHN DOE,"                      )
7                                    )
                  Defendants.        )
8   _____)

9

10
```

```
1                                         MERCER COUNTY COURT
                                          LAW DIVISION
2                                         DOCKET NO.

3   RALPH BENNETT,                   )
                                     )
4                 Plaintiff,         )         Civil Action
                                     )
5        v.                          )           SUMMONS
                                     )
6   CROCKETT, INC.,                  )
    and DOE ONE and DOE TWO,         )
7                                    )
                  Defendants.        )
8                                    )

9

10
```

```
 1   IN THE CIRCUIT COURT OF _____COUNTY, WEST VIRGINIA

 2   RALPH BENNETT,
                     Plaintiff
 3
     v.                                Civil Action No. _____
 4
     DOE ONE, DOE TWO, AND
 5   CROCKETT, INC., a corporation
                     Defendants
 6
                          COMPLAINT
 7

 8

 9

10
```

```
 1   STATE OF WYOMING )              IN THE DISTRICT COURT
                      )ss.
 2   COUNTY OF _____ )              FIRST JUDICIAL DISTRICT

 3
     RALPH BENNETT,             )
 4                             )    No._____
                    Plaintiff  )
 5                             )
                              )
 6      vs.                    )
                              )
     CROCKETT, INC., a Florida )
 7   corporation, and DOE ONE  )
     and DOE TWO,              )
 8                             )
                    Defendants )
 9

10
```

```
 1   STATE OF WISCONSIN     CIRCUIT COURT        _____ COUNTY

 2   _____
     Ralph Bennett,
 3
                    Plaintiff
 4                                                   COMPLAINT
        VS.
 5
     Crockett, Inc., and
 6   Doe One and Doe Two,

 7                  Defendants

 8

 9

10
```

**Venue and jurisdiction**    *Venue* refers to the geographical area of the court, *jurisdiction* to the name of the court itself. The phrasing of the caption depends to a great extent on the structure of the courts—whether they are organized by county, for instance, or by numbered districts. Stylings such as the following, where venue and jurisdiction are combined and centered on the page, are the most common:

IN THE DISTRICT COURT OF THE FIRST JUDICIAL DISTRICT OF THE
STATE OF MONTANA, IN AND FOR THE COUNTY OF LEWIS AND CLARK

IN THE DISTRICT COURT IN AND FOR
THE COUNTY OF GUNNISON
STATE OF COLORADO

The venue and jurisdiction are separated in some caption stylings:

STATE OF VERMONT                                             COUNTY COURT
RUTLAND COUNTY,        SS

**Case title**    The names of the parties to a lawsuit are typed all in capital letters and identified as to their role in the lawsuit (whether plaintiff, respondent, etc.). In some instances lowercased explanatory phrases must follow the name:

1. When a suit is brought or defended on behalf of a minor or an incompetent, the guardian's name is given in the caption. Example:

   JEFFERY JOHNSON, guardian ad litem of
   AMANDA JONES, a minor

2. When a person sues or is sued not as an individual but in his or her capacity as trustee, executor, or administrator. Example:

   JEFFERY JOHNSON, as executor of
   the last will and testament of
   JASON JONES, deceased

3. When husband and wife join in a suit. Example:

   LEE K. ALYSON and
   MARVIN R. ALYSON, her husband

4. When the party is a partnership and frequently when it is a corporation. Examples:

   HENRY MARKHAM and MELVIN SISITSKY,
   doing business as a partnership
   under the name of MARKHAM & SISITSKY
   XYZ CORPORATION, a domestic corporation

The names of the parties to the action usually appear on the left half of the page, opposite the title of the document, and some kind of boxing for the names is customary. The boxing is frequently indicated by a vertical row of closing parentheses, colons, or a combination of closing parentheses and colons. However, there is a trend toward eliminating boxing because of the time involved.

A case title may become lengthy when there is more than one defendant or plaintiff or when it includes identifying phrases such as those listed above. When typing case titles in pleadings that occur after the complaint, and also when typing the endorsement on a legal back, you are permitted to save space by typing only the names of the principal plaintiff and principal defendant. In these instances you should substitute the following Latin abbreviations for the omitted names and phrases:

*et al.*—*et alia*, and the others (the additional parties)
*etc.*—*et cetera*, and so forth
*et ux.*—*et uxor*, and wife
*et vir*—and husband

Runover lines in a case title are usually single-spaced.

**Index numbers**   When typing the caption for the first document in any proceeding, leave space for the index number or docket number, which will be assigned by the clerk of court when the first pleading in the case is filed. It is important to obtain this number as soon as it is available. You may ask for the number or look it up in the clerk's cross-index, which is arranged alphabetically by the plaintiff's name in each case. (The index or docket number should not be confused with the *calendar number,* which is usually assigned later when the case is ready for trial and which refers to the sequence in which cases appear on the court's calendar.) Once the index number has been assigned, you should conform all copies of the document by copying the number in the proper place. This number is then typed on <u>all</u> future documents prepared in the case for that particular court.

**Title of the document**   Each document bears a title indicating the purpose and often the type of action involved in a case. The document title is generally typed in solid capitals on the right side of the page, opposite the case title, but some offices prefer to center it between the caption and the body of the document. If it is long, it may be separated into sections that may be centered or blocked. The longest line will be centered in the space between the center point of the page and the right margin. The center point of the page is usually set five spaces to the right of the actual center of the paper (42 for pica type on 8½-inch paper). This places the center approximately equidistant from the margins.

**Introductory statement or paragraph**   Each court document bears an opening statement that introduces the statements to follow. Forms for introductory statements to all court documents are available in form books. The attorney follows these forms carefully, making only minor deviations that may be required by the circumstances of a particular case. Certain requirements must be met in this paragraph. For example, where litigants are identified in the caption as trustees or officers of corporations, these capacities must be restated in the introductory paragraph.

**Body style**   The sample complaint on pages 446–450 illustrates a common styling. In this complaint, the statements and allegations are separated and identified first by headings (FIRST CAUSE OF ACTION), then by centered Roman numerals.

**Prayer**   The prayer is the closing paragraph of a pleading. It states the relief or remedy sought and usually begins, WHEREFORE . . . . Example:

WHEREFORE, plaintiff prays:
1. Demand for relief claimed by plaintiff;
2. For plaintiff's costs of suit incurred herein;
3. For such other and further relief as the Court deems proper.

**Signature line**   Signatures must never appear alone on the final page of a legal document. At least two lines of the last paragraph of the document must be carried over to the top of the last page with the signature lines below them. To accomplish this, you may have to use a Z-mark.

Style and individual preferences, as well as rules of court, regulate the format of signature lines; and these rules and preferences vary greatly. The signature line usually begins at the center or just to the right of center and continues to the right margin. Two widely used forms are shown below.

JOHNSON & WITKOWSKI, P.C.

By _____          _____
        THOMAS CARTER                          THOMAS CARTER
      Attorney for Plaintiff                   Attorney for Plaintiff

# A Complaint for Damages

```
1   Law Offices of Leon H. Rountree, Jr.
    3283 Lake Shore Avenue, Suite 209
2   Oakland, CA 94610

3   (415) 465-7744

4

5   Attorneys for Plaintiff

6

7

8           SUPERIOR COURT OF THE STATE OF CALIFORNIA

9               IN AND FOR THE COUNTY OF ALAMEDA

10

11  JOHN BROWN,                    )
                                   )
12            Plaintiff,           )   NO. 499305-2
                                   )
13     vs.                         )   COMPLAINT FOR DAMAGES
                                   )   (ASSAULT AND BATTERY)
14  SWAN AND COMPANY,              )   (FALSE IMPRISONMENT)
    a corporation, and DOES I      )   (INTENTIONAL INFLICTION
15  through DOES VIII, Inclusive,  )    OF EMOTIONAL DISTRESS)
                                   )
16            Defendants.          )   (CC Secs. 3293, 3333)
                                   )
17

18          Plaintiff alleges:

19                     FIRST CAUSE OF ACTION

20                      Assault and Battery

21                             I

22          Defendant SWAN AND COMPANY is and at all times herein

23  mentioned was a corporation existing under the laws of the State

24  of California and having a principal place of business in

25  Oakland, California.

26                            II

27          Plaintiff is ignorant of the true names and capacities

28  of defendants and sued herein as DOES I-VIII, inclusive, and
```

-1-

1   therefore sues these defendants by such fictitious names.

2   Plaintiff will amend this complaint to allege their true names

3   and capacities when ascertained. Plaintiff is informed and

4   believes and thereon alleges that each of the fictitiously named

5   defendants is responsible in some manner for the occurrence herein

6   alleged, and that plaintiff's damages as herein alleged were

7   proximately caused by their conduct.

8                            III

9       At all times herein mentioned, defendants DOES I-VIII

10   were the agent and employee of defendant SWAN AND COMPANY and in

11   doing the things hereinafter alleged were acting within the scope

12   and course of such agency. Plaintiff is informed and believes

13   and thereon alleges that defendant SWAN AND COMPANY authorized

14   the acts of defendants DOES I-VIII by failing to stop the acts of

15   DOES I-VIII.

16                            IV

17       On or about October 20, 19--, in Oakland, California,

18   defendants DOES I-VIII maliciously and willfully assaulted and

19   battered plaintiff by threatening to and beating, kicking,

20   wounding, and ill-treating plaintiff by striking blows with their

21   fists on plaintiff's head and body and by knocking plaintiff to

22   the ground and jumping on plaintiff's body with their feet and

23   knees.

24                            V

25       As a result of the aforementioned assault and battery,

26   plaintiff sustained the following injuries: multiple bruises and

27   contusions over various parts of the body; concussion; traumatic

28   cervical, thoracic lumbar sprain with concomitant bruised

-2-

1 musculature surrounding these areas and left shoulder; cephalgia;

2 and a contusion of the left forefoot with possible tendonitis and

3 periostitis, all to plaintiff's damage.

VI

5 By reason of the wrongful acts of defendants, plaintiff

6 was required to and did employ physicians and surgeons to examine,

7 treat, and care for him, and other incidental medical expenses in

8 an amount which has not yet been ascertained. Plaintiff is

9 informed and believes and thereon alleges that he will incur some

10 additional medical expenses, the exact amount of which is unknown.

11 Plaintiff will ask leave of court to amend his complaint to insert

12 the correct amount of such medical expenses when the case has been

13 ascertained.

VII

15 By reason of the wrongful acts of defendant, plaintiff

16 was prevented from attending to his usual occupation as a butcher

17 and thereby lost earnings. Plaintiff is informed and believes

18 and thereon alleges that he will thereby be prevented from

19 attending to his usual occupation for a period in the future that

20 he cannot now ascertain and will thereby sustain further loss of

21 earnings. Plaintiff will ask leave of court to amend this

22 complaint to set out the exact amount of such additional damages

23 when the same is ascertained.

VIII

25 The aforementioned acts of defendant were willful,

26 wanton, malicious, and oppressive and justify the awarding of

27 exemplary and punitive damages.

28 /// /// 

-3-

1      SECOND CAUSE OF ACTION

2          FIRST COUNT

3       (False Imprisonment)

4          I

5          Plaintiff refers to and incorporates, as though fully

6  set forth herein, Paragraphs I-III, inclusive, and Paragraphs VI-

7  VIII, inclusive, of the First Cause of Action.

8          II

9          On October 20, 19--, at or about 6 p.m., and within

10  defendant SWAN AND COMPANY'S retail store, while plaintiff was

11  peacefully and in a law-abiding manner shopping and walking in the

12  store, defendants DOES I-VIII seized plaintiff, accused him of

13  theft of certain property belonging to defendant SWAN AND COMPANY,

14  and detained and imprisoned plaintiff by threats of force and

15  violence.  Defendants, and each of them, accused plaintiff

16  publicly of having stolen certain items from defendant; and

17  plaintiff denied having stolen any items and demanded to be

18  released.  Defendants, and each of them, continued to detain

19  plaintiff and forced him to move about in the store under their

20  supervision and control and thereafter continued to imprison and

21  confine plaintiff for a period of three hours, during which time

22  defendants, and each of them, assaulted and battered plaintiff.

23          SECOND COUNT

24       (Negligent Entrustment)

25          I

26          Plaintiff refers to and incorporates, as though fully

27  set forth herein, Paragraphs I-III, inclusive, and Paragraphs VI-

28  VIII, inclusive, of the First Cause of Action.

-4-

II

Defendant SWAN AND COMPANY negligently hired and entrusted defendants DOES I-VIII to protect its property and premises and to investigate possible harm to its property or premises and to perform other related functions.

WHEREFORE, plaintiff prays judgment as follows:

1. For general damages;

2. For medical and related expenses according to proof;

3. For lost earnings, past and future, according to proof;

4. For exemplary and punitive damages;

5. For costs of suit incurred herein;

6. For such other and further relief as the court may deem proper.

_____
GAIL D. BREWSTER
Attorney for Plaintiff

Court documents are usually signed by the attorney on behalf of the firm. Occasionally, though not often, the client may also sign. If the address of the firm was not typed or printed at the beginning of the document, it is typed below the signature lines. Though most states require a handwritten signature on the original copy, some states require only the typewritten firm name and address.

## VERIFICATION

When a pleading or supporting document contains statements of fact or belief, it must be verified by the client. The verification is a statement that the party involved has read the document and knows or believes that the facts stated within it are true. In some law offices all pleadings are routinely verified, whether required or not. Complaints and answers are normally verified, as are petitions and bills of particulars, since these documents usually contain a recitation of facts. The client generally signs the verification, though when the client is not available to sign in person, the attorney may sign on behalf of the client. When an attorney signs any document other than an affidavit, it is usually not notarized, since the attorney is an officer of the court. An attorney's signature is called an *attorney's affirmation*.

In some states, in some jurisdictions, and on certain types of documents, the verifications must be sworn to in the presence of a notary public, who then signs and seals the document. In other instances, when the verification does not need to be notarized, the format and wording differ and the document is referred to as a *declaration* or a *certificate*.

**Typing the verification**  Sometimes printed forms are used for verification. These may be printed on the legal back or attached to the final page of the document. If it is not already printed, the verification must be typewritten, either beginning four lines of space below the signature lines or on a separate sheet. Verifications are most commonly typewritten on separate sheets of paper. The secretary who is told to verify a document must find out whether a formal verification or a declaration is required. Because the formal verification is a sworn document, it requires a statement of venue and a jurat (the notary's statement, as described in section 14.1 of Chapter 14). In preparing the document, the secretary must plan the placement of the verification or declaration. The declaration simply requires enough space for the signature of the party involved, while a notarized verification also requires space for the jurat below.

As with acknowledgments, there are different forms of verification to be used for individuals, officers of foreign and domestic corporations, and attorneys. The verification illustrated on page 452 is styled for an individual signature. Other forms may be obtained from office form books and practice manuals.

The verification is headed by the venue, which states the county and state in which the verification was made. Three lines of space are left below the venue and above the body of the statement, which begins with the name of the verifier typed in fully capitalized letters. A rule for the signature is prepared. There is no need to type the verifier's name below the signature line, since it appears in the body of the document. The jurat usually begins about three lines of space below the signature on the left half of the page. The notary public fills in the date and administers the oath to the verifier, as described in connection with affidavits in Chapter 12.

## PROOFREADING

As court documents must be absolutely accurate, the secretary must proofread carefully. It may be necessary to proofread a document more than once. Secretaries often read property descriptions and technical matters aloud to another person who reads silently from the rough draft copy to verify the accuracy of the typed information. Proofreading techniques are described in detail on page 180.

## A Verification

```
 1                  VERIFICATION (CCP Secs. 446, 2015.5)

 2

 3          I, JOHN BROWN, am the plaintiff in the above entitled

 4   action.  I have read the foregoing complaint and know the

 5   contents thereof.  The same is true of my own knowledge, except

 6   as to those matters which are therein alleged on information and

 7   belief; and, as to those matters, I believe it to be true.

 8          I declare under penalty of perjury that the foregoing

 9   is true and correct and that this declaration was executed on

10   November 5, 19--, at Oakland, California.

11

12
                                        _____
13                                           JOHN BROWN
```

## CONFORMING COPIES

The secretary has the responsibility of putting on all copies of the original document any additions—such as index number, dates, or signatures—or later revisions that are made to the original document after it is typed. Making these additions is called *conforming*. To indicate that the original document has been signed, the secretary types the name above the signature line and types the symbol S/, /S/, or s/ before it as shown below:

/S/   JAMES T. JONES
_____

        JAMES T. JONES, Plaintiff

The conforming of copies is described in greater detail in Chapter 14.

## LEGAL BACKS

In some jurisdictions original court documents must be stapled to a heavy backing sheet called a legal back. The backing sheet is usually colored, often blue and thus sometimes called a *blue back*; it is ¾ to 1 inch longer than the paper on which the document is typed. The extra length is folded over the top of the document, and two staples are used to fasten the document within the fold of the backing sheet. Chapter 12 gives a detailed explanation of how to fold and staple backing sheets.

On one of the folds of the backing sheet the *endorsement* is typed or printed. This information includes:

1. The name and address of the law firm
2. The party that the firm represents, as "Attorneys for the Defendants"
3. The name of the court
4. The title of the case (names of the parties to the action)
5. The index number
6. The titles of all the documents bound in the legal back
7. The name and address of the opposing attorney to whom the papers are addressed, if applicable
8. (Sometimes) the date

If the title of the case is lengthy, you may use an abbreviated form of the litigants' names, such as "LEE K. ALYSON et vir."

Sometimes the blanks to be filled in are printed on the fold; otherwise, the endorsement must be fully typewritten on the proper fold. In both cases the endorsement must be typed *before* the document is stapled into the backing sheet. If the document requires an acknowledgment or verification, a form printed on the backing sheet may be used.

Frequently more than one document is stapled in a backing sheet. It is important to know the order in which the papers should be stapled. The primary document is normally placed on top with support documents beneath. A proof of service form may be printed on the backing sheet; if so, it should be used. If a proof of service must be typed separately, it should be stapled beneath the other documents. Ask the attorney if you are not familiar with the court rules in this matter.

Fewer courts now require legal backs than formerly because of the inconvenience of filing them. Consequently, many firms today use legal cap with the name and address of the firm printed in an upper or lower corner as a substitute for the information that normally appears on the endorsement panel of a legal back.

# 13.3

## HOW TO PREPARE PLEADINGS

The division of responsibility in an office that employs both legal secretaries and legal assistants depends upon the training and experience of each, the current work load of the office, and frequently the type of legal work in which the firm specializes. Typically, legal assistants involved in litigation work may interview clients and witnesses, prepare interrogatories, do legal research, and prepare drafts of court documents. The legal secretary normally assumes responsibility for the preparation and filing of documents: transcribing pleadings from dictation or other sources, obtaining signatures, conforming copies, filing, and mailing copies to interested parties. The secretary may also schedule appointments with clients and witnesses, arrange for court hearings, maintain the office litigation calendar, and keep official case progress records.

### SOURCES OF INFORMATION FOR THE PREPARATION OF PLEADINGS
The law office that handles a large volume of litigated cases will usually provide checklists and form books to assist both lawyer and secretary to perform all steps in the litigation process correctly and on time.

**Checklists** Law offices frequently prepare detailed checklists that allow each step in a particular legal proceeding to be listed and checked off with the initials of the person completing the task and the date it was completed. State bar associations, legal secretaries' associations, and other groups often prepare such checklists as a service to lawyers in a particular state. These checklists can be adapted to the individual purposes of each law office.

A multipage checklist for the defense of tort cases that is used by a Texas law firm is shown on the following pages. It lists every possible task to be done by the legal secretary, legal assistant, or lawyer in this type of defense action. Not all of the steps are applicable to every case, but the sequence is designed to include all potential steps in the defense of a tort case. When certain types of cases are frequently handled, it is worthwhile to take the time to prepare such a list and duplicate it so that a copy may be attached to the cover of each client's litigation file.

# Sample Pages from a Checklist for the Defense of Tort Cases

CASE:_____   CLIENT_____

| Date | Initial |
|------|---------|

**A.  Initial File Procedure:**

_____ _____   1.  Preliminary review of file
_____ _____       a.  Calendar appearance day
_____ _____   2.  Acknowledgment letter
_____ _____   3.  File opened
              4.  Responsive pleadings:
_____ _____       a.  Prepared
_____ _____       b.  Filed
_____ _____       c.  Mailed to opposing attorney
_____ _____       d.  Mailed to company
_____ _____   5.  Letter to Defendant(s) (pleadings, conference-phone call)

**B.  File Review Procedure:**

_____ _____   1.  Review file material
_____ _____   2.  Letter to company requesting original statements and photographs
_____ _____   3.  Type longhand statement
_____ _____   4.  Check our Card Index File
_____ _____       a.  Letter to company
_____ _____   5.  Check Plaintiff-Defendant Indexes: requested
_____ _____       a.  Obtained
_____ _____       b.  Letter to company
_____ _____   6.  Police reports & supplements (in file)
_____ _____       a.  Requested
_____ _____       b.  Obtained
_____ _____       c.  Reviewed
_____ _____       d.  Photographs (requested_____: obtained_____)
_____ _____       e.  Letter to company
_____ _____   7.  Recent medical records ordered if authorized
_____ _____   8.  Scene subject to change: Yes_____ No _____
_____ _____       a.  Photographs: Yes _____ No _____
_____ _____       b.  Plat:        Yes_____ No _____
              9.  Complete witness sheet
              10. Driving records:
_____ _____       a.  Requested
_____ _____       b.  Obtained
_____ _____       c.  Letter to company
              11. Southwest Index Bureau Report:
_____ _____       a.  File: Yes_____ No_____
_____ _____   12. Medical report reviewed and summarized
_____ _____   13. File review outline prepared

1

| Date | Initial | |
|------|---------|---|
| ____ | ____ | 14. File review outline prepared & file returned to attorney |
| ____ | ____ | 15. Preliminary conference with attorney |
| ____ | ____ | 16. File review report to company |

C. Discovery and Trial Preparation

| Date | Initial | |
|------|---------|---|
| ____ | ____ | 1. Conference with Defendant(s) |
| ____ | ____ |    a.  Summary prepared |
| ____ | ____ |    b.  Report to company |
| ____ | ____ | 2. Preliminary Interrogatories to Plaintiff |
| ____ | ____ |    a.  Reply date calendared |
| ____ | ____ |    b.  Reminder letter to attorney |
| ____ | ____ |    c.  Reply received |
| ____ | ____ |    d.  Reviewed |
| ____ | ____ |    e.  Interrogatories and reply (copies) to company |

3. ORAL DEPOSITIONS

| Name | Date Taken | Date Rec'd | Out-lined | Report to Co. |
|------|-----------|-----------|-----------|---------------|
| a. _____ | ____ | ____ | ____ | ____ |
| b. _____ | ____ | ____ | ____ | ____ |
| c. _____ | ____ | ____ | ____ | ____ |
| d. _____ | ____ | ____ | ____ | ____ |

4. MEDICAL AND HOSPITAL RECORDS

| Name | Date Taken | Date Rec'd | Out-lined | Report to Co. |
|------|-----------|-----------|-----------|---------------|
| a. _____ | ____ | ____ | ____ | ____ |
| B. _____ | ____ | ____ | ____ | ____ |
| c. _____ | ____ | ____ | ____ | ____ |
| d. _____ | ____ | ____ | ____ | ____ |
| e. _____ | ____ | ____ | ____ | ____ |
| f. _____ | ____ | ____ | ____ | ____ |

| Date | Initial | |
|------|---------|---|
| ____ | ____ | 5. Request for admissions to Plaintiff |
| ____ | ____ |    a.  Reply date calendared |
| ____ | ____ |    b.  Reminder letter to attorney |
| ____ | ____ |    c.  Reply received |
| ____ | ____ |    d.  Reviewed |
| ____ | ____ |    e.  Interrogatories and reply (copies) to company |
| | | 6. Discovery motions: |
| ____ | ____ |    a.  Income tax returns |
| ____ | ____ |    b.  Business records |
| ____ | ____ |    c.  _____ |
| ____ | ____ | 7. Counterclaim considered |
| | | 8. Employment information obtained |
| ____ | ____ |    a.  Employer(s) contacted |
| ____ | ____ |    b.  Records obtained |
| ____ | ____ |    c.  Interrogatories |

2

Date    Initial
_____

                 D.   Incoming Discovery

                      1.   Interrogatories received from Plaintiff (other adverse party)

_____  _____       a.   Received

_____  _____       b.   Reviewed and calendared

_____  _____            1.   Request for extension

_____  _____       c.   Preliminary draft of answers

_____  _____       d.   Copy to company/insured

_____  _____       e.   Answer/Information received from company/insured

_____  _____       f.   Reminder to company/insured

_____  _____       g.   Comparison of preliminary/received information

_____  _____       h.   Conference with attorney

_____  _____       i.   Final reply drafted

                      2.   Demands for admissions from Plaintiff (others)

_____  _____       a.   Received

_____  _____       b.   Reviewed and calendared

_____  _____            1.   Request for extension

_____  _____       c.   Preliminary draft of **answers**

_____  _____       d.   Copy to company/insured

_____  _____       e.   Answer/Information received from company/insured

_____  _____       f.   Reminder to company/insured

_____  _____       g.   Comparison of preliminary/received information

_____  _____       h.   Conference with attorney

_____  _____       i.   Final reply drafted

                E.   Trial Settings             (Subsequent)

_____  _____       1.   Notice received    ____ ____ ____ ____

_____  _____       2.   Notice to company    ____ ____ ____ ____

_____  _____       3.   Notice to insured    ____ ____ ____ ____

_____  _____       4.   Notice to principal witnesses    ____ ____ ____ ____

_____  _____       5.   Check completion of list and discovery

_____  _____       6.   Pre-trial conference with attorney

_____  _____       7.   Notice of cancellation

               F.   Final Trial Preparations (Trial **assistant** to inquire)

_____  _____       1.   Amend pleadings

_____  _____       2.   Alert witnesses and client

_____  _____       3.   Demand jury

_____  _____       4.   Pre-trial interrogatories to Plaintiff(s)

_____  _____       5.   Enlargement of photographs

Date  Initial

_____  _____     6.  Instructions to witnesses
_____  _____     7.  Trial report to company
_____  _____     8.  Demonstrative evidence
_____  _____     9.  Trial pleading prepared
_____  _____    10.  Material witnesses interviewed
_____  _____    11.  Scene of accident inspected
_____  _____    12.  Legal memo prepared
_____  _____    13.  Defendant(s) interviewed
_____  _____    14.  Status of case on docket
_____  _____    15.  Jury list obtained
_____  _____    16.  Subpoenas  issued
_____  _____    17.  Special issues
_____  _____    18.  Motions in limine
_____  _____    19.  Trial notebook completed

      G.  Case Settled

_____  _____     1.  Draft requested
_____  _____     2.  Draft received
_____  _____     3.  Settlement papers prepared
_____  _____     4.  Hearing arranged
_____  _____     5.  Hearing held
_____  _____     6.  Papers drafted and sent to attorney
_____  _____     7.  Signed papers received from attorney
_____  _____     8.  Order dismissal entered
_____  _____     9.  Cost bill requested
_____  _____    10.  Cost bill received
_____  _____    11.  Closing report and bill to company
_____  _____    12.  Check for cost received
_____  _____    13.  Check for cost mailed
_____  _____    14.  Fee received
_____  _____    15.  File closed

4

**Form books and other references**    All those involved in preparing legal documents should be aware of form books that cover all subjects and phases of the law. Some well-known form books are *American Jurisprudence Legal Forms Annotated* and *American Jurisprudence Pleading and Practice Forms Annotated*. States also issue form books covering the procedures of the state courts. There are many other references that are either essential or at least helpful to the legal secretary. Among them are publications of various Continuing Legal Education organizations, state and national bar associations, and local courts. Other references include legal dictionaries, legal secretaries' manuals, and office form books and style manuals.

## THE COMPLAINT

Section 13.1 summarized pleadings as steps in a civil litigation proceeding, while section 13.2 provided guidelines for transcribing court documents in general. The following paragraphs describe the major types of pleadings, beginning with the complaint, in greater detail and explain how the secretary handles each one.

To initiate an action, the plaintiff must file a complaint in the proper court. This document is a written petition or declaration setting forth the cause of the action. The plaintiff's attorney is responsible for preparing a complaint that is complete and clear and that is worded so that the defendant's attorney cannot object to it on the grounds that it is inadequate or legally indefensible. After obtaining all the information needed to prepare a complaint, the attorney dictates the following items: the names of the parties to the action, the facts or allegations constituting the cause of action, and the prayer or closing statement. The legal secretary must transcribe the document accurately, following the form prescribed by the rules of the court and the customs of the law office, and must also know how to file it with the court and how to serve it on the defendant. The plaintiff's attorney will sign the original complaint, and the plaintiff will sign the original verification. As soon as the papers have been signed, all copies are conformed. In most jurisdictions the complaint is assembled by placing a copy of the summons on top of a copy of the complaint and exhibits, if any.

**Summons**    The official notice that tells the defendant he is being sued and that informs him of his legal rights is known as the *summons*. This document is usually a printed legal blank. In some cases the clerk of court issues and serves the summons when the complaint is filed. In other states the secretary prepares and serves the summons. The summons is usually served with a copy of the complaint, but in some jurisdictions it is served alone.

When a printed form is used, the secretary should follow the guidelines for typing on a printed form that are outlined in Chapter 11, make sure that the name of the court is correct, and find out whether photocopies are allowed. When a printed form is not available, the summons must be typewritten. It should also be typewritten when the listing of defendants is lengthy and does not fit on the blank. (Rules of court do not allow abbreviated forms of the parties' names in the caption of a summons.) The printed form should be copied exactly on legal-size paper. A typewritten summons is usually attached to a legal back that has a preprinted affidavit of service. The names of the parties may be abbreviated on the endorsement. If summons and complaint are stapled together in the backing sheet, the summons goes on top and the endorsement reads, "Summons and Complaint."

Service of the summons is outlined in Chapter 14. Both the plaintiff's and the defendant's attorneys must note the return date of the summons, i.e., the last day by which an *appearance* (an answer, a notice of appearance, or other official response) must be made. This date is calculated according to court rules from the date of service, is noted on both the attorney's and the secretary's calendars, and is incorporated in the office reminder system.

**Case progress record**   Chapter 14 gives detailed directions on how to file and serve the first pleading in a case. An equally important responsibility of the secretary is starting a record (often called a *suit register* or *case progress record*) of every important step connected with the case. This record is usually kept on sheets in a loose-leaf notebook, where pages can be added as needed or removed after the case is closed.

If you are preparing a complaint and summons, you will need to record the following information in the progress record: the court, the title of the case, the type of case (use the terminology developed for your office filing system), and the attorney in charge. The court index number, the name and address of the opposing attorney, and the court calendar number should be added as they are learned. Each important step in the litigation process is recorded and dated in the progress record.

**The elements of a complaint**   A typewritten complaint that illustrates all the elements described below is shown on pages 446–450.

1. **Caption**   Captions and titles are used on all court documents. They are described and illustrated in section 13.2. As emphasized there, the format of the caption varies according to court rules and office preference.
2. **Introductory clause**   The form of the introduction is not prescribed by statute. Many lawyers, for example, introduce the body of the complaint with a simple indented line placed below the caption:

Plaintiff alleges:

Other lawyers continue to use the stately but archaic:

Comes now the plaintiff and complains against the above-named defendant, and for cause of action alleges:

Still others prefer phrasing such as the following:

Plaintiffs by their attorneys, Kepler and Clark, complaining of the defendants above named, allege:

If different plaintiffs assert different causes of action against different defendants, it is helpful to use a separate introduction under each cause of action heading:

FIRST CAUSE OF ACTION
Plaintiffs Tom Jones and Alex Adams, for a cause of action against defendant Walter Morton, allege:

3. **Cause or causes of action**   The plaintiff may allege that he or she has been harmed in more than one way. Each way is set forth in a separate *cause of action* or *count* in the complaint. Each cause of action alleges the kind and amount of damage suffered and lists these allegations. If there are several plaintiffs, each cause of action may contain the allegations of one plaintiff. Each cause of action is numbered, and each allegation is numbered consecutively.
4. **Prayer**   The final paragraph of the complaint is the prayer, which consists of an introductory statement followed by an enumeration of the damages or, in equity actions, a request for the desired relief.
5. **Signature**   The complaint is customarily signed by the attorney on a line under which his or her name or the name of the firm has been typed in capital letters, followed by a phrase such as "Attorney for the plaintiff." There may be rules regarding the signature styling. In some jurisdictions, for example, both attorney and plaintiff must sign the complaint. In New York, only the firm's name is typed, followed by "Attorneys for Plaintiff" and the firm's address. The attorney must sign his or her individual name rather than the firm's name in pleadings prepared for federal courts.
6. **Verification**   Because a complaint contains allegations of fact or belief, some

state laws require that it be verified by the client, either by declaration under penalty of perjury or by notarized affidavit. If for some reason the client is not available to sign the verification, it may be signed by the attorney.

**Petition**   The initial document filed in chancery courts or courts of equity is usually called a petition rather than a complaint. In the majority of jurisdictions, however, equity and law are combined and a complaint is filed even in equity cases.

## THE DEFENDANT'S ANSWER

The summons may merely direct the defendant to make an appearance, in which case he or she does so by filing an appearance with the clerk of court. Or, if a complaint accompanies the summons, the defendant must file and serve an *answer* to avoid a judgment by default. An answer is a pleading in a civil action filed by the defendant to state objections and defenses to a complaint or cross-complaint. In addition to following the proper format for preparing an answer, the secretary to the defendant's attorney must keep an up-to-date record of the various deadlines for filing replies and check it regularly. A case progress record is kept for the defendant's file just as for the plaintiff's file described on page 459. The number of copies required is the same as for a complaint.

**Elements of an answer**   The answer is typewritten according to the general guidelines for court documents detailed in section 13.2. It has the following parts:
1. **Caption**   The caption is identical to the caption of the complaint except for the title of the document, which will usually be *Answer to Complaint*. If the listing of the parties' names in the case title is long, an abbreviated form such as those described on page 444 may be used. The index number will now be available and must be included in the caption.
2. **Introductory clause**   The following is a typical introduction to an answer:
   Defendant answers plaintiff's complaint as follows:
3. **Denial of allegations**   The answer contains a response to the allegations in the complaint. Some allegations may be denied and some admitted, or all may be denied. Each separate cause of action in the complaint must be answered, though each allegation does not have to be. Each statement in the answer is numbered consecutively.
4. **Counterclaim**   In some jurisdictions court rules permit the answer to contain a *counterclaim* against the plaintiff. This counterclaim arises out of the subject of the complaint and is more conveniently included in the answer than as the subject of a separate suit. This claim alleges that the plaintiff's actions in some way caused injury to the defendant. When a counterclaim is included in the answer, it becomes a separate section of the document.
5. **Prayer**   The prayer is similar in format and purpose to that of the complaint. It begins with the word "WHEREFORE."
6. **Dateline**   The answer often has a dateline typed three lines of space below the last line of the prayer and above the signature.
7. **Signature**   Signature stylings are the same as those in a complaint.
8. **Verification**   If the complaint was verified, the answer must be verified and notarized.

The law firm's name, address, and telephone number should be printed or typed on the answer or on the legal back. Legal backs, if used, are endorsed much like those used for backing complaints, except that the index number is included and both the attorneys for the plaintiff and the attorneys for the defendant are identified. Methods of serving the answer are detailed in Chapter 14.

## NOTICE OF APPEARANCE

The defendant files a notice of appearance rather than an answer with the clerk of court in those jurisdictions where the summons is served without the complaint attached. This notice simply states that the defendant "appears" through his or her attorney; it usually requests that copies of the complaint and other pleadings and supporting papers be served on the attorney from that point on. A notice of appearance is ordinarily a printed form, but it may be typed on plain bond. Depending on court rules, it may be addressed to the clerk of court or to the plaintiff's attorney. If addressed to the plaintiff's attorney, it typically begins in this fashion:

S I R:

PLEASE TAKE NOTICE that the defendant ARLENE P. MILLER hereby appears in the above entitled action and that we are retained . . . .

If addressed to the clerk of court, the notice may follow this styling:

TO THE CLERK OF THE ABOVE COURT:

We hereby enter our appearance as attorneys for the defendant ARLENE P. MILLER in the above entitled suit . . . .

Frequently a dateline appears on the left side of the page below the body of the notice. The attorney's signature is typically preceded by a complimentary close.

## OTHER COMMON TYPES OF PLEADINGS

Opposing attorneys may file a long series of pleadings before the trial is set or the issue otherwise settled. Some of these pleadings are described below. For each pleading, the original document is filed with the court and conformed copies served on the opposing party's attorney. In each case the secretary must see that filing deadlines are not missed and that the proper parties receive copies of the document.

**Demurrer**   Many states permit the defense attorney to object to the complaint on the grounds that it is improper, uncertain, unintelligible, or ambiguous. This objection asserting the complaint to be legally indefensible is called a *demurrer*. The demurrer raises only questions of law, not of fact; that is, it does not respond to the facts alleged in the case. The Federal Rules of Civil Procedure do not allow for demurrers; therefore, states that have adopted the federal rules do not accept demurrers. In those states, the defense attorney may use a document entitled *motion to make complaint more definite and certain* or *motion to dismiss for failure to state a case*.

In the body of a demurrer, which is fairly standardized, each ground is stated in a separate paragraph identified by Roman numerals. The numerals are frequently centered on a separate line above each paragraph. A demurrer is often supported by an accompanying document called a *memorandum of points and authorities*. The title of the demurrer is *Demurrer to Complaint*, or to whatever pleading is thought to be legally indefensible.

No verification is required, but in some jurisdictions a separate attorney's certificate of good faith must be added to the demurrer. This certificate is typically a brief form that states the following:

I hereby certify that this demurrer is filed in good faith and not for the purpose of delay. In my opinion the grounds are well taken.

The attorney signs the certificate. If a supporting list of points and authorities is attached, it should begin on a separate page.

**Motion to strike**   In some jurisdictions the defense attorney may file a motion to strike (i.e., to strike the entire complaint or a portion of it). This motion may be filed with a demurrer or with a motion to make complaint more definite and certain.

**Memorandum of points and authorities**   The demurrer, the motion to strike, and the motion to make complaint more definite and certain are based on points of law. In many states a memorandum of points and authorities is prepared to accompany and support the motions. Sometimes this document is typed in abbreviated form on the final page of the document and consists only of the citations to the sources. In other cases, it is typed on a separate sheet headed *Memorandum of Points and Authorities*, as in the illustration on pages 463–465. If it is long and detailed, it may be typed as a separate document bearing the same caption as the other pleadings.

**Cross-claim or cross-complaint**   A cross-claim is a claim that may be litigated among co-defendants or among co-plaintiffs. For example, the defendant may believe that another party is either fully or partially responsible for the damages alleged by the plaintiff. In this case the defendant's attorney will respond to the complaint with an answer and cross-claim or cross-complaint. The cross-claim may be filed separately from the answer, or it may be combined with the answer into one document. When the answer and cross-claim form a single document, it is common to use a double box as a caption. The top half of the double box indicates the parties exactly as they were designated in the original complaint. This section is normally separated from the lower portion by a ruled line. In the lower half of the double box, the parties involved in the cross-claim may be designated as Cross-Complainant(s) and Cross-Defendant(s), as in the example below:

**IN THE SUPERIOR COURT OF THE STATE OF CALIFORNIA
IN AND FOR THE COUNTY OF ALAMEDA**

| | | |
|---|---|---|
| ROSCOE BARNES,<br>                    Plaintiff,<br><br>          vs.<br><br>MCKENZIE CLEANERS, INC.,<br>A Los Angeles corporation, and<br>DOE ONE and DOE TWO,<br>                    Defendants. | )<br>)<br>)<br>)<br>)<br>)<br>) No. 100804<br>)<br>) | |
| MCKENZIE CLEANERS, INC.,<br>a Los Angeles corporation,<br>                    Cross-Complainant,<br><br>          vs.<br><br>ALLEN TRUCKING CO.<br>                    Cross-Defendant. | )<br>)<br>)<br>)<br>)<br>)<br>)<br>) | ANSWER<br>AND<br><u>CROSS-COMPLAINT</u> |

**Motion**   Outside the courtroom every request made by an attorney for court action requires a written motion, which is typed in the format of all court documents. The motion is a request for a specific court order, which is an official instruction by the judge to do or refrain from doing something. When a motion is made, opposing counsel must be notified through service of a *notice* of motion.

Motions are typewritten unless made orally during a trial or hearing. Notice must be given to opposing counsel so that objections may be filed. In some jurisdictions only a detailed notice of motion, accompanied by an affidavit and supporting papers, and not the motion itself, must be written and served on opposing counsel; the motion itself is made later before the judge. In many courts motions are heard only during specified days.

## A Memorandum of Points and Authorities

```
 1 │ Law Offices of Arthur Burns
   │ 1919 21st Street, Suite 111
 2 │ Oakland, CA 94609
   │
 3 │ (415) 222-5056
   │
 4 │
   │
 5 │ Attorneys for Defendant
   │
 6 │
   │
 7 │
   │
 8 │           MUNICIPAL COURT OF THE STATE OF CALIFORNIA
   │
 9 │                 LOS ANGELES JUDICIAL DISTRICT
   │
10 │
   │
11 │ MARY SMITH,                    )
   │                                )
12 │            Plaintiff,          )    NO. 567933
   │                                )
13 │      vs.                       )    MEMORANDUM OF POINTS AND
   │                                )    AUTHORITIES IN SUPPORT OF
14 │ JOHN DOW,                      )    MOTION FOR CHANGE OF VENUE
   │                                )
15 │            Defendant.          )    (CCP Secs. 397(3), 398)
   │                                )
16 │
   │
17 │         THE COURT MAY PROPERLY ORDER A CHANGE IN THE
   │
18 │         PLACE OF THE TRIAL OF AN ACTION WHEN THE
   │
19 │         CONVENIENCE OF WITNESSES, LITIGANT, AND ENDS
   │
20 │         OF JUSTICE WOULD BE PROMOTED BY THE CHANGE.
   │
21 │
   │
22 │         According to CCP Sec. 397(3), the Court may, on motion,
   │
23 │ change the place of trial when the convenience of witnesses and
   │
24 │ the ends of justice would be promoted by the change.
   │
25 │         Moreover, the convenience of a party will be considered
   │
26 │ when due to serious illness of a party to an action he will be
   │
27 │ prevented from traveling to attend trial in another county and
   │
28 │ his testimony is material.  Such facts may justify an order
```

-1-

1    changing the place of trial to the county of his residence; in

2    such circumstances, the ends of justice would be promoted by the

3    transfer.   Simonian v. Simonian (1950) 97 Cal. App.2d 68, 69,

4    217 P.2d 157.

5    In Simonian, supra, defendant appealed from an order

6    granting a change of venue from the City and County of

7    San Francisco to the County of Los Angeles.  The Appellate Court

8    affirmed.  Plaintiff was a resident of Los Angeles and moved for

9    a change of venue on the ground that the convenience of witnesses

10   and the ends of justice would be promoted thereby.  The case

11   involved a dissolution of partnership in which testimony of the

12   parties was material and crucial.  Plaintiff's affidavit recited,

13   inter alia, that he had had a heart attack, was confined to a

14   sanatorium, and might suffer serious consequences to his life if

15   compelled to go to San Francisco to prosecute the action.

16   In the present case defendant JOHN DOW is a resident of

17   Alameda County.  The case involves a claim to insurance proceeds,

18   one-half of which has already been distributed to plaintiff.

19   Defendant asserts sole ownership to the remaining proceeds on the

20   ground that he is the natural father of the insured - deceased,

21   PAUL DOW.  Testimony by defendant in the case is critical and

22   material.

23   Defendant is an elderly man of 80 years.  He suffers

24   various physical ills including diabetes.  (See attached

25   affidavit.)  He is unable to walk well or stand for long periods

26   of time.  Such physical condition makes it difficult for him to

27   travel long distances without appropriate medical supervision.

28   Compelling defendant to travel to Los Angeles County to defend

-2-

```
 1   this action could result in serious consequences to his life.

 2   It is therefore submitted that due to the defendant's inability

 3   to safely travel to Los Angeles County to give his testimony by

 4   reason of his physical condition, the ends of justice would be

 5   promoted by transferring the trial to the county of his residence.

 6

 7                               Respectfully submitted,

 8                               LAW OFFICES OF ARTHUR BURNS

 9

10                               By_____
                                       ARTHUR BURNS
11                                   Attorney for Defendant
```

**Notice**   Notices are used to advise others of a wide variety of things, some related to court proceedings and others to non-court activities. Notices of motion are commonly used to advise opposing counsel of the fact that a motion is being filed with the court. A notice is typed according to the rules of the court in that jurisdiction.

Notices are normally addressed to opposing counsel. They may begin, below the caption, with the following conventional salutation to the opposing attorney:

SIR:   *if addressed to an attorney*
*or*
SIRS:   *if addressed to a law firm*
   PLEASE TAKE NOTICE that . . . .

Alternate forms of introduction are

DEFENDANT and KEPLER & CLARK, HER ATTORNEYS:
*or*
TO: Leslie R. Muldrew
   123 Center Building
   Townville, ST 98765
   Attorney for Defendants

Notices are ordinarily dated about three lines below the body of the document. A complimentary close may precede the attorney's signature. The name and address of the law firm to which the notice is directed is usually typed on the bottom left of the page.

Notices are typically typewritten, although printed forms can be used. If a notice must be addressed to a large number of people, legal-size paper should be used so that all the names will fit on one page.

Notices are frequently accompanied by other documents. An affidavit may accompany a notice of motion, for instance, or an order will accompany a notice of entry of order. In these cases, the papers are stapled together in a legal back with the notice on top. (An exception to this rule occurs when one of the papers is an order for the judge's signature, in which case the order itself is on top.) Endorsements on the legal back usually reverse the order of the stapled documents, naming the most important paper first, as in "Order and Notice of Entry."

## A Notice of Hearing

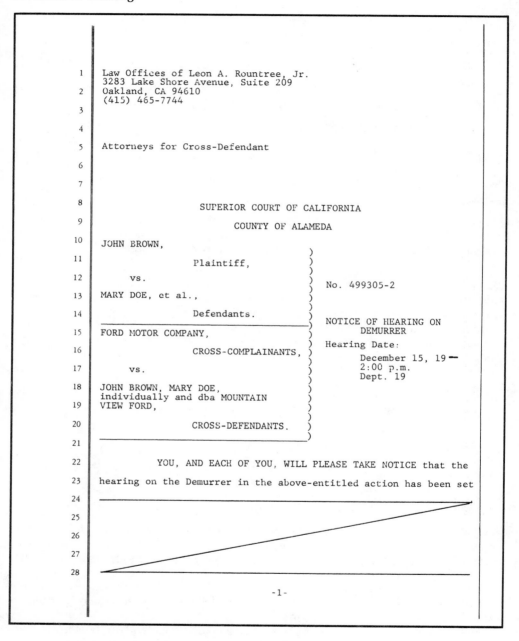

```
1    for December 15, 19--, at 2.00 p.m. in the above-entitled court.

2    DATED:  November 25, 19--

3                        LAW OFFICES OF LEON A. ROUNTREE, JR.

4

5                        By_____
                                GAIL D. BREWSTER
6                            Attorneys for Cross-Defendant

7
```

**Subpoena**  A writ issued under the authority of a court and requiring that a person appear at a specified time and place to give testimony is known as a subpoena. Federal and state laws specify the circumstances under which a subpoena is necessary. Witnesses required for trial testimony are subpoenaed. Subpoenas are generally prepared on printed forms supplied by the court, though they may be typed. The subpoena includes the following information:

1. The name and address of the attorney requesting the appearance
2. The title of the case
3. The name and address of the party required to appear
4. The name of the party on whose behalf the witness is to testify and whether that party is the plaintiff or the defendant
5. The time and place the witness is to appear

Some states require that witnesses who are to give a deposition be subpoenaed; in these cases a *subpoena re deposition* is served on the witness. An attorney who knows that a witness may refer to certain items in testimony or who wants such items admitted as evidence prepares a *subpoena duces tecum*, which requires the witness to bring specified documents to the hearing or trial.

**Stipulation**  A stipulation is an agreement between opposing attorneys which is legally binding on their clients. It may be used in order to agree to extend a deadline, to amend a complaint, to take a deposition, or to come to an agreement on some similar matter. A stipulation made in open court may be an oral agreement. Commonly prepared stipulations—such as those to extend deadlines—may be copied from a practice manual. Others are dictated.

Stipulations differ from other litigation papers in that they are dated and signed by attorneys for all the interested parties; the attorney seeking the stipulation prepares it. The caption is the same as for other documents in the case. The following are conventional openings for a stipulation:

IT IS HEREBY STIPULATED AND AGREED by and between the undersigned attorneys that . . . .

IT IS HEREBY STIPULATED that time for the defendant to answer, or make any motion with relation to the complainant in this act be and the same hereby is extended to . . . .

Each separate stipulation forms a complete paragraph. The signatures of all concerned attorneys follow the list of stipulations, along with the name of each law firm, a notation as to whom each attorney represents, and the date.

Because a stipulation is signed by attorneys from different offices, special procedures are necessary to arrange for signature. The attorney who prepares the stipulation signs the original and a copy for each attorney involved. The original and the copies are then delivered to the other attorneys, who are asked to sign each one and retain one copy. When the signed original is returned, office copies are conformed. If the stipulation is to be filed with the court, the original copy is filed. A conformed copy is retained for the office files. As with all court papers, a notation of the terms of the stipulation, the date, and other pertinent information is recorded on the office's case progress record.

## COURT ORDERS

A court order differs from other court documents in litigation in that it is prepared for the judge's signature. It is a directive made in writing by a court or judge, upon motion of counsel for a party in a case, and it is usually prepared by the attorney's secretary. An actual *court order* is made while the court is in session; when an order is made by a judge while the court is not sitting, it is called a *judge's order*. In some jurisdictions this is an important distinction because the formats of the two types of order may differ.

**Court order**   A court order typically begins with the term and name of the court (which is in session) and the date single-spaced in the upper right corner of the page. The name of the presiding judge is typed *above* the boxed caption:

PRESENT:                 *or*    PRESENT:
     HON. MARGARET CHANG,            HONORABLE LEON PIERCY,
                 Judge.                 United States Circuit Judge.

At the end of the document a signature line is typed, and below it the initials of the judge's title, as *J.S.C.* for Justice of the Supreme Court or *J.C.C.* for Judge of County Court. In some jurisdictions the judge's signature is preceded by the phrase ENTER:

ENTER

                _____

                      U.S.D.J.

**Judge's order**   A judge's order is styled more like a regular pleading. The judge's name does not appear in the caption, and ENTER is not used. The judge's title is typed in full below the signature line; an abbreviation is not used.

**Injunction**   An injunction is a court order that protects a legal right by requiring a party to take or to refrain from taking some specified action. This type of order is usually issued only after a showing that the legal remedy is inadequate and that irreparable injury will otherwise result. Injunctive relief may be either provisional (a temporary restraining order or preliminary injunction) or permanent.

A *temporary restraining order* is an interim order issued to preserve the status quo pending a hearing on application for preliminary injunction. Although it has the same force and effect, a restraining order technically is not an injunction. With some variations as specified in both federal and state law, the order usually (1) expires automatically at the end of a specific period of time, (2) terminates if a preliminary injunction is denied, or (3) is superseded by the issuance of a preliminary injunction.

A *preliminary injunction* is usually prohibitory in effect and is issued to preserve the status quo pending the final determination of an action. After a trial on the merits, a preliminary injunction is either merged into a permanent injunction or extinguished if a permanent injunction is denied. A sample preliminary injunction appears on the following pages. It is dated on the last line and signed by the judge.

## A Judge's Order

```
 1  Law Offices of Leon H. Rountree, Jr.
    3283 Lake Shore Avenue, Suite 209
 2  Oakland, CA 94610

 3  (415) 465-7744

 4

 5  Attorneys for Plaintiff

 6

 7

 8         IN THE SUPERIOR COURT OF THE STATE OF CALIFORNIA

 9              IN AND FOR THE COUNTY OF ALAMEDA

10

11  JOHN S. DOE,                  )
                                  )
12              Plaintiff,        )   NO. 55555
                                  )
13      vs.                       )   PRELIMINARY INJUNCTION
                                  )   AND ORDER FOR UNDERTAKING
14  MARY SMITH,                   )
                                  )
15              Defendant.        )
    _____)
16

17         The application of plaintiff for the preliminary

18  injunction made herewith came on regularly for hearing by the

19  court this date pursuant to an order to show cause issued by

20  this court on September 19, 19—.  Plaintiff appeared by counsel

21  ANTHONY PORTER; defendant appeared by counsel ANNA MOORE.

22         Upon proof made to the satisfaction of the court, and

23  good cause appearing therefor,

24         IT IS ORDERED that during the pendency of this action

25  the above-named defendant and her officers, agents, employees,

26  representatives, and all persons acting in concert or

27  participating with them, shall be and they are hereby enjoined

28  and restrained from engaging in, committing, or performing,
```

-1-

1   directly or indirectly, by any means whatsoever, any of the

2   following acts:

3           a.  From selling, or otherwise transferring, property

4               located at 159 Eighth Street, Oakland, California

5               94610;

6           IT IS FURTHER ORDERED that the above-named defendant

7   shall be and is hereby required and ordered forthwith:

8           a.  Maintain the property located at 159 Eighth

9               Street, Oakland, California 94610

10          b.  Pay all taxes due on the property;

11          IT IS FURTHER ORDERED that, before the foregoing order

12  shall take effect, plaintiff herein shall file a written

13  undertaking in the sum of $10,000, as required by Section 529 of

14  the Code of Civil Procedure, for the purpose of indemnifying

15  defendant for such damages as she may sustain by reason of this

16  preliminary injunction if the court finally decides that plaintiff

17  is not entitled thereto;

18          IT IS FURTHER ORDERED that the preliminary injunction

19  as set forth above shall issue upon plaintiff's filing a written

20  undertaking in the sum specified above.

21          The court reserves jurisdiction to modify this

22  injunction as the ends of justice may require.

23  Dated: _____, 19____

24

25

26                          _____
                                Judge of the Superior Court

27

28

-2-

A *permanent* (or *final*) *injunction* is issued after a trial on the merits. A permanent injunction may be later modified or vacated, however, if a judgment is made on a motion disclosing changed circumstances that make continued enforcement of the injunction unjust.

To obtain a judge's signature on a restraining order or a preliminary injunction, the attorney ordinarily needs to produce the following documents:

1. Complaint (or cross-complaint) and summons
2. Affidavits or declarations in support of the order or preliminary injunction
3. A memorandum of points and authorities
4. The restraining order and an order to show cause (to be filed with proof of service after being signed by the judge)

**Judgments and other orders**    Other court papers that require the judge's signature include findings of fact and conclusions of law, which are prepared by counsel at the end of a trial; and judgments and decrees, which are the Court's decisions at the conclusion of litigation. *Judgments* normally decide a case in law; *decrees* usually decide cases in equity. Judgments may require a greater number of copies than most court documents, since copies may be necessary for the parties as well as their attorneys. Extra copies may also be required so that one may be served with the notice of entry *before* the judgment is signed and another served *after* the judgment is signed. After it is signed, the clerk of court enters it. The secretary may need to check with the clerk or a legal newspaper to find out whether and when the judgment was signed.

**Typing court orders**    It is important to know the judge's correct title (Chief Judge, Associate Justice, Circuit Judge, etc.) before preparing a court order; whether or not the court is in session must also be determined. Practice manuals and form books will supply the correct format. In general, the court order is styled like other documents in litigation, with a complete caption; however, a dateline is often typed about three lines below the body of the document, and a signature line is typed for the judge. Below the signature line appears the title of the judge, either in full or abbreviated, but not the judge's personal name.

The body of a court order is conventionally divided into paragraphs that begin:

IT IS ORDERED that . . . .
IT IS FURTHER ORDERED that . . . .

Orders are frequently placed in legal backs. When notices are attached, as they frequently are, the set that is delivered to the judge should have the order on top to facilitate its signing.

## DOCUMENTS IN DISCOVERY

There are a variety of proceedings whereby an attorney can obtain needed information about a case from the opposing side. Two common discovery documents—bills of particulars and interrogatories—are discussed in the following paragraphs.

**Bill of particulars**    A document called a *demand for a bill of particulars* is used in many jurisdictions, although it has been abolished by the Federal Rules of Civil Procedure. It is a demand for further details about a specified claim; the desired details are listed and numbered separately. The caption is styled like the caption in the original complaint but, like a notice, the demand is addressed to the opposing attorney (SIR: or SIRS:), often begins with the phrase "PLEASE TAKE NOTICE that . . . ," and concludes with a dateline and complimentary close. The name and address of the attorney to whom the bill is addressed is usually typed in the lower left corner of the page. No verification is required.

If your office receives a demand for a bill of particulars, you may be asked to prepare it. The bill of particulars is formatted much like the demand, with a numbered listing of the particulars demanded. It is verified, however, because it contains statements of fact.

**Interrogatories** Interrogatories are a set of written questions directed to the opposing party; they may be filed by either party. Interrogatories are more commonly used than bills of particulars. An affidavit is always attached, either on the last page of the interrogatories or on a separate page, asserting that the questions are material to the case. Answers to interrogatories are verified. Many courts require that the answers be typed directly on the copy; in these instances the secretary who prepares the interrogatories must type lines for the answers.

## AFFIDAVIT

An affidavit, as explained in Chapter 12, is a written statement of fact made voluntarily under oath in which the affiant swears to the truth of the statements made in the affidavit. Affidavits are legal instruments. They may be used for a variety of purposes, such as in real estate transactions, applications for licenses, and affirmation of birth, citizenship, or age. Affidavits are also commonly used to support court documents such as motions for a change of venue.

The format for an affidavit that accompanies a court document is the same as that described on pages 416–420, except that the affidavit is headed with the caption of the case to which it pertains. The title of the affidavit is usually specific, such as *Affidavit of Service by Mail* or *Affidavit of Proof of Property Damage*. Unlike verifications, in which the verifier swears to the truth of statements made in an attached pleading, the affidavit itself contains the facts sworn to. The affidavit is an independent document and is frequently stapled in a legal back.

Below the heading, the affidavit begins with a statement of venue, indicating the state and county in which the affidavit is made. The venue is boxed by closing parentheses or brackets and may be followed by *ss*, the abbreviation for *scilicet* (meaning "to wit" or "namely") typed in capital or lowercase letters and followed by a period. The statement of venue is followed by the name of the affiant and a statement that the affiant appeared before a notary and swore under oath to the statements contained in the document. The statements of fact—which may be written in the first or third person—are followed by the affiant's signature.

The notary public also signs the document and may imprint a notarial seal on the paper. The section of the document bearing the notary's signature and seal and the statement that the document was signed in the presence of the notary and sworn to under oath is known as the *jurat*. The jurat, which is essential to the affidavit, may be either stamped or typed on the document. It is usually typed below and to the left of the signature, but it may also be typed margin-to-margin below the signature. An affidavit with jurat is illustrated on pages 473–474.

## ACKNOWLEDGMENT

An acknowledgment is a statement attached to a document stating, in effect, that the person who signed the document is the person mentioned in that document and did, in fact, sign the document. The person making the acknowledgment signs the document; the notary public or other official signs the acknowledgment.

Acknowledgments are more commonly used with client documents than with court documents because client documents require the client's signature while the attorney normally signs court documents. However, an acknowledgment is sometimes needed to affirm a signature on a document used in court proceedings. Acknowledgments are explained in detail in Chapters 11 and 12.

## An Affidavit with Jurat

```
 1   Law Offices of Leon H. Rountree, Jr.
     3283 Lake Shore Avenue, Suite 209
 2   Oakland, CA 94610

 3   (415) 465-7744

 4

 5   Attorneys for Plaintiff

 6

 7

 8                  SUPERIOR COURT OF CALIFORNIA

 9                      COUNTY OF ALAMEDA

10

11   JOHN DOW,                    )
                                  )
12              Plaintiff,        )     NO. 56790
                                  )
13        vs.                     )     AFFIDAVIT OF JOHN DOW
                                  )     IN SUPPORT OF MOTION
14   MARY BROWN,                  )     FOR CHANGE OF VENUE
                                  )
15              Defendant.        )
     _____)

16

17   STATE OF CALIFORNIA    )
                            )ss.
18   COUNTY OF LOS ANGELES )

19           JOHN DOW, being first duly sworn on his oath says:

20        In 19-- and again in 19-- I suffered from a stroke.  I

21   also suffer from high blood pressure, sugar diabetes, and

22   hypertension.  Three to four times per day I consume various

23   types of prescribed drugs for hypertension, diabetes, and my

24   blood pressure.  By doctor's orders I am required to take an

25   injection of insulin each morning.

26           These conditions prevent me from traveling long

27   distances and from engaging in activities that may easily tire me

28   including walking or standing for long periods.  I am in no
```

-1-

```
 1   condition to travel to defend on the matter herein.

 2          If compelled to travel without appropriate medical

 3   supervision, my health will be seriously affected; and such

 4   effects may result in adverse consequences to my life.

 5

 6                                    _____
                                              JOHN DOW
 7

 8          Subscribed and sworn to before me this 5th day of

 9   November, 19--.

10

11
                                     _____
12        (SEAL)                             DEBORAH SMITH
                                       111 North Street, Oakland
                                       Notary Public in and for said
13                                     County and State

14                                   My commission expires March 30, 19--

15

16

17
```

# 13.4

## PROBATE, ADOPTION, AND GUARDIANSHIP

This section describes some common court proceedings for which the legal secretary must prepare court documents. The secretary should follow the attorney's instructions and seek the attorney's guidance at all times. Although many of these proceedings are highly technical and can be handled only by the attorney, others are relatively routine. In these latter cases the secretary can assume considerable responsibility, using comprehensive checklists as guides. If the secretary understands the basic requirements for preparing, filing, and serving notice of court documents and, in addition, knows what resources are available, these matters should proceed smoothly.

### PROBATE

Probate is a proceeding brought in an appropriate court to prove the validity of a will and to facilitate administration of a decedent's estate and other matters related to the estate. Probating a will frequently involves a large amount of documentation.

Probate may be either formal (supervised) or informal (unsupervised). The formal administration of estates is the more common practice. However, states following the Uniform Probate Code in the administration of decedents' estates permit the use of both formal and informal probate proceedings. Formal probate proceedings are conducted in probate court.

The county and state in which the decedent resides at death is the proper place for the administration of the decedent's estate. In some states special probate courts or surrogate's courts handle the proving of wills and the settling of estates. Courts of general jurisdiction may handle probate cases when no court of special jurisdiction has been established. The probate court's jurisdiction—that is, the authority or power the court has to hear and decide matters related to the decedent's estate—continues until the proceeding is finished.

Probate proceedings consist of two phases: (1) proving the validity of the will and (2) carrying out the terms of the will. Formal probate proceedings require the petitioner for the probate of a will to give notice to all parties with an interest—heirs, devisees, and so on—so that they may be present at the initial hearing to contest the validity of the will if they choose.

In probate proceedings the attorney, the executor (the person named in the will to carry out its terms), and the secretary work closely together in a special team effort. The attorney makes sure that every step taken is legally correct and that all documents are properly prepared. As a representative of the executor and the estate, the attorney attends all court hearings related to the probate proceedings. The executor, within the authority provided by statute, handles many practical problems that arise in conjunction with the estate, from making payments on the decedent's mortgage to managing a portfolio of stocks and bonds. The executor provides the attorney with a great deal of information about the estate, including a list of personal possessions such as furnishings, jewelry, and cars. The executor must also keep careful records of all money received or paid out on behalf of the estate during the probate period. The executor will need certified copies of the death certificate—a document that is signed by a physician or coroner and that indicates the date, time, and place of death—in order to handle certain responsibilities, especially the collecting of money from sources such as insurance policies. The executor or the attorney's office secures these certified copies from the proper county office.

The legal secretary with probate experience significantly contributes to the successful handling of the entire proceeding. The secretary may prepare documents, watch deadlines, schedule appointments, and answer routine questions from clients. Clients are often distraught, and the attorney and secretary must be tactful, sympathetic, and understanding.

## CHECKLIST OF PROBATE PROCEDURES

Although probate is not usually a difficult legal proceeding, it does involve many steps. It is usually the secretary's responsibility to see that each step is taken at the proper time and in proper sequence. A checklist should be followed to make sure that no step is omitted. Many offices prepare their own list, and some use lists published by state bar associations. A sample list based on California procedures is reproduced on pages 476–477. This checklist can be used as a model for the preparation of checklists in other jurisdictions by making the modifications necessary to make the list comply with local customs and requirements. When probating a will, one should check off each step on the list to ensure that no step has been overlooked. As with any checklist, it is wise to include the date and the initials of the person completing the task.

Probate handbooks are available in many states. These can be of great assistance because they indicate the required steps and also answer many other questions about probate procedures.

# A Sample Checklist for Probate Procedures

PROBATE CHECKLIST

Name of decedent_____

Name of executor or administrator_____

_____
            Address                        **Tel.:**   Home        Business
Appointment for conference with executor or admin._____

Certified copies of death certificate obtained_____Number_____

### PREPARATION FOR HEARING AND ADMITTING WILL TO PROBATE WITH LETTERS

Will filed_____Petition filed_____Date of Hearing_____

Notices of hearing prepared_____ Sent to clerk_____

Affidavit of mailing prepared_____ Sent to clerk_____

Bond required?_____Amount_____Obtained_____ Cost_____

Affidavit of subscribing witnesses required? _____Prepared_____Signed___

Order admitting will to probate prepared_____Date signed_____

Order appointing appraiser prepared _____Date signed_____

Name and address of appraiser_____

Letters prepared_____Signed_____Original filed____

Certified copies obtained_____Number_____Cost_____

### SAFE-DEPOSIT BOX AND BANK ACCOUNTS

Location of safe-deposit box_____No._____

Date with treasurer_____List of contents prepared_____

Banks notified of death_____ Trans. accounts in joint tenancy_____

After hearing, arrangements to release cash to executor_____

### FAMILY ALLOWANCE

Petition filed_____Signed ex parte_____

Or signed on notice_____Notice prep._____Hearing date_____

Order for family allowance prepared_____Signed_____Filed_____

### NOTICE TO CREDITORS

Published_____Where_____

Date of first publication_____Late date for return of claims_____

Proof of publication prepared_____ __Filed_____

### INVENTORY AND APPRAISEMENT AND DOCUMENTS FOR INHERITANCE TAX

Inv. and apprais. form prepared_____Inventory typed_____

Sent to appraiser_____Signed and returned_____Fee_____

Copies conformed_____Original filed_____

Inheritance tax affidavit prepared_____Signed_____

Sent to controller's office_____Objections due_____

Community property aff. needed?_____Prepared_____Filed_____

Federal estate tax required_____Preliminary notice due_____

Final return due_____Prepared_____Filed_____

Federal income tax return prepared_____Filed_____

State income tax return prepared_____Filed_____

SALE OF PROPERTY

Petition for sale of real property_____Filed_____Hearing_____

Notice published_____Where_____When_____

Order prepared_____Approved and signed_____Sale price_____

If notice not required, arrangements made for sale_____

Order prepared_____Approved and signed_____Filed_____

Petition for sale of personal property prepared_____Filed_____

If notice required, prepared_____Filed_____Hearing_____

Order for sale of personal property prepared_____Signed_____Filed_____

CREDITORS' CLAIMS--List each on a schedule that shows:

1.   Claimant
2.   Amount
3.   Date filed
4.   Date approved by executor or administrator
5.   Date approved by court
6.   Date paid or other disposition

PETITION FOR DISTRIBUTION AND FINAL DISCHARGE

Petition for distribution prepared_____ _____Filed_____Hearing_____

Accounting prepared_____Notices sent and filed_____

Order for final distribution prepared_____Date signed_____

Prepared receipts of distributees_____Date signed and returned_____

Petition and order for final discharge_____Date signed_____

## PROVING THE WILL

After the death of the testator, the attorney will meet with the person or persons closest to the decedent, often the executor, to discuss the terms of the will. During this meeting the attorney will obtain information necessary to probating the will. After the initial meeting, the next step often is the opening of the decedent's safe-deposit box, which in some jurisdictions takes place in the presence of a specified public official. The attorney is responsible for notifying this official and arranging the time and place where the box will be opened. The secretary often makes this arrangement, making certain that the attorney will be present.

The attorney, assisted by the executor, obtains a complete list of the estate's assets. This information may come from various sources, such as the papers in the safe-deposit box, relatives, or the executor. In states with community property laws, the attorney must determine which of the assets are community property in order to determine inheritance taxes. The attorney makes complete notes of his findings, and these notes become part of the file on the proceeding. This file will then be available to both the attorney and the legal secretary for reference as various documents are prepared.

After the attorney has obtained all the information required, the secretary will establish a file and prepare papers as needed. A checklist or a register should be prepared so that each step of the probate proceeding will be recorded as it occurs. Photocopies of the will are made and held until needed. (Photocopying should be accomplished <u>without</u> unfastening the original staples that hold the pages of the will together. The original will should remain intact.)

**Petition for probate**   In some jurisdictions the law specifies the time limit within which one or more copies of the will must be filed with the clerk of the court. With the will a document that in some states is called a *petition for probate of will and for letters testamentary* will be filed. The court may provide a form for this petition. If it does not, the petition is typed in the format that court documents take in that jurisdiction. A sample typewritten petition that conforms to California statutes is shown on the following pages.

Depending upon statutory requirements and local customs, the petition may include the following:

1. The executor's name, address, and citizenship
2. The name, address, domicile, and citizenship of the decedent on the date of death
3. The date and place the will was signed and the names and addresses of witnesses to the will and to the codicil if there is one
4. The names and addresses of the next of kin (those who would inherit in the event of intestacy, as prescribed in the state law of intestate succession)
5. The names and addresses of testamentary trustees, guardians, substitutes, or successor executors or trustees, if included in the will
6. The names and addresses of all beneficiaries named in the will and possibly the amount of each bequest
7. The names and addresses of any of the above who are infants (minors or persons below a specified age—usually 21 but in some states 18) or incompetents so that guardians or conservators may be appointed for them
8. The type and estimated value of the real and personal property in the estate

Like most documents in probate, the petition is signed by the executor on the signature line at the right. In this document the executor is the petitioner, and the word *petitioner* may be typed below the signature lines. The petition may have to be verified.

# Petition for Probate of Will and Issuance of Letters Testamentary

```
1  Abrahms & Foster
   1169 Grand Avenue
2  Oakland, CA 94621

3  (415) 444-2376

4

5  Attorneys for Petitioner

6

7

8          SUPERIOR COURT OF THE STATE OF CALIFORNIA

9              COUNTY OF CONTRA COSTA

10  Estate of              )
    ARTHUR M. NATHANSON,   )           No. 867644
11           Deceased.     )
                           )

12

13          PETITION FOR PROBATE OF WILL AND
            ISSUANCE OF LETTERS TESTAMENTARY
14

15          To the Honorable Superior Court of the State of

16  California in the County of Contra Costa:

17          The petition of ROBERT L. DEAN respectfully shows:

18          That ARTHUR M. NATHANSON died on the 24th day of

19  October, 19--, in the City of Richmond, County of Contra Costa,

20  State of California; that said decedent was at the time of his

21  death a resident of the County of Contra Costa, State of

22  California, and left an estate therein consisting of real and

23  personal property;

24          That said decedent left a will dated the 15th day of

25  August, 1968, which your petitioner believes and therefore

26  alleges to be the Last Will and Testament of said decedent; that

27  said will is herewith presented to this court, and a copy of

28  same is annexed to this petition.
```

-1-

1    At the time said Will was executed, to wit, on the 15th

2  day of August, 1968, said decedent was over the age of 18 years,

3  was of sound and disposing mind and not acting under duress,

4  menace, fraud, or undue influence, and was in every respect

5  competent by Last Will to dispose of all of his estate.

6    Your petitioner, ROBERT L. DEAN, is named as executor

7  in said Will and consents to act.

8    The names and residences of the heirs, devisees, and

9  legatees of the decedent, so far as known to petitioner, are:

10    CAROLINE NATHANSON, wife of decedent, 1324 Barrett
         Avenue, Richmond, CA 94801

11

12    JAMES NATHANSON, adult son of decedent, 1489 Jules
         Avenue, San Francisco, CA 94110

13    WHEREFORE, your petitioner prays that said Will be

14  admitted to probate and that Letters Testamentary be issued to

15  your petitioner; for that purpose a time be appointed for proving

16  said Will and that all persons interested be notified and

17  directed to appear at the time for proving same in the manner

18  provided by law; and that all other necessary and proper audits

19  be made in the premises.

20

21    _____
                                        ROBERT L. DEAN
22                                      Petitioner

23

24  ABRAHMS & FOSTER

25

26  By_____
            JOHN E. STONER
27    Attorney for Petitioner

28  ///                                        ///

-2-

**Filing the petition**   The petition and will are filed together in the office of the clerk of court, and the originals of both are retained there. It is general practice to send the original and one copy of the petition with a request that the copy be endorsed and returned for the office files. This endorsed copy constitutes proof of filing and verifies the filing date for both the petition and the will. Some courts request that at least two copies of the will be filed. The following items should be packaged and sent together to the clerk's office:

1. The original will and the number of copies required by the court
2. The original petition and one copy
3. The check for the filing fee
4. A letter of transmittal requesting that the will and petition be filed and that one copy of the petition be endorsed and returned
5. The death certificate, if required
6. A bond, if required
7. Other papers as required by state statutes
8. A self-addressed, stamped envelope

In most areas the court clerk will assign a file number to the petition. This number must be placed on all subsequent papers filed in the matter.

**Letters testamentary and letters of administration**   The petition to the court for admission of the will is usually called a *petition for admission of will to probate and for letters testamentary* (or *letters of administration*). Letters testamentary are orders of the court, signed by the judge, that authorize the executor to manage the estate and eventually to terminate it. When an administrator rather than an executor manages the estate, letters of administration provide the same authority for the administrator. (An administrator is a person appointed by the court to handle an estate when there is no will.) *Letters of administration, c.t.a.* are similar to letters of administration except that, although there is a will, no one has been named executor, the named executor cannot or will not serve, or the named executor has died or dies before completing service as executor. The abbreviation c.t.a. is for *cum testamento annexo*, which means "with will annexed." Such "letters" are actually one-page documents that are often prepared on court-supplied printed forms.

**The hearing on the petition**   The petition is filed with the probate court and the court establishes its jurisdiction over the estate and sets a date and time for a hearing. The clerk's office usually notifies the attorney of the date, time, and place for the hearing, and the secretary immediately calendars the date and prepares notices of the hearing.

**Notice of hearing**   Everyone who has an interest in the estate of the deceased must be sent a notice of the hearing on the petition. This document, which may be titled *notice of hearing on admission of will to probate* or simply *notice of probate* or *citation*, informs the parties of the date, time, and place of the hearing. The people receiving such notices may attend the hearing if they wish. Usually, unless the will is contested, only the attorney for the petitioner and one of the witnesses to the signing of the will, if needed, attend the hearing.

The secretary must prepare the correct number of copies of the notice—one for each person who must be informed of the hearing and one for the office files. If many copies are needed, they may be photocopied.

**Mailing the notices**   If court rules specify that the attorney's office must mail the notices, the secretary will mail them and file a proof of mailing with the clerk of the court. Proof of mailing is an affidavit containing a list of the names and addresses of all parties to whom the notice was sent, together with a sworn statement that the notice was sent. An affidavit of mailing is illustrated on page 514 of Chapter 14. If court rules specify that the notices must be mailed by the clerk's office, they are sent or taken there with stamped envelopes, one of which is addressed to the law office. The clerk's office prepares the affidavit and sends a certified copy to the attorney for the office files. In some instances, in addition to mailing notices to the interested parties, the court requires publication in a local newspaper. Two forms usually required by the court in connection with publication are *proof of publication of notice of hearing* and an affidavit stating when and where the notice was published.

**Declaration of subscribing witnesses**    In some jurisdictions one of the witnesses to the will must appear at the hearing to attest to the fact that he or she did indeed witness the will and knew it was the last will and testament of the decedent. The secretary contacts witnesses and arranges for them to be present in court.

**Required court orders**    At the hearing on the petition in some jurisdictions, the attorney must have all the documents that require the Court's signature. These may include the certificate of probate, the order to admit the will, the order appointing an appraiser, an order appointing a trustee or guardian if appropriate, a notice to the surviving spouse, and copies of letters testamentary or letters of administration. It is the secretary's responsibility to see that all these papers have been prepared and assembled. The wording of these documents is standardized, and they can easily be prepared by adapting file copies of similar documents. If the petition is approved, the Court signs the various orders and the original of the letters.

**Filing the orders**    After the hearing on the petition, the signed copies of the various orders and letters are taken to the clerk's office. The originals are filed with the clerk, and a copy of each order is endorsed for placement in the office file. The attorney also requests several certified copies of the letters for the executor, who needs the certified copies to establish a bank account in the name of the estate, collect insurance policies, and carry out other functions for the estate. The attorney's secretary conforms all office copies with the information supplied by the court, including the name of the appraiser, and files them.

## ADMINISTRATION OF THE ESTATE

The signed order and the letters legally authorize the executor to take charge of the decedent's property within the state. With the help of the attorney and the appraiser, the executor will see that a value is placed on all assets so that the total value of the estate may be determined.

**Notices to creditors**    In some states all creditors must receive proper notice of the testator's death. The secretary prepares a *notice to creditors*, which must be published, as prescribed by law, a certain number of times and for a specified period in one of the newspapers in the area where the deceased lived.

**Inventory and appraisement**    The secretary must type a detailed inventory of assets to accompany an official printed form that is sometimes called an *inventory and appraisement*. The appraiser fills in the form, which indicates the total value of the property in the estate, and signs one portion. The completed typewritten inventory and the original copy of the inventory and appraisement are filed with the clerk of the court after they have been signed by the appropriate people, including the executor. The secretary must be familiar with the required forms for declaring the value of the estate for court and tax purposes.

**Federal and state income taxes**   Federal and state income taxes must be paid on the decedent's income up to the date of death. Also, these same taxes must be paid by the estate from the date of death until the estate has been finally distributed. The secretary may assist in the preparation of the tax forms, or this work may be done by a legal assistant who has had special training in probate proceedings including the tax requirements. Secretaries for attorneys who specialize in or who do a good deal of probate work should learn to prepare tax forms.

**Federal and state inheritance and estate taxes**   Federal and state laws specify that estates in which the assets exceed a legally established amount must pay estate and/or inheritance taxes. The cutoff points vary from state to state and occasionally are changed. The attorney will determine whether state or federal estate or inheritance taxes must be paid, and the secretary will assist with the preparation of the federal or state forms. Federal and state governments provide the forms required for these taxes. The time limits within which these forms must be submitted are also established by federal and state laws. The secretary must know these time limits in order to calendar them and make sure that deadlines are met.

## CLOSING THE ESTATE
When all the obligations of the estate have been paid, all tax forms completed, taxes paid and, where necessary, property sold to obtain needed cash, the attorney must prepare for the executor's signature a petition to the court for approval of the manner in which the estate has been administered and for an order permitting distribution of assets according to the terms of the will. An order that may be called *settling first and final account and decree of distribution* must be prepared and ready for the hearing on the petition. A *notice of hearing on the final accounting and order for distribution*—or a similarly titled document—must be sent to all heirs so that they may be present at the hearing if they choose. If the will provided for trusts, guardianships, or conservatorships, the appropriate documents should be available for the judge's signature at the same time, unless this was done earlier in order to provide custody for minors or incompetents.

**Distributing the assets**   When the order permitting distribution of assets has been signed and the original filed with the court, the secretary conforms all office copies. Then the executor proceeds with the distribution of assets. If personal property or amounts of money must be sent to heirs, the secretary prepares for each heir a document which may be called *receipt of distributee, receipt and release,* or a similar title. These are sent to the heirs together with a letter of transmittal requesting that the recipient sign the receipt and send it back to the attorney. After these documents are signed and, in some states, acknowledged, the checks or personal property is delivered to the heirs.

**Discharging the executor**   When all the requirements of the will have been met, the judge signs an order or decree that affirms the proper actions of the executor and discharges him from any further responsibility to the estate.

## PROBATE PROCEEDINGS AND THE LEGAL SECRETARY
It is helpful for the secretary to be familiar with the probate process. Manuals are available that deal exclusively with probate procedures, and copies of these should be available in the office. These and other reference books, along with checklists, will serve as guides. The secretary who watches the checklist, follows the attorney's instructions, calendars deadlines carefully, and uses model documents from a form file or from the office files will be a valuable assistant to the attorney during probate.

## ADOPTION

Adoption may be defined as the legal process by which a child acquires parents other than his or her natural parents and parents acquire a child other than a natural child. Each state has statutes designating which court will grant adoptions. Jurisdiction to grant adoption may reside in a court of general jurisdiction, such as a superior court, or in a specialized court, such as a probate, juvenile, or domestic relations court.

An adoption proceeding is not an adversary proceeding; therefore, the caption in the adoption papers is different from that in litigation. Instead of being styled like THOMAS ATKINS vs. MARTHA MORTON, for example, the caption might read, "In the Matter of the Adoption Petition of THOMAS ATKINS and ALICE ATKINS, Adopting Parents."

While adoption proceedings vary somewhat from state to state, they are usually initiated by the filing of a *petition for adoption*. The parents sign a *consent and agreement* form stating that they agree to adopt the child and give the child every right of a natural child including the right of inheritance. If an agency manages the adoption, the agency signs a *consent of agency to adoption* form. If the child is over a certain age, he or she may be required to sign a consent and agreement form. Nearly every state requires the consent of natural parents, guardians, and others as a prerequisite to adoption.

The final document filed in the adoption proceeding may be called a *decree of adoption* or *certificate of adoption*. This decree is dated and signed by the judge and indicates the name by which the child will be subsequently known. A copy of this decree must be sent to the appropriate state office so the child's birth certificate may be sealed and a new certificate issued that shows the child's new name and the new parents as the legal parents.

## GUARDIANSHIP AND CONSERVATORSHIP

Sometimes it becomes necessary for the court to appoint a person to assume responsibility for a minor or an incompetent adult. This procedure is usually accomplished by a court-initiated action and the issuance of *letters of guardianship* or *letters of conservatorship*—legal papers authorizing a person to act for or on behalf of another. If a minor is involved in the action, the minor is referred to as a *ward*.

**Guardianship**    The guardianship relationship may require that the guardian be responsible for the custody and care of the minor or simply for the management of the minor's financial affairs. Guardianship proceedings are initiated when the person desiring to become the guardian of the minor files a form often entitled *petition for appointment of guardian*. The names and addresses of close relatives who may be concerned with the welfare of the minor must be included in the petition. Thus, their names become a matter of record, and they must be given written notice of the guardianship proceedings. At the same time that the petition for guardianship is prepared, an *order setting petition for appointment of guardian for hearing* may be made. The petition and order are filed with the court, and the judge signs the order. Conformed copies of the order, along with an affidavit or declaration of service, should be sent to all the persons listed on the petition.

The secretary may also be asked to prepare an *order appointing guardian* and several copies of the letters of guardianship for the attorney to take to the hearing. The judge signs the original order, and the clerk issues the letters of guardianship. Certified copies of the letters should be made for the guardian's use. These letters provide authorization for the guardian to carry out his or her responsibilities.

**Conservatorship**    A conservator is a person appointed to manage the property of another person. The procedures for appointing a conservator are essentially the same as those for appointing a guardian. A conservator may be appointed upon the request of the conservatee if the conservatee realizes that he or she is no longer capable of handling business affairs. All close relatives must be notified at the time of the hearing on the petition. The Court decides if the conservatee is making a wise decision in the appointment of the conservator and thereby protects the conservatee against fraud or undue influence.

# 13.5

## THE PREPARATION OF BRIEFS

A *brief* is an argument written by the attorney that sets forth the facts and legal issues of a case, the attorney's interpretation of the law involved, and the pertinent authorities that support that interpretation. Attorneys may prepare trial briefs or appeal briefs. Both types are described in the following pages.

### TRIAL COURT BRIEFS

Trial court briefs are filed in the trial court after a hearing or whenever the judge orders them to be filed. Sometimes an attorney files a trial brief at his or her own discretion during the trial. When the supporting points and authorities are numerous and detailed, they may be typed as a separate document with the caption *Points and Authorities in Support of (Name of Document), Memorandum of Law,* or *Brief.*

One type of trial brief is referred to as a *trial book, trial manual, trial file,* or *trial schedule.* It is a compilation of all the papers that the lawyer will use in the preparation and conduct of a trial. In a typical jury case the lawyer's trial brief will contain notes relating to the impaneling of the jury, an opening statement, data for the examination of witnesses, exhibits to be introduced, arguments and authorities on anticipated legal points on which judicial rulings may be required, possible motions, and requests for charges to the jury. The trial brief just described serves as a guide and resource for the attorney in conducting the trial. Frequently an abridged version is prepared for submission to the court.

In addition to the trial brief, either for the attorney's own use or for the court, lawyers often prepare trial memoranda on the law involved in a case. A separate memorandum is often prepared in advance for each legal issue that reasonably can be anticipated. These memoranda are then held in readiness until needed to justify a legal position or approach, to validate motions, to furnish authority for the admissibility of types of evidence, or to guide the court on the legal soundness of requested instructions.

As the above discussion suggests, trial briefs vary considerably in their form, content, and use. The trial court may prescribe the form and content of trial briefs that are submitted. However, the requirements are usually less rigid than for appeal briefs. Trial briefs are submitted most often when the case involves highly technical legal issues, unusual or relatively obscure points of law, or a new and untried interpretation of law. The trial brief may be long and detailed, in which case its format may be similar to that of an appeal brief. In other instances the brief may be relatively short and consist of a simple list of points and authorities. Because these documents vary widely according to the jurisdiction, the case, and the attorney's preference, the secretary's responsibility is usually to respond to the instructions of the attorney, transcribe the dictation, verify citations at the attorney's direction, and type the material accurately.

## APPEAL BRIEFS

An appeal brief, often called an appellate brief, is filed in the appropriate appellate court when the losing party in litigation chooses not to accept the decision of a lower court. The attorney usually dictates the text of the document to the legal secretary, who then transcribes a triple-spaced draft of the document for the attorney to review and revise. (Take-ins of quoted material may be single-spaced on rough drafts, since they will not need revision.) A complicated brief may undergo more than one rough draft. When the final draft is approved, the secretary prepares the final copy of the document. The final copy is frequently sent to a printer for printing the requisite number of briefs to be filed with the appellate court.

**Typing a brief**   Court rules are very specific about the manner in which appeal briefs may be submitted. Some courts prefer or permit typewritten briefs, while others require that briefs be printed. The court rules also specify the size and type of paper, the method of reproducing or printing to be used, the width of margins, the number of lines to a page, the size of type, the method of handling quotations, the method of citing references, and other details. These rules may differ from jurisdiction to jurisdiction. It is extremely important that the brief conform precisely to court specifications. For assistance, the secretary can refer to form files, copies of briefs in the office files, office reference books, the published rules of the court in which the brief is to be filed and, of course, to the attorney.

**Copies**   Most appeal briefs require a fairly large number of copies; for example:

1. One filed with the clerk of the appellate court
2. A copy for each justice or judge of the court
3. Additional copies for court files or the judges' assistants
4. A copy for each attorney of record
5. A copy for the client
6. An office copy

It is necessary to determine the exact number of copies required before sending the document to the printer. When typing a manuscript for the printer, make at least two extra copies—one for the files and one for the lawyer to use while the original is at the printer's.

## PARTS OF AN APPEAL BRIEF

Most appellate courts require that every brief include the following:

1. A cover'sheet
2. A table of contents
3. A table of authorities
4. Properly typed points in the argument, each numbered and supported by references to legal authorities (citations)
5. Some type of signature line

**Cover sheet**   The cover sheet generally includes the following information:

1. The name of the court including, where applicable, the number of the division if it is a state court or the number of the circuit if it is a federal court of appeals
2. The docket number, if assigned; or space for it if unassigned (the number will differ from the old docket number because the case is in a different court)
3. Often, though not always, the state and county and the name of the presiding judge
4. The name, address, and telephone number of the attorney filing the brief
5. The purpose or title of the document (as "Brief of Respondent")
6. The title of the case

## Cover Sheet for an Appeal Brief

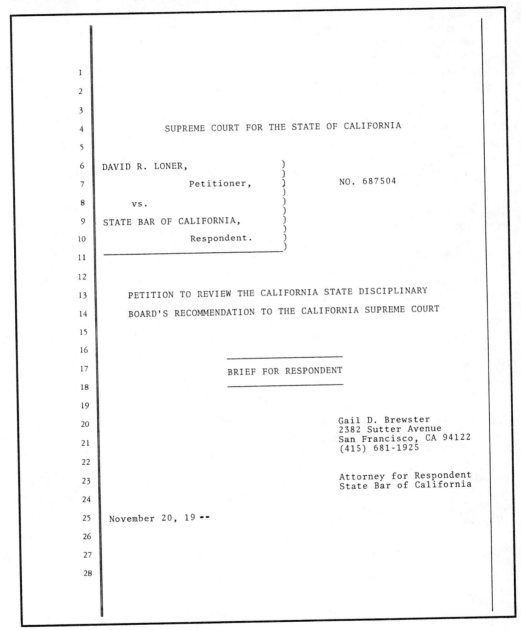

1
2
3
4        SUPREME COURT FOR THE STATE OF CALIFORNIA
5
6   DAVID R. LONER, )
7             Petitioner, )     NO. 687504
                    )
8     vs. )
                    )
9   STATE BAR OF CALIFORNIA, )
10         Respondent. )
11
12
13   PETITION TO REVIEW THE CALIFORNIA STATE DISCIPLINARY
14   BOARD'S RECOMMENDATION TO THE CALIFORNIA SUPREME COURT
15
16
17               BRIEF FOR RESPONDENT
18
19
20                      Gail D. Brewster
                        2382 Sutter Avenue
21                        San Francisco, CA 94122
                        (415) 681-1925
22
23                      Attorney for Respondent
                      State Bar of California
24
25   November 20, 19 --
26
27
28

The title of the case will not be the same in the appellate court as it was in the general trial court. The party who appeals the case, whether formerly plaintiff or defendant, is now called the *appellant*; the prevailing party in the trial court is now called the *appellee* or the *respondent*. (Where the review is not by appeal but rather by petition for a writ, the appellant is referred to as the *petitioner*, the opposing party as *respondent*.) The names may also be reversed: if the former defendant is now the appellant, in most jurisdictions his or her name will be listed first, whereas in the captions of trial court documents it was listed second.

**Table of contents**   A formal list of the contents of the brief follows the cover sheet. It may be called Table of Contents, Index, Subject Index, or something similar. It is typed in the format of the table of contents of any manuscript, indicating the page number on which each subject begins. Pages in the table of contents and table of authorities are generally numbered with lowercase Roman numerals: i, ii, iii, iv, etc., whereas the pages in the body of the brief are numbered with Arabic numbers.

**Table of authorities**   A table of authorities is a complete, alphabetical list of all the legal sources used to support the attorney's arguments. It may include the page on which the source is referred to in the brief. The list may be divided into categories, as in the illustration on page 490, where sources are noted as cases, articles, or texts. Within each section the list is alphabetical.

**Text**   The text consists of the attorney's arguments with supporting information. Each point is numbered and supported by arguments including the citations. It is customary to repeat much of the information included on the cover page as a heading on the first page of the text, as illustrated on page 491.

**Signature**   Briefs do not usually bear a handwritten signature. Some court rules require only the name of the attorney typed at the end of the brief; others require the name and address of the firm to be added below the name of the attorney.

**Citations**   Citations occur as footnotes in appellate briefs as well as in the running text. Refer to section 13.6 for directions on typing citations and to Chapter 18, section 18.4, for suggestions on how to check and verify citations.

**Printed briefs**   Once the brief has been completed and the final draft approved, the secretary may be required to send it to the printer. The printer sets the brief in type and sends back *galley proofs*. These are on long sheets with no page divisions. The galley proofs must be checked carefully against the original material to ensure absolute accuracy. Corrections on the proofs are made by writing the correction in the margin and indicating by a caret or underline the point where the correction is to be made. The illustration on page 492 gives a standardized list of abbreviated marks commonly used by proofreaders. One copy of the corrected proof is sent to the printer, and one copy is retained in the office. After the corrections have been made, the printer divides the material into pages and prints *page proofs*, which are sent to the office. Once again, the material must be carefully proofread to make sure that the printer has made all the requested corrections. When the final proof has been approved by the attorney, the printer is given the order to print the required number of copies and file them with the appropriate court.

When the brief is typewritten on legal-size paper, it is affixed to a legal back, endorsed with the information listed above for the cover sheet. When the brief is typewritten on letter-size paper, it may be placed between a front and back cover and stapled at the side.

## Table of Contents for an Appeal Brief

TABLE OF CONTENTS

Page Number

-i-

## Table of Authorities for an Appeal Brief

1

2

3

4

5

6

7

8

9

10

11

12

13

14

15

16

17

18

19

20

21

22

23

24

25

26

27

28

TABLE OF AUTHORITIES

STATUTES AND CONSTITUTION

Business and Professions Code, Sections 6076 and 6083

Business and Professions Code, Article 1, Section 6001

California Constitution, Article 1, Section 9

CASES

Abeles v. State Bar of California, 9 C.3d 603, 108 Cal. Rptr. 359, 510 P.2d 719 (1973)

Barton v. State Bar of California, 209 Cal. 677 (1976)

Belli v. State Bar of California, 10 C.3d 841, 112 Cal. Rptr. 527, 519 P.2d 575 (1974)

Bigelow v. Virginia, 421 U.S. 809 (1975)

Virginia State Bd. of Pharmacy v. Va. Cit. Consumers' Council, 425 U.S. 748 (1976)

ARTICLES

Cheatham, Availability of Legal Services: The Responsibility of the Individual Lawyer and of the Organized Bar, 12 U.C.L.A. L. Rev. 438 (1965)

Christensen, Lawyer Referral Services: An Alternative to Lay-Group Legal Services? 12 U.C.L.A. L. Rev. 341 (1965)

Comment, Advertising by Lawyers, 15 A.B.A.J. 116 (1929)

TEXTS

7 American Jurisprudence, 2d Section 43

Cohen, Julius Henry, The Law: Business or Profession? New York, 1916

-ii-

## First Page of the Text of an Appeal Brief

```
 1              SUPREME COURT FOR THE STATE OF CALIFORNIA
 2   DAVID R. LONER,            )
                               )
 3              Petitioner,     )        NO. 687504
                               )
 4        vs.                   )
                               )
 5   STATE BAR OF CALIFORNIA,   )
                               )
 6              Respondent.     )
                               )
 7   _____
 8        PETITION TO REVIEW THE CALIFORNIA STATE DISCIPLINARY
          BOARD'S RECOMMENDATION TO THE CALIFORNIA SUPREME COURT
 9
10              _____
11              BRIEF FOR RESPONDENT
                _____
12                              Gail D. Brewster
                                Attorney for Respondent
13
14                   STATEMENT OF THE CASE
15        Disciplinary proceedings were instituted against
16   DAVID R. LONER by the California State Bar Disciplinary Board.
17   The Board has recommended to the California Supreme Court that
18   Loner be placed on three years probation, with three months
19   actual suspension from the practice of law for an alleged
20   intentional violation of the Rules of Professional Conduct 2-101
21   and 2-102.  Loner petitions the California Supreme Court to
22   review the Board's recommendation.
23        The California State Bar Disciplinary Board heard the
24   case pursuant to American Bar Association rules and regulations.
25   The California Supreme Court is authorized to hear this petition
26   for review under Business and Professions Code Section 6083.
27                   STATEMENT OF FACTS
28        Petitioner, DAVID R. LONER, placed advertisements in
                              -1-
```

## PROOFREADERS' MARKS

| | |
|---|---|
| ℰ or ɤ or ⁊ | delete; take it out |
| ◡ | close up; print as one word |
| ℰ | delete and close up |
| ∧ or ˃ or ⅄ | caret; insert here *(something)* |
| # | insert a space |
| eq # | space evenly where indicated |
| stet | let marked text stand as set |
| tr | transpose; change order the |
| / | used to separate two or more marks and often as a concluding stroke at the end of an insertion |
| [ ⌊ | set farther to the left |
| ⌉ set⌊ | farther to the right |
| ⌒ | set æ or fl as ligatures æ or fl |
| = | straighten alignment |
| ‖ ‖ | straighten or align |
| X | imperfect or broken character |
| ▯ | indent or insert em quad space |
| ⁋ | begin a new paragraph |
| ⓈⓅ | spell out ⟨set 5 lbs as five pounds⟩ |
| cap | set in capitals ⟨CAPITALS⟩ |
| sm cap or s.c. | set in small capitals ⟨SMALL CAPITALS⟩ |

| | |
|---|---|
| lc | set in lowercase ⟨lowercase⟩ |
| ital | set in italic ⟨*italic*⟩ |
| rom | set in roman ⟨roman⟩ |
| bf | set in boldface ⟨**boldface**⟩ |
| = or -/ or ≐ or /H/ | hyphen |
| $\frac{1}{N}$ or en or /N/ | en dash ⟨1965–72⟩ |
| $\frac{1}{M}$ or em or /M/ | em — or long — dash |
| V | superscript or superior ⟨$^2$as in $\pi r^2$⟩ |
| ∧ | subscript or inferior ⟨∧as in $H_2O$⟩ |
| ∨ or ⅄ | centered ⟨for a centered dot in $p \cdot q$⟩ |
| ⌄ | comma |
| ⌄ | apostrophe |
| ⊙ | period |
| ; or ;/ | semicolon |
| : or ⊙ | colon |
| ❝❞ or ⌄⌄ | quotation marks |
| (/) | parentheses |
| [/] | brackets |
| OK/? | query to author: has this been set as intended? |
| ⌐ or ⌐¹ | push down a work-up |
| ⑨¹ | turn over an inverted letter |
| wf¹ | wrong font; a character of the wrong size or esp. style |

¹ The last three symbols are unlikely to be needed in marking proofs of photocomposed matter.

The appeal brief is an extremely important document, one that cannot be prepared with too much care. The secretary's major responsibility is to type the information accurately—especially citations, quotations, page and volume numbers, and names. An equally important responsibility is the calendaring of all steps in appellate procedure so that no deadlines are missed.

# 13.6

## HOW TO INTERPRET AND TYPE CITATIONS

A citation is a reference to a legal authority that is used as support for a statement made within a text. A citation may also be used to reveal the source of a quotation. These references are usually cited to statutory sources (constitutions, statutes, codes, and regulations), to reports of cases in official and unofficial reporters, and sometimes to secondary sources such as encyclopedias, books, and periodicals. Citations are used to support opinion letters and memoranda of law. They appear as the closing section of supporting documents that are submitted to the court along with a motion. They are always included in appeal briefs—in the text, as footnotes, and in summary form in a section of the brief called a table of authorities.

A legal citation is conventionally designed to give a great amount of information in concentrated form so that the reader may easily find the source and determine its relative authority. <u>Consistency of form</u> is important: the writer and reader must accept the same conventions of styling to facilitate communication. A consistent form, however, is secondary to the primary consideration of <u>absolute accuracy.</u> While the lawyer or legal assistant is normally responsible for the content of a citation—determining which sources to cite and the order in which to list them—the legal secretary is responsible for (1) double-checking, or *verifying,* all parts of the citation before typing the final memorandum, opinion letter, or brief; and (2) typing the citation in a form that is consistent with those in other documents produced by the office and also with any rules laid down by state or federal courts. Some courts are very particular about the form of citations in court papers; others prescribe very few rules.

Chapter 18 provides a useful overview of the sources that lawyers use and describes the procedures by which a secretary might check citations in the original sources. (Citations should be checked against actual sources whenever possible; it is not always safe to check them against the lawyer's dictation.) Especially in briefs and in any papers having to do with an appeal, accurate citations are imperative.

Citation forms are complex enough that whole books have been written to explain how to write citations. Some of these books are listed in the Appendix; the most well-known is *A Uniform System of Citation,* published by the Harvard Law Review Association and popularly known as the "Blue Book." The section that follows provides guidelines for the typist who interprets the dictation or the drafts of the lawyer. Together with Chapter 18, it is designed to give the new secretary a familiarity with basic citation forms. It is by no means a thorough presentation of this complex subject but rather a primer on how to read a citation and what the different parts of a citation mean. The final paragraphs of this section review the stylistic considerations—abbreviation, italicization, and so forth—that are normally the responsibility of the transcriber.

## CITATIONS TO STATUTORY SOURCES

Statutory sources of law include constitutions, statutes, codes, and administrative regulations. Citations to each type are described here.

**Constitutions**    Citations to constitutions have four parts: (1) the jurisdiction or name of the constitution, usually abbreviated, (2) the article or amendment number, usually in Roman numerals preceded by the abbreviation *art.* or *amend.,* (3) the section, chapter, or clause number, if applicable, in Arabic numerals, and (4) the date of the constitution in parentheses if it is no longer in force.

U.S. Const. amend. XIII
Ind. Const. art. III, § 2, cl. 4

Note that punctuation is minimal; frequently no comma separates the name of the constitution and the article or amendment number. Some alternate stylings capitalize *Art.* and *Amend.* Instead of the section symbol, the abbreviation *Sec.* is occasionally used. To type the section symbol on a typewriter that lacks a key for the symbol, strike a capital *S,* backspace, turn the platen up slightly and strike another *S.* A simpler method is to strike the capital *S,* backspace, and strike a lowercase *s* on the same line.

**Federal statutes**    Federal statutes appear in both codified and uncodified form, as described in Chapter 18. Those statutes in slip law form (that is, those that have not yet been published in the *Statutes at Large* or in the *United States Code*) are usually cited in the following order: (1) name of statute if known, (2) public law number,

(3) chapter and section number if applicable, (4) (sometimes) the congress that passed the law, (5) published source, if the slip law itself is not available, and (6) date of enactment in parentheses, if necessary.

Trade Agreements Act, Pub. L. 96-39, § 32, 96th Cong., 1st Sess. (July 26, 1979)

When the statute is found in the *Statutes at Large,* the information is listed in the citation as follows: (1) name of statute if applicable, (2) chapter and section number of the statute if applicable, (3) volume number of the *Statutes at Large* in Arabic numerals, (4) the official abbreviation *Stat.,* (5) the number of the page on which the law begins, but *not* the word "page" or its abbreviation, and (6) the date of the *Statutes at Large* edition in parentheses.

National Swine Flu Immunization Program of 1976, § 56, 90 Stat. 1113
*or*
90 Stat. 1113 (1976)

Federal statutes that have been codified—i.e., published in the *United States Code* in a subject-matter arrangement—are usually cited in the following order: (1) volume number of the code, in Arabic numerals, (2) name of the code abbreviated—U.S.C. or U.S.C.A., (3) section number of the code, (4) date of the codification or date of the code volume when necessary in parentheses, (5) any needed supplementary information, including further identification of the codification in parentheses and other information as needed, such as the original session law number.

28 U.S.C. § 17
28 U.S.C. § 17 (1964)
28 U.S.C. § 17 (1964), as amended (Supp. II, 1966)

**State statutes**    Like federal statutes, state statutes are published in both uncodified and codified form. The precise titles of the various statutory compilations are listed in Part III of *A Uniform System of Citation,* along with their recommended citation forms. Each state has determined the form or forms that are acceptable for citing its statutes. The session laws of Oklahoma, for example, should be cited "19-- Okla. Sess. Laws," while the statutory compilation of Colorado is cited "Colo. Rev. Stat. § ---." Frequently the preface to a compilation of state laws gives a method for citing the statutes in that volume. If it does, you should use that method. Styling conventions vary widely among the states in such matters as capitalization, the use of commas between elements of the citation, and the use of abbreviations.

A complete citation to the session laws of a state might include the following items: (1) name of the state compilation, properly abbreviated, (2) year of the session, usually not preceded by a comma, (3) chapter, title, or section number of the law (only the abbreviation *No.* for *Number* is normally capitalized), (4) page number, usually preceded by the word *at* if it immediately follows a section number, (5) additional information, if needed, in parentheses.

Ark. Acts 1922, No. 198, at 45 (expired 1940)

Citations to state code compilations typically follow this order: (1) name of the compilation, properly abbreviated, (2) number of the statute, (3) date of the compilation, usually in parentheses, and (4) additional information as needed:

La. Civil Code, Arts. 1495 and 1499 (1870)

When citing the statutes of the states in which they practice, lawyers may omit the name of the state: instead of the proper form *Minn. Stat., Sec. 289.23,* for instance, a Minneapolis lawyer might use *Stat., Sec. 289.23.*

**Administrative regulations**    The regulations of federal administrative agencies are cited to the *Code of Federal Regulations* (C.F.R.), to the *Federal Register* (Fed. Reg.), or to the exact form in which they were originally issued:

33 C.F.R. § 403.2 (1980)
43 Fed. Reg. 54221 (1978)
Treas. Reg. 118, § 28.04 (1953)

The numbers preceding *C.F.R.* and *Fed. Reg.* in the examples above refer to the volume numbers of those two sources; the number following *Fed. Reg.* is the page on which that statute begins in volume 43.

## CITATIONS TO CASES
Court decisions are cited to either official reporters or unofficial reporters. Segments of case citations are described in the following paragraphs.

**The name of the case**   The case title is italicized: *Surner v. Kellogg.* Cases that do not involve two opposing parties have titles such as *In re Watson* or *In the matter of John Watson;* these case titles are also italicized. Only the surnames of individuals are included in the case title, but the full names of business firms are used, although they may be abbreviated. The first word of a litigant's name, however, is never abbreviated. When it is a party to an action, *United States* is always spelled in full: *Marston v. United States.*

The proper form of the case name can be obtained in most cases from the running head (the title at the top of the pertinent reporter pages). For example, a case whose caption reads: "Mary P. Reams, Plaintiff-Appellee, v. Tulsa Cable Television, Inc., an Oklahoma corporation, Defendant-Appellant, and Stephen M. Fike, Defendant-Appellee," is shortened to *Reams v. Tulsa Cable Television, Inc.* in the running heads of the pertinent reporter pages and is also the proper form in which to cite the case.

**The reporter source**   The names of the reporters in which court decisions are found refer to the jurisdiction of the courts included in those reporters, as *Minn.* for *Minnesota Reports* and *S.W.* for *South Western Reporter.*

The reporter in which the case is found is always identified in this order: (1) volume number, (2) official abbreviation of the reporter title, and (3) page number at which the opinion begins. For example, a case that begins on page 450 of volume 277 of the second series of the *Pacific Reporter* would be cited as "277 P. 2d 450." If more than one reporter cites the same case, as happens frequently, the two citations are separated by a comma:

*A Minor v. State,* 85 Nev. 323, 454 P. 2d 895 (1969)

The case cited above can be found in both *Nevada Reports* and the *Pacific Reporter, Second Series.*

In some citations an additional page number follows the first page reference, as "277 P. 2d 450, 462." The first number is always the page on which the case begins; the second number pinpoints a specific reference to the court's opinion.

It is important not to omit the *2d* in those reporter titles that include the number. It denotes the second series of a reporter—S.W. 2d, for instance, represents an entirely different set of volumes from *S.W.*

**Court and date of opinion**   At the end of the citation to a case, in parentheses, may be listed the name of the court and the date of its decision. It is not necessary to include the name of the court, however, if it is obvious from the name of the reporter. A case cited to *U.S.*—the official abbreviation for *United States Supreme Court Reports*—to take one example, obviously involves the U.S. Supreme Court and need not be identified further. On the other hand, a case cited to *F. 2d* (the abbreviation for *Federal Reporter,* Second Series) must be further identified because it could have been decided in any one of the several U.S. courts of appeals. The citation would then identify a specific circuit of the court of appeals, for example: 354 F. 2d 546 (8th Cir. 1965).

It is important to use the proper abbreviations for the courts, especially for the lower state courts, whose names vary considerably. Refer to the official abbreviations listed in *A Uniform System of Citations*. United States district courts are identified by district and state, but not by their divisions. S.D.N.Y., for example, is used to identify the district court of the Southern District of New York.

## CITATIONS TO SECONDARY SOURCES

Interpretative or analytical sources that may be cited include legal encyclopedias, periodical articles, and books and treatises on law.

**Legal encyclopedias**   Citations to major legal encyclopedias include the following segments: (1) the volume number of the encyclopedia, in Arabic numerals, (2) the official abbreviation for the publication, as *C.J.S.* for *Corpus Juris Secundum* or *Am. Jur. 2d* for the second edition of *American Jurisprudence*, the two major legal encyclopedias, (3) the title of the article cited, (4) page and section numbers, and (5) the date of the edition.

88 C.J.S., Trial § 192 (1955)

**Periodical articles**   Segments of citations to articles published in legal periodicals—which are typically law reviews—are listed in the following order: (1) last name of the author, without first name or initial, (2) title of the article, (3) volume number of the periodical, or year if the volume number is not known, (4) name of the publication, typically abbreviated, (5) number of the page on which the article begins, and (6) year of publication, in parentheses, unless it already appears in place of the volume number.

Owen, Punitive Damages in Products Liability Litigation, 74 Mich. L. Rev. 1257 (1976)

Sometimes the citation is to a law review article written anonymously by a student. In these cases, the author's name is omitted and the article is called "Note," "Comment," or some such title.

There are numerous variants in the styling of citations to law reviews and other periodicals. You may see the title of the article italicized and the title of the periodical printed in all-capital letters. Or the article title may be roman, perhaps also enclosed in quotation marks, while the periodical title is italicized.

**Books and treatises**   The styling of citations to texts, like that of citations to legal periodicals, differs from the styling generally used for bibliographies in non-legal fields. The normal order of the segments of these citations is (1) volume number, if applicable, in Arabic numerals, (2) the last name of the author or, if needed, only the first initial and the last name, (3) the title of the book, unabbreviated, (4) section or page number if needed, and (5) sometimes the edition and date of publication. A subtitle that follows a colon may be omitted if it would make the title unduly long. The book title is usually italicized to make it stand out in the citation, but many lawyers prefer to have the entire citation, including the title, printed in roman.

C. Wright, Handbook of the Law of Federal Courts § 50, at 29 (Supp. 1972)

## CONVENTIONS AND VARIATIONS IN THE STYLING OF CITATIONS

Variant forms of citation are widespread; they result from the individual preferences of lawyers as well as from disparate court rules. There are also differences that arise from the context of the citation: those that appear in the body of a text, for instance, especially those in appeal briefs, tend to have fewer abbreviations and to be more generous with spacing than citations used as footnotes.

**Italicization**    Italics are indicated on the typewriter by underscoring. Except when listed in a table of authorities, the names of the parties to a case are always underscored or italicized. The *v.* (for *versus*) may or may not be italicized. Printers usually set it in roman type. On typewritten copy, however, a continuous underline seems to improve the appearance of the page.

*In re Sumner*
*Ex parte John Chase*
*Hart v. Community School Board of Education*
Hart v. Community School Board of Education

Other citation elements—such as titles of articles in legal encyclopedias and legal periodicals or titles of periodicals—may be italicized by some individuals or in some jurisdictions or in accordance with the rules of some law reviews. You should check to see which styles are used in your law office.

You will also need to consult the attorney or the court rule book on whether to italicize bibliographical signals and related terms. More often than not, law offices italicize traditional bibliographical signals such as *ibid.* (*ibidem;* the same reference), *infra* (below), *vide* (see), *supra* (above), and the like. Words and phrases that show relationships between different cases or that indicate the history of a case (such as *appeal denied, certiorari granted, sub nomine, rev'd, aff'd, aff'g*), whether Latin or English, have traditionally been italicized; however, the trend now is to eliminate the typewritten underscoring in the interest of more efficient typing.

*United States v. School District of Omaha,* 521 F. 2d 530 (8th Cir.), *cert. denied,* 423 U.S. 946 (1975)
*or*
*United States v. Lee Wilson & Co.,* D.C. Ark. 1914, 214 F. 630, affirmed 227 F. 827

**Abbreviation**    *A Uniform System of Citation* provides quick reference for the proper abbreviation of the titles of statute compilations, reporters, law reviews, and other sources of citations. Tables of abbreviations may also be found in *Black's Law Dictionary* and in other references. The Blue Book also gives rules for abbreviating the names of corporate litigants in case titles. Acceptable abbreviations in company names include *Co., Inc., Corp., RR., Ry., Ltd., Assn.,* and *Commn.* The first word of the party name, however, is never abbreviated.

Plurals of abbreviations are most often formed by adding *-s* before the period, as in *arts.* for *articles.* However, some abbreviations deviate from this rule, as *pp.* for *pages* and §§ for *sections.* In some jurisdictions the periods may be omitted from abbreviations in order to save time and space: NE2d, NY Jur, etc. In texts that are not briefs, familiar government agencies are styled without periods and spaces (FTC, ICC, NLRB). Finally, where contractions (*aff'g, rev'd*) are used instead of abbreviations, the period should be omitted.

Abbreviations are used sparingly in briefs. Whereas the names of government agencies and labor unions tend to be abbreviated in other legal writings, they are spelled out in a brief. Similarly, signals such as *certiorari granted* are spelled in full in most court briefs.

**Spacing**    There is considerable lack of uniformity in the spacing of abbreviations in citations. In briefs, where the appearance of the document is important, abbreviations tend to be spaced: N. E. 2d; Yale L. J. In footnotes as in most other legal writing, however, the practice is to close up the abbreviation: N.E.2d; Yale L.J. Closed abbreviations, which allow for more efficient typing, have become widely used in citations. A guideline followed in many offices is to close up all abbreviations except where the elements of the abbreviation consist of more than one letter:

S.D.N.Y.    D. Del.
N.Y.S.2d    N.Y. Supp.
C.C.P.A.    S. Ct.

In footnote citations, on the other hand, where space is at a premium and appearance is not so important, all abbreviations may be closed up: S.D.Minn.; Mo.Ct.Ap.(1975); App.Div.1969.

The initials of a personal name are always spaced, as: J. H. Jones. Subdivisions of sections of statutes and constitutions are indicated in closed-up parentheses, as: §7(a).

**Punctuation**    Citations do not normally require terminal punctuation unless they appear in the text of a document run in with other sentences. Most, but not all, of the elements of a citation are separated by commas. You should consult the court rule books or office form files to see if there are any rules for the use of commas between the parts of a citation. Many citation forms omit dividing marks of punctuation when the division is noticeable without the help of a comma or other punctuation mark:

74 Mich. L. Rev. 1257 (1956)
U.S. Const. art. VII

Certain citation forms require that the titles of legal encyclopedias, legal periodicals, and books be typed or printed in all-capital letters: 5 TEX. JUR. 2d; 49 CAL. L. REV. 344 (1949). A more widespread practice is to fully capitalize the names of constitutions: U.S. CONST. amend. XIV.

**Placement of citations**    In the running text of a brief or memorandum, citations should appear as if they were a new sentence, preceded and terminated by a period. Such a natural position makes it easy to read the citations and to associate them with the statements that they support. But citations may also be preceded by commas, semicolons, or colons in a running text, or they may be separated from the text in footnote form. When a citation is used to give the source of a quotation, however, it is indented and placed on the line following the quotation.

It is usually not a good idea to enclose a citation in parentheses. If one of the citations includes a parenthetical phrase, as is likely, a set of brackets will have to be typed to indicate parentheses within parentheses; brackets used for this purpose can appear ungainly.

There are rules for the order in which parallel citations, or citations to the same case, occur. The official source (see Chapter 18 for a discussion of official and unofficial sources) is always given first, followed by any unofficial sources. If more than one of the unofficial West reporters are included in a case citation, the local reporter precedes the regional one, as in the following citation, where the Maryland reporter precedes the Atlantic:

*Baltimore Foundry & Machinery Corp. v. Comptroller,* 211 Md. 316, 127 A. 2d 386 (1956)

Parallel citations are useful because they serve as a check against error and also increase the chance that the reader has one of the sources available.

A series of citations to the same case, as in the *Baltimore Foundry* example above, are separated by commas. String citations, on the other hand, are a run-in series of citations to *different* cases. String citations are separated by a semicolon, a mark of stronger separation than a comma. An alternative to using string citations is to list the different citations on separate lines.

## CONSISTENCY AND PRECISION IN THE TYPING OF CITATIONS

The secretary who transcribes legal citations should adhere to whatever styling conventions are preferred by the law office or required by the court. In most instances the reader of the memorandum or brief will not care what styling is used as long as it is used consistently throughout the document and as long as the citation can be understood. More important than consistency is that the citation direct the reader in the most efficient manner to the intended source. For this reason, numerals—page, volume, section, and supplement numbers—<u>must</u> be correct. Numbers can be easily misread from a draft, misinterpreted during dictation, and mistyped during transcription. The citation must also be precise in its inclusion of information directing the reader to a second series, a supplement, or other specific volume of a work. The spelling of names, of course, should always be verified. The correct spelling of a case name may not be vital, but if the reader notices the misspelling, he or she may distrust the accuracy of the citation as a whole. The secretary should keep in mind that everything typewritten for use outside the office—including briefs for judges to read—reflects upon the reputation of the law firm.

# 14

# EXECUTING LEGAL DOCUMENTS: Signature, Recording, Filing, and Service

## CONTENTS

# 14.1

## EXECUTING LEGAL DOCUMENTS

The three preceding chapters focused on the preparation of formal papers for clients and for courts, either as legal blanks with fill-ins or as originally created documents. The present chapter summarizes the procedures necessary to turn these completed documents into valid legal instruments: execution and, where appropriate, recording and filing with a public office and service on the parties involved in a legal action.

A legal instrument is not valid until it is executed. The word *executing* is used informally in law offices to refer only to the signing of a document, but in formal terms execution includes everything necessary to make the instrument valid including, where appropriate, signature, seal, attestation, acknowledgment, verification, notarization, and delivery.

Once a document has been properly signed, the legal secretary's responsibilities are far from over. It is the secretary who prepares letters of transmittal to accompany the document for filing or recording and who arranges delivery to the office of the clerk of court or the recorder. In addition, the secretary may be expected to prepare certificates of mailing, instructions for service, and other accompanying papers without further instruction from the attorney. If a filing fee, recording fee, or other fee is needed, the secretary draws the check, keeps a record for client billing, and places the check, forwarding letter, signed instrument, and other required enclosures on the attorney's desk for signature.

The first section of this chapter reviews the secretary's responsibilities in the execution of legal documents: seeing that they are properly signed and, where required, acknowledged, witnessed, or verified. The following sections explain how to record legal instruments, file court documents, and serve papers on the parties involved in court actions.

## TESTIMONIUM CLAUSE

In many legal instruments or client documents a testimonium clause immediately precedes the signature block. The testimonium clause is a declaration by the parties to the instrument that their signatures are affixed in testimony of the contents of the instrument. The introductory phrase of the testimonium clause is usually capitalized, as in the following examples:

IN WITNESS WHEREOF, the parties hereto have hereunto set their hands the day and year first above written.

IN TESTIMONY WHEREOF, [Named Corporation] has caused its corporate seal to be affixed hereto and attested by its secretary, and these presents to be signed by its president, this fifth day of June, 19--.

A styling similar to the first example is normally used when the date appears in the first paragraph of the document. The secretary must note whether the testimonium clause mentions a seal; if it does, there must be a seal next to the signature. Testimonium clauses should be inserted in the secretary's form file for future reference.

## SIGNATURE

By the act of signing a legal document, the signer gives it effect as his or her act and avows knowledge, approval, acceptance, and/or obligation. The parties to a legal instrument normally sign it, and in most cases the body of the instrument will indicate who is to sign. Court documents, on the other hand, are usually signed by the attorney or, in the case of court orders and judgments, by the judge in accordance with state statutes or the rules of the court. You should become familiar with the signature requirements for each type of document you prepare, and your form file should contain examples of the proper signature blocks for all types of legal documents.

The legal secretary assumes the following responsibilities for the execution of legal documents:

1. making certain that the papers are correctly prepared for execution
2. determining exactly who is to sign the document so that the number of signature lines is accurate and the parties correctly identified
3. typing the party's name below the signature line, if required, exactly as it appears in the document
4. helping the attorney ensure that the document is signed exactly as the names appear in the document
5. typing *SEAL* or *L.S.* at the end of the signature line if required
6. ensuring that corporate seals are imprinted where needed
7. if attestation is required, ensuring that witnesses actually witness the signature
8. ensuring that the correct number of copies are signed
9. following the attorney's instructions concerning the acknowledgment or verification of the document

In some states, corporations are required to use a corporate seal or to state on corporate documents that the corporation has no seal. The seal is an engraved metal plate with which an imprint may be made on paper.

## HOW TO CONFORM LEGAL DOCUMENTS

It is important to make a practice of conforming all copies of documents immediately after the originals are signed. If postponed, conforming may be unintentionally neglected.

Many law offices simply make photocopies of the executed document so that the signature, date, and additional notations are picked up automatically on the copies. If the copies are to be conformed manually, you must type or write on each copy all pertinent information from the original that was added after the document was typed; this includes signatures, seals, dates, initials, and any material added in the margins or between the lines.

To conform signatures, type or write in the signature space /s/ (or /S/, or S/) followed by the name to indicate that that is where and how the person signed the document.

/s/              Nicole Robbins
                 NICOLE ROBBINS

To conform signatures in pen, the same procedure is used.

---

/s/ James L. Doe
       JAMES L. DOE

---

To indicate that a document has been sealed, type *Corporate Seal, Notarial Seal,* or *Official Seal* in brackets at the appropriate location.

To conform a stapled copy on the typewriter without removing the staples, follow these steps:

1. Insert a No. 10 envelope into your typewriter in its normal position for typing. Roll it forward until an inch of the envelope is visible.
2. Insert from the front the page that needs to be conformed by placing the bottom edge of the page between the envelope and the platen (roller).
3. Turn the platen in a reverse motion so that the page is drawn into the machine.
4. Align the page and begin typing.

Sometimes copies, such as those made on text-editing machines and some photocopiers, are of such high quality that they could be mistaken for originals. It is a good idea to prevent any mix-ups by typing COPY across the top of each copy at the time they are conformed, if it has not already been done.

## EXECUTED COPIES

Legal documents must often be prepared with duplicate or triplicate original copies. In the case of a multiparty contract, for example, each signatory receives an "original" that is signed by all parties to the contract. With the photocopying machines in law offices today it is seldom necessary to type more than one ribbon copy. Instead, the usual practice is for one ribbon original to be typed and additional copies made on the photocopier. Each photocopy can then be treated as an executed copy by having the signers sign the required number of duplicate originals. Carbon copies may also be treated as duplicate originals.

Executed copies differ from conformed copies in that an executed copy of an instrument is a valuable legal document and should be kept in a safe place. A conformed copy does not have the same legal value and need not be as carefully safeguarded.

## ACKNOWLEDGMENT

Acknowledgment of an instrument is a formal declaration before an authorized official—who may be a notary public, judge, clerk of court, or other public officer—that the instrument is the free act of the person who executed it. Documents that must be recorded, such as deeds, mortgage notes, liens, and leases, require acknowledgment with an acknowledgment clause, or certificate of acknowledgment, annexed to the document. The form of an acknowledgment varies from state to state. It may be a very short form:

STATE OF KANSAS   )
                           )  ss

COUNTY OF BLANK )

The foregoing instrument was acknowledged before me this 15th day of August, 19--, by ROY J. CLARK.

_____
(Notary's Signature)

[seal]                                        Notary Public
                                       My commission expires _____.

In some states a longer and more formal acknowledgment is used:

STATE OF CALIFORNIA )
                               )  ss

COUNTY OF BLANK    )

On this 15th day of August of the year 19--, before me, Nancy R. Contini, a Notary Public of said State, duly commissioned and sworn, personally appeared ROY J. CLARK, known to me to be the person whose name is subscribed to the within instrument, and acknowledged that he executed the same.

IN WITNESS WHEREOF, I have hereunto set my hand and affixed my official seal the day and year in this certificate first above written.

_____

[seal]                                        Notary Public in and for Said State

Acknowledgments are of two kinds: individual and corporate. The acknowledgment on an instrument executed by a corporation must contain the name of the corporation, the corporate office held by the person or persons signing the instrument, and a statement that the corporation has authorized that person to execute the instrument on behalf of the corporation. A corporate acknowledgment form is illustrated on page 399 of Chapter 12; section 12.2 of that chapter also gives suggestions on the typing of acknowledgments.

**Authentication**   It is sometimes necessary to acknowledge an instrument in one state and file it in another. In these cases, some states require a certificate of authentication that certifies the validity of the notary public's commission. The notary may obtain these printed forms, when necessary, from the local courthouse. One such form is illustrated on page 386.

## ATTESTATION

Some client documents require that signatures be witnessed. An attestation clause is used to introduce the witnesses' signatures. This clause is a brief statement by the witnesses that the instrument was executed before them; it is signed by the witnesses at the request of the party signing the instrument. The attestation clause is sometimes necessary to make the instrument legal, and its form varies; it may be simply "In the presence of:" or it may be in the lengthy style commonly used in wills. The secretary must determine before typing the document whether attestation is required in order to plan the spacing of the signature page.

Spaced rules are drawn for the witnesses' signatures. The will shown on pages 425–427 contains an attestation clause that requires the addresses of the witnesses as well as their signatures. The facsimile on the next page represents a common styling that is used in many legal documents. Note that proper names are *not* typed below the signature lines. Witnesses' signatures typically appear on the left half of the page, opposite the signature lines of those executing the document.

```
Signed, sealed, and delivered

in the presence of:


_____


_____
```

## VERIFICATION

A verification is a sworn confirmation of the truth or authenticity of a writing, most commonly a pleading. It is accomplished by affidavit, oath, or deposition. In some jurisdictions, all litigation pleadings which contain new affirmations must be verified, in which case the verification is usually made by a party to the litigation but may in certain instances be made by the party's agent or attorney. Whenever a complaint is verified, the answer must also be verified.

To administer the oath to a person signing a verification, both the person administering the oath and the verifier stand and raise their right hands. The person administering the oath asks, "Do you solemnly swear that the contents of this instrument subscribed by you are the truth, the whole truth, and nothing but the truth?" The verifier answers "Yes," or "I do." If the verifier cannot swear because his or her religion forbids it, say, "Do you *affirm* . . .?" and substitute the word *affirmed* for *sworn* in the jurat.

The format of a verification varies, but it always contains the venue and a jurat. A typical form is illustrated on page 452 in Chapter 13.

## AFFIDAVIT

An affidavit is a statement of fact that is sworn to in order to help prove that fact. Like a verification, it is signed by the affiant and made under oath. The affidavit contains both venue and jurat. Affidavits are illustrated and discussed in greater detail in section 12.3 of Chapter 12.

## THE NOTARY PUBLIC

Since many legal documents require notarization, legal secretaries usually obtain notarial commissions. Information on how to become a notary public is available from the secretary of state or a similar designated state official. A bond is required in some states, which is usually paid for by the employing law firm. Some states have additional requirements such as passing a written examination.

Once you have been commissioned, you may purchase a notary's kit which includes a seal bearing your name, license number, the county in which you are commissioned, and the expiration date of your commission. The seal may be either a rubber stamp or a metal plate. Some states now allow the use of a rubber stamp in place of the engraved plate traditionally used in sealing documents. The rubber stamp is, of course, less expensive and easier to carry, but many notaries public still prefer the formality and official appearance of the imprint made by an engraved metal plate.

The notary public must register a new commission with the county clerk or other designated official. Then, whenever the notary's signature and commission need to be authenticated for use in another state, the clerk can issue the required certificate of authentication.

The powers and duties of a notary public are governed by state statute. Generally, they include administering oaths and affirmations and taking acknowledgments, depositions, verifications, and affidavits. When a notary administers an oath to the signer of an affidavit, verification, or deposition, the oath is documented in the form of a *jurat*. A jurat is illustrated on page 420. To *notarize* a document, on the other hand, means to attach a certificate of acknowledgment that the signature on a document is authentic. Acknowledgments are not made under oath and therefore do not require the jurat. Both the jurat and the certificate of acknowledgment require the notary's signature.

When notarizing a document, the secretary should (1) check to make sure that a seal is included with the signature if required, (2) date the acknowledgment with the exact date, (3) check to make certain that all other blanks are filled in where required, such as the date of the expiration of the notary's commission, (4) check to see if an authentication is required (see page 503), and (5) take the acknowledgment: that is, ask the person if he or she signed the instrument in question. It is important to adhere to the statutes governing the taking of acknowledgments. For example, the person making the acknowledgment must appear personally before the notary to attest that the signature on the document is genuine; acknowledgments should not be taken over the telephone. If the person making the acknowledgment is not a client and is a stranger, the notary should ask for evidence of identity. Some states require that husband and wife make separate acknowledgments.

A notary public may act only within the territory (usually a state or county) authorized by the statutes and may be required to keep a record of instruments acknowledged. Most states set maximum notarial fees and require that a notarial seal or stamp be impressed on documents authenticated by a notary public. Some states also require that the notary's name and the date of expiration of the notary's commission be printed or typed below the notary's signature.

There are civil and criminal penalties for errors, omissions, or misconduct in the official duties of a notary public, and the bonding company as well as the notary may be held liable. You should become thoroughly familiar with the statutes governing notaries public in your state. Whenever possible, notarize documents only when they have been signed in your presence. Only then will you be able to testify (as you may be called upon to do) that the signature is genuine. You must also be sure that the date is accurate.

The notarial duties of a legal secretary most often involve verifications and acknowledgments.

# 14.2

## RECORDING LEGAL DOCUMENTS

The prompt recording of certain legal instruments after execution is an important secretarial responsibility. Recording documents is the act of entering them in the public land records to preserve authentic evidence of their existence and thus to protect the interests of those involved. Promptness in recording is essential, because an unrecorded conveyance of title may be void. These records are kept by the county recorder, who may also be known as the register of deeds.

The recorder's office records each instrument by making a photocopy or microfilm record and placing that copy in its official records. The date and the page and volume numbers that indicate where it is entered in the record book are noted on the original document, which is then returned to the person who presented it for recording. Certain documents in certain states, for example a divorce judgment affecting real property, may be recorded in abstract form. Valuable documents such as deeds, however, are recorded in full so that if the original is lost it may be replaced by a photostatic copy upon application to the recorder's office.

Papers which <u>must</u> be recorded are those having an effect on ownership of real property, including both land and buildings—such as transfers of title, mortgages, easements, liens, and any court judgment affecting ownership of property. Articles of incorporation may also have to be recorded in a local government office.

Documents are recorded in the county in which the property is located, regardless of the residence of the parties or where the papers are executed.

When preparing a document for recording, remember that in order to be recorded a document must first be acknowledged before a notary public or other public officer. Note on the face of the document the name and address of the party to whom the recorded document is to be returned, or, if the document is in a legal back, write above the firm's name and address printed on the endorsement: "Please record and return to." Deliver or mail it by Certified Mail, Return Receipt Requested, to the appropriate recorder's office with a letter of transmittal and a check for the recording fee. Recording fees are fixed by state statute. The fee normally depends on the length of the document and the number of party names to be indexed. A telephone call to the recorder's office is the simplest way to determine the amount of the fee. (As always, keep a record of the fee for client billing.) When mailing documents to be recorded, use Certified Mail as described in Chapter 4.

When the document is returned by the recorder's office, *immediately* conform on all copies the numbers stamped on it by the recorder. Then forward the original to the client, again by Certified Mail, and keep a conformed copy for your file.

# 14.3

## FILING LEGAL DOCUMENTS WITH THE COURT

Filing legal papers is simply placing them in the custody of a court through delivery to the clerk of court. Whereas legal instruments are recorded to preserve them in order to establish ownership, documents are filed with the court to begin and maintain litigation and to preserve a record of legal actions. And while the registry of deeds keeps only copies of original documents, the court retains the originals.

### FILING THE INITIAL PLEADINGS
A lawsuit is commenced by filing an initial pleading (which may be termed a claim, complaint, petition, declaration, or libel; see Chapter 13 for a discussion of pleadings) with the court of proper jurisdiction and serving it, with a summons, on the defendant. An attorney decides in which court to commence a lawsuit after considering the subject matter of the lawsuit, the amount of money at issue, and the residence of the parties. Subsequent pleadings and supporting papers are also filed with the court.

When the first pleading is filed with the clerk of court, the clerk notes on the document the date it was received, assigns an index, docket, or case number to the lawsuit, and returns to the attorney a copy of the pleading marked with the date of receipt and the index number. The original is retained in the clerk's office, where it may be inspected by concerned parties.

Filing fees for litigation are set by statute or court rules. They often differ from court to court and are subject to change. Questions concerning the fee can be answered by a telephone call to the clerk of court. You should keep a current list of fees

## Letter of Transmittal to the County Recorder

MITCHELL, MUMFORD & ZUBROSKI
Counselors at Law
1200 Northgate Building
Southville, State 53421
Telephone: (123) 456-7890

September 2, 19—
File No. 76-109

CERTIFIED MAIL

Register of Deeds
Mendota County Courthouse
124 Main Street
Centerville, ST 65432

Dear Sir:

   Re: Sale of Market Building

Enclosed for recording is _____(Name of Document)_____

and our check in the amount of $_____

for the recording fee.  Please return the recorded

document to the party indicated on the face of the docu-

ment (or to this office).

     Very truly yours,

     *Vivian Gray*

     (Mrs.) Vivian Gray
     Assistant to Mr. Mumford

Enclosures (2)

of the courts in which the lawyers in the office practice; you will find it convenient to add to that list the standard witness fee, the mileage rate for subpoenaed witnesses, and the other fees you often pay.

When the copy of the initial pleading is returned to you, or when the attorney is served a pleading that requires an answer, you should make a record of the index or case number assigned to the case by the clerk of court. If you do not know the number, ask the clerk for it and immediately note it on your copy of the pleading. That number must appear on all pleadings and papers filed in the action and should be given in any telephone calls to the clerk of court about the case.

**Calendaring**  The legal secretary's calendaring responsibilities begin even before the case is filed. As soon as a prospective case is received in the law office, the date on which the statute of limitations runs out should be determined and noted in the case file, in the case progress record or suit register, and on the attorney's calendar. Once the action is commenced, the date of service of the papers determines the date on which the response is due. Refer to a practice manual or the rules of the court for the number of days in which the response is due and the method for computing the days. If the due date falls on a Sunday or holiday (or in some jurisdictions on Saturday), the response is due the next working day. Take care to note the date of receipt of any legal documents which are delivered to the law office and the date of mailing (the postmark) of any legal documents served by mail, since several days are usually added to the time for response to documents served by mail. Immediately calculate the date on which the response is due and calendar it. See section 5.3 of Chapter 5 for a description of calendaring methods and techniques for reminding the lawyer of upcoming matters.

**Summons and complaint**  A summons is usually prepared on a form available from and to be signed by the clerk of the court, although in some instances it is prepared and signed by the plaintiff's attorney. In the latter case, the summons and complaint may have to be authenticated by the court before they are served on the defendant. While in some instances only the summons is served to commence an action and the plaintiff then "demands" a copy of the complaint either from the court or from the attorney for the filing party, most jurisdictions require that the summons and complaint be served together. A check for the filing fee must accompany the summons and complaint when they are filed with the court.

Some courts require a cover sheet to be filed with the initial papers. Cover sheets are forms that provide a description of the lawsuit; they are available from the clerks of courts which require them. They are filed only with the court and are not served on the defendant.

Once filed with the court, the summons and complaint are then served on the defendant (except in those jurisdictions where only the summons is served). Clerks of court are usually willing to deliver to the server of process the copies of the summons and complaint which are to be served on the defendant, but many law offices prefer to deliver these pleadings to the process server themselves.

## CHECKLIST OF FILING PROCEDURES
Even if your office files all actions by mail or employs messengers to deliver them, you should file at least one action with the court yourself so that you will be familiar with the procedure. Before a summons and complaint leave your office, make sure that all these steps have been taken:

1. The complaint must be properly signed, dated, and, if necessary, verified.
2. The summons must be signed by the plaintiff's attorney in jurisdictions where it is necessary.

3. Sufficient copies must be made: the original (and sometimes more) for the court; one copy to be served on each defendant; one copy to which the process server will attach the certificate of service in those jurisdictions where it is required; one copy for the client; and one copy for your files.

4. All exhibits must be attached to the complaint.

5. Blue backs should be attached to the copies which will be filed and served, if required in the jurisdiction.

6. A check must be written to the order of the clerk of the court in the amount of the filing fee.

7. A letter or memo of instructions for serving should be prepared.

8. A check for advance payment of service fees must be written if the process server requires advance payment.

After the proper preparations have been made, you are ready to file the papers:

1. Take the original summons and complaint to the office of the clerk of court along with the check for the filing fee.

2. Obtain from the clerk a receipt for the filing fee.

3. Note the case number and, in some courts, the name of the judge to whom the case is assigned.

4. In jurisdictions where it is required, present copies with the original. The clerk will authenticate them and immediately return them to you.

5. Deliver copies of the initial papers to the process server with a check for advance payment of fee, if required, and instructions for service.

The initial pleadings may also be mailed by Certified Mail to the clerk of court with a letter of transmittal and a stamped, addressed envelope. The clerk will often forward to the process server the copies to be served. A sample letter of transmittal is illustrated on page 510.

Papers subsequent to the initial pleading are served on the other party first, then filed with the court along with an affidavit of service where required. There are exceptions to this rule; for instance, in some jurisdictions sufficient copies of the papers are filed with the clerk of the court, who then serves them on other parties. You should check a practice manual or ask the attorney for the correct procedure in your jurisdiction.

# 14.4

## SERVING COURT DOCUMENTS

Service of court documents gives notice to concerned parties of the actions that involve them. Service is accomplished by giving a conformed copy of the court document to the party in question (who may be an individual or an agent of a corporation or association) and by returning to the court a form stating that the papers were properly delivered to that party at a particular time. Summonses, complaints, and subpoenas are served directly on the party, while other litigation papers subsequent to the complaint are ordinarily served on the party's attorney.

As suggested in the preceding section, local practice regulations govern service of the initial papers in a lawsuit. In most jurisdictions, copies of the summons and complaint are served together, the summons stapled to the top of a copy of the complaint. In others only the summons is served, and the party served is required to pick up a copy of the complaint at the clerk's office. In still other jurisdictions, the complaint is filed <u>after</u> the summons is served on the defendant.

## Letter of Transmittal to the Clerk of Court

MITCHELL, MUMFORD & ZUBROSKI
Counselors at Law
1200 Northgate Building
Southville, State 53421
Telephone: (123) 456-7890

November 23, 19—

CERTIFIED MAIL

The Honorable Mary C. Piercy
Clerk of Court
State Superior Court
123 First Street
Centerville, ST 65432

Dear Ms. Piercy:

RE TYNING v. JOHNSON
Index No. 123-4567

Enclosed for filing in the captioned action is the
defendant's Answer to the Complaint, together with the
corresponding Certificate of Service.

Please charge the filing fee to our account:  No. 678-K.

Very truly yours,

*Nancy Baines*

Nancy Baines
Secretary to
Attorney Barry Zubroski

2 encs.

## PROCESS SERVERS

The server of process may be a public officer such as a United States marshal or deputy marshal or a sheriff or deputy sheriff; or it may be a professional process server.

**Public officers**   It is usually the legal secretary's responsibility to obtain a process server. In federal jurisdictions, the United States marshal nearest the court in which the action is filed serves process within his jurisdiction and forwards papers to be served outside his jurisdiction to the United States marshal in the area in which the paper is to be served. An advance fee is usually required by the United States marshal. In state and local actions, the sheriff may serve legal documents, although in some jurisdictions the sheriff's department does so only for criminal actions.

**Professional process servers**   Professional process servers may serve legal papers in most jurisdictions, and you should have a list of dependable professional process servers in your area. If you need to serve a paper in another geographical area, local process servers can usually give you names of authorized process servers in other places. You can also go to the public library to check the Yellow Pages of telephone books for other cities. If all else fails, you can call a legal secretary at a law firm in the area where the paper is to be served to request the name of a dependable process server.When serving a subpoena duces tecum, which requires the recipient to provide certain documents as evidence, professional process servers are sometimes authorized to obtain those papers, copy them, notarize and deliver the copies to the attorney, and return the originals.

## THE SECRETARY'S RESPONSIBILITIES

When delivering papers to a process server, you should advise the server how and where to serve the papers. You should furnish the addresses of the recipient's residence and place of employment and any information you have about working hours or probable location at any specific time. Let the process server know if the party is to be served as the representative of a corporation. Be sure to state the time limits within which service must be made, and follow up to ensure that service is accomplished before that date.

The server of process may require advance payment of part of the service fee. Each time you forward papers to be served, you should find out whether an advance is necessary and, if so, attach a check for that amount to the papers.

In some jurisdictions, the certificate of service contains a statement to the effect that the "attached" document was served. In such cases, an extra copy of the paper to be served must be included with the papers sent to the process server.

You should be aware that some states have special laws for serving certain parties. For instance, in some states an insurance company or a defunct corporation is served by serving the secretary of state. A fee for this service is payable to the office through whom service is made, and an extra copy is usually required.

## PROOF OF SERVICE

After service of process has been made, the process server returns a proof of service (often called a certificate or affidavit of service) to the court or to the attorney. When proof of service is returned, it is your responsibility to check it carefully to be sure that it is filled out properly. You may need to notarize the signature, as provided for on the form reproduced on page 512. The affidavit of service may be made directly on a copy of the document served, or it may have to be attached to a copy of that document.

The returned proof of service will be accompanied by a statement for the server's fee. These statements should be paid promptly and a record kept for client billing.

## Proof of Service

---

PROOF OF SERVICE BELOW IS TO BE COMPLETED BY THE SHERIFF OR CONSTABLE MAKING SERVICE

**PROOF OF SERVICE**

I hereby certify that on the date below I served a copy of this summons and a copy of the complaint received herewith upon the above named defendant by delivering or leaving these papers in the following manner:

☒ to the defendant personally (Personal service required in all Divorce Actions)

☐ at his dwelling house at the address entered below, with a person of suitable age and discretion then residing therein.

☐ at his usual place of abode at the address entered below, with a person of suitable age and discretion then residing therein.

☐ to an agent named below authorized by appointment of law to receive service of process. Further notice as required by statute was given as noted below.

| ADDRESS OF DWELLING OR USUAL PLACE OF ABODE |
| --- |
| 101 Parsons Street, Providence, RI |

| NAME OF AUTHORIZED AGENT |
| --- |

| FURTHER NOTICE GIVEN |
| --- |

| DATE OF SERVICE | DEPUTY SHERIFF/CONSTABLE |
| --- | --- |
| August 5, 19-- | Thomas Meehan |

FOR SERVICE BY A PERSON OTHER THAN A SHERIFF OR DEPUTY

| DATE | PLACE | NOTARY PUBLIC |
| --- | --- | --- |

Dates of service should be recorded at once on your calendar, since the time for response begins to run on the date of service. Compute the date on which the response is due and calendar it. If the response does not arrive on or before that date, notify the attorney immediately.

Conform a copy of the proof of service or make a photocopy for your files, and file the original with the clerk of court.

## SERVICE BY PUBLICATION

In most cases, actual personal delivery of an initial pleading is required in order to effect service. However, when a party cannot be found through proper diligence, sufficient notice of a lawsuit may be made by publishing the summons in an officially designated newspaper. The intervals and the duration of publication are designated by statute. Notice by mail to the last known address of the party may also be required.

To accomplish service by publication, the summons is mailed to the newspaper designated in the state statutes with a letter setting forth the dates and number of times it should be published and asking the newspaper to return a proof of publication. When the proof of publication is returned, check it carefully, make a copy for your files, and file the original with the court. If the proof of publication is not promptly received, contact the newspaper and ask that it be sent.

## PAPERS SUBSEQUENT TO THE SUMMONS AND COMPLAINT

Copies of pleadings and other court documents subsequent to the summons and complaint are served on the attorneys for the parties rather than directly on the parties. Some jurisdictions require that a certificate of service accompany these documents when they are filed with the court. Other jurisdictions consider that filing the document with the court constitutes certification that a copy has been timely served on all parties required to be served. Answers and subsequent documents may be delivered to the opposing attorney's office in person, or they may be mailed. Process servers are not required to deliver these papers in most jurisdictions.

**Service by personal delivery**   When an answer is served on the opposing attorney, the recipient (who is often the attorney's secretary) may be required to write or stamp on the back of the original document a notation that indicates (1) the date the copy was received, (2) the name of the recipient firm, and (3) the name of the client represented by the firm. A form for this purpose may already be printed on the legal back. Many attorneys advise their secretaries who receive preprinted forms to read them carefully and cross out any words such as "timely" or "due and proper" service before signing the form. After receiving the document, the secretary should immediately calendar the date.

**Service by mail**   Court papers that follow the summons and complaint are frequently served by mail. Certificates of mailing—formal affidavits that are required in many jurisdictions—are signed by the person who mailed the documents and should be notarized. A typical form of a certificate of mailing follows. It contains a list of the names and addresses of all parties to whom the papers were sent together with a sworn statement that the papers were sent.

### Certificate of Mailing

STATE OF _____ )
                               ) ss

COUNTY OF _____ )

____(Name)____, being first duly sworn on oath, deposes and says that (s)he is employed by the law firm of ____(Name of Firm)____, that (s)he is not a party to this action, and that on the _____ day of _____, 19___, (s)he served a copy of the attached _(Name of_ _Document)_ on the following named parties, by depositing the same in the United States Mails in the City of ____(City)____, securely enclosed in an envelope with sufficient postage attached thereto, addressed as follows:

     (Here are listed the names and addresses of the parties served by mail.)

Subscribed and sworn to before me

this _____day of _____, 19___.

_____

Name of Affiant

_____

Notary Public, State of _____

My commission expires _____.

A printed form such as the one reproduced on the following page may also be used. The secretary who mails a document requiring such an affidavit must adhere to the terms of the affidavit, which usually require that the affiant—the secretary or a messenger—deposit the document "in the United States Mails"—<u>not</u> in an OUT box to be picked up by someone else.

    Copies of legal papers in a lawsuit are served on attorneys for all parties in the action, whether they represent opposing parties or co-parties. When serving papers by mail, send them with a short transmittal letter stating the name of the action, the case number, and the titles of the documents being served.

    You will need to conform all copies of the document, record the date served, and calendar the date on which response is due. After service is completed and the certificate filled in, the original is then mailed or delivered to the clerk of court for filing, together with the proof of mailing.

## Proof of Mailing

---

*Attorney(s):*    Mitchell, Mumford & Zubroski
*Office Address & Tel. No.:* 1200 Northgate Building
                                   Southville, ST 54321
*Attorney(s) for*  the Defendant

---

Southville Hardware, Inc.
                              *Plaintiff(s)*
                  *vs.*

Gary Marks

                              *Defendant(s)*

*Docket No.*  123-xyz

*CIVIL ACTION*

*PROOF OF MAILING*

1. *I, the undersigned, am*  secretary to Barry Mitchell,

*attorney(x) for*    Gary Marks, the Defendant

*in the above entitled action.*

2. *On*    **August 21,**        *19* -- *, I mailed in the U.S. Post Office in*  **Southville,**
*New Jersey, a sealed envelope with postage prepaid thereon, by*  **Certified**    *mail, return receipt*
*requested, addressed to*  **Mary Monahan, Counselor at Law**

*at said addressee's last known address at*    123 Main Street
                                                       Southville, ST 54321
*containing*    Notice of Motion to Dismiss
                  Motion to Dismiss
filed in the above action in Superior Court.

R. 1:5-3    *The return receipt card is attached to the original hereof.*

*I certify that the foregoing statements made by me are true. I am aware that if any of the foregoing state-*
*ments made by me are wilfully false, I am subject to punishment.*

*Dated:*  **August 21,**        *19* -- .

*Janet Dow*
JANET DOW

Reprinted by permission of All-State Legal Supply Co.

# 15

CHAPTER FIFTEEN

# TEXT-EDITING SYSTEMS IN LAW OFFICES

## CONTENTS

# 15.1

## INTRODUCTION: Text-editing Machines

A revolution in typing began in the 1930s with the availability of the Autotypist®, a technologically advanced machine which assisted the secretary in the production of routine, repetitive letters. The revolution manifested itself more dramatically in the mid 1960s with the introduction of the IBM Magnetic Tape/Selectric Typewriter (MT/ST), followed a few years later by Mag Cards I and II.

These machines were the forerunners of even more advanced electronic type-writers that store digitally encoded keystrokes and page format codes (such as spacing, tab, carriage return, centering, and underscoring commands) on *magnetic media*. The MT/ST uses magnetic tape, Mag Card units use magnetic cards, and more recent equipment uses floppy disks to record a typist's original keystrokes in electronic form. The magnetic media permit the data to be recalled for editing or correcting without retyping the entire document.

Typing on a text-editing machine (called *input*) is performed much as it would be on a standard typewriter. Typographical errors are corrected in almost all instances by a simple backspace/strikeover process. Through the use of special machine in-struction codes, material is *formatted* (that is, certain lines centered, underscored, or indented or the right-hand margin adjusted) and then recorded.

Documents to be revised are recalled, or *read,* from the medium into the ma-chine memory. Characters, words, and variously sized blocks of text can be inserted into or deleted from the original material by using keys provided for these functions. A final document (*hard copy* or *output*) is then typed automatically, or *printed,* at speeds which generally range from 15.5 to 55 characters per second or more, de-pending upon the sophistication of the equipment.

Since the early 1970s, the technology of text-editing equipment has advanced at a phenomenal rate. Recent machines that are equipped with cathode-ray tubes (TV-like display screens also known as CRTs), microprocessors (the ubiquitous computers on chips), and communications capabilities resemble small business computers. Such equipment often can be interfaced through cables or communications techniques with many types of electronic office machines to form a totally integrated office system that performs both word and data processing applications. Communicating text-editing machines can also be used to transmit electronic mail (described on page 82) over telephone lines and receive messages from remotely situated equipment.

Although text-editing machines can handle all typing tasks, they are generally used for document assembly (the merging of pre-stored paragraphs into "new" text documents), the preparation of repetitive correspondence, and other text-oriented applications. Short letters without revisions and single envelopes are more economically produced on standard electric typewriters.

The legal secretary should be familiar with text-editing equipment, its effect on legal personnel, and its most efficient uses. The next section of this chapter deals with the equipment and its applications as well as the organization necessitated by automating a law office. A discussion of typical legal word-processing procedures follows in section 15.3. Finally, the proper selection, care, and utilization of equipment, supplies, and furnishings are explained in the fourth section. Because of the diverse uses of text-editing equipment, this chapter deals with general concepts, methods, and techniques of accomplishing work rather than descriptions of specific machine functions.

# 15.2

## TEXT-EDITING EQUIPMENT IN THE LAW OFFICE

Literally hundreds of companies manufacture text-editing equipment. These machines can be arranged into two categories: stand-alone units and clustered configurations. Within these groups, further classifications form a hierarchy of machines categorized according to their degree of automation. The following paragraphs describe each category from the simplest to the most sophisticated and most expensive.

### STAND-ALONE UNITS

Text-editing machines that function on their own without being connected to a computer are called *stand-alones*. They include electronic and memory typewriters, *blind* (non-display) machines, linear-display units, and video-display equipment with varying levels of intelligence.

**Electronic and memory typewriters** Resembling standard electric typewriters in appearance, these machines can be used to automate repetitive typing functions such as the preparation of form letters. They can also be used, within limits, for document revision. Their internal memories will store up to several pages of information. This stored material can be recalled for simple editing and error-free printout.

Electronic and memory typewriters are suitable for the preparation of one- or two-page original documents and repetitive correspondence. Original material is produced by *keyboarding* (typing) from dictation media, handwriting, or shorthand. The keyboarded text, stored in the machine's memory, can be revised lightly and then printed. Repetitive correspondence is created by typing or (on more advanced models) automatically merging previously recorded, variable information into a pre-recorded text or by reassembling pre-stored paragraphs in the desired sequence.

Although electronic and memory typewriters are often called text-editing machines, they really cannot be considered as such. Not only are their editing capabilities limited, but their fixed, internal memories limit the amount of data they can store. When full, the memory must be purged in order to receive new text. Machines with removable magnetic storage media are more versatile.

**Blind text-editing machines**  Machines in this category are called "blind" because textual content and format cannot be visually verified on a screen or other type of display before a document is printed. Blind machines consist of a keyboard/printer mechanism (like a typewriter) equipped with removable magnetic media housed either in the typewriter unit itself or in a cable-connected console. Typed information is stored in digital form on the media. The use of removable media enables these machines to store more information than is possible with electronic and memory typewriters. In addition, the editing capabilities of blind text-editing machines are often more extensive than on the less costly electronic and memory typewriters.

On machines that utilize magnetic cards and tapes as media, each page of typed information is stored on a separate card or sequential tape segment. Thus, although it is possible to make light-to-medium revisions on each page, heavy editing—which often necessitates right-hand margin adjustments and extensive repagination—cannot be handled efficiently on these devices. By contrast, machines that record multiple pages on floppy disks (flat, flexible media the size of a 45 rpm record which frequently offer random storage and access to data) allow quicker retrieval of information and greater flexibility in editing the material.

A major limitation of non-display machines is the necessity of using the same unit for both typing and printing. Thus, operators cannot perform both tasks simultaneously, as they can on more expensive and complex equipment. Moreover, the machine instruction codes, which are needed as references should further editing ever be necessary, are visible to the operator only when a document is printed with the codes. This situation often requires the preparation of two copies—one for the lawyer and one containing the editing commands, which the operator files with the medium.

**Linear-display machines**  Whereas blind text-editing machines do not allow an operator to see typed characters and machine instruction codes except on the printed form, linear-display units provide a window into the machine's memory, showing approximately 30 characters and codes at a time. Text can be moved through the window to verify spelling and word placement as well as the location of instruction codes before the document is printed in its final form. As is the case with blind units, linear-display machines that are equipped with magnetic cards or miniature disks store one page on each medium. This restricts their editing capability in comparison with machines that store multiple pages randomly on floppy disks.

Linear-display units, like their blind counterparts, generally use the same device for both keyboarding and printing. This means that operators have to wait for printout to occur before they begin a new project. Also like the blind machines, partial-line display units do not allow page formats to be reviewed before a hard copy is generated.

**Video-display equipment**  Consisting of a keyboard, full- or partial-page CRT, removable media storage unit, and a printer, video-display equipment allows multiple lines of text to be viewed on the screen (with or without accompanying machine codes), usually in the same format as the printed copy assumes. Moreover, CRT-based devices offer many more features than the equipment described in the preceding categories.

When a document is typed onto the display screen (as opposed to paper, which is used on the less sophisticated non-display models) or recalled from the storage medium, the operator usually can *scroll*, or move, through the entire contents to make extensive revisions, adjust formats, rearrange blocks of text, search for and replace particular words or phrases, and add footnotes and headings to the stored material. The magnetic medium used is generally the floppy disk, which permits many pages of text to be stored and accessed quickly. A separate printer, which is connected by cable to the main console, automatically types the hard copy. With this hardware configuration the operator can begin another input or revision operation in a foreground mode while the printer is operating simultaneously in a background mode. (The term *foreground* is used to describe the actions of the operator, who is making decisions at the keyboard; *background* describes the automatic working of the printer.)

These comparatively sophisticated text-editing machines are most effectively utilized to prepare lengthy documents or those requiring heavy revision. Using CRT equipment to generate repetitive or boilerplate material is often overkill. These applications would be handled at a better cost/performance ratio by less sophisticated machines.

**Intelligent text-editing machines**    Thanks to modern-day technology, most text-editing machines now are equipped with powerful microprocessors that control their operating functions. These "intelligent" units offer various advantages. They can be programmed, their storage capacity may be expanded, and they are generally available with communications capabilities.

Software programs for special applications (such as entering data into forms, sorting lists, performing mathematical calculations, or displaying or printing statistical equations with special symbols) are contained on floppy disks. When one of these application disks is loaded into the machine memory, the program replaces or augments the original text-editing operations and enables the intended function.

Special application programs are limited to the amount of material that can be handled by the machine at one pass, which varies from as little as a single page of text to an entire disk's contents—in some cases up to 125 pages. When these limitations need to be exceeded, some intelligent machines can be expanded by increasing their memory and storage capacity. Innovations like the Winchester disk, bubble memory, and laser technologies are expected to produce larger, faster, and more sophisticated memories and storage by the end of the 1980s.

## SYSTEM CONFIGURATIONS

Stand-alone equipment can be interfaced to supplementary work stations and/or computers through cable connections or communications techniques and thus become part of a larger system. Through *local-area* (in-house) and *long-haul* (interoffice) networks, large organizations are now expanding their word-processing operations into extensive information-processing systems. These groupings or *configurations,* known as distributed-logic, clustered, or integrated office systems, are beginning to replace traditional shared-logic systems and time-sharing services. A description of each of these systems follows.

**Shared-logic systems**    When several relatively "dumb" visual-display units (that is, units that cannot operate in a stand-alone mode), letter-quality character printers, and high-speed line printers for rough-draft copy are connected to a minicomputer, and when all these components operate together with the computer-based central processing unit, the result is a shared-logic system. Although prices depend upon the specific equipment configuration ordered, they are substantially higher than the prices of even the most sophisticated stand-alones. However, shared-logic systems provide extensive document handling capabilities at a lower price per station than can usually be achieved with a similar number of stand-alone display machines. One disadvantage of shared-logic systems is that they are entirely dependent upon the computer to which they are connected. Thus, when the central processing unit or disk operating system goes down, or fails, the work stations cannot operate.

**Time-sharing services**    Text-editing machines capable of communicating can be used to access remote computers for extensive textual manipulation. This is done by connecting the machine to an acoustic coupler or similar device that transmits information over telephone lines. Firms can use these stand-alone terminals for standard text-editing purposes. When special applications (such as sorting lengthy lists by multiple parameters and merging numerous variables into lengthy documents) are required, the terminals can have a remote computer accomplish these tasks. *On-line* text-editing machines (those in direct communication with computer equipment) can also be used to perform library research. Customers of time-sharing services are charged for the time they are on-line to the computer as well as for information storage and other provided services.

One problem that arises in using remote computing services is that of security. Law firms with highly confidential material prefer to keep the work in-house rather than let an outside company handle it. Other problems include slow response time when the terminals of many different firms contend for computer time simultaneously. And computer failures leave the entire network inoperative.

**Distributed-logic systems**    In order to circumvent the downtime of shared-logic and time-sharing service, some manufacturers provide backup computers that take over system operations when the main computer goes down. But this is an expensive solution compared with the more recent use of intelligent terminals connected with a computer which together form a distributed-logic system. When intelligent terminals are clustered around a minicomputer, each terminal has the ability to perform standard functions on its own and can continue to operate when a portion of the central system fails.

It should be noted that there is much confusion in distinguishing between shared- and distributed-logic systems. As an alternative to these terms, manufacturers variously refer to their configurations as shared-cluster and shared-resource systems. In the final analysis, if the terminal's ability to function is completely dependent upon a central processing unit and/or a large-storage, hard-disk operating system, neither of which is integrally contained in the terminal being utilized, then "shared-logic" is the proper designation. Machines having local intelligence and using a computer and/or central storage area to augment their capabilities should be referred to as "distributed-logic" systems.

True distributed-logic systems can also perform multiple tasks involved in word and data processing. As recently as 1980, however, virtually no single vendor of text-editing equipment offered equipment that could handle and exchange word and data processing files upon command. The unavailability of such configurations necessitates the purchase or lease of dissimilar equipment from different manufacturers in order to obtain a system that merges all the applications a law office might need.

**Integrated office systems**    Starting with programmable, expandable, communicating text-editing machines *(intelligent machines)*, firms can expand their original equipment into integrated office systems for word and data processing. These office systems will consist of dissimilar devices, including optical character recognition (OCR) units, photocomposition equipment, intelligent copiers or copier-printers, and computers.

OCR units, sometimes called page readers (OCR is frequently used to abbreviate optical character *reader* as well as optical character *recognition*), are machines that scan typewritten copy and automatically convert it to electrical signals that can be transmitted to word processing, data processing, and communications systems. A firm automating its document preparation through an OCR and text-editing machine combination might, for example, have all material prepared on standard electric typewriters equipped with OCR-readable type elements. Hard copy would then be read into the text-editing machines via the OCR device. This procedure eliminates the need to type documents on the text-editing machine and frees it for the revision work to which it is better suited. It is generally agreed that initially keyboarding material on a text-editing machine is counterproductive because the original typing takes almost as long as it would on an ordinary typewriter. An additional advantage of using an OCR device is that rough drafts are typically prepared not by the machine operator but by a secretary who is more familiar with the lawyer's work requirements.

As the firm's needs expand, the OCR/text-editing machine installation could then be interfaced with a small business computer. Billing information could be prepared on the former and transmitted to the latter to generate records of accounts receivable. Alternatively, the text-editing machine could send material to a printer, intelligent copier, or photocomposition unit for printout. The firm could also exchange documents with clients and branch offices that have compatible equipment, using electronic mail procedures. The text-editing equipment might also access a computer data base for research purposes.

**Communications networks**    Large organizations may wish to expand their word-processing operations even further into extensive information-processing systems through local-area and long-haul communications networks. A local network is a data communications system for the interconnection of terminals and computers for text-editing, graphics, and management functions that are within one building, in several buildings on the same property, or in close proximity. Long-haul networks, on the other hand, carry information across geographical boundaries at high speeds through private lines, public switched services, private switched systems, and satellites.

A multi-vendor equipment installation requires a great deal of knowledge and preparation to implement correctly. Special software or equipment interfaces may be required. In addition, the firm must have developed personnel policies and operational procedures governing the equipment and its use.

## DISTRIBUTION OF EQUIPMENT

With the installation of text-editing equipment, law firms often find it necessary to reorganize their office systems to take advantage of the increased efficiency and productivity afforded by the equipment. Typical changes involve the distribution of equipment and the roles of the work originators and the personnel involved in word processing. Text-editing machines are usually grouped together. Operations may be centralized or decentralized.

**Centralized work stations**    In a centralized environment, all the text-editing machines and their operators are located in a common area available to all attorneys. Work may be dictated into a central dictation system by attorneys at their desks or, with some systems, from telephones outside the office. Alternatively, handwritten copy may be delivered to the word-processing center. Operators may handle the work as it comes into the center or they may be assigned specific tasks. Where responsibilities are divided, some operators prepare only short documents and boilerplate materials while others specialize in lengthy documents and heavy revisions.

This type of centralized word-processing operation has several advantages. It facilitates the implementing of standard procedures. It also makes it easier to file hard copy and media, to cross-train operators on equipment, and to schedule second-shift operations. On the other hand, the centralized word-processing center is typically production-oriented and operators have little contact with attorneys and other work originators. Although this situation permits the mass production of routine correspondence, it is not as suitable for personalized work.

**Decentralized work stations**    In a decentralized word-processing environment, operators and machines are grouped in small clusters, each serving several attorneys. Thus the litigation, corporate, and estate planning departments in the firm may have their separate text-editing operations, where each cluster specializes in the department's work. Being familiar with a particular legal specialty, these operators tend to assume more responsibility for setting priorities and tailoring documents to attorneys' specific requirements than they would in a centralized operation. A primary problem with the decentralized plan, however, is the inability of the firm to develop standard procedures for the use of the equipment.

## PERSONNEL ROLES

The introduction of text-editing machines has had a major impact on the traditional role of the legal secretary in many law offices. One reason for this is that a skilled operator of a text-editing machine can produce at least two or three times the correspondence generated by a legal secretary using a standard electric typewriter. By keeping machines active, law firms can offset the relatively high cost of automated typing equipment. Therefore, in an effort to reduce the time that expensive machines lie idle, many firms have divided typing and non-typing tasks between equipment operators and administrative support personnel. The equipment operators, or *word-processing support* group, are usually responsible for typing, revising, and printing office correspondence and legal documents. On the other hand, *administrative support* secretaries generally answer the telephones, schedule appointments, relieve attorneys of routine dictation, engage in some paralegal research tasks, and do the proofreading, filing, and copying. In short, the traditional duties of the legal secretary have, in some offices, been split into two separate job categories.

The size of a law firm also affects the secretary's involvement in word-processing systems. In small offices the secretaries with the heaviest typing load generally receive automated typing equipment. Transcribing from dictation equipment, they prepare a variety of documents ranging from correspondence, court forms, legal briefs, and pleadings to attorney calendars, timekeeping records, and billing statements. They may also be involved in computerized legal research and in the distribution of electronic mail. In larger firms where the equipment is more diverse, tasks may be more specialized. In a typical large firm, for example, a secretary with a standard electric typewriter may type material for input, via an OCR unit, to a display-based text-editing machine. Or a legal assistant using a blind or linear-display, mag-card-based machine may store certain information which is to be read into the word-processing system through a mag-card reader. A text-editing machine operator then adapts the information and prints it out. Or the operator may turn the information over to a computer for further preparation of documents pertaining to the attorney's clients or for billing. The computer, in turn, can be called upon to monitor copier or telephone usage.

## OPERATOR TRAINING

No matter how word-processing operations may be structured within a firm, the operators of text-editing equipment must be fully trained. Most manufacturers of text-editing equipment offer complete courses in machine functions and their applications for specific work situations. Courses are usually limited to one or two people for each unit installed. Some companies provide self-paced instruction through audio-visual or taped materials and programmed manuals. Such instruction can take place in the work environment where the equipment is installed. Other manufacturers arrange classroom instruction on their own premises.

When vendor courses have been completed, some law firms develop subsequent training programs. In small offices these may take the form of a skilled operator instructing a new employee at the text-editing station. Larger firms often establish classroom sessions for employees entering the word-processing operation.

After formal training, the text-editing machine operator is likely to require anywhere from a few weeks to several months to become fully familiar with the machine's functions and optimally productive. This is a very important period because it is when the basis for efficiency and high productivity is established.

Operators who follow the manufacturer's directions carefully for recording, editing, playback, and all other equipment functions discover shortcuts which increase efficiency and raise productivity to higher levels. In order to develop these skills, it is often necessary to review the operator's manual, try out new applications, and experiment with various combinations of coding. Frequently, operators will uncover useful machine functions that have not been suggested by the manufacturer. In order to learn the potential of a machine, it is helpful to attend advanced training sessions and make contact with other operators. Both of these activities can be accomplished by joining user groups established by individual vendors or becoming a member of a word-processing association. These organizations are active in most major U.S. cities.

**Building efficiency**   Operators should prepare well-organized notes on machine functions and keep them in a handy place for easy reference. New applications should be added to the list as they are learned. Whenever a phase of machine operation has been forgotten or a new task is encountered, the operators should review their notes.

Depending on the capabilities of the text-editing equipment, the information that should be recorded includes setting up page beginnings, endings, and formats; handling hyphenations; repaginating lengthy material; making insertions and deletions; moving and copying text; controlling footnotes and headings; recording and recalling information; justifying right-hand margins; searching for and replacing words and phrases; flagging changes; and working with special math, sorting, and timekeeping applications. Because a series of machine instructions required to complete a complex function often can be stored in the machine's memory unit and recalled with one or two keystrokes and executed at the point of need, the exact combination of commands and codings used for each function should also be contained in the reference notes. Standard stored phrases, handled in a similar manner to eliminate repetitive typing, should also be listed.

## CAREER PATHS

Basic typing skills and the related knowledge acquired by people working in word-processing operations have gained new importance and are recognized as essential by many law offices that rely on text-editing equipment. Although speed and accuracy are still the keys to productivity and quality in typing, the ability to apply the rules of English grammar and considerations of good style to proofreading and editing is considered to be essential.

Recognizing the importance of such skills, many firms have established within their word-processing operations a hierarchy of job responsibilities ranging from trainee to manager. This structure forms an effective career path through which employees can advance. Legal secretaries may become involved at entry-level typist, operator, and proofreader positions. As their skills develop, they can work their way up to applications specialists, paralegals, supervisors, and managers.

# 15.3

## TEXT-EDITING PROCEDURES IN A LAW OFFICE

Law firms which have automated their offices through word-processing operations and have developed appropriate applications and procedures are much more efficient in dealing with proliferating paperwork than firms still utilizing manual methods. The faster turnaround of documentation allows attorneys to handle more matters with the help of fewer people. This results in substantial cost savings to the firm. However, in order to reap these benefits, the office must maintain standards of quality through established procedures. This section outlines some of the most important standards that a law firm should implement and describes the role of text-editing procedures in maintaining those standards.

### DOCUMENTATION

Because of the significance of an attorney's tangible product—the paperwork produced—it is necessary to prepare documents that enhance a lawyer's professional image and maintain the personal relationship with clients. Even where standard phrases are utilized, each document must appear to be an original and must contain accurate information. Achieving such high standards requires quality control based on a clear understanding of a law firm's documentation and work organization.

A variety of paperwork is generated in a law office, much of it repetitive. Some is original text that requires proofreading. All documents, however, are highly stylized to meet the requirements of the legal profession. Therefore, it is necessary to keep sample copies of documents for reference in order to ensure conformity of content and format.

**Boilerplate material**    Many legal documents—wills, trusts, workers' compensation claims, routine court pleadings, and corporate and real estate agreements—utilize standard paragraphs and forms into which variable information must be inserted. Chapter 11 describes many of these forms. Storing the paragraphs, forms, and variables on magnetic media allows these documents to be generated almost instantly. Even wills sometimes can be prepared by assembling standard paragraphs into the desired sequence and merging variables like names and dollar amounts. Client correspondence can be generated by incorporating particular names and addresses, dates, client or matter reference numbers, and related facts into standard letters. Court forms can be completed by calling pre-stored information into appropriate fields. Being routine by nature, these materials generally require little or no revision.

**Original documents**    Briefs, opinions, contracts, reports, some pleadings, and lengthy correspondence are frequently and extensively revised. Many are edited by several attorneys before the final draft is approved. In some instances, a document can be revised up to 20 times before it is acceptable. Initial revisions may be substantial, with whole paragraphs being rewritten or rearranged. This process results in extensive right-hand margin adjustments and repagination. Subsequent editing may involve less extensive textual manipulation. The ability of a text-editing machine to store the original document and recall it for revisions without having the entire document retyped is particularly helpful in law offices.

**Proofreading**    The operator of text-editing equipment is responsible for proofreading typewritten material. The importance of this task should never be underestimated. Each word should be read carefully to ensure that the spelling is correct, and every sentence should be checked to make sure that no words or punctuation marks have been omitted. On blind stand-alone equipment, this must be done on the printed copy. Errors detected must be corrected and a new page reprinted. On linear- and visual-display machines, the copy can be verified for correctness on the display and corrected before printing. The same proofreading techniques described on page 180 apply here. Those general suggestions should be expanded to include specific requirements identified by the operators.

**Docket control**    The lifeline of a law firm is its docket control system and resulting attorney calendar that remind lawyers of statutes of limitation, various court filing deadlines, appearances, and appointments. Text-editing machines with sorting capabilities can simplify the preparation of these calendars. For example, entries denoting the initials of the attorney concerned, the date by which action is to be taken, the client file number, the class of item (for example, court designation or statute of limitations), and a description of what needs to be done can be keyboarded at random and stored on a magnetic medium. Periodically the list can be sorted by time and date and then photocopied and distributed to the attorneys. (Some law firms copy the calendar on brightly colored paper stock to make it easy to locate on a cluttered desk.) Additionally, the material may be sorted alphabetically by attorney so that each lawyer receives an individual calendar as well as the master calendar for the entire office.

**Litigation support**    Another use for sorting routines on systems that possess extensive memory and storage facilities is litigation support. This capability helps attorneys prepare for witness depositions, answer interrogatories, complete research, plan trial strategies, and otherwise cope with voluminous evidentiary materials. Exact input depends upon whether the firm prefers to work with full text, abstracts, or indexes. A running printout given to the lawyers can prove helpful in permitting quick review of the subject matter without going to the files. When more details are needed as a deposition or trial date approaches, for example, a computerized search can locate all documents pertaining to a meeting which took place on a specific date. A search might also reveal the number of people who recall that an event happened on that date and, conversely, how many people deny the occurrence. Information can be further sorted by witness or by document type in order to prepare exhibit lists, annotate findings of facts, and organize supporting legal briefs.

**Timekeeping and billing**    One of the most tedious jobs in a law office is keeping track of how attorneys spend their time and billing clients for work performed on their behalf. Text-editing machines simplify this task to some extent by performing sorting and mathematical functions. These functions are included in legal timekeeping and billing software packages. In general, however, timekeeping and billing are at best semi-automatic processes on text-editing machines. A text-editing machine may be capable of entering time slips; sorting them by attorney, client, date, and amount; adding fees and figuring percentages; deducting amounts paid; and merging this information with preformatted statements. However, when a firm requires complete automation of its timekeeping and billing practices, including comprehensive analyses of various staff members' time-effectiveness, it must utilize a computer.

Combining text-editing machines and computers into one office system through compatible communications and software so that material entered and manipulated on the former can be translated into billing statements and reports on the latter is usually more effective than establishing separate word- and data-processing operations. The size of the law firm or the volume of its transactions will determine when this step should be taken.

**Document styling**   Legal documents are highly stylized. Many of them must adhere to pre-established formats acceptable in court. The use of numbered paper and court forms also requires close attention to margins and tab settings. By storing formats along with text, some text-editing equipment permits choice among several levels of indention and enables an operator to proceed from one document to another without having to preset the formats each time.

**Document and form books**   Operators should know which documents are repetitive form letters requiring variable information; which are created from boilerplate material; what information is to be filled into forms; how pleadings, minutes, contracts, agreements, wills, and real property descriptions are organized; and what formats should be used in each case. For help, operators rely on their form books. Document and form books are prepared by saving sample copies of the various types of documents generated in the office. These samples should include any recorded codes which are invisible on hard copy or the display screen, such as margin, tab, and spacing requirements; variable information to be inserted in the text; and boilerplate paragraphs with reference numbers. In addition, copies of correspondence pertinent to each lawyer's practice, along with checklists of variable and boilerplate information, should be distributed to attorneys to help them present material to the operators.

In preparing a boilerplate document, for instance, an attorney would use a checklist to indicate the appropriate paragraph numbers or variables and send it to the word-processing center. An operator would look up the paragraphs or variables in the document or form book, locate the corresponding magnetic medium, load it into the machine, call the paragraphs in sequence into the machine memory or onto the display screen, add selected information, and print the document. When an original text is received, the operator could locate a similar document in the form book and prepare the original according to the specifications noted there.

Establishing a system of forms may take many months. Some offices prefer to obtain standard legal blanks from a publishing company. Legal blanks may be purchased in both hard-copy form and in magnetic-media form. A lawyer can select a blank, indicate the necessary changes, and present it to a word-processing operator. The typist can read the material into a text-editing machine from the appropriate magnetic medium, edit it from the lawyer's notes, and print a final copy.

## WORK ORGANIZATION
Because of the vast differences in preparing repetitive and original copy, not to mention numerous special applications, word-processing personnel need to establish organized work methods. Grouping the day's work according to type and priority is one method of improving work-flow patterns.

**Work grouping**   The term *work grouping* refers to organizing and setting priorities for work according to type of task. Advantages of work grouping include increased productivity and efficiency, a heightened sense of accomplishment, and reduced fatigue. Work grouping takes only a few minutes and can be accomplished in the following ways:

1. At the beginning of the work day and at various intervals during the day, review the tasks to be done.
2. Sort the tasks into categories such as recording, revising, printing, proofreading, copying, and filing.
3. Decide which categories must be completed first, second, third, and so on according to their importance and urgency.
4. Whenever possible, complete all tasks in each category before proceeding to the next one. Of course, any single task which must take priority over all others should be handled first.

Work grouping must be flexible enough so that the operators can handle nonstandard tasks whenever they occur.

**Work-flow patterns**   A smooth work flow is important so that the productive capabilities of the text-editing machine are fully used and backlogs avoided. The time taken to process typewritten work completely is known as *turnaround* (or *throughput*) time; it comprises the time it takes for a document to proceed from *input* (author's dictation) to *output* (completed document). The goal is to keep turnaround time to a minimum without sacrificing the quality of the work.

To analyze work-flow patterns, one should follow documents through all stages of production, including author origination, delivery to the word-processing center, typing, author or operator revision, and distribution. Some steps can usually be streamlined. Providing attorneys with self-explanatory forms or dictation units, for example, can speed the input process. Designating pickup and delivery points and times for documents entering and leaving the center allows work to be handled in batches. In addition, by using OCR equipment, mag-card readers, and similar peripheral equipment for input, a firm can allocate keyboarding functions to standard electric typewriters or blind stand-alone text-editing machines. Typed material in hard-copy or digital form can then be read into text-editing equipment for revision or printing, thus relieving the more expensive equipment of the manual typing task. To improve the output cycle, draft copy can be prepared on high-speed line printers equipped with continuous forms, and final copy can be generated on letter-quality printers with automatic sheet paper feeders. Some firms may take further steps, utilizing communications options to speed the distribution of mail.

Whatever guidelines the firm establishes for these matters should be compiled in a procedures manual and distributed to all involved staff.

## DEVELOPING A PROCEDURES MANUAL
Obtaining peak efficiency in the word-processing environment requires standardized operating procedures. Otherwise, confusion, duplication of effort, and great amounts of wasted time can result. Therefore, when an office installs text-editing equipment, it should also establish a set of standardized procedures. A good procedures manual covers every task performed by a text-editing equipment operator in the office. Such a manual, along with a document or form book, can be used as a training tool for new operators as well as a reference for present operators. Separate manuals might also be prepared for attorneys and administrative support secretaries. The exact format, of course, depends upon the firm's size, type of practice, and equipment and the applications the firm requires of the equipment.

**Gathering information**   The most time-consuming activity in preparing a manual is determining what topics to include and how they can be presented and organized most effectively. If possible, it is a good idea to examine a few manuals prepared by other law firms. These can be obtained by calling law office administrators, who are often willing to supply a sample copy to serve this purpose.

With several different manuals in hand, one can read through the contents and make a list of tentative items that might be included in the office manual. The next step is to interview colleagues to learn the kind of work they do and how current equipment is used. In addition, one should review office memorandums and other materials that explain office policies and procedures and take complete notes of all information gathered from these various sources. When sufficient information has been gathered, it should be organized into appropriate categories according to the previously created list. Categories may be added and deleted where needed, and all the material that has general application should be separated into subtopics.

**Procedures manual checklist**  Some items that might be included in a legal word-processing procedures manual are listed below.

1. Documentation: letters, memos, briefs, proposals, contracts, pleadings, manuals, statistics, speeches. The manual should include samples of each.
2. Applications: paragraph assembly; the merging of variables; wide documents; math, sorting, and timekeeping routines; document storage.
3. Input: handwritten and typed material, dictation, priorities, confidential material.
4. Revisions: media storage, handling of revisions, repagination.
5. Proofreading: techniques, proof marks, editing limitations, punctuation and grammar, use of reference materials.
6. Printing: type styles, type pitch, stationery, use of paper feeders.
7. Production logs: use, compilation, evaluation.
8. Supplies: media, ribbons, print elements, and paper; location, use, and care.
9. Equipment: use, care, service.
10. Distribution: order for listing names, number of copies, envelopes and labels, enclosures, binding methods, distribution methods (interoffice, branch, outgoing), mail alternatives (regular, parcel post, messenger, Special Delivery, express, facsimile, telex, Mailgram, electronic mail via text-editing machines).

Separate manuals for administrative support secretaries might include, in addition to routine assignments like manning the telephone, procedures in the following areas related to word processing: light typing tasks; proofreading, copying, and filing correspondence and documents; dictation and transcription techniques; research; and billing and docket control procedures.

A procedures manual for the attorney might include the following items: submitting material to the word-processing operator, using sample forms, turnaround time and special needs, handling priority documents and confidential material, dictation equipment and dictation techniques, methods of revision, and proofreading marks.

**Writing procedures**  In preparing the manual, present the material in the clearest, most readable, and most easily accessible manner possible. This can be accomplished by allocating one or more pages to each procedure. Working on one item at a time, write an introduction to the subject, stating its purpose and objectives. Then prepare a description of how the procedure is to be performed. Arrange the information in logical steps that explain the task from start to finish.

When writing directions, pay careful attention to style. Be sure that your sentences are concise, direct, and clear. Do not make several long words do the work of a single short one or strings of noun and adjective phrases struggle to take the place of a verb. Let several people, including the users, read the original draft of the manual. Encourage them to make comments, suggestions, and changes. Naturally, the more people involved in the process of writing the procedures manual, the more cooperation will be given when the document is put to use.

**Final form of the manual**  After making the necessary revisions, prepare the manual for its final form. Develop an efficient system for numbering the pages in order to make allowance for future revisions and updates. Compile a table of contents and plan an indexing system. Leave plenty of white space around the copy to make the contents legible.

When the manual goes into production, it should be printed on 20-pound, quality paper stock that will resist wear and tear. Finished pages, table of contents, and index dividers should be bound in an attractive, colorful, durable binder with the name of the firm and "Word-Processing Procedures Manual" on the cover. Quality production lends an air of importance to a manual. Users tend to keep a binder with other reference books such as dictionaries and telephone directories, while pages stapled together generally wind up in a pile of other papers on the desk. A bright color, such as persimmon, turquoise, or even shocking pink, will make the manual easy to locate quickly. Heavy-duty covers and binder rings will keep the manual serviceable for many years. Binders bearing the firm's name will remain behind when an employee departs.

**Distribution and evaluation of the manual**   When the manuals are ready for distribution, it is necessary to develop a control system. A log should be maintained showing the date a manual is issued to an employee. When the employee is terminated, the manual should be retrieved and logged in. The log can also serve to check off the name of each employee receiving revised and updated pages.

The person in charge of producing the manual should make periodic evaluations of how well procedures are working and make revisions as necessary.

The completed procedures manual is a useful tool for a number of purposes. It can be used to orient new employees and temporary personnel to their job responsibilities and to provide material for training programs. It is also helpful in preparing job descriptions. Its chief purpose, however, is to ensure maximum efficiency, productivity, and cost control in the overall word-processing operation.

# 15.4

## SELECTION, CARE, AND USE OF EQUIPMENT, SUPPLIES, AND FURNISHINGS

Skillful operators and efficient procedures are major factors in the productivity of a word-processing operation, but their ultimate effectiveness depends upon reliable and well-organized equipment. Of utmost importance are machines that handle the law firm's applications with minimal downtime, supplies that produce high-quality results, and furniture that is comfortable, good-looking, and practical. Therefore, the selection, care, and use of these elements deserve careful consideration.

### EQUIPMENT
Although the decision to obtain text-editing equipment is generally made by a managing partner and/or the law office manager, operators are frequently involved in determining what kind of machines are acquired. In firms where a word-processing expert (who may be an attorney, the office manager, a vendor, or a consultant) makes a recommendation for appropriate equipment to be installed, secretaries and operators are often asked to keep detailed records of all work processed for a one- or two-week period in order to help determine the firm's actual needs. In other firms, legal secretaries may contact manufacturers to arrange equipment demonstrations. The secretaries may then make recommendations to attorneys based upon the facts they have gathered.

**Selection of equipment**   If a firm's legal documents average less than one or two pages in length and are not ordinarily revised to a great extent, text-editing equipment is warranted only when the material is virtually boilerplate in character. When documents are longer than two or three pages and are primarily standardized, repetitive, or heavily revised, acquisition of automated equipment is worthwhile.

Because machines, once installed in a law firm, are often called upon to handle many applications, they should be flexible enough to meet future requirements. Such machines will usually have a certain amount of intelligence (provided through microprocessors) as well as communications options and the capability of being programmed and expanded. With an expandable machine, memory, storage, and additional work stations can be added to the basic configuration. Programmable machines can accept software packages for an increasing number of applications. Communications options allow a machine to exchange information with similar and, in some cases, dissimilar electronic office equipment. Above all, an expandable, programmable, and communicating text-editing machine avoids the obsolescence caused by new technology because it can transmit information to and receive material from more advanced machines as they are developed. In addition, there are features that make certain machines especially useful in preparing legal correspondence and documents. These features include the following:

1. Large screen with clear, well-defined characters. The screen should display at least half a page of text so that the operator can verify both the content and format of the document being produced.

2. Random-access removable media (such as floppy disks) for convenient storage and retrieval of information. Floppy disks are available in many versions: standard (8-inch) or mini (5¼-inch), single-sided or dual-sided, single-density or dual-density. Obviously, the more storage available, the better.

3. Letter-quality character printer that produces at least 45 characters per second. The printer should also be able to handle extra-wide documents as well as accept an automatic paper feeder controlled from the keyboard, if needed.

4. Index of stored documents displayed on the screen. If possible, the list should be arranged in alphabetical sequence for quick reference.

5. Multiple tab and margin settings within one document. This feature allows material to be indented right and left with an unlimited number of levels.

6. Horizontal scrolling (scanning of the text) on the screen. This permits the viewing and printing of extra-wide documents. Some text-editing machines can scroll across lines up to 256 characters long. For easy readability, the movement should be continuous rather than by blocks of text.

7. Automatic repagination that controls the number of lines on a page and prevents a single line of a paragraph appearing at the bottom or the top of a page. Ideally, this task is accomplished in a background mode, freeing the operator to continue work on another document in foreground.

8. Automatic page numbering, starting with any preselected number. An operator should be able to start printing a revised document at any page rather than having to start from the beginning.

9. Automatic control and placement of headings and footnotes. When a document is revised, the "headers" and "footers" travel to the page on which they are referenced.

10. Ability to search for specified strings of characters and replace them with new information. Control over the matching or disregarding of upper- and lower-case characters is desirable.

11. Glossary or vocabulary that can enter frequently used phrases into the text with one keystroke. Lengthy client names or document titles can then be called into a document each time they occur without their having to be typed in full.

12. Proofreading aids that flag lines of text on the display or print text in boldface type to signal information added or changed in a document. Spelling dictionaries that highlight misspelled words on the display screen are also available.

13. Ability to merge variables into a standard text automatically. Operators can program instruction codes, store them on a disk, and execute them with one keystroke.

14. Ability to accept special mathematics and sorting or selecting programs. Mathematical programs should be at least able to perform the four arithmetic functions (add, subtract, multiply, divide) across rows and down columns of figures as well as to store several in-

structions for automatic execution when attorney fees are calculated. Sorting and selecting programs may help produce management reports and litigation-support records.

15. Double underscoring for mathematical applications. A double underscore character on the print wheel can be used below a column of figures to highlight the total amount.

16. Legal timekeeping and billing programs. A few vendors have developed software programs that meet the needs of some law firms in preparing bills and printing statements.

17. Ability to accept communications programs. The machine selected must be able to support several *protocols* (procedures that contain all the criteria and parameters necessary for two devices to exchange data). Machines that can program the parameters (such as speed, direction of transmission, and error-checking capabilities) score extra points.

18. Multiple communications *ports* that enable peripheral equipment to be connected by cable to the text-editing machine. Then mag-card readers, OCR units, printers, communications *modems* (i.e., equipment that couples the machine to a telephone receiver so that data can be transmitted over telephone lines), and additional work stations can be added as needed.

19. Ability to accept additional memory and storage. Expandability supports additional features and applications as they are added by the manufacturer.

Of course, not all text-editing equipment manufacturers offer all the features outlined above, nor would a law office necessarily require all of them. The basic principle in the selection of text-editing equipment is this: machines that are expandable and software-programmable and that provide communications options do not need to be replaced when a more complex system is needed. Through the addition of memory, storage, peripheral equipment, and software programs, their functions can be enhanced.

A word of caution should be noted. Some vendors promise features they cannot provide. Therefore, it behooves a prospective buyer to obtain demonstrated proof that all functions advertised can actually be performed. It is a far sounder practice to install equipment with a small number of actual features than to trust a vendor to meet verbal commitments to provide more.

Prospective buyers should also be forewarned that sophisticated text-editing machines equipped with many features are generally difficult to operate. Law office personnel should evaluate not only the ease of operating the machine but also the vendor's support and service policies in helping customers use the equipment for their specific applications.

**Buying or leasing equipment**    Considering that sophisticated text-editing machines are very expensive, it becomes essential to determine the lowest net cost arrangements for obtaining the equipment. In the final analysis, an office must choose between buying, leasing, or renting. Although the decision depends upon each firm's situation, in most cases an outright purchase is seldom the best alternative.

One factor which tends to limit a firm's choices is the limited number of alternatives offered by prospective suppliers. For example, most minicomputer manufacturers and vendors do not offer cancelable rental plans. The buyer, in this event, must choose between outright purchase or a plan by which the buyer first leases, then purchases the equipment. The latter alternative is usually available through a third party, with maintenance billed separately under a service agreement. Other vendors prefer rental customers and, as a result, set the list price of their equipment inordinately high in order to make their rental plans seem more attractive.

Nevertheless, it does not necessarily follow that a law firm should deal only with those vendors who offer a wide assortment of acquisition plans. Generally, the most desirable alternative is one that is offered by almost all potential suppliers: a lease/purchase arrangement. It offers protection against price increases, allows tax credits, and is usually less expensive than the other alternatives.

**Maintenance**   To ensure the greatest benefits from text-editing equipment, the law firm should obtain a maintenance agreement from the manufacturer or a third-party service organization. As part of the installation and service arrangement, the vendor should perform the following functions:

1. Instruct the customer in the use and care of the equipment.
2. Offer a regularly scheduled preventive maintenance program to ensure cleaning, lubrication, and replacement of parts as needed.
3. Respond quickly to service calls.

**Care**   Operators can take certain precautions to keep text-editing machines in good working condition:

1. Call for service if equipment is not functioning properly.
2. Wipe the typefaces with a clean, dry cloth as needed, unless instructed otherwise by the manufacturer.
3. Use an acoustical hood as a dust cover as well as a noise reducer.
4. Keep food, beverages, and paper clips away from the equipment.
5. Cover the text-editing machine when the equipment is not in use.
6. Discourage the use of the equipment by personnel who are not properly trained in its operation.
7. Be sure the on/off switch is set at "off" at the end of the work day or when the equipment is to be idle for long periods of time.

## CHOOSING A SUPPLIER

Electronic text-editing equipment requires top-quality supplies in order to function properly. Media, ribbons, elements, paper, and accessories must be chosen and used carefully.

The number of organizations to which an office can turn for its word-processing production tools has expanded at a phenomenal rate over the past few years. In spite of the growing number of firms offering various supplies, only a handful are in the business of manufacturing the products. These manufacturers, in turn, sell to equipment vendors and to independent suppliers. Therefore, one manufacturer's supplies may be available through several sources.

The person responsible for ordering word-processing supplies should choose a supplier carefully, qualifying the prospective candidates in the following manner:

1. How long has the item been carried and how well has it been received by other customers?
2. How quickly can the company fill orders?
3. What guarantees are provided on the products sold?
4. What product lines and what special services are offered?
5. Does the company have word-processing expertise, and is it able to offer solutions to the problems users have with media, ribbons, print elements, and other supplies?

## MAGNETIC MEDIA

Fundamental to any text-editing and dictation equipment is the removable medium (card, tape, or disk) on which digital information is stored. Because of the highly sensitive nature of these products, great care should be exercised in their selection. Recommendations for the selection of media include the following:

1. Identification—An area on the sleeve, plastic box, or envelope should be provided for control notes to aid in retrieving the correct medium for revision and updating. In some cases removable, color-coded labels serve this purpose. Cards, which can become numerous and unwieldy, require a six-digit pre-numbering system and self-numbering corners to write on.

2. Certification—All media should be certified 100 percent error-free in the package and be guaranteed for an optimum number of passes (at least 1,000 passes is recommended for cards, 10 million for disks).
3. Function—Cassette tapes for audio and digital applications should be splice-free to prevent breaking and have magnetic leaders for immediate recording. Cassette tapes wear and function well when packaged in low-friction plastic cases with no-squeal tape corner guides, multi-layer pressure pads, and low-abrasion rollers.

Most manufacturers of text-editing equipment offer magnetic media for purchase in any quantity. Some companies offer a lower price for large orders. Even better price advantages can be obtained from dealers and supply houses. It is wise to have extra supplies of media on hand in case an unusually large volume of work must be processed or a special project must be handled at the text-editing machine. The media reorder number should be kept close at hand to facilitate quick replenishment of supplies. A reorder number file located at the work station is very useful.

**Care and maintenance**    With normal use, most magnetic media are virtually indestructible and can be reused indefinitely for recording and playing back information. However, one must maintain their serviceability through proper maintenance.

1. Store the media where there is as little dust as possible. Wipe visible dust from the media with a clean, dry cloth.
2. Fingerprints may impair record and playback functions of some media. Wipe the affected area with a clean cloth.
3. Store and handle media in such a manner that the possibility of physical damage is minimized. If irreparable damage occurs, record information on new media and discard the old.

**Storage of media**    Media storage is a critical element in a successful word-processing operation. It is important for word-processing personnel to set up a filing system for the center's printed and stored documents. For efficient use, media should be separated into three categories: daily, temporary, and permanent storage.

1. Daily media are those which are used repeatedly for one-time documents, items which do not need to be stored for long periods. Many firms allow one to five work days for editing, revising, and printing the recorded materials before purging the media for other work. These media should be stored within fingertip reach of the operator.
2. Temporarily stored media should contain those documents, such as reports and manuscripts, which have short-term usefulness. These materials may be played back repeatedly or revised over an extended period of time. The media may therefore be kept in a file drawer located in an area close to the work station, but they need not be within immediate reach.
3. Permanently stored media should contain materials which are useful over a long period. Address lists, legal instruments that seldom change in content, and manuscripts in a constant process of revision are among the kinds of materials that are permanently stored. These should be accessible to all operators. For protection against loss of important records (such as software programs and material that would be difficult to re-create in the event of erasure or fire), duplicate copies of permanent media should be placed in a safe. It is also advisable to retain media containing classified information in drawers or files which can be locked.

**Logging, filing, and record-keeping**    A system of control that permits the rapid location of all recorded material and the making of hard copies of that material is important in a time-sensitive legal environment. In designing a record-keeping system, simplicity and convenience should be kept in mind. The specific design of such a system is determined in every instance by the nature and volume of the work. The following suggestions, however, will aid in establishing effective controls:

1. Identify magnetic cards, tapes, or disks by means of numbers or some other identifying codes. Some media are pre-numbered by the manufacturer and adapt easily to any control system.

2. Create a brief coding system to appear on hard copy produced by text-editing machines that do not create their own index. The coding system should indicate the media and the location of documents on the media. File copies of the documents in a daily file folder in the order of their location on the media. Store the folder in the secretarial desk or within immediate reach in the work station area.

3. Print out an index of documents recorded on media when text-editing machines provide this capability. Attach the index to the medium before filing it away.

4. Group media according to author, client/matter, contents, or operator in a filing system designed for easy retrieval.

5. File copies of temporarily and permanently stored documents, showing all special codes and format information, in a special drawer or binder. Use transparent page protectors or page lamination to protect copies of permanently stored documents and to ensure a long shelf life.

6. Keep files and binders up-to-date; that is, once the stored information is out-of-date or no longer useful, eliminate the obsolete copies. Update media according to the manufacturer's instructions, deleting old or unused information and adding any new material. File updated hard copies in the file or binder.

**Media organizers**   As long as a firm utilizes only a few magnetic media, they can be retained in the boxes in which they were packaged. Once the data base becomes extensive, however, it is necessary to store the media in containers that keep them indexed for easy retrieval. Important considerations in selecting media organizers (which include folders, binders, trays, rotary files, and filing cabinets) include:

1. Ease of use—Media housing should be engineered so that it can fit on the top of a text-editing machine console or shelf. It should also be accessible to more than one operator at a time.

2. Durability—Organizers should be constructed of heavy-duty materials that are resistant to the wear of frequent handling. They should also be tip-proof, unbreakable, and washable.

3. Design—Media should be retained in a static-free environment to prevent accumulation of dust.

4. Method of indexing—An indexing system that is easy to use and update should allow work to be coded by job, client, or department for fast retrieval. Cards should be held on end in a staggered fashion to keep the numbering system visible. Provision should also be made for referencing hard copy for retrieval along with the media.

5. Expandability—Storage units should be modular or interchangeable in various housing devices for expansion into larger systems as needs dictate.

## RIBBONS
Most word-processing suppliers have standards or limits to which all manufacturers must conform, but the ribbon industry is an exception. Ink formulas, inking methods, quality controls, and packaging vary with each company.

**Selection**   Most companies make ribbons available for the text-editing machines which they manufacture and market. Ribbons can usually be ordered and paid for singly or in quantity; the cost per ribbon is often less when a sizable quantity is ordered. Some companies offer an ordering plan that features automatic, periodic shipment of and billing for necessary supplies. Prepaid coupon systems are also available from some manufacturers of ribbons and other office supplies, whereby reorders are processed when a coupon is forwarded to the company with whom the ribbon order was placed. This coupon contains all the information necessary to ensure delivery of the proper items.

A rule of thumb for purchasing ribbons is to remember that single- or multi-strike film ribbons provide the crisp impression important to professional-looking correspondence. Less costly fabric ribbons, which tend to produce fuzzy characters, are suitable for draft documents.

While paper is normally absorbent enough to produce a good quality impression, stock with a high finish might cause the ink to lie on the surface, thus producing an easily smudged impression. Adapting ribbon inks to the end use can be accomplished by consulting with a knowledgeable manufacturer of inked ribbons.

For ease in selecting the proper ribbon for each application, many ribbon companies issue catalogs describing the most appropriate use of each of their products. Among items listed are extra-length sheer polyethylene films and multi-strike ribbons that release their ink gradually to provide up to 50 percent more impressions than standard ribbons. OCR ribbons with a specially formulated ink coating are also available. Lift-off tape with low-tack properties can remove typed errors without tearing or damaging the paper or depositing unwanted residue into the printer.

**Recycling methods**    To reduce expenses, used carbon/film ribbon cartridges can be reloaded and used fabric ribbons can be reinked. When fabric ribbons are recycled, they should be used for approximately 90 percent of their normal life; at that point they begin to dry out and print quality degrades. Ribbons can be reinked once or twice. To help get as much use as possible from fabric ribbons, it is recommended that a line counter be installed on the printer. The counter, which is set for a given number of lines, will flash an alarm signal when the line count is reached, indicating that the ribbon is ready for recycling.

## PRINT ELEMENTS

There are many different kinds of print elements. Ball-shaped elements are used in some text-editing machines, daisy wheels are employed in others, and thimble elements are used in still others. Regardless of the element used, their selection depends on four criteria: material, type style, pitch, and sequence.

**Material**    When selecting daisy wheels, it is important to know whether they are available with metal or plastic characters. Because of their different weights, metal and plastic wheels usually are not interchangeable on a printer. A document prepared with a metal-plated serif type style (serifs are short lines stemming from and at an angle to the upper and lower ends of the strokes of a letter) provides exceptional print quality. For rough-draft copy or a multi-part form, however, it will probably be better to substitute a less-expensive plastic wheel for the metal one. Of course, if the form consists of many carbon and paper layers, the metal print element will make a stronger impression.

**Type style**    Descriptive names are used for the design of characters. These include *letter gothic* (a sans serif style, that is, one without serifs), *courier* (with serifs), *italic* (characters slanted upward to the right), *bookface* (boldface), *OCR* (type styles specially designed for recognition by OCR scanners), and *Greek/math* (containing the Greek alphabet plus symbols for printing mathematical equations).

**Pitch**    Pitch defines character size and the spacing for which characters were originally designed. For example, 12 pitch means that 12 characters are printed per linear inch; 10 pitch has 10 characters to the inch.

**Sequence**    Characters are positioned on the print element according to a specific arrangement. Standard or WP sequence places characters in the same relationship to each other as they appear on the keyboard. Foreign language sets contain special characters with accents, cedillas, and umlauts. Some manufacturers of type heads and print wheels can make individual letter changes on regular elements, reproduce virtually any special symbols (including engineering, electronics, chemical, and computer symbols), and provide foreign-language character sets. Some of these companies also repair elements by replacing old caps, mending damaged teeth, and repairing broken hubs.

## PAPER PRODUCTS

The medium that carries the printed message is paper. Used in word-processing operations as output from a variety of impact printers, ink-jet printers, and copiers, or as input through OCR scanners that are usually equipped with automatic feeding devices, paper is processed at extremely high speeds. Under these conditions, top-grade papers containing excellent paper feeding properties, providing little or no lint buildup on machine parts, and resulting in excellent quality print must be used. This applies to all paper, including cut sheets, carbonless sets, continuous paper, business forms, and the carrier packs described below.

**Cut sheets**   Papers used in impact and ink-jet printing, OCR scanning, and copying applications must meet stringent requirements. High-quality rag-content bond is ideal for impact units. Its nonporous surface prevents ink from spreading through the fibers and improves print quality. However, because rag-content paper is considerably more expensive than sulfite bonds, it should be reserved principally for professional correspondence. Sulfites, which are more porous and absorbent, are adequate for interoffice memorandums, drafts, and forms. Cut sheets can be fed through a printer manually or automatically by means of a paper feeder.

In ink-jet printing, it is important that the paper be free of iron scale, which can become magnetized along with the ink beads and thereby confuse the printer. OCR bond requires an exceptionally clean sheet so as to eliminate needless scanning errors caused by dirt particles. Copy paper must have a scorch-resistant finish that will stand up to high heat in the fixing stage. It should also have a smooth finish to receive optimum transfer of the image.

**Carbonless sets**   The ability to make multiple copies without carbon paper is important in a word-processing system. NCR (no carbon required) paper, available through many paper merchants, accomplishes this task; its paper sets are coated on the front and/or back sides to transfer the impression from the previous sheet to the next sheet under it.

Another type of NCR paper, called self-contained, combines coated front and back ingredients on the same side of the paper, thus enabling the sheet to become self-imaging. Self-contained paper may be used behind non-NCR paper original sheets (like OCR bond or cotton content letterheads) to obtain carbonless copies.

**Continuous forms paper**   Gaining ever wider use in word-processing systems, continuous forms paper eliminates the need to insert individual sheets of paper into high-speed printers. This type of paper requires the use of a pin-feed platen or forms tractor to prevent skewing. Users are encouraged to select paper with minimal curl properties. Marginal pin-hole alignment, bursting and decollating properties, and refoldability are other factors to be considered.

**Business forms**   Cut sheet paper, NCR forms, carbon sets, and continuous forms paper can be imprinted with business forms on which operators fill in the blanks. Paper companies can help customers design forms to their exact specifications.

**Carrier packs** Continuous forms paper can be used alone or as carrier sheets for letterheads, envelopes, carbon sets, snap-out forms, and NCR forms, giving them a personalized appearance with no tell-tale perforations. Printed, engraved, thermographed, or embossed papers or forms are mounted on continuous carrier sheets with special glues that cannot be detected after the pages have been removed. The carrier strip can be used to print draft copy after the letterheads or envelopes have been removed.

## FURNISHINGS

Text-editing machines are often installed in an effectively organized work station enclosed by soundproof panels where operators can concentrate on the work at hand. In addition, storage spaces afford operators close proximity to supplies and reference materials.

To provide maximum operator comfort and to decrease fatigue, the insights of ergonomics, or human engineering, can be incorporated in the work station in a number of ways:

1. Brightly colored panels with tackboards provide a pleasant environment which can be personalized to an individual's taste.
2. Fireproofing in the panels provides important protection.
3. Task (direct) and ambient (indirect) lighting, incorporated into the work station, illuminates the work surface and prevents screen glare.
4. Rounded corners on desks prevent bruises.
5. Lockable storage areas secure confidential materials as well as personal property.
6. Channels located in desks and/or panels conceal equipment cords and cables.
7. Padded chairs with arm rests are adjustable to heights that suit individual operators.
8. Static control to eliminate shocks that cause data loss on magnetic media is provided by the carpeting.
9. Proper heating, air-conditioning, and ventilation are additional considerations.

In summary, the work station should utilize space to best advantage, yet keep materials within easy reach of the operator for maximum efficiency and create a pleasant, safe environment in which to work.

# 16

CHAPTER SIXTEEN

# OFFICE COPYING EQUIPMENT: How to Make It Work for You

## CONTENTS

# 16.1

## REPROGRAPHICS EQUIPMENT AND PROCESSES

### INTRODUCTION

Paper-based communications are the staple of a law office's services, the tangible product of an attorney's labors. More than almost any other type of business, law firms generate paperwork. In addition to the proliferation of original material, the use of multiple copies of documents is increasing. These easily produced multiple copies have fundamentally altered the law office as they have altered the general business scene. The production and handling of this paper barrage is dependent on the ever-increasing technological evolution of office machines which goes on at an almost unbelievable pace. Every issue of the business magazines bombards its readers with "the newest" and "the best" in office copiers. The term designating this field is *reprographics*: this includes all the processes, techniques, and equipment employed in the multiple copying or reproduction of documents in a graphic form—hence *repro* plus *graphics*.

Not only have technological advancements created an impact on offices, but they have also expanded the responsibilities and duties of secretaries. Now the secretary must understand the capabilities of each reprographic process, know how to operate commonly used copying equipment, and be aware of the costs of each copying process. Often a secretary selects the reprographics equipment for the office; therefore, it is vital that the secretary understand which process will provide the office with the best copy quality in minimum time and at minimum cost.

No single office reproduction method can be described as the best for handling all situations, and requirements of each particular situation will suggest the appropriate reprographic process. However, the selection of a reprographic process should be based principally on quality/quantity/budget requirements with consideration given to one or more of the following factors:

1. **Appearance of copy desired**  If the copy will be distributed within an organization, generally a lower quality of reproduction is acceptable; however, if the copy is mailed to someone outside the office, a higher quality product is usually desired.

2. **Quantity needed**   If a large number of copies is needed, a process specifically applicable to large-volume reproduction requirements would probably be used.
3. **Cost**   In general, the higher the quality of the copy, the higher the cost in materials and labor. However, some of these costs can be substantially lowered where a large output is usual.
4. **Time demands**   If a copy is needed instantly with no setup time, this limitation will determine the reprographic method to be used.
5. **Additional considerations**   Standard equipment cannot always accommodate unusual jobs. Such additional factors might include unusual sizes of copy, special copy design, and the need for color reproduction.

Though the priority of the factors may be determined by the office management, the secretary often determines the most appropriate method in each situation.

Reprographics encompasses five basic processes of duplication:
1. Carbon Process (conventional and film)
2. Fluid Process
3. Stencil Process
4. Printing Process
5. Photocopy Process

In addition, the five basic processes have been integrated in a variety of ways to serve additional needs. Each of the processes is described in the following paragraphs.

## CARBON PROCESS

The carbon process can be effectively used to make from 2 to 15 copies of a document. Two types of carbon are available—conventional carbon paper and carbon film. Conventional carbon paper has long been a staple supply in offices. The selection of the grade and weight of conventional carbon paper depends on the number of copies that are required. A lighter weight carbon paper should be used as the number of copies increases. The table below provides guidelines for the selection of conventional carbon paper.

### Carbon Paper Recommendations for Typewriters

| Electric Typewriters | | Manual Typewriters | |
|---|---|---|---|
| Number of Copies | Weight Recommended | Number of Copies | Weight Recommended |
| 1–5 | Heavy (standard) | 1–3 | Heavy (standard) |
| 6–8 | Medium | 4–5 | Medium |
| 8–10 | Light | 6–8 | Light |

Film carbon is a newer development that has gained enthusiastic acceptance in the office. Film carbon is a tough polyester film coated with a plastic solvent. The increased durability of film carbon prevents tearing and eliminates wrinkling and curling. This strong but pliant carbon will produce up to 15 legible copies. It has the added advantage of not smearing or smudging hands or paper.

Additional factors affecting the suitability of carbon paper or carbon film include the weight of the original stationery and the second sheets, the sharpness of the typewriter typeface, the kind and condition of the typewriter platen, and the touch of the typist, particularly if a manual typewriter is being used.

An impression control device on electric typewriters regulates the pressure of the typeface striking the paper. This mechanism allows for a setting of one to ten, with the *one* setting being suitable for typing one or two copies and the *five* (or more) setting appropriate when the typist is making many copies. Electric typewriters also have a carbon copy lever which interacts with the impression control regulator to ensure that multiple copy impressions are properly made.

**Carbon pack**   A carbon pack contains the original, the carbon paper, and the copy sheets. Since the pack tends to slip while being inserted into the typewriter, secretaries have developed methods to keep the edges of the pack even. One method is to insert the pack into the fold of an envelope or into the crease of a folded piece of paper. The pack with the envelope or folded paper is then inserted into the typewriter with a quick turn of the cylinder and rolled around. The envelope is then removed. A second method is the machine assembly method:

1. Assemble one sheet of letterhead or bond stationery in front of the required number of copy sheets and begin inserting them into the typewriter.
2. Turn the cylinder to a point where all of the sheets are gripped securely by the feed rolls. (Approximately seven-eighths of the paper will not have entered the typewriter.)
3. Then, flip all of the sheets except the last sheet of copy paper toward you over the top of the typewriter.
4. Place one sheet of carbon paper (with the glossy carbon side facing you) between each of the sheets of paper. Lay each sheet back as the carbon sheet is added.
5. After all carbon sheets have been inserted, continue rolling the pack into the regular typing position.
6. Use the paper-release lever on the typewriter to avoid wrinkling the carbon pack and to allow you to straighten it.

After the typing is completed, the carbon pack can be removed from the typewriter by pulling the paper bail forward and using the paper-release lever. The carbon paper can be removed in one swift motion by giving the pack a quick downward shake. If the machine assembly method is used, the carbon extensions may be grasped and the carbon sheets pulled out all in one motion.

Previously assembled carbon sets may be purchased. These sets consist of a lightweight sheet of carbon paper attached to the top of a sheet of copy paper. These carbon sets may be stacked to make several copies at one typing. A newer development, treated carbonless paper, available as NCR (no carbon required) sets, is popular in many offices. The pressure-sensitive top sheets and duplicate sheets allow the reproduction of several copies without the use of carbon paper. Telephone message pads, billing statements, legal forms, and other preprinted material can be purchased with this feature. Even customized office forms may be printed on NCR paper, either in pads or in individual multi-part sets. The cost of preassembled carbon sets is somewhat higher than do-it-yourself packs, and the cost of carbonless forms is even higher. Many secretaries, however, believe that the ease of use and the savings in time more than compensate for the added cost.

**Correction of errors**   Quality typing demands careful correction of errors. Although some typists follow the practice of correcting an error on all copies of a document, a growing trend today is to correct the errors only on the original and on those copies being sent outside the firm. An exception to this practice occurs when an error is made on a number or date, or when the error might cause the message to be misunderstood. In those cases, corrections should be made on all copies. Errors should be corrected on all copies of statistical/technical typing, including citations.

In the absence of a self-correcting typewriter, a hard, abrasive typing eraser works best when one is correcting errors on an original. A soft pencil eraser is most effective when one is correcting carbon copies. Erasures will be neat if the typist (1) makes sure that the hands are clean before making an erasure (2) checks to see that the eraser is clean (one can clean it by rubbing it on a rough surface such as sandpaper or an emery board) (3) erases with the grain of the paper (4) erases each letter separately with a light, short stroke, and (5) camouflages the erased area by applying a white charcoal film or by using a special white charcoal pencil. Also, a good quality white liquid correction fluid can be used to cover up difficult corrections, punctuation marks, and others. Tinted liquid correction fluid is available to match colored shades of stationery, but should be ordered at the time the stationery order is placed. If an erasing shield is used, it should be placed in front of the carbon paper. When correcting subsequent copies, the typist should transfer the shield, making sure that it is placed in front of the carbon each time.

When errors are discovered after the carbon pack has been removed from the typewriter, the typist inserts each sheet into the machine individually to make the correction. If it is important to keep the shading similar, a small piece of carbon can be placed over the erased spot before the correction is typed on the copy.

The typist ought to use the typewriter alignment scale and the variable line spacer to align the typing when reinserting typewritten work into the machine for correction. A good practice is to check the positioning of the typewriter typeface in relation to the alignment scale by first typing a few words on a sheet of scratch paper.

**Storage of carbon paper**   Carbon paper should be stored in a flat folder with the carbon side down and away from heat. Used carbon paper should be put away as soon as possible to avoid the possibility of getting carbon marks on other papers, on clothing, or on the desk top. Carbon paper should be discarded as soon as it no longer makes good, clean copies. Wrinkled carbon paper should not be reused, since any characters striking the wrinkled section will be distorted.

**Problem-solving tips for working with conventional (non-film) carbon paper**   The following table describes some of the more common problems encountered with conventional (non-film) carbon paper and suggests some ways these problems may be solved (note that the characteristics of film carbon differ markedly from those of conventional carbon; therefore, the table that follows does not apply to film carbon):

## Problem-solving Tips—Carbon Process

| Condition | Probable Cause(s) | Guideline(s)/Solution(s) |
|---|---|---|
| **Curling** | usually the result of a change in temperature or humidity | Store carbon paper face down in a flat folder away from extreme temperature or excessive moisture; purchase curl-free carbon paper. |
| **Limited durability** | possibly due to poor-quality carbon paper or a soft finish on the carbon paper, or excessive wear caused by the use of the high impression settings on the typewriter | Select carbon paper having a hard finish; alternate the carbon sheets within the carbon pack for more even wear. |
| **Illegibility** | often due to excessive use of carbon paper beyond the manufacturer's recommendations | Typewriter may need cleaning; discard worn carbon paper and replace it with unused sheets; determine whether the finish and weight of the carbon paper are suitable for the number of copies being typed. |
| **Cutting** | results when the typewriter's typeface is excessively sharp | Use a heavier weight of carbon paper; if lightweight bond paper is used for the original, insert a second sheet of bond between the original and the first carbon. |

| | | |
|---|---|---|
| **Slippage** | may be caused by using copy sheets with a slick finish | Slip the carbon pack into the fold of an envelope before inserting it into the typewriter; when typing near the bottom of a page, insert an extra sheet of bond paper between the last copy and the cylinder. |
| **Smudging** | may be caused by careless handling of carbon copies; may be aggravated by using glossy copy paper | Use carbon paper having a hard finish; select copy paper that will absorb carbon. |
| **Treeing** | results from wrinkled carbon paper | When inserting or removing a carbon pack, use the paper-release lever. This procedure tends to smooth out potential wrinkles. |
| **Offsetting image** | usually caused by excessive pressure on the carbon pack | Adjust the impression control mechanism on the typewriter; use lightweight carbon paper and copy paper; discourage roller marks by moving the rollers to the edge of the paper. |

**Advantages and disadvantages of the carbon process**  Every reprographic process has superior features as well as limitations, and the carbon process is no exception. The following table describes some of the advantages and disadvantages most evident in this process:

**Advantages**
1. a relatively inexpensive method of producing copies
2. process can be used on a wide variety of papers relative to color, quality, and weight
3. all copies made at same time as original
4. entire process completed in one location; secretary does not have to leave work station
5. additional equipment not needed to make copies
6. file copies reproduced on lightweight paper, creating less bulk in files

**Disadvantages**
1. only a limited number of copies reproduced from one typing
2. time needed to make corrections on the original and all copies

Although reprographics is often associated with copier equipment, one should recognize that carbon paper or film is often superior for preparing a small number of copies. It is tempting for a legal secretary to disregard carbon packs when the office has convenient copy machines, but one should always consider the total cost of time and equipment. A major disadvantage of the carbon process—the time required to correct errors—is eliminated on the perfect copies produced by text-editing typewriters. These machines could be used to greater advantage in producing carbon copies for law office use.

## FLUID PROCESS
Fluid duplicating is one of the older reprographic processes. Other well-known terms for this kind of duplication include *liquid, spirit,* and *direct-process.* The fluid process

involves the interaction of five elements: the carbon sheet, the master sheet, the moistening fluid, the duplicating paper, and a duplicator machine. The material is typed directly onto the spirit master. After the carbon sheet is removed, the master sheet is placed on the outside of the machine cylinder (sometimes called the *drum*) with the carbon copy side up. The paper is then fed through the moistening unit and between the cylinder and impression roller. As each sheet of moistened paper makes contact with the master on the cylinder, the moistening fluid on the paper dissolves a thin layer of the carbon deposit from the master. The copy that appears on the sheet of paper is the result of this layer of carbon deposit.

**The master unit**    The master unit consists of the original sheet of special glossy white paper (*master*) attached to a sheet of paper coated with a waxlike substance (*direct process/hectograph carbon*) which gives the appearance of carbon. Typewriting, handwriting, drawing, or printing on the face of the master causes this waxlike carbon to be transferred to the back of the master. A protective tissue slip-sheet separates the master from the carbon sheet and must be removed before any impressions are made on the master. After the master sheet has been completed, the protective sheet should be replaced behind it to protect its content and to avoid unwanted carbon transfer that will stain other surfaces.

Thermal spirit masters can now be made with photocopying machines that use the heat-transfer process (see page 548). Of course, a special thermal spirit master pack is required, but these packs are not expensive. The original to be copied is inserted into the thermal carbon pack; then the pack is passed through the photocopying machine. This flexibility allows thermal spirit masters to be made of typewritten copy, handwritten copy, or printed matter. In addition, correction fluid and paste-ups may be used on the original without affecting the quality of the master. The master made by this process will produce from 40 to 50 legible copies.

**Advantages and disadvantages of the fluid process**    The following table shows some of the advantages and disadvantages of using the fluid process.

| Advantages | Disadvantages |
|---|---|
| 1. an inexpensive process | 1. a master must be prepared before any copies can be made |
| 2. master usable on a variety of paper weights and colors | 2. about 300 copies can be made from a standard master and no more than 50 from a thermal master |
| 3. several colors usable simultaneously on a single copy | 3. copies do not have a high-quality appearance when compared with more sophisticated copy work |
| 4. copies that can be made at a rate of over 100 a minute | 4. copies are not usually legible enough to be satisfactorily reproduced on a photocopying machine |
| 5. equipment that is easy to use and that requires a minimum of training time | 5. carbon is messy and requires careful handling |
| | 6. black masters tend to reproduce in a dull, gray shade rather than in black |

The fluid process is used primarily for work to be distributed within a large organization. Few law firms now use this process. However, the new thermal spirit masters, which are so conveniently produced on copying machines, may answer the need for inexpensive interoffice communications in some law offices.

Information on preparing a spirit master, correcting errors, and running the duplicator may be obtained from the manufacturer of the duplicator or by consulting a general secretarial manual such as *Webster's Secretarial Handbook*.

## STENCIL PROCESS

One of the better-known reprographic processes involves the use of a stencil and is technically referred to as the *stencil process*. This method of duplication is more versatile than the carbon paper process or the fluid process because electronic stencil-cutting equipment that allows one to reproduce photographs is available. The stencil process relies on four elements: the stencil, the ink, the paper, and the stencil duplicator machine. The stencil is prepared and placed on the cylinder of the stencil duplicator over an ink pad. Ink flows from the inside of the cylinder onto the ink pad and through the openings in the stencil. As paper is fed between the cylinder and the impression roller, the roller causes the paper to touch the stencil. Simultaneously, the ink flows from the ink pad through the openings in the stencil and produces a copy on the paper.

**Stencil pack**   A stencil pack usually has four parts: (1) the stencil sheet, (2) the backing sheet, (3) the cushion sheet, and (4) the typing film (optional). The stencil sheet is made of a fine but tough fibrous tissue covered on both sides with a wax coating that will not allow ink to pass through the surface. This coating is pushed aside when the typewriter key or stylus strikes the stencil. The backing is the heavy, smooth sheet on which the stencil is mounted. The cushion sheet is placed between the stencil and the backing sheet. It supports the stencil, cushions the blow of the typeface, and makes the typed stencil easier to read. The typing film, considered an optional feature, is a thin sheet of plastic film lightly attached to the top of the stencil sheet. Use of the typing film sheet tends to make the copy more bold in appearance and minimizes the cutting out of letters on the stencil sheet.

**Stencil selection**   Stencils are available to accommodate varying conditions relative to copies required, durability, guide markings, cushion coating, and preprinted designs. Because of the variety of stencils available, it is important that the intended use of a stencil be carefully considered. For instance, if 1,000 copies or less are required, an average-run stencil is suitable; however, if more than 1,000 copies are planned or if the stencil will be run at a later time, it is advisable to select a long-run stencil which can produce 5,000 or more satisfactory copies.

Manufacturers offer a variety of special stencils designed for specific kinds of jobs. Some of the special stencils available are:

1. **Addressing stencil**   This stencil provides 33 grid spaces in which names and addresses are to be typed. The stencil can be run off on regular paper or on sheets of gummed labels.
2. **Continuous stencil**   This stencil has control holes punched along one or both sides and is used with automated data processing printout machines.
3. **Document stencil**   This stencil is intended for use when typing oversized documents.
4. **Electronic stencil**   This stencil is electronically produced and permits the reproduction of letterheads, office forms, and bulletin or memo headings with the use of an electronic scanner. An electronic scanner is an office machine that can create a stencil producing up to 10,000 copies. The scanner reproduces any original copy including typewritten copy, line drawings, hand lettering, and photographic halftones. Simple scanners recognize all colors as black, but more expensive models can be set to ignore specific colors in the original copy. Although these devices may require as much as 12 minutes to make one stencil, the machine can be left unattended.
5. **Thermal stencil**   This stencil is cut by running an original copy with a heat-sensitive stencil through a special thermal photocopier, thereby eliminating the need to type the stencil. This process can reproduce copy which is prepared in black ink. Photographic halftones cannot be reproduced. Care must be taken in order not to smudge the original copy, since this process reproduces all shades of any color as definite black impressions.

**Storage of stencils**    Stencils that will be used again should be stored individually in stencil folders (sometimes called *filing wrappers*) and ought to be kept in a cool, dry area. The stencil should be placed in the folder with the ink side up. The stencil must be carefully straightened to avoid wrinkling. Any excess ink on the stencil will be absorbed by closing the folder and firmly rubbing the outside of the folder. After five minutes, the folder should be opened and the stencil turned over to prevent it from sticking to the folder when it dries. Stencils may be cleaned with various special preparations or they may be washed (depending on the kind of ink used) so that handling and storage are facilitated (washed stencils may be hung on racks). The contents of each stencil folder should be identified for filing purposes. Simple techniques for doing so are these: (1) run the stencil folder through the stencil duplicator before removing the stencil for storage, (2) remove the stencil and blot it on the stencil folder, thus reproducing a copy, or (3) tape one copy from the stencil duplication on the outside of the folder.

**Stencil maker**    This piece of equipment will automatically transfer printed, typewritten, or pasted-up copy to an electronic stencil. The original and a blank electronic stencil are placed side-by-side on the cylinder of the stencil maker. When the machine is activated, the image of the original is transferred to the blank stencil.

**Advantages and disadvantages of the stencil process**    The following table lists some of the advantages and disadvantages of the stencil process.

| Advantages | Disadvantages |
|---|---|
| 1. inexpensive process | 1. stencil must be prepared before copies can be made |
| 2. stencil duplicator generally uncomplicated; operator can be easily trained | 2. color can be produced, but the process is time-consuming and untidy |
| 3. easy-to-type stencils; corrections easy to make | 3. machine operation somewhat difficult if operator is improperly trained |
| 4. legible copies with excellent contrast between black ink and paper | 4. stencils may be cleaned for later runs, but doing so is a messy process |
| 5. stencils repeatedly usable on paper of different weights and colors | |
| 6. from 11 to 5,000 or more copies may be made from one stencil at a production rate of 7,500 to 12,000 copies an hour | |

The stencil process is used primarily in small or medium-sized businesses. However, the convenience of the electronic stencil and recent improvements in the quality of the copies produced have made the stencil duplicator a useful adjunct to the photocopying machine in many large law offices. Interoffice forms, for example, may be duplicated in large numbers by the relatively inexpensive stencil process. Rough, absorbent paper was formerly required, but some of the newer machines allow copies to be printed on standard bond.

Information on preparing a stencil, correcting errors, and running the stencil duplicator may be obtained from the manufacturer of the duplicator or by consulting a general secretarial manual such as *Webster's Secretarial Handbook*.

## PRINTING PROCESS
The five basic printing methods are: (1) letterpress, (2) gravure, (3) engraving, (4) screen, and (5) offset. Since the offset process is the one most often used in offices, it is described here. Small, tabletop offset machines—very popular in offices today—are capable of producing quality copies, and they are relatively simple to operate. Some models are self-cleaning.

The fundamental parts of an offset duplicator are the master (or the *plate*) cylinder, the blanket cylinder, the impression cylinder, the ink fountain, and the water fountain. When the offset duplication process is begun, the master contacts the blanket cylinder leaving a mirror image. When paper passes between the blanket cylinder and the impression cylinder, the image is mirrored a second time and appears on the copy in correct, original form.

**Classification of offset masters**    The offset duplicating master may be paper, plastic, or metal. Paper masters are less durable and are normally used for short runs (from 50 to 1,000 copies) while plastic masters are designed for producing as many as 25,000 copies. Metal masters are the most durable, and the same metal master may be used repeatedly over a period of several years to produce 50,000 and more copies. Masters are available in a variety of sizes and weights, mountings (as straight-edge, slotted, or pin), and come in rolls, individual sheets, and fan-fold pockets. Each of these is designed for specific applications.

**Imaging offset masters**    Several methods can be used to transfer an image to a paper offset duplicating master:

1. **Direct image**    The image is made on an offset master by writing, drawing, or typing directly on the offset master. Special tools containing an oil-based substance that will attract ink must be used. Special pencils, crayons, ball-point pens, and rubber stamps can be purchased for this purpose. Typewriter ribbons suitable for use in the offset process are carbon ribbons (paper, polyethylene, and Mylar) or fabric ribbons (cotton, nylon, and silk).

2. **Electrostatic**    This method uses a copying feature available on many photocopying machines. The original copy is inserted into the machine and is projected onto a positive-charged photoconductive plate. This plate is passed through a toner solution and the emerging image is transferred, and then fused by the application of heat, onto a master. Many machines have the capability to produce paper and plastic masters, and several models of photocopying machines can also image metal masters. Masters can be made in seconds from any printed, typed, drawn, or bound original and will produce a minimum of 100 high-quality copies.

3. **Transfer**    This method uses a photographic camera process without the use of a separate negative. An image from an original is projected onto a light-sensitive sheet by way of gelatin transfer and photo-transfer methods. This process images a master. Self-contained photocopy units can deliver several masters a minute using this method.

4. **Pre-sensitized**    A photocopying machine is utilized in this process. An original and a special pre-coated master sheet are inserted into the machine. This master sheet has been pre-coated with a highly sensitive substance which is acted on by the photocopying machine and results in a master ready for use on an offset duplicator.

Two methods can be used to produce an image on a metal master:

1. **Pre-sensitized**    A graphic camera is used to make a film negative of an original. This film negative is exposed to a concentrated light source and onto a metal master. These film negatives can be stored and used many times to make additional metal masters when needed. Metal masters produce very high-quality copies. Photographs can be effectively reproduced through the capability of this method to reproduce halftones.

2. **Transfer**    This method is basically the same as the one described for imaging paper and plastic masters. Photocopying machines can produce metal masters of the same size as the original, while a camera process can accommodate the enlargement or reduction of the original before imaging the metal master.

**Typing paper offset masters**    Secretaries are directly involved in writing or typing on paper offset masters. A discussion concerning the correct procedures to follow when typing paper offset masters is included in this section. Paper offset masters must be handled with care. The following steps outline a satisfactory procedure in preparing typewritten offset masters:

1. Clean the typeface on your typewriter.
2. Check the typewriter fabric ribbon to make certain that it is suitable for typing on a paper offset master; certain kinds of film ribbon may be used in offset master preparation.
3. Push the paper bail rollers to the margin area of the master.
4. Type directly on the paper master with the same amount of pressure that is used in regular typing, but at a slightly slower pace. (A heavy touch tends to encourage the appearance of hollow characters on copies.)
5. The paper master should be handled with the utmost care. One's fingers should touch only the edges of the master to avoid smearing. Nail polish or hand lotion containing lanolin can produce smudge marks on copies. Also, paper offset masters should never be folded or creased.
6. If the paper master must be reinserted into the typewriter, slip a clean sheet of paper over the master to prevent it from being smudged by the feed rollers.
7. After typing the master, allow it to rest for a minimum of 30 minutes. This waiting period will provide time for the image to become fixed so that the master will produce a darker, sharper image when run on the offset duplicator.

Special offset pens, pencils, and crayons should be used when drawing, writing, or ruling on an offset master. When one is tracing a design on a paper master, offset carbon paper must be used. (The manufacturer of the offset duplicating equipment can provide the necessary information concerning the drawing tools needed for preparing various kinds of artwork on an offset master.)

**Correction of errors on a paper offset master**   For best results, errors should be corrected with a special eraser designed for use on paper offset masters. Offset erasers are very soft and do not contain abrasives that will mar the surface of the master. (If absolutely necessary, any soft nonabrasive eraser may be substituted; however, this practice is not recommended.) A light, quick stroke should be used in erasing an error. The eraser should be cleaned after each stroke by rubbing it on a clean sheet of paper or on a piece of sandpaper. One should not erase too heavily since the carbon deposit is removed rather easily. A slightly visible ghost image may remain on the master, but this image will not be reproduced on the copies. Only the surface ink should be removed. Deep erasures will remove the surface coating on the paper master, and these spots will reproduce in black. Offset deletion fluid can be used to make a correction which covers a large area of the master. The secretary can then type over the erased area with the same pressure used originally. Only a single erasure can be made in any one spot.

**Storage of offset masters**   Offset paper masters should be filed and stored in a plain paper folder and placed in a flat position. If more than one master is stored in a folder, each of the paper masters should be separated with a sheet of paper to prevent them from absorbing ink from each other. A cotton pad moistened with water can be used to remove any smudges left on the edges of a master before it is stored. If proper care is taken of paper offset masters, they can be rerun many times with excellent results. The same methods that have been suggested on page 544 for identifying the folders in which stencils are stored can be used in filing paper offset masters. Plastic and metal masters can be stored in paper folders in the same manner as paper masters; however, special cabinets are available in which these plates may be hung so that there is little danger of their touching each other.

**Problem-solving tips for working with offset masters**   Some common problems encountered in working with offset masters are identified in the following table.

## Problem-solving Tips—Offset Process

| Condition | Probable Cause(s) | Guideline(s)/Solution(s) |
|---|---|---|
| **Black correction smudges** | errors erased too deeply on offset master, thereby removing surface coating | Typist must prepare a new offset master. |
| | dirty eraser | Use fountain solution on the eraser to try to clean the master error area. |
| **Fingerprints** | improper handling of offset master | Only the edges of the offset master should be touched; avoid using hand lotion with lanolin before touching the offset master. |
| **Roll marks** | excess pressure from typewriter rollers | Push the paper bail rollers to the margin area of the offset master; if reinserting the master, place a sheet of paper over the master. |
| **Light image** | offset master run immediately after preparation | Allow the offset master to rest from 30 minutes to two hours to allow the image to set. |
| | typing strokes too light | Type the master using a slightly heavier pressure or install a new offset fabric ribbon. |
| **Uneven drawing** | uneven pressure used when making outlines | Make all drawings on a flat, hard surface; use a firm, even pressure when making lines; use the artwork tool that is appropriate for the desired effect. |

**Advantages and disadvantages of the offset process**   Like other duplicating processes, offset printing is excellent for certain uses but inappropriate for others. The following table lists the advantages and disadvantages of the offset process.

**Advantages**
1. high-quality printing closely resembling original
2. all copies of equal quality
3. copy reproducible on both sides of the paper
4. printing can be in color
5. hourly production rate of 9,000 or more copies
6. only one metal master needed for more than 50,000 copies
7. copies made on almost any kind of paper

**Disadvantages**
1. equipment relatively expensive when compared with that used in fluid and stencil processes
2. more training required for operating personnel
3. equipment requires more maintenance than fluid and stencil process equipment
4. higher material costs than those used in fluid and stencil processes
5. more time needed both in preparing the machine for operation and in cleaning the machine after copies have been run off

Use of the offset printing process can result in excellent reproduction. If appearance is a primary requirement, offset duplication offers many advantages. A law firm might wish to use an offset duplicator to print letterhead, office manuals, or forms that are distributed outside the office.

## PHOTOCOPY PROCESS

Fluid, stencil, and offset processes are *duplicating* processes; that is, they create many copies from a master that first has to be specially prepared. A *copying* machine creates a few copies directly from an original document through an image-forming process. No intermediate master is needed. The copying machine has rapidly become a necessity in the office. Copiers are now used in virtually all offices, large or small.

Copiers are usually classified in two ways. One classification is based on the chemical process by which the copier works; the second, which is used more frequently, concerns the type of paper used for making copies. The major copier classifications are the *wet process* and the *dry process*. These are divided into a number of secondary processes. The wet processes—diazo, diffusion transfer, stabilization, and dye transfer—use liquid or vapor chemicals. Copying machines employing a wet process are rarely used today in law offices.

The dry photocopying processes that have largely replaced the wet processes are (1) thermal, (2) dual spectrum, and (3) electrostatic, but chiefly electrostatic.

1. **Thermal** is a process by which an original and a heat-sensitive sheet are joined and exposed to an infrared light source. Because dark material absorbs more heat than light material does, this exposure images the dark outlines and produces a copy. Unfortunately, the copies made with this process have a tendency to become brittle as time passes. Thermal copiers are used today chiefly to prepare stencils, direct-process masters, and overhead transparencies.

2. **Dual spectrum** is a process in which a light-sensitive copy paper and a heat-sensitive copy paper are both needed to produce a copy. The original and the light-sensitive paper are exposed to a light source. Then, the original is removed and the light-sensitive copy paper and the heat-sensitive copy paper are placed together and are exposed to a source of heat. This step transfers the image to the heat-sensitive paper which becomes the final copy.

3. **Electrostatic** involves a *transfer* electrostatic process which is based on light reflecting an original through lenses and exposing a charged drum. The resulting particles of toner left on the drum become the image, which is then transferred and fused by heat onto the copy. A *direct* electrostatic process follows the same principles as the transfer electrostatic process except that the image appears directly on the copy paper and does not need to be transferred.

Photocopying machines are more often categorized as *coated-paper copiers* or *plain-paper copiers,* depending on the copy paper required for duplication. Earlier machines used coated papers, and although these photocopiers are still prevalent, the present trend is definitely toward an increased use of plain-paper copying equipment. Some of the reasons given for the current popularity of plain-paper copiers include the following:

1. The appearance of the copies closely resembles the original, since the same grade and weight of paper is used in the duplication process.

2. Plain-paper copies can be produced on letterhead stationery.

3. The slightly higher per-copy cost of plain-paper copies is often considered to be justified, because of the higher quality copies that can be made. The appearance of plain-paper copies is especially suitable and desirable for documents that will be sent outside the company.

4. Photocopying equipment manufacturers continue to develop special peripheral equipment used with plain-paper copiers that can easily and quickly produce offset masters, transparencies, and two-sided copies; that can automatically sort and collate copies; and that can provide for the cassette-loading of paper. Other available features include: slitters, perforators, folders, staplers, stitchers, and binding devices. Often, these mechanisms can be operated independently of the copier.

5. The ease of operating a plain-paper copier is appealing to office employees.

6. Special supply requirements are kept to a minimum.

Though coated-paper copiers are used in many offices, the copies made with these machines do have some limitations: (1) coated-paper copies do not resemble or feel like bond stationery, (2) writing is difficult on coated-paper copies, and (3) equipment tends to be complex and requires special materials for its use. Efforts are being made by manufacturers of coated-paper copiers to overcome some of these disadvantages. Even though the present costs of plain-paper copies are higher than the coated-paper copies, the prices of the plain-paper machines relative to coated-paper machines are being reduced, and an estimated six out of every seven copies are now being produced on plain-paper copiers.

**Selecting a copying machine**    A legal secretary is often involved in the selection of an office copier. Copier manufacturers offer a great variety of features, and it makes no sense to pay for elaborate features that will not be used. Therefore, before making a choice, the secretary, along with the attorney and the office manager, should precisely determine the copying needs of the office by answering these questions:

1. **What kinds of documents need to be copied? Single pages? Multiple-page documents? Law books?**
   Some machines feed one sheet at a time; others feature multiple copy control with automatic document feeding and automatic repeat. Some machines can copy only flat pages; others are also capable of reproducing pages from books.

2. **What type of paper will the copies be reproduced on?**
   This is an important factor in determining whether to select a plain-paper copier or a coated-paper copier. In addition, one should consider the number of loading drawers for the different sizes or types of paper copies that will be needed in the office.

3. **How large are the documents to be copied?**
   Many machines will reproduce large computer printouts and ledger sheets as well as legal-size documents.

4. **Is there a need for reducing the size of a copy?**
   Many copiers can reduce a legal-size original, for example, to a letter-size copy.

5. **Does the office frequently need copy on both sides of a sheet?**
   Many copiers offer this "duplexing" feature. It is especially convenient for making space-saving file copies and for copying double-sided law blanks.

6. **Is speed of operation important?**
   Copiers vary in the number of seconds it takes for them to produce the first copy, and also in the number of copies per minute produced after the first copy is made.

7. **Is it worthwhile to pay for the extra capabilities that some copiers offer? These may include:**
   Making full-size reproductions from microfilm
   Making offset masters
   Making thermal spirit masters
   Making transparencies for overhead projection
   Additional equipment such as automatic collaters and staplers, paper cutters, binding machines, addressing machines.

8. **Will the machine be operated by many people, or will a trained operator be available?**
   If the copier is to be operated by a secretary who must leave her work station to make copies, certain convenience features are desirable to save the secretary's time. Such convenience features include:
   pushbutton operation
   LED displays
   counter to keep track of the number of copies being made

toner and developer supply indicators

paper jam indicator

paper supply indicator

cassette in use indicator

interruption feature to allow copying a few pages of a different original in the middle of a long run

operating instructions visible on the machine

large capacity of paper loaders

ease of replacing paper

ease of replacing toner.

Additional questions about a specific copier under consideration should also be asked:

1. **Does the copier have automatic shutoff? Does it require a warm-up time?**

   These features should be considered in determining whether the machine will be left on or turned off between uses.

2. **How well does the copier fit into the office?**

   The exact dimensions of the machine should be determined, along with where the machine will be placed and how accessible it will be to its users. Some copiers are portable desktop models, some are movable consoles on casters, others are stationary. The color scheme of the room, the availability of storage space for paper and other supplies, and special electrical requirements should also be considered.

3. **Are supplies and suppliers for this particular machine easily available?**

4. **Most important, what is the quality of the copies reproduced?**

   Is the background white?

   Is the background free of specks, streaks, and smudges?

   Does the machine compensate for originals with a colored background or with light type?

   Do blue colors reproduce well?

   Do pencil marks and other handwritten copy reproduce well?

   Do the lines on ruled legal paper reproduce well?

   If half-tones are to be copied, do they reproduce well?

   Does the copier make good-quality copies on all types of paper that the office plans to use—letterhead, card stock, labels, etc.?

**Control of photocopying machines**    The total volume of copies produced on an individual copying machine depends on the size of the office, the type of material copied, the availability of the copier, and whether or not use of the machine is supervised. The duplicating costs associated with a copier can be astonishingly high. An abnormally large part of a law firm's reprographics budget is often spent on photocopiers, and it has been said that, next to telephone expenditures, copying expenses may be the largest part of a firm's total operations budget. When copiers are very convenient and easy to operate, their use is often diverted to activities unrelated to business. Several plans have been devised to discourage the personal use of copying machines as well as the indiscriminate copying of office communications. The use of these systems has reduced the copying expenses of some firms as much as 20 percent. The following copy control systems are in use today:

1. **Key control plan**    A key must be inserted into the photocopying machine in order to make copies.

2. **Card control method**    A small card (plastic or computer) must be placed into the photocopier before it will function properly and produce copies.

3. **Coin control method**    A pay-as-you-go practice is followed by which the insertion of a coin is required in order to activate the machine.

4. **Supervisory control plan**   One person is placed in charge of the copying machine(s), and all work to be copied must be submitted to this person before copying is allowed.

5. **Audit system**   A machine-recorded tally is kept of all work being processed on the copier. An audit system can be used independently or in conjunction with any of the previously mentioned plans.

Sensible office practices such as the following may also serve to reduce copying expenditures:

1. Making carbon copies instead of machine copies whenever feasible
2. Using a duplicating machine or commercial printer for large runs
3. Watching the supply of forms so that one does not have to make photocopies when forms run out
4. Routing a single copy to several people in the office

It is illegal to photocopy driver's licenses, auto registrations, passports, U.S. government securities, postage stamps, copyrighted materials, and citizenship, naturalization, or immigration papers.

**Problem-solving tips for working with copiers**   Although most copiers work quite satisfactorily, an occasional problem may arise during their operation. The table on page 552 lists a few problems associated with some photocopiers, offers possible causes of the trouble, and suggests a few solutions.

**Advantages and disadvantages of the photocopying process**   The following table provides an overall view of some of the strengths and weaknesses often associated with using a photocopying process.

**Advantages**
1. copies easy to make
2. copies reproducible very quickly
3. machine that is easy to operate and requires little training
4. no master needed—only a legible original
5. quality on all copies remains the same throughout a run
6. pages from books (with copyright permission) can be copied on many machines

**Disadvantages**
1. higher costs per copy than with other duplicating processes
2. very attractive for copying material for personal use
3. tendency toward making too many unnecessary copies of material
4. rather slow functioning of some copiers

Photocopiers have become indispensable in most law offices. They are ideal for fast reproduction of legal documents, incoming correspondence, and filled-in forms. Copies of incoming papers can be sent quickly to several members of a firm in those instances when routing would cause an unwanted delay. The table of contents of a publication may be copied and routed to office personnel while the publication itself is sent directly to the office library. Other uses ideally suited to copiers include (1) copying the front and back of incoming checks, (2) copying items needed for tax reports, (3) making copies of incoming correspondence and legal documents for clients, (4) copying from law books, (5) reproducing ledger cards as part of a client's statement, (6) reducing legal size documents to letter size for filing, (7) making small quantities of address labels, and (8) making duplicator stencils, spirit masters, and offset masters without time-consuming retyping.

A common practice in business is to write a reply directly on an incoming letter, have a photocopy made, return the original to the sender, and keep the copy for filing. A notation is often stamped on the letter calling the sender's attention to the reply. This method, which saves secretarial time as well as file space, is catching on in American law offices. It is used chiefly in the efficiently managed small firm.

## Problem-solving Tips—Photocopying Machines

| Condition | Probable Cause(s) | Guideline(s)/Solution(s) |
|---|---|---|
| **Feeding difficulties** | dimensional stability and tolerance of the paper affected feeding—perhaps paper was too stiff | Use 20-pound paper for best results; lighter paper is more difficult to handle. |
| | moisture content in the paper too high | Check your packaging and storing facility—humidity must be controlled. |
| **Paper curls** | inadequate weight of paper being used | Read the instruction manual to determine whether the proper kind of copy paper is being used. If so, call the sales office of the firm selling the equipment for further advice. |
| **Poor duplication** | attempting to copy show-through originals | Use only opaque originals. |
| **Machine malfunction** | any one of many mechanical difficulties | Call the authorized service representative. |

## IN-HOUSE REPROGRAPHICS CENTERS

The immense popularity of photocopiers as well as many new developments in the reprographics field have resulted in the initiation of some changes in the reprographic approaches used by many law offices. Those firms with medium-volume or high-volume reproduction needs have discovered that they can often lower their reprographics budget to a substantial extent and yet continue to maintain a high level of service by following such practices as: (1) comparing available pricing plans of equipment and selecting the one that is most reasonable for the firm's operation (2) centralizing all duplication equipment in one area in order to more fully use the greater volume capacity and faster equipment available (3) switching from plain-paper copiers to the lower-cost coated-copy systems for all internal documents (4) purchasing copying machines or leasing them from a third party not directly associated with the manufacturer, and (5) instituting a copy control system which encourages a charge-back policy to the user department. Experience indicates that greater savings have resulted from the installation of a copy control system than any other single procedure.

Reprographics departments have been organized in several ways to meet the needs of law offices. Some firms prefer to have one centralized reprographics center in which all duplication work is done. Others employ one center for the principal reprographics workload but have installed satellite copy areas throughout the building to provide fast service for lower-volume jobs. Still other offices prefer to continue employing the services of an outside firm for major high-volume work but install satellite copy centers easily accessible to the office personnel in the immediate vicinity of each center for lower-volume work. Libraries in larger law firms are furnished with their own copiers that are capable of reproducing pages from bulky books.

A law firm's reprographics center should probably include duplicating machines—fluid, stencil, or offset process—as well as copiers. Multiple copies can be produced on duplicators at up to one-third less than the cost of reproduction on copiers. Offset has increased in use because its reprographic quality is superior, but all three duplicating processes have vastly improved in the ease of preparing the master and in the ease of operating the equipment. Of course, there would have to be a need for enough multiple-copy documents in an office to justify the expense of buying or leasing a duplicating machine.

Law firms frequently employ commercial firms for printing items such as appeal briefs. In comparing the costs of a commercial service with in-house reproduction, the secretary should consider (1) the charge per copy, (2) the quality of the copies, (3) extra costs of collating and binding, (4) the time required to complete the work, and (5) the accessibility of the printer's services.

# 16.2

## NEW DEVELOPMENTS IN REPROGRAPHICS

Technological developments cause frequent changes in reprographic techniques; even the best copying method for a particular office application may become obsolete or too expensive overnight. A few of the technological developments that in time will probably change or alter office copying procedures are described here. Some of these processes are already in use in larger law offices.

**Copier-duplicators**   Like copiers, these new machines directly image the original without the intermediate step of employing a master. Like duplicators, they are designed for high-volume production and will reproduce up to 5,000 copies per hour. To the speed and cost advantage of duplicators they have added the convenience of copiers, together with several automated features that are found on copiers but not on duplicators. Copier-duplicators are expensive, however, and require trained operators. They are used in very large word-processing and reprographics departments.

**Facsimile copying**   Images of telegram-size messages have been transmitted between offices over teletype telephone lines for years. The recent application of laser technology has broadened the size and volume capabilities as well as the speed with which messages can be transmitted. Facsimile copiers are designed for use anywhere that a telephone and an electric outlet are available. One master at the source office can cause single or multiple copies to be transmitted to many other offices which may be geographically separated. Documents, charts, and pictures can be transmitted or received within two to six minutes. Recent improvements in facsimile transmission have ensured the increased use of facsimile as a means of reproducing copy. The quality of the copies is improving, and some machines will now print on bond paper. With digital technology, speeds of under a minute are now possible, reducing the cost of telephone transmission time. In addition, automation now permits unattended sending and receiving of messages, as described in the discussion of telecommunications on page 62. Law firms may employ facsimile devices to transmit documents to branch offices, client offices, or courts.

**Intelligent copiers**   These new copiers eliminate the preparation of a typewritten original that has to be taken manually to a copying machine. They are equipped to take raw data from text-editing machines or computers and to create an original by means of their own programmed logic. They are able to create specified formats, mix type styles, and reproduce signatures from memory. They can even transmit hard copy to other locations quickly, although as long-distance transmitters they are not yet a viable alternative to facsimile copying.

**Word-processing and printing integration**    Many large organizations have begun to integrate the text-editing work stations of their word-processing operations with their own phototypesetting systems or with those of a commercial printer. If the two systems of a law office and a printer are compatible, word-processed material may go, via telephone lines, directly into print without the intermediate steps of typesetting or keyboarding.

**Micrographic copies**    Many offices use microfilm as a relatively inexpensive method of storing large files. This photoreduction process, discussed in Chapter 6, allows individual records to be retrieved, viewed, and copied. The pages stored on microfilm or microfiche are retrieved through the use of a special reader. When this reader is attached to certain models of photocopying machines, printed copies of the stored pages may be made.

# 17

CHAPTER SEVENTEEN

# TRIPS AND MEETINGS

## CONTENTS

# 17.1

## INTRODUCTION: The Mobile Attorney

Today's lawyers, like their counterparts in business, have become increasingly mobile. An attorney may be employed by an international conglomerate or represent clients dealing with one or several of the multitude of federal and state agencies. The attorney may travel to defend antitrust violations, take depositions, handle labor negotiations, serve in the legislature, or argue before an appellate court. In addition, intense competition requires the practicing attorney to be alert to new developments through participation in seminars, workshops, and professional associations.

Even though the firm may have an in-house travel department, the legal secretary should know how to plan a business trip. The secretary's scope of responsibility goes beyond making plane reservations and typing itineraries to include the understanding of what information is needed for various kinds of business trips, where to obtain current information quickly, and how to isolate and discard extraneous data. Good secretarial support may mean the difference between a successful trip and a failure.

Maintaining efficiency in the office in the attorney's absence is also a vital part of the secretary's role. It is the secretary's duty to see that clients' problems receive the necessary attention. The secretary should be aware of the attorney's travel schedule and organize the office workload to minimize disruption.

# 17.2

## TRAVEL ARRANGEMENTS

Some attorneys are spur-of-the-moment travelers who dash to the airport an hour before departure; others may insist that the legal secretary attend to each minute detail of the trip well in advance. Some lawyers travel frequently, others rarely. No matter how often the attorney travels, the same care in preparation must be exercised. The best trip is one without surprises, which only careful planning can eliminate.

## PREPARING FOR THE ATTORNEY'S TRIP

If the attorney travels regularly, the secretary may be able to anticipate travel arrangements; however, a notice of hearing or an emergency conference request will necessitate immediate trip plans. It is important to make travel plans efficiently to ensure that convenient transportation and hotel facilities are available and that the requirements of the client can be met. The secretary making an attorney's travel arrangements should know <u>in advance</u> the following:

1. *Office policies and procedure relative to attorney travel*
   procedure for making a formal travel request
   how to coordinate the attorneys' schedules and provide for covering the absent attorney
   procedure for cash advances and/or prepayment or reimbursement of expenses
   procedure for charging the proper account and billing the client
   whether travel arrangements are made by the in-house travel department, a travel agent, or the secretary

2. *The attorney's personal preferences*
   means of transportation—specific carrier, class, time of day, meal service, and special services
   hotel accommodations—chain affiliation, required facilities, and special arrangements
   entertainment and sightseeing activities
   ground transportation services
   amount of leisure time
   personal interests
   medical problems

3. *Methods for keeping records of the trip*
   dictation equipment, telephone communication, secretary's attendance, outside clerical assistance, or dictation upon the attorney's return

Although the gathering and organization of this information may involve conferences with the attorney, your co-workers or predecessors, and members of the attorney's family in addition to a review of previous travel folders, the result—routine and effortless travel arrangements—will make the investment in time worthwhile.

In addition to knowing general office policies and the lawyer's preferences, for each trip you must determine specifics as follows:

1. The purpose of the trip, the departure and return dates, and the number of people traveling
2. The most convenient and expedient means of transportation to the destination from the attorney's home city, the mileage, and the estimated travel time
3. The hotel most completely equipped and closest to trip activities (Personal experience, a call to the local hotel chain representative, or a quick check of the American Hotel and Motel Association's *Hotel and Motel Red Book* should provide an answer.)
4. Selection of co-counsel at the destination
5. Arrangements and facilities for meetings
6. Forms to be completed prior to departure
7. Information for and instructions to the clients involved
8. Memoranda and background information for co-counsel or opposing attorney
9. The availability of necessary supplies such as dictation equipment, reference books or research facilities, files, and handout materials; also the availability of clerical, reproduction, and other special services
10. Allocation of free time and designated activities
11. Additional arrangements for family and traveling companions
12. Notes on climate, time zones, and accepted modes of dress

**Arrangements with travel agents**    If it is the policy of the firm and the attorney to use a travel agency, the skilled travel agent can be the most effective tool at the secretary's disposal. Travel agents will refer to the *Official Airline Guide* for schedules, fares, and information about airport facilities, and they also have current information about special rates, package trips, and promotions. The agent relies on the airlines' computers, which provide split-second flight confirmations, waitlisting, and in some cases seat assignments. The travel agent can also obtain information as to distances from terminal to hotel, available ground transportation, and comparative rates for such services. Certain airports are notorious for delays, and the agent will be aware of these. A travel agent may, but does not generally, reserve theater and sporting event tickets or dinner facilities, arrange clerical assistance or package delivery service, reserve hospitality suites, and provide ground transportation.

The selection of a travel agent may result from personal recommendations, established reputation, or spot usage to determine competency. You should try to use the same agent to arrange all trips. In this way, the agent can become familiar with the traveler's habits, and a rapport can develop between the agent and the secretary that works to the attorney's advantage.

To maintain such rapport, you should have all necessary information at hand <u>before</u> calling the agent and be courteous and friendly yet completely candid about the attorney's desires. When you call the agent, you should supply the following information:

1.  The attorney's name, office address, and office telephone number
2.  The secretary's name
3.  The times and dates of departure and return
4.  The attorney's preferences as to travel arrangements—airline, first class or coach, smoking or non-smoking, etc.
5.  The attorney's home telephone number

The agent will provide confirmation; suggest an acceptable method of payment; tell you the check-in time, the travel time, and the estimated time of arrival; and arrange either to send the tickets to you or have you pick them up.

The travel agent is indispensable for an attorney who is involved in international travel. The secretary should verify with the agent such things as passport and visa regulations, required inoculations, fluctuating luggage restrictions and currency exchange rates, general political conditions in the host country, consulate facilities, and entry and departure requirements. A variety of useful information may be obtained from the *Directory of International Business Travel and Relocation,* published by Knowledge Industry Publications, White Plains, New York. See also Chapter 15 of *Webster's Secretarial Handbook.* Should the attorney's work be so highly specialized as to require extensive travel abroad, the secretary should obtain travel reference books such as *Pan Am's World Guide* or *Fielding's Travel Guide to Europe.* Reading the travel sections of certain periodicals regularly will provide extra hints. The efficient secretary will maintain a current passport for the attorney.

**Making travel arrangements directly**    If the secretary makes travel reservations without the help of an agent, preparation is more complex. It involves obtaining and keeping current the appropriate schedules and brochures from airlines, bus lines, railroads, travel clubs, motor clubs, and various travel agencies. You should know the full particulars of the trip before placing any call for reservations. If time is not a consideration, you may write to the chamber of commerce, convention bureau, or travel department of the destination city for brochures and special information. Another source of information is the local newspaper of the destination city. There you can find special events calendars, weather reports, and service and facility advertisements.

**Airline reservations**   If you do not rely on an agent for airline reservations, a call to the airline will provide information about its schedules, rates, and special promotions. Reservations and even seat assignments may be made instantly. You can confirm flights and in some cases make hotel reservations through the airline, but you should always confirm hotel reservations yourself. Clip the special service announcements and schedules that are often published in newspapers. Allot enough time between connecting flights. Inquire specifically as to (1) the space available for carry-on luggage, (2) methods of payment, (3) how to pick up the ticket, and (4) check-in time at the airport.

Most major airlines have private clubroom facilities in the larger airports. An annual membership charge enables the club member to avoid the turmoil of a busy airport, find a quiet place to work during layovers, learn of equipment problems and delays, change reservations if necessary, and obtain seat assignments well in advance of the gate's opening. Information about such facilities is available from ticket agents and flight attendants.

**Railroad travel**   Rail travel is limited to certain cities at only certain times of the day. Such leisurely transportation is feasible only when time and access to Amtrak terminals are available. Rail travel requires more time than the busy attorney is likely to have, but some lawyers prefer to travel by train. You can obtain a schedule for Amtrak trains as well as for connecting or commuter lines from the nearest Amtrak station. A call to a ticket agent will answer any additional questions. If the attorney drives to the nearest Amtrak station to board the train, provisions for parking must be made.

**Automobile travel**   In some instances the attorney may choose to travel by automobile. Membership in a major automobile or oil company travel club provides guides and maps, towing and repair service, and detailed road trip plans. A phone call to the state police will inform you of current road conditions.

**Hotel reservations**   It is essential to make hotel reservations as soon as possible. Hotels in major cities may be fully booked for several weeks in advance. Reservations are normally made by telephone and confirmed in writing. When making hotel reservations, you should provide the name, address, and telephone number of the guest and your own name for reference. Many hotels hold reservations only until a certain hour, usually 6 p.m. You may frequently hold a reservation beyond that hour by guaranteeing payment whether or not the guest arrives. If the room is to be guaranteed, you will need to give the full name and address of the firm or the number and expiration date of a major credit card.

On the telephone, the secretary advises the hotel as to the attorney's preferences and inquires about the hotel's guarantee that such accommodations will be available. The secretary will find out about the extent of valet and laundry services and the availability of hairdressers, masseurs, health clubs, and shoe shining and repair facilities and make notes of these services on the attorney's itinerary. It may be desirable to make advance appointments for certain services. Written confirmation of all hotel reservations should be requested that include arrival and departure dates, guarantee, rates, and applicable tax percentages. In addition, the secretary should ask about check-out times, standard payment procedures, requirements for the establishment of credit and check-cashing privileges, meeting facilities, and other needed services.

The reservations clerk should be asked about complimentary limousine service from the airport or rail station to the hotel and the comparative rates and times of other means of ground transportation. The clerk should also be able to tell you how to secure ground transportation upon arrival if arrangements cannot be made beforehand. There may be a direct telephone line from the baggage claim area of the airport, for example, or an agent at a desk or curbside, or posted notices of available transportation.

**Renting a car**   If the attorney prefers to rent a car for use on business trips, the type of car and rate should be guaranteed with the preferred agency. The secretary should determine the acceptable method of payment, special discounts available, insurance coverage requirements, and driver's license stipulations. The attorney's arrival time should be relayed to the rental agency so that no unnecessary delays are encountered at the destination. The attorney may wish to review the contract form and maps secured from the agency prior to departure. Most rental agents will gladly give detailed directions to your destinations.

**Travel club services**   If the attorney travels often, the secretary may want to obtain information about one of the travel clubs sponsored by major airlines, oil companies, and credit card suppliers. Their monthly newsletters contain helpful hints as to types of travel; ratings of various airlines, hotel chains, automobile rental agencies, and travel services; descriptions of little-known vacation spots; and offerings of package trips at substantial discounts.

**Special arrangements**   The attorney with health problems must wear appropriate identification, carry sufficient prescribed medication, and have access to a local physician. Provision for special diets or storage facilities may have to be made.

It may be necessary for the attorney to engage another attorney in the destination city as co-counsel. Such co-counsel would advise as to applicable state laws and local rules of practice and may make many of the arrangements at the destination city. The attorney may rely on acquaintances in the area, or the local bar association may have referral lists for selecting the co-counsel. The name of a competent attorney may also be obtained from the *Martindale-Hubbell Law Directory,* described in Chapter 2. The Sullivan Directory (NAPCO Graphic Arts, Inc., Chicago) and Legal Directories, Inc., of Los Angeles publish individual state and regional directories.

If the trip involves the deposing of a key witness, the attorney must confirm that the required subpoenas or notices have been served and that co-counsel has arranged for conference rooms and a court reporter.

## PREPARING A TRAVEL FOLDER
The secretary files all notes on the various arrangements in one folder to facilitate the typing of an itinerary and appointment schedule. When the arrangements are completed, the secretary marks a deadline on the calendar for receipt of confirmations. If confirmations are not received by that date, the secretary must follow up with a phone call.

**The itinerary**   A typewritten itinerary is invaluable in guiding an attorney through a hectic day in a distant city. The itinerary is planned with the traveler's convenience in mind; that is, it should be logically and neatly arranged so that the attorney can review it at a glance, be completely organized, and accomplish the trip's purpose with as little effort as possible. A brief description of activities is listed with dates and specific times. Departure and arrival are detailed and airports, ports, or railway stations named. Hotels are listed and confirmed reservations indicated, and social engagements are itemized with comments as to suggested dress. The itinerary might also contain pertinent data about individuals, reference to files or reports and correspondence, reminders to reconfirm flight reservations and meeting arrangements, and comments on climate and social amenities.

In preparing the itinerary, the legal secretary considers the length of the stay, the estimated travel times, the time periods for each hearing or appointment, and the pressure on the attorney. Flexibility is a prerequisite for the manageable itinerary. It is difficult to anticipate the length of an afternoon court hearing or the amount of time to be spent with clients before departure. (If time is limited, the secretary might arrange for co-counsel or the client to meet the attorney at a hotel near the airport or in an airport conference room.)

Some of the items which might appear on an itinerary are shown below.

**ITINERARY**

Deposition of Haynes case witnesses, Minneapolis, MN, September 17–20

WEDNESDAY, September 17

*Flight*

| | | |
|---|---|---|
| Lv. Quad City Airport | 4:13 p.m. OA# 916 | Ticket at airport |
| Ar. Minneapolis/St. Paul | 5:05 p.m. | Perkins Transfer to hotel |
| | | Tele. 666-0200 |
| | | Fare—$5.75 cash |

*Accommodations*      Radisson Hotel Guaranteed
45 South Seventh Street, Minneapolis
Tele. 575-2800
Four nights at $39–45 plus 10% tax

*Dinner Meeting*—Atty. Gillespie      8:00 p.m.      Radisson Club
Res. with Pierre 9/1

THURSDAY, September 18

*Deposition of Carrie Haynes*      9:00 a.m.      Gillespie Law Office
to      123 State Street, Minn.
4:00 p.m.      (Taxi necessary—10 min.)

Travel agents also provide itineraries, but these are usually in the form of a printout from a computerized reservation service and thus should be carefully reviewed and supplemented with additional appointments and information. In some cases a separate appointment schedule is advisable with notes for the attorney on each meeting— the participants, the papers needed, etc. After the draft itinerary is approved by the attorney, the final itinerary is typed and filed in the attorney's travel folder and copies distributed as directed by the attorney to partners and family members. The secretary, of course, retains a copy so that the attorney may be reached when necessary.

**Expense account records**   In preparing for any business trip, the secretary needs an understanding of the firm's expense account records, time sheets, and billing procedures. These records are needed to charge travel expenses to the proper client and to comply with U.S. Internal Revenue Service regulations. Many law firms design their own expense account records. However, the secretary might wish to examine IRS Publication 463, "Travel, Entertainment and Expense," which sets forth the conditions for making deductions on federal tax returns for travel, entertainment, and gifts and which also outlines bookkeeping rules. Copies of this booklet are available from a local IRS office or from the Superintendent of Documents, U.S. Government Printing Office, Washington, DC 20402. Expenses can be deducted only when they are exact figures which can be substantiated. Therefore, some system must be agreed upon whereby the attorney can record the expenses of the trip. These forms belong in the travel folder.

**Time sheets**   Lawyers should keep records of their working time away from the office as well as in the office. The secretary can put into the travel folder a time sheet, such as the one illustrated here, for each working day of the trip.

**Attorney's Time Sheet**

| Name | | Day | Date |
|---|---|---|---|
| 9:00–9:15 | 9:15–9:30 | 9:30–9:45 | 9:45–10:00 |
| Account | Account | Account | Account |
| 10:00–10:15 | 10:15–10:30 | 10:30–10:45 | 10:45–11:00 |
| Account | Account | Account | Account |
| 11:00–11:15 | 11:15–11:30 | 11:30–11:45 | 11:45–12:00 |
| Account | Account | Account | Account |
| 12:00–12:15 | 12:15–12:30 | 12:30–12:45 | 12:45–1:00 |
| Account | Account | Account | Account |

**The final travel folder**    The final step in making travel arrangements is compiling the attorney's travel folder. The travel folder might contain the following items:

Luggage tags with the office address

Traveler's checks, office checks, or credit cards; letters of credit (If the attorney carries these items, the traveler's check receipt can be filed in the folder.)

Final itinerary

Airline tickets (The attorney may wish to carry these.)

Confirmation of hotel accommodations noting any special provisions

Confirmation of rental car

Diary or journal with space for comments and a pocket for receipts

Daily time sheets

Expense account record forms

List of names, addresses, and telephone numbers of persons to contact

Copy of registration form for a conference or other meeting, with acknowledgment

Copy of agenda and pre-publicity material for a meeting

Copy of notice of deposition or hearing

Copies of pertinent information from client files or individual folders for each person contacted

Speech and handout materials or oral arguments and exhibits

A note as to the location of reference books in the destination city

Map of the destination city showing meeting places

Sightseeing information, special events calendar, activity tickets

Supplies of stationery, postage stamps, writing tools, and business cards

Portable dictation equipment may also be provided for the attorney; if so, it should be labeled with the name and address of a service agency. The carrying case should contain an instruction booklet, extra tapes, the maintenance agreement, and mailing labels.

Except for the supplies and equipment, the secretary should maintain duplicate materials in the office.

Just before the attorney's departure, the secretary should check the travel folder's contents with the attorney, discuss pending matters in the office that require attention, and make provision for handling office correspondence and emergencies during the attorney's absence.

## TRAVEL DIARIES

A separate diary may be provided for each trip, or the same one may be used for successive trips. Within the diary the efficient secretary will list items from the itinerary and the names, addresses, and telephone numbers of contacts in the destination city. Care should be taken that all information is correct. The diary should provide ample space for notes and comments by the attorney. Upon return the diary may be filed in the client's file or in a general travel folder by geographical location. If the attorney prefers not to take notes on the trip, you should provide portable dictation equipment and ask the attorney to return the tapes periodically. In this way transcription can begin prior to the attorney's return. It is important to transcribe the tapes in order and listen first for special instructions. Tapes usually provide a space for the date, subject matter, and sequence number. General information can be inserted on the tape by the secretary before the attorney's departure.

## CHECKLIST OF FOLLOW-UP PROCEDURES

As soon as possible upon the attorney's return, the secretary needs to attend to the following:

1. Read instructions and information from the attorney and transcribe any machine dictation.
2. Review the travel folder for notes and comments.
3. Review the client file or seminar materials for labeling and filing.
4. Arrange receipts chronologically, cross-checking with expense claims; arrange billing to the proper client.
5. Review the trip diary and make notes for future reference.
6. File all materials.

## CANCELLING A PLANNED TRIP

When it becomes necessary to cancel a planned trip, the legal secretary must notify all parties—including clients, co-counsel, and special assistants—as quickly as possible. Transportation arrangements as well as hotel accommodations should be cancelled promptly by telephone with a follow-up letter to confirm the cancellation. Meeting arrangements are cancelled with the catering manager or meeting coordinator.

If the tickets have been prepaid, application for a refund (accompanied by the unused tickets if you have them) is made directly with the carrier or travel agent with whom you made the reservation. If hotel accommodations have been paid in advance, you need to apply for a refund to the hotel by letter promptly after telephoning the cancellation. If hotel reservations are guaranteed, *prompt* cancellation is crucial to avoid charges. If any payment has been made by charge card, application for credit should be made through the carrier, the hotel reservations clerk, or the travel agent with whom you made the reservation. Care must be taken to verify that the correct credit has been allowed on the monthly statement.

# 17.3

## MEETINGS, CONFERENCES, AND CONVENTIONS

A *conference* is a meeting for discussion or consultation; its scope may range from the intra-office meeting for the discussion of office procedures or problems to meetings on a nationwide or international scale. By contrast, the term *convention* regularly refers to large formal meetings such as state, regional, national, or international gatherings of representatives from local groups.

Regardless of the scope of the meeting, the legal secretary may be asked to assist with preparations, provide services during the course of the meeting, and help with follow-up matters. The legal assistant may perform a leading role in the setup and conduct of regular and special meetings of the professional corporation and the corporate client. A large organization that holds several meetings a year may even hire a legal assistant just to coordinate these meetings. Certain meetings of corporations are required by statute, and in most cases the legal assistant or the legal secretary can do many of the tasks involved in planning the meetings.

The extent to which a secretary plans meetings depends upon the size and type of law practice and the attorney's degree of personal involvement in outside activities. A secretary is not ordinarily expected to plan a convention because doing so requires a great deal of time. However, an attorney's practice may necessitate meetings with other attorneys or clients for the purpose of discovery or negotiation, and small conferences of this sort may require the secretary's help in arranging them. Also, if an attorney represents numerous corporate clients, regular and special meetings of the directors and stockholders are frequently called. The secretary can anticipate many of these meetings through tickler files and diary or calendar notations.

There are several types of meetings which the secretary may be asked to plan for the attorney and for the attorney's corporate clients:

1. In-house meetings and conferences—held within the law firm or corporation and usually relating to normal business activity; informal or formal depending upon the participants' preference or the corporate bylaws. (On occasion meetings for such purposes might be held outside of the firm.)
2. Outside meetings, conferences, and conventions—held outside the firm, either locally or in distant cities, and sponsored by law firms or professional associations for the benefit of attorneys. One of the firm's attorneys may have responsibility because of personal affiliation.
3. Local business and professional meetings—held as a rule within the local community.

### NOTICES OF IN-HOUSE MEETINGS

The legal secretary—or, in some firms, the legal assistant—plays a key role in getting the right people together at the right time. To announce official hearings and depositions, for example, the secretary sends legal notices. No less important to the smooth-running and efficient office is the in-house business meeting or conference, which the secretary may be asked to help plan. These meetings should be scheduled to avoid conflicts with the attorneys' calendars and court schedules. Secretaries and legal assistants may, in the course of their regular duties or at the direction of the attorney, issue notices for (1) regular meetings for attorneys and/or staff, (2) special meetings for attorneys and/or staff, (3) annual stockholders' meetings, (4) board of directors' meetings, and (5) other corporate meetings.

**Regular staff meetings**   For those meetings scheduled on a weekly or monthly basis, the legal secretary, office manager, or legal assistant in charge of such meetings will remind participants by distributing an interoffice memorandum one or more days before the scheduled meeting. A form similar to the one which appears below might be used. (Additional information on the preparation of interoffice memorandums may be found on pages 352–354.)

**Notice of Staff Meeting**

---

STAFFORD LAW OFFICES, P.C.   INTER-OFFICE CORRESPONDENCE
     To: Gary Smith, Attorney          From: S. Majors

   Subject: Staff meeting:                Date: September 20, 19--
            Computerized billing

This note is to remind you that the regularly scheduled attorneys'

meeting to discuss the aforementioned subject will be held at

8:00 a.m. tomorrow (Tuesday) in the office conference room.   The

following topics are on the agenda:

_____

_____

_____

Please notify Ms. Young if you cannot attend.   _SM_

---

The responsible secretary should verify attendance by telephone and reschedule the meeting when the presiding officer directs. The presiding officer or senior partner should be advised of any staff member's anticipated absence so that the voting process will not be hampered by the lack of a quorum.

**Special staff meetings**   Attorneys frequently find themselves in situations which call for immediate decisions. If procedures have not been adopted to handle such a crisis, the secretary, legal assistant, or office manager will have to contact individuals personally for an immediate meeting. Should a special meeting be scheduled for some date in the near future, personal contact would be followed by written confirmation of the date, time, location, and subject of the meeting.

**Notice of annual stockholders' meetings**   Invitations or notices of the annual meeting of the stockholders of a corporation must meet statutory requirements. They are formal and usually issued in printed form by the corporate secretary or corporate counsel. The following form may be adapted for such use.

---

### CALL AND NOTICE OF ANNUAL
### MEETING OF SHAREHOLDERS

TO THE SHAREHOLDERS OF JONES LAW OFFICE, LTD.

NOTICE IS HEREBY GIVEN that the annual meeting of the shareholders of JONES LAW OFFICE, LTD., an Illinois professional corporation, is hereby called and will be held at the corporate offices at 123 State Street, in the City of Rockford, Illinois, on the fifteenth day of January, 19--, at the hour of 8:00 a.m. for the purpose of electing directors and transacting such other business as may come before the meeting.

                                        /s/
                              _____
                                        Secretary

---

The legal secretary routinely prepares the invitation or notice for the attorney's approval. The notice is then printed and mailed in accordance with corporate bylaws, or at least three to four weeks before the meeting. Proxy forms are routinely mailed to stockholders together with the notice of meeting. If the stockholder is unable to attend, he or she may be represented in the voting by completing and returning the proxy form. The proxy may be prepared as a form with blanks for the date, as illustrated below, so that it can be used for more than one meeting:

---

### PROXY FOR ANNUAL MEETING
### OF SHAREHOLDERS

KNOW ALL MEN BY THESE PRESENTS:

That the undersigned shareholder of ACE CORPORATION, an Ohio corporation, does hereby constitute and appoint JAMES MORRISON the true and lawful attorney of the undersigned, for and in the name, place and stead of the undersigned, to appear and act as the proxy of the undersigned at the annual meeting of shareholders of said corporation to be held at Cleveland, Ohio, on the           day of             , 19    , at the hour of 10:00 a.m., and to vote all shares of said corporation standing in the name of the undersigned, or which the undersigned may be entitled to vote, in the transaction of such business as may come before said meeting, as fully as the undersigned might or could do if personally present, hereby ratifying and confirming all that said attorney shall lawfully do or cause to be done by virtue hereof, hereby revoking any proxy or proxies heretofore given by the undersigned to vote and act at such meeting.

IN WITNESS WHEREOF, the undersigned has executed this proxy this                      day of
     19

_____ (SEAL)

Shareholder

---

A reply card as well as a proxy form may be included with the invitation or notice of meeting.

**Notice of board of directors' meetings**   Corporate bylaws may state the provisions for notifying the directors of meetings and the procedure for securing waivers of notice. The "Call and Notice" form on page 564 for stockholders' meetings may be adapted for board of directors' meetings. Frequently, the bylaws require the secretary to prepare an affidavit such as the one shown on the next page, certifying that notices were properly mailed. Should the call for a special meeting not allow time to meet the notice requirements of the bylaws, a corporate director might execute a Waiver of Notice of the Special Meeting, a signed form which would be filed in the corporate records. Waivers of notice may also be signed and filed when the directors are in close touch and agree that a formal notice is not required.

It is helpful to maintain a list of the names, addresses, and telephone numbers of the directors of each corporation which the attorney represents, with space for the date on which a notice was sent or a waiver received, attendance plans, and the number that constitutes a quorum. A printed form such as the one shown on page 567 prepared for each meeting will be a time-saver.

**Notice of other meetings and conferences**   Meeting notices that are sent to large numbers of office personnel are normally printed or duplicated. The legal secretary's initial task is to assemble all the pertinent data relative to the meeting and arrange the data in an attractive format. As previously illustrated, notices of in-house meetings and other routine meetings may be set up on interoffice correspondence forms. All-inclusive captions such as "All Attorneys," "Personal Injury Attorneys and Support

**Affidavit of Mailing of Notice**

```
        STATE OF FLORIDA )
                            ss.
        COUNTY OF DADE    )

                I, ROBERT HERSCH, being of full age, depose and
        say:
                That I caused copies of a Notice of Meeting, in the
        form hereto annexed and made part of this Affidavit, to be
        deposited on the 20th day of March, 19--, in the United States
        mail, postage prepaid, Certified Mail, addressed to the
        following persons at the addresses shown next to their names:

                JAY THOMAS, 25 Roscoe Road, Miami, Florida
                ROBIN THOMAS, 25 Roscoe Road, Miami, Florida
                MICHAEL KRAFT, 3 College Road, Miami, Florida
                GERI KRAFT, 3 College Road, Miami, Florida


                _____
                                ROBERT HERSCH

        Sworn and subscribed to before
        me this       day of April, 19--.


        _____
            Notary Public
        My commission expires        19--.
```

Staff," or "Bookkeeping Department" may be used. The secretary must verify all information included in the notice and ensure that it is clearly stated. Depending upon the number in the group and the importance of the event, the secretary may be requested to send original typewritten letters to specific individuals.

## INVITATIONS TO OUTSIDE MEETINGS, CONFERENCES, AND OTHER FUNCTIONS

The secretary whose employer is a leader in professional and community affairs may be asked to include informal meeting notices as part of a newsletter setting forth the correct details of the meeting. Where required, a self-addressed postal card with a reply form on the back might be included which would later serve as a list of names for the reservations list (as for a luncheon or dinner meeting).

The secretary may be involved in preparing and issuing formal and informal invitations to social or business functions. These events may be part of convention activities extending over one or more days. For such functions, invitations are usually extended to the attorney and spouse. The secretary should refer to a good etiquette book for the proper way to issue formal invitations.

**Use of mailing lists for invitations and notices** The secretary ought to devise a system for keeping mailing lists current. If name and address changes are infrequent, corrections may be noted directly on the list. With a list requiring frequent changes,

**Directors' Meeting Notification and Attendance Form**

### WATERMAN ENTERPRISES, INC.
#### BOARD OF DIRECTORS

Name of Chairperson: William Theodore Waterman, Presiding Officer

Meeting Date: October 19, 19—     Time: 9:30 a.m.

Meeting Place: Board Room

| Names of Board Members (Listed in order of years on the Board) | Date Notice Sent | Will Attend | Will Not Attend |
|---|---|---|---|
| Charles France | 10/5/19— | X | |
| Henry G. Johnson | " | X | |
| Willard Hazelett | " | X | |
| Ralph Knepshield | " | X | |
| Mark McKallip | " | X | |
| Myron Klingensmith | " | X | |
| Andrew Konietzko | " | X | |
| Harald Rasmusson | " | X | |
| Roger Wayne Johnson | " | X | |
| William Kiersey | " | | X |
| Inga Konietzko | " | X | |
| Elmer Wolfe | " | X | |
| Lawrence Slack | " | X | |
| Leonard Wolfe | " | X | |
| Cuvier Best | " | X | |

Total Members to Attend 14

Regular Meeting X

Special Meeting _____

Quorum Assured: X Yes _____ No

_____
Secretary

---

however, index cards are helpful. Individually addressed envelopes may be prepared within the firm for small or medium-sized group functions. Volume envelope addressing is normally done by addressing machines or other automated processes. On computerized name and address lists, changes should be reported on special cards or directly on the work in process (WIP) sheets in order to update future printouts.

## PLANS FOR CONFERENCES AND CONVENTIONS

In addition to preparing and distributing invitations and notices, the secretary may work closely with an attorney who directs, chairs, or sponsors a meeting, convention, or conference. In these cases, preplanning frequently involves confirmation of the meeting site and the speaker, editing and preparing conference materials, and special arrangements for services. Each of these responsibilities is discussed below.

**Meeting site and speaker confirmation**    The secretary should contact the site manager to reserve a block of rooms for conference participants. Room size (single or double) and price range should be specified. In some cases the manager will discount the sleeping room prices if the group is very large. Also, the catering manager or meeting coordinator should be asked to reserve the appropriate meeting rooms, including both the general-session auditorium and smaller group discussion rooms. Seating plans may also be prepared. Provision should be made for a smoking section if smoking is to be permitted. A thermos or pitcher of water and glasses should be

## Newsletter Meeting Notice

J A N U A R Y   M E E T I N G

Monday, January 19, 19--

TOPIC:    "The Law Office of Tomorrow"

PANEL:

Ruth Anderson, Anderson Associates    Vivian Heald, Legal Consultants, Inc.
Arline Basarab, Pilson & Curie        Ola Knapp, Latch Insurance Co.
Cecelia Orr, Legal Services, Ltd.     Alice Ralph, Mercer, Mason & Otto

CHAIRPERSON:  Alta Hazelett, Past President
              Arnold Chapter, Secretary's Forum;
              Supervisor, Secretarial Services
              Mason, Kupinski and Pelham, P.C.

PLACE:    Devon Country Club

TIME:     6:00 p.m. Social

          6:30 p.m. Dinner

MENU:     Smorgasbord

COST:     $10.50

RETURN:   Enclosed reservation card by January 12, please

## Reservation Postal Card

PLEASE --

Send this reservation card to our Secretary
on or before Wednesday of this week.

_____Yes, I plan to attend the next Forum
      dinner meeting.

_____Yes, I'll bring _____ guests.

      Guest Names: _____

_____Sorry, I'll miss the Forum this month.

          Signature_____

          Office_____

available for the speaker, panelists, board members, and the audience when possible. Arrangements for coat checking may be necessary. Tables and writing tools should be provided for all participants if the facilities permit.

Advance arrangements for large or small meetings or conferences are important. It is a good idea to visit unfamiliar meeting sites to ensure that there is adequate space for the event. Firsthand knowledge of the meeting or conference layout is helpful in placing the registration desk, in locating electrical outlets and fixtures, and in directing guests to the meeting area. A letter confirming the reservation of all necessary meeting or conference facilities must be sent to the site manager. (In the case of in-house requests, the reservation may be made by telephone and confirmed by a written memorandum.)

The date and time of the event should be promptly entered on both secretary and attorney calendars.

Letters of invitation may be sent to speakers as soon as the date is firm. An attorney will often invite speakers by telephone to save time. If the invitation is accepted, a follow-up letter confirming the engagement and requesting information about the speaker's background and experience (and perhaps asking for a glossy print for news releases) may be sent.

**Preparing meeting and conference materials**  The preparation of an agenda is basic to the success of a professional meeting. A workshop agenda similar to one that a secretary might be asked to prepare is shown below. Supporting materials such as outlines, reports, and checklists may be needed at some meetings, too. The secretary may be asked to prepare a copy of each of these items for the meeting participants. Often these items are assembled and placed in a folder or envelope for distribution during registration. The planning for formal conferences and conventions is complex. Program information must be carefully edited to ensure that the names, titles, topics, sections, and meeting times and places are correct.

**A Sample Workshop Agenda**

A Workshop in Computerized Docket Control
International Law Office Management Society
September 24, 19--

SCHEDULE

| | | |
|---|---|---|
| 8:00 a.m. | Arrive Doyle, Inc. | Education Center |
| 8:15 a.m. | Breakfast | Conference Room 8 |
| 9:00 a.m. | Workshop | Conference Room 6 |
| | Welcome | Stella Williams, Legal Division Manager |
| 9:05 a.m. | Introduction, Comparison of Different Systems, and Advantages of Service Bureau | Stanley Lindberg, Public Relations Manager |
| 9:20 a.m. | Demonstration of Procedures Applicable to Law Offices | Elwin Young, Docket Control Supervisor |
| 10:15 a.m. | Facility Tour (optional) or Departure | |
| 11:15 a.m. | Departure | |

**Arrangements for special services**  Large conventions and conferences require a wide variety of special services. For example, the secretary may be asked to do the following:

Attend to printing and engraving arrangements
Organize tours and special events for conferees and/or spouses
Arrange for refreshments and meals
Handle pre-registration and registration
Assemble conference folders or packets
Request audiovisual equipment and materials
Mail pre-conference materials
Ship supplies and printed materials to conference site
Arrange for press coverage
Inform security offices and parking attendants of pertinent conference details
Prepare meeting files for the attorney

Assembling all the information needed for a complete conference program is a demanding task. The secretary may have to coordinate all the information, type the final copy, and send it to the printer on time. This material usually includes programs, booklets, reports, brochures, name tags, tickets, and other items. Banquet and special event tickets should be ready early. The pre-numbering of tickets will aid in accounting for them. Special office numbering machines may be secured for this purpose. Orders for special items (as award plaques and other engraved gifts) should be placed well in advance. The secretary may be given assistants to help with arrangements, and they will need to be assigned tasks and supervised.

It is important to confirm with the catering manager the number of conference participants for refreshments, social hours, luncheons, and banquets.

As conference reservations and registration fees come in, each conferee's name, title, firm, address, and other important information may be typed on a card. Conference fee payment may be recorded on the card for accounting purposes. Later, the cards may be grouped and filed. After the cut-off date for pre-registration and usually one week before the meeting, the rooming list of conference participants should be sent to the site manager.

The secretary should arrange the staffing of the registration desk well in advance and remind assistants the day before the conference begins to assure the continuity of plans for handling duties at the registration desk. Registration personnel are responsible for accepting registrations on the day of the conference and integrating these registrations into the system. Orders should be placed early for attractive signs to be located at the registration desk so that registrants may quickly find information.

Whenever possible, conference name tags or badges should be prepared and arranged ahead of time. They might be placed in conference folders or packets which contain the program and other papers and which have been labeled with the name of the conference, the dates, and the location. If time permits, the participants' names might also be added and the packets arranged alphabetically to facilitate distribution. Special packets for speakers and honored guests with complimentary tickets to luncheons, banquets, and other special events should be prepared.

Arrangements should be made with the facility manager for audiovisual equipment and operators if needed. Frequently used pieces of equipment are as follows:

| | |
|---|---|
| Chalkboards or feltboards | Extra projector bulbs and extension cords |
| Filmstrip or overhead projector | Projection screen (specify size) |
| Hook-and-loop board | Record or tape player |
| Lectern or podium | Slide projector (specify tray design) |
| Microphones (floor or lapel) | Tape recorder (specify size) |
| Movie projector (specify size) | Television (specify screen size) |
| Newsprint with easel | Videotape machine |

Use of a reservation request form supplied by the facility will simplify ordering audiovisual aids and other items; the items and services desired are simply checked off on the form. The chairperson or the secretary should be familiar with the location of all electrical outlets and light switches to assure smooth presentations.

Training sessions often require participants to prepare in advance. In these cases, the secretary should mail the materials at least two weeks before the conference.

It will be necessary to call the catering manager and request that all conference supplies and materials shipped to the conference site be held for pickup by the chairperson. A confirmation letter should also be sent.

Security police should be aware of the locations and times of meetings. They should also be informed if VIP guests (as high government officials requiring extra protection) will be in attendance. In-house events create special parking problems if large numbers attend. These problems may be alleviated if parking attendants are told in advance of the numbers expected. It is also helpful to prepare and send in advance maps showing the conference site and directions to reach it.

The secretary should prepare a tabbed notebook for the attorney who is leading the conference. It should contain all pertinent materials—programs, reports, minutes of previous meetings, correspondence, and other important information. Separate file folders relating to different segments of a large meeting may also be prepared. Tabs should contain the name of the conference, individual topics, and the location and dates of the conference.

## DUTIES DURING MEETINGS, CONFERENCES, OR CONVENTIONS

At the event, the secretary should meticulously check to ensure that all plans are carried through. Good organization and follow-through are essential to effective meetings and conferences.

**In-house meeting room readiness**   The secretary should visit the conference room prior to the in-house meeting to make a final check of room arrangements, cleanliness, correct lighting, proper heating, and ventilation and to distribute printed materials, pens, note pads, pencils, and conference folders. Fresh water and glasses should be available, and required audiovisual equipment or materials should be in place.

**Checklist of arrangements for outside meetings**   Conference facility inspections are expedited through the use of a conference arrangements checklist prepared by the secretary and given to the catering manager. A sample conference arrangements checklist is illustrated on page 572.

**Hospitality arrangements for conference guests**   A pleasant welcome to conference guests builds the goodwill of the firm and the individual attorney. The secretary's precise role depends upon the number of guests. If there are only a few guests, they may be individually escorted to the meeting room. Large numbers of guests may be given directions to the check rooms, the registration desk, and the meeting room.

**Secretarial services during meetings and conferences**   Some of the duties commonly delegated to the secretarial staff during meetings or conferences are listed below:

1. Supervise registration desk; alert registration desk personnel as to the identity and arrival time of speakers, guests, and dignitaries.
2. Prepare a list of participants including the names and addresses of firms or associations they represent. Know the number of participants attending each event.
3. Take minutes of certain meetings, either in shorthand or by taping.

## A Sample Checklist for Conference Arrangements

DAILY CONFERENCE/CONVENTION ARRANGEMENTS CHECKLIST

TO: Catering Manager

FROM: Beatrice Pomerance
Administrative Secretary

DATE: October 19, 19--

KIND OF MEETING: Missouri Bar Association Seminar

MEETING SITE: Kansas Hotel, Kansas City, MO

MEETING DATES: October 19-21, 19--

| DATE | TIME | AM | PM | NAME OF ROOM | NAME OF FUNCTION | ROOM SETUP | NO. OF GUESTS | MENUS/AUDIOVISUAL AIDS |
|---|---|---|---|---|---|---|---|---|
| 10/19/19-- | 9:00–12:00 | AM | | McKenzie | Bankruptcy | U-formation Tables for 30 | 30 | 1 Lectern<br>1 Overhead projector<br>1 Cassette recorder<br>1 Easel with newsprint paper |
| | 10:30–10:45 | AM | | McKenzie | Coffee break | Serving table Self-service | 30 | Coffee Danish |
| | 12:15–1:15 | | PM | Kansas Star | Luncheon | 5 tables of 6 each | 30 | French onion soup<br>Chicken à la king<br>Green beans amandine<br>Butternut squash<br>Apple pie à la mode<br>Coffee/tea |
| | 1:30–4:30 | | PM | McKenzie | Creditors' rights | 6 tables of 5 each | 30 | Same as 9:00–12:00 |
| | 3:00–3:15 | | PM | McKenzie | Coffee break | Serving table Self-service | 30 | Coffee Donuts |

4. Handle specific correspondence requests of convention officers, executive personnel, or special guests; place special telephone calls when requested.

5. Assemble and typewrite information for a conference news sheet, coordinate duplicating services, and distribute the news sheets to participants.

6. Coordinate and synchronize convention events, as by transmitting messages to attendees.

7. Meet and direct media representatives and photographers to room locations for group pictures and other events; distribute prepared news releases to them.

8. Arrange place cards for seating officers and guests on the dais or at the head table for luncheons and banquets; assign guides or hostesses to escort guests to the dais.

9. Remain available to handle last-minute changes or decisions.

## FOLLOW-UP AFTER MEETINGS, CONFERENCES, OR CONVENTIONS

The follow-up duties after a meeting, conference, or convention often become the secretary's responsibility. The secretary may be asked to do the following at the meeting site:

1. Remove any remaining conference literature from the meeting room and prepare it for return to the office.

2. Ask the catering manager to service the meeting room.

3. Supervise the transfer of audiovisual equipment to locked storage areas.

4. Return any lost-and-found items to the firm's receptionist or to the appropriate convention authorities.

5. Make a list of people entitled to letters of appreciation and give it to the attorney; upon returning to the office, note future meeting dates, deadlines for reports, appointments, and other meeting- or conference-related information on the secretary's and attorney's calendars.

**Conference correspondence, reports, minutes, and notations**    Letters of appreciation are written to those persons who assisted with the conference. Letters of congratulation may also be in order for newly elected officers or directors. Minutes taken at the conference should be transcribed as soon as possible and the attorney reminded of any unassigned tasks spelled out in the minutes.

# 17.4

## THE PREPARATION OF MINUTES

Unless the attorney requests it, full minutes need not be taken of in-house staff meetings, but a summary record should be made, distributed to the participants, and filed. The format could be similar to that of the meeting summary shown on the next page. Formal meetings, on the other hand, require the preparation of a formal record in conventional minute form.

### PREPARATION FOR TAKING MINUTES

The secretary should arrive early at the meeting site to organize the area where minutes will be taken. You will need adequate supplies of paper, pens, pencils, and notebooks for manual note-taking and an adequate supply of paper tape for the shorthand machine. Recording machines are often used to supplement secretarial note-taking when verbatim minutes are required, as with public hearings. In the latter case, you will need a good supply of recording tapes of the proper size.

## Format of a Meeting Summary

SUMMARY                                                    CONFIDENTIAL

STAFFORD LAW OFFICES, P.C.
PERSONAL INJURY DIVISION MEETING
November 22, 19--

ATTENDANCE:          Messrs. Jones, Carter, Dunn; Ms. Carroll

ATTORNEY'S CONTRACT:  Mr. Carter discussed the effect of revised
                      legislation, submitted a proposed contract
                      form, and cautioned all attorneys to
                      provide copies to clients.

COSTS ADVANCED:      Ms. Carroll reported that costs advanced
                      during October exceeded $10,000, which is
                      hurting total profits.

DECISIONS:           The proposed contract form was adopted.
                      It was determined that costs must be billed
                      to the client, when possible, before they
                      are paid.

**Materials needed**   The presiding officer and the secretary should discuss the materials which will be needed at the meeting, and there should be clear understanding as to what materials the secretary must provide. The corporate secretary, for instance, will need to take the following items to shareholders' and directors' meetings:

Agenda with extra copies

Membership and committee lists, including attendance data

Current meeting file (current papers relating to the meeting)

Minute book or books

Corporate seal

Copy of meeting notice sent to stockholders or directors with a notation of the mailing date or waivers of notice

Copy of corporation laws of the state in which the firm is incorporated

Copy of the certificate of incorporation, including amendments

Copy of the bylaws plus amendments

Blank forms for affidavits, oaths, and other purposes

Reference book on parliamentary procedure

## KNOWLEDGE OF MEETING PROCEDURES

Reading and referring to previous minutes and talking with secretaries who have taken notes at similar meetings will aid you in note-taking. Before a meeting it is also a good idea to consult the presiding officer about a means of having motions or statements clarified or repeated. An adequate knowledge of all meeting procedures is essential.

Meetings may be conducted formally or informally. At informal meetings such as committee meetings, the presiding officer joins in the discussion and some parliamentary procedures are waived. Formal meetings, on the other hand, call for strict adherence to the rules of parliamentary procedure as defined in *Robert's Rules of Order* and in the bylaws governing the meeting. Annual stockholders' meetings, directors' meetings, and professional association meetings are typical examples of formal meetings.

**Familiarity with the order of business**   A meeting agenda or order of business may or may not be used at informal meetings. An agenda is required, however, for formal meetings. Agenda items are determined by the presiding officer. A list of possible agenda items follows; some of the items are optional, depending upon the nature of the meeting and the desires of the participants.

**Agenda**

1. Call to order
2. Roll call or verification of members or stockholders present
3. Minutes of the previous meeting for correction and/or approval
4. Reading of correspondence
5. Report of the treasurer
6. Report of the directors
7. Report of the officers
8. Report of standing committees
9. Report of special committees
10. Unfinished business (from previous meeting or meetings)
11. New business (normally items submitted in advance)
12. Appointment of committees
13. Nominations and elections
14. Programs, if appropriate
15. Announcements (including date of next meeting)
16. Adjournment

**Recording basic facts about the meeting**   It is essential for the secretary to record the following basic facts concerning a meeting:

1. The date, location, and time of day that the meeting was held
2. The name of the presiding officer
3. The kind of meeting (as regular, special, board, executive, or committee)
4. The names of members present for small groups of under 20 persons or the names of members absent; a quorum check is needed for larger groups (Representation at corporate stockholders' meetings is usually based upon shares of stock owned and not upon the number of individual stockholders. Thus, it is necessary to have information about the number of shares outstanding and represented at the meeting.)
5. The order of business as indicated on the agenda
6. The motions made, their adoption or rejection, and the names of the originators of the motions (It is not necessary to record the names of those who second motions unless one is requested to do so.)

For a discussion of the use of the stenographic notebook and for suggestions on how to handle revisions in the taking of shorthand minutes, refer to pages 165–168.

**The wording of minutes**   Minutes should be brief and factual. The illustration on the facing page shows how the minutes of an annual meeting might be phrased.

**Resolutions**   At any corporate meeting, but most particularly at the first meeting, numerous resolutions will be enacted concerning the bylaws, the payment of expenses, the designation of a depository, and other actions of the corporation. The minutes might then include paragraphs such as the following:

Thereupon on motion duly made by John Carter and seconded by Gilbert Smith, the following resolution was unanimously adopted:

> RESOLVED that the following bylaws be and they are hereby adopted as the bylaws of this corporation.

Thereupon on motion duly made by John Carter and seconded by Gilbert Smith, the following resolution was unanimously adopted:

> RESOLVED that the officers of this corporation be and they are hereby authorized and directed to pay all organization expenses of this corporation out of the funds of said corporation.

Many variations of such resolutions are possible, and they may be contained either in the body of the minutes or as clearly denoted attachments. Printed forms are frequently used to record resolutions. These are attached to the typewritten minutes.

**Recording special actions**   In some instances, the board of directors or the executive committee, in lieu of holding a meeting, may act by unanimous consent in writing unless the articles of incorporation or bylaws prohibit that course. In these cases, care should be taken to record the action in the official records.

Some states allow the shares of a corporation to be owned by one person. These corporations are held to the same recording requirements as other corporations.

**Certification of minutes**   On occasion, the corporate secretary will have to certify to the authenticity of a certain set of minutes or of a resolution. In this case a certificate like the one shown on page 419 might be used.

**Preparing to type minutes**   Materials should be organized before you begin to type. You should have available the materials and supplies listed on page 575 and, in addition, copies of the reports and materials distributed at the meeting, a copy of motions and resolutions voted, reference books on style and parliamentary procedure, a dictionary, and the official corporate record sheets from a commercially printed rec-

## Sample Minutes of an Annual Meeting

ANNUAL MEETING OF SHAREHOLDERS

The Annual Meeting of the Shareholders of ACE CORPORATION for the year 19-- was held at the corporate offices at 509 Elm Street, Cleveland, Ohio, on Thursday, September 25, 19-- at 10:00 a.m., pursuant to notice distributed in accordance with the bylaws hereof (or pursuant to waiver of notice signed by all the shareholders and annexed to the minutes of this meeting). The meeting was called to order by President John Carter.

Present were the following shareholders, being the owners of a majority of the outstanding shares and constituting a quorum, namely:

|  | Shareholder | Number of Shares |
|---|---|---|
| IN PERSON: | John Carter | 500 |
|  | Gilbert Smith | 250 |
| BY PROXY: | Carrie Alford | 250 |
|  | Total shares represented | 1,000 |

The President reported on the activities of the corporation since the last annual meeting and its prospects for the ensuing year. The Treasurer gave a report of the corporation's financial condition, a copy of which is annexed to the minutes of this meeting. Both reports were approved upon motion duly made, seconded, and carried.

Upon motion of Gilbert Smith, seconded by John Carter, and by unanimous vote, the following persons were elected directors, to hold office until the next annual meeting of shareholders, and until the election and qualification of their respective successors, namely:

| John Carter | 612 Carolee Lane, Cleveland, OH |
| Gilbert Smith | 433 Aspen Drive, Cleveland, OH |
| Carrie Alford | 1632 Oak Street, Cleveland, OH |

A general discussion then followed on the affairs of the corporation, after which the meeting was adjourned.

Respectfully submitted,

_____
Secretary

APPROVED:

_____
President

ord book or official printed stationery and continuation sheets with preprinted subject headings. The spelling of names, the correct use of titles, and other items should be verified before typing.

**Format** Since the format of the minutes is determined in most cases by the standards set by one's organization, you should carefully examine the setup of previous minutes. Some organizations have special printed stationery for minutes, but if special paper is not available, you need to select the appropriate quality of plain white bond. The typed minutes should closely follow the agenda of the meeting, with the appropriate introductory comments such as the name of the group, its address, the type of meeting, the date and time of the meeting, and attendance data. With a preprinted form, you simply fill in the blanks, taking care not to type directly on the printed lines so that the typescript is obscured.

**Guides for typing minutes** The secretary who types the minutes or summaries of any meeting and maintains corporate records has an important responsibility. Because these serve as the official records of the corporation, accuracy is essential. Tape recorders are valuable in checking the precise wording of motions and resolutions, the order of business, and so forth. Frequently the attorney will want to review the rough draft of the minutes before they are typed in final form. For the secretary preparing minutes on plain paper, the following guidelines are suggested:

1.  Leave a two-inch top margin and type the title all in capital letters on line 13.
2.  Center the date two lines beneath the title.
3.  Use all-capitalized side headings or side headings that are typed in underscored capital and lowercase letters. Choice of side-heading style will vary according to organization guidelines.
4.  Single-space the text paragraphs to save paper.
5.  Use a 60-space typing line for textual matter.
6.  Include a complimentary close (as *Respectfully submitted*) followed by the secretary's and the chairman's signatures.
7.  Make the necessary copies for distribution and filing.

The following illustration shows how a secretary might follow these guidelines in writing minutes for a corporate board meeting. When the minutes are very brief, a simple form such as that illustrated on page 577 is acceptable.

## Sample Minutes of a Board Meeting

```
                                                        117
                                                        19—#4

            INTERNATIONAL TRACTORS, INC.

                   DIRECTORS' MEETING

MINUTES OF APRIL 6, 19—                     REGULAR MEETING, No. 4

             A regular meeting of the Board of Directors
        of International Tractors, Inc., was held on
        Thursday, April 6, 19—.  The meeting was called
        to order by John Elmer Wolfe, Chairman, at 10 a.m.
        in the Founder's Conference Room of the Corporate
        Office on Gilpin Road in Leechburg, Pennsylvania.
```

|  |  |
|---|---|
| PRESENT | Thirteen members of the Board were present: Pauline Alt, Charles Filip, Glenn France, Robert Hazer, Joseph Latina, Richard Linamen, Lorraine Perejda, Ismail Perez, Ethel Rasmusson, Irene Stanick, Elizabeth Walden, Forest Wolfe, and John Zalesny. These members constitute a quorum. |
| ABSENT | One member was absent: Louis Jones. |
| MINUTES APPROVED | The minutes of the March 5, 19—, special Directors' meeting were read and approved. |
| REPORT OF THE CHAIRMAN | The chairman reported on the period of growth in sales during the last quarter, especially in international business with a 12 percent increase as compared with a year ago. However, mention was made of the increasing difficulties in bidding for critical material supplies against strong and affluent foreign competitors. |

A plan for Organizing for Growth was submitted to the Board for study:

First, decentralize from our corporate headquarters into each operating company responsibility for its sales, marketing, and accounting operations.

Next, reinstitute the dual management posts of chairman and chief executive officer and of president and chief operating officer. This will assure that undivided attention will be given to current operations and to future growth.

---

MINUTES OF APRIL 6, 19—

118
19—#4

|  |  |
|---|---|
| REPORT OF THE TREASURER | James McKallip, Treasurer, submitted a quarterly profit and loss statement, dated March 31, 19—, with a net profit of $......... The surplus available for dividends is $......... as determined by a general balance sheet, dated March 31, 19—. These reports were accepted and placed on file. |
| ADJOURNMENT | A motion for adjournment was made by Mr. France and seconded by Ms. Stanick. The meeting was adjourned at 11:45 a.m. |

Charlotte Charpnak, Secretary          John Elmer Wolfe, Chairman

# 18

CHAPTER EIGHTEEN

# THE LAW LIBRARY

## CONTENTS

# 18.1

## INTRODUCTION TO THE LAW LIBRARY

The first chapter of this handbook summarized the sources of American law—constitutions, statutes, regulations, and case law. This "law," created by legislative and judicial bodies, is disseminated through a variety of legal publications. Law books are extremely important tools for the practicing attorney, and they have a character, an organizational pattern, and a system of identification that are unlike those of the publications of most other professional disciplines.

A well-known law librarian used to say that a good law library, regardless of its size or type, is distinguished by three qualities: order, system, and discipline. To allow the user to locate and retrieve material and information efficiently and expeditiously, there must be *order* in the arrangement of things, and the order must be based on a *system*—a scheme which brings like materials together in a reasonable way. Finally, *discipline* is needed to ensure that order and system prevail and that the library client is properly served.

When a law collection begins to approach an appreciable size—about 10,000 volumes or more—many law firms turn to a professional librarian for assistance in managing the collection and providing services. Until such a professional is hired, however, it is often the secretary who administers the library. With initiative and the will to learn, it is possible for secretarial personnel to maintain the law firm library quite effectively.

Attorneys normally expect their assistants to be able to deal with citations to legal publications quickly and accurately, and a natural extension of that requirement is familiarity with the law books themselves—what they contain, what their physical formats are, how they are identified bibliographically, and how they are arranged.

## SOURCES OF INFORMATION

One of the first things a new librarian should do is to become familiar with two publications: (1) *Legal Research in a Nutshell,* by Morris L. Cohen (3d edition, 1978); and (2) *A Uniform System of Citation* (12th edition, 1976), published by the Harvard Law Review Association. Although you may not be expected to read either from cover to cover, the more you refer to them the more familiar you will become with legal publications. You will become proficient in constructing, interpreting, and verifying citations to a myriad of legal sources. You will learn that absolute accuracy in the identification and transcription of legal citations is not a goal just to aspire to but one that <u>must</u> be achieved in all assignments.

Other sources of information are courses in legal bibliography and legal research, which are frequently offered as part of paralegal or legal secretarial education programs. In addition, a visit to the library of a law school, bar association, court, or even a nearby law firm will give you an excellent opportunity to see the variety of law books being published and the method of their arrangement.

There may be a chapter of the American Association of Law Libraries or some other locally organized group of law librarians in your city or state. Although certain professional requirements may prevent full membership, it may be possible to attend the meetings, seminars, and workshops of these organizations as a guest to benefit from the expertise of those who address their full energies to law library administration and service. A call to the librarian at the nearest law library should supply the information you need regarding existing organizations. In addition, you can get a wealth of information from the latest edition of the *Directory of Law Libraries,* published by Commerce Clearing House, Inc., for the American Association of Law Libraries. A copy can be ordered from AALL Headquarters, 53 West Jackson Boulevard, Chicago, IL 60604.

## AN OVERVIEW OF LAW LIBRARIES

A perusal of the *Directory of Law Libraries* reveals several types of law libraries: academic libraries, the predominant group; government libraries, an equally large group spanning city, county, state, and federal levels; court libraries that also exist at various judicial levels; bar association libraries, which are less numerous now than previously; and the private law libraries of law firms and corporations. The size and number of private law libraries are increasing steadily; the Private Law Libraries Special Interest Section (SIS) of the American Association of Law Libraries represents the fastest growing segment of that organization's membership. For additional information on law firm and corporate law libraries, two publications may be consulted: the latest edition of the *Directory* of the Private Law Libraries SIS of the AALL, and the latest edition of its *Corporate Law Libraries.*

Accompanying the growth of law libraries in the private sector is a movement toward shared or joint library facilities, especially among attorneys in small law firms. The impetus is primarily financial. Law books are essential but very expensive professional tools, and many lawyers starting practice have found that it is more economical to pool financial resources and provide one facility to serve several firms. No extensive literature is available on such arrangements, but they have been successful in Minneapolis/St. Paul, Los Angeles, and other cities.

## AN OVERVIEW OF LIBRARY MATERIALS

The following paragraphs outline the principal publications you are likely to find in a law office or corporate law department library.

**Primary and secondary sources**    You should be aware that most legal publications divide themselves into two broad categories known as *primary* and *secondary* sources. Primary sources consist of statutory material, including administrative regulations and court decisions. Secondary sources are generally interpretative, analytical, theoretical, philosophical, or practical publications. The distinction is important because primary sources are said to be authoritative or mandatory; that is, legislative enactments and/or judicial decisions within a given jurisdiction *must* be applied to resolve legal conflicts unless strong circumstances warrant a departure from them. Secondary sources are merely persuasive, although they can and often do influence the drafting of statutes and the application of statutory provisions and judicial decisions. For further discussion of this concept, see the introduction to *Effective Legal Research* by Miles O. Price, et al. (4th edition, 1979).

**Official and unofficial publications**   The terms *official* and *unofficial* also distinguish legal publications. Official sources are those whose publication has been sanctioned or approved by a governmental or judicial body. For example, the *United States Statutes at Large* is the official source of all the statutory enactments of the United States Congress. These same statutes are also found in the *United States Code Congressional and Administrative News*, but because the latter is a commercial publication, it is not considered an official source. Similarly, the *United States Reports* is the official edition of the cases and decisions of the United States Supreme Court. There are two other publications containing the same decisions—the *Supreme Court Reporter* and *United States Supreme Court Reports*, Lawyers' Edition—but again, because these are published commercially, they are considered unofficial.

The publications mentioned in the preceding paragraph are *primary* source materials, even though some are official and others are unofficial. The two ways of classifying should not be confused. The primary/secondary distinction applies to the *contents* of the publications, while the official/unofficial distinction applies to the *body responsible for the publication* of the material.

**Updating law publications**   Legal publications require continuous updating and supplementation. Legal precedents, whether statutory or judicial, are always changing and always subject to change. The United States is a common law country, which means that legal precedent is a cornerstone of its legal system. As a common law country, it historically retains and applies the pronouncements of its judicial and legislative bodies so long as circumstances do not mandate a change. However, when these principles no longer provide equitable resolutions to legal conflicts, they do change. Publications that contain legal information must therefore be adaptable in order to accept frequent changes.

You should learn about publications in slip form, pocket parts, advance sheets, loose-leaf services, and citators and their importance to legal research and legal materials. The lawyer must always be aware of what has occurred in the past, what the current status of the law is, and what developments taking place may augur for change in the future. As a legal secretary, you too must develop this same kind of sensitivity to the past, the present, and the future.

# 18.2

## PRIMARY SOURCE MATERIALS

This section deals chiefly with the primary materials that relate to the federal government. The scheme that emerges, however, is generally applicable to state materials, with obvious jurisdictional adjustments.

## FEDERAL STATUTES

The United States Congress passes all federal legislation. Once a bill becomes a law, it is published in three different forms: first in *slip* form (hence the expression "slip law"), next in the chronologically arranged, official *United States Statutes at Large,* and finally in three *code* editions.

**Slip laws and *Statutes at Large*** As a slip law, a statute is published all by itself. A subscription to the slip laws is available from the United States Government Printing Office in Washington, D.C. When the law is later incorporated into a volume of the *Statutes at Large,* it is listed there in chronological order according to its public law number. Today the public law number, which is an important identifier, consists of two parts. For example, Pub. L. No. 94-1, a proper form of citation, refers to the first law (-1) enacted in the Ninety-fourth Congress (94); Pub. L. No. 94-588 happens to be the last law passed in that congress. The first example appears in 89 Stat. 3 and the latter in 90 Stat. 2949, which are the proper, official citations to a federal law once it is published in the *Statutes at Large.* It is important to note that the volume number of the *Statutes at Large* does *not* correspond to the number of the congress in which the public law was enacted.

Because the publication of each *Statutes at Large* volume is quite slow, it is useful to know about a commercial publication, the *United States Code Congressional and Administrative News,* which is the unofficial equivalent of the *Statutes at Large.* It contains the identical text of the public laws arranged in the same chronological order, but its publication is faster. This series began publication in 1941 with the first session of the Seventy-seventh Congress.

**Code formats** The publications described above are arranged chronologically and numbered sequentially. Another way to arrange U.S. statutes is in code form. Codes employ the numeric designations but primarily provide a *subject* arrangement of all the laws currently in force in the jurisdiction which the code covers. At the federal level there are three code editions: the *United States Code* (U.S.C.), which is the official edition; and two unofficial editions, the *United States Code Annotated* (U.S.C.A.) and the *United States Code Service* (U.S.C.S.). The unofficial codes are also called *annotated* editions.

There are many reasons why a subject arrangement of the laws is needed. For one thing, researching applicable law through a myriad of chronologically arranged volumes is cumbersome and time-consuming. Also, as already mentioned, laws change; they may be frequently amended and sometimes repealed. Such changes are not easy to trace in chronologically arranged volumes. What the lawyer needs is a publication that brings together all the relevant law on a particular subject and that can also accommodate changes as they occur.

**The *United States Code*** The *United States Code,* the official, unannotated edition, is divided into fifty titles which designate the broad subject categories into which the various federal statutes fall. A list of these titles appears on page 4 of this book. A proper citation to the code looks like this: 20 U.S.C. §236 (1976). The number preceding *U.S.C.* signifies the title (not the volume, because Title 20 happens to be in volume 5), and § (section) 236 is a particular provision of that title. The year in parentheses indicates the edition of *United States Code.* This date is important because the code is republished in a new edition every six years. Annual supplements, designated in Roman numerals, are issued between editions to update the basic material. If pertinent statutory language is taken from a supplement, it is so indicated in the citation: for example, 20 U.S.C. §236 (Supp. II 1978). From this citation you know that the provision appears in the second supplement, dated 1978.

**Unofficial codes**    The two unofficial, annotated code compilations are virtually identical in content to the *United States Code* but have a number of added features that
enhance their value as research aids. For one thing, they are annotated. This means
that where there exist case decisions that interpret, apply, analyze, or distinguish any
provision in the code, they will be referred to in that section so that, in doing research, the attorney will be alerted to these cases.

Another very important research feature of the annotated codes is that all the volumes in these editions are supplemented by annual pocket parts and by additional
supplementary pamphlets that are issued as necessary to reflect new legislation and
changes' in or repeal of existing statutes. Pocket parts are pamphlet inserts that get
placed in a pocket constructed in the back of each code volume. Pocket parts are
almost always updated annually. When they become too numerous for adequate retention in the pocket, the publisher issues an entirely new volume or volumes that
incorporate the supplements. To locate or verify a statutory citation, therefore, you
must do more than just consult the basic code volumes. You must press on to the
latest supplemental material to be absolutely certain that your information is current
and reliable and therefore authoritative. The checking is not difficult, however, because the arrangement remains the same from one supplementary source to another;
that is, after locating 20 U.S.C.A. §236 or 20 U.S.C.S. §236, you check for the same
citation number in the pocket parts of both editions and in their respective supplementary pamphlets.

## FEDERAL ADMINISTRATIVE REGULATIONS

Administrative regulations are, in a sense, a by-product of statutory enactments. They
are promulgated by the myriad of administrative agencies in our federal government
organization. Some of these agencies that you may have encountered are the Securities and Exchange Commission, the Internal Revenue Service, and the Federal Trade
Commission. These and other agencies are the creation of statutory enactments of
Congress which define the scope of their respective authority and the nature of the
functions they may exercise. Some agencies are strictly regulatory bodies but most
are hybrids, which means that they exercise quasijudicial powers (they render decisions) as well as quasilegislative powers (they promulgate regulations).

**The *Code of Federal Regulations***    Administrative regulations function and are applied in much the same way as statutes; however, the publications in which they are
located are a bit more difficult to manipulate and are not as easy to update. Federal
administrative regulations currently in force are located in a subject compilation
called the *Code of Federal Regulations* (C.F.R.). It constitutes primary source material; it is official, and there is no unofficial equivalent. Like the federal codes, it is
divided into fifty titles, but there is *not* a one-to-one correspondence between its titles
and those of the *United States Code*. There are differences.

Of all the volumes in the C.F.R., you should become most familiar with Title 3,
The President; and the last volume, the CFR Index and Finding Aids. The presidential
volume is important because in a small library it is the one place where you can locate the Proclamations and Executive Orders of the government's chief executive officer. Inside the cover of the latest annual you will find a listing of all the Title 3 compilations, which date back to 1936. Executive Orders and Proclamations can also be
found in *United States Code Congressional and Administrative News* and in U.S.C.S.,
but they are most conveniently located in the C.F.R.

The Index and Finding Aids volume is your key to learning how to use the C.F.R.
The Index is now being extensively revised and enlarged and should be much more
useful as terms and cross-references are further refined. One of the most important
tables—which should be familiar to attorneys—is Table 1, Parallel Table of Statutory

Authorities and Rules. It lists all the sections of the *United States Code* and the *Statutes at Large,* which together are the authority for the regulations promulgated in the C.F.R. as well as for any presidential Proclamations or Executive Orders. There is also an alphabetical list of all the agencies named in the C.F.R. and where their regulations will be found.

**The *Federal Register*** Regulations, like statutes, may be amended, revised, or repealed. Since the C.F.R. titles are revised only once each year, another tool must be consulted to update the information found in the annual volumes. This tool is the *Federal Register,* a government publication which is issued daily, Monday through Friday, by the National Archives and Records Service of the General Services Administration in Washington, D.C. A subscription may be placed with the Superintendent of Documents, United States Government Printing Office.

The cover of each issue begins a "Highlights" listing of the most important regulatory information contained within, followed by a full Contents section. Presidential documents such as Proclamations and Executive Orders are always given first in both lists. There is also, at the front of each issue, a compilation of the C.F.R. titles and sections affected by the regulations in the issue at hand; at the back of each issue this information is cumulated for the days in a given month. This "List of CFR Sections Affected" (or LSA) also appears in quarterly cumulative pamphlets containing updated references to C.F.R. titles and sections that may have been changed subsequent to their annual revision dates. Monthly pamphlets are also issued between the quarterlies.

**Using the *Federal Register*** Suppose you wish to check the status of a particular regulation in the C.F.R.—for example, 24 C.F.R. §571.100 (revised as of 4-1-80). Since Title 24 has been revised as of April 1, 1980, you want to check this citation in the "List of CFR Sections Affected"(LSA) for dates after that date through the latest quarterly cumulation and monthly pamphlet of that list that is available to you. If you should happen to find a reference to 24 C.F.R. §571.100, you would note the page references to the *Federal Register.* You would then check your page references against those listed in the "Table of Federal Register Issue Pages and Dates," found at the back of each LSA pamphlet, in order to get the exact date of the *Federal Register* in which the new information will be found.

If in the above example the latest quarterly cumulation was through June 1980 and the latest monthly pamphlet was July 1980, you would check for changes to 24 C.F.R. §570.100 in those two pamphlets first, jot down what you found, and get the dates of the *Federal Register* for your pages. If you were searching in the month of September, you would next go to the *last* issue for the month of August and the last daily issue available to you in the month of September. In the last daily issue of August you would find the LSA cumulated for all of August. After checking it you would then go to the latest daily issue of September, where you would find the LSA cumulated for September through that date. If the latest monthly issue of the LSA was August 1980, you would check it and then check the latest daily for September.

Having recorded your references to the *Federal Register,* or having found none, you would have completely verified your C.F.R. citation right up to the date of your search.

To summarize:

1. Find the regulation in C.F.R. and note the pamphlet's revision date.
2. Check the regulation in the latest quarterly and latest monthly issues of the LSA subsequent to its revision date.
3. Check the regulation in the LSA in the last daily issue of each month of the *Federal Register* as necessary.

4. Check the regulation in the last daily issue of the *Federal Register* preceding the date on which the searching is done.

The route will cover all four steps or just the first, second, and fourth, depending on the dates of the publications being consulted.

For a more detailed explanation see *The Federal Register: What It Is and How to Use It: A Guide for the User of the Federal Register—Code of Federal Regulations System,* published in Washington, D.C., by the U.S. Office of the Federal Register.

## FEDERAL CASE LAW

The hierarchical structure of state and federal courts in the United States is described in the first chapter of this book. A case begins in a lower court which has original jurisdiction, and it can end in an appellate court. Usually a case will proceed to an intermediate appellate court before going up to the highest court of appeal, but there are circumstances when the intermediate step can be bypassed.

**Law reports**   The opinions of all of these courts and others discussed here are published in volumes called law reports. There are many series of law reports; some cover many courts in one jurisdiction, and some cover several jurisdictions. The official/unofficial distinction discussed in connection with statutory publications applies in some but not all cases of law report publishing.

The decisions of the U.S. District Courts are found in a set of law reports called *Federal Supplement* (F. Supp.). Although considered unofficial because of its commercial publication, it is the only place where these decisions are consistently published. The opinions of the U.S. Courts of Appeal are published in a single set called the *Federal Reporter* (F. or F.2d), which is also commercially produced and, therefore, unofficial. An important point to remember is that the *Federal Reporter* is now in a second series.

Decisions of the United States Supreme Court constitute an exception to the publishing scheme at the federal level because they are reproduced in not just one but three series of law reports: one official and two unofficial. The official edition is called, simply, *United States Reports* (U.S.). One unofficial set is called *United States Supreme Court Reports,* Lawyers' Edition (L. Ed.), and the other is titled *Supreme Court Reporter* (S. Ct.). The unofficial editions have indexing, tabular, and annotation features which enhance their value as research tools, and thus they are more popular.

**Slip opinions**   Before being published in bound editions as law reports, the opinions of the U.S. Supreme Court, like statutes of the U.S. Congress, are first published in "slip" form. So also are the decisions of many other federal and state courts. This means that the opinion is printed individually so that it may be arranged either by date of decision or by a docket or index number. The docket number is an important identifier for any case decision even after it has been reported and printed in a law report series. A docket number is assigned to a case when it is filed in a particular court; each court has its own docketing system. The case is then placed on a calendar where its status is periodically updated as it moves closer to hearing and disposition by the court. A federal case may have several docket numbers: one in a U.S. District Court, one in a U.S. Court of Appeals, and one in the U.S. Supreme Court. All documents filed with the court relating to the case will be identified by its docket number and in the majority of instances will forever be filed under that number in the archival depositories of the court. Most law office libraries subscribe to the slip opinions of the U.S. Supreme Court and perhaps also to those of the U.S. Court of Appeals for the circuit in which they are located; they may also subscribe to the slip opinions of a state court. Cost is the determining factor because slip opinion subscriptions can be very expensive.

**Advance sheets**   A sequence of slip opinions is cumulated to appear eventually in what is called an *advance sheet*. Advance sheet publications generally accompany each law report series. Advance sheets also are eventually cumulated and superseded by bound volumes of law reports, at which time the sheets can be discarded. Advance sheet services can be subscribed to by themselves or as part of a subscription to the bound volumes. Some of the larger law offices arrange to get multiple subscriptions to the advance sheets for circulation to various attorneys so that they can keep current on the decisions of certain courts.

## CITATIONS TO CASES IN LAW REPORTS

Citations to cases are determined by the series of law reports in which the cases are reported. As a general rule, all parallel citations to a case (different citations to the *same* case) should be given with the official citation (if there is one) indicated first because the official citation is always the preferred one. The following are illustrations of citations to federal court cases:

### U.S. District Court
Name of case: *Bonney* v. *Upjohn Co.*
Citation: 487 F. Supp. 486 (W.D. Mich. 1980)
U.S. District Court docket number: No. K75-86 CA4

Name of case: *United States* v. *Nelson*
Citation: 486 F. Supp. 464 (W.D. Mich. 1980)
U.S. District Court docket number: No. G78-115 CR5

### U.S. Court of Appeals
Name of case: *Wabash Ry. Co.* v. *Huelsmann*
Citation: 290 F. 165 (C.C.A. 8th 1923)
U.S. Court of Appeals docket number: No. 6167

Name of case: *Republic of U.S. of Brazil* v. *Markland, The*
Citation: 290 F. 2d 165 (5th Cir. 1961)
U.S. Court of Appeals docket number: No. 18681

### U.S. Supreme Court
Name of case: *Regents of the University of California* v. *Bakke*
Official citation: 438 U.S. 265 (1978)
Unofficial citations:  98 S.Ct. 2733 (1978)
                                    57 L.Ed. 2d 750 (1978)
U.S. Supreme Court docket number: No. 76-811

The numbers preceding the abbreviations for all law report series indicate the *volume* in which the decision will be found; the numbers following the abbreviation designate the page at which the case begins. The abbreviated information in parentheses at the end of a citation identifies the specific federal district or appeals court in which the case was decided and the year of the decision. For instance, *W.D. Mich.* refers to the U.S. District Court for the Western District of Michigan. *5th Cir.* refers to the 5th circuit of the U.S. Court of Appeals, while *C.C.A. 8th* refers to the older name for the same courts, the U.S. Circuit Court of Appeals. The docket number does not appear in the citation but may be found in the prefatory material preceding the actual text of the decision.

Searching and verifying citations to a case requires precision. Notice how a slip of the typing finger can alter the information. In the *Bonney* case, for example, if you typed 486 rather than 487 for the volume number, the reader would be sent not to the *Bonney* case but to the *Nelson* case, which continues at page 486 in Volume 486. In the *Brazil* case, inadvertently omitting the *2d* after *F.* would send the reader to the *Wabash* case instead. Judges and law clerks and supervising attorneys do not excuse such errors very lightly. Accuracy is critically important in identifying legal sources, especially primary ones such as law reports.

## STATE STATUTES AND ADMINISTRATIVE REGULATIONS

Federal statutory publications have their equivalents at the state level. In the following paragraphs those features which are common to all or most state materials are generalized; however, you must keep in mind that there are fifty jurisdictions with which to contend and that each state's body of law is different. In researching state law, if the general principles given here do not seem to apply, seek the assistance of someone who is familiar with the state's system and its publication sources.

**State statutory publications**   State statutes, like federal statutes, are published both in a numeric/chronological order and in a subject compilation called a code. They are published in numeric/chronological order in a series generally called Session Laws, although in some states they are called Public Acts, General Laws, or a similar term. In addition, all states have at least one code representing a subject arrangement of the law currently in force in their respective jurisdictions. You should become quite familiar with those in your own state.

State code compilations vary in the number of volumes in each set, the subject headings used, and the way in which the subjects are broken down. Most state codes include sections on topics like Agriculture, Civil Procedure, and Taxation. California's code includes a segment on Water because that topic is subject to much legislation in California. All the state codes are supplemented regularly, mostly by annual pocket parts inserted at the end of each volume and additional pamphlet material issued during the course of a state legislative session. All have some sort of a numeric breakdown—title, chapter, section, etc.—for their code material.

All state session laws are primary source materials, as are all state codes. However, the distinction between official and unofficial publications is not so clear-cut. The attorney should advise you as to which form of citation is required or preferred. You may also consult *A Uniform System of Citation*, Section III: "Specific Citation Forms and Abbreviations."

**State administrative regulations**   Sources of state administrative regulations are, in most cases, not well organized. A few jurisdictions—California, New Jersey, New York, and several others—have fairly well-organized administrative codes, but many states do not. A good source of information about these publications is an article by Henry P. Tseng and Donald B. Pedersen, "Commentary: Acquisition of State Administrative Rules and Regulations—Update 1979," which appears in 31 *Administrative Law Review* 405 (1979).

## STATE LAW REPORTS

Law reports at the state level are numerous because they represent the judicial product of fifty jurisdictions. Another problem is that the distinction between official and unofficial publications applies to some state law report series but not to others.

With some exceptions, such as *New York Miscellaneous Reports* (cited Misc., Misc. 2d), decisions of the state courts where cases originate are generally not published in any formal law report series. If a local legal newspaper is published regularly, however, it is likely to print the text of the more important cases from lower courts or at least summaries of the cases. At the intermediate appellate level, in a considerable number of the more litigious states like New York, Pennsylvania, California, Illinois, and Ohio, there are many law report series, and most states publish official reports of their supreme appellate court decisions. However, some states have found it too expensive to maintain official editions of these opinions.

At least two commercial vendors provide published sources for state court decisions. One set is called the *National Reporter System;* the other is known as *American Law Reports* (A.L.R.).

**The National Reporter System**    The National Reporter System is comprehensive in that it contains decisions of the supreme appellate courts of all the fifty states. It is subdivided into seven regional reporters and two individual state reporters. The two separate reporters are the *New York Supplement* (N.Y.S., N.Y.S.2d) and *West's California Reporter* (Cal.Rptr.). The regional reporters are the *Atlantic* (A., A.2d), *Northeastern* (N.E., N.E.2d), *Northwestern* (N.W., N.W.2d), *Southern* (So., So.2d), *Southeastern* (S.E., S.E.2d), *Southwestern* (S.W., S.W.2d), and *Pacific* (P., P.2d). The *2d* indicates that each one is now in a second series. Their geographic breakdown is as follows:

| | |
|---|---|
| Atlantic: | Connecticut, Delaware, District of Columbia, Maine, Maryland, New Hampshire, New Jersey, Pennsylvania, Rhode Island, Vermont |
| Northeastern: | Illinois, Indiana, Massachusetts, New York, Ohio |
| Northwestern: | Iowa, Michigan, Minnesota, Nebraska, North Dakota, South Dakota, Wisconsin |
| Pacific: | Alaska, Arizona, California, Colorado, Hawaii, Idaho, Kansas, Montana, Nevada, New Mexico, Oklahoma, Oregon, Utah, Washington, Wyoming |
| Southeastern: | Georgia, North Carolina, South Carolina, Virginia, West Virginia |
| Southern: | Alabama, Florida, Louisiana, Mississippi |
| Southwestern: | Arkansas, Kentucky, Missouri, Tennessee, Texas |

The groupings are intended to bring decisions from the courts of sister states—those with like or common interests—together. Note that, in addition to the individual state reporters, California is also covered by the Pacific and New York by the Northeastern reporters. Hence there may be at least three places where texts of court decisions in these states can be found: in the official state reports (both have several), their individual reporters, and the regional reporters.

Court decisions in the National Reporter System are initially published in advance sheet pamphlets, which are then cumulated and superseded by bound volumes. In all cases these commercially published law reports are considered to be unofficial sources of case decisions even in those states which have abandoned official editions.

**American Law Reports**    *American Law Reports* (A.L.R.) is a much less comprehensive law report series, although it spans many volumes (it is now in its third series) and has a distinguished history as a research tool. The difference in coverage between A.L.R. and the National Reporter System is its selectivity. The editorial board of its publisher selects, out of the thousands of reported cases decided in the courts of the 50 states, those which illustrate a unique application or development of a legal principle of interest to lawyers beyond the jurisdiction of the rendering court. The selected cases are carefully evaluated by legal experts, and their analyses are published as "annotations" to the cases chosen. These annotations are often lengthy pieces of documentary research, and they are sometimes revised and updated. A small office law library may not subscribe to A.L.R.; attorneys are well aware of its usefulness, however, and may often request volumes from a neighboring law library.

# 18.3

## SECONDARY SOURCE MATERIALS

Beyond primary sources such as statutes and law reports are the research tools which an attorney must use and which the legal secretary should be familiar with. These tools are secondary source materials—indexes and citators, form books, loose-leaf services, legal periodicals, texts, encyclopedias, and miscellaneous reference works.

## INDEXES AND CITATORS

Given the array of legal publications that must be consulted when one is researching a point of law and the attorney's continuing need to get reliable, current information, the need becomes clear for sophisticated indexing tools.

**The American Digest**   Indexes to legal publications, especially to those on case law, are chiefly in the form of *digests*. The most important one is the American Digest, which accompanies the National Reporter System described in the last section. It is cumulated over ten-year periods so that, with the exception of the earliest and the most current ones, its volumes are identified by a particular decennial period. The initial volumes, covering the period 1658–1896, are known as the *Century Edition of the American Digest*. Volumes which are being currently cumulated for the next decennial are called *West's General Digest*. So far there have been eight decennial cumulations beyond the Century Edition period in the American Digest System.

What this huge digest system does is to break down the spectrum of law into a series of very broad topics such as Bankruptcy, Constitutional Law, Evidence, Liens, and Torts. These broad topics are then broken down by narrower, often very precise subheadings which are assigned what are popularly known as "key numbers." The *key* derives from the fact that the publisher actually uses a trademark symbol of a key preceding the numerical assignments to a particular topic. Thus, once a researcher has isolated the key numbers assigned to the broader subject area being analyzed, he or she can then consult the body of the volume containing that information and scan *abstracts* or *squibs* of cases from many jurisdictions that relate to the subject matter. The squibs provide enough information regarding the cases digested so that they can be easily located in the National Reporter System.

There are a few additional volumes in the Digest which enhance its utility and make access to the system easier. These are the *Descriptive-Word Index* and the *Table of Cases*. The former indexes factual and legal terminology used in the cases digested; the latter is an alphabetical listing of all the cases covered for a particular period. This table also provides the key numbers assigned to the case. So, for example, if an attorney learned that a particular unfamiliar case might be relevant to the problem at hand, the researching attorney would look up the case in the Table of Cases, get its citation and also all the key numbers under which it has been digested. The digest could then be consulted under those key numbers for additional information about the case.

The single most significant research contribution that the American Digest makes is its universality. By that is meant that all case law, regardless of its originating jurisdiction, is digested by the application of the same broad subject headings and the assignment of pertinent key-numbered subheadings. This feature is augmented by the publication and availability of six regional digests that correspond to six of the seven regional reporters of the National Reporter System (only the Southwestern is no longer published). In addition, there are key number digests for a majority of the states, and at the federal level there is one covering all the federal courts—the *Modern Federal Practice Digest* and its successor, *West's Federal Practice Digest 2d*—and also one which covers only the decisions of the United States Supreme Court—the *United States Supreme Court Digest*.

To understand how this digest system works you must get a feel for it through some hands-on experience. The key numbers under which each case reported in the National Reporter System is digested always appear preceding the full text of the cases in both the advance sheets and the bound volumes. For practice, you can pick a case at random, examine the entries listed under it in the digest volume for your state or geographic region or in any of the decennial volumes. Also check the case in any of the Tables of Cases appearing after its date of decision and see just what information you find. The more experience you get in looking up cases in these indexes, the easier it will become to use digests efficiently.

**Words and Phrases** *Words and Phrases* is another research tool which attorneys find useful when dealing with legal terms or general phrases that may develop legal connotations in case law. It is basically a 46-volume annotated dictionary whose definitions are based on judicial interpretations of the terms. For example, if you wanted to know whether the expression "about one year" had ever been judicially interpreted or defined, you could check the phrase in this set. *Words and Phrases* is supplemented annually by pocket parts.

**Citators** From the moment a case is decided by some court or a statute is enacted by some legislature, it becomes subject to the process of change. The decision of the court may be applied identically again and again to similar situations, or it may be distinguished, modified, or even reversed in whole or in part. The same is true of a statute: it may stand for a long time or be amended or repealed in whole or in part. Such changes in the law occur daily; thus, whatever legal authority an attorney locates to support a legal argument has to be tested to see if it is still "good law." The tool which allows the lawyer to do that is a *citator,* and the publisher whose name is virtually synonymous with legal citators is Shepard, so much so that the process of updating a case or statute is known as Shepardizing.

Shepardizing a case or statute involves finding all the references to it in subsequent cases. These subsequent citations are then analyzed as to their effect on the judicial precedent that the case or statute represents. Shepardizing provides a historical summary of the case or statute from the date of its rendition to the present.

The mechanics of Shepardizing are quite simple. A full explanation is given at the front of every Shepard's citator. There are many citators in the system of *Shepard's Citations.* There is one for every unit of the National Reporter System and for all the reports and statutes of the federal system, including a number of administrative agency report series and now the *Code of Federal Regulations.* There are citators for each of the fifty states, covering both statutory and case law. In addition, there are a few other special Shepard's which are fully described in Chapter 18 of *Effective Legal Research.*

In order to Shepardize a case, statute, or federal regulation, you must have a *completely accurate* citation with which to start. One wrong digit could lead to the wrong item and cause you to miss noting that a case has been reversed or a statute repealed. For purposes of illustration, take the citation to the *Bakke* case: 438 U.S. 265 (1978). Since it was decided in 1978, we must consult volume five of *Shepard's United States Citations,* which is the Case Edition Supplement 1976–1980. Because we are working with the official citation, we turn to the first section covering United States Supreme Court Reports and look for "Vol. 438." The volume numbers appear on the upper outside corners of the left and right pages. Each page consists of eight columns of numbers and letters. Having located Vol. 438 on page 647 of the citator, beginning in the second column from the left, we watch for *265,* the starting page for the case—in the lower part of the sixth column. Immediately below 265, we see *in parentheses* the two alternate unofficial citations to *Bakke:* 57 LE2d 750 and 98 SC 2733. (Note that the abbreviations for *Lawyers' Edition* and *Supreme Court Reporter* are different from the ones recommended earlier in this chapter. That is because Shepard's uses its own forms of abbreviations. They are *not* to be used in citing any legal writing.)

Following the alternate citations you will see a string of citations to cases which have cited *Bakke.* Some have small letters preceding them; the significance of these letters and of all symbols used in the citator is explained at the front of the volume.

After you have checked the bound volume, if it was your starting point, you must check the citation in any supplementary pamphlets that may be available. There are two kinds: red ones and white ones. If neither or just the red one is available, check with someone responsible for the services to see what the complete holdings should be. <u>You must verify the status of the case as good law through the most current pamphlet</u>. The white pamphlet tells you, on its front cover, what each Shepard's citator should contain, so you need only verify that you have consulted all the parts listed.

You can also begin Shepardizing with one of the two unofficial citations if it is correct. Always remember to check your information, and if you are copying it out to give back to the attorney, do so with the utmost care.

The following steps summarize the process of Shepardizing for the legal secretary:

1. Find the Shepard's citator which corresponds to your citation. All Shepard's volumes are clearly labelled. Also locate all the supplementary pamphlets you will need.
2. Find the series, volume number, and page number corresponding to your citation.
3. Copy all the information following the page number exactly as you see it.
4. If the attorney wants to see the cited materials, assemble and present them as instructed.

Shepardizing statutes requires the same procedure as Shepardizing cases except that you begin with a different kind of citation. As with cases, it is essential to begin with the correct citation. The one additional point to keep in mind when dealing with statutes is that citations to them can be changed in form as well as in substance. The form of a case—its citation—never changes, but a statute may be recompiled and thus renumbered, or it can be transferred to another section in the code. Therefore, you must be especially careful in dealing with statutory citations.

## FORM BOOKS AND LOOSE-LEAF SERVICES

A good portion of a lawyer's time is spent drafting legal documents to serve the various needs of clients. Whether these forms are substantive (a commercial note or contract, a will, a trust agreement, or sale of property) or procedural (a motion, an affidavit, or a complaint), the attorney will frequently check sample forms whose composition is generally acceptable and based on principles developed in case law.

Two general, multivolume form book sets commonly used by attorneys for this purpose are *American Jurisprudence Legal Forms Annotated* and *American Jurisprudence Pleading and Practice Forms,* which is also annotated. The first set contains substantive legal forms and the second one covers procedural forms. Both refer to cases where the forms have been subjected to judicial scrutiny. In addition, the jurisdiction in which the attorney practices may have published form books dealing exclusively with forms accepted and recognized by its courts. Also, volumes of forms often accompany texts on certain legal subjects such as probate. The attorney (and the many publishers' sales representatives) will most likely call these to your attention.

**Loose-leaf services**   A loose-leaf service is a form of publication that is particularly associated with supplying current legal information in a particular field of law. A publication in loose-leaf form makes it easy to continuously insert new or revised pages into its basic text. At least one and often several loose-leaf services exist for any specialty.

For reference use, each service almost always has introductory material which states the extent of its coverage and gives detailed explanations on how to use the service. Each time you file or handle one for the first time, you should read through this introductory material carefully and examine all the parts of the publication to become familiar with it. The list in Appendix D of the third edition of Morris Cohen's *Legal Research in a Nutshell* gives a comprehensive list of loose-leaf services up to

1977. A list of abbreviations to be used in referring to loose-leaf services appears on pages 95–99 of *A Uniform System of Citation,* 12th edition.

Interfiling in a loose-leaf publication is not difficult, but it is a recurring responsibility that should not be postponed. Filing more than one supplement at a time increases the possibility of error in a publication where such error can be disastrous. All loose-leaf services have precise, easy-to-understand filing instructions printed on numbered transmittal sheets to make checking, verifying, and filing simple if one pays attention.

## ENCYCLOPEDIAS, TEXTS, AND PERIODICALS

Among the many secondary sources important in the practice of law are legal encyclopedias, major textbooks, and legal periodical literature.

**Legal encyclopedias**   There are two major legal encyclopedias: *Corpus Juris Secundum* (C.J.S.) and *American Jurisprudence,* Second Edition (Am. Jur. 2d). They are similar to general encyclopedias except that their coverage is devoted to legal subjects. Both are filled with references to cases and statutory sources, and both present extensive explanatory material that elucidates generally accepted legal principles. They provide good starting points for initial research into unfamiliar areas. Many of the states also have encyclopedic sets covering the development of legal principles within their own jurisdictions. Most often the word *jurisprudence* is part of their titles, as in *Texas Jurisprudence, Ohio Jurisprudence,* and *California Jurisprudence III.*

**Texts**   Single- and multivolume legal texts are numerous. All the major legal publishers will, upon request, provide catalogs listing the most significant ones which they sell. Among the most widely used law texts are the following:

*Administrative Law,* by Kenneth Culp Davis—a 1958 text that is supplemented irregularly.

The 15th edition of *Collier on Bankruptcy*—a multivolume, loose-leaf text.

*Model Business Corporation Act Annotated,* published by the Section of Corporation, Banking and Business Law, Committee on Corporate Laws of the American Bar Association—a three-volume work that is supplemented irregularly.

*A Treatise on the Law of Contracts,* by Samuel Williston—supplemented with annual pocket parts and popularly known as "Williston on Contracts."

*Evidence in Trials at Common Law,* by John Henry Wigmore—supplemented with annual pocket parts and popularly known as "Wigmore on Evidence."

*American Jurisprudence Proof of Facts,* 2d series—a multivolume text supplemented with annual pocket parts.

*Computer Law Service,* edited by Robert P. Bigelow—a six-volume text with a supplementary volume that is updated regularly.

*Personal Injury: Actions, Defenses, Damages,* edited by Louis R. Frumer, et al.—a multivolume, loose-leaf text.

*The Law of Trusts and Trustees,* by George Gleason Bogert—supplemented with annual pocket parts and popularly known as "Bogert on Trusts."

*Page on the Law of Wills,* by William H. Page—supplemented with annual pocket parts.

*Restatement of the Law,* 1st and 2d, published by the American Law Institute—a multivolume set resembling a legal encyclopedia but confined to certain subject areas. It is nevertheless an important, highly recognized, and much used research tool.

The items listed above represent a very small sampling of the large number and variety of legal texts available. There are many single-volume casebooks, hornbooks, and handbooks that are equally of value and importance to attorneys. The contents of a law office library reflect the areas of the firm's practice and the personal preferences of its lawyers. Catalogs of law book publishers are good sources of information about basic legal publications.

**Legal periodicals**   Other research publications of value to attorneys are the legal periodical and the legal newspaper. There are numerous periodical publications in the field of law, the bulk of them originating with the law schools. These are known as *law reviews,* which is an apt term since their primary function is to review legal developments in a variety of subjects. Examples are the *Cornell Law Review, Duke Law Journal,* and *University of Chicago Law Review.* Some law reviews concentrate on specific subject areas such as urban law, civil rights, and employee relations. There are many private publishers of legal periodicals as well.

**Periodical indexes**   There are several indexing tools for searching legal periodicals. The oldest and one of the best-known is the *Index to Legal Periodicals.* There is also the *Index to Periodical Articles Related to Law* and the *Harvard Current and Annual Legal Bibliography.* The newest index to legal periodical literature is *Current Law Index,* which is available in hard copy, on microfiche, and on-line.

**Legal newspapers**   Legal newspapers are also fairly numerous. Until a few years ago most of them were local, published primarily for readers in metropolitan areas or in certain states. The best known of these are the *New York Law Journal* and the *Los Angeles Daily Journal.* In addition, national legal newspapers are now available to the legal community. Among them are the *Legal Times of Washington,* the *National Law Journal,* and the *American Lawyer.* The first two focus on issues important to the substantive practice of law as well as to the profession itself. The third one focuses more on personalities and information about the profession.

   In a small law office library you are unlikely to find many law reviews. While periodicals are not terribly expensive to purchase, their cost is a factor when retention is permanent and binding is necessary. You can expect a small library to have local legal newspapers and at least one of the national newspapers.

## OTHER REFERENCE TOOLS
Included in this category are primarily legal directories and dictionaries, which are standard secondary source materials.

**Directories**   Of the legal directories, the *Martindale-Hubbell Law Directory* is the best-known. It is found in almost every law office. Published annually, it consists of several volumes with the majority of its information dedicated to listing names of attorneys engaged in practice throughout the United States. It is geographically organized, so that a user must know the city and state where an attorney is practicing in order to find the listing. Each directory volume has a biographical section in which lawyer personnel are listed under the names of the law firms where they practice with biographical data generally added. Not all firms are listed in the biographical section, however, and this kind of extended information is not provided for government or corporate attorneys. There are listings, by city and country, of many prominent foreign attorneys. The last Martindale-Hubbell volume is known as the Digest volume because it contains a summary of the most important statutory and common law provisions of each jurisdiction. It is a handy place to first check something like what the statute of limitations period is on a breach of contract action in a particular jurisdiction. Although the answer must be verified, a reference to the statutory source is always given, thus making it easy to check the language of the state code section.

   In addition to Martindale-Hubbell, many state lawyer directories are published by bar associations, often as supplements to bar publications. These directories may carry other useful information such as the state's code of conduct for lawyers and judges, a list of important public officers with their telephone numbers, and many more items of information needed in the daily practice of law.

**Dictionaries**    The best-known legal dictionaries are *Black's Law Dictionary* and Ballentine's *Law Dictionary*. Both have pronunciation guides along with the definitions, and both supply lists of accepted forms of abbreviation. Black's has particularly good coverage of definitions of legal maxims, which are sometimes difficult to find. In addition, it features a chart which tells the composition of the United States Supreme Court at any given time as well as a list of British regnal years to help persons doing research on English law.

**Other reference aids**    Although not technically a legal reference tool, it is recommended that every law office have a copy of the latest *United States Government Manual,* which can be purchased from the Superintendent of Documents, United States Government Printing Office, Washington, D.C. It is the single most comprehensive source of information on all three branches of the federal government including the many executive and independent agencies functioning in each branch. It lists key personnel and telephone numbers, provides organization charts, describes functions and authority, and refers to statutes creating and governing each of the agencies. You might also wish to have a copy of the latest edition of the *Statistical Abstract of the United States,* prepared by the Bureau of the Census of the United States Department of Commerce. It is also available from the Government Printing Office.

If the lawyers in your office have regular business with congressional personnel, one or two additional publications may be useful: the latest *Congressional Staff Directory* (published in Mount Vernon, Virginia, by the Congressional Staff Directory, Inc.) and the *Congressional Directory* for the present Congress, available from the Government Printing Office.

A trio of publications that may be useful if you have need of out-of-state information is the latest edition of (1) *Book of the States,* which contains much official information on government structure and organization for the fifty states; (2) *State Administrative Officials Classified by Function,* which supplies information about many state administrative agencies; and (3) *State Elective Officials and the Legislatures.* All three are published by the Council of State Governments, located in Lexington, Kentucky.

Some additional reference aids are listed in the Appendix to this book. It is difficult to make further recommendations because needs are always dictated by the nature of an attorney's practice and the availability of funds. Law publications are very expensive compared to publications in most other disciplines. Reference librarians in any library can recommend materials to you if you supply an adequate explanation of the information you need.

# 18.4

## CITATIONS

This section reviews the library materials discussed in the preceding sections by illustrating the construction of citations to the major types of primary and secondary source materials. For details of punctuating citations, see section 13.6 of Chapter 13.

### CONSTITUTIONS
**United States Constitution**    Citations to the U.S. Constitution give article, section, and clause numbers:

U.S. Constitution, Article II, Section 1, Clause 3
*or* U.S. Const. Art. II, § 1, cl. 3

**State constitutions**   Citations to state constitutions follow a similar form:

Michigan Constitution, Article 6, Section 6
or Mich. Const. Art. 6, §6

Most states have reenacted their constitutions from time to time. References to the one currently in force need not be dated, but references to *prior* constitutions must carry a date:

Michigan Constitution, Article 6, Section 6 (1850)

The same rule applies to footnote references.

## FEDERAL STATUTES

**Slip laws**   Citations to slip laws give the public law number, the Congress and session, and the date of enactment:

Pub. L. No. 96-39, 96th Cong., 1st Sess. (July 26, 1979)

**Statutes at Large**   You must give volume and page number as well as the year of the *Statutes at Large:*

90 Stat. 1113 (1976)

**Official code**   For titles reenacted into positive law, you must give the number of the title, the code initials, the section number, and in parentheses the date of the latest edition or volume of the code and the date of the supplement where applicable:

17 U.S.C. §107 (Supp. II 1978)

**Unofficial codes**   Citations to the unofficial codes must give the number of the title, the title, the code initials, the section number, and in parentheses the publisher and the date of the supplementary pamphlet if applicable:

42 U.S.C.A. §2000e(k) (West, Supp. Pam. 1974 to 1979)

**Popular name**   Citations to statutes may be preceded by the popular name of the act:

Automobile Dealers Day in Court Act, Act of August 8, 1956, c.1038, 70 Stat. 1125
*or*
Automobile Dealers Day in Court Act, 15 U.S.C. §1221 (1976).

In text and footnote citing the generally acceptable form is to give the name of the act and the *Statutes at Large* citation or, for those titles enacted into positive law, the *United States Code* citation.

**Verification of statutes**   To verify the accuracy of a statute you must actually check the sources cited to be sure that they are correct. When you have only the name of a statute, you can consult the Popular Name Tables in U.S.C., U.S.C.A., and U.S.C.S. or you may consult *Shepard's Acts and Cases by Popular Name, Federal and State*. If you are not successful in any of these sources, you must search for the statute through the general indexes of the code compilations.

## FEDERAL REGULATIONS

**Code of Federal Regulations**   A citation to the C.F.R. must give title number, section number, and year of compilation:

22 C.F.R. §709.1 (1980)

**Federal Register**   The citation must give volume and page number and year:

45 Fed. Reg. 61550 (1980)

## STATE STATUTES

Forms of citation for both session laws and code compilations vary from state to state. Your best course of action is to check *A Uniform System of Citation*, 12th edition, for the recommended citation format for each state or Miles O. Price, et al., *Effective Legal Research*, 4th edition, Section 32.8, "State Legislation." In many of the state code compilations the publishers give you the accepted citation form at the front of each code volume; some states have uniform citation rules promulgated and recognized by the courts.

To verify citations to state statutes, you must actually go to the sources. If you have only the name of the statute, you can first check a Popular Name Table in the Shepard's citator for that state to see if it is listed there. Otherwise, a search of the state's code indexes must be made.

## FEDERAL CASES

**United States Supreme Court**    A citation to the official source for *Gideon* v. *Wainwright* would take this form:

372 U.S. 335 (1963)

while a citation to unofficial sources would be formatted thus:

83 S. Ct. 792, 9 L. Ed. 2d 799
93 A.L.R. 2d 733

To verify citations to U.S. Supreme Court decisions, check the Table of Cases volumes in *United States Supreme Court Digest* (West or Lawyers' Edition) or *West's Federal Practice Digest 2d.*

**United States District Court and Court of Appeals cases**    For *Abercrombie* v. *Lum's Inc.* the citation is:

345 F. Supp. 387 (S.D. Fla. 1972)

For *Tarutis* v. *United States*, the citation is:

354 F. 2d 546 (8th Cir. 1965)

To verify these citations, check the Table of Cases volumes in *West's Federal Practice Digest 2d.* If you are not sure of the date of the case, check all components of the Digest including any supplementary pamphlets. Regarding the *Tarutis* case, if you knew that the subject matter is bankruptcy, you could also verify it in *Collier on Bankruptcy* or in a loose-leaf service called *Consumer Credit Guide.* Both happen to have Tables of Cases as features of their publications. The same is true for the *Abercrombie* case. If you knew that it concerns an aspect of antitrust or trade regulation law, you could verify it by checking the Table of Cases in the *Trade Regulation Reporter.*

## STATE CASES

A landmark products liability case, *Greenman* v. *Yuba Power Products, Inc.,* is cited in the official source as follows:

59 Cal. 2d 57 (1962)

and in the unofficial sources as follows:

27 Cal. Rptr. 697, 377 P. 2d 897
13 A.L.R. 3d 1049

To verify this case, you would check the Table of Cases in any of the digests that cover California case law—obviously *West's California Digest*, the regional *Pacific Digest*, or the decennial digests of the National Reporter System. If you were fairly sure of the year of the decision, then you would know enough to consult the *Seventh*

*Decennial Digest's* Table of Cases; if you didn't know the approximate date, you would have to search in several places. This case is a good illustration of the availability of multiple sources.

When cases have possible alternate citations and if you know one of them, then Shepard's will supply the alternates. This is especially important to keep in mind when the citation that you have is an unofficial one and you must get to the official one. In the case of multiple citations, the official one with the year of decision in parentheses is always given first.

## PERIODICAL ARTICLES

In the field of law the periodical citation form used is brief and logical. The last name of the author is given, then the title of the article, the volume number and abbreviated title of the periodical, and the page where the article begins; finally, the year is given in parentheses. Example:

Fisher, "Multiple regression in legal proceedings," 80 *Colum. L. Rev.* 702 (1980)

Colum. L. Rev. is the official abbreviation for Columbia Law Review. Abbreviations for periodical titles should follow those suggested in *A Uniform System of Citation,* 12th edition, especially for words like *Review* (Rev.), *Journal* (J.), *University* (U.), and *Association* (A.). If the article is an editor's contribution, it will be called a Note, Case Comment, Comment, Recent Case, Recent Development, or a similar title. In that case, instead of giving the author's surname, you substitute whatever label is indicated in the article:

Note, "Connolly v. Connolly: Antenuptial Agreements Settling Alimony," 24 *S.D. L. Rev.* 494 (1979)

# 18.5

## MICROFORMS AND COMPUTERIZED LEGAL DATA BASES

Given the need to retain information in other than book form in order to conserve space and retain retrospective resources, more and more libraries are turning to new technological formats: microforms (microfilm, microfiche, and ultrafiche) and computerized data bases.

The microformat is increasingly replacing long runs of legal publications including certain law report series, legal periodicals, government documents, and other space-consuming serial publications. Microfilm, used primarily for displacement of bound volumes of legal periodicals, is film that is contained on reels to be mounted on a viewer for reading and copy production. There are two sizes—16mm and 35mm. In addition, 16mm formats are available in cartridge containers that do not have to be threaded on viewers like roll film. Microfiche has a smaller reduction ratio than microfilm and is usually available in sizes approximating a 3 × 5 card. The cards are easier to manipulate than roll film. Fiche of the smallest reduction ratio are called ultrafiche.

The entire first series of the National Reporter System is available on ultrafiche. Records and briefs of United States Supreme Court cases and of other court cases are now available on fiche, as are the *Code of Federal Regulations,* the *Federal Register,* and Congressional reports, hearings, prints, and other documents. Microform equipment is also useful in a law library because an attorney may use it to read documents—especially financial records—in discovery, as suggested in section 6.6 of Chapter 6. Equipment may be purchased or leased.

**Computerized data bases**   Computerized legal data bases with the ability to do legal research via a computer have been slowly developing in the field of law. At the present time, the systems and equipment available are quite sophisticated and improvements, expansion of coverage, and cost reductions are occurring continuously. The two most important systems are Lexis, prepared and marketed by Mead Data Control, Inc., a subsidiary of Mead Corporation, and Westlaw, prepared and marketed by the West Publishing Company of St. Paul, Minnesota. Lexis and Westlaw cover federal and state case law going back to different dates, but their coverage is almost identical from about 1970 to the present. Sources for data in the Lexis system are official; that is, texts of opinions come directly from the courts. The Westlaw system derives from the network of the West Publishing Company's law reports, which were described in the preceding section, and incorporate the key number index and research features.

Lexis has an additional service feature called "Auto-cite," developed by the Lawyers Co-operative Publishing Company, which provides a fast way of checking the accuracy of citations and the validity of cases as precedent. It is a tool that the legal secretary should learn to use if access to Lexis is available. Auto-cite supplies the name of the case, the date and place of the decision, its official citation, any parallel citations that exist, and citations to cases that directly affect the validity of the case. Similarly, Westlaw is making all the Shepard's citing capability available on its system so that information can be verified by using the Shepardizing techniques adapted to the computer.

You must receive training on one or both data bases from representatives of the marketing corporations if you are to carry out these research tasks. You and the attorneys in your firm should explore the arrangements necessary for you to access one or both of these systems in your community if you do not have a computer terminal in your law office. If you are accustomed to using text-processing equipment or other computerized systems, you should find it quite easy to learn to use Lexis or Westlaw. There is now a considerable body of material designed to educate interested persons in the use and usefulness of both systems. A good place to begin is Chapter 31 in the 4th edition of *Effective Legal Research*.

# 18.6

## THE MANAGEMENT OF A SMALL LAW LIBRARY

This section is directed to the legal secretary whose responsibilities may include the management of a small law office library. The discussion is based on the premise that the library collection does not exceed 10,000 volumes, regardless of its composition, and that the number of attorneys served is less than 25. Under certain circumstances both parameters may be varied, but in most cases once these numbers are reached, a professional librarian is needed to oversee the management and reference functions which the law library must provide.

### ESTABLISHING ORDER
The secretary whose duties include managing the law library must first of all develop order. If the library is not already in order, the first thing you must do is sort and group like things together: statutes, law reports, periodicals, loose-leaf services, texts, citators, and other groups with similar formats. The next step is to form subgroups according to jurisdiction. What you can't recognize or categorize you should set aside.

The next step is to check the currency of your materials and make a note of items with missing pocket parts or advance sheets. Find out if anyone has maintained records of the materials. If any missing materials turn up, check them against your inventory of the physical holdings and attempt to assess their usefulness and currency.

## MAINTAINING RECORDS

A record must be made and filed for each publication in the library. You should record the following information for each title in order to develop a *system* for the library's continued organization:

1. Author—personal or corporate
2. Title—as complete as possible
3. Publisher, place of publication, and date
4. Number of volumes; number of pages for single-volume titles
5. Format and method of supplementation (i.e., periodical, loose-leaf, pocket parts, advance sheets/pamphlets, bound volumes); frequency of publication, if indicated
6. Source, if other than publisher
7. Price
8. Standing order—whether you wish to receive the title and/or future supplements on a continuing basis

With the exception of items 6, 7, 8, and possibly 5, the data should come from the publications themselves. Data for items which you order will be supplied by a publisher's catalog or by a phone call to the publisher's representative. In addition to the eight items listed, you will want to record the date on which you order an item and reserve space for recording the date when it is received. You might also add an entry for "Requested by" where you can record the name of the attorney requesting the material.

You will need to create two files initially: an Orders Outstanding file for those items being awaited and an Orders Received file or a shelflist. If you call the second file an Orders Received file, then the entries will be arranged by either author or title; if you call it a shelflist, then the order should be by shelf arrangement categories—e.g., Law Reports, Texts, Statutes, etc., if form is to govern or by subject categories such as the National Reporter System, Administrative Law, Constitutional Law, etc. You may want to have three separate files: Orders Outstanding, Orders Received, and a shelflist file, but your choice should be the simplest, easiest method for you to execute and monitor. Try to avoid creating multiple files; instead, concentrate as much information as you can into a minimum of locations and use aids such as tags, color codes, dividers, and colored cards to provide the checks needed to keep you informed of changes and updating requirements.

**Continuations records**   The vast majority of legal publications are updated at some time. Receipt of the additional volumes and supplements must be carefully and conscientiously recorded. You may provide extensions in the shelflist to accommodate this duty, or you may create what is often called a "continuations" record. To extend the shelflist, insert supplemental cards immediately following the main card for each title. If you prefer to create a separate continuations record, you will include most of the data listed above on a form that provides space on which to record items that are received or supplemented daily, weekly, monthly, quarterly, annually, or irregularly. For those supplements that are irregular, you should create a free form where you can record in chronological order whatever is received and adequately describe the supplement. These records should indicate the date on which the item is received in the library and the date of the supplement itself so that you can see the interval between the two. You can also let the continuations record act as a record of payment, binding, and routing (with a list of names of staff to whom supplements are circulated). Make cross-reference cards for those items whose identity is misleading or difficult to recognize and remember.

For publications that are issued in pamphlet form first and later in bound volumes, you really need two continuations records for each main entry: one to record the single pamphlets and the other the bound volumes. Records for the bound volumes of the *Atlantic Reporter* are illustrated on the following pages. In the first example, the number above the slash is the number of the volume received; below the slash is the date in 1979/80 when it was received. Note that these records are somewhat unstructured and allow for receipt of multiple volumes in the same month. The form is equally adaptable for advance sheets, as shown at the bottom of page 603. In this form, the year and volume numbers are recorded in the labelled columns on the left. The numbers 1 to 5, numbered vertically in three groups, represent advance sheet issue numbers. Note that a slash joins no. 5 of vol. 390 and no. 1 of vol. 391. That is because the advance sheet incorporates the end of one volume and the beginning of another. The numbers in each square are the receipt dates for each advance sheet issue.

However you set up the continuations records, you should record the volume or part with which the library's subscription begins if it is other than number one. You may also wish to indicate special retention policies for publications which the library does not keep permanently. The goal is to accumulate as much data on these records as is useful to you and can be most conveniently found in one place.

Payments can be recorded on the continuations records or in the Orders Received file or the shelflist; or a record of them can be maintained separately. Your payment procedures will largely be determined by the accounting and billing procedures developed by your firm.

## ARRANGEMENT OF MATERIALS

In a small law office library, legal publications are probably best grouped by form in combination with jurisdiction where applicable. That is, all United States materials should be shelved together with primary statutory sources first, followed by case law sources, related digests, and *Shepard's Citations*. All state materials should be similarly organized. Textbooks should be grouped together and arranged by author entry. Division by subjects and then by author is justifiable where there are many titles.

Periodicals and loose-leaf services should be grouped together and arranged by title or author. Legal encyclopedias, form books, dictionaries, and the like can be grouped to form the core of a reference collection. The preferences of the attorneys will usually dictate the arrangement scheme, but you should try to see that it is logical, responsive to their needs, and easy for you to implement and maintain.

**Work areas**   Most law libraries try to provide comfortable work stations, but even the finest private law libraries quickly outgrow their facilities. The librarian must consider good lighting, adequate ventilation, comfortable temperatures, and the absorption of sound. Tables should be large enough so that many materials can be assembled and spread out, chairs should be sturdy and of a good height to avoid back strain, and work areas should be as private and as free from distractions as possible. Photocopying machines should be placed where the noise will not bother those who are reading.

## CIRCULATION

You need to have a circulation system in order to know where a given item is at any given moment. Whatever system you decide to implement, the cardinal rule is "Keep It Simple." The best method is to equip every circulating item with a charge card and

## Continuations Records for Bound Volumes

| Title | **Atlantic Reporter** | Frequency **irreg.** Date due |
|---|---|---|
| Publisher | **West Publ. Co.** | Subscrip. date **Jan. 1** |
| Address | **50 Kellogg Blvd., St. Paul, MN** | Nos. per vol. |
| Bound | **yes** | Vols. per year |

| Year | Ser. | Vol. | Jan. | Feb. | Mar. | Apr. | May | June | July | Aug. | Sept. | Oct. | Nov. | Dec. | | |
|---|---|---|---|---|---|---|---|---|---|---|---|---|---|---|---|---|
| '79 | | | 390 1/12 | 391 2/12 | 392 2/28 | 393 3/5 | 394 3/31 | 395 | | | → | | | | | |
| | | | 408 10/2 | 409 11/19 | 410 12/6 | | | | → | | | | | | | |
| '80 | | | | | | | | | | | | | | | | |

| Title | **Atlantic Reporter** | Frequency **irreg.** Date due |
|---|---|---|
| Publisher | **West Publ. Co.** | Subscrip. date **Jan. 1** |
| Address | **50 Kellogg Blvd., St. Paul, MN** | Nos. per vol. |
| Bound | **yes** | Vols. per year |

| Year | Ser. | Vol. | Jan. | Feb. | Mar. | Apr. | May | June | July | Aug. | Sept. | Oct. | Nov. | Dec. | | |
|---|---|---|---|---|---|---|---|---|---|---|---|---|---|---|---|---|
| '79 | | 1 | 390 | 391 | 393 | 395 | 398 | 399 | 401 | 403 | 406 | 408 | 409 | 410 | | |
| | | 2 | | 392 | 394 | 396 | | 400 | 402 | 404 | 407 | | | | | |
| | | 3 | | | | 397 | | | | 405 | | | | | | |
| | | 4 | | | | | | | | | | | | | | |
| | | 5 | | | | | | | | | | | | | | |
| '80 | | 1 | 411 | 413 | | | | | | | | | | | | |
| | | 2 | 412 | 414 | | | | | | | | | | | | |
| | | 3 | | 415 | | | | | | | | | | | | |
| | | 4 | | | | | | | | | | | | | | |
| | | 5 | | | | | | | | | | | | | | |
| | | 1 | | | | | | | | | | | | | | |
| | | 2 | | | | | | | | | | | | | | |
| | | 3 | | | | | | | | | | | | | | |
| | | 4 | | | | | | | | | | | | | | |
| | | 5 | | | | | | | | | | | | | | |

**Cumulative Bound Volume Record**

| Atlantic Reporter | | | | | Volumes | |
|---|---|---|---|---|---|---|

| | | | | | | |
|---|---|---|---|---|---|---|
| **1st series:** | 315 | 334 | 353 | 372 | 391 | 410 |
| **v. 1-200** | 316 | 335 | 354 | 373 | 392 | 411 |
| | 317 | 336 | 355 | 374 | 393 | 412 |
| | 318 | 337 | 356 | 375 | 394 | 413 |
| **2d series:** | 319 | 338 | 357 | 376 | 395 | 414 |
| **v. 1-300** | 320 | 339 | 358 | 377 | 396 | |
| 301 | 321 | 340 | 359 | 378 | 397 | |
| 302 | 322 | 341 | 360 | 379 | 398 | |
| 303 | 323 | 342 | 361 | 380 | 399 | |
| 304 | 324 | 343 | 362 | 381 | 400 | |
| 305 | 325 | 344 | 363 | 382 | 401 | |
| 306 | 326 | 345 | 364 | 383 | 402 | |
| 307 | 327 | 346 | 365 | 384 | 403 | |
| 308 | 328 | 347 | 366 | 385 | 404 | |
| 309 | 329 | 348 | 367 | 386 | 405 | |
| 310 | 330 | 349 | 368 | 387 | 406 | |
| 311 | 331 | 350 | 369 | 388 | 407 | |
| 312 | 332 | 351 | 370 | 389 | 408 | |
| 313 | 333 | 352 | 371 | 390 | 409 | |
| 314 | | | | | | |

**Continuations Record for Advance Sheets**

| Title | **Atlantic Reporter** | Frequency | **irreg.** | Date due |
|---|---|---|---|---|
| Publisher | **West Publ. Co.** | Subscrip. date | **Jan. 1** | |
| Address | **50 Kellogg Blvd., St. Paul, MN** | Nos. per vol. | | |
| Bound | **no** | Vols. per year | | |

| Year | Ser. | Vol. | Jan. | Feb. | Mar. | Apr. | May | June | July | Aug. | Sept. | Oct. | Nov. | Dec. | | |
|---|---|---|---|---|---|---|---|---|---|---|---|---|---|---|---|---|
| '79 | | 390 | 1 1/12 | 393 | 20 | | | | | | | | | | | |
| | | | 2 2/6 | 1/1 | | | | | | | | | | | | |
| | | | 3 3/1 | 1/15 | | | | | | | | | | | | |
| | | | 4 3/15 | 1/30 | | | | | | | | | | | | |
| | | | 5 4 | 8 | | | | | | | | | | | | |
| | | 391 | 1 2 | 394 | 5 | | | | | | | | | | | |
| | | | 2 4/15 | | | | | | | | | | | | | |
| | | | 3 4/30 | | | | | | | | | | | | | |
| | | | 4 5/2 | | | | | | | | | | | | | |
| | | | 5 5 | | | | | | | | | | | | | |
| | | 392 | 1 17 | | | | | | | | | | | | | |
| | | | 2 5/ | | | | | | | | | | | | | |
| | | | 3 4/1 | | | | | | | | | | | | | |
| | | | 4 4/10 | | | | | | | | | | | | | |
| | | | 5 5 | | | | | | | | | | | | | |

**Circulation Card and Pocket**

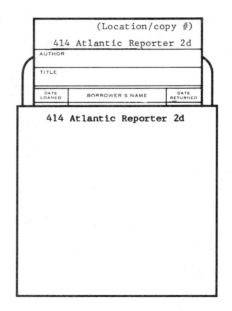

preferably also with a pocket in which to store it. Items like Shepard's citators, indexes, and other reference books should be stamped "Does Not Circulate" so that attorneys are discouraged from walking off with them. When a new item is received in the library, it should be stamped with an ownership stamp in several places to show that it is the property of the law firm. This procedure is extremely important and should be done immediately after making the decision to retain the item.

A small card and pocket like the one illustrated should be used for bound material which is to be permanently retained. The pocket should be affixed to the book just inside the front or the back cover but on the same place in each volume in the library. For monographs, the card should indicate the author and title, copy number, and location. The pocket itself should also identify the book. Getting patrons to fill out the card should not be a problem if the library's entire collection is in one place that has only one entry/exit point. You should have a sign near the exit reminding users to sign out for the materials being taken. Always have pens and pencils handy.

A tall card like the one illustrated on the opposite page can have many uses and can even be reused. It is best used for material that is temporarily held or in an interim format such as periodical issues and advance sheets. The illustration shows how a tall card may be used for a certain issue of a law review and reused for the same numbered issue in the next volume of the next year. Just type in only the information that is not likely to change over time: title, issue number and, sometimes, partial issue date. The volume number and the year would be penciled in. Then, after issue number 8 has been removed for bindery, the card can be retained in a file for next year's issue. You can very easily create such a rotating reserve of charge cards to have for use at all times. These cards stand out prominently above the height of most publications to remind users to sign them out, but their height is also a drawback because a separate circulation file must be maintained for them; they cannot be interfiled with the shorter card illustrated above.

It is doubtful that in a small law firm you would want to impose time restrictions on materials withdrawn. On the other hand, you must get management's attention regarding any recurring abuses of the charge-out system and seek out their solutions. The file of charge-out cards should be maintained in alphabetical order by author or title. You can purchase letter dividers and maybe even make your own for such items as reporters in the National Reporter System, which are always in circulation.

## Tall Circulation Card

| Harvard Law Review | | |
|---|---|---|
| **Title** | | |
| **Vol.** | Issue No. 8 | |
| **Date** | | |
| June | | |
| **Date** | Borrower's Name | Tel.Ext. |
| | | |
| | | |
| | | |
| | | |
| | | |
| | | |
| | | |
| | | |
| | | |
| | | |
| | | |
| | | |
| | | |
| | | |
| | | |

## CATALOGING

Cataloging a law collection is a highly technical, demanding, and detailed undertaking. It is best left to trained professional librarians who can handle the many questions and problems that arise in the course of doing this work. If you must undertake the job yourself, you will have to study the topic thoroughly before you begin. Two books are recommended, but with the caution that their contents are not easy to assimilate: (1) Chapter X, "Cataloging," in Elizabeth Finley's *Manual of Procedures for Private Law Libraries*, and (2) *Akers' Simple Library Cataloging*, by Susan Grey Akers. Another approach you might consider, after you have inventoried your holdings and recorded them as completely as possible, is to visit another law library in your area whose collection is already cataloged and replicate their system and style with modifications to meet your needs. The chances are that your library will consist of fairly standard texts and primary and secondary source materials for which you will find cataloging in almost any law library.

**Catalog cards**   The following are main entry cards, or master cards, for two types of publications, monographic and serial, to illustrate how a catalog record is prepared—what data must be recorded and how it should appear. The main entry card is the one upon which all other catalog entries are built. The substantive subject headings, that is, those which reflect the contents of the item being cataloged, are designated by the Arabic numerals and are listed first. The publication itself will often suggest these headings. The headings with Roman numerals are called added entries; they are descriptive extensions of the item, that is, additional elements by which users may identify it. All subject headings should be kept simple.

Enough copies of these cards must be made so that each subject and added entry heading can be typed on a card above the first line of the main entry card and then interfiled in the catalog. The catalog may be structured either as a divided catalog or as a dictionary catalog. In a divided catalog, all subject entries are filed together and all author/title entries are filed together. In a dictionary arrangement, all entries are interfiled together in one alphabet.

Cataloging increases the usefulness of a collection, but it must be done properly to serve well. You may wish to explore the possibility of contracting the work out to a professional. With some clerical help, a professional librarian can catalog a collection in anywhere from three to six months, depending on its size and condition.

**Main Entry Card for a Monograph**

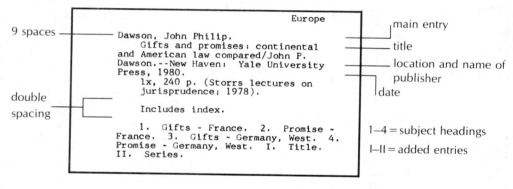

**Main Entry Card for a Serial Publication**

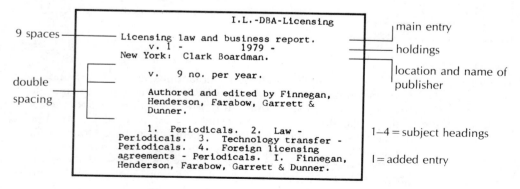

# APPENDIX

## SELECTED REFERENCES

The following books and periodical articles, listed in alphabetical order within categories, will provide the secretary with further information in specific fields of knowledge. Many of the items listed in this bibliography are part of the growing field of law office economics and management, and the majority of these references were written for the lawyer or the law firm administrator rather than for the legal secretary. However, a familiarity with the economics of law firm management is a definite advantage for the legal secretary: first, because efficient office managers usually delegate many administrative tasks to the secretary or legal assistant; and second, because the secretary who understands and accepts the goals of office management will make a greater contribution to the attainment of those goals.

### Abbreviations Dictionaries/General

Crowley, Ellen T., ed. *Acronyms, Initialisms, and Abbreviations Dictionary.* 7th ed., 3 vols. Detroit: Gale Research Co., 1980.

DeSola, Ralph. *Abbreviations Dictionary.* 5th ed., rev. New York: Elsevier-North Holland Publishing Co., 1977.

Paxton, John, ed. *Dictionary of Abbreviations.* Totowa, NJ: Rowman & Littlefield, 1973.

Pugh, Eric. *Third Dictionary of Acronyms and Abbreviations.* Hamden, CT: Shoe String Press, 1977.

Rybicki, Stephen A. *Abbreviations: A Reverse Guide to Standard and Generally Accepted Abbreviated Forms.* Ann Arbor, MI: The Pierian Press, 1971.

Spillner, Paul. *World Guide to Abbreviations.* 2d ed., 3 vols. New York: R. R. Bowker Co.

### Abbreviations Dictionaries/Legal

Bieber, Doris M. *A Dictionary of American Legal Abbreviations.* Buffalo, NY: William S. Hein, 1979.

*Dictionary of Legal Words and Phrases.* Binghamton, NY: Gould Publications, 1981.

—see also DICTIONARIES/LAW DICTIONARIES

### Abbreviations Dictionaries/Medical

Roody, Peter, et al. *Medical Abbreviations and Acronyms.* New York: McGraw-Hill, 1977.

Schertl, Albrecht. *Abbreviations in Medicine.* Ridgewood, NJ: K. G. Saur Publishing, 1977.

Steen, E. B. *Abbreviations in Medicine.* 4th ed. New York: Macmillan Company, 1978.

### Bibliographies on Law Office Management

Bigelow, Robert. "Where to Go for Help on Law Office Management," *Legal Economics,* vol. 6, no. 4 (July–August 1980), pp. 25–40. Supplement, vol. 7, no. 4 (July–August 1981), pp. 37–38.

Engholm, C. Rudy and Darcy J. Engholm, eds. *Law Office Information Service: A Bibliography of Material on Law Office Economics* (LOIS). Published quarterly by the Section of Economics of Law Practice of the American Bar Association and the Institute of Continuing Legal Education. Ann Arbor, MI: Institute of Continuing Legal Education. A computerized bibliography containing, in each issue, listings of some 3,000 articles, books, cassettes, and audio-visual materials on particular aspects of managing a law practice. Dated materials, especially those dealing with changing office technologies, are removed from each issue, and each issue supersedes previous ones.

*Index to Legal Periodicals.* New York: The H. W. Wilson Company. Monthly, with quarterly cumulations and bound annual cumulations.

Rikli, Donald C. "A Bibliography of Systems for the Law Office," *Legal Economics,* vol. 6, no. 3 (May–June 1980), pp. 27–30. Supplement, vol. 7, no. 4 (July–August 1981), pp. 39–40.

## Computers in the Law Office

Cwilko, William E., ed. *Computers in Litigation Support.* Princeton, NJ: Petrocelli Books, 1979.

Hildebrandt, Bradford W. "Computer Has Place with Small Firms," *New York Law Journal,* January 9, 1979. Reprinted in *Law Office Economics and Management,* Spring 1979, p. 62.

Laventhol and Horwath. *Law Office Automation.* Section of Economics of Law Practice. Chicago: American Bar Association.

Moses, Albert L. "Microcomputers in the Law Office," *Legal Economics,* vol. 6, no. 5 (September–October 1980), pp. 21–30.

—see also LAW OFFICE MANAGEMENT; LEGAL RESEARCH WITH COMPUTERS

## Correspondence

Bovee, Courtland L. *Techniques of Writing Business Letters, Memos and Reports.* 2d ed. La Mesa, CA: Roxbury Publishing Co., 1979.

Brock, Luther A. *How to Communicate by Letter and Memo.* New York: McGraw-Hill, 1974.

DeMeo, J. N. "A Dignified Mini-Letter for Speed and Economy," *Practical Lawyer,* vol. 17, no. 1 (1971), pp. 49–52.

————. "A Paper-Saving Formula for Law Office Correspondence," *Practical Lawyer,* vol. 22, no. 7 (1976), pp. 7–69.

DeVries, Mary A. *The Prentice-Hall Complete Secretarial Letter Book.* Englewood Cliffs, NJ: Prentice-Hall, 1978.

Ellenbogen, Abraham. *Letter Perfect: A Business Person's Guide to More Effective Correspondence.* New York: Macmillan Co., 1978.

Gilson, Goodwin. *Letter-Perfect: the Accurate Secretary.* New York: Arco Publishing/Prentice-Hall, 1977.

Prentice-Hall Editorial Staff. *Manual for Managing the Law Office.* Englewood Cliffs, NJ: Prentice-Hall. See the following chapters:

"How Your Secretary Prepares Letters and Other Written Correspondence," pp. 10051–10061.

"Save Practice Time by Using Informal Memo-Letters" and "Save Even More Time with Stickers, Stamps and Photocopies," pp. 7191–7193.

Reid, James M., and Robert M. Wendlinger. *Effective Letters: A Program for Self-Instruction.* 3d ed. New York: McGraw-Hill, 1978.

Smith, Robert S. *Lawyer's Model Letter Book.* Englewood Cliffs, NJ: Prentice-Hall, 1978.

Strong, Kline, and Arben O. Clark. "Handling Correspondence" and "Rapid Response Method" in Chapter XVI, *Law Office Management.* St. Paul, MN: West Publishing Co., 1974.

Vermes, Jean C. *Secretary's Book of Instant Letters.* Englewood Cliffs, NJ: Prentice-Hall, 1971.

—see also HUMAN RELATIONS/ETIQUETTE

## Dictation and Transcription/General

Bates, Jefferson D. *Dictating Effectively: A Time Saving Manual.* Washington, DC: Acropolis Books, 1980.

Kupsch, Joyce, et al. *Machine Transcription and Dictation.* New York: John Wiley & Sons, 1978.

Meyer, Lois, and Ruth Moyer. *Machine Transcription in Modern Business.* New York: John Wiley & Sons, 1978.

Sabin, William A. *The Gregg Reference Manual.* 5th ed. New York: Gregg Division, McGraw-Hill, 1977.

Zoubek, Charles E., and Morris W. Rifkin. *Gregg Reporting Shortcuts.* 2d ed. New York: Gregg Division, McGraw-Hill, 1959.

## Dictation and Transcription/Legal

Adams, Dorothy, and Margaret A. Kurtz. *Legal Terminology and Transcription.* New York: Gregg Division, McGraw-Hill, 1981.

Arco Editorial Board. *Law and Court Stenographer.* 3d ed. New York: Arco Publishing/Prentice-Hall, 1971.

Carr, A. Allen. *Practice in Legal Stenog-*

*raphy.* Belmont, CA: Pitman Learning, 1967.

Craft, Bernice. *An Introduction to Legal Typing.* Indianapolis: Bobbs-Merrill, 1978.

Craft, Bernice, et al. *Speedwriting for the Legal Secretary.* Indianapolis: Bobbs-Merrill, 1979.

DuPree, Garland Crowe, and Dorothy S. Namanny, *Legal Office Typing.* Cincinnati: South-Western Publishing Co., 1975.

Grahm, Milton, et al. *Legal Typewriting.* New York: Gregg Division, McGraw-Hill, 1968.

Rudman, Jack. *Law Stenographer.* Career Examination Series No. C-436. Syosset, NY: National Learning Corporation.

————. *Legal Stenographer.* Career Examination Series No. C-1344. Syosset, NY: National Learning Corporation.

*Shorthand Guide to Legal Terminology.* Binghamton, NY: Gould Publications, 1981.

Schoepfer, Virginia B. *Legal Secretarial: Typewriting and Dictation.* Portland, OR: National Book Co., 1974.

## Dictionaries/Law Dictionaries for Lawyers

Anderson, William S. *Ballentine's Law Dictionary with Pronunciations.* 3d ed. Rochester, NY: The Lawyers Co-operative Publishing Company, 1969. With pronunciation guides, abbreviations, descriptions of federal statutes and uniform acts, and tax terms.

Black, Henry Campbell. *Black's Law Dictionary.* 5th ed. St. Paul, MN: West Publishing Co., 1979. With pronunciation guides, abbreviations, the U.S. Constitution, and other addenda.

## Dictionaries/Law Dictionaries for Laymen

Bander, Edward J. *Dictionary of Selected Legal Terms and Maxims.* 2d ed. First published in 1966 as *Law Dictionary of Practical Definitions.* Dobbs Ferry, NY: Oceana Publications, Inc., 1979.

Flynn, William J. *A Handbook of Canadian Legal Terminology.* Don Mills, ON: new press, 1976.

*Glossary of Terms Used in the Federal Courts.* Rev. ed. Washington, DC: The Administrative Office of the United States Courts, 1980.

Hamilton, Harper. *Harper Hamilton's Law Dictionary for Laymen.* Briarcliff Manor, NY: Stein & Day, 1978.

Hemphill, Charles F., Jr., and Phyllis D. Hemphill. *The Dictionary of Practical Law.* Englewood Cliffs, NJ: Prentice-Hall, 1979.

Oran, Daniel. *Law Dictionary for Non-Lawyers.* St. Paul, MN: West Publishing Co., 1980.

Radin, Max, and Lawrence G. Greene, eds. *Law Dictionary.* Revised edition. Dobbs Ferry, NY: Oceana Publications, 1970.

Redden, Kenneth R., and Enid L. Veron. *Modern Legal Glossary.* Charlottesville, VA: Michie Company, 1980.

Roshton, Mabel R., ed. *Legal Secretary's Concise Dictionary.* Rev. ed., compiled by Louisiana Association of Legal Secretaries. Baton Rouge, LA: Claitor's Publishing Division, 1974.

Sturgess, H., and A. Hewett. *A Dictionary of Legal Terms and Citations.* New York: Gordon Press, 1980.

## Dictionaries/General and Specialized

Osler, Robert W., and John S. Bickley. *Glossary of Insurance Terms.* Santa Monica, CA: The Merritt Company, 1972.

Ross, Martin J. *New Encyclopedic Dictionary of Business Law with Forms.*

*Webster's New Collegiate Dictionary.* Springfield, MA: Merriam-Webster Inc., 1973.

*Webster's Third New International Dictionary.* Springfield, MA: Merriam-Webster Inc., 1961.

## Dictionaries/Medical

Blakiston. *Blakiston's Gould Medical Dictionary.* 4th ed. McGraw-Hill Book Co., 1979.

Byers, Edward E. *Gregg Medical Shorthand Dictionary.* New York: Gregg Division, McGraw-Hill Book Co., 1975.

Critchley, Macdonald, ed. *Butterworth's Medical Dictionary.* 2d ed. Woburn, MA: Butterworths Publishing, 1978.

*Dorland's Illustrated Medical Dictionary.*

25th ed. Philadelphia: W. B. Saunders Co., 1974.

Schmidt, J. E. *Schmidt's Attorneys' Dictionary of Medicine and Word Finder.* 3 vols. with irregular supplements. New York: Matthew Bender & Co.

Stedman. *Stedman's Medical Dictionary.* 23d ed. Baltimore, MD: Williams and Wilkins, 1976.

Stegeman, Wilson. *Medical Terms Simplified.* St. Paul, MN: West Publishing Co., 1975.

Thomas, Clayton L., ed. *Taber's Cyclopedic Medical Dictionary.* 13th ed. Philadelphia: F. A. Davis Co., 1977.

Thomson, William A., ed. *Black's Medical Dictionary.* 32d rev. ed. Totowa, NJ: Barnes & Noble Books, 1979.

Windholz, Martha, ed. *The Merck Index: An Encyclopedia of Chemicals and Drugs.* 9th ed. Rahway, NJ: Merck & Co., Inc., 1976.

## Directories/General Legal Reference

*United States Lawyers Reference Directory.* Los Angeles: Legal Directories Publishing Company, Inc. Federal courts, U.S. Department of Justice. State offices, bar associations, district and county personnel. Digests of courts.

Wasserman, Paul, and Marek Kaszubski, eds. *Law and Legal Information Directory: A Guide to National and International Organizations, Bar Associations, Federal Court System, Federal Regulatory Agencies, Law Schools, Continuing Legal Education, Scholarships and Grants, Awards and Prizes, Special Libraries, Information Systems and Services, Research Centers, Etc.* Detroit: Gale Research Co., 1980.

## Directories/Lawyers

*The American Bar, the Canadian Bar, the International Bar.* Minneapolis, MN: Reginald Bishop Forster & Associates, Inc. Annual. Includes individual biographies, sketches of law firms, and bank listings.

*The American Bar Reference Handbook: Including the Canadian Bar and the International Bar.* Minneapolis, MN: Reginald Bishop Forster & Associates,

Inc. Annual. A condensed compilation of the lawyers and firms listed in the above title.

*The Lawyer's Directory.* Annual. Selected list of leading lawyers in the United States and Canada; corporate law department counsel; foreign embassies and legations in Washington, D.C.; U.S. embassies, legations, and consular offices throughout the world.

*The Lawyer's List: A List of Counsel in General, Corporation and Trial Practice; Patent, Trademark and Copyright Practice.* Mount Vernon, NY: The Law List Publishing Co., Inc. Selected listings, updated irregularly.

*The Martindale-Hubbell Law Directory.* Multivolume. Summit, NJ: Martindale-Hubbell, Inc. Annual. The first volumes, comprising the Geographical Section, provide a roster of the bar of the United States and Canada, including U.S. Government lawyers, patent and trademark attorneys, and foreign attorneys. The final volume includes (1) digests of law for the fifty states; also of U.S. copyright, patent, and trademark law; (2) information on U.S. District Courts and other courts in various jurisdictions; (3) digests of the laws of Canada, the Canadian provinces, and many other countries; (4) uniform and model acts, including the complete text of the Uniform Commercial Code and the Uniform Probate Code; (5) information on international treaties to which the United States is a party; (6) the ABA Model Code of Professional Responsibility and Code of Judicial Conduct.

## Directories/State and Regional Lawyers

The Legal Directories Publishing Co. of Los Angeles publishes many directories listing attorneys in specified states or regions, such as the *Mountain States Legal Directory.* Each of these contains sections on federal and state officials and federal, state, and local courts.

## Directories/Specialty Practice

A number of directories are published which list only those attorneys practicing a certain specialty, as in the *Juvenile Law Litigation Directory* or *The Probate Counsel*. Professional groups also publish directories of members. A few directories are specialized in a different way, such as the *Directory of Women Attorneys in the United States*.

## Directories/Judicial
In addition to the national directories listed below, some states compile directories of state and local judges.

*Federal Court Directory*. Washington, DC: WANT Publishing Company. Annual.

National College of the State Judiciary. *Directory of State and Local Judges*. Reno, NV: National Judicial College, 1975.

*Register of the U.S. Department of Justice and the Federal Courts*. Washington, DC: U.S. Department of Justice. Annual.

*United States Court Directory*. Washington, DC: The Administrative Office of the United States Courts. Semiannual.

—see also DIRECTORIES/GENERAL LEGAL REFERENCE and the *Martindale-Hubbell Law Directory*.

## Directories of Corporations
Bottin International. *International Business Register*. 2 vols., 182d ed. New York: International Publications Service, 1979.

*Marconi's International Register*. Larchmont, NY: Telegraphic Cable and Radio Registrations. Revised annually.

*Standard & Poor's Register of Corporations, Directors and Executives*. 3 vols. New York: Standard & Poor's Corporation. Annual, with supplements.

*Standard Directory of Advertisers*. Skokie, IL: National Register Publishing, 1980.

*Thomas Register of American Manufacturers*. 16 vols., 70th ed. New York: Thomas Publishing Co. Volumes 9 and 10 contain company names listed alphabetically with addresses and telephone numbers, branch offices, and company officials.

## Directories of Federal and State Agencies
*Braddock's Federal-State-Local Government Directory*. Washington, DC: Braddock Publications, 1977.

*Congressional Directory*. Washington, DC: U.S. Government Printing Office. Published at the convening of each new Congress. Supplements published in alternate years.

*Congressional Staff Directory*. Mount Vernon, VA: Congressional Staff Directory.

Lukowski, Susan, and Cary T. Grayson, Jr., eds. *State Information Book*. 3d rev. ed. Washington, DC: Potomac Books, 1980. Biennial.

*State Administrative Officials Classified by Functions*. Lexington, KY: The Council of State Governments. Biennial.

*State Elective Officials and the Legislatures*. Lexington, KY: The Council of State Governments. Biennial.

*United States Government Manual*. Washington, DC: Office of the Federal Register, National Archives and Records Service, General Services Administration. Annual. Comprehensive coverage of the programs and agencies of the legislative, judicial, and executive branches of the federal government, including quasi-official agencies.

Wright, Nancy D., and Gene P. Allen, eds. *The National Directory of State Agencies*. Arlington, VA: Herner and Company for Information Resources Press. Biennial.

## Ethics
American Bar Association. *Code of Professional Responsibility* and *Code of Judicial Conduct*. Chicago: American Bar Association. Adopted in 1969 by the ABA and, with amendments, by various state bars. There are nine Canons, each followed by Disciplinary Rules and Ethical Considerations. (Also printed in the final volume of *The Martindale-Hubbell Law Directory*.)

American Bar Association, Standing Committee on Ethics and Professional Responsibility. *Code of Professional Responsibility by State*. Chicago: American Bar Association. How each state has amended the ABA Code of Professional Responsibility.

Aronson, Robert H., and Donald T. Weckstein. *Professional Responsibility in a Nutshell.* Nutshell Series. St. Paul, MN: West Publishing Co., 1980.

Brown. "Confidentiality: A Responsibility of the Legal Secretary," *Legal Economics,* vol. 1, no. 2 (Summer 1975), p. 34.

"Confidentiality Pledge for Secretaries," 19 *Law Office Economics and Management* 453.

Ream, Davidson, ed. *Professional Responsibility: A Guide for Attorneys.* Professional Education Publications. Chicago: American Bar Association, 1978.

**Financial Management/General**

*Accounting Fundamentals for Nonfinancial Managers.* AMACOM Reprint Collections Series. New York: American Management Association, 1972.

Brock, Horace R., et al. *College Accounting for Secretaries.* New York: McGraw-Hill Book Company, 1971.

Dyer, Mary L. *Practical Bookkeeping for the Small Business.* Chicago: Contemporary Books, 1976.

Keeling, B. Lewis. *Payroll Records and Accounting.* Cincinnati: South-Western Publishing Co., 1976.

Nickerson, Clarence B. *The Accounting Handbook for Non-Accountants.* 2d ed. Boston: CBI Publishing, 1979.

United States Treasury Department. *Tax Guide for Small Business.* Internal Revenue Service Pub. No. 334. Annual.

————. *Travel, Entertainment and Expense.* Internal Revenue Service Publication No. 463.

————. *Your Federal Income Tax.* Internal Revenue Service Pub. No. 17. Annual.

**Financial Management/Law**

Avery, Luther J. "Financial Records and Controls," in G. Grissom, ed., *The Lawyer's Handbook.* Ann Arbor, MI: Institute of Continuing Legal Education, 1975.

Burke, William J., ed. *Accounting Systems for Law Offices.* New York: Matthew Bender, 1978--. Loose-leaf service with periodic supplements.

Editors of the National Notary Magazine of the National Notary Association. *Journal of Notarial Acts and Record-keeping Practices.* 8th ed. Woodland Hills, CA: National Notary Association, 1979.

Ferst, Barton E. *Basic Accounting for Lawyers.* 3d ed. Philadelphia: American Law Institute-American Bar Association Committee on Continuing Professional Education, 1976.

Giuliani, Peter A., and Duane E. Watts. *Financial Management of Law Firms.* Monograph Series, Section of Economics of Law Practice. Chicago: American Bar Association, 1979.

Herwitz, David R. *Materials on Accounting for Lawyers.* University Casebook Series. St. Paul, MN: Foundation Press, 1980.

Hildebrandt, Bradford W. *Financial Management for Law Firms.* New York: Law Journal Press, 1975.

*Law Firm Administrative and Accounting Manual.* Fort Washington, PA: Safeguard Business Systems, Inc., 1975.

*Model Accounting System for Individual Practitioners and Small, Medium and Large Law Firms.* Section of Economics of Law Practice booklet. Chicago: American Bar Association, 1977.

Sellin, Henry, ed. *Attorney's Handbook of Accounting.* 3d ed. New York: Matthew Bender, 1979. Originally published as *Attorney's Practical Guide to Accounting,* 1965. Loose-leaf service.

—see also manuals listed in LAW OFFICE MANAGEMENT, especially the section "Law Office Technology" in *Manual for Managing the Law Office;* also articles in *Legal Economics.*

**Financial Management/Billing**

"Billing Procedures, Collection Methods, Legal Services Insurance, Attorneys' Liens, Prepaid Legal Services," in P. Hoffman, ed., *Law Office Economics and Management Manual,* vol. 1, sec. 26. Wilmette, IL: Callaghan & Company.

"Fees, Fee Determination, Schedules, Retainers, Trust Accounts, Bank Financing Plans," in Hoffman, *op. cit.*, vol. 1, sec. 25.

Henson, Gene. "Monthly Billing on the Mag Card II: Automation without Computerization," *Legal Economics,* vol. 2, no. 4 (Winter 1977), pp. 44–45.

Moldenhauer, Howard H. "Fees and Billing," in G. Grissom, ed., *The Lawyer's Handbook,* section C3. Ann Arbor, MI: Institute of Continuing Legal Education, 1975.

Pinna, William P., and Samuel T. Wyrick III. "Fee Collections," *Legal Economics,* vol. 5, no. 2 (March–April 1979), pp. 17–24.

Shellenberger, Fran. "How to Send a Bill Your Client is Willing to Pay," 19 *Law Office Economics and Management* 326.

## Financial Management/Timekeeping

"How Time Records Can Boost Your Income," in Prentice-Hall Editorial Staff, *Manual for Managing the Law Office,* pp. 5201–5205. Englewood Cliffs, NJ: Prentice-Hall.

Orren, Harding. "How to Save Time Keeping Time," in P. Hoffman, ed., *Law Office Economics and Management Manual,* vol. 1, sec. 24. Wilmette, IL: Callaghan & Company.

Regan, Ray R. "Timekeeping Systems," in G. Grissom, ed., *The Lawyer's Handbook,* sec. C1. Ann Arbor, MI: Institute of Continuing Legal Education, 1975.

Strong, Kline D. "How Timeslip Keeping Can Make Your Time Count for More," in Prentice-Hall Editorial Staff, *Manual for Managing the Law Office,* pp. 5211–5222.

————, and Arben O. Clark. "Timekeeping, Minimum Fee Schedules and Computers," Chapter V of *Law Office Management.* St. Paul, MN: West Publishing Co., 1974.

"Time Records and Timekeeping, Time Planning," in P. Hoffman, ed., *Law Office Economics and Management Manual,* vol. 1, sec. 24. Wilmette, IL: Callaghan & Company.

Weil, Robert I. "Safe, Simple and Efficient Timekeeping with a Paste-up System," in Prentice-Hall Editorial Staff, *Manual for Managing the Law Office,* pp. 5251–5257.

Wells, William E. *Automated Timerecord Accounting System and Legal Forms File for the Small Law Office.* Des Moines, IA: 1973.

## Forms/Legal Form Books

*American Jurisprudence Legal Forms 2d.* 23 vols. Rochester, NY: The Lawyers Co-operative Publishing Company. Forms for client documents.

*American Jurisprudence Pleading and Practice Forms, Revised.* 25 vols. Rochester, NY: The Lawyers Co-operative Publishing Company. Practice documents covering all phases of court proceedings and all jurisdictions. With annotations and procedural timetables.

Dawson, Townes L. *Mounce's Legal Forms Workbook.* 6th ed. Dubuque, IA: William C. Brown, 1979.

*Federal Procedural Forms, Lawyers Edition.* 18 vols. Rochester, NY: The Lawyers Co-operative Publishing Company, 1975--.

Heller, Marjorie K. *Working Papers in the Matter of Training The Legal Secretary.* Bayside, NY: Marjorie K. Heller, 1977.

Jones, Leonard A. *Jones Legal Forms.* 3 vols., 10th ed. Bobbs-Merrill Law Series. Michie, 1962.

*Modern Legal Forms.* 17 vols. St. Paul, MN: West Publishing Co.

Nichols, Clark A. *Nichols Cyclopedia of Legal Forms Annotated.* Wilmette, IL: Callaghan & Company. Supplements.

Rabkin, Jacob, and Mark H. Johnson. *Current Legal Forms with Tax Analysis.* New York: Matthew Bender, 1948--. A multivolume loose-leaf service.

Read, W. *Corporate Officer's Desk Book—with Model Documents, Agreements and Forms.* Englewood Cliffs, NJ: Prentice-Hall, 1980.

Sletwold, Evangeline. *Sletwold's Manual of Documents Forms for the Legal Secretary.* Englewood Cliffs, NJ: Prentice-Hall.

—Callaghan & Company of Wilmette, Illinois, publishes automated legal forms contained in hard-copy format and stored on floppy disk for editing and printout on text-editing machines. Matthew Bender & Co. also sells an automated system for custom-drafting wills.

## Forms/Specialty Form Books

Many form books are published to cover general practice within a particular state, such as *Baldwin's Ohio Legal Forms.* Other form books are confined to a special subject such as banking, criminal law, and private corporations. Another source for specialty forms is treatises on law, such as the multivolume *Thompson on Real Property.*

## Forms/Use in the Law Office

DeMeo, J. N. "Check-in Forms for Instant Drafting," *The Practical Lawyer,* vol. 16, no. 7 (November 1970), pp. 57–60. Reprinted in *The Practical Lawyer's Law Office Management Manual* No. 3, 1972.

Foonberg, Jay. "Administrative Forms," *Legal Economics,* Winter 1976, p. 10.

Grutzner, Edward, "How to Use Your Copying Machine to Build and Maintain an Up-to-the-Minute Forms Bank," in Prentice-Hall Editorial Staff, *Manual for Managing the Law Office,* pp. 7151–7164. Englewood Cliffs, NJ: Prentice-Hall.

Seward, Peter G., "How to Save Time with a Letter Form Book," in Prentice-Hall Editorial Staff, *Manual for Managing the Law Office,* pp. 13515–13521.

Tilton, Linda B., and James T. Tilton. "Basic Considerations in Designing Forms," *The Practical Lawyer,* vol. 26, no. 5 (July 15, 1980), pp. 55–69.

## Human Relations

Contemporary Programs, Inc. *Woman's Contemporary Image: A Personal and Professional Guide.* Englewood Cliffs, NJ: Prentice-Hall, 1975.

DuBrin, Andrew J. *Human Relations: A Job Oriented Approach.* Reston, VA: Reston, 1978.

———. *Managerial Devices: How to Deal with Problem People in Key Jobs.* New York: Van Nostrand Reinhold, 1978.

Fulmer, Robert M. *Practical Human Relations.* Homewood, IL: Richard D. Irwin, 1977.

Johnson, David W. *Human Relations and Your Career: A Guide to Interpersonal Skills.* Englewood Cliffs, NJ: Prentice-Hall, 1978.

*The Practice of Supervision: Achieving Results Through People.* Business Publications, 1980.

Torrington, Derek. *Face to Face: Techniques for Handling the Personal Encounter at Work.* New York: Beekman Publishers, 1972.

Vermes, Jean. *Secretary's Guide to Dealing with People.* Englewood Cliffs, NJ: Prentice-Hall, 1964.

## Human Relations/Etiquette

Baldridge, Letitia. *The Amy Vanderbilt Complete Book of Etiquette: A Guide to Contemporary Living.* New York: Doubleday & Company, 1978.

Vermes, Jean. *Complete Book of Business Etiquette.* Englewood Cliffs, NJ: Prentice-Hall, 1976.

Watson, Lillian E. *The Standard Book of Letter Writing and Correct Social Forms.* Rev. ed. Englewood Cliffs, NJ: Prentice-Hall, 1958.

## The Law and the Courts

Bonsignore, John J., et al. *Before the Law: An Introduction to the Legal Process.* 2d ed. Boston: Houghton Mifflin, 1979.

Cataldo, Bernard F., et al. *Introduction to Law and the Legal Process.* 3d ed. John Wiley and Sons, 1980.

Ehrenzweig, Albert A., et al. *Jurisdiction in a Nutshell, State and Federal.* 4th ed. Nutshell Series. St. Paul, MN: West Publishing Co., 1980.

Fisher, Bruce D. *Introduction to the Legal System: Theory—Overview—Business Applications.* St. Paul, MN: West Publishing Co., 1972.

Houston, A. A. *The Court System.* Corte Madera, CA: Anthelion Press, 1979.

Jacob, Herbert. *Justice in America: Courts, Lawyers, and the Judicial Process.* 3d ed. Boston: Little, Brown, 1978.

Klein, Fannie J., ed. *Federal and State Court Systems: A Guide.* Cambridge, MA: Ballinger Publishing, 1977.

*Law for the Legal Secretary and Paraprofessional.* Illinois Institute for Continuing Legal Education, 1979.

Marks, F. R., et al. *The Lawyer, The Public and Professional Responsibility.* Chicago: American Bar Foundation, 1972.

Mayers, Lewis. *The Machinery of Justice: An Introduction to Legal Structure and Process.* Quality Paperback No. 261. Totowa, NJ: Adams, Littlefield, 1976.

Payler, Frederick. *Law Courts, Lawyers and Litigants.* Reprint of 1926 ed. Littleton, CO: Fred B. Rothman, 1980.

Reynolds, William L. *Judicial Process in a Nutshell.* Nutshell Series. St. Paul, MN: West Publishing Co., 1980.

Schussler, Theodore. *Federal Courts: Jurisdiction and Practice.* Binghamton, NY: Gould Publications, 1980.

Schwartz, Helene. *Lawyering.* New York: Farrar, Strauss & Giroux, 1976.

Ulmer, S. S., ed. *Courts, Law and Judicial Processes.* New York: Free Press, 1981.

Weinerman, Chester S. *Practical Law: A Layperson's Handbook.* Englewood Cliffs, NJ: Prentice-Hall, 1980.

## Law Office Management

Altman, Mary Ann, and Robert I. Weil. *How to Manage Your Law Office.* New York: Matthew Bender, 1973--. Loose-leaf service with annual supplements.

Cantor, Daniel J., and Co. *Law Office Employment Guide.* 2d ed. 1980.

————. *Law Office Management and Economics.* Loose-leaf text with cassettes.

Grissom, Garth C., et al., ed. *The Lawyer's Handbook.* Rev. ed. Ann Arbor, MI: Published for the Section of Economics of Law Practice, American Bar Association, by the Institute of Continuing Legal Education, 1975. Loose-leaf with irregular supplements.

Hoffman, Paul S., ed. *Law Office Economics and Management Manual.* 2 vols. Wilmette, IL: Callaghan & Company, 1970--. Loose-leaf service with quarterly and annual supplements. (*See* listed under LAW OFFICE MANAGEMENT/PERIODICALS.)

*An Institute on Law Firm Management: Course Handbook.* Ann Arbor, MI: The Institute for Continuing Legal Education, 1974. Loose-leaf.

*Law Office Efficiency.* Published by the American Bar Association and the Canadian Bar Association, 1972.

*The Practical Lawyer's Law Office Management Manual.* Philadelphia: American Law Institute-American Bar Association Committee on Continuing Professional Education. No. 1 (1956), No. 2 (1959), No. 3 (1972), No. 4 (1974).

Wilkins, Robert P., ed. *New Tricks for Old Dogs.* Monograph Series, Section of Economics of Law Practice. Chicago: American Bar Association.

Practising Law Institute. Commercial Law and Practice Course Handbook Series. New York: Practising Law Institute.

Prentice-Hall Editorial Staff. *Manual for Managing the Law Office: Systems and Procedures.* Englewood Cliffs, NJ: Prentice-Hall, 1971--. A loose-leaf service with monthly new and replacement pages.

Strong, Kline D., and Arben O. Clark. *Law Office Management.* St. Paul, MN: West Publishing Co., 1974.

## Law Office Management/Periodicals

*Law Office Economics and Management.* Quarterly; edited by Paul Hoffman. Wilmette, IL: Callaghan & Company. Designed to be used in conjunction with Hoffman, ed., *Law Office Economics and Management Manual.*

*The Lawyer's Newsletter.* Bimonthly; edited by S. Z. Katzan. Los Angeles: Law Publications, Inc.

*Legal Economics.* Bimonthly. Published by the Section of Economics of Law Practice of the American Bar Association. Received by section members.

*Legal Economics, Automation and Management.* Monthly newsletter; editor in chief: Norman M. Martin. New York. *Newsletter* of the Association of Legal Administrators.

*The Practical Lawyer.* Eight issues annually. Philadelphia: American Law Institute-American Bar Association Committee on Continuing Professional Education.

*Report to Legal Management.* Bimonthly. Ardmore, PA: Altman & Weil Publications, Inc.

## Law Office Management/Profit-Making

Silver, Bertram S., and Martin J. Rosen. *How to Make a Better Profit in the Law Office—Year after Year.* San Francisco: Three L Press, 1978.

Stevenson, Noel C. *How to Build a More Lucrative Law Practice.* Englewood Cliffs, NJ: Prentice-Hall, Inc., 1978.

Strong, Kline D. *Practicing Law Profitably.* Rev. ed. Boston: American Press, 1979.

## Law Office Management/State Manuals

Many state bar associations publish office manuals for their members. These manuals are concerned mainly with practice and procedure matters, but many of them also contain sections on the economics of law practice. See especially those of Connecticut, Nebraska, North Carolina, Indiana, and Washington.

## Lawyers and Clients

Gillers, Stephen. *The Rights of Lawyers and Clients.* New York: Avon Books, 1979.

McGinn, Joseph C. *Lawyers: A Client's Manual.* Englewood Cliffs, NJ: Prentice-Hall, 1979.

Wehringer, Cameron K. *When and How to Choose an Attorney.* 2d ed. Legal Almanac Series No. 63. Dobbs Ferry, NY: Oceana Publications, 1979.

## Lawyers and Law Offices

Blaustein, Albert P., and Charles O. Porter. *The American Lawyer: A Summary of the Survey of the Legal Profession.* Westport, CT: Greenwood Press, 1972. Reprint of the 1954 University of Chicago Press edition.

Maron, Davida. "Legal Clinics," *Legal Economics,* vol. 3, no. 4 (Winter 1978), pp. 46–48.

Mayer, Martin. *The Lawyers.* Westport, CT: Greenwood Press, 1980. Reprint of 1967 Harper & Row edition.

O'Brien, John E. "Organization and Direction in the Operation of a Law Firm," *Legal Economics,* vol. 2, no. 2 (Summer 1976), pp. 45–50.

Rabin, Robert L. *Lawyers for Social Change: Perspectives on Public Interest Law.* Edited by the American Bar Foundation Staff. Chicago: American Bar Foundation, 1976.

Schwartz, Murray L. *Lawyers and the Legal Profession.* Contemporary Legal Education Series. Indianapolis: Bobbs-Merrill, 1979.

Smigel, Erwin O. *Wall Street Lawyer.* Rev. ed. Midland Books No. 130. Bloomington, IN: Indiana University Press, 1970.

Strong, Kline D., and Arben O. Clark. "Forms of Practice: Sole Proprietorship, Office Arrangements, Partnerships and Professional Corporations," Chapter II in *Law Office Management.* St. Paul, MN: West Publishing Co., 1974.

Vogel, Harold. *Corporate Law Department Practice.* Englewood Cliffs, NJ: Prentice-Hall, 1972.

Yale Law Journal Staff. *The New Public Interest Lawyers.* Law Review Research Project Series. Chicago: American Bar Foundation, 1971.

## The Legal Assistant

Anderson, Austin G., "Nonlegal Personnel," in Grissom, ed., *The Lawyer's Handbook,* sec. B4. Ann Arbor, MI: Institute of Continuing Legal Education, 1975.

Blackstone Associates. *Paralegals and Administrative Assistants.* Chicago: National District Attorney's Association.

Deming, Richard. *The Paralegal: A New Career.* New York: Elsevier/Nelson Books, 1980.

Eimermann, Thomas E. *Fundamentals of Paralegalism.* Boston: Little, Brown, & Co., 1980.

"Legal Assistants," 15 *Law Office Economics and Management* 333–367.

"Secretary/Legal Assistant: A New Answer to an Old Problem," 19 *Law Office Economics and Management* 179.

"Selected Checklist of Materials on Paralegals/Legal Assistants," *Records of the Association of the Bar of the City of New York,* vol. 33, no. 1/2 (January–February 1978), pp. 91–97.

Shayne, Neil T. *The Paralegal Profession: A Career Guide.* Dobbs Ferry, NY: Oceana Publications, 1977.

Statsky, W. P. *Introduction to Paralegalism.* St. Paul, MN: West Publishing Co., 1974.

Terhune, Jane H., et al., "Law Office and Personnel Management," in *Manual for Legal Assistants,* p. 240. St. Paul, MN: West Publishing Co., 1979.

Ulrich, Paul G., and Robert S. Mucklestone. *Working with Legal Assistants: A Team Approach for Lawyers and Legal Assistants.* Monograph Series, Section of Economics of Law Practice. Chicago: American Bar Association.

## The Legal Assistant/Manuals

Bruno, Carole. *Paralegal's Litigation Handbook.* Englewood Cliffs, NJ: Institute for Business Planning, 1979.

Grapp, V. *Paralegal's Encyclopedic Dictionary.* Englewood Cliffs, NJ: Prentice-Hall, 1979.

Heller, Marjorie K. *Paralegal Practical Handbook with 1979 Extensive Revision.* Bayside, NY: Marjorie K. Heller/ Lawyers Bookshelf, 1979.

Larbalastrier, Deborah E. *Paralegal Practice and Procedure: A Practical Guide for the Legal Assistant.* Englewood Cliffs, NJ: Prentice-Hall, 1977.

National Association of Legal Assistants, Inc. *Manual for Legal Assistants.* Edited by William R. Park. St. Paul, MN: West Publishing Co., 1979.

—see also SYSTEMS FOR LAW OFFICES

## The Legal Secretary/Manuals

Baranov, Alvin B. *Manual of Procedures for the Legal Secretary.* Los Angeles: Legal Publications, Inc., 1976.

Blackburn, Norma Davis. *Legal Secretaryship.* 2d ed. Englewood Cliffs, NJ: Prentice-Hall, 1981.

Crawford, Lois A. *The Legal Secretary's Litigation Office Manual: A How-to Handbook on Filings and Service of Federal Pleadings.* 1979.

Heller, Marjorie K. *Guide and Compendium for a Lawyer's Secretary.* 2d rev. ed. Bayside, NY: Marjorie K. Heller, 1979. Loose-leaf, revised periodically.

———. *Law Office Portfolio of Tips and Helpful Hints.* 2d ed. Bayside, NY: Marjorie K. Heller, 1976.

Krogfoss, Robert B., ed. *Manual for the Legal Secretarial Profession.* 2d ed. National Association of Legal Secretaries, Inc. St. Paul, MN: West Publishing Co., 1974.

Leslie, Louis A., and Kenneth B. Coffin. *Handbook for the Legal Secretary.* Diamond Jubilee Series. New York: McGraw-Hill Book Co., 1968.

Malone, Gerry. *The Career Legal Secretary.* St. Paul, MN: Published for the National Association of Legal Secretaries by West Publishing Co., 1981.

———. *The Career Legal Secretary—Advanced.* St. Paul, MN: Published for the National Association of Legal Secretaries by West Publishing Co., 1981.

Miller, Besse May. *Legal Secretary's Complete Handbook.* 3d ed., rev. by Mary A. DeVries. Englewood Cliffs, NJ: Prentice-Hall, 1980.

Nicholson, M. *Corporate Secretary's Complete Forms Handbook.* Englewood Cliffs, NJ: Prentice-Hall, Inc., 1980.

Prentice-Hall Editorial Staff. *Legal Secretary's Encyclopedic Dictionary.* 2d ed., rev. by Betty Kennedy Thomae. Englewood Cliffs, NJ: Prentice-Hall, 1977.

Thomae, Betty Kennedy. *Legal Secretary's Desk Book—With Forms.* West Nyack, NY: Parker/Prentice-Hall, 1973.

Many state legal secretarial associations publish office manuals. Noteworthy among these are *Legal Secretary's Handbook* (California), 11th ed., edited by Marian Freeman; *Handbook for Legal Secretaries in Virginia,* 2d ed.; and *Texas Law Office Handbook.*

## The Legal Secretary/Practice and Procedure

Bate, Marjorie Dunlap, and Mary C. Casey. *Legal Office Procedures.* New York: Gregg and Community College Division/McGraw-Hill Book Company, 1981.

Heller, Marjorie K. *Working Papers for Training the Legal Secretary.* 2d ed., rev. Bayside, NY: Marjorie K. Heller, 1979.

Heller, Marjorie K., and Betty Cohen. *Complete Course in Legal Secretarial Practice.* New York: Monarch Press/Simon & Schuster, 1977.

Morton, Joyce. *Legal Secretarial Procedures.* Englewood Cliffs, NJ: Prentice-Hall, 1979.

Rudman, Jack. *Legal Secretary.* Career Examination Series: C-1343. Syosset, NY: National Learning Corporation, 1979. A programmed learning booklet.

## The Legal Secretary/Office Tasks

Altman, Mary Ann, and Robert Weil, "The Legal Secretary," Chapter 15 in *How to Manage Your Law Office.* Wilmette, IL: Callaghan & Company.

"Do You Set a High Enough Standard for Your Legal Secretary?" 19 *Law Office Economics and Management* 368.

McArthur, Scott. "Nine Points to Discuss with Your New Secretary," *Legal Economics,* vol. 6, no. 5 (September–October 1980), pp. 49–50.

O'Brien, John E. "Answering Written Interrogatories," *Legal Economics,* vol. 3, no. 2 (Summer 1977), pp. 51–52.

Practising Law Institute. Commercial Law and Practice Course Handbook Series. New York: Practising Law Institute.

No. 11: *The Lawyer's Secretary,* 1968.

No. 41: Constance Pirnie, ed. *The Lawyer's Secretary 2d.,* 1970.

No. 50: Constance Pirnie and Mary C. Casey, eds. *The Lawyer's Secretary 3rd.,* 1971.

No. 76: *The Lawyer's Secretary 4th,* 1972.

No. 113: *The Lawyer's Secretary 5th: Office Management and Legal Support,* 1974.

Nos. 190–192: *Lawyer's Assistant:*
*Paraprofessional and Secretary 1978.*

Prentice-Hall Editorial Staff. *Manual for Managing the Law Office: Systems and Procedures.* Englewood Cliffs, NJ: Prentice-Hall, Inc. See chapters under "The Legal Secretary."

## Library/Legal Research Aids

Bander, Edward, and David F. Bander. *Legal Research and Education Abridgment: A Manual for Law Students, Paralegals and Researchers.* Cambridge, MA: Ballinger Publishing/Harper and Row, 1978.

Cohen, Morris L. *Legal Research in a Nutshell.* 3d ed. Nutshell Series. St. Paul, MN: West Publishing Co., 1978.

Jacobstein, J. Myron, and Roy M. Mersky. *Fundamentals of Legal Research.* Mineola, NY: The Foundation Press, 1977.

Price, Miles O., et al. *Effective Legal Research.* 4th ed. Boston: Little, Brown and Co., 1979.

*A Uniform System of Citation.* 12th ed. Cambridge, MA: The Harvard Law Review Association. General rules and citation forms; specific citation forms and abbreviations.

## Library/Research Aids from Publishers

*The Federal Register: What It Is and How to Use It; A Guide for the User of the Federal Register-Code of Federal Regulations System.* Washington, DC: U.S. Office of the Federal Register.

*How to Use Shepard's Citations.* Colorado Springs, CO: Shepard's Inc., 1979.

*The Living Law.* The Lawyers Co-operative Publishing Company/Bancroft-Whitney Company, 1980.

*Reporter Services and their Use.* Washington, DC: The Bureau of National Affairs, 1980.

*West's Law Finder: A Research Manual for Lawyers.* St. Paul, MN: West Publishing Co., 1978.

## Library Management

Altman, Devra L. *A Manual for Small and Medium-Sized Law Libraries.* Chicago: American Bar Foundation, 1976.

Bird, Viola, et al. *Order Procedures.*

American Association of Law Libraries Publication Series No. 2. Littleton, CO: Fred B. Rothman & Co., 1960.

Broghan, Anthony. *Manual and Code of Rules for Simple Cataloging.* 2d ed. New York: Jeffrey, 1974.

Curley, Arthur, and Jana Varlejs. *Akers' Simple Library Cataloging.* 6th rev. ed. Metuchen, NJ: Scarecrow Press, 1977.

Finley, Elizabeth. *Manual of Procedures for Private Law Libraries.* American Association of Law Libraries Publication Series No. 8. Littleton, CO: Fred B. Rothman & Co., 1966.

Gates, Jean K. *Introduction to Librarianship.* 2d ed. Library Education Series. New York: McGraw-Hill, 1977.

Head, Anita K. "The Law Firm Library: Today and Tomorrow," *Legal Economics,* vol. 2, no. 4 (Winter 1977), pp. 31–39.

Helburn, Judith, and Judith K. Mahrer. "The Law Library Consultant: Help When You Need It," *Legal Economics,* vol. 7, no. 3 (May–June 1981), pp. 23–27.

"The Law Library," Chapter 7 of *The American Courthouse, Planning and Design for the Judicial Process,* pp. 67–70. Ann Arbor, MI: The Institute of Continuing Legal Education, 1973.

Marke, Julius J. "The Law Librarian and You—Are You Missing the Boat?" 40 *New York State Bar Journal* 340–349 (1968).

Moyes, Elizabeth, ed. *Manual of Law Librarianship: The Use and Organization of Legal Literature.* Boulder, CO: Westview Press, 1976.

"Private Law Libraries in the 1970's," 63 *Law Library Journal* 453–470 (1970).

*Private Law Libraries—1980's and Beyond.* Commercial Law and Practice Course Handbook No. G4-3653. New York: Practising Law Institute.

Sloane, Richard. "The Law Office Library," in G. Grissom, ed., *The Lawyer's Handbook,* 1980 supplement. Ann Arbor, MI: published by the Institute of Continuing Legal Education for the Section of Economics of Law Practice of the American Bar Association, 1975.

Strable, Edward G., ed. *Special Libraries: A Guide for Management.* New York: Special Libraries Association, 1975.

Strong, Kline D., and Arben O. Clark, "Library and Retrieval Systems," in *Law Office Management,* sec. 10. St. Paul, MN: West Publishing Co., 1974.

## Legal Research with Computers

Greguras, Fred M., and Larry L. Carlisle. "Computer-Assisted Legal Research— The Present and the Future," *Legal Economics,* vol. 5, no. 6 (November–December 1979), pp. 32–39.

Musselman, Francis H., and Harding A. Orren. "How Computers Can Be Used in Legal Research," in Prentice-Hall Editorial Staff, *Manual for Managing the Law Office,* pp. 1571–1580. Englewood Cliffs, NJ: Prentice-Hall.

Sprowl, James A., ed. *A Manual for Computer Assisted Legal Research.* New edition by Bette Sikes. Chicago: American Bar Foundation, 1976.

## Mail Systems

*Everything You Need to Know about Mail.* Dallas: The Drawing Board, 1978.

"How to Keep Your Postage Costs Under Control," in Prentice-Hall Editorial Staff, *Manual for Managing the Law Office,* pp. 13601–13606. Englewood Cliffs, NJ: Prentice-Hall.

"Letters, Mail and Postal Service, Delivery Services," in Hoffman, ed., *Law Office Economics and Management Manual,* vol. 2, sec. 38. Wilmette, IL: Callaghan & Company.

Marshall, Kathryn S. "Prioritizing Office Communications," *Legal Economics* vol. 6, no. 1 (January–February 1980), pp. 41–43.

United States Postal Service Publications. Washington, DC: Superintendent of Documents, U.S. Government Printing Office.

No. 13: *Mailing Permits.* Free.

No. 42: *International Mail.* Subscription includes revisions as they occur.

No. 51: *International Postage Rates and Fees.* Free.

No. 59: *Domestic Postage Rates, Fees,*

*and Information.* Free.

No. 65: *U.S. Postal Service National ZIP Code and Post Office Directory.* Revised annually. Complete information on mailing procedures.

*Domestic Mail Manual* (DMM). Subscription includes revisions as they occur.

"What You May Not Know about Metered Mail," 18 *Law Office Economics and Management* 543.

## Mail Systems/Electronic Mail

"Electronic Mail Delivers," 18 *Law Office Economics and Management* 227.

*Electronic Mail in the 1980's.* Norwalk, CT: International Resource Development.

Martin, Norman E. "Electronic Mail: Digital Facsimile Machines and Intelligent Copiers Speed the Flow of Information," *Legal Economics,* vol. 5, no. 6 (November–December 1979), pp. 22–27.

## Office Administration

Anderson, Ruth I., et al. *The Administrative Secretary.* 2d ed. New York: McGraw-Hill, 1976.

Hanna, J. Marshall, et al. *Secretarial Procedures and Administration.* 6th ed. Cincinnati: South-Western Publishing Co., 1973.

Leaming, Marjorie P., and Robert J. Motley. *Administrative Office Management: A Practical Approach.* Dubuque, IA: William C. Brown, 1979.

Place, Irene, et al. *Office Management.* 3d ed. New York: Canfield Press/Harper & Row, 1974.

Terry, George R., and John J. Stallard. *Office Management and Control.* 8th ed. Homewood, IL: Richard D. Irwin, 1980.

—see also WORD PROCESSING; SECRETARIAL MANUALS

## Office Administration/Periodicals

*Administrative Management.* New York: Geyer-McAllister Publications, Inc. Monthly.

*Infosystems.* Wheaton, IL: Hitchcock Publishing Co. Monthly.

*Journal of Systems Management.* Cleveland, OH: Association of Systems Management. Monthly.

*Management World.* Willow Grove, PA: Administrative Management Society. Monthly.

*Modern Office Procedures.* Cleveland, OH: Industrial Publishing Co. Monthly.

*The Office.* Stamford, CT: Office Publications, Inc. Monthly.

*Office Equipment and Methods.* Maclean-Hunter Publications. Monthly.

*Office Products News.* Garden City, NY: United Technical Publications, Inc. Monthly.

## Office Design and Layout/General

Davison, D. J. *The Environmental Factor: An Approach for Managers.* New York: Halsted Press, 1978.

Duffy, Francis, et al. *Planning Office Space: A New Approach to Office Planning.* Architectural Press/Nichols, 1976.

Palmer, A. *Planning the Office Landscape.* New York: McGraw-Hill Book Co., 1977.

Ripnen, Kenneth. *Office Space Administration.* New York: McGraw-Hill Book Co., 1974.

## Office Design and Layout/Law Offices

Albertini, Eugene J. "Considerations in Planning a Law Office," *Legal Economics,* Summer 1976, pp. 40–42.

Altman, Mary Ann. "Office Location and Design," in Grissom, ed., *The Lawyer's Handbook,* sec. B1. Ann Arbor, MI: The Institute of Continuing Legal Education, 1975.

Hoffman, Paul, ed. *Law Office Economics and Management Manual.* Wilmette, IL: Callaghan & Company. See volume 2, sections 39–43.

Strong, Kline D., and Arben O. Clark. "Essential Equipment and Law Office Layout," Chapter XII in *Law Office Management.* St. Paul, MN: West Publishing Co., 1974.

Sussna. "Your Law Office Design," *New Jersey State Bar Journal,* November 1978. Reprinted in 20 *Law Office Economics and Management* 43.

## Office Equipment

Arentowicz, Frank, and Ward Bower, eds. *Law Office Automation and Technology.* New York: Matthew Bender, 1980--. Loose-leaf service with supplements.

Gensler, M. Arthur, and Peter B. Brandt. *A Rational Approach to Office Planning.* New York: American Management Association, 1978.

Hanson, Richard E. *The Manager's Guide to Copying and Duplicating.* New York: McGraw-Hill Book Co., 1980.

Martin, Norman. "Copiers Get Smart," *Legal Economics,* vol. 7, no. 4 (July–August 1981), pp. 25–28.

McKenzie, Jimmy C., and Robert J. Hughes. *Office Machines: A Practical Approach.* Dubuque, IA: William C. Brown, 1978.

*The Office Products Analyst.* Newsletter concentrating on word-processing and reprographics equipment.

Shellenberger, Fran. "OCR—A New Way with Words," *Legal Economics,* vol. 5, no. 3 (May–June 1979), pp. 14ff.

Walshe, Willoughby Ann. "Versatile Dictation Equipment Improves Productivity," 66 *American Bar Association Journal* 56–62 (January 1980).

—see also selected chapters in manuals listed under LAW OFFICE MANAGEMENT and articles in periodicals listed under LAW OFFICE MANAGEMENT/PERIODICALS. Business periodicals such as *Modern Office Procedures, Word Processing World,* and *The Office* frequently publish comparison tables of office products test results.

## Office Manuals

*A Blueprint for Preparing Your Own Law Office Staff Manual.* Pamphlet No. 511-0022. Chicago: American Bar Association, 1975.

Cantor, Daniel J. "Developing a Law Office Manual for Administrative Policies and Procedures," *The Practical Lawyer,* vol. 20, no. 2 (March 1974), pp. 35ff.

DeMeo, J. N. "How to Develop Manuals of Forms and Procedures," *The Practical Lawyer,* vol. 18, no. 8 (December 1972), pp. 33–39.

Eisenstatt, Leo. *Create-A-System for the Law Office Style Manual.* Monograph Series, Section of Economics of Law Practice. Chicago: American Bar Association, 1978.

*Guidelines for Corporate Law Department Manual.* Section of Corporation Banking and Business Law. Chicago: American Bar Association, 1980.

*How to Write a Successful Office Manual.* Management Information Center, 1972.

Light, Terry. "The Why and How of a Law Office Procedure Manual," *The Practical Lawyer,* vol. 25, no. 8 (December 1979), pp. 65–69.

## Parliamentary Procedure

Evans, William J. *The Scott, Foresman Robert's Rules of Order.* Glenview, IL: Scott, Foresman, 1980.

Shepard, David W., and Edward S. Strother. *The Practical Guide to Parliamentary Procedure.* Dubuque, IA: Kendall-Hunt Publishing Co., 1977.

## Purchasing Guides

*Lawyer's Directolog.* Chicago: American Bar Association, 1981.

## Records Management/General

Borko, Harold, and Charles L. Bernier. *Indexing Concepts and Methods.* New York: Academic Press, 1978.

General Services Administration. *A Guide to Record Retention Requirements.* Washington, DC: U.S. Government Printing Office. Annual.

Kahn, Gilbert, et al. *Filing Systems and Records Management.* 2d ed. New York: McGraw-Hill Book Co., 1971.

Knight, G. Norman. *Indexing: The Art of.* Winchester, MA: Allen and Unwin, 1979.

Place, Irene M., and E. L. Popham. *Filing and Records Management.* Englewood Cliffs, NJ: Prentice-Hall, 1966.

*Rules for Alphabetical Filing as Standardized by ARMA.* Prairie Village, KS: Association of Records Managers and Administrators.

Stewart, Jeffrey R., et al. *Progressive Fil-*

*ing.* 9th ed., edited by Ella Pezzuti. New York: McGraw-Hill Book Co., 1980.

## Records Management/Law

Dimitriou, Demetrios. "Client Files: To Destroy or Not to Destroy?" *Legal Economics,* vol. 7, no. 1 (January–February 1981), pp. 17–21.

"Filing Equipment and Storage Space," 15 *Law Office Economics and Management,* 377–393.

"Filing Equipment and Systems, Microfilm," in P. Hoffman, ed., *Law Office Economics and Management Manual,* vol. 2, sec. 49. Wilmette, IL: Callaghan & Company.

"Filing Problems—A Boston Solution," 18 *Law Office Economics and Management* 116.

Hutzler, Laurie H. "Basic Rules for a Filing System (with a form)," *The Practical Lawyer,* vol. 26, no. 6 (September 1980), pp. 77–86.

Luvera, Paul N., Jr. "Organize Your File Folders," *Legal Economics,* vol. 1, no. 4 (Winter 1976), pp. 34–38.

Mathwich, Alfred J. "File Planning and Selection," *Legal Economics,* vol. 2, no. 2 (Summer 1976), pp. 32–35.

Orren, Harding A. "Filing, Docket Control and Information Retrieval," in Grissom, ed., *The Lawyer's Handbook,* sec. C5. Ann Arbor, MI: The Institute of Continuing Legal Education, 1975.

Prentice-Hall Editorial Staff. *Manual for Managing the Law Office.* Englewood Cliffs, NJ: Prentice-Hall. See the following chapters:

Hillman, William C. "Computerized File Control for the Small Law Office," pp. 1599–1606.

"How Your Secretary Can Set Up an Efficient and Accurate Filing System," pp. 10075-10085.

King, Edward M. "How to Set Up a Controlled Filing System in a Decentralized Mode," pp. 7201–7205.

Strong, Kline D. "New Techniques for Handling Client Files," pp. 7215–7226.

Rose, Joel A. "File Indexing and Maintenance—A Systems Approach, " *Legal Economics,* vol. 7, no. 2 (March-April 1981), pp. 12ff.

Strong, Kline D. *How to Implement Your Very Own Retrieval System by the Numbers.* Section of Economics of Law Practice. Chicago: American Bar Association.

———. *Retrieval Systems for Lawyers: How to Index and Store Research and Other Office Created Documents for Future Use.* Monograph Series, Section of Economics of Law Practice. Chicago: American Bar Association, 1980.

Strong, Kline D., and Arben O. Clark. "Client Files: Open, Maintain and Close," Chapter 8 of *Law Office Management.* Wilmette, IL: Callaghan & Company, 1974.

*Yardstick for Legal Records and Information Retrieval.* Section of Economics of Law Practice Pamphlet No. 010. Chicago: American Bar Association.

## Records Management/Microfilm

Costigan, Daniel M., ed. *Guide to Micrographic Equipment.* 2 vols., 7th ed. Silver Spring, MD: National Micrographics Association, 1979.

———. *Micrographic Systems.* Silver Spring, MD: National Micrographics Association, 1975.

Iezzi, John G. "How to Initiate a Microfilm Program in Your Law Firm," in Prentice-Hall Editorial Staff, *Manual for Managing the Law Office,* pp. 1655–1659. Englewood Cliffs, NJ: Prentice-Hall.

Johnson, Albert Sidney. "Cut Storage Costs, Facilitate Retrievability, with Microfilm," *Legal Economics,* vol. 3, no. 4 (Winter 1978), pp. 20–25.

Saffady, William. *Micrographics.* Library Science Text Series. Littleton, CO: Libraries Unlimited, 1978.

## Secretarial Manuals

Clark, Freda. *Secretary's Desk Book of Shortcuts and Timesavers.* Englewood Cliffs, NJ: Prentice-Hall, Inc., 1978.

Dallas, Richard J., and James M. Thompson. *Clerical and Secretarial Systems for the Office.* Office Occupations Series. Englewood Cliffs, NJ: Prentice-Hall, 1975.

Doris, Lillian, and Besse M. Miller. *Complete Secretary's Handbook*. 4th ed. Englewood Cliffs, NJ: Prentice-Hall, 1977.

Ettinger, Blanche. *A Secretary's Reference Guide*. Manhasset Hills, NY: Avery Publications, 1978.

Hanna, J. Marshall, et al. *Secretarial Procedures and Administration*. 7th ed. Cincinnati: South-Western Publishing Co., 1978.

Janis, J. Harold, and Margaret Thompson. *New Standard Reference for Secretaries and Administrative Assistants*. New York: Macmillan Co., 1972.

McCabe, Helen M., and Estelle L. Popham. *Word Processing: A Systems Approach to the Office*. New York: Harcourt Brace Jovanovich, 1977.

Merriam-Webster Editorial Staff. *Webster's Secretarial Handbook*. Springfield, MA: Merriam-Webster Inc., 1976.

Nanassy, Louis C., et al. *Reference Manual for Office Workers*. New York: Macmillan Company, 1977.

Place, Irene, and Edward E. Byers. *Executive Secretarial Procedures*. 5th ed. New York: Gregg Division, McGraw-Hill Book Co., 1980.

Prentice-Hall Editorial Staff. *Common Secretarial Mistakes and How to Avoid Them*. Englewood Cliffs, NJ: Prentice-Hall, 1963.

Whalen, Doris. *Secretary's Handbook*. 3d ed. New York: Harcourt Brace Jovanovich, 1978.

## Systems for the Law Office

Brill, James E. "Rubber Stamps Can Make an Impression," *Legal Economics*, vol. 2, no. 4, pp. 56–59. Available from the ABA as a reprint.

Hoffman, Paul, ed. *Law Office Economics and Management Manual*, vol. 2. Wilmette, IL: Callaghan & Company. See sections 31 and 35.

*Non-conventional Systems*. Section of Economics of Law Practice pamphlet No. 014. Chicago: American Bar Association.

Ramo, Roberta Cooper. "Bibliography of Systems Manuals" in "How to Find Your Way Down the Yellow Brick Road: Systems for Lawyers," *American Bar Association Journal*, vol. 65 (March 1979).

————, ed. *How to Create-A-System for the Law Office*. Chicago: The American Bar Association, 1975. With optional cassette.

Smith, Cullen. "Developing Effective Office Systems," in *An Institute on Law Firm Management*, pp. 38–119. Ann Arbor, MI: Institute of Continuing Legal Education, 1974.

Wilkins, Robert P. "Drafting a Divorce Complaint: Using the Mini-System of How to Create-A-System for the Law Office," *Legal Economics*, vol. 2, no. 2 (Summer 1976), pp. 23–29.

—see also numerous recent publications that offer the lawyer and the legal assistant practical guides through a particular field of practice such as probate. These are typically loose-leaf in form so that they can be updated and notes added; they contain checklists and sample forms and documents. Continuing Legal Education programs frequently publish these guides for a particular jurisdiction.

## Systems for the Law Office/Docket Control

Brown, Thomas P. "Ways and Means to Reduce Vulnerability to Malpractice Claims and Recoveries," *Legal Economics* vol. 3, no. 2 (Summer 1977), pp. 26–30.

"Docket and Case Control, Tickler Files, Court Delays," in P. Hoffman, ed., *Law Office Economics and Management Manual*, vol. 2, sec. 32. Wilmette, IL: Callaghan & Company.

Light, Terry W. "The Many Faces of a Tickler File," *The Practical Lawyer*, vol. 26, no. 7 (October 1980), pp. 75–80.

Strong, Kline D., and Arben O. Clark, "Calendar and Monitor Systems," Chapter 9 of *Law Office Management*. St. Paul, MN: West Publishing Co., 1974.

Strong, Kline D., and Duke Nordlinger Stern. *Docket Control—the Most Effective Means to Avoid Malpractice Claims.* Monograph Series, Section of Economics of Law Practice. Chicago: The American Bar Association, 1981.

## Telecommunications Equipment

*Business Communications Review.* Bimonthly periodical.

Hoffman, Paul S., and Jerry W. Mills, eds. *Communications Handbook for Attorneys: Telephone Systems and Facsimile.* Section of Economics of Law Practice. Chicago: American Bar Association, 1978.

Prentice-Hall Editorial Staff. *Manual for Managing the Law Office.* Englewood Cliffs, NJ: Prentice-Hall. See chapters in section entitled "Law Office Technology."

Sunier, John H. *The Handbook of Telephones and Accessories.* Blue Ridge Summit, PA: Tab Books, 1978.

## Telecommunications in the Office

Bailey, Mead. "Have You Called Yourself Up Lately?" *Legal Economics,* vol. 7, no. 2 (March–April 1981), pp. 25–27.

Gough, Vera, and B. R. Grier. *Better Telephoning: A Plan to Improve Your Telephone Technique.* Elmsford, NY: Pergamon Press, 1970.

Griesinger, Frank K. *How to Cut Costs and Improve Service of Your Telephone, Telex, TWX, and Other Telecommunications.* New York: McGraw-Hill Book Co., 1974.

Kuehn, Richard A. *Cost-Effective Telecommunications.* New York: American Management Association, 1975.

"Reducing Your Firm's Phone Bill," 19 *Law Office Economics and Management* 22.

Rosenweig, "Fighting Telephone Inflation," 79 *Commercial Law Journal* 119 (1974).

"Telecommunications," 19 *Law Office Economics and Management* 475.

*The Telephone and Your Professional Image.* California Bar Association. Cassette with syllabus.

"Telephone, Intercom, Telegram, Mailgram," in Hoffman, ed., *Law Office Economics and Management Manual,* vol. 2, sec. 37. Wilmette, IL: Callaghan & Company.

*Using the Telephone Effectively.* Section of Economics of Law Practice booklet No. 511–0020. Chicago: American Bar Association.

Waterford, Van. *All About Telephones.* Blue Ridge Summit, PA: Tab Books, 1979.

## Word Books and Spellers/Legal

Gordon, Frank S., and Thomas M. S. Hemnes. *The Legal Word Book.* Boston: Houghton Mifflin, 1978.

Merriam-Webster Editorial Staff. *Webster's Legal Speller.* Springfield, MA: Merriam-Webster Inc., 1978.

Reilly, Theresa M. *Legal Secretary's Word Finder and Desk Book.* West Nyack, NY: Parker Publishing/Prentice-Hall, 1974.

Sloane, Sheila B. *The Legal Speller With Useful Medical Terms.* Philadelphia: W. B. Saunders, 1977.

## Word Books and Spellers/Medical

Byers, E. E. *Ten Thousand Medical Words.* New York: McGraw-Hill, 1972.

Carlin, H. L. *Medical Secretary Medi-Speller: A Transcription Aid.* Springfield, IL: Charles C Thomas, 1973.

Johnson, C. E. *Medical Spelling Guide: A Reference Aid.* Springfield, IL: Charles C Thomas, 1966.

Lee, R. V., and Doris Hofer. *How to Divide Medical Words.* Carbondale, IL: Southern Illinois University Press, 1972.

Merriam-Webster Editorial Staff. *Webster's Medical Speller.* Springfield, MA: Merriam-Webster Inc., 1975.

Prichard, Robert W., and Robert E. Robinson, *Twenty Thousand Medical Words.* New York: McGraw-Hill, 1972.

Sloane, Sheila B. *The Medical Word Book: A Spelling and Vocabulary Guide to Medical Transcription.* Philadelphia: William Saunders, 1973.

Willeford, George. *Medical Word Finder.* 2d ed. Englewood Cliffs, NJ: Prentice-Hall, 1976.

## Word Processing

The International Word Processing Association, in Willow Grove, Pennsylvania, has chapters in major cities and publishes information helpful to text-editing equipment users.

Cecil, Paula B. *Management of Word Processing Operations.* Reading, MA: Addison-Wesley, 1980.
————. *Word Processing in the Modern Office.* 2d ed. Menlo Park, CA: Benjamin-Cummings, 1980.
Kleinschrod, Walter. *Management's Guide to Word Processing.* Dartnell Corporation, 1975.
Kleinschrod, Walter, et al. *Word Processing Operations, Applications, and Administration.* Indianapolis: Bobbs-Merrill Co., 1980.
Martin, D. *Practical Guides for Word Processing.* Booklet series. Atlanta, GA: Word Processing Informational Management Corp.
Waterhouse, Shirley. *Word Processing Fundamentals.* New York: Harper and Row, 1978.

## Word Processing in the Law Office

Parkin, Frank E., and Peter G. Seward. "Word Processing for the Law Office," in Grissom, ed., *The Lawyer's Handbook,* sec. B2. Ann Arbor, MI: The Institute of Continuing Legal Education, 1975.
Sternin, Bernard S. *The Practical Lawyer's Manual for Automatic Law-Office Typing and Word Processing.* Philadelphia: American Law Institute-American Bar Association, 1979.
Strong, Kline D. *Word Processing Equipment: A Guide to Understanding, Evaluating and Selecting.* Section of Economics of Law Practice. Chicago: American Bar Association, 1979.
Walshe, Willoughby Ann. "What to Consider When Selecting Text-editing Equipment," 67 *American Bar Association Journal* (January 1981), 45–49.
"Word Processing and Micrographics: Natural Allies for Storage and Retrieval Systems," *Word Processing Systems,* October 1979, p. 22.

—*see also* articles in *Legal Economics, The Practical Lawyer,* and *Law Office Economics* and *Management;* also chapters under "Law Office Technology" in Prentice-Hall Editorial Staff, *Manual for Managing the Law Office.*

## Word Processing/Periodicals

*Impact: Information Technology.* Willow Grove, PA: Administrative Management Society. Monthly.
*Information and Word Processing Report.* New York: Geyer-McAllister Publications. Semimonthly newsletter.
*Legal Economics, Automation and Management.* New York: Legal Economics, Automation and Management. Monthly newsletter.
*vieWPoint.* Willow Grove, PA: International Word Processing Association. Monthly.
*Word Processing and the American Office.* Office Management Systems Corp. Semimonthly.
*Word Processing and Information Systems.* New York: Geyer-McAllister Publications. Monthly magazine.
*Words.* Willow Grove, PA: International Word Processing Association. Quarterly.

## Writing Guides/Business

Aurner, Robert R., and Morris P. Wolf. *Effective Communication in Business.* 6th ed. Cincinnati: South-Western Publishing Co., 1974.
Barry, R. *Basic Business English.* Englewood Cliffs, NJ: Prentice-Hall, 1981.
Dow, Roger W. *Business English.* New York: John Wiley and Sons, 1979.
Janis, J. Harold. *Writing and Communicating in Business.* 3d ed. New York: Macmillan Co., 1978.
Whalen, Doris H. *Handbook of Business English.* New York: Harcourt Brace Jovanovich, 1980.

## Writing Guides/General

Barzun, Jacques. *Simple & Direct: A Rhetoric for Writers.* New York: Harper & Row, 1975.
Bernstein, Theodore M. *The Careful Writer: A Modern Guide to English Usage.* New York: Atheneum, 1977.

————. *Dos, Don'ts and Maybes of English Usage.* New York: New York Times Books, 1977.

Copperud, Roy H. *American Usage and Style.* New York: Van Nostrand Reinhold, 1979.

Evans, Bergen, and Cornelia Evans. *A Dictionary of Contemporary English Usage.* New York: Random House, 1957.

Flesch, Rudolf. *The Art of Readable Writing.* Rev. and enlarged ed. New York: Harper and Row, 1974.

Follett, Wilson. *Modern American Usage: A Guide.* Edited by Jacques Barzun. New York: Hill & Wang, 1979.

Graves, Robert, and Alan Hodge. *The Reader Over Your Shoulder: A Handbook for Writers of English Prose.* 2d ed. New York: Random House, 1979.

Shaw, Harry. *Dictionary of Problem Words and Expressions.* New York: McGraw-Hill, 1975.

Strunk, William. *Elements of Style.* 3d ed., with revisions, introduction, and chapter on writing by E. B. White. New York: Macmillan Company, 1979.

Timmons, Christine, and Frank Gibney, eds. *Britannica Book of English Usage.* Doubleday-Britannica Books. Garden City, NY: Doubleday & Co., 1980.

*Webster's Collegiate Thesaurus.* Springfield, MA: Merriam-Webster Inc., 1976.

Zinsser, William. *On Writing Well: An Informal Guide to Writing Nonfiction.* 2d ed. New York: Harper and Row, 1980.

## Writing Guides/Legal

Biskind, Elliott L. *Simplify Legal Writing.* New York: Arco/Prentice-Hall. Portions published previously as *Legal Writing Simplified.*

Flesch, Rudolf. *How to Write Plain English: A Book for Lawyers and Consumers.* New York: Harper and Row, 1979.

MacDonald, Duncan A., ed. *Drafting Documents in Plain Language.* Commercial Law and Practice Course Handbook Series No. 203. New York: Practising Law Institute, 1979.

Till, Paul, and Albert Gargiulo. *Plain Language Acts.* New York: American Management Association, 1979.

Wincor, Richard. *Contracts in Plain English.* New York: McGraw-Hill, 1975.

Wydick, Richard C. *Plain English for Lawyers.* Durham, NC: Carolina Academic Press, 1979.

## Writing Guides/Style Manuals

Gibaldi, Joseph, and Walter S. Achtert. *MLA Handbook for Writers of Research Papers, Theses, and Dissertations.* New York: Modern Language Association of America, 1977.

Keithley, Erwin M., and Philip S. Shreiner. *A Manual of Style for the Preparation of Papers and Reports.* Cincinnati: South-Western Publishing Co., 1971.

McNaughton, Harry H. *Proofreading and Copyediting: A Practical Guide to Style for the 1970's.* Communications Arts Books. New York: Hastings House, 1973.

Skillin, Marjorie E., and Robert M. Gay. *Words into Type.* 3d ed. Englewood Cliffs, NJ: Prentice-Hall, 1974.

Turabian, Kate L. *A Manual for Writers of Term Papers, Theses, and Dissertations.* 4th ed. Chicago: University of Chicago Press, 1973.

*U.S. Government Printing Office Style Manual.* Rev. ed. Washington, DC: U.S. Government Printing Office, 1973.

University of Chicago Press. *A Manual of Style.* 12th ed., rev. Chicago: The University of Chicago Press, 1969.

## Writing Guides/Usage and Grammar

Ebbitt, Wilma R., and David R. Ebbitt. *Writer's Guide and Index to English.* 6th ed. Glenview, IL: Scott, Foresman and Co., 1978.

Irmscher, William F. *The Holt Guide to English.* New York: Holt, Rinehart and Winston, 1976.

Keithley, Erwin, and Margaret H. Thompson. *English for Modern Business.* 3d ed. Homewood, IL: Richard D. Irwin, 1977.

Shaw, Harry. *Handbook of English.* 4th ed. New York: McGraw-Hill, 1977.

# INDEX